THE

PUBLIC GENERAL ACTS

AND GENERAL SYNOD MEASURES

1998

[IN FOUR PARTS]

PART IV

TABLES & INDEX

£280

Published by The Stationery Office Limited
and available from:

The Publications Centre
(Mail, telephone and fax orders only)
PO Box 276, London SW8 5DT
General enquiries 0870 600 5522
Order through the Parliamentary Hotline Lo-call 0847 7 023474
Fax orders 020 7873 8200

The Stationery Office Bookshops
123 Kingsway, London WC2B 6PQ
020 7242 6393 Fax 020 7242 6394
68–69 Bull Street, Birmingham B4 6AD
0121 236 9696 Fax 0121 236 9699
33 Wine Street, Bristol BS1 2BQ
0117 9264306 Fax 0117 9294515
9–21 Princess Street, Manchester M60 8AS
0161 834 7201 Fax 0161 833 0634
16 Arthur Street, Belfast BT1 4GD
028 9023 8451 Fax 028 9023 5401
The Stationery Office Oriel Bookshop
The Friary, Cardiff CF1 4AA
029 2039 5548 Fax 029 2038 4347
71 Lothian Road, Edinburgh EH3 9AZ
0131 228 4181 Fax 0131 622 7017

The Parliamentary Bookshop
12 Bridge Street, Parliament Square,
London SW1A 2JX
Telephone orders 020 7219 3890
General enquiries 020 7219 3890
Fax orders 020 7219 3866

Accredited Agents
(see Yellow Pages)

and through good booksellers

ISBN 0 11 840373 7

THIS PUBLICATION

relates to

the Public General Acts
and General Synod Measures
which received the Royal Assent in 1998
in which year ended the FORTY-SIXTH YEAR
and began the FORTY-SEVENTH YEAR
of the Reign of HER MAJESTY
QUEEN ELIZABETH THE SECOND
and
ended the First session
and began the Second session
Of the Fifty-Second Parliament
Of the United Kingdom of Great Britain
and Northern Ireland

CONTENTS

TABLE I
Alphabetical List of
the Public General Acts of 1998

h

i

TABLE II

Chronological List of

the Public General Acts of 1998

* Consolidation Act

TABLE III
Alphabetical List of
the Local and Personal Acts of 1998

There were no personal acts passed during the year 1998

l

TABLE IV
Chronological List of
the General Synod Measures of 1998

Measures passed by the General Synod of the Church of England which received the Royal Assent during the year 1998

		Part	Page
No. 1.	National Institutions Measure	III	2471

TABLE V

Tables of the Derivations and Destinations
of the Consolidation Acts of 1998

These Tables have no official status. They are intended only as a help in tracing the derivation of the Consolidation Acts and the destination of the enactments consolidated.

CONTENTS

PETROLEUM ACT 1998 (c. 17)
TABLE OF DERIVATIONS

(For Table of Destinations see page viii)

Notes:

1. This Table shows the derivation of the provisions of the Act.

2. The following abbreviations are used in the Table:—

Acts of Parliament

1934	= The Petroleum (Production) Act 1934 (c. 36)
1964	= The Continental Shelf Act 1964 (c. 29)
1975	= The Petroleum and Submarine Pipe-lines Act 1975 (c. 74)
1982	= The Oil and Gas (Enterprise) Act 1982 (c. 23)
1987	= The Petroleum Act 1987 (c. 12)
1992	= The Offshore Safety Act 1992 (c. 15)

Subordinate legislation

1992 N.I.	= The Offshore, and Pipelines, Safety (Northern Ireland) Order 1992 (S.I. 1992/1728 (N.I. 17))
1993	= The Offshore Safety (Repeals and Modifications) Regulations 1993 (S.I. 1993/1823)
1993 N.I.	= The Offshore Safety (Repeals and Modifications) Regulations (Northern Ireland) 1993 (S.R. (N.I.) 1993 No.384)
1995	= The Offshore Installations and Pipeline Works (Management and Administration) Regulations 1995 (S.I. 1995/738)
1995 N.I.	= The Offshore Installations and Pipeline Works (Management and Administration) Regulations (Northern Ireland) 1995 (S.R. (N.I.) 1995 No.340)

3. The functions of the Board of Trade under 1934 were transferred to the Minister of Fuel and Power by the Ministers of the Crown (Minister of Fuel and Power) Order 1942 (S.R. & O. 1942 No. 1132) Art.2(1)(a) and the Ministry of Fuel and Power Act 1945 (c. 19) s.1.

4. The style and title of the Minister of Fuel and Power was changed to "the Minister of Power" by the Minister of Fuel and Power (Change of Style and Title) Order 1957 (S.I. 1957/48) Art.1.

5. The functions of the Minister of Power under 1934 were transferred to the Minister of Technology by the Minister of Technology Order 1969 (S.I. 1969/1498) Art.2(1).

6. The functions of the Minister of Technology under 1934 were transferred to the Secretary of State by the Secretary of State for Trade and Industry Order 1970 (S.I. 1970/1537) Art.2(2).

7. The functions of the Minister for the Civil Service under section 27 of 1975 were transferred to the Treasury by the Transfer of Functions (Minister for the Civil Service and Treasury) Order 1981 (S.I. 1981/1670) Art.2(1).

8. The functions of the Treasury under section 27 of 1975 were transferred to the Minister for the Civil Service under the Treasury and Minister for the Civil Service) Order 1995 (S.I. 1995/269) Art.2(1).

Provision	Derivation
1	1934 s.1(4)
2(1)	1934 s.1(1); 1982 s.18(1).
(2), (3)	1934 s.1(2); 1982 s.18(1).
(4)	1934 s.1(3); 1982 s.18(1); drafting.
3(1)	1934 s.2(1); 1982 s.18(3).
(2)	1934 s.2(1); 1964 s.1(3).
(3)	1934 s.2(2).

PETROLEUM ACT 1998 (c. 17)
—continued

Provision	Derivation
	TABLE OF DERIVATIONS—*continued*
(4)	Drafting.
4(1)(a)	1934 s.6(1)(a).
(b)	Drafting.
(c) to (e)	1934 s.6(1)(b) to (d).
(2)	1934 s.6(1).
(3)	1934 s.6(2); Statutory Instruments Act 1946 (c.36) s.5(2).
(4)	1934 s.2(3).
(5)	1975 s.19(2).
5	Drafting.
6(1)	1975 s.41(3).
(2)	1982 s.30(1).
(3)	1975 s.41(3).
7(1)	1934 s.3(1); Mines (Working Facilities and Support) Act 1966 (c.4) Sch.2 para.1(a); 1987 s.19(2).
(2)	1934 s.3(1)(a).
(3)	1934 s.3(1)(b); Mines (Working Facilities and Support) Act 1966 (c.4) Sch.2 para.1(b).
(4)	1934 s.3(2); Railway and Canal Commission (Abolition) Act 1949 (c.11) s.1(1).
8	1934 s.7; Section 7 of the Petroleum (Production) Act 1934 and Section 2(1)(a) of the Petroleum Act 1987 (Modification) Regulations 1997 (S.I. 1997/2703) reg.2.
9(1), (2)	1934 s.10(2), (3).
(3)	1975 s.19(5).
10(1)	1982 s.22(1).
(2), (3)	1982 s.22(2).
(4) to (6)	1982 s.22(3) to (3B); 1987 s.24(5).
(7), (8)	1982 s.22(4), (5).
(9)	1982 s.22(6); Territorial Sea Act 1987 (c.49) Sch.1 para.7(1).
(10)	1982 s.22(7).
(11)	1982 s.32(2).
11(1) to (5)	1982 s.23 (1) to (5).
(6)	1982 s.22(7).
(7)	1982 s.32(2).
(8)	1982 s.23(6).
12(1)	1982 s.27(1)(a), (c).
(2)	1982 s.27(2); 1987 s.13(7); Merchant Shipping Act 1995 (c.21) Sch.13 para.65(1); Interpretation Act 1978 (c.30) s.17(2); 1992 s.3(1)(d); 1992 N.I. Art.5(1)(b); Value Added Tax Act 1994 (c.23) Sch.13 para.1(3).
(3)	1982 s.27(3), (4).
(4)	1982 s.27(5).
(5)	1982 s.27(6); 1992 s.3(1)(d); 1992 N.I. Art.5(1)(b); 1993 reg.6; 1993 N.I. reg.6; drafting.
13	1982 s.28(1).

Provision	Derivation
	TABLE OF DERIVATIONS—*continued*
14(1)	1975 s.20(1); Petroleum and Submarine Pipe-lines Act 1975 (Commencement) Order 1975 (S.I. 1975/2120).
(2)	1975 s.20(2).
15(1) to (4)	1975 s.21(1) to (4).
(5) to (8)	1975 s.21(5).
16(1), (2)	1975 s.22(1); 1982 s.25(2).
(3), (4)	1975 s.22(2), (3).
17(1), (2)	1975 s.23(1).
(3), (4)	1975 s.23(2).
(5)	1975 s.23(3); 1982 s.25(3).
(6)	1975 s.23(3).
(7) to (9)	1975 s.23(4) to (6).
18(1)	1975 s.24(1).
(2) to (4)	1975 s.24(2).
(5)	1975 s.24(3).
(6) to (8)	1975 s.24(4).
(9)	1975 s.24(5).
19(1)	1975 s.25(1).
(2), (3)	1975 s.25(2).
20(1)	1975 s.27(1).
(2)	1975 s.27(2).
(3)	1975 s.27(2A); 1993 reg.5(3).
(4)	1993 N.I. reg.5(3).
(5)	1975 s.46(1).
21(1)	1975 s.28(1); Interpretation Act 1978 (c.30) Sch.1; Magistrates' Courts Act 1980 (c.43) s.32(2); Criminal Procedure (Consequential Provisions) (Scotland) Act 1995 (c.40) sch.1 para.2; Criminal Procedure (Scotland) Act 1995 (c.46) s.225(8); Fines and Penalties (Northern Ireland) Order 1984 (S.I. 1984/703 (N.I.3)) Art.4(1).
(2)	1975 s.28(2)(a).
(3) to (5)	1975 s.28(3) to (5).
22(1)	1975 s.29(1); drafting.
(2), (3)	1975 s.29(2).
(4)	1992 s.3(1)(c); 1992 N.I. Art.5(1)(a).
(5)	1975 s.29(3).
(6), (7)	1975 s.29(4).
(8), (9)	1975 s.29(5), (6).
23(1), (2)	1975 s.30(1); Fatal Accidents Act 1976 (c.30) Sch.1 para.2; Fatal Accidents (Northern Ireland) Order 1977 (S.I. 1977/1251 (N.I. 18)) Sch.1 para.8.
(3) to (6)	1975 s.30(2) to (5).
24(1), (2)	1975 s.31(1), (2).
(3), (4)	1975 s.31(3).

PETROLEUM ACT 1998 (c. 17)
—continued

Provision	Derivation
	TABLE OF DERIVATIONS—*continued*
(5)	1975 s.46(1).
25(1), (2)	1975 s.32(1), (2).
(3)	1975 s.32(3); Criminal Justice Act 1988 (c.33) s.51(4); Criminal Procedure (Consequential Provisions) (Scotland) Act 1995 (c.40) Sch.1 para.7; Criminal Justice (Northern Ireland) Order 1994 (S.I. 1994/2795 (N.I.15)) Art.6(4).
(4)	1975 s.32(4).
(5)	1975 s.32(4); 1993 reg.4(3).
(6)	1993 N.I. reg.4(3).
(7) to (10)	1975 s.46(1); drafting.
26(1), (2)	1975 s.33(1); 1982 s.25(1).
(3)	1975 s.33(2).
27	1975 s.33(3).
28(1)	1975 s.33(5), s.48(1).
(2), (3)	1975 s.33(6), (7).
(4), (5)	1975 s.48(2).
(6), (7)	1975 s.48(3).
29	1987 s.1.
30(1) to (4)	1987 s.2(1) to (4).
(5) to (7)	Mineral Workings (Offshore Installations) Act 1971 (c.61) s.12(2), (3); 1982 Sch.3 para.11(2).
(8), (9)	1987 s.2(5), (6)
31	1987 s.3(2) to (7).
32	1987 s.4.
33	1987 s.5.
34	1987 s.6.
35	1987 s.7.
36	1987 s.8.
37	1987 s.9.
38	1987 s.10.
39	1987 s.11.
40	1987 s.12.
41	1987 s.13.
42	1987 s.14.
43	1987 s.15.
44	1987 s.16(1); Mineral Workings (Offshore Installations) Act 1971 (c.61) s.1; 1982 s.24; drafting.
45	1987 s.16(1).
46	1982 s.29.
47	1975 s.42.
48(1)	Mineral Workings (Offshore Installations) Act 1971 (c.61) s.1(4); 1982 ss.24(1), 28(1); Territorial Sea Act 1987 (c.49) Sch.1 paras.2, 7.

PETROLEUM ACT 1998 (c. 17)
—continued

Provision	Derivation
	TABLE OF DERIVATIONS—*continued*
(2)	Drafting.
(3)	1975 s.33(9); 1982 s.28(2); 1987 s.16(2); drafting.
49 to 51	—
52(1)	—
(2)	1982 s.38(2).
(3), (4)	—
(5)	1982 s.32(1); drafting.
53	—
Sch. 1	Drafting.
Sch. 2	
para.1(1), (2)	1975 Sch.4 para.1.
(3)	1975 s.46(1).
para.2, 3	1975 Sch.4 para.2, 3.
para.4(1), (2)	1975 Sch.4 para.4.
(3)	1975 Sch.4 para.6.
para.5 to 10	1975 Sch.4 para.5 to 10.
Sch. 3	
para.1, 2	Drafting.
para.3	1934 s.1(1); 1982 s.18(1).
para.4	Drafting.
para.5(1), (2)	1934 s.11(2) proviso.
(3)	1934 s.1(3); 1982 s.18(1).
para.6(1)	1975 s.19(6).
(2)	1975 s.19(3).
para.7, 8	Drafting.
para.9	1993 reg.6(1); 1993 N.I. reg.6(1).
para.10, 11	Drafting.
para.12	1982 s.25(4).
para.13	Fatal Accidents Act 1976 (c.30) Sch.1 para.2.
Sch. 4	
para.1	1934 s.9.
para.2(1), (2)	Drafting.
(3)	1982 Sch.3 para.2.
(4)	1975 s.45(1).
para.3	—
para.4	1975 s.45(2).
para.5 to 7	—
para.8	1982 Sch.3 para.24.
para.9	—
para.10, 11	1982 Sch.3 para.35, 36.
para.12	—

PETROLEUM ACT 1998 (c. 17)
—continued

Provision	Derivation
	TABLE OF DERIVATIONS—*continued*
para.13	1982 Sch.3 para.38.
para.14 to 19	—
para.20	1975 s.45(3).
para.21 to 33	—
para.34	Trade Union and Labour Relations (Consolidation) Act 1992 (c.52) Sch.2 para.29.
para.35 to 39	—
para.40	Employment Rights Act 1996 (c.18) Sch.1 para.18.
para.41	—
Sch. 5	1982 Sch.4 (repeal of Employment (Continental Shelf) Act 1978 (c.46)); remainder drafting.

PETROLEUM ACT 1998 (c. 17)
TABLE OF DESTINATIONS

Notes:

1. This Table shows how the enactments proposed to be repealed are dealt with by the consolidation.

2. The following abbreviations are used in the Table:—

Acts of Parliament

1934	= The Petroleum (Production) Act 1934 (c. 36)
1964	= The Continental Shelf Act 1964 (c. 29)
1975	= The Petroleum and Submarine Pipe-lines Act 1975 (c. 74)
1982	= The Oil and Gas (Enterprise) Act 1982 (c. 23)
1987	= The Petroleum Act 1987 (c. 12)
1992	= The Offshore Safety Act 1992 (c. 15)

Subordinate legislation

1992 N.I.	= The Offshore, and Pipelines, Safety (Northern Ireland) Order 1992 (S.I. 1992/1728 (N.I. 17))
1993	= The Offshore Safety (Repeals and Modifications) Regulations 1993 (S.I. 1993/1823)
1993 N.I.	= The Offshore Safety (Repeals and Modifications) Regulations (Northern Ireland) 1993 (S.R. (N.I.) 1993 No.384)
1995	= The Offshore Installations and Pipeline Works (Management and Administration) Regulations 1995 (S.I. 1995/738)
1995 N.I.	= The Offshore Installations and Pipeline Works (Management and Administration) Regulations (Northern Ireland) 1995 (S.R. (N.I.) 1995 No.340)

3. The functions of the Board of Trade under 1934 were transferred to the Minister of Fuel and Power by the Ministers of the Crown (Minister of Fuel and Power) Order 1942 (S.R. & O. 1942 No. 1132) Art.2(1)(a) and the Ministry of Fuel and Power Act 1945 (c.19) s.1.

4. The style and title of the Minister of Fuel and Power was changed to "the Minister of Power" by the Minister of Fuel and Power (Change of Style and Title) Order 1957 (S.I. 1957/48) Art.1.

5. The functions of the Minister of Power under 1934 were transferred to the Minister of Technology by the Minister of Technology Order 1969 (S.I. 1969/1498) Art.2(1).

6. The functions of the Minister of Technology under 1934 were transferred to the Secretary of State by the Secretary of State for Trade and Industry Order 1970 (S.I. 1970/1537) Art.2(2).

7. The functions of the Minister for the Civil Service under section 27 of 1975 were transferred to the Treasury by the Transfer of Functions (Minister for the Civil Service and Treasury) Order 1981 (S.I. 1981/1670) Art.2(1).

8. The functions of the Treasury under section 27 of 1975 were transferred to the Minister for the Civil Service under the Treasury and Minister for the Civil Service) Order 1995 (S.I. 1995/269) Art.2(1).

Existing Provision	Subject matter	Provision of 1998 Act	Remarks
	THE PETROLEUM (PRODUCTION) ACT 1934 (c.36)		
1(1)	Vesting of petroleum in His Majesty.	2(1); Sch. para.3	Substituted 1982 s.18(1).
(2)		2(2), (3)	Substituted 1982 s.18(1); repealed in part 1987 s.19(1).
(3)		2(4); Sch. para.5(3)	Substituted 1982 s.18(1).
(4)	Meaning of "petroleum".	1	Renumbered 1982 s.18(1).

PETROLEUM ACT 1998 (c. 17)
—continued

Existing Provision	Subject matter	Provision of 1998 Act	Remarks
	THE PETROLEUM (PRODUCTION) ACT 1934 (c.36)—continued		
2(1)	Licences to search for and get petroleum.	3(1), (2)(a)	Amended 1982 s.18(2); unnecessary in part.
(2)		3(3)	
(3)		4(4)	
3(1)	Provisions as to compulsory acquisition of rights to enter on land, etc.	7(1) to (3)	Repealed in part Public Utilities Street Works Act 1950 (c.39) Sch.5; extended 1964 s.1(3); amended Mines (Working Facilities and Support) Act 1966 (c.4) Sch.2 para.1; 1987 s.19(2); proviso spent (see Water Act 1989 (c.15) Sch.27).
(2)		7(4)	Modified Railway and Canal Commission (Abolition) Act 1949 (c.11) s.1(1).
4	Power to supply natural gas.	—	Repealed 1982 s.12(2).
5	Account of receipts and expenditure under Act.	—	Repealed 1975 s.16(3).
6(1)	Power to make regulations	4(1)(a), (c) to (e), (2)	Extended 1964 s.1(3); spent in part.
(2)		—	Superseded Statutory Instruments Act 1946 (c.36) s.5(2).
7	Power to inspect plans of mines.	8	Substituted Section 7 of the Petroleum (Production) Act 1934 and Section 2(1)(a) of the Petroleum Act 1987 (Modification) Regulations 1997 (S.I. 1997/2703) reg.2.
8	Exercise of powers and duties of Board of Trade.	—	Repealed Ministry of Fuel and Power Act 1945 (c.19) Sch.3.
9	Definition of minerals in Mining Industry Act 1926.	Sch. para.1.	
10(1)	Savings.	—	Repealed 1982 Sch.4.
(2), (3)		9(1), (2)	
11(1)	Short title, repeal and extent.	—	Spent.
(2)		Sch. para.5(1), (2)	Spent in part.
(3)		—	Repealed 1987 Sch.3.
Schedule	Licences in force under the Petroleum (Production) Act 1918.	Sch. para.5(1)	Repealed in part Statute Law (Repeals) Act 1978 (c.45) Sch.1 Pt.XVII.
	THE MINES AND QUARRIES ACT 1954 (c. 70)		
Sch.4 para. relating to 1934	Amended 1934 s.7.	—	Spent (see Section 7 of the Petroleum (Production) Act

PETROLEUM ACT 1998 (c. 17)
—continued

Existing Provision	Subject matter	Provision of 1998 Act	Remarks
	THE MINES AND QUARRIES ACT 1954 (c. 70)—*continued*		
			1934 and Section 2(1)(a) of the Petroleum Act 1987 (Modification) Regulations 1997 reg.2 which substituted 1934 s.7).
	THE CONTINENTAL SHELF ACT 1964 (c. 29)		
1(3)	Exploration and exploitation of petroleum in continental shelf.	3(2)(b)	
Words in (8)		—	Spent.
	THE MINES (WORKING FACILITIES AND SUPPORT) ACT 1966 (c. 4)		
15(5)	Introduces Sch.2.	—	Spent.
Sch.2			
para.1		7	Amends 1934 s.3.
para.2, 3		—	Para.2 repealed Coal Industry Act 1994 (c.21) Sch.11 Pt.II; para.3 repealed Town and Country Planning Act 1971 (c.78) Sch.25, Town and Country Planning (Scotland) Act 1972 (c.52) Sch.23.
	THE OIL TAXATION ACT 1975 (c. 22)		
21(5)	Construction of references to licences under section 2 of the Petroleum (Production) Act 1934.	—	Unnecessary (see (1) and (2)(b) and Sch. para.7).
	THE PETROLEUM AND SUBMARINE PIPE-LINES ACT 1975 (c. 74)		
Part I	The British National Oil Corporation.	—	S.1 repealed Oil and Gas Act 1985 (c.62) Sch.4 Pt.II; remainder repealed ibid. Pt.I.
17	Modification of model clauses for incorporation in petroleum production licences.	—	Superseded ; spent in part.
18(1), (2)	Incorporation of modified model clauses into existing licences.	—	Superseded 5.
(3)		—	Superseded 5.
(4)		—	
(5)		5(8)	Para.(a) unnecessary; para.(b) amended Requirements of Writing (Scotland) Act 1995 (c.7) Sch.4 para.48.
19(1)	Provisions supplementary to section 18.	—	Superseded 5.
(2)		4(5)	
(3)		Sch. 3 para.6(2)	
(4)		—	Superseded 5(9).
(5)		9(3)	

PETROLEUM ACT 1998 (c. 17)
—continued

Existing Provision	Subject matter	Provision of 1998 Act	Remarks
THE PETROLEUM AND SUBMARINE PIPE-LINES ACT 1975 (c. 74)—*continued*			
(6)		Sch. para.6(1)	
(7)		—	Unnecessary.
20	Control of construction and use of pipe-lines in territorial and continental-shelf waters.		
21(1) to (4)	Authorisations for pipe-lines.	15(1) to (4)	
(5)		15(5) to (8)	
22(1)	Compulsory increases in capacity etc. of pipe-lines.	16(1), (2)	Amended and repealed in part 1982 s.25(2).
(2), (3)		16(3), (4)	
23(1)	Acquisition by persons of rights to use pipe-lines belonging to others.	17(1), (2)	
(2)		17(3), (4)	
(3)		17(5), (6)	Para.(d) amended 1982 s.25(3).
(4) to (6)		17(7) to (9)	
24(1)	Termination of authorisations.	18(1)	
(2)		18(2) to (4)	
(3)		18(5)	
(4)		18(6) to (8)	Unnecessary in part.
(5)		18(9)	
25(1)	Vesting of pipe-lines on termination or subsequent issue of authorisations.	19(1)	
(2)		19(2), (3)	
(3)		—	Amended 1982 s.8(2); unnecessary.
26	Safety.	—	Repealed 1993 reg.3(2)(a), 1993 N.I. reg.3(2)(a).
27(1), (2)	Inspectors etc.	20(1), (2)	Subs.(2) repealed in part 1993 reg.3(2)(b), 1993 N.I. reg.3(2)(b).
(2A) (for England and Wales and Scotland)		20(3)	Inserted 1993 reg.5(3).
(2A) (for Northern Ireland)		20(3), (4)	Inserted 1993 N.I. reg.5(3).
(3) to (6)		—	Repealed 1993 reg.3(2)(b), 1993 N.I. reg.3(2)(b).
28	Enforcement.	21	Subs.(1) modified Magistrates' Courts Act 1980 (c.43) S.32(2), Criminal Procedure (Consequential Provisions) (Scotland) Act 1995 (c.40) Sch.1 para.2, Criminal Procedure (Scotland) Act

PETROLEUM ACT 1998 (c. 17)
—continued

Existing Provision	Subject matter	Provision of 1998 Act	Remarks
THE PETROLEUM AND SUBMARINE PIPE-LINES ACT 1975 (c. 74)—*continued*			1995 (c.46) s.224(8), Fines and Penalties (Northern Ireland) Order 1984 (S.I. 1984 (N.I.3)) Art.4(1); para.(b) unnecessary in part; subs.(2)(b) repealed 1992 s.3(1)(c), 1992 N.I. Art.5(1)(a).
29(1)	Criminal proceedings.	22(1)	
(2)		22(2), (3)	Repealed in part 1992 s.3(1)(c), 1992 N.I. Art.5(1)(a) (see 22(4)).
(3)		22(5)	
(4)		22(6), (7)	
(5), (6)		22(8), (9)	
30(1)	Civil liability for breach of statutory duty.	23(1), (2); Sch. para.13	Extended Fatal Accidents Act 1976 (c.30) Sch.1 para.2; amended Fatal Accidents (Northern Ireland) Order 1977 (S.I. 1977/1251 (N.I.18)) Sch.1 para.8.
(2) to (5)		23(3) to (6)	
31	Exclusion of application of Part III.	24	
32(1), (2)	Regulations.	25(1), (2)	
(3)		25(3)	Modified Criminal Justice Act 1988 (c.33) s.51(4); Criminal Procedure (Consequential Provisions) (Scotland) Act 1995 (c.40) Sch. 1 para.7; Criminal Justice (Northern Ireland) Order 1994 (S.I. 1994/2795 (N.I.15)) Art.6(4).
(4)		25(4), (5)	Modified 1993 reg.4(3), 1993 N.I. reg.4(2).
33(1), (2)	Interpretation etc. of Part III.	26	Subs.(1)(aa) inserted 1982 s.25(1).
(3)		27	
(4)		—	Unnecessary (see Interpretation Act 1978 (c.30) s.14).
(5) to (7)		28(1) to (3)	
(8)		—	Unnecessary.
(9)		48(3)	
Part IV	Refineries.	—	Repealed 1987 s.28.
40	The National Oil Account.	—	Subs.(1), (4) repealed 1982 s.8(3); subs.(2), (3) amended

PETROLEUM ACT 1998 (c. 17)
—continued

Existing Provision	Subject matter	Provision of 1998 Act	Remarks
	THE PETROLEUM AND SUBMARINE PIPE-LINES ACT 1975 (c. 74)—*continued*		
			and repealed in part 1982 s.4(1), (6), 8(2), (3); unnecessary.
41(1), (2)	Payments to petroleum licence holders.	—	Repealed 1982 s.30(2).
(3)		6(1), (3)	
(4)		—	Amended 1982 s.8(2)(b); repealed in part 1982 s.30(2); unnecessary.
42(1)	Loans etc. to promote development of United Kingdom resources.	47(1)	
(2)		47(2), (3)	Unnecessary in part.
(3)		47(4), (5)	
(4)		47(6)	
43	Payments in respect of Burmah Oil Co. Ltd.	—	Spent.
44	Extension of Mineral Workings (Offshore Installations) Act 1971 (c.61) s.6.		Subs.(1) to (4) repealed 1982 Sch.3 para.30; subs.(5) spent (extends Mineral Workings (Offshore Installations) Act 1971 (c.61) s.6 which was repealed 1993 reg.3(1)(e), 1993 N.I. reg.3(1)(e)).
45(1)	Amendments of enactments.	Sch. 4 para.2(3).	Modifies 1964 s.8.
(2)		Sch. para.4	Amends Prevention of Oil Pollution Act 1971 (c.60) s.23.
(3)		Sch. para.20	Modifies Food and Environment Protection Act 1985 (c.48) Pt. II; amended ibid. s.15(3), (4)(b); repealed in part 1982 Sch.3 para.31.
46	Orders and regulations.	20(5), 24(5), 25(7) to (9), Sch. para.1(3)	Subs.(1) repealed in part and subs.(2) repealed Oil and Gas Act 1985 (c.62) Sch.4 Pt.I; unnecessary in part; spent in part.
47	Expenses.	—	Unnecessary.
48(1)	Interpretation etc.—general.	28(1) ("controlled pipe-line", "controlled waters", "enactment", "notice", "prescribed")	Unnecessary in part ("functions", "regulations"); repealed in part Oil and Gas Act 1985 (c.62) Sch.4 Pt.I ("the Corporation", "relevant subsidiary", "subsidiary").
(2)		28(4), (5)	
(3)		28(6), (7)	

PETROLEUM ACT 1998 (c. 17)
—continued

Existing Provision	Subject matter	Provision of 1998 Act	Remarks
	THE PETROLEUM AND SUBMARINE PIPE-LINES ACT 1975 (c. 74)—*continued*		
(4)		—	Unnecessary (see Interpretation Act 1978 (c.30) s.20(2)).
(5)		—	Unnecessary.
49(1), (2)	Short title, commencement and extent.		Spent.
(3)		53(1)	Unnecessary in part.
Sch.1	Additional provisions relating to constitution etc. of British National Oil Corporation.	—	Repealed Oil and Gas Act 1985 (c.62) Sch.4 Pt.II.
Sch.2	Production licences for seaward areas.	—	Superseded ; amended 1982 Sch.2; 1987 Sch.1, 2.
Sch.3	Production licences for landward areas.	—	Superseded ; amended 1982 Sch.2; 1987 Sch.1, 2.
Sch.4	Authorisations in pursuance of section 20(1).	Sch.	
	THE FATAL ACCIDENTS ACT 1976 (c. 30)		
Words in sch.1 para.2(2)	Extension of reference to Fatal Accidents Act 1846.	23(1); Sch. para.13	
	THE EMPLOYMENT (CONTINENTAL SHELF) ACT 1978 (c. 46)		
1	Powers to apply employment legislation in relation to foreign sectors of continental shelf.	—	Prospectively repealed 1982 Sch.4; subs.(1) repealed Trade Union and Labour Relations (Consolidation) Act 1992 (c.52) Sch.1.
2	Interpretation	—	Prospectively repealed 1982 Sch.4.
	THE OIL AND GAS (ENTERPRISE) ACT 1982 (c. 23)		
1 to 7	The British National Oil Corporation.	—	Repealed Oil and Gas Act 1985 (c.62) Sch.4 Pt.I.
8	Abolition of the National Oil Account.	—	Spent.
9 to 17	Gas.	—	Repealed Gas Act 1986 (c.44) Sch.9.
18(1)	Amendment of 1934.	2; Sch. para.3, 5(3).	Unnecessary in part.
(2)		—	Amends 1934 s.2; unnecessary.
19(1)	Modification of model clauses in existing licences.	—	Superseded 5.
(2)		5(8)	Amended Requirements of Writing (Scotland) Act 1995 (c.7) Sch.4 para.50.
(3)		—	Superseded 5(9).
20	Modification of model clauses for incorporation in future licences.	—	Superseded 5.
21	Safety zones around installations.	—	Repealed 1987 s.24(4).
22(1)	Application of criminal law etc.	10(1)	
(2)		10(2), (3)	

PETROLEUM ACT 1998 (c. 17)
—continued

Existing Provision	Subject matter	Provision of 1998 Act	Remarks
	THE OIL AND GAS (ENTERPRISE) ACT 1982 (c. 23)—*continued*		
(3), (3A), (3B)		10(4) to (6)	Substituted 1987 s.24(5).
(4), (5)		10(7), (8)	
(6)		10(9)	Definition of "cross-boundary field" substituted Territorial Sea Act 1987 (c.49) Sch.1 para.7(1).
(7)		10(10), (6)	
(8)		—	Spent.
23	Application of civil law.	11(1) to (5), (8)	
25(1)	Extended meaning of "pipe-line" etc. in the 1975 Act.	26(2)(b)	Inserts 1975 s.33(1)(aa).
(2)		16(1)(b)	Amends 1975 s.22(1); spent in part.
(3)		17(5)(d)	Amends 1975 s.25(3)(d).
(4)		Sch. para.10	
(5)		—	Spent.
27(1)	Prosecutions.	12(1), (5)	Para.(b) spent in part; para.(d) repealed 1987 s.24(6)(a).
(2)(a)		12(2)(e)	Substituted Merchant Shipping Act 1995 (c.21) Sch.13 para.65.
(b)		12(2)(c)	Substituted ibid.
(c)		12(2)(d)	
(d)		12(2)(f)	
(e)		12(2)(a)	
(f)		12(2)(b)	
(g)		12(2)(f)	Inserted 1987 s.13(7).
(3)		12(3)(a)	Amended 1987 s.24(6)(b); repealed in part 1992 s.3(1)(d).
(4)		12(3)(b)	Amended 1987 s.24(6)(b); repealed in part 1992 N.I. Art.5(1)(b).
(5)		12(4)	
(6)		12(5)(b)	Regulations under Mineral Workings (Offshore Installations) Act 1971 (c.61) saved by 1993 reg.6, 1993 N.I. reg.6.
(7)		—	Spent.
28(1)	Interpretation of Part IV.	48(1); ("instal-lation")	Definition of "foreign sector of the continental shelf" substituted Territorial Sea Act 1987 (c.49) Sch.1 para.7(2); definition of

Tables of Derivations and Destinations

PETROLEUM ACT 1998 (c. 17)
—continued

Existing Provision	Subject matter	Provision of 1998 Act	Remarks
	THE OIL AND GAS (ENTERPRISE) ACT 1982 (c. 23)—*continued*		
			"statutory maximum" repealed Statute Law (Repeals) Act 1993 (c.50) Sch.1 Pt.XIV. Gp.2; remainder (definitions of "submersible apparatus", "vessel") unnecessary.
(2)		48(3)	
29	Northern Ireland and Isle of Man shares of petroleum revenue.	46	
30(1)	Payments to petroleum production licence holders etc.	6(2)	
(2)		—	Spent.
32(1)	Provisions as to regulations, orders etc.	52(5)	Repealed in part Gas Act 1986 (c.44) Sch.9 Pt.I, II.
(2)		10(11), (7)	Repealed in part Oil and Gas Act 1985 (c.62) Sch.4 Pt.I; Gas Act 1986 (c.44) Sch.9 Pt.II.
(3)		—	Repealed Gas Act 1986 (c.44) Sch.9 Pt.II.
33	Stamp duty.	—	Repealed ibid.
34	Application of Trustee Investments Act 1961.	—	Repealed ibid.
35	Financial provisions.	—	Unnecessary.
36	General interpretation.	—	Repealed in part Oil and Gas Act 1985 (c.62) Sch.4 Pt.I; Gas Act 1986 (c.44) Sch.9 Pt.II; unnecessary.
Sch.1	Provisions as to transfers of property, rights and liabilities.	—	Repealed Gas Act 1986 (c.44) Sch.9 Pt.II.
Sch.2	Petroleum production licences: modification of model clauses.	—	Superseded 5.
Sch.3			
para.2		—	Superseded Sch. para.2(2).
para.5, 6		—	Repealed Gas Act 1986 (c.44) Sch.9 Pt.I.
paras.7, 8 (part), 9, 10		—	Spent.
paras.12 to 20		—	Repealed Gas Act 1986 (c.44) Sch.9 Pt.I.
para.21		—	Repealed Social Security (Consequential Provisions) Act 1992 (c.6) Sch.1.
para.22		—	Spent.
para.23		—	Repealed (for England and Wales and Scotland) Local

PETROLEUM ACT 1998 (c. 17)

—continued

Existing Provision	Subject matter	Provision of 1998 Act	Remarks
\multicolumn{4}{c}{THE OIL AND GAS (ENTERPRISE) ACT 1982 (c. 23)—*continued*}			
			Government Act 1988 (c.41) Sch.13; unnecessary otherwise.
para.24		—	Superseded Sch. para.8.
para.25		—	Repealed Trade Union and Labour Relations (Consolidation) Act 1992 (c.52) Sch.1.
para.26		—	Repealed Oil and Gas Act 1985 (c.62) Sch.4 Pt.II.
paras.27, 28		—	Repealed ibid Pt.I.
para.29		—	Repealed 1987 Sch.3.
paras.30, 31		—	Spent.
para.32		—	Repealed Oil and Gas Act 1985 (c.62) Sch.4 Pt I.
para.33		—	Repealed ibid Pt.II.
paras.35, 36, 38, 39		—	Superseded Sch. paras.10, 11, 13, 14.
para.40		—	Repealed Employment Rights Act 1996 (c.18) Sch.3.
para.41		—	Repealed Wages Act 1986 (c.48) Sch.5 Pt.II.
para.42, 43		—	Superseded Sch. para.17.
para.44		—	Repealed Social Security (Consequential Provisions) Act 1992 (c.6) Sch.1.
para.45		—	Inserted Trade Union and Labour Relations (Consolidation) Act 1992 (c.52) Sch.2 para.29(3); superseded Sch. para.34.
para.46		—	Inserted Employment Rights Act 1996 (c.18) Sch.1 para.18(1); superseded Sch. para.40.
Sch.4	Repeals	Sch. 5 (repeal of Employment (Continental Shelf) Act 1978 (c.46))	Remainder spent.
\multicolumn{4}{c}{THE TELECOMMUNICATIONS ACT 1984 (c. 12)}			
107(3)	Application to territorial waters and the continental shelf etc.	—	Spent.
\multicolumn{4}{c}{THE FOOD AND ENVIRONMENT PROTECTION ACT 1985 (c. 48)}			
15(4)(b)	Amends 1975 s.45(3).	—	Superseded Sch. para.20.

PETROLEUM ACT 1998 (c. 17)
—*continued*

Existing Provision	Subject matter	Provision of 1998 Act	Remarks
	THE PETROLEUM ACT 1987 (c. 12)		
1	Preparation of programmes.	29	
2(1)	Persons who may be required to submit programmes.	30(1), (5) to (7)	Para.(a) repealed in part Section 7 of the Petroleum (Production) Act 1934 and Section 2(1)(a) of the Petroleum Act 1987 (Modification) Regulations 1997 (S.I. 1997/2703) reg.3, Section 2(1)(a) of the Petroleum Act 1987 (Modification) Regulations (Northern Ireland) 1997 (S.R. (N.I) No.528).
(2) to (4)		30(2) to (4)	
(5), (6)		30(8), (9) 3(1)	
3(1)	Section 1 notices: supplementary provisions.	—	Spent.
(2) to (7)		31	
4	Approval of programmes.	32	
5	Failure to submit programmes.	33	
6	Revision of programmes.	34	
7	Withdrawal of approval.	35	
8	Duty to carry out programmes.	36	
9	Default in carrying out programmes.	37	
10	Financial resources.	38	
11	Regulations.	11	Subs.(2)(a) repealed in part 1993 reg.3(3), 1993 N.I. reg.3(3).
12	Offences: penalties.	40	
13(1) to (6)	Offences: general.	41	
(7)		12(2)(f)	
14	Validity of Secretary of State's acts.	42	
15	Notices.	43	
16(1)	Interpretation of Part I.	44, 45	
(2)		48(3)	
17	Existing licences.	—	Superseded 5.
18	Future licences.	—	Superseded 5.
19	Northern Ireland territorial waters.	48(1)	Subs.(1) spent.
20	Annual reports.	—	Spent.
24(4)		—	Spent.
(5)	Amends 1982 s.22.	10(4) to (6)	
(6)			Spent.
28	Construction of refineries.	—	Repeals 1975 ss.34 to 39; spent.
31(2)(a)	Commencement.	—	Spent.

PETROLEUM ACT 1998 (c. 17)
—continued

Existing Provision	Subject matter	Provision of 1998 Act	Remarks
	THE PETROLEUM ACT 1987 (c. 12)—continued		
Sch.1	Amendment of existing licences.	—	Superseded 5.
Sch.2	Amendment of model clauses.	—	Superseded 5.
	THE PILOTAGE ACT 1987 (c. 21)		
Sch.2			
para.5		—	Spent (amends 1982 s.27(2)(a), which was substituted Merchant Shipping Act 1995 (c.21) Sch.13 para.65(a)).
	THE TERRITORIAL SEA ACT 1987 (c. 49)		
Sch.1			
para.7(1)		10(9)	Amends 1982 s.22(6).
(2)		48	Amends 1982 s.28.
	THE OFFSHORE SAFETY ACT 1992 (c. 15)		
Words in 1(3)(c)		—	Spent (see 1993 reg.3(3)).
(5)(b)		Sch. para.33(2)(d); 1992 s.1(5)(d)	
words in (c)		Sch. para.33(2)(d); 1992 s.1(5)(d)	
3(1)(c)		22(4)	
(d)		12(4)	Spent in part.
	THE TRADE UNION AND LABOUR RELATIONS (CONSOLIDATION) ACT 1992 (c. 52)		
287(5)		—	Prospectively repealed 1982 Sch.3 para.45.
Sch.2		Sch.	Inserts 1982 Sch.3 para.45.
para.29		para.34	
	THE REQUIREMENTS OF WRITING (SCOTLAND) ACT 1995 (c. 7)		
Sch.4			
para.48		5(8)	Amends 1975 s.18(5)(b).
para.50		5(8)	Amends 1982 s.19(2).
	THE MERCHANT SHIPPING ACT 1995 (c. 21)		
Sch.13			
para.65(1)		12(2)(c), (e)	Substitutes 1982 s.27(2)(a), (b).
(2)		—	Amends definition of "submersible apparatus" in 1982 s.28(1); spent.
	THE CRIMINAL PROCEDURE (CONSEQUENTIAL PROVISIONS) (SCOTLAND) ACT 1995 (c. 40)		
Sch.4			
para.40		—	Amends definition in 1982 s.28(1) of "the statutory maximum" which was

PETROLEUM ACT 1998 (c. 17)
—continued

Existing Provision	Subject matter	Provision of 1998 Act	Remarks
**THE CRIMINAL PROCEDURE (CONSEQUENTIAL PROVISIONS) (SCOTLAND) ACT 1995 (c. 40)—continued**			
			repealed Statute Law (Repeals) Act 1993 Sch.1 Pt.XIV Gp.2; spent.
**THE EMPLOYMENT RIGHTS ACT 1996 (c. 18)**			
201(5)		—	Prospectively repealed 1982 Sch.3 para.46.
Sch.1			
para.18		Sch. para.40	Inserts 1982 Sch.3 para.46.
**THE FATAL ACCIDENTS (NORTHERN IRELAND) ORDER 1977 (S.I. 1977/1251 (N.I. 18))**			
Sch.1			
para.8		23(2)	Amends 1975 s.30(1).
**THE OFFSHORE, AND PIPELINES, SAFETY ORDER 1992 (S.I. 1992/1972 (N.I. 17))**			
Words in Art. 3(3)(c)		—	Spent (see 1993 N.I. reg.3(3)).
(5)(b)		Sch. para.35(d); 1992 N.I. Art.3(5)(d)	
words in (c)		Sch. 4 para.35(d); 1992 N.I. Art.3(5)(d)	
Art.5(1)(b)		12(4)	Spent in part.
**THE OFFSHORE SAFETY (REPEALS AND MODIFICATIONS) REGULATIONS 1993 (S.I. 1993/1823)**			
Reg.4(3)		25(5)	Modifies 1975 s.32(4).
**THE OFFSHORE SAFETY (REPEALS AND MODIFICATIONS) REGULATIONS (NORTHERN IRELAND) 1993 (S.R. (N.I.) 1993 No. 384)**			
Reg.4(2)		25(6)	Modifies 1975 s.32(4).
**THE SECTION 7 OF THE PETROLEUM (PRODUCTION) ACT 1934 AND SECTION 2(1)(a) OF THE PETROLEUM ACT 1987 (MODIFICATION) REGULATIONS 1997 (S.I. 1997/2703)**			
Reg.1	Citation, commencement and extent.	—	Spent in part;; unnecessary in part.
Reg.2		8	substitutes 1934 s.7.
Reg.3		—	Repeals in part 1987 s.2(1)(a).
**THE SECTION 2(1)(a) OF THE PETROLEUM ACT 1987 (MODIFICATION) REGULATIONS (NORTHERN IRELAND) 1997 (S.R. (N.I.) 1997 No.528)**			
Reg.1	Citation and commencement.	—	
Reg.2		—	Repeals in part 1987 s.2(1)(a).

AUDIT COMMISSION ACT 1998 (c. 18)
TABLE OF DERIVATIONS

(For Table of Destinations see page xxviii)

Notes:

1. This Table shows the derivation of the provisions of the Act.

2. The following abbreviations are used in the Table:

1982	=	Local Government Finance Act 1982 (c. 32)
1988	=	Education Reform Act 1988 (c. 40)
1990	=	National Health Service and Community Care Act 1990 (c. 19)
1991	=	Local Government Finance (Publicity for Auditors' Reports) Act 1991 (c. 15)
1992	=	Local Government Act 1992 (c. 19)
1996	=	Audit (Miscellaneous Provisions) Act 1996 (c. 10)

3. The Table does not separately acknowledge the provisions in the Criminal Justice Act 1982 (c.48) and the Criminal Justice Act 1991 (c.53) by virtue of which references to the amount of the maximum fines to which persons are liable in respect of offences were translated into levels on the standard scale and the financial penalties imposed for the commission of offences were increased.

Provision	Derivation
1(1)	1982 s.11(1); 1990 Sch. 4 para. 1(1).
(2)	1982 s.11(2) (part); 1990 Sch. 4 para. 1(2)(a), (b).
(3)	1982 s.11(3) (part).
(4)	1982 s.11(2), (3) (part); 1990 Sch.4 para.1(2)(c).
(5)	1982 s.11(4).
2(1)	1982 s.12(1).
(2)	1982 s.12(2) to (3A) (part), s.31(1) (part).
3(1), (2)	1982 s.13(1), (2).
(3), (4)	1982 s.13(3), (4); 1990 Sch. 4 para. 3(1).
(5)	1982 s.13(5) (part), (5A); 1990 Sch. 4 para. 3(2), (3).
(6)	1982 s.13(5) (part).
(7), (8)	1982 s.13(6), (7).
(9)	1982 s.13(8) (part), (9); 1992 s.29(1).
(10)	Drafting.
(11)	1982 s.13(8) (part).
4(1)	1982 s.14(1) (part); 1992 s.29(1).
(2)	1982 s.14(1) (part); 1990 Sch. 4 para. 4(1).
(3) to (6)	1982 s.14(2) to (5).
(7)	1982 s.14(6), (7); 1990 Sch. 4 para. 4(2).
5(1)	1982 s.15(1); 1990 Sch. 4 para. 5; 1992 s.3(1).
(2)	1982 s.15(2).
6(1), (2)	1982 s.16(1); Local Government Act 1988 (c.9) s.30(2); 1992 s.29(1).
(3)	1982 s.16(1A); 1990 Sch. 4 para. 6.
(4), (5)	1982 s.16(2), (3); Local Government Act 1988 (c.9) s.30(2); 1992 s.29(1).
(6), (7)	1982 s.16(4), (5).
7(1)	1982 s.21(1).
(2)	1982 s.21(2), (2A); 1990 Sch. 4 para. 11.

AUDIT COMMISSION ACT 1998 (c. 18)
—continued

Provision	Derivation
	TABLE OF DERIVATIONS—*continued*
(3), (4)	1982 s.21(3), (4).
(5), (6)	1982 s.21(5).
(7), (8)	1982 s.21(6), (7).
(9)	1982 s.35(3) (part).
8	1982 s.15(3).
9(1), (2)	1982 s.18(1), (2).
10(1)	1982 s.18(3) (part).
(2)	1982 s.18(4); 1990 Sch.4 para. 8.
(3)	1982 s.18(3) (part); 1992 s.5(5).
(4), (5), (6)	1982 s.18(5); Local Government (Access to Information) Act 1985 (c.43) Sch. 2 para. 7.
11(1)	1992 s.5(1) (part).
(2)	1992 ss.5(6)(a), 28(2); Environment Act 1995 (c.25) Sch.7 para.19(1).
(3)	1992 s.5(1) (part).
(4), (5)	1992 s.5(2)(a), (b).
(6), (7)	1992 ss.5(3).
(8), (9)	1992 s.5(4), (7).
12(1)	1992 s.6(1).
(2)	1992 s.6(2), (4)(a).
(3), (4)	1992 s.6(3), (5).
13(1)	1982 s.18A(6); 1991 s.1(2); drafting.
(2), (3)	1982 s.18A(1), (2); 1991 s.1(2).
(4)	1982 s.18A(5); 1991 s.1(2).
(5), (6)	1982 s.18A(3), (4); 1991 s.1(2).
(7)	1982 s.18A(7); 1991 s.1(2).
14(1)	1982 s.24(1); 1990 Sch. 4 para. 14; 1991 s.1(3).
(2) to (4)	1982 s.24(2) to (4).
15(1)	1982 s.17(1); 1990 Sch. 4 para. 7.
(2)	1982 s.17(2).
(3)	Local Government and Housing Act 1989 (c.42) s.11(1) (part), (3) ("relevant body").
(4)	Local Government and Housing Act 1989 (c.42) s.11(2) (part).
(5)	Local Government and Housing Act 1989 (c.42) s.11(3) (part).
16(1) to (3)	1982 s.17(3) to (5).
17(1)	1982 s.19(1); 1990 Sch. 4 para. 9.
(2) to (5)	1982 s.19(2) to (5)
(6)	1982 ss.19(6); The High Court and County Courts Jurisdiction Order 1991 (S.I. 1991/724) Sch.
(7)	1982 ss.19(7), 36(3)(b); Norfolk and Suffolk Broads Act 1988 (c.4) s.17(12); Police and Magistrates' Courts Act 1994 (c.29) Sch. 4 para.26; Environment Act 1995 (c.25) Sch. 7 para. 19(2); Police Act 1996 (c.16) Sch. 7 paras. 1(1), (2)(s); Police Act 1997 (c.50) Sch.6 para.20.

AUDIT COMMISSION ACT 1998 (c. 18)
—continued

Provision	Derivation
	TABLE OF DERIVATIONS—*continued*
18(1)	1982 s.20(1) (part); 1990 Sch. 4 para. 10.
(2)	1982 s.20(1) (part).
(3)	1982 s.20(2) (part), (3) (part).
(4)	1982 s.20(3) (part).
(5)	1982 s.20(2) (part), (3) (part).
(6)	1982 s.20(3) (part).
(7) to (11)	1982 s.20(4) to (8).
(12)	1982 s.20(9); The High Court and County Courts Jurisdiction Order 1991 (S.I. 1991/724) Sch; 1982 ss.20(10), 36(3)(b); Norfolk and Suffolk Broads Act 1988 (c.4) s.17(12); Police and Magistrates' Courts Act 1994 (c.29) Sch. 4 para.27; Environment Act 1995 (c.25) Sch. 7 para. 19(2); Police Act 1996 (c.16) Sch. 7 paras. 1(1), (2)(s); Police Act 1997 (c.50) Sch.6 para.21.
19	1990 s.20(3).
20(1), (2)	1982 s.25A(1); Local Government Act 1988 (c.9) s.30(1), Sch. 4; 1990 Sch. 4 para. 16.
(3) to (8)	1982 s.25A(2) to (7); Local Government Act 1988 (c.9) s.30(1) and Sch. 4.
21(1) to (3)	1982 s.25AA(1) to (3); Local Government Finance Act 1988 (c.41) Sch. 12 para. 3(3).
22(1) to (6)	1982 s.25B(1) to (6); Local Government Act 1988 (c.9) s.30(1), Sch. 4.
23(1), (2)	1982 25C(1), (2); Local Government Act 1988 (c.9) s.30(1), Sch. 4.
24(1)	1982 s.25D(1); Local Government Act 1988 (c.9) s.30(1), Sch. 4; 1990 Sch. 4 para. 17.
(2),(3)	1982 s.25D(2), (3); Local Government Act 1988 (c.9) s.30(1), Sch. 4.
25(1)	1982 s.22(1), (4A) (part); 1990 Sch. 4 para. 12(1), (2) (part).
(2)	1982 s.22(2).
(3)	1982 s.22(3), (4A) (part); 1990 Sch. 4 para. 12(1), (2) (part).
(4), (5)	1982 s.22(4), (5).
26(1)	1982 s.25(1) (part).
(2)	1982 s.25(1) (part), (2); 1990 Sch. 4 para. 15.
27(1)	1982 s.23(1); 1990 Sch. 4 para. 13.
(2)	1982 s.23(2).
(3)	1982 s.35(3) (part).
(4), (5)	1982 s.23(3), (4).
28(1)	1982 s.29(1); Local Government Finance Act 1988 (c.41) Sch. 12 para. 3(4); Local Government and Housing Act 1989 (c.42) s.184(2).
(2)	1982 s.29(5) (part).
29(1)	1982 s.29(3); 1990 Sch. 4 para. 20(2).
(2), (3)	1982 s.29(4).
(4)	1982 s.29(5) (part).
30(1)(a) to (c)	1982 s.31(1)(a) to (c); drafting.
(d)	1982 s.31(1)(ca); Local Government Finance (Publicity for Auditors' Reports) Act 1991 (c.15) s.1(4).

AUDIT COMMISSION ACT 1998 (c. 18)
—*continued*

Provision	Derivation
	TABLE OF DERIVATIONS—*continued*
(e)	1982 s.31(1)(d).
(2)	1982 s.31(3).
(3)	1982 s.31(2).
31(1)	1982 s.31(4); Transport Act 1985 (c.67) Sch. 7 para. 22(1).
(2)	1982 s.31(6); Transport Act 1985 (c.67) Sch. 7 para. 22(2).
(3)	1982 s.31(5); Companies Consolidation (Consequential Provisions) Act 1985 (c.9) Sch. 2.
32(1), (2)	1982 s.28F(1), (2); Police Act 1997 (c.50) Sch.6 para.22.
33(1)	1982 s.26(1).
(2)	1992 s.3(3) (part); Environment Act 1995 (c.25) Sch.7 para.19(1).
(3)	1982 s.27(6); 1990 Sch. 4 para. 19(2).
(4)	1982 s.26(2).
(5)	1982 s.26(3); 1990 Sch. 4 para. 18(1).
(6)	1982 s.26(4); 1990 Sch. 4 para. 18(2); 1992 s.3(3) (part).
34(1)	1982 s.27(1); 1990 Sch. 4 para. 19(1).
(2)	1982 s.27(2).
(3), (4)	1982 s.27(3).
(5), (6)	1982 s.27(4), (5).
35(1)	1982 s.29(2) (part).
(2)	1982 s.29(2) (part); 1990 Sch. 4 para. 20(1).
(3)	1982 s.29(5) (part).
36(1)	1988 s.220(1), (2); Further and Higher Education Act 1992 (c.13) Sch. 8 para. 51(2), (3); Education Act 1994 (c.30) Sch. 2 para. 8(5); Education Act 1996 (c.56) Sch.37 para.78.
(2)	1988 s.220(3); Further and Higher Education Act 1992 (c.13) Sch. 8 para. 51(4).
(3)	1988 ss.123(1), 220(4); Further and Higher Education Act 1992 (c.13) Sch. 8 para. 51(5).
(4)	1988 s.220(5); Further and Higher Education Act 1992 (c.13) ss.17(1), 90(1) ("higher education corporation").
(5)	1988 s.220(6).
(6)	1988 s.235(7); Education Act 1996 (c.56) s.578, Sch.37 para.81(4).
37(1) to (9)	1982 s.28AA(1) to (9); 1996 s.1(1).
38(1) to (9)	1982 s.28AB(1) to (9); Social Security Administration (Fraud) Act 1997 (c.47) s.6(2).
39(1), (2)	1982 s.28AC(1), (2); Social Security Administration (Fraud) Act 1997 (c.47) s.6(3).
40	1982 s.28B; Housing Act 1996 (c.52) Sch.3 para.2(1).
41(1) to (3)	1982 s.28C(1) to (3); Housing Act 1996 (c.52) Sch.3 para.2(1).
(4)	1982 s.28C(4) (part); Housing Act 1996 (c.52) Sch.3 para.2(1).
42	1982 s.28D; Housing Act 1996 (c.52) Sch.3 para.2(1).
43	1982 s.28E; Housing Act 1996 (c.52) Sch.3 para.2(1).
44(1)	1992 s.1(1).
(2)	1992 s.1(2), (6); 1996 s.5(1).

AUDIT COMMISSION ACT 1998 (c. 18)
—continued

Provision	Derivation
	TABLE OF DERIVATIONS—*continued*
(3)	1992 s.1(3) (part).
(4)	1992 s.1(4), (6).
(5)	1992 s.1(5)
(6)	1992 s.1(7)(a); Environment Act 1995 (c.25) Sch.7 para.19(1).
(7)	1992 s.1(8).
45(1) to (5)	1992 s.1A(1) to (5); 1996 s.5(2).
46(1) to (6)	1992 s.2(1) to (6).
47(1), (2)	1992 s.4(1), (3).
48(1)	1982 s.28(1); 1992 s.29(1).
(2)	Drafting.
(3)	1982 s.28(2).
(4), (5)	1982 s.28(3).
49(1)	1982 ss.30(1), (1A), 28C(4) (part); 1990 Sch. 4 para. 21; 1996 s.2(1); Housing Act 1996 (c.52) Sch.3 para.2(1); Social Security Administration (Fraud) Act 1997 (c.47) s.6(4)
(2)	Drafting.
(3)	1982 s.30(2); Interpretation Act 1978 (c. 30) Sch. 1 ("statutory maximum"); Criminal Justice Act 1988 (c.33) Sch. 15 para. 58(b).
50	1982 s.30A; Social Security Administration (Fraud) Act 1997 (c.47) s.6(5).
51(1)	1992 s.7(1), (2); Environment Act 1995 (c.25) Sch.7 para.19(1).
(2)	1992 s.7(3).
(3), (4)	1992 s.7(5), (6).
52(1)	1982 s.35(1); 1992 ss.1(3) (part), 4(2) (part).
(2)	1982 Sch.3 para.10(2) (part).
(3)	1982 s.35(2); 1992 ss.1(3) (part), 4(2) (part).
53(1)	
"the 1972 Act"	1982 s.18(6); Local Government (Access to Information) Act 1985 (c.43) Sch. 2 para. 7; 1992 s.28(1); drafting.
"allotted sum"	1982 s.12(3C), 16(1A) (part); 1990 Sch. 4 para. 2(2), 6.
"auditor"	1982 s.36(1); Transport Act 1985 (c.67) Sch. 7 para. 22(3); 1992 s.28(1), (2).
"body subject to audit"	Drafting.
"the Commission"	1982 s.36(1); 1990 Sch. 4 para. 23(a); drafting.
"the health service"	1982 s.14(7)(a) (part); 1990 Sch. 4 para. 4(2); drafting.
"health service body"	1982 s.12(5), 36(1); 1990 Sch. 4 paras. 2(3), 23(b).
"recognised fund-holding practice"	1982 s.36(1); 1990 Sch. 4 para. 23(b).
"statutory provision"	1982 s.36(1).

AUDIT COMMISSION ACT 1998 (c. 18)
—continued

Provision	Derivation
	TABLE OF DERIVATIONS—*continued*
(2)	1982 s.36(2); 1988 s.235(1); 1992 s.1(6) (part), s.28(1) ("financial year"); 1996 s.3(2).
(3)	1982 s.12(3) (part) and 12(3A) (part); Local Government Finance Act 1988 (c.41) Sch. 12 para. 3(2); 1990 Sch. 4 para. 2(2).
(4)	1982 ss.36(3) (part), (3A); Norfolk and Suffolk Broads Act 1988 (c.4) s.17(12); Environment Act 1995 Sch. 7 para. 19(3).
54	—
55	—
Sch. 1	
paras. 1, 2	1982 Sch. 3 paras. 1, 2.
para. 3	1982 Sch. 3 para. 3; 1990 Sch. 4 para. 24(1).
paras. 4, 5	1982 Sch. 3 paras. 4, 5.
para. 6	1982 Sch. 3 para. 6; 1990 s.20(8).
para. 7	1982 Sch. 3 para. 7(1) to (6).
para. 8(1)	1982 Sch. 3 para. 9; 1990 Sch. 4 para. 24(2).
(2)	1982 Sch. 3 para. 9(2); 1990 Sch. 4 para. 24(2); 1996 s.2(2); Housing Act 1996 (c.52) Sch.3 para.2(2); Education Act 1997 (c.44) Sch.7 para.5; Social Security Administration (Fraud) Act 1997 (c.47) Sch.1 para.1.
para. 9(1) to (5)	1982 Sch. 3 para. 10(1), (2) (part), (3) to (5).
para. 9(6)	1982 Sch. 3 para. 10(6); 1996 s.3(3)(a).
para. 9(7)	1982 Sch. 3 para. 10(7).
para. 10(1)	1982 Sch. 3 para. 11(1); Miscellaneous Financial Provisions Act 1983 (c.29) s.4(1), Sch. 2.
(2) to (5)	1982 Sch. 3 para. 11(2) to (5).
para. 11(1), (2)	1982 Sch. 3 para. 12(1), (2).
(3)	1982 Sch. 3 para. 12(3); 1996 s.3(3)(b).
(4)	1982 Sch. 3 para. 12(4).
(5)	1982 s.36(1A); 1996 s.3(1).
paras. 12 to 14	1982 Sch. 3 paras. 13 to 15.
Sch. 2	
para 1(a)	1982 s.12(2)(a).
(b)	1982 s.12(2)(aa); Local Government Act 1985 (c.51) s.72(3).
(c) to (f)	1982 s.12(2)(b) to (e).
(g)	1982 s.12(2)(ea); 1990 Sch. 4 para. 2(1).
(h)	1982 s.12(2)(f).
(i)	1982 s.12(2)(ff); Norfolk and Suffolk Broads Act 1988 (c.4) s.17(10).
(j)	1982 s.12(2)(fg); Environment Act 1995 (c.25) Sch. 7 para. 19(1).
(k)	1982 s.12(2)(g); Police and Magistrates' Courts Act 1994 (c.29) Sch. 4 para. 25; Police Act 1996 (c.16) Sch. 7 para. 1(1), (2)(s).
(l)	1982 s.12(2)(ga); Police Act 1997 (c.50) Sch.6 para.19.
(m) to (o)	1982 s.12(2)(h) to (j).

AUDIT COMMISSION ACT 1998 (c. 18)
—continued

Provision	Derivation
	TABLE OF DERIVATIONS—*continued*
(p)	1982 s.12(2)(l); Criminal Justice Act 1982 (c.48) s.65(1); Criminal Justice Act 1988 (c.33) Sch. 11 para. 8; Probation Service Act 1993 (c.47) Sch. 3 para. 6.
para. 2	
(a)	1982 s.12(3)(a); Local Government Finance Act 1988 (c.41) Sch. 12 para. 3(2).
(b)	1982 s.12(3)(b); Local Government Finance Act 1988 (c.41) Sch. 12 para. 3(2); Local Government Pension Scheme Regulations 1995 (S.I.1995/1019), Interpretation Act 1978 (c.30) ss.17(2)(a), 23(2).
para. 3(1)	1982 s.12(3A) (part); 1990 Sch. 4 para. 2(2); drafting.
(2)	1982 s.12(3B); 1990 Sch. 4 para. 2(2); Health Authorities Act 1995 (c.17) Sch. 1 para. 106.
para.4	1982 s.31(1) (part).
Sch. 3	—
Sch. 4	
paras.1 to 6	—
para.7	1982 s.12(4).
para.8	1990 s.20(8).
para.9	1982 Sch.3 para.8(3); 1990 s.20(6); Employment Rights Act 1996 (c.18) Sch.1 paras.19, 45(3)(a).
para.10	1996 s.3(5) (part).
Sch. 5	—

AUDIT COMMISSION ACT 1998 (c. 18)

TABLE OF DESTINATIONS

Notes:

1. This Table shows how the enactments proposed to be repealed are dealt with by the consolidation.

2. The following abbreviations are used in the Table:—

1982	= Local Government Finance Act 1982 (c. 32)
1988	= Education Reform Act 1988 (c. 40)
1990	= National Health Service and Community Care Act 1990 (c. 19)
1992	= Local Government Act 1992 (c. 19)
1996	= Audit (Miscellaneous Provisions) Act 1996 (c. 10)

3. The Table does not separately remark on the provisions in the Criminal Justice Act 1982 (c.48) and the Criminal Justice Act 1991 (c.53) by virtue of which references to the amount of the maximum fines to which persons are liable in respect of offences were translated into levels on the standard scale and the financial penalties imposed for the commission of offences were increased.

Existing Provision	Subject matter	Provision of 1998 Act	Remarks
	THE LOCAL GOVERNMENT FINANCE ACT 1982 (c.32)		
11(1)	Establishment of Audit Commission.	1(1)	Amended 1990 Sch.4 para.1(1).
(2)		1(2), (4)	Amended 1990 Sch.4 para.1(2).
(3)		1(3), (4)	
(4)		1(5)	
12(1)	Accounts subject to audit.	2(1)	
(2)		2(2)	
para.(a)		Sch.2 para.1(a)	
para.(aa)		Sch. 2 para.1(b)	Inserted Local Government Act 1985 (c.51) s.72(3).
para.(ab)		—	Inserted Local Government Act 1985 (c.51) s.72(3), repealed 1988 Sch.13 Pt.I.
paras.(b) to (e)		Sch. 2 para.1(c) to (f)	
para.(ea)		Sch. 2 para.1(g)	Inserted 1990 Sch.4 para.2(1).
para.(f)		Sch. 2 para.1(h)	
para.(ff)		Sch. 2 para.1(i)	Inserted Norfolk and Suffolk Broads Act 1988 (c.4) s.17(10).
para.(fg)		Sch. 2 para.1(j)	Inserted Environment Act 1995 (c.25) Sch.7 para.19(1).
para.(g)		Sch. 2 para.1(k)	Substituted Police and Magistrates' Courts Act 1994 (c.29) Sch.4 para.25, amended Police Act 1996 (c.16) Sch.7 para.1(1), (2)(s).
para.(ga)		Sch. 2 para.1(l)	Inserted Police Act 1997 (c.50) Sch.6 para.19.
paras.(h) to (j)		Sch. 2	

AUDIT COMMISSION ACT 1998 (c. 18)
—continued

Existing Provision	Subject matter	Provision of 1998 Act	Remarks
THE LOCAL GOVERNMENT FINANCE ACT 1982 (c.32)—*continued*			
		para.1(m) to (o)	
para.(k)		—	Superseded Health and Social Services and Social Security Adjudications Act 1983 (c.41) s.4.
para.(l)		Sch. 2 para.1(p)	Amended Criminal Justice Act 1982 (c.48) s.65(1), Criminal Justice Act 1988 (c.33) Sch.11 para.8, Probation Service Act 1993 (c.47) Sch.3 paras.1, 6.
(3)		2(2), (3)(a), Sch. 2 para.2	Substituted Local Government Finance Act 1988 (c.41) Sch.12 para.3(2); 1974 Regulations consolidated, see now Local Government Pension Scheme Regulations 1995 (S.I.1995/1019), Interpretation Act 1978 (c.30) ss.17(2)(a), 23(2).
(3A)		2(2), 53(3)(b), Sch. 2 para.3(1)	Inserted 1990 Sch.4 para.2(2).
(3B)		Sch. 2 para.3(2)	Inserted 1990 Sch.4 para.2(2); amended Health Authorities Act 1995 (c.17) Sch.1 para.106.
(3C)		53(1) ("allotted sum")	Inserted 1990 Sch.4 para.2(2).
(4)		Sch. para.7	
(5)		53(1) ("health service body")	Inserted 1990 Sch.4 para.2(3).
13(1), (2)	Appointment of auditors.	(1), (2)	
(3), (4)		3(3), (4)	Amended 1990 Sch.4 para.3(1).
(5)		3(5), (6)	Amended 1990 Sch.4 para.3(2).
(5A)		3(5)(c)	Inserted 1990 Sch.4 para.3(3).
(6), (7)		3(7), (8)	
(8)		3(9), (11)	
(9)		3(9)	
14(1)	Code of audit practice.	4(1), (2)	Amended 1990 Sch.4 para.4(1).
(2) to (5)		4(3) to (6)	
(6)		4(7)(b), (c)	
(7)		4(7)(a), (c),	Inserted 1990 Sch. 4 para.4(2).

AUDIT COMMISSION ACT 1998 (c. 18)
—*continued*

Existing Provision	Subject matter	Provision of 1998 Act	Remarks
	THE LOCAL GOVERNMENT FINANCE ACT 1982 (c.32)—*continued*		
		53(1) ("the health service")	
15(1)	General duties of auditors.	5(1)	Subs.(1)(a) amended 1990 Sch.4 para.5; subs.1(d) inserted 1992 s.3(1).
(2)		5(2)	
(3)		8	
16(1)	Auditor's right to obtain documents and information.	6(1), (2)	Amended Local Government Act 1988 (c.9) s.30(2).
(1A)		6(3), ("allotted sum")	Inserted 1990 Sch.4 para.6.
(2), (3)		6(4), (5)	Amended Local Government Act 1988 (c.9) s.30(2).
(4), (5)		6(6), (7)	
17(1)	Public inspection of accounts and right of challenge.	15(1)	Amended 1990 Sch.4 para.7.
(2)		15(2)	
(3) to (5)		16(1) to (3)	
8(1), (2)	Auditor's report.	9(1), (2)	
(3)		10(1), (3)	Amended 1992 s.5(5).
(4)		10(2)	Amended 1990 Sch.4 para.8.
(5)		10(4), (5), (6)	Amended Local Government (Access to Information) Act 1985 (c.43) Sch.2 para.7.
(6)		53(1) ("the 1972 Act")	Inserted Local Government (Access to Information) Act 1985 (c.43) Sch.2 para.7.
18A	Additional publicity for auditors' immediate reports.		Inserted Local Government Finance (Publicity for Auditors' Reports) Act 1991 (c.15) s.1(2).
(1), (2)		13(2), (3)	
(3), (4)		13(5), (6)	
(5)		13(4)	
(6)		13(1)	
(7)		13(7)	
19(1)	Declaration that item of account is unlawful.	17(1)	Amended 1990 Sch.4 para.9.
(2) to (5)		17(2) to (5)	
(6)		17(6)	Substituted The High Court and County Courts Jurisdiction Order 1991 (S.I.1991/724) Sch.
(7)		17(7)	Amended London Government Reorganisation

AUDIT COMMISSION ACT 1998 (c. 18)
—continued

Existing Provision	Subject matter	Provision of 1998 Act	Remarks
THE LOCAL GOVERNMENT FINANCE ACT 1982 (c.32)—*continued*			
			(Miscellaneous Provisions) (No. 7) Order 1986 (S.I. 1986/2293) Art.2, Police and Magistrates' Courts Act 1994 (c.29) Sch.4 para.26, Police Act 1996 (c.16) Sch.7 para.1(1), (2)(s), Police Act 1997 (c.50) Sch.6 para.20; repealed in part 1988 Sch.13 Pt.I; modified 1982 s.36(3)(b), Norfolk and Suffolk Broads Act 1988 (c.4) s.17(12), Environment Act 1995 (c.25) Sch.7 para.19(2).
20(1)	Recovery of amount not accounted for etc.	18(1), (2)	Amended 1990 Sch.4 para.10.
(2)		18(3)(a), (5)(a)	
(3)		18(3)(b), (4), (5)(b), (6)	Part unnecessary.
(4) to (8)		18(7) to (11)	
(9)		18(12)	Substituted The High Court and County Courts Jurisdiction Order 1991 (S.I.1991/724) Sch.
(10)		18(12)	Amended London Government Reorganisation (Miscellaneous Provisions) (No. 7) Order 1986 (S.I. 1986/2293) Art.2, Police and Magistrates' Courts Act 1994 (c.29) Sch.4 para.27, Police Act 1996 (c.16) Sch.7 paras.1(1) and 1(2)(s), Police Act 1997 (c.50) Sch.6 para.21; repealed in part 1988 Sch.13 Pt.I; modified 1982 s.36(3)(b), Norfolk and Suffolk Broads Act 1988 (c.4) s.17(12), Environment Act 1995 (c.25) Sch.7 para.19(2).
21(1)	Fees for audit.	7(1)	
(2)		7(2)(b), (c)	
(2A)		7(2)(a), (c)	Inserted 1990 Sch.4 para.11.
(3), (4)		7(3), (4)	
(5)		7(5), (6)	

AUDIT COMMISSION ACT 1998 (c. 18)
—continued

Existing Provision	Subject matter	Provision of 1998 Act	Remarks
	THE LOCAL GOVERNMENT FINANCE ACT 1982 (c.32)—continued		
(6), (7)		7(7), (8)	
22(1)	Extraordinary audit.	25(1)	Amended 1990 Sch.4 para.12(1).
(2)		25(2)	
(3)		25(3)(a)	Amended 1990 Sch.4 para.12(1).
(4)		25(4)	
(4A)		25(1)(b), (3)(b)	Inserted 1990 Sch.4 para.12(2).
(5)		25(5)	
23(1)	Regulations as to accounts.	27(1)	Amended 1990 Sch.4 para.13.
(2)		27(2)	
(3), (4)		27(4), (5)	
24(1)	Right to inspect statements of accounts and auditor's reports.	27(1)	Amended 1990 Sch.4 para.14, Local Government Finance (Publicity for Auditors' Reports) Act 1991 (c.15) s.1(3).
(2) to (4)		14(2) to (4)	
25(1)	Audit of accounts of officers.	26(1), (2)(b)	
(2)		26(2)(a)	Inserted 1990 Sch.4 para.15.
25A	Power of auditor to issue prohibition order.		Inserted Local Government Act 1988 (c.9) s.30(1), Sch.4.
(1)		20(1), (2)	Amended 1990 Sch.4 para.16.
(2) to (7)		20(3) to (8)	
25AA	Restriction on power to issue prohibition order.	21	Inserted Local Government Finance Act 1988 (c.41) Sch.12 para.3(3).
25B	Effect of and appeals against prohibition orders.	22	Inserted Local Government Act 1988 (c.9) s.30(1), Sch.4.
25C	Supplementary provisions as to prohibition orders.	23	Inserted Local Government Act 1988 (c.9) s.30(1), Sch.4.
25D	Power of auditor to apply for judicial review.		Inserted Local Government Act 1988 (c.9) s.30(1), Sch.4.
(1)		24(1)	Amended 1990 Sch.4 para.17.
(2), (3)		24(2), (3)	
26(1), (2)	Studies for improving economy etc. in services.	33(1), (4)	
(3)		33(5)	Amended 1990 Sch.4 para.18(1).
(4)		33(6)	Amended 1990 Sch.4 para.18(2).
27(1)	Reports on impact of statutory provisions etc.	34(1)	Amended 1990 Sch.4 para.19(1).
(2)		34(2)	

AUDIT COMMISSION ACT 1998 (c. 18)
—*continued*

Existing Provision	Subject matter	Provision of 1998 Act	Remarks
	THE LOCAL GOVERNMENT FINANCE ACT 1982 (c.32)—*continued*		
(3)		34(3), (4)	
(4), (5)		34(5), (6)	
(6)		33(3)	Inserted 1990 Sch.4 para.19(2).
28(1), (2)	Furnishing of information and documents to Commission.	48(1), (3)	
(3)		48(4), (5)	
28A	Functions of Commission in relation to national health service.	—	Repealed Health Authorities Act 1995 (c.17) Sch.3.
28AA	Collaborative studies of social services.	37	Inserted 1996 s.1(1).
28AB	Studies of benefit administration at request of Secretary of State.	38	Inserted Social Security Administration (Fraud) Act 1997 (c.47) s.6(2).
28AC	References and reports to Secretary of State.	39	Inserted Social Security Administration (Fraud) Act 1997 (c.47) s.6(3).
28B	Delivery of documents relating to police authorities to Secretary of State.	—	Inserted Police and Magistrates Courts Act 1994 (c.29) Sch.4 para.28; amended Police Act 1996 (c.16) Sch.7 para.1(1), (2)(s); s.28F substituted Police Act 1997 (c.50) Sch.6 para.22.
28B	General functions of Commission in relation to registered social landlords.	40	Inserted Housing Act 1996 (c.52) Sch.3 para.2(1).
28C	Provisions supplementary to s.28B.		Inserted Housing Act 1996 (c.52) Sch.3 para.2(1).
(1) to (3)		4(1) to (3)	
(4)		41(4), (1)(e)	
28D	Functions of Commission in relation to audit of accounts of registered social landlords.	42	Inserted Housing Act 1996 (c.52) Sch.3 para.2(1).
28E	Meaning of "the Corporation" and "registered social landlord".	43	Inserted Housing Act 1996 (c.52) Sch.3 para.2(1).
28F	Delivery of documents relating to police authorities etc. to Secretary of State.	32	Substituted by Police Act 1997 (c.50) Sch.6 para.22 for s.28B as inserted by Police and Magistrates Courts Act 1994 (c.29) Sch.4 para.28.
29(1)	Miscellaneous functions of Commission.	28(1)	Subs.(1)(c) inserted Local Government Finance Act 1988 (c.41) Sch.12 para.3(4); subs.(1)(d) and words after it inserted and subs.(1)(a) amended Local Government and Housing Act 1989 (c.42) s.184(2).

AUDIT COMMISSION ACT 1998 (c. 18)
—continued

Existing Provision	Subject matter	Provision of 1998 Act	Remarks
THE LOCAL GOVERNMENT FINANCE ACT 1982 (c.32)—continued			
(2)		35(1), (2)	Amended 1990 Sch.4 para.20(1).
(3)		29(1)	Amended 1990 Sch.4 para.20(2).
(4)		29(2), (3)	
(5)		28(2), 29(4), 35(3)	
30(1)	Restriction on disclosure of information.	49(1)	Subs.(1)(b) amended 1990 Sch.4 para.21; subs.(1)(ba) inserted Social Security Administration (Fraud) Act 1997 (c.47) s.6(4).
(1A)		49(1)(e)	Inserted 1996 s.2(1).
(2)		49(3)	
30A	Supply of benefit information to Commission.	50	Inserted Social Security Administration (Fraud) Act 1997 (c.47) s.6(5).
31(1)	Passenger transport executives and their subsidiaries.	30(1), Sch. 2 para.4	Subs.(1)(ca) inserted Local Government Finance (Publicity for Auditors' Reports) Act 1991 (c.15) s.1(4); part repealed London Regional Transport Act 1984 (c.32) Sch.6 para.26(a).
(2)		30(3)	Part repealed London Regional Transport Act 1984 (c.32) Sch.6 para.26(b).
(3)		30(2)	Part repealed London Regional Transport Act 1984 (c.32) Sch.6 para.26(c).
(4)		31(1)	Substituted Transport Act 1985 (c.67) Sch.7 para.22(1).
(5)		31.(3)	Amended Companies Consolidation (Consequential Provisions) Act 1985 (c.9) Sch.2; part unnecessary.
(6)		31(2)	Amended Transport Act 1985 (c.67) Sch.7 para.22(2).
32	Water authorities and National Water Council.	—	Repealed Water Act 1989 (c.15) Sch.27 Pt.I.
33(1) to (3)	Commencement of Part III and transitional provisions.	—	Spent.
(4)		—	Repealed in part London Regional Transport Act 1984 (c.32) Sch.7, Water Act 1989 (c.15) Sch.27 Pt.I; spent.

AUDIT COMMISSION ACT 1998 (c. 18)
—continued

Existing Provision	Subject matter	Provision of 1998 Act	Remarks
THE LOCAL GOVERNMENT FINANCE ACT 1982 (c.32)—continued			
(4A)		—	Inserted 1990 Sch.4 para.22(1); spent.
(5)		—	Amended 1990 Sch.4 para.22(2); spent.
34(1)	Consequential amendments.	—	Unnecessary.
(2)		—	Spent.
35(1), (2)	Orders and regulations.	52(1), (3)	
(3)		7(9), 27(3).	
36(1)	Interpretation.	53(1)	"the first appointed day" and "the second appointed day" spent; "auditor" amended Transport Act 1985 (c.67) Sch.7 para.22(3); "the Commission" amended 1990 Sch.4 para.23(a); "health service body" and "recognised fund-holding practice" inserted 1990 Sch.4 para.23(b).
(1A)		Sch. 1 para.11(5)	Inserted 1996 s.3(1).
(2)		53(2)	Amended 1996 s.3(2).
(3)		17(7)(c), (d), 18(12), 53(4)(a)	Inserted Norfolk and Suffolk Broads Act 1988 (c.4) s.17(12).
(3A)		53(4)(b)	Inserted Environment Act 1995 (c.25) Sch.7 para.19(3).
38(5), (6)	Savings for repeals.	—	Spent.
Sch.3		The Audit Commission.	
paras.1, 2		Sch. 1 paras.1, 2	
para.3		Sch. 1 para.3	Amended 1990 Sch.4 para.24(1).
para.4		Sch. 1 para.4	
para.5		Sch. 1 para.5	Sub-para.(4) repealed 1996 s.6(1).
para.6		Sch. 1 para.6	
para.7		Sch. 1 para.7	Sub-para.(7) spent.
para.8(1), (2)		—	Spent.
para.8(3)		Sch. 4 para.9(1)(a), (2)	Amended Employment Rights Act 1996 (c.18) Sch.1 para.19.
para.8(4)		—	Spent.
para.9		Sch. 1	Amended 1990 Sch.4

AUDIT COMMISSION ACT 1998 (c. 18)
—continued

Existing Provision	Subject matter	Provision of 1998 Act	Remarks
THE LOCAL GOVERNMENT FINANCE ACT 1982 (c.32)—*continued*			
		para.8	para.24(2), 1996 s.2(2), Housing Act 1996 (c.52) Sch.3 para.2(2), Education Act 1997 (c.44) Sch.7 para.5, Social Security Administration (Fraud) Act 1997 (c.47) Sch.1 para.1.
para.10		52(2), Sch. 1 para.9	Amended 1996 s.3(3)(a).
para.11		Sch. 1 para.10	Amended Miscellaneous Financial Provisions Act 1983 (c.29) s.4(1), Sch.2.
para.12		Sch. 1 para.11(1) to (4)	Amended 1996 s.3(3)(b).
paras.13 to 15		Sch. 1 paras.12 to 14	
Sch.5	Consequential amendments.		
para.1		Sch. 3 para.1	
para.2		—	Repealed Police and Magistrates' Courts Act 1994 (c.29) Sch.9 Pt.I.
para.3		Sch. 3 para.2	
para.4		—	Repealed London Regional Transport Act 1984 (c.32) Sch.7.
para.5		Sch. 3 para.3	
para.6		—	Repealed Water Act 1989 (c.15) Sch.27 Pt.I.
para.7		—	Repealed Water Consolidation (Consequential Provisions) Act 1991 (c.60) Sch.3 Pt.I.
para.8		Sch. 3 para.5	Sub-para.(3) repealed Local Government and Housing Act 1989 (c.42) Sch.12 Pt.I.
Sch.6 Pt.IV	Repeals	—	Spent
THE MISCELLANEOUS FINANCIAL PROVISIONS ACT 1983 (c.29)			
Sch.2 (the entry relating to the 1982 Act)	Amends 1982 Sch.3 para.11(1).	Sch.1 para.10(1)	
THE LONDON REGIONAL TRANSPORT ACT 1984 (c.32)			
Sch.6 para.26	Repeals 1982 s.31 in part	—	

AUDIT COMMISSION ACT 1998 (c. 18)
—continued

Existing Provision	Subject matter	Provision of 1998 Act	Remarks
THE COMPANIES CONSOLIDATION (CONSEQUENTIAL PROVISIONS) ACT 1985 (c.9)			
Sch.2 (the entry relating to the 1982 Act)	Amends 1982 s.31(5)	31(3)	
THE LOCAL GOVERNMENT (ACCESS TO INFORMATION) ACT 1985 (c.43)			
Sch.2 para.7	Amends 1982 s.18(5) and inserts s.18(6).	10(5), (6), 53(1)("the 1972 Act")	
THE LOCAL GOVERNMENT ACT 1985 (c.51)			
s.63(6)	Adaptation for pre-1982 accounts.	—	Spent.
s.72(3)	Inserts 1982 s.12(2)(aa), (ab).	Sch. 2 para.1(b)	
THE TRANSPORT ACT 1985 (c.67)			
Sch.3 para.8	Amends Transport Act 1968 (c.73) s.14(3)	Sch. 3 para.2	
Sch.7			
para.22(1)	Substitutes 1982 s.31(4).	31(1)	
para.22(2)	Amends 1982 s.31(6).	31(2)	
para.22(3)	Amends 1982 s.36("auditor").	53(1)("auditor")	
THE NORFOLK AND SUFFOLK BROADS ACT 1988 (c.4)			
s.17(10)	Inserts 1982 s.12(2)(ff).	Sch. 2 para.1(i)	
(12)	Inserts 1982 s.36(3).	17(7)(c), (d), 18(12), 53(4)(a)	
THE LOCAL GOVERNMENT ACT 1988 (c.9)			
30(1)	Introduces Sch.4	—	
(2)	Amends 1982 s.16.	6(1), (2), (4), (5)	
(3)	Commencement.	—	Spent.
(4)	Extent.	55(3)	
Sch.4	Inserts 1982 s.25A, 25B, 25C, 25D.	20,22,23,24	
THE CRIMINAL JUSTICE ACT 1988 (c.33)			
Sch.11 para.8	Amends 1982 s.12(2)(l).	Sch. 2 para.1(p)	
THE EDUCATION REFORM ACT 1988 (c.40)			
220(1)	Extension of functions of the Audit Commission.	36(1)	Amended Further and Higher Education Act 1992 (c.13) Sch.8 para.51(2), Education Act 1993 (c.35) s.10(2), Education Act 1994 (c.30) Sch.2 para.8(5)(a), Education Act 1996 (c.56) Sch.37 para.78(2).

AUDIT COMMISSION ACT 1998 (c. 18)
—*continued*

Existing Provision	Subject matter	Provision of 1998 Act	Remarks
	THE EDUCATION REFORM ACT 1988 (c.40)—*continued*		
(2)(a), (b)		36(1)	Substituted Further and Higher Education Act 1992 (c.13) Sch.8 para.51(3)(a).
(2)(ba), (bb)		36(1)	Inserted Further and Higher Education Act 1992 (c.13) Sch.8 para.51(3)(b).
(2)(bc), (bd)		36(1)	Inserted Education Act 1993 (c.35) s.10(3), Education Act 1996 (c.56) Sch.37 para.78(3).
(2)(c)		36(1)	Amended Education Act 1993 (c.35) s.10(4), Education Act 1996 (c.56) Sch.37 para.78(4).
(2)(d), (e)		36(1)	Inserted Education Act 1994 (c.30) Sch.2 para 8(5)(b).
(3)		36(2)	Substituted Further and Higher Education Act 1992 (c.13) Sch.8 para.51(4).
(4)		36(3)	Amended Further and Higher Education Act 1992 (c.13) Sch.8 para.51(5).
(5), (6)		36(4)(b), (5)	
	THE LOCAL GOVERNMENT FINANCE ACT 1988 (c.41)		
Sch.12			
para.3(1)	Introduces amendments.	—	
para.3(2)	Substitutes 1982 s.12(3).	2(2), 53(3)(a), Sch. 2 para.2	
para.3(3)	Inserts 1982 s.25AA.	21	
para.3(4)	Inserts 1982 s.29(1)(c).	28(1)(c)	
para.3(5)	Commencement.	—	Spent.
	THE LOCAL GOVERNMENT AND HOUSING ACT 1989 (c.42)		
11	Confidentiality of staff records	15(3), (4), (5)	Repealed only as applies to 1982 s.17.
66(5)(b)	Meaning of references to proper practices.	—	Reference to 1982 Pt.III: unnecessary.
184(2)	Amends 1982 s.29(1)	28(1)	
	THE NATIONAL HEALTH SERVICE AND COMMUNITY CARE ACT 1990 (c.19)		
20	Extension of functions etc. of Audit Commission to cover the health service.		
(1)	Introduces Schedule 4	—	
(3)		19	
(4), (5)		—	Spent.

AUDIT COMMISSION ACT 1998 (c. 18)
—continued

Existing Provision	Subject matter	Provision of 1998 Act	Remarks
THE NATIONAL HEALTH SERVICE AND COMMUNITY CARE ACT 1990 (c.19)—*continued*			
(6)		Sch. 4 para.9(1)(b), (2)	Amended Employment Rights Act 1996 (c.18) Sch.1 para.45(3)(a).
(7)		—	Spent.
(8)	Construction of enactments.	Sch. 4 para.8	
Sch.4			
para.1(1)	Amends 1982 s.11(1).	1(1)	
para.1(2)	Amends 1982 s.11(2).	1(2), (4)	
para.2(1)	Inserts 1982 s.12(2)(ea).	Sch. 2 para.1(g)	
para.2(2)	Inserts 1982 s.12(3A), (3B), (3C).	2(2), 53(1) ("allotted sum"), (3)(b), Sch. 2 para.3	
para.2(3)	Inserts 1982 s.12(5).	53(1) ("health service body")	
para.3(1)	Amends 1982 s.13(3), (4).	3(3), (4)	
para.3(2)	Amends 1982 s.13(5).	3(5)(c)	
para.3(3)	Inserts 1982 s.13(5A).	3(5)(c)	
para.4(1)	Amends 1982 s.14(1).	4(2)	
para.4(2)	Inserts 1982 s.14(7).	4(7)(a), (c), ("the health service")	
para.5	Amends 1982 s.15(1)(a).	5(1)(a)	
para.6	Inserts 1982 s.16(1A).	6(3), ("allotted sum")	
para.7	Amends 1982 s.17(1).	15(1)	
para.8	Amends 1982 s.18(4).	10(2)	
para.9	Amends 1982 s.19(1).	17(1)	
para.10	Amends 1982 s.20(1).	18(1)	
para.11	Inserts 1982 s.21(2A).	7(2)(a), (c)	
para.12	Amends 1982 s.22(1), (3), inserts 1982 s.22(4A)	25(1)(b), (3)(b)	
para.13	Amends 1982 s.23(1).	27(1)	
para.14	Amends 1982 s.24(1).	14(1)	
para.15	Inserts 1982 s.25(2).	26(2)(a)	
para.16	Amends 1982 s.25A(1).	20(1)	
para.17	Amends 1982 s.25D(1).	24(1)	
para.18(1)	Amends 1982 s.26(3).	33(5)	
para.18(2)	Amends 1982 s.26(4).	33(6)	

AUDIT COMMISSION ACT 1998 (c. 18)
—continued

Existing Provision	Subject matter	Provision of 1998 Act	Remarks
THE NATIONAL HEALTH SERVICE AND COMMUNITY CARE ACT 1990 (c.19)—*continued*			
para.19(1)	Amends 1982 s.27(1).	34(1)	
para.19(2)	Inserts 1982 s.27(6).	33(3)	
para.20(1)	Amends 1982 s.29(2).	35(2)(b)	
para.20(2)	Amends 1982 s.29(3).	29(1)(a)	
para.21	Amends 1982 s.30(1).	49(1)(c)	
para.22(1)	Inserts 1982 s.33(4A).	—	
para.22(2)	Amends 1982 s.33(5).	—	
para.23	Amends 1982 s.36(1).	53(1)	
para.24(1)	Amends 1982 Sch.3 para.3(3).	Sch.1 para.3(4)	
para.24(2)	Amends 1982 Sch.3 para.9 and inserts para.9(2).	Sch.1 para.8	
THE LOCAL GOVERNMENT FINANCE (PUBLICITY FOR AUDITORS' REPORTS) ACT 1991 (c.15)			
1(1)	Introduces amendments.	—	
(2)	Inserts 1982 s.18A.	13	
(3)	Amends 1982 s.24(1).	14(1)	
(4)	Inserts 1982 s.31(1)(ca).	30(1)(d)	
(5)	Saving.	—	Spent.
2(1)	Short title.	—	Unnecessary.
(2)	Commencement.	—	Spent.
(3)	Extent.	53(3)	
THE FURTHER AND HIGHER EDUCATION ACT 1992 (c.13)			
Sch.8			
para.51(1)	Introduces amendments.	—	
para.51(2)	Substitutes 1988 s.220(1)(a), (b), (c).	36(1)	
para.51(3)	Substitutes 1988 s.220(2)(a), (b) and inserts s.220(2)(ba), (bb).	36(1)	
para.51(4)	Substitutes 1988 s.220(3).	36(2)	
para.51(5)	Amends 1988 s.220(4).	36(3)	
THE LOCAL GOVERNMENT ACT 1992 (c.19)			
1(1)	Publication of information as to standards of performance.	44(1)	
(2)		44(2)	Amended 1996 s.5(1).
(3)		44(3), 52(1), (3)	
(4), (5)		44(4), (5)	
(6)		44(2), (4)	
(7)		44(6)	Modified Environment Act 1995 (c.25) Sch.7 para.19(1).
(8)		44(7)	
1A	Permitted methods of publishing information.	45	Inserted 1996 s.5(2).
2	Directions under s.1.	46	

AUDIT COMMISSION ACT 1998 (c. 18)
—continued

Existing Provision	Subject matter	Provision of 1998 Act	Remarks
	THE LOCAL GOVERNMENT ACT 1992 (c.19)*—continued*		
3	Functions of auditor and studies by the Commissions.		
(1)		5(1)(f)	Inserts 1982 s.15(1)(d).
(2)		—	Unrepealed: applies to Scotland only.
(3)		33(2), (6)	
4(1)	Application to parish and community councils and charter trustees.	47(1)	
(2)		52(1), (3)	
(3)		47(2)	
5(1)	Duty to consider auditor's report or recommendation.	11(1), (3)	
(2)		11(4), (5)	
(3)		11(6), (7)	
(4)		11(8)	
(5)		10(3)	Amends 1982 s.18(3).
(6)		11(2)	Para.(a) modified Environment Act 1995 (c.25) Sch.7 para.19(1); para.(b) unrepealed: applies to Scotland only.
(7)		11(9)	
6(1), (2), (3)	Publicity requirements for meetings under s.5.	12(1), (2), (3)	
(4)		12(2)	Paras.(b) and (c) unrepealed: apply to Scotland only.
(5)		12(4)	
7(1), (2)	Publication of information by the Commission.	51(1)	Modified Environment Act 1995 (c.25) Sch.7 para.19(1).
(3)		51(2)	
(4)		—	Spent.
(5), (6)		51(3), (4)	
28(1)	Interpretation		
"the 1982 Act"		—	Unnecessary.
"the Audit Commission"		53 ("the Commission"); Sch. para.24	
"auditor"		53 ("auditor")	
(2)		53 ("body subject to audit"); Sch. para.24	

AUDIT COMMISSION ACT 1998 (c. 18)
—continued

Existing Provision	Subject matter	Provision of 1998 Act	Remarks
	THE LOCAL GOVERNMENT ACT 1992 (c.19)—*continued*		
29(1)	Consequential amendment	3(9), 4(1), 6(1), (2), (4), (5), 48(1), Sch. 3 para.24	
30(2)	Commencement	—	Spent.
	THE PROBATION SERVICE ACT 1993 (c.47)		
Sch.3			
para.6	Amends 1982 s.12(2)(l).	Sch. 8 para.1(p)	
	THE POLICE AND MAGISTRATES' COURTS ACT 1994 (c.29)		
Sch.4			
para.25	Substitutes 1982 s.12(2)(g).	Sch. 2 para.1(k)	
para.26	Amends 1982 s.19(7).	17(7)(f)	
para.27	Amends 1982 s.20(10).	17(7)(f), (12)	
para.28	Inserts 1982 s.28B.	—	
	THE EDUCATION ACT 1994 (c.30)		
Sch.2			
para.8(1)	Introduces amendments.	—	Unnecessary: para.8(2) to (4) repealed Education Act 1996 (c.36) Sch.38 Pt.I.
para.8(5)(a)	Inserts 1988 s.220(1)(aa).	36(1)	
para.8(5)(b)	Inserts 1988 s.220(2)(d), (e).	36(1)	
	THE HEALTH AUTHORITIES ACT 1995 (c.17)		
Sch.1 para.106	Amends 1982 s.12(3B)	Sch. 2 para.3(2)	
	THE ENVIRONMENT ACT 1995 (c.25)		
Sch.7			
para.19(1)	Inserts 1982 s.12(2)(fg), modifies 1992 ss.1 to 7.	Sch. 2 para.1(j)	
para.19(2)	Modifies 1982 s.19, 20.	17(7)(e), 18(12)	
para.19(3)	Inserts 1982 s.36(3A).	53(4)(b)	
	THE LONDON LOCAL AUTHORITIES ACT 1995 (c. x)		
Sch. Pt.I	Application of 1982 s.16.	Sch. 3 para.30	
	THE AUDIT (MISCELLANEOUS PROVISIONS) ACT 1996 (c.10)		
1(1)	Inserts 1982 s.28AA.	37	
(2)	Commencement.	—	Spent.
2(1)	Inserts 1982 s.30(1A).	49(1)(e)	Part 1982 s.30(1A) unnecessary.
(2)	Amends 1982 Sch.3 para.9(2).	Sch.1 para.8(2)	

AUDIT COMMISSION ACT 1998 (c. 18)
—continued

Existing Provision	Subject matter	Provision of 1998 Act	Remarks
	THE AUDIT (MISCELLANEOUS PROVISIONS) ACT 1996 (c.10)—*continued*		
3(1)	Inserts 1982 s.36(1A).	Sch. 1 para.11(5)	
(2)	Amends 1982 s.36(2).	53(2)	
(3)	Amends 1982 Sch.3 paras.10(6) and 12(3).	Sch.1 paras.9(6) and 11(3)	
(4)	Commencement	—	Spent
(5)	Transitional provision	Sch. 4 para.10	Part spent.
5(1)	Amends 1992 s.1(2)(b).	44(2)(b)	
(2)	Inserts 1992 s.1A.	45	
6(1)	Repeals 1982 Sch.3 para.5(4).	—	Spent.
(2)	Commencement.	—	Spent.
	THE POLICE ACT 1996 (c.16)		
Sch.7 para.1(2)(s)	Amends 1982 ss.12(2)(g), 19(7), 20(10), 28B(1), (2)(a).	17(7)(f), 18(12), Sch. 2 para.1(k)	For 1982 s.28B see 1982 s.28F.
	THE EMPLOYMENT RIGHTS ACT 1996 (c.18)		
Sch.1 para.19	Amends 1982 Sch.3 para.8(3)	Sch. para.9	
para. 45(3)(a)	Amends 1990 s.20(6)	Sch. para.9	
	THE HOUSING ACT 1996 (c.52)		
Sch.3 para.2(1)	Inserts 1982 ss.28B, 28C, 28D, 28E	40, 41, 42, 43, 49(1)(e)	
para.2(2)	Inserts 1982 Sch.3 para.9(2)(aa), (ab)	Sch. 1 para.8(2)(c), (d)	
	THE EDUCATION ACT 1996 (c.56)		
Sch.37 para.78	Amends 1988 s.220	36	Continues effect of Education Act 1993 (c.35) s.10.
	THE EDUCATION ACT 1997 (c.44)		
Sch.7 para.5	Inserts 1982 Sch.3 para.9(2)(ac)	Sch. 1 para.8(2)(e)	
	THE SOCIAL SECURITY ADMINISTRATION (FRAUD) ACT 1997 (c.47)		
s.6(1)	Introduces amendments.	—	
(2)	Inserts 1982 s.28AB	38	
(3)	Inserts 1982 s.28AC	39	
(4)	Inserts 1982 s.30(1)(ba)	49(1)(d)	
(5)	Inserts 1982 s.30A	50	
Sch.1 para.1	Inserts 1982 Sch.3 para.9(2)(aza)	Sch. 1 para.8(2)(b)	
	THE POLICE ACT 1997 (c. 50)		
Sch.6			

Tables of Derivations and Destinations

AUDIT COMMISSION ACT 1998 (c. 18)
—continued

Existing Provision	Subject matter	Provision of 1998 Act	Remarks
THE POLICE ACT 1997 (c. 50)—*continued*			
para.19	Inserts 1982 s.12(2)(ga).	Sch. 2 para.1(l)	
para.20	Amends 1982 s.19(7).	17(7)(g)	
para.21	Amends 1982 s.20(10).	18(12)	
para.22	Substitutes 1982 s.28F.	32	
THE HIGH COURT AND COUNTY COURTS JURISDICTION ORDER 1991 (S.I.1991/724)			
In the Schedule, in Part 1, the entry relating to 1982	Substitutes 1982 s.19(6), 20(9).	17(6), 18(12)	

TABLE VI

Acts and Measures (in chronological order)
repeated, amended or otherwise affected
by those Acts, Measures and Statutory Instruments
which received the Royal Assent or were made during 1998

LIST OF ABBREVIATIONS

am................	amended	ext................	extended	restr..............	restricted
appl..............	applied	GSM.............	General Synod Measure	(*retrosp.*).......	retrospectively
appt. day/days	appointed day/days	incorp.	incorporated	SI..................	Statutory Instrument
CAM	Church Assembly Measure	(L.)...............	local (S.I.)	subst.	substituted
cont..............	continued	mod..............	modified	(*temp.*)..........	temporarily
defn/defns. of	definition/definitions of	(mods.)..........	with modifications	trans.............	transfer
excl...............	excluded	(*prosp.*)..........	prospectively	spec. provns. .	specified provisions
expld.	explained	rep................	repealed	in pt.	in part/partially

Year and Chap. or No. of Measure	Short title	How affected	1998, Chapter of Act or Number of Measure or Statutory Instrument
1533 (25 Hen. 8) c.34	Attainder of John Wolff and others Act 1533	rep. (Isle of Man)	43, s.1(1), Sch.1, Pt.X, Group 5
1571 (13 Eliz. 1) c.10	Ecclesiastical Leases Act 1571	rep.	43, s.1(1), Sch.1, Pt.II, Group 1
1572 (14 Eliz. 1) c.11	Ecclesiastical Leases Act 1572	rep.	43, s.1(1), Sch.1, Pt.II, Group 1
1575 (18 Eliz. 1) c.11	Ecclesiastical Leases Act 1575	rep.	43, s.1(1), Sch.1, Pt.II, Group 1
1662 (14 Cha. 2) *c.34* (private)	Bengeworth Bridge (Worcestershire) Repair Act 1662	rep.	43, s.1(1), Sch.1, Pt.V
1700 (12 & 13 Will. 3) c.2	Act of Settlement 1700	s.3 excl.	12, s.4(4)
		s.3 excl.	38, s.13(2)
		s.3 restr.	46, s.16(2)
		s.3 excl. (*prosp.*)	47, s.36(7)
1702 (1 Ann. St. 2) c.21	Treason Act 1702	s.3 rep.in pt. (EW)	37, s.36(2)(c)
1706 (6 Ann.) c.11	Union with Scotland Act 1706	am. (25.1.1999)	46, s.37
		arts.4,6 saved (1.7.1999)	46, ss.29,53(4), Sch.4, Pt.I, paras.1(2)(a),9
1708 (7 Ann.) c.27	Morrison's Haven and Fort, East Lothian Act 1708	rep.	43, s.1(1), Sch.1, Pt.X, Group 5

Year and Chap. or No. of Measure	Short title	How affected	1998, Chapter of Act or Number of Measure or Statutory Instrument
1722 (9 Geo.1) c.17	An Act to inflict Pains and Penalties on Francis Lord Bishop of Rochester 1722	rep. (Isle of Man)	43, s.1(1), Sch.1, Pt.X, Group 5
1737 (11 Geo. 2) c.5	Church of All Saints Worcester Act 1737	rep.	43, s.1(1), Sch.1, Pt.V
1738 (12 Geo. 2) c.4	Saint Nicholas Church Worcester Act 1738	rep.	43, s.1(1), Sch.1, Pt.V
1769 (9 Geo. 3) c.84	Worcester Bridge Act 1769	rep.	43, s.1(1), Sch.1, Pt.V
1774 (14 Geo. 3) c.48	Life Assurance Act 1774	s.6(1) excl.	SI 633, art.K4(3)
1779 (19 Geo. 3) c.42	Worcester Bridge Act 1779	rep. (except s.9)	43, s.1(1), Sch.1, Pt.V
		s.9 rep.in pt.	43, s.1(1), Sch.1, Pt.V
1782 (22 Geo. 3) c.112	Hereford Roads Act 1782	rep.	43, s.1(1), Sch.1, Pt.V
1785 (25 Geo.3) c.94	Kidderminster Parish Church Act 1785	rep.	43, s.1(1), Sch.1, Pt.V
1786 (26 Geo. 3) c.31	National Debt Reduction Act 1786	s.14 am.	11, s.9(1)
1789 (29 Geo. 3) c.42	Cockburnspath Bridge, Berwick Act 1789	rep.	43, s.1(1), Sch.1, Pt.X, Group 5
1790 (30 Geo. 3) c.48	Treason Act 1790	rep.	37, ss.36(3)(a),120(2), Sch.10
1795 (35 Geo. 3) c.78	Bewdley Bridge Act 1795	rep. (except s.27)	43, s.1(1), Sch.1, Pt.V
		s.27 rep.in pt.	43, s.1(1), Sch.1, Pt.V
c.133	Worcester Roads Act 1795	rep.	43, s.1(1), Sch.1, Pt.V
1795 (36 Geo. 3) c.7	Treason Act 1795	rep.	37, ss.36(3)(b),120(2), Sch.10
1797 (37 Geo. 3) c.70	Incitement to Mutiny Act 1797	rep.	43, s.1(1), Sch.1, Pt.I, Group 2
1800 (39 & 40 Geo. 3) c.41	Ecclesiastical Leases Act 1800	rep.	43, s.1(1), Sch.1, Pt.II, Group 1
c.88	Crown Private Estate Act 1800	saved (6.5.1999)	46, s.30, Sch.5, Pt.I, paras.1,4(2)

Year and Chap. or No. of Measure	Short title	How affected	1998, Chapter of Act or Number of Measure or Statutory Instrument
1800—*cont.*			
c.iii	Edinburgh Poor Relief Act 1800	rep.	43, s.1(1), Sch.1, Pt.VII, Group 1
1803			
(43 Geo. 3) c.143	Public Officers Protection (Ireland) Act 1803	rep. (saving)(*prosp.*)	32, s.74(2)(3), Schs.5,6
c.cvii	Writers to the Signet Widows' Fund Act 1803	rep.	43, s.1(1), Sch.1, Pt.VII, Group 1
1805			
(45 Geo. 3) c.xxxi	Excise Incorporation in Scotland Act 1805	rep.	43, s.1(1), Sch.1, Pt.VII, Group 1
1808			
(48 Geo. 3) c.142	Life Annuities Act 1808	s.32 am.	11, s.9(1)
c.cxlviii	Leominster and Luston Inclosure and Improvement Act 1808	rep.	43, s.1(1), Sch.1, Pt.V
1814			
(54 Geo. 3) c.146	Treason Act 1814	s.1 am.	37, s.36(4)
c.ccxviii	Ombersley Church and Workhouse Act 1814	rep. (except s.32)	43, s.1(1), Sch.1, Pt.V
		s.32 rep.in pt.	43, s.1(1), Sch.1, Pt.V
1815			
(55 Geo. 3) c.ix	Hereford County Offices Act 1815	rep.	43, s.1(1), Sch.1, Pt.V
1817			
(57 Geo. 3) c.6	Treason Act 1817	rep.	37, s.120(2), Sch.10
1818			
(58 Geo. 3) c.lxxiv	Writers to the Signet Widows' Fund Act 1818	rep.	43, s.1(1), Sch.1, Pt.VII, Group 1
1821			
(1 & 2 Geo. 4) c.cxv	Portmadoc Harbour Act 1821	rep. (saving)	SI 683(L), art.4, Sch.
1823			
(4 Geo. 4) c.xxxii	Worcester Severn Bridge Act 1823	rep. (except ss.35,39,40)	43, s.1(1), Sch.1, Pt.V
1824			
(5 Geo. 4) c.83	Vagrancy Act 1824	s.4 appl. (NI)	SI 261, art.13(2)
c.113	Slave Trade Act 1824	ss.3-9 rep.	43, s.1(1), Sch.1, Pt.VIII
		s.10 am. (GB)	43, s.1(2), Sch.2, para.1
		s.11 am.	43, s.1(2), Sch.2, para.2
		ss.12,39,40,47 rep.	43, s.1(1), Sch.1, Pt.VIII
c.lxvii	Evesham Improvement Act 1824	rep. (except ss.66,95,96 and Schs.A,B & C)	43, s.1(1), Sch.1, Pt.V
1825			
(6 Geo. 4) c.lx	Kerne Bridge over River Wye Act 1825	rep. (except ss.2, 3)	43, s.1(1), Sch.1, Pt.V
1826			
(7 Geo. 4) c.64	Criminal Law Act 1826	s.28 proviso rep.	43, s.1(1), Sch.1, Pt.I, Group 2

Year and Chap. or No. of Measure	Short title	How affected	1998, Chapter of Act or Number of Measure or Statutory Instrument
1826—*cont.*			
		s.29 rep.in pt.	43, s.1(1), Sch.1, Pt.I, Group 2
c.lix	Holt Fleet Bridge over River Severn Act 1826	rep. (except ss.48,49 & 107)	43, s.1(1), Sch.1, Pt.V
		s.107 rep.in pt.	43, s.1(1), Sch.1, Pt.V
1829			
(10 Geo. 4) c.cii	Kington (Herefordshire) Improvement Act 1829	rep.	43, s.1(1), Sch.1, Pt.V
1830			
(11 Geo. 4 & 1 Will. 4) c.xii	Axmouth Harbour Act 1830	ext.	SI 2228(L), art.3, Sch.
		s.41 rep.	SI 2228(L), art.6
1831			
(1 & 2 Will. 4) c.xlviii	Worcester County Hall and Courts of Justice Act 1831	rep.	43, s.1(1), Sch.1, Pt.V
1833			
(3 & 4 Will. 4) c.13	Public Revenue (Scotland) Act 1833	s.2 am. (1.7.1999)	46, s.125, Sch.8, para.1
c.41	Judicial Committee Act 1833	power to appl. (6.5.1999)	46, s.103(3)(b)
		power to appl. (*prosp.*)	47, s.82(3)(b)
c.73	Slavery Abolition Act 1833	rep.	43, s.1(1), Sch.1, Pt.VIII
c.lxiv	Faculty of Procurators of Glasgow Widows' Fund Act 1833	rep.	43, s.1(1), Sch.1, Pt.VII, Group 1
1835			
(5 & 6 Will. 4) c.i	Ledbury High Street Act 1835	rep.	43, s.1(1), Sch.1, Pt.V
c.lxxxiii	Gateshead and Monks Wearmouth Railway Act 1835	excl. (13.1.1999)	SI 3269(L), art.16(1)(6)
1836			
(6 & 7 Will. 4) c.13	Constabulary (Ireland) Act 1836	rep. (saving)(*prosp.*)	32, s.74(2)(3), Schs.5,6
c.71	Tithe Act 1836	rep. (except ss.12,64,96)	43, s.1(1), Sch.1, Pt.II, Group 2
c.lvii	Brandling Junction Railway Company Act 1836	excl. (13.1.1999)	SI 3269(L), art.16(1)(6)
1837			
(7 Will. 4 & 1 Vict.) c.88	Piracy Act 1837	s.2 am.	37, s.36(5)
c.iii	Worcester County Hall and Courts of Justice Act 1837	rep.	43, s.1(1), Sch.1, Pt.V
1838			
(1 & 2 Vict.) c.64	Tithe Act 1838	rep.	43, s.1(1), Sch.1, Pt.II, Group 2
c.110	Judgments Act 1838	s.17 renumbered (as s.17(1)) (26.4.1999)	SI 2940, art.3(a)
		s.17 referred to (26.4.1999)	SI 3132, rule 44.12(2)
		s.17 power to excl. (26.4.1999)	SI 3132, rules 47.8(3), 47.14(5)

Year and Chap. or No. of Measure	Short title	How affected	1998, Chapter of Act or Number of Measure or Statutory Instrument
1838—*cont.*			
		s.17 appl.	22, s.2(1) (adding 1993 c.39, s.10A)
		s.17(1) am. (26.4.1999)	SI 2940, art.3(b)
		s.17(2) added (26.4.1999)	SI 2940, art.3(c)
c.xiv	Leominster Improvement (Amendment) Act 1838	rep.	43, s.1(1), Sch.1, Pt.V
1839			
(2 & 3 Vict.) c.45	Highway (Railway Crossing) Act 1839	excl.	SI 1936(L), art.3(6)
c.47	Metropolitan Police Act 1839	s.75 subst.	43, s.1(2), Sch.2, para.3
		s.76 rep.in pt.	43, s.1(1), Sch.1, Pt.I, Group 2
c.62	Tithe Act 1839	rep. (except ss.1,37)	43, s.1(1), Sch.1, Pt.II, Group 2
c.75	Constabulary (Ireland) Act 1839	rep. (saving)(*prosp.*)	32, s.74(2)(3), Schs.5,6
1840			
(3 & 4 Vict.) c.15	Tithe Act 1840	rep.	43, s.1(1), Sch.1, Pt.II, Group 2
c.84	Metropolitan Police Courts Act 1840	s.6 rep.	43, s.1(1), Sch.1, Pt.I, Group 2
c.97	Railway Regulation Act 1840	excl.	SI 1936(L), art.3(5)
c.110	Loan Societies Act 1840	rep.	43, s.1(1), Sch.1, Pt.IV, Group 4
c.xciii	Glasgow Poor Act 1840	rep.	43, s.1(1), Sch.1, Pt.VII, Group 1
c.cxxv	Lord Scudamore's Charity Act 1840	s.29 rep.	43, s.1(1), Sch.1, Pt.V
1841			
(4 & 5 Vict.) c.30	Ordnance Survey Act 1841	saved (6.5.1999)	46, s.30, Sch.5, Pt.II, s.L4
c.38	School Sites Act 1841	s.14 mod. (*prosp.*)	31, s.22, Sch.3, Pt.I, para.2(8)
		s.14 mod. (*prosp.*)	31, ss.28,29,31, Sch.6, Pt.IV, para.16(7)
c.l	Scrabster Harbour Act 1841	ss.2,3,4,6 subst.	SI 1221(L), art.19, Sch.2, paras.1-5
		s.7 subst.	SI 1221(L), art.19, Sch.2, para.6
		s.8 subst.	SI 1221(L), art.19, Sch.2, paras.1-5
		s.12 rep.in pt. & am.	SI 1221(L), art.19, Sch.2, para.7
		s.14 rep.in pt.	SI 1221(L), art.19, Sch.2, para.8
		s.99 am.	SI 1221(L), art.19, Sch.2, para.9
c.lxxii	Kidderminster Poor Rates Act 1841	rep.	43, s.1(1), Sch.1, Pt.V
c.xcvi	Scottish Marine Insurance Company Act 1841	rep.	43, s.1(1), Sch.1, Pt.VII, Group 4

Year and Chap. or No. of Measure	Short title	How affected	1998, Chapter of Act or Number of Measure or Statutory Instrument
1842			
(5 & 6 Vict.) c.54	Tithe Act 1842	rep.	43, s.1(1), Sch.1, Pt.II, Group 2
1843			
(6 & 7 Vict.) c.90	Public Notaries Act 1843	rep. (Isle of Man) (*prosp.*)	43, s.1(1), Sch.1, Pt.X, Group 5
(6 & 7 Vict.) c.98	Slave Trade Act 1843	s.1 rep.in pt.	43, s.1(1), Sch.1, Pt.VIII
		s.4 rep.	43, s.1(1), Sch.1, Pt.VIII
c.cvii	Glasgow Marine Insurance Company Act 1843	rep.	43, s.1(1), Sch.1, Pt.VII, Group 4
1844			
(7 & 8 Vict.) c.vi	Edinburgh Charity Workhouse Act 1844	rep.	43, s.1(1), Sch.1, Pt.VII, Group 1
1845			
(8 & 9 Vict.) c.18	Lands Clauses Consolidation Act 1845	excl.	iv, s.4(4)
c.19	Lands Clauses Consolidation (Scotland) Act 1845	incorp.(mods.) (except ss.120-125)	iii, s.1, Sch.
		ss.120-125 excl.	iii, s.1, Sch., O., s.4(1)
c.20	Railways Clauses Consolidation Act 1845	s.24 incorp. (13.1.1999)	SI 3269(L), art.3(1)(2)
		s.46 appl.(mods.)	SI 1936(L), art.3(1)-(3)
		s.58 appl.in pt.(mods.)	SI 1936(L), art.3(1)(2)
		s.58 incorp. in pt. (13.1.1999)	SI 3269(L), art.3(1)(2)
		s.61 appl.(mods.)	SI 1936(L), art.3(1)(2)
		s.68 appl.(mods.)	SI 1936(L), art.3(1)(2)(4)
		s.68 incorp. (13.1.1999)	SI 3269(L), art.3(1)(2)
		s.71 appl.in pt.(mods.)	SI 1936(L), art.3(1)(2)
		s.71 incorp. in pt. (13.1.1999)	SI 3269(L), art.3(1)(2)
		s.72 appl.(mods.)	SI 1936(L), art.3(1)-(3)
		s.72 incorp. (13.1.1999)	SI 3269(L), art.3(1)(2)
		s.73 appl.(mods.)	SI 1936(L), art.3(1)-(3)
		s.73 incorp. (13.1.1999)	SI 3269(L), art.3(1)(2)
		ss.75,77 appl.(mods.)	SI 1936(L), art.3(1)-(3)
		s.77 incorp. (13.1.1999)	SI 3269(L), art.3(1)(2)
		ss.78-85E appl.(mods.)	SI 1936(L), art.3(1)-(3)
		ss.78-85E,103-105 incorp. (13.1.1999)	SI 3269(L), art.3(1)(2)
		s.145 appl.(mods.)	SI 1936(L), art.3(1)-(3)
		ss.145,154 incorp. (13.1.1999)	SI 3269(L), art.3(1)(2)
		Schs.1-3 appl.(mods.)	SI 1936(L), art.3(1)-(3)
c.118	Inclosure Act 1845	s.9 rep.in pt.	43, s.1(1), Sch.1, Pt.VI
		ss.12, first proviso,28- 48 rep.	43, s.1(1), Sch.1, Pt.VI
		s.49 rep.in pt.	43, s.1(1), Sch.1, Pt.VI
		ss.50-55,57,59,60 rep.	43, s.1(1), Sch.1, Pt.VI
		s.61 rep.in pt.	43, s.1(1), Sch.1, Pt.VI
		ss.62-66 rep.	43, s.1(1), Sch.1, Pt.VI
		s.68 rep.in pt.	43, s.1(1), Sch.1, Pt.VI
		ss.69-71 rep.	43, s.1(1), Sch.1, Pt.VI
		ss.72,73 rep.in pt.	43, s.1(1), Sch.1, Pt.VI

Year and Chap. or No. of Measure	Short title	How affected	1998, Chapter of Act or Number of Measure or Statutory Instrument
1845—*cont.*			
		ss.76,77,79-82 rep.	43, s.1(1), Sch.1, Pt.VI
		s.83 rep.in pt.	43, s.1(1), Sch.1, Pt.VI
		ss.84-92,95,97,99-104 rep.	43, s.1(1), Sch.1, Pt.VI
		s.107 rep.in pt.	43, s.1(1), Sch.1, Pt.VI
		s.113 rep.	43, s.1(1), Sch.1, Pt.VI
		ss.114,115,123 rep.in pt.	43, s.1(1), Sch.1, Pt.VI
		ss.124-129,133-138,140-144,152-154,156,157 rep.	43, s.1(1), Sch.1, Pt.VI
		s.162 rep.in pt.	43, s.1(1), Sch.1, Pt.VI
		Sch., Form of Conveyance by Commissioners rep.	43, s.1(1), Sch.1, Pt.VI
c.xcii	Newcastle and Darlington Junction Railway Act 1845	excl. (13.1.1999)	SI 3269(L), art.16(1)(6)
1846			
(9 & 10 Vict.) c.70	Inclosure Act 1846	ss.1-5 rep.	43, s.1(1), Sch.1, Pt.VI
c.73	Tithe Act 1846	rep.	43, s.1(1), Sch.1, Pt.II, Group 2
c.cxxiv	Bromsgrove Improvement and Small Tenements Act 1846	rep.	43, s.1(1), Sch.1, Pt.V
c.cccxxxv	Cornwall Railway Act 1846	referred to	iv, s.21(b)
1847			
(10 & 11 Vict.) c.27	Harbours, Docks and Piers Clauses Act 1847	incorp.(mods.) (except ss.6-22,24-27,42,43,48-50,79,80,84-90,95-102)	SI 683(L), art.3
		incorp.(mods.) (except ss.6-25,31, proviso to s.32, ss.42,48-50,60-63, 66,67,73,77-82)	SI 1016(L), art.3
		incorp.(mods.) (except ss.6-13,16-19,22,25,26, 48,79-82,95,97,98,99, 101,103)	SI 1215(L), art.3
		ss.27-41 appl.	SI 1209(L), art.7(4)
		s.33 excl.	SI 980(L), art.4(1)(2)
		s.33 excl.	SI 980(L), arts.4(3),5
		ss.44-46 appl.	SI 1209(L), art.7(4)
		s.58 appl.(mods.)	SI 980(L), art.5(2)(b)
c.104	Tithe Act 1847	rep.	43, s.1(1), Sch.1, Pt.II, Group 2
c.111	Inclosure Act 1847	ss.3,5,6 rep.	43, s.1(1), Sch.1, Pt.VI
		s.7 rep.in pt.	43, s.1(1), Sch.1, Pt.VI
c.xxxiv	Scottish Union Insurance Company Act 1847	rep.	43, s.1(1), Sch.1, Pt.VII, Group 4
1848			
(11 & 12 Vict.) c.12	Treason Felony Act 1848	s.2 rep.	37, s.120(2), Sch.10
c.72	Constabulary (Ireland) Act 1848	rep. (saving)(*prosp.*)	32, s.74(2)(3), Schs.5,6

Year and Chap. or No. of Measure	Short title	How affected	1998, Chapter of Act or Number of Measure or Statutory Instrument
1848—*cont.*			
c.99	Inclosure Act 1848	ss.1-3 rep.	43, s.1(1), Sch.1, Pt.VI
		s.4 rep.in pt.	43, s.1(1), Sch.1, Pt.VI
		ss.5,8,9,11,13,14 rep.	43, s.1(1), Sch.1, Pt.VI
1849			
(12 & 13 Vict.) c.83	Inclosure Act 1849	ss.1-6 rep.	43, s.1(1), Sch.1, Pt.VI
		s.7 rep.in pt.	43, s.1(1), Sch.1, Pt.VI
		ss.8,9,10 rep.	43, s.1(1), Sch.1, Pt.VI
c.xii	Kidderminster Union Small Tenements Rating Act 1849	rep.	43, s.1(1), Sch.1, Pt.V
1851			
(14 & 15 Vict.) c.42	Crown Lands Act 1851	s.21 power to delegate functions	SI 215, art.2
c.53	Inclosure Commissioners Act 1851	rep.	43, s.1(1), Sch.1, Pt.VI
c.xcvi	Malvern Improvement Act 1851	rep. (except ss.2,14,36, 50,62 & the Sch.)	43, s.1(1), Sch.1, Pt.V
1852			
(15 & 16 Vict.) c.79	Inclosure Act 1852	s.1 rep.in pt.	43, s.1(1), Sch.1, Pt.VI
		ss.3-13,15,16,20,23-27,30- 32 rep.	43, s.1(1), Sch.1, Pt.VI
1853			
(16 & 17 Vict.) c.20	Evidence (Scotland) Act 1853	s.3 ext.	14, s.16(5)(b)
c.xvi	Evesham Bridge Act 1853	rep.	43, s.1(1), Sch.1, Pt.V
c.lxxvii	Leominster Markets and Fairs Act 1853	rep. (except ss.1-3,5,24-26,28,35,36,43,44,46,49, 50,51)	43, s.1(1), Sch.1, Pt.V
1854			
(17 & 18 Vict.) c.97	Inclosure Act 1854	ss.1,2,6,7 rep.	43, s.1(1), Sch.1, Pt.VI
c.xxxi	Hereford Improvement Act 1854	rep. (except ss.1,3-5,7, 12,20,21,28-31,43,47,48, 51,52,66,67,103 & Sch.A)	43, s.1(1), Sch.1, Pt.V
c.clxiv	Jarrow Dock and Railway Act 1854	s.1 (defn. of "the Undertaking") rep.in pt. (6.1.1999)	SI 3277(L), art.4, Sch.
		s.1 (defn. of "Docks") rep. (6.1.1999)	SI 3277(L), art.4, Sch.
		s.2 rep.in pt. (6.1.1999)	SI 3277(L), art.4, Sch.
		ss.3,4 rep. (6.1.1999)	SI 3277(L), art.4, Sch.
		ss.5,7-59 rep.in pt. (6.1.1999)	SI 3277(L), art.4, Sch.
		Sch.(A)(B) rep. (6.1.1999)	SI 3277(L), art.4, Sch.
1855			
(18 & 19 Vict.) c.81	Places of Worship Registration Act 1855	s.5 am. (1.4.1999)	SI 3171, art.2, Sch.
c.v	Hoarwithy Bridge Act 1855	rep. (except ss.2,25-28)	43, s.1(1), Sch.1, Pt.V

Year and Chap. or No. of Measure	Short title	How affected	1998, Chapter of Act or Number of Measure or Statutory Instrument
1855—*cont.*			
c.clxxix	Hereford Improvement Act 1854 (Correction of Oversight) Act 1855	rep.	43, s.1(1), Sch.1, Pt.V
1857 (20 & 21 Vict.) c.31	Inclosure Act 1857	s.3 rep.in pt.	43, s.1(1), Sch.1, Pt.VI
		s.13 rep.	43, s.1(1), Sch.1, Pt.VI
c.44	Crown Suits (Scotland) Act 1857	ss.1-3 am. (20.5.1999)	46, s.125, Sch.8, para.2(2)(3)(4)
		s.4A added (20.5.1999)	46, s.125, Sch.8, para.2(5)
		s.5 am. (20.5.1999)	46, s.125, Sch.8, para.2(6)
c.81	Burial Act 1857	s.25 excl.	38, s.127, Sch.13, para.3 (adding 1975 c.70, at Sch.4, Pt.III, para.7(9))
		s.25 excl. (pt.prosp.)	45, s.23, Sch.6, para.3(8)
c.xi	Chester Waterworks Act 1857	s.3 rep.	SI 281, art.4, Sch.2, Pt.I
		s.4 rep.in pt.	SI 281, art.4, Sch.2, Pt.I
		ss.5-7 rep.	SI 281, art.4, Sch.2, Pt.I
		s.8 rep.in pt.	SI 281, art.4, Sch.2, Pt.I
		ss.10-12,14-16,19-27,34, 36-39,41,70-88,90,91 rep.	SI 281, art.4, Sch.2, Pt.I
c.xlviii	Fownhope and Holme Lacy Bridge Act 1857	rep. (except ss.1,34)	43, s.1(1), Sch.1, Pt.V
1858 (21 & 22 Vict.) c.xxxi	Malvern Improvement Amendment Act 1858	rep. (except ss.1,9-13)	43, s.1(1), Sch.1, Pt.V
1859 (22 & 23 Vict.) c.43	Inclosure Act 1859	ss.1,2 rep.	43, s.1(1), Sch.1, Pt.VI
		s.7 rep.in pt.	43, s.1(1), Sch.1, Pt.VI
		ss.8-11,13,14 rep.	43, s.1(1), Sch.1, Pt.VI
c.xlix	Scottish National Insurance Company's Incorporation Act 1859	rep.	43, s.1(1), Sch.1, Pt.VII, Group 4
1860 (23 & 24 Vict.) c.93	Tithe Act 1860	rep. (except s.24)	43, s.1(1), Sch.1, Pt.II, Group 2
c.clxxvi	Royal College of Surgeons of Edinburgh (Widow's Fund) Act 1860	rep.	43, s.1(1), Sch.1, Pt.VII, Group 1
1861 (24 & 25 Vict.) c.39	Local Government Supplemental Act 1861	s.4, Sch. Bromsgrove Order rep.	43, s.1(1), Sch.1, Pt.V
c.82	Durham University Act 1861	rep.	43, s.1(1), Sch.1, Pt.III, Group 2
c.100	Offences against the Person Act 1861	excl.	SI 1936(L), art.3(7)
c.101	Statute Law Revision Act 1861	rep.	43, s.1(1), Sch.1, Pt.IX, Group 1

Year and Chap. or No. of Measure	Short title	How affected	1998, Chapter of Act or Number of Measure or Statutory Instrument
1861—*cont.*			
c.cxlv	City of Glasgow Life Assurance Company's Act 1861	rep.	43, s.1(1), Sch.1, Pt.VII, Group 4
1863			
(26 & 27 Vict.) c.32	Local Government Supplemental Act 1863	Sch. Bromsgrove Order rep.	43, s.1(1), Sch.1, Pt.V
1864			
(27 & 28 Vict.) c.24	Naval Agency and Distribution Act 1863	s.12 rep.in pt.	43, s.1(1), Sch.1, Pt.VIII
c.cccxix	Exmouth Docks Act 1864	ss.22,24-27,29-34, Schs. (A)(B) rep.	SI 980(L), art.6, Sch.
1865			
(28 & 29 Vict.) c.25	Local Government Supplemental (No.2) Act 1865	Sch. Bromsgrove Order rep.	43, s.1(1), Sch.1, Pt.V
c.cviii	Ross Improvement Act 1865	rep. (except ss.1,3-5,23, 26,28(pt.),29(pt.),30, 31,32(pt.))	43, s.1(1), Sch.1, Pt.V
1866			
(29 & 30 Vict.) c.39	Exchequer and Audit Departments Act 1866	s.3 am. (*prosp.*)	38, s.125, Sch.12, para.1
		s.10 am.	36, s.145(1)(2)(3)
		s.10 mod. (6.5.1999)	46, s.78(8)
c.107	Local Government Supplemental Act (No.4) 1866	Sch. Leominster Order rep.	43, s.1(1), Sch.1, Pt.V
c.111	Ecclesiastical Commissioners Act 1866	saved (1.1.1999)	GSM 1, s.5(1), Sch.2, Pt.I
c.xix	Bromsgrove and Droitwich Waterworks Act 1866	rep.	43, s.1(1), Sch.1, Pt.V
1867			
(30 & 31 Vict.) c.83	Local Government Supplemental (No.5) Act 1867	s.1 rep.in pt.	43, s.1(1), Sch.1, Pt.V
		Sch. Malvern Order rep.	43, s.1(1), Sch.1, Pt.V
c.xxiii	Worcester Prison Act 1867	rep.	43, s.1(1), Sch.1, Pt.V
1868			
(31 & 32 Vict.) c.37	Documentary Evidence Act 1868	mod.	SI 1340, reg.9(6), Sch.2, para.6(c)
		am. (*prosp.*)	47, s.88
		Sch. mod.	SI 1340, reg.9(6), Sch.2, para.6(a)(b)
c.72	Promissory Oaths Act 1868	appl. (6.5.1999)	46, s.84(4)(a)
c.89	Inclosure, etc., Expenses Act 1868	ss.4,5 rep.	43, s.1(1), Sch.1, Pt.VI
c.118	Public Schools Act 1868	s.4A added	43, s.1(2), Sch.2, para.4
		s.5 rep.in pt.	43, s.1(1), Sch.1, Pt.III, Group 1
		s.27 cont. (amendment by 1869, c.58 cont.)	43, s.1(2), Sch.2, para.5

Year and Chap. or No. of Measure	Short title	How affected	1998, Chapter of Act or Number of Measure or Statutory Instrument
1868—cont.			
c.lxxxvi	Local Government Supplemental (No.5) Act 1868	Sch. Malvern Order rep.	43, s.1(1), Sch.1, Pt.V
1869			
(32 & 33 Vict.) c.19	Stannaries Act 1869	rep.	43, s.1(1), Sch.1, Pt.X, Group 1
c.58	Public Schools Act 1869	rep.	43, s.1(1), Sch.1, Pt.III, Group 1
c.lxx	Oyster and Mussel Fisheries Order Confirmation Act 1869	rep.	43, s.1(1), Sch.1, Pt.VII, Group 7
c.lxxix	Ross Improvement Act (Amendment Act) 1869	rep.	43, s.1(1), Sch.1, Pt.V
1870			
(33 & 34 Vict.) c.71	National Debt Act 1870	s.55 am.	11, s.9(2)
c.xxvii	Oyster and Mussel Fisheries Orders Confirmation Act 1870 No.2	rep.	43, s.1(1), Sch.1, Pt.VII, Group 7
c.cxiv	Local Government Supplemental Act 1870	s.4, Sch. Kidderminster Order rep.	43, s.1(1), Sch.1, Pt.V
1871			
(34 & 35 Vict.) c.60	Public Schools Act 1871	rep.	43, s.1(1), Sch.1, Pt.III, Group 1
c.i	Local Government Supplemental Act 1871	Sch., Kidderminster Order No.1 rep.	43, s.1(1), Sch.1, Pt.V
c.ii	Oyster and Mussel Fisheries Order Confirmation Act 1871	rep.	43, s.1(1), Sch.1, Pt.VII, Group 7
c.xxi	Lloyd's Act 1871	power to H.M.Treasury to contract out certain functions	SI 2842, art.2, Sch., Pt.II, para.62
c.li	Bromsgrove Waterworks Act 1871	rep.	43, s.1(1), Sch.1, Pt.V
c.clxxxvii	Local Governmental Supplemental (No.4) Act 1871	Sch. Malvern Order rep.	43, s.1(1), Sch.1, Pt.V
1872			
(35 & 36 Vict.) c.97	Statute Law Revision (No.2) Act 1872	rep.	43, s.1(1), Sch.1, Pt.IX, Group 1
c.i	Oyster and Mussel Fisheries Orders Confirmation Act 1872	Greshernish Fishery Order rep.	43, s.1(1), Sch.1, Pt.VII, Group 7
c.cxix	Hereford Improvement Act 1872	rep. (except ss.1,2,5,10, 24,33)	43, s.1(1), Sch.1, Pt.V
1873			
(36 & 37 Vict.) c.41	Public Schools (Shrewsbury and Harrow Schools Property) Act 1873	rep.	43, s.1(1), Sch.1, Pt.III, Group 1
c.88	Slave Trade Act 1873	ss.2,3 rep.in pt. s.3 am.	43, s.1(1), Sch.1, Pt.VIII 43, s.1(2), Sch.2, para.6

Year and Chap. or No. of Measure	Short title	How affected	1998, Chapter of Act or Number of Measure or Statutory Instrument
1873—*cont.*			
		s.3(a)(b) rep.in pt.	43, s.1(1), Sch.1, Pt.VIII
		ss.4-16 rep.	43, s.1(1), Sch.1, Pt.VIII
		s.17 rep.in pt.	43, s.1(1), Sch.1, Pt.VIII
		ss.18-23 rep.	43, s.1(1), Sch.1, Pt.VIII
		s.24 rep.in pt.	43, s.1(1), Sch.1, Pt.VIII
		s.25 rep.	43, s.1(1), Sch.1, Pt.VIII
		s.26 rep.in pt.	43, s.1(1), Sch.1, Pt.VIII
		ss.28,29, Sch.1 rep.	43, s.1(1), Sch.1, Pt.VIII
1874			
(37 & 38 Vict.) c.80	Constabulary (Ireland) Act 1874	rep. (saving)(*prosp.*)	32, s.74(2)(3), Schs.5,6
c.96	Statute Law Revision (No.2) Act 1874	rep.	43, s.1(1), Sch.1, Pt.IX, Group 1
c.lxv	Chester Waterworks Act	s.3 rep.in pt.	SI 281, art.4, Sch.2, Pt.1
		ss.5-10,12,13,15-19,46,48- 50 rep.	SI 281, art.4, Sch.2, Pt.I
1875			
(38 & 39 Vict.) c.55	Public Health Act 1875	s.265 am.	18, s.54(1), Sch.3, para.1
c.vi	Glasgow Faculty of Procurators Widows Fund Act 1875	rep.	43, s.1(1), Sch.1, Pt.VII, Group 1
c.clxviii	Local Government Board's Poor Law Provisional Orders Confirmation (Oxford, &c.) Act 1875	Sch. Sutton Saint Michael and Sutton Saint Nicholas Order rep.	43, s.1(1), Sch.1, Pt.V
c.cxciii	Local Government Board's Provisional Orders Confirmation (Leyton, &c.) Act 1875	Sch. Redditch Order rep.	43, s.1(1), Sch.1, Pt.V
1876			
(39 & 40 Vict.) c.56	Commons Act 1876	ss.2-6,9,12-14,18,21-23, 32 rep.	43, s.1(1), Sch.1, Pt.VI
c.59	Appellate Jurisdiction Act 1876	s.25 (defn. of "high judicial office") appl.	38, s.109, Sch.8, Pt.V, para.33(b)
		s.25 (defn. of "high judicial office") appl. (6.5.1999)	46, s.103(2)(b)
		s.25 (defn. of "high judicial office") appl. (*prosp.*)	47, s.82(2)(b)
c.clxi	Local Government Board's Provisional Orders Confirmation (Carnarvon, &c.) Act 1876	s.2, Sch. Tenbury Wells Order rep.	43, s.1(1), Sch.1, Pt.V
1877			
(40 & 41 Vict.) c.2	Treasury Bills Act 1877	ext.	36, s.160, Sch.26, paras.1(3),3 (adding 1968 c.13,Sch.5A, para.4(4))
		s.5 excl.	36, s.160, Sch.26, paras.1(3),3 (adding 1968 c.13,Sch.5A, para.4(6))

Year and Chap. or No. of Measure	Short title	How affected	1998, Chapter of Act or Number of Measure or Statutory Instrument
1877—*cont.*			
		s.8(1) subst.	36, s.159(1)(2)
c.48	Universities of Oxford and Cambridge Act 1877	ss.52-55 rep.	43, s.1(1), Sch.1, Pt.III, Group 2
c.59	Colonial Stock Act 1877	rep. (saving)	43, s.1(1)(2), Sch.1, Pt.IV, Group 1, Sch.2, para.7
c.ccxlii	Local Government Board's Provisional Orders Confirmation (Atherton, &c.) Act 1877	Sch. Evesham Order rep.	43, s.1(1), Sch.1, Pt.V
1878			
(41 & 42 Vict.) c.42	Tithe Act 1878	rep.	43, s.1(1), Sch.1, Pt.II, Group 2
c.56	Commons (Expenses) Act 1878	s.3 rep.	43, s.1(1), Sch.1, Pt.VI
c.73	Territorial Waters Jurisdiction Act 1878	s.3 excl.	SI 968, reg.16(10)
		s.3 excl. (*prosp.*)	17, ss.12(4),22(9),41(6)
		s.3 power to excl.	39, s.42(3)(d)
c.79	Statute Law Revision Act 1878	rep.	43, s.1(1), Sch.1, Pt.IX, Group 1
c.lvii	Local Government Board's Provisional Orders Confirmation (Droitwich, &c.) Act 1878	Sch. Droitwich Order rep.	43, s.1(1), Sch.1, Pt.V
1879			
(42 & 43 Vict.) c.11	Bankers' Books Evidence Act 1879	appl. (*prosp.*)	v, s.12(2)(3)
		s.9(2) (defn. of "books") appl. (*prosp.*)	v, s.12(1)
c.58	Public Offices Fees act 1879	s.8(2) rep.	43, s.1(1), Sch.1, Pt.IV, Group 5
c.lxxvii	Local Government Board's (Highways) Provisional Orders Confirmation (Buckingham, &c.) Act 1879	Sch. county of Worcester Order rep.	43, s.1(1), Sch.1, Pt.V
c.lxxxiv	Local Government Board's (Highways) Provisional Orders Confirmation (Gloucester and Hereford) Act 1879	Sch. county of Hereford Order rep.	43, s.1(1), Sch.1, Pt.V
1880			
(43 & 44 Vict.) c.xxxii	Faculty of Physicians and Surgeons of Glasgow Widows Fund Act 1880	rep.	43, s.1(1), Sch.1, Pt.VII, Group 1
c.lviii	Local Government Board's Provisional Orders Confirmation (Abergavenny, &c.) Act 1880	Sch. Bromsgrove Order rep.	43, s.1(1), Sch.1, Pt.V

Year and Chap. or No. of Measure	Short title	How affected	1998, Chapter of Act or Number of Measure or Statutory Instrument
1881			
(44 & 45 Vict.) c.41	Conveyancing Act 1881	defn. of "convey" appl. (NI) (*prosp.*)	v, ss.2(1),14(2)(a)
c.lxii	Local Government Board's Provisional Orders Confirmation (Poor Law No.2) Act 1881	Sch. Bromsgrove Union Orderon Order rep.	43, s.1(1), Sch.1, Pt.V
c.clxiv	Tramways Orders Confirmation (No.3) Act 1881	Sch. Worcester Tramways Order 1881 rep. (except arts.1,3,4,9)	43, s.1(1), Sch.1, Pt.V
1882			
(45 & 46 Vict.) c.ccxxxi	Ross District Water Act 1882	rep.	43, s.1(1), Sch.1, Pt.V
1883			
(46 & 47 Vict.) c.14	Constabulary and Police (Ireland) Act 1883	rep. (saving)(*prosp.*)	32, s.74(2)(3), Schs.5,6
c.22	Sea Fisheries Act 1883	rep. (saving)	43, s.1(1)(2), Sch.1, Pt.X, Group 2, Sch.2, para.8
c.37	Public Health Act 1875 (Support of Sewers) Amendment Act 1883	rep.	43, s.1(1), Sch.1, Pt.X, Group 3
c.xxxvii	Faculty of Procurators in Paisley Act 1883	rep.	43, s.1(1), Sch.1, Pt.VII, Group 8
c.lxxx	Local Government Board's Provisional Orders Confirmation (Poor Law) Act 1883	Sch. Ross Union Orders rep.	43, s.1(1), Sch.1, Pt.V
c.lxxxix	Local Government Board's Provisional Orders Confirmation ((No.3) Act 1883	Sch. Improvement District of Kington Order Evesham Joint Hospital District Order rep.	43, s.1(1), Sch.1, Pt.V
c.cxxxviii	Local Government Board's Provisional Orders Confirmation (Poor Law) (No.2) Act 1883	Sch. Ross and Westbury-upon-Severn Unions Order rep.	43, s.1(1), Sch.1, Pt.V
1884			
(47 & 48 Vict.) c.xxiii	Scottish Imperial Insurance Company's Act 1884	rep.	43, s.1(1), Sch.1, Pt.VII, Group 4
c.xlviii	Local Government Board's Provisional Orders Confirmation (Poor Law) (No.7) Act 1884	rep.	43, s.1(1), Sch.1, Pt.V
c.clviii	Local Government Board's Provisional Orders Confirmation (No.2) Act 1884	Sch. Malvern Order rep.	43, s.1(1), Sch.1, Pt.V
c.ccl	Scotch Education Department Provisional Order Confirmation (Ardchattan and Muckairn) Act 1884	rep.	43, s.1(1), Sch.1, Pt.VII, Group 3

Year and Chap. or No. of Measure	Short title	How affected	1998, Chapter of Act or Number of Measure or Statutory Instrument
1885			
(48 & 49 Vict.) c.32	Tithe Rentcharge Redemption Act 1885	rep.	43, s.1(1), Sch.1, Pt.II, Group 2
c.lxii	Local Government Board's Provisional Orders Confirmation (No.5) Act 1885	Sch.Bromsgrove Order rep.	43, s.1(1), Sch.1, Pt.V
c.lxvi	Tramways Orders Confirmation (No.1) Act 1885	Sch. Worcester Tramways Order 1881 Amendment Order 1885 rep.	43, s.1(1), Sch.1, Pt.V
c.cvii	Local Government Board's Provisional Orders Confirmation (No.7) Act 1885	Sch. Evesham Borough Order rep.	43, s.1(1), Sch.1, Pt.V
1886			
(49 & 50 Vict.) c.v	Local Government Board's Provisional Orders Confirmation (Gas) Act 1886	Sch. Droitwich Gas Order 1886 rep.	43, s.1(1), Sch.1, Pt.V
1887			
(50 & 51 Vict.) c.40	Savings Banks Act 1887	s.10 am. (1.4.1999)	SI 3171, art.2, Sch.
c.43	Stannaries Act 1887	rep.	43, s.1(1), Sch.1, Pt.X, Group 1
c.55	Sheriffs Act 1887	s.6(1) rep.in pt.	43, s.1(1), Sch.1, Pt.I, Group 1
		ss.11,16(2),20(1) rep.	43, s.1(1), Sch.1, Pt.I, Group 1
		s.20(3) rep.in pt.	43, s.1(1), Sch.1, Pt.I, Group 1
		ss.20(4),21,22,23(2) rep.	43, s.1(1), Sch.1, Pt.I, Group 1
		s.27(1) rep.in pt.	43, s.1(1), Sch.1, Pt.I, Group 1
		s.28 rep.	43, s.1(1), Sch.1, Pt.I, Group 1
		s.29(1)(2) rep.in pt.	43, s.1(1), Sch.1, Pt.I, Group 1
		ss.30(2),31 rep.	43, s.1(1), Sch.1, Pt.I, Group 1
		ss.33(4),39 rep.in pt.	43, s.1(1), Sch.1, Pt.I, Group 1
		s.40(2) rep.	43, s.1(1), Sch.1, Pt.I, Group 1
c.lxxxiv	Local Government Board's Provisional Orders Confirmation (No.2) Act 1887	Sch. Borough of Evesham Order rep.	43, s.1(1), Sch.1, Pt.V
c.cxxiii	Tramways Orders Confirmation (No.2) Act 1887	Sch. Worcester Tramways Order 1887 rep.	43, s.1(1), Sch.1, Pt.V
1888			
(51 & 52 Vict.) c.45	Victoria University Act 1888	rep.	43, s.1(1), Sch.1, Pt.III, Group 2

Effects of Legislation

Year and Chap. or No. of Measure	Short title	How affected	1998, Chapter of Act or Number of Measure or Statutory Instrument
1888—*cont.*			
c.clxvi	Oyster and Mussel Fisheries (West Loch Tarbet) Order Confirmation Act 1888	rep.	43, s.1(1), Sch.1, Pt.VII, Group 7
1889			
(52 & 53 Vict.) c.69	Public Bodies Corrupt Practices Act 1889	am.	38, s.79
		ext. (6.5.1999)	46, s.43
1890			
(53 & 54 Vict.) c.21	Inland Revenue Regulation Act 1890	s.4A ext.	36, s.117, Sch.18, Pt.XI, para.95(5)
c.27	Colonial Courts of Admiralty Act 1890	ss.2, proviso, para.(b), 9(2) proviso, para.(a) rep.in pt.	43, s.1(1), Sch.1, Pt.VIII
		s.13 rep.	43, s.1(1), Sch.1, Pt.VIII
c.39	Partnership Act 1890	mod. (1.1.1999)	GSM 1, s.6(4)
		defn. of "partnership" appl. (1.1.1999)	GSM 1, s.6(4)(a)
		s.1(2) rep.in pt.	43, s.1(1), Sch.1, Pt.X, Group 1
		s.23(4) rep.	43, s.1(1), Sch.1, Pt.X, Group 1
c.clxxxi	Tramways Orders Confirmation (No.1) Act 1890	Sch. Worcester Tramways (Abandonment and Release of Deposit) Order 1890 rep.	43, s.1(1), Sch.1, Pt.V
c.clxxxvi	Electric Lighting Orders Confirmation Act 1890	Sch. Worcester Electric Lighting Order 1890 rep.	43, s.1(1), Sch.1, Pt.V
c.clxxxviii	Electric Lighting Orders Confirmation (No.3) Act 1890	Sch. Malvern Electric Lighting Order 1890 rep.	43, s.1(1), Sch.1, Pt.V
1891			
(54 & 55 Vict.) c.37	Fisheries Act 1891	s.6(3) subst.	43, s.1(2), Sch.2, para.9
c.38	Stamp Duties Management Act 1891	s.22 am.	36, s.150(3)
c.39	Stamp Act 1891	s.15 excl.	36, s.150(2)
c.43	Forged Transfers Act 1891	s.5 rep.	43, s.1(1), Sch.1, Pt.IV, Group 1
c.xxvii	Oyster and Mussel Fishery (Loch Sween) Order Confirmation Act 1891	rep.	43, s.1(1), Sch.1, Pt.VII, Group 7
c.lii	Electric Lighting Orders Confirmation (No.4) Act 1891	Sch. Kidderminster Electric Lighting Order 1891 rep.	43, s.1(1), Sch.1, Pt.V
c.xcvi	Malvern Water Act 1891	ss.18-20,56,59, Sch. rep.	43, s.1(1), Sch.1, Pt.V
1892			
(55 & 56 Vict.) c.19	Statute Law Revision Act 1892	rep.	43, s.1(1), Sch.1, Pt.IX, Group 1
c.35	Colonial Stock Act 1892	rep. (saving)	43, s.1(1)(2), Sch.1, Pt.IV, Group 1, Sch.2, para.7
c.iii	City of Glasgow Life Assurance Company Act 1892	rep.	43, s.1(1), Sch.1, Pt.VII, Group 4

Year and Chap. or No. of Measure	Short title	How affected	1998, Chapter of Act or Number of Measure or Statutory Instrument
1892—*cont.*			
c.xxiii	Stourport Bridge Transfer Act 1892	rep.	43, s.1(1), Sch.1, Pt.V
c.ccxxvi	Water Orders Confirmation Act 1892	Sch. arts.15,16 of Ross Water Order 1892 rep.	43, s.1(1), Sch.1, Pt.V
1893			
(56 & 57 Vict.) c.14	Statute Law Revision Act 1893	s.1 rep.	43, s.1(1), Sch.1, Pt.IX, Group 1
c.54	Statute Law Revision (No.2) Act 1893	rep.	43, s.1(1), Sch.1, Pt.IX, Group 1
c.cv	Oyster and Mussel Fishery (Loch Creran) Order Confirmation Act 1893	rep.	43, s.1(1), Sch.1, Pt.VII, Group 7
c.cx	Local Government Board's Provisional Order Confirmation (No.3) Act 1893	rep.	43, s.1(1), Sch.1, Pt.V
c.cxxxii	Local Government Board's Provisional Orders Confirmation (No.16) Act 1893	Sch. Hereford and Monmouth and Hereford and Worcester Orders rep.	43, s.1(1), Sch.1, Pt.V
1894			
(57 & 58 Vict.) c.li	Mussel Fishery (Cockenzie) Order Confirmation Act 1894	rep.	43, s.1(1), Sch.1, Pt.VII, Group 7
1895			
(58 & 59 Vict.) c.16	Finance Act 1895	s.12 restr. (pt.prosp.)	45, s.39(3)
c.xxx	Ayr Faculty of Solicitors Widows' Fund Society Act 1895	rep.	43, s.1(1), Sch.1, Pt.VII, Group 1
c.lxxxvi	Local Government Board's Provisional Orders Confirmation (No.5) Act 1895	Sch. County of Worcester (Dowles and Upper Arley) Order 1895 rep.	43, s.1(1), Sch.1, Pt.V
1895			
(59 Vict.) c.v	Local Government Board's Provisional Orders Confirmation (No.3) Act 1895	Sch. Upton upon Severn (Hanley Castle and Welland) Order 1895 rep.	43, s.1(1), Sch.1, Pt.V
1896			
(59 & 60 Vict.) c.lxxii	Malvern Link (Extension and Water) Act 1896	rep. (except ss.1,3,41-43,45,47,49,57,58,60)	43, s.1(1), Sch.1, Pt.V
c.cii	Local Government Board's Provisional Orders Confirmation (No.7) Act 1896	Sch. Evesham Joint Hospital Order 1896 rep.	43, s.1(1), Sch.1, Pt.V
c.ccxxviii	Kidderminster and Stourport Electric Tramway Act 1896	rep.	43, s.1(1), Sch.1, Pt.V
1897			
(60 & 61 Vict.) c.30	Police Property Act 1897	rep. (NI) (saving) (*prosp.*)	32, s.74(2)(3), Schs.5,6

Year and Chap. or No. of Measure	Short title	How affected	1998, Chapter of Act or Number of Measure or Statutory Instrument
1897—*cont.*			
c.lxv	Electric Lighting Orders Confirmation (No.5) Act 1897	Sch. Redditch Electric Lighting Order rep.	43, s.1(1), Sch.1, Pt.V
c.lxxv	Local Government Board's Provisional Orders Confirmation (No.10) Act 1897	rep.	43, s.1(1), Sch.1, Pt.V
c.lxxvi	Local Government Board's Provisional Order Confirmation (Gas) Act 1897	rep.	43, s.1(1), Sch.1, Pt.V
c.lxxx	Pier and Harbour Orders Confirmation (No.5) Act 1897	Scrabster Harbour Order am.	SI 1221(L), art.17
c.cxxxvi	Malvern Link Gas Act 1897	rep. (except ss.1,3,20)	43, s.1(1), Sch.1, Pt.V
1898			
(61 & 62 Vict.) c.22	Statute Law Revision Act 1898	rep.	43, s.1(1), Sch.1, Pt.IX, Group 1
c.37	Local Government (Ireland) Act 1898	saving (*prosp.*)	47, s.95(3)
c.xxxi	Local Government Board's Provisional Orders Confirmation (No.1) Act 1898	Sch. Tewkesbury Rural Order rep.	43, s.1(1), Sch.1, Pt.V
c.xxxix	Electric Lighting Orders Confirmation (No.3) Act 1898	Sch. Hereford Electric Lighting Order 1898 rep.	43, s.1(1), Sch.1, Pt.V
1901			
(1 Edw. 7) c.cli	Local Government Board's Provisional Orders Confirmation (No.10) Act 1901	Sch. Upton -upon-Severn and Pershore Joint Hospital District Order rep.	43, s.1(1), Sch.1, Pt.V
c.cxci	Worcester Tramways Act 1901	rep. (except ss.1,3,13(A) (D))	43, s.1(1), Sch.1, Pt.V
1902			
(2 Edw. 7) c.14	University of Wales Act 1902	rep.	43, s.1(1), Sch.1, Pt.III, Group 2
1903			
(3 Edw. 7) c.37	Irish Land Act 1903	ss.27-42,47 rep. (*prosp.*)	47, s.100(2), Sch.15
c.lix	Local Government Board's Provisional Orders Confirmation (No.2) Act 1903	Sch. Yardley Rural Order 1903 rep.	43, s.1(1), Sch.1, Pt.V
c.lx	Local Government Board's Provisional Orders Confirmation (No.3) Act 1903	rep.	43, s.1(1), Sch.1, Pt.V
c.cxlix	Scottish Episcopal Clergy Widows' and Orphans' Fund Order Confirmation Act 1903	rep.	43, s.1(1), Sch.1, Pt.VII, Group 6

Year and Chap. or No. of Measure	Short title	How affected	1998, Chapter of Act or Number of Measure or Statutory Instrument
1904			
(4 Edw. 7) c.11	University of Liverpool Act 1904	rep.	43, s.1(1), Sch.1, Pt.III, Group 2
c.12	Leeds University Act 1904	rep.	43, s.1(1), Sch.1, Pt.III, Group 2
c.lxv	Local Government Board's Provisional Order Confirmation (Poor Law) Act 1904	rep.	43, s.1(1), Sch.1, Pt.V
c.cxlviii	Scotch Education Department Provisional Order Confirmation (Edinburgh) Act 1904	rep.	43, s.1(1), Sch.1, Pt.VII, Group 3
1905			
(5 Edw. 7) c.cxxxiii	Worcestershire County Council (Bridges) Act 1905	rep.	43, s.1(1), Sch.1, Pt.V
c.clxxxiv	Malvern Water Act 1905	ss.2,7,8,23,27, Schs.1,2 rep.	43, s.1(1), Sch.1, Pt.V
1906			
(6 Edw. 7) c.xxx	Norwich Union Life Insurance Society (Scottish Imperial Fusion) Act 1906	rep.	43, s.1(1), Sch.1, Pt.VII, Group 4
1907			
(7 Edw. 7) c.24	Limited Partnership Act 1907	defns. of "limited partner" and "general partner" appl. (1.1.1999)	GSM 1, s.6(5)
c.51	Sheriff Courts (Scotland) Act 1907	s.14 mod.	42, s.18(4)(e)
c.cl	Dumbarton Burgh Order Confirmation Act 1907	rep.	43, s.1(1), Sch.1, Pt.VII, Group 6
c.clxi	Local Government Board's Provisional Orders Confirmation (No.11) Act 1907	Sch. Evesham Order 1907 rep.	43, s.1(1), Sch.1, Pt.V
1908			
(8 Edw. 7) c.49	Statute Law Revision Act 1908	rep.	43, s.1(1), Sch.1, Pt.IX, Group 1
c.i	Transfer of Training Colleges (Scotland) Order Confirmation Act 1908	rep.	43, s.1(1), Sch.1, Pt.VII, Group 3
1909			
(9 Edw. 7) c.i	Zetland Masonic Sick and Widows and Orphans Fund Order Confirmation Act 1909	rep.	43, s.1(1), Sch.1, Pt.VII, Group 6
c.xlii	University of Bristol Act 1909	s.9 rep.	43, s.1(1), Sch.1, Pt.III, Group 2
c.xci	Stourbridge and District Water Board Act 1909	ss.51,54, Sch. rep.	43, s.1(1), Sch.1, Pt.V
1910			
(10 Edw. 7 & 1 Geo. 5) c.cxxxii	Oyster and Mussel Fishery (Bay of Firth) Order Confirmation Act 1910	rep.	43, s.1(1), Sch.1, Pt.VII, Group 7

Year and Chap. or No. of Measure	Short title	How affected	1998, Chapter of Act or Number of Measure or Statutory Instrument
1911			
(1 & 2 Geo. 5) c.28	Official Secrets Act 1911	saved (6.5.1999)	46, s.30, Sch.5, Pt.II, s.B8(a)
c.xxxiii	St.Andrew's Ambulance Association Order Confirmation Act 1911	rep.	43, s.1(1), Sch.1, Pt.VII, Group 1
c.lxxvii	Chester Waterworks Act	s.2 rep.in pt.	SI 281, art.4, Sch.2, Pt.I
		ss.41-48,50-56,60,61,63, 64,70,71 rep.	SI 281, art.4, Sch.2, Pt.I
c.cxxix	Partick Burgh Order Confirmation Act 1911	rep.	43, s.1(1), Sch.1, Pt.VII, Group 6
c.cxlix	Local Government Board's Provisional Orders Confirmation (No.14) Act 1911	Sch. Hereford Order 1911 rep.	43, s.1(1), Sch.1, Pt.V
c.clii	Local Government Board's Provisional Order Confirmation (Gas) (No.2) Act 1911	rep.	43, s.1(1), Sch.1, Pt.V
c.cliv	Education Board Provisional Orders Confirmation (Durham, &c.) Act 1911	Sch. Worcestershire County Council order rep.	43, s.1(1), Sch.1, Pt.V
c.clix	Pier and Harbour Order Confirmation (No.3) Act 1911	rep.	43, s.1(1), Sch.1, Pt.VII, Group 6
1912			
(2 & 3 Geo. 5) c.cxxix	Local Government Board's Provisional Orders Confirmation (No.3) Act 1912	Sch. Kington Order 1912 rep.	43, s.1(1), Sch.1, Pt.V
c.cxxxi	Local Government Board's Provisional Order Confirmation (No.5) Act 1912	rep.	43, s.1(1), Sch.1, Pt.V
1913			
(3 & 4 Geo. 5) c.cxlvii	Pier and Harbour Orders Confirmation (No.2) Act 1913	rep.	43, s.1(1), Sch.1, Pt.VII, Group 6
1914			
(4 & 5 Geo. 5) c.4	Sheffield University Act 1914	rep.	43, s.1(1), Sch.1, Pt.III, Group 2
c.lxviii	Lanarkshire Gas Order Confirmation Act 1914	rep.	43, s.1(1), Sch.1, Pt.VII, Group 6
1915			
(5 & 6 Geo. 5) c.32	Irish Police (Naval and Military Service) Act 1915	rep. (saving)(*prosp.*)	32, s.74(2)(3), Schs.5,6
1917			
(7 & 8 Geo. 5) c.21	Venereal Disease Act 1917	rep.	43, s.1(1), Sch.1, Pt.X, Group 5
1918			
(8 & 9 Geo. 5) c.53	Constabulary and Police (Ireland) Act 1918	rep. (saving)(*prosp.*)	32, s.74(2)(3), Schs.5,6

Year and Chap. or No. of Measure	Short title	How affected	1998, Chapter of Act or Number of Measure or Statutory Instrument
1918—*cont.*			
c.54	Tithe Act 1918	rep.	43, s.1(1), Sch.1, Pt.II, Group 2
c.xlii	Bristol Corporation Act 1918	s.64 rep.	SI 1209(L), art.19, Sch.
1919 (9 & 10 Geo. 5) c.19	Local Government (Ireland) Act 1919	saving (*prosp.*)	47, s.95(3)
c.50	Ministry of Transport Act 1919	s.17(1) trans.of functions (1.7.1999)	46, ss.53,56(1)(a)
c.68	Constabulary and Police (Ireland) Act 1919	rep. (saving)(*prosp.*)	32, s.74(2)(3), Schs.5,6
c.lxxi	Pier and Harbour Orders Confirmation Act 1919	rep.	43, s.1(1), Sch.1, Pt.VII, Group 6
c.cx	Scottish Amicable Life Assurance Society's Order Confirmation Act 1919	rep.	43, s.1(1), Sch.1, Pt.VII, Group 6
1920 (10 & 11 Geo. 5) c.65	Employment of Women, Young Persons and Children Act 1920	s.1(2) excl.	31, s.112(2)
c.67	Government of Ireland Act 1920	rep. (*prosp.*)	47, ss.2,100(2), Sch.15
		s.29 rep. & superseded (in part)	36, ss.150(1)(4),165, Sch.27, Pt.V(2)
		s.61 saving (*prosp.*)	47, s.95(2)
c.75	Official Secrets Act 1920	saved (6.5.1999)	46, s.30, Sch.5, Pt.II, s.B8(a)
1921 (11 & 12 Geo. 5) c.32	Finance Act 1921	ss.50,51 rep.	SI 1446, art.30(2), Sch.2, Pt.I
c.xii	Dundee Gas Order Confimation Act 1921	rep.	43, s.1(1), Sch.1, Pt.VII, Group 6
1922 (12 & 13 Geo. 5) c.55	Constabulary (Ireland) Act 1922	rep. (saving)(*prosp.*)	32, s.74(2)(3), Schs.5,6
1923 (13 & 14 Geo. 5) c.33	Universities of Oxford and Cambridge Act 1923	ss.7(1)(2)(3),8(2) rep.in pt.	43, s.1(1), Sch.1, Pt.III, Group 2
		Sch., paras.6-11,33,35,56 rep.	43, s.1(1), Sch.1, Pt.III, Group 2
c.xxxvi	Ministry of Health Provisional Orders Confirmation (No.3) Act 1923	Sch. Hereford Order 1923 rep.	43, s.1(1), Sch.1, Pt.V
c.xli	Ministry of Health Provisional Orders Confirmation (No.8) Act 1923	Sch. Stourbridge and District Water Board Order, Sch.r, art.8(3) rep.	43, s.1(1), Sch.1, Pt.V
1924 (14 & 15 Geo. 5) c.iv	Leith Harbour and Docks Order Confirmation Act 1924	rep.	43, s.1(1), Sch.1, Pt.VII, Group 6

Year and Chap. or No. of Measure	Short title	How affected	1998, Chapter of Act or Number of Measure or Statutory Instrument
1925			
(15 & 16 Geo. 5) c.18	Settled Land Act 1925	s.73(1)(xvi) rep.	43, s.1(1), Sch.1, Pt.II, Group 2
c.20	Law of Property Act 1925	defn. of "convey" appl. (*prosp.*)	v, s.2(1)
c.21	Land Registration Act 1925	appl. (*prosp.*)	31, s.76, Sch.22, Pt.III, para.9(1)
c.24	Universities and College Estates Act 1925	s.26(1)(xiv) rep.	43, s.1(1), Sch.1, Pt.II, Group 2
c.86	Criminal Justice Act 1925	s.11(3) rep.	43, s.1(1), Sch.1, Pt.VIII
c.87	Tithe Act 1925	rep.	43, s.1(1), Sch.1, Pt.II, Group 2
c.88	Coastguard Act 1925	saved (6.5.1999)	46, s.30, Sch.5, Pt.II, s.E3(a)
1926			
(16 & 17 Geo. 5) c.28	Mining Industry Act 1926	s.23(6) added (*prosp.*)	17, s.50, Sch.4, para.1
c.xxxvii	Glasgow Education Authority (Juvenile Delinquency) Order Confirmation Act 1926	rep.	43, s.1(1), Sch.1, Pt.VII, Group 3
c.lxxiii	Kidderminster and Stourport Electric Tramway Act 1926	rep.	43, s.1(1), Sch.1, Pt.V
c.lxxxiv	University of Reading Act 1926	s.7 rep.	43, s.1(1), Sch.1, Pt.III, Group 2
No.4	Ecclesiastical Commissioners Measure 1926	saved (1.1.1999)	GSM 1, s.5(1), Sch.2, Pt.I
1927			
(17 & 18 Geo. 5) c.35	Sheriff Court and Legal Officers (Scotland) Act 1927	ss.1(2),2,3,5,12 rep.in pt. (1.7.1999)	46, s.125, Sch.8, para.3, Sch.9
c.xxxviii	Ministry of Health Provisional Orders Confirmation (No.9) Act 1927	Sch. Hereford Order 1927 rep.	43, s.1(1), Sch.1, Pt.V
1928			
(18 & 19 Geo. 5) No.2	Tithe (Administration of Trusts) Measure 1928	rep.	43, s.1(1), Sch.1, Pt.II, Group 2
1929			
(19 & 20 Geo. 5) c.29	Government Annuities Act 1929	ss.32(4),62(3)(4) rep.in pt.	43, s.1(1), Sch.1, Pt.X, Group 5
1929			
(20 & 21 Geo. 5) c.5	Colonial Development Act 1929	rep.	43, s.1(1), Sch.1, Pt.IV, Group 1
c.xi	Leith Harbour and Docks Order Confirmation Act 1929	rep.	43, s.1(1), Sch.1, Pt.VII, Group 6
c.xxx	Ministry of Health Provisional Orders Confirmation (No.11) Act 1929	Sch. Upton upon Severn Order 1929 rep.	43, s.1(1), Sch.1, Pt.V

Year and Chap. or No. of Measure	Short title	How affected	1998, Chapter of Act or Number of Measure or Statutory Instrument
1929—*cont.* c.xxxiii	Ministry of Health Provisional Orders Confirmation (Bristol and Ross Water)Act 1929	Sch. Ross Water Order, arts.46,51 rep.	43, s.1(1), Sch.1, Pt.V
1930 (20 & 21 Geo. 5) c.lvii	Chester Waterworks Act	s.2 rep.in pt.	SI 281, art.4, Sch.2, Pt.I
		ss.17,29,30,32,34-45,51-56,69,70 rep.	SI 281, art.4, Sch.2, Pt.I
c.cv	Ministry of Health Provisional Orders Confirmation (Kidderminster and Llanelly) Act 1930	rep.	43, s.1(1), Sch.1, Pt.V
1931 (21 & 22 Geo. 5) c.24	Sentence of Death (Expectant Mothers) Act 1931	rep.	37, ss.36(6)(a),120(2), Sch.10
c.28	Finance Act 1931	s.28(6) rep.	43, s.1(1), Sch.1, Pt.IV, Group 2
		Sch.2 subst.	43, s.1(2), Sch.2, para.10
c.49	Finance (No.2) Act 1931	s.22 ext.	36, s.161(1)
1932 (22 & 23 Geo. 5) c.xxii	St Andrews Links Order Confirmation Act 1932	rep.	43, s.1(1), Sch.1, Pt.VII, Group 6
1933 (23 & 24 Geo. 5) c.12	Children and Young Persons Act 1933	defn. of "guardian" appl.	37, s.106, Sch.7, para.25 (adding 1973 c.62, s.46(3))
		defn. of "guardian" appl.	37, s.106, Sch.7, para.45 (adding 1991 c.53 s.58(9))
		defn. of "guardian" appl.	37, s.106, Sch.7, para.52 (adding 1997 c.43 s.50(7))
		s.1(7) am. (*prosp.*)	31, s.140(1), Sch.30, para.1
		s.18(1)(a) am.	SI 276, reg.2(1)(2)(a)
		s.18(1)(aa) added	SI 276, reg.2(1)(2)(b)
		s.18(1)(f) rev.	SI 276, reg.2(1)(2)(c)
		s.18(1)(f) rep.	SI 2857, reg.1(2)(a)
		s.18(1)(g)-(j) added	SI 276, reg.2(1)(2)(d)
		s.18(2)(a) added	SI 276, reg.3(1)(3)(b)
		s.18(2)(a)(i) am.	SI 276, reg.2(1)(3)(a)
		s.18(2)(ia) added	SI 276, reg.3(1)(3)(b)
		s.18(2A) added	SI 276, reg.2(1)(4)
		s.18(3) am.	SI 276, reg.2(1)(5)(a)
		s.18(3)(b) am.	SI 276, reg.2(1)(5)(b)
		s.21(2A) added	SI 276, reg.3
		s.23 am.	SI 276, reg.4
		s.25(1) am.	SI 276, reg.5(a)

Year and Chap. or No. of Measure	Short title	How affected	1998, Chapter of Act or Number of Measure or Statutory Instrument
1933—*cont.*			
		s.25(1)(b) added	SI 276, reg.5(b)
		s.25(2) am.	SI 276, reg.5(c)(d)
		s.25(3) am.	SI 276, reg.5(e)
		s.25(4)-(8) am.	SI 276, reg.5(d)
		s.25(7) am.	SI 276, reg.5(f)
		s.25(9) rep.	SI 276, reg.5(g)
		s.26(2) am.	SI 276, reg.6(a)
		s.26(2)(b) added	SI 276, reg.6(b)
		s.28(1) am.	SI 276, reg.7(a)
		s.28(1)(2) excl.	31, s.112(2)
		s.28(2)(a) am.	SI 276, reg.7(b)
		s.28(2)(b) am.	SI 276, reg.7(c)
		s.47(2) rep.in pt.	37, ss.47(6),120(2), Sch.10
		s.49(4A)(e) subst. (*prosp.*)	37, s.119, Sch.8, para.1
		s.53 am.	37, s.107(5) (adding 1997 c.43 s.9A)
		s.55(1A)(a) am.	37, s.106, Sch.7, para.1(1)
		s.55(1A)(b) replaced (by s.55(1A)(b)(bb))	37, s.106, Sch.7, para.1(2)
		s.55(1A)(d) mod. (*temp.*)	SI 2327, art.5(2)(a)
		s.55(1A)(d) subst.	37, s.119, Sch.8, para.2
		s.55(6) added	37, s.106, Sch.7, para.1(3)
		s.56(1A) added (4.1.1999)	37, s.119, Sch.8, para.3
		s.58 am.	37, s.119, Sch.8, para.4
		Sch.2, para.15(a) am.	37, s.48(1)(a)
		Sch.2, para.15(a) rep.in pt.	37, ss.48(1)(a),120(2), Sch.10
		Sch.2, para.15(b) am.	37, s.48(1)(b)
		Sch.2, para.15(c) am.	37, s.48(1)(c)
		Sch.2, para.17 rep.in pt.	37, ss.48(2),120(2), Sch.10
c.36	Administration of Justice (Miscellaneous Provisions) Act 1933	s.2(2)(ac) added (4.1.1999)	37, s.119, Sch.8, para.5(1)(a)
		s.2(2)(c) added (4.1.1999)	37, s.119, Sch.8, para.5(1)(b)
		s.2(2) proviso, para.(iB) added (4.1.1999)	37, s.119, Sch.8, para.5(2)
c.41	Administration of Justice (Scotland) Act 1933	ss.24(7),25 rep.in pt. (1.7.1999)	46, s.125, Sch.8, para.4, Sch.9
c.xvii	Ministry of Health Provisional Orders Confirmation (Hereford and West Kent Main Sewerage District) Act 1933	Sch. Hereford Order 1933 rep.	43, s.1(1), Sch.1, Pt.V
1934			
(24 & 25 Geo. 5) c.36	Petroleum (Production) Act 1934	rep. (saving)(*prosp.*)	17, ss.49,51, Sch.3, Pt.II, para.3, Sch.5, Pt.I
c.56	Incitement to Disaffection Act 1934	s.2(4) am. (NI) (*prosp.*)	32, s.74(1), Sch.4, para.1

Year and Chap. or No. of Measure	Short title	How affected	1998, Chapter of Act or Number of Measure or Statutory Instrument
1935 (25 & 26 Geo. 5) c.xix	Chester Waterworks Act	s.3 rep.	SI 281, art.4, Sch.2, Pt.I
1935 (26 Geo. 5 & 1 Edw. 8) c.2	Government of India Act 1935	rep.	43, s.1(1), Sch.1, Pt.X, Group 5
1936 (26 Geo. 5 & 1 Edw. 8) c.43	Tithe Act 1936	s.30, Sch.6 rep.	43, s.1(1), Sch.1, Pt.II, Group 2
c.52	Private Legislation Procedure (Scotland) Act 1936	saved (1.7.1999) s.1(5) added (1.7.1999)	46, ss.29,53(4), Sch.4, Pt.I, paras.1(2)(b),9 46, s.125, Sch.8, para.5
c.cxiii	Hereford Corporation Act 1936	rep. (except ss.1,4,11, 12,66-72,76(pt.),165, 167,169,171 and Schs.1, 2)	43, s.1(1), Sch.1, Pt.V
1937 (1 Edw. 8 & 1 Geo. 6) c.33	Diseases of Fish Act 1937	s.1 excl.	SI 190, reg.34, Sch.6
c.37	Children and Young Persons (Scotland) Act 1937	s.28(1)(a) am. s.28(1)(aa) added s.28(1)(f) rep. s.28(1)(f) rep. s.28(1)(g)-(j) added s.28(2)(a) added s.28(2)(a)(i) am. s.28(2)(ia) added s.28(2A) added s.28(3) am. s.28(3)(b) am. s.31(2A) added s.33 am. s.36(1) am. s.36(2)(a) am. s.36(2)(b) am.	SI 276, reg.8(1)(2)(a) SI 276, reg.8(1)(2)(b) SI 276, reg.8(1)(2)(c) SI 2857, reg.1(2)(b) SI 276, reg.8(1)(2)(d) SI 276, reg.8(1)(3)(b) SI 276, reg.8(1)(3)(a) SI 276, reg.8(1)(3)(b) SI 276, reg.8(1)(4) SI 276, reg.8(1)(5)(a) SI 276, reg.8(1)(5)(b) SI 276, reg.9 SI 276, reg.10 SI 276, reg.11(a) SI 276, reg.11(b) SI 276, reg.11(c)
c.48	Methylated Spirits (Sale by Retail) (Scotland) Act 1937	ss.1(1),2,4 rep. s.5 rep.in pt. s.6 (defn. of "local authority") rep.	SI 1602, art.2(1) SI 1602, art.2(2) SI 1602, art.2(3)
c.iv	Ministry of Health Provisional Order Confirmation (Evesham and Pershore Joint Hospital District) Act 1937	rep.	43, s.1(1), Sch.1, Pt.V
1937 (1 & 2 Geo. 6) c.iv	Empire Exhibition (Scotland) Order Confirmation Act 1937	rep.	43, s.1(1), Sch.1, Pt.VII, Group 8
1939 (2 & 3 Geo. 6) c.69	Import, Export and Customs Powers (Defence) Act 1939	saved (6.5.1999)	46, s.30, Sch.5, Pt.II, s.C5

Year and Chap. or No. of Measure	Short title	How affected	1998, Chapter of Act or Number of Measure or Statutory Instrument
1939—*cont.*			
c.83	Pensions (Navy, Army, Air Force and Mercantile Marine) Act 1939	ss.3-5,7 saved (6.5.1999)	46, s.30, Sch.5, Pt.II, s.F4
c.100	Government and other Stocks (Emergency Provisions) Act 1939	s.1(1)(2)(4) rep.in pt.	43, s.1(1), Sch.1, Pt.IV, Group 1
1940 (3 & 4 Geo. 6) c.42	Law Reform (Miscellaneous Provisions) (Scotland) Act 1940	s.3 mod. (*prosp.*)	42, s.8(5)(a)
1942 (5 & 6 Geo. 6) c.21	Finance Act 1942	s.47(1ZA) added	11, s.34
		s.47(4)(c) rep.	SI 1446, art.30(2), Sch.2, Pt.I
		Sch.11, Pt.II rep.in pt.	SI 1446, art.30(2), Sch.2, Pt.I
1943 (6 & 7 Geo. 6) No.2	Episcopal Endowments and Stipends Measure 1943	saved (1.1.1999)	GSM 1, s.5(1), Sch.2, Pt.I
1944 (7 & 8 Geo. 6) c.10	Disabled Persons (Employment) Act 1944	saved (6.5.1999)	46, s.30, Sch.5, Pt.II, s.H3(a)
1945 (9 & 10 Geo. 6) c.17	Police (Overseas Service) Act 1945	ext. (to Northern Ireland) (*prosp.*)	32, s.74(1), Sch.4, para.2
		s.3(4) rep. (*prosp.*)	32, s.74(1)(3), Sch.4, para.2, Sch.6
c.18	Statutory Orders (Special Procedure) Act 1945	defn. of "any order" appl.	38, s.44(3)(e)
		s.8(2) rep. (S)	43, s.1(1), Sch.1, Pt.X, Group 5
		s.10 appl.(mods.)	iii, s.1, Sch. O., s.59(3) (b)
1946 (9 & 10 Geo. 6) c.27	Bank of England Act 1946	s.1(4) am.	11, s.8(1)
		s.1(6) added	11, s.8(2)
		s.2 rep.	11, s.43, Sch.9, Pt.I
		s.3(3) am.	11, s.9(3)
		s.4(1) am.	11, s.10
		s.4(2) rep.	11, s.43, Sch.9, Pt.I
		Sch.1, para.11A added	11, s.8(3)
		Sch.1, para.14 subst.	11, s.8(4)
		Sch.2 rep.	11, s.43, Sch.9, Pt.I
c.36	Statutory Instruments Act 1946	ext. (1.1.1999)	GSM 1, s.1(5)
		appl.(mods.) (1.1.1999)	GSM 1, s.5(8)
		mod. (1.7.1999)	46, s.118(5)
		s.1(1A) added (*prosp.*)	38, s.125, Sch.12, para.2
		s.7(1) appl.	35, s.19(3)(c)

Year and Chap. or No. of Measure	Short title	How affected	1998, Chapter of Act or Number of Measure or Statutory Instrument
1946—*cont.*			
		s.8 am. (*prosp.*)	47, s.85(11)
c.45	United Nations Act 1946	s.1(4) am. (1.7.1999)	46, s.125, Sch.8, para.6
c.64	Finance Act 1946	s.66 rep.	SI 1446, art.30(2), Sch.2, Pt.I
1947			
(10 & 11 Geo. 6) c.19	Polish Resettlement Act 1947	s.1 saved (6.5.1999)	46, s.30, Sch.5, Pt.II, s.F4
c.30	Indian Independence Act 1947	s.18(2) rep.	43, s.1(1), Sch.1, Pt.X, Group 5
c.37	Northern Ireland Act 1947	ss.8,9(1)(5),14(1)(2) rep. (*prosp.*)	47, s.100(2), Sch.15
c.40	Industrial Organisation and Development Act 1947	s.9 trans.of functions (1.7.1999)	46, ss.53,56(1)(c)
c.44	Crown Proceedings Act 1947	defn. of "authorised government department" appl. (*prosp.*)	42, s.21(1)
		defn. of "Minister of the Crown" appl. (*prosp.*)	42, s.21(1)
		s.38(2) (defns. of "His Majesty's aircraft", "His Majesty's ships" and "officer") am. (20.5.1999)	46, s.125, Sch.8, para.7(2)
		s.38(3) appl. (*prosp.*)	7, s.14(4)
		s.38(3) appl. (*prosp.*)	33, s.28(4)
		s.40(2) am. (20.5.1999)	46, s.125, Sch.8, para.7(3) (a)
		s.40(3A) added (20.5.1999)	46, s.125, Sch.8, para.7(3) (b)
		s.44 am. the proviso (20.5.1999)	46, s.125, Sch.8, para.7(4)
		s.50 am. (20.5.1999) (S)	46, s.125, Sch.8, para.7(5) (a)
		s.50(2)(e) added (20.5.1999)	46, s.125, Sch.8, para.7(5) (b)
		s.51(2)(ii) am. (20.5.1999)	46, s.125, Sch.8, para.7(6)
No.2	Church Commissioners Measure 1947	s.4(2)(b) rep. (1.1.1999)	GSM 1, s.7(1), Sch.4, para.2
		s.5(1) subst. (1.1.1999)	GSM 1, s.7(1), Sch.4, para.3(a)
		s.5(4)(a) subst. (1.1.1999)	GSM 1, s.7(1), Sch.4, para.3(b)(i)
		s.5(4)(b)(c) rep.in pt. (1.1.1999)	GSM 1, s.7(1), Sch.4, para.3(b)(ii)
		s.5(4A) added (1.1.1999)	GSM 1, s.7(1), Sch.4, para.3(c)
		s.5(5) rep. (1.1.1999)	GSM 1, s.7(1), Sch.4, para.3(d)
		s.6(1) subst. (1.1.1999)	GSM 1, s.7(1), Sch.4, para.4(a)
		s.6(2) rep. (1.1.1999)	GSM 1, s.7(1), Sch.4, para.4(b)

Year and Chap. or No. of Measure	Short title	How affected	1998, Chapter of Act or Number of Measure or Statutory Instrument
1947—*cont.*			
		s.6(3B)(3C) added (1.1.1999)	GSM 1, s.7(1), Sch.4, para.4(c)
		s.6(4) rep.in pt. (1.1.1999)	GSM 1, s.7(1), Sch.4, para.4(d)
		s.7(2) am. (1.1.1999)	GSM 1, s.7(1), Sch.4, para.5
		s.10(1) am. (1.1.1999)	GSM 1, s.7(1), Sch.4, para.6
		ss.10(2)(3),13(1),14 rep. (1.1.1999)	GSM 1, s.13(2)
		s.17(1) am. (1.1.1999)	GSM 1, s.7(1), Sch.4, para.7
		Sch.II rep. (1.1.1999)	GSM 1, s.13(2)
		Sch.IV, para.1,2 am. (1.1.1999)	GSM 1, s.7(1), Sch.4, para.9
		Sch.IV, para.3 subst. (1.1.1999)	GSM 1, s.7(1), Sch.4, para.9(c)
		Sch.IV, para.4 am. (1.1.1999)	GSM 1, s.7(1), Sch.4, para.9(d)
		Sch.IV, para.5, proviso rep. (1.1.1999)	GSM 1, s.7(1), Sch.4, para.9(e)
		Sch.IV, para.7 am. (1.1.1999)	GSM 1, s.7(1), Sch.4, para.9(f)
		Sch.1, para.1 power to am. (1.1.1999)	GSM 1, s.5(2)(a)
		Sch.1, para.1 subst. (1.1.1999)	GSM 1, s.7(1), Sch.4, para.8(a)
		Sch.1, para.2 subst. (1.1.1999)	GSM 1, s.7(1), Sch.4, para.8(b)
		Sch.1, para.3 am. (1.1.1999)	GSM 1, s.7(1), Sch.4, para.8(c)
		Sch.1, para.5 subst. (1.1.1999)	GSM 1, s.7(1), Sch.4, para.8(d)
		Sch.1, para.5A subst. (1.1.1999)	GSM 1, s.7(1), Sch.4, para.8(e)
1948 (11 & 12 Geo. 6) c.29	National Assistance Act 1948	s.21(2A)(2B) added (EW)	19, s.1
		s.22(4) am.	SI 498, reg.2
c.47	Agricultural Wages Act 1948	excl. (*prosp.*)	39, s.46(3)(4)(a)
		power to am. (*prosp.*)	39, s.47(2)(a)(3)
		s.2(1)(c) added	38, s.149
		s.3(2B)(2C) added (*prosp.*)	39, s.47, Sch.2, Pt.I, para.2(2)
		s.3(8)-(15) added (*prosp.*)	39, s.47, Sch.2, Pt.I, para.2(3)
		s.3A added (*prosp.*)	39, s.47, Sch.2, Pt.I, para.3
		s.4(1) rep.in pt. (*prosp.*)	39, ss.47,53, Sch.2, Pt.I, para.4(1)(a)(ii), Sch.3
		s.4(1)(a)(b)(d) rep. (*prosp.*)	39, ss.47,53, Sch.2, Pt.I, para.4(1)(a)(i), Sch.3

Year and Chap. or No. of Measure	Short title	How affected	1998, Chapter of Act or Number of Measure or Statutory Instrument
1948—*cont.*			
		s.4(2) rep. (*prosp.*)	39, ss.47,53, Sch.2, Pt.I, para.4(1)(b), Sch.3
		s.4(3) rep.in pt. (*prosp.*)	39, ss.47,53, Sch.2, Pt.I, para.4(1)(c), Sch.3
		s.4(4) rep. (*prosp.*)	39, ss.47,53, Sch.2, Pt.I, para.4(1)(d), Sch.3
		s.4, sidenote am. (*prosp.*)	39, s.47, Sch.2, Pt.I, para.4(2)
		s.5(1) am. (*prosp.*)	39, s.47, Sch.2, Pt.I, para.5(2)
		s.5(1A)(1B) added (*prosp.*)	39, s.47, Sch.2, Pt.I, para.5(3)
		s.5(2) am. (*prosp.*)	39, s.47, Sch.2, Pt.I, para.5(4)
		s.7 power to am. (*prosp.*)	39, s.47(4)(a)
		s.7(2) rep. (*prosp.*)	39, s.53, Sch.3
		s.11(1)(a) rep. (*prosp.*)	39, ss.47,53, Sch.2, Pt.I, para.6, Sch.3
		s.12(5)(a) rep.in pt. (*prosp.*)	39, ss.47,53, Sch.2, Pt.I, para.7(2), Sch.3
		s.12(8)(9) added (*prosp.*)	39, s.47, Sch.2, Pt.I, para.7(3)
		s.15A added (*prosp.*)	39, s.47, Sch.2, Pt.I, para.8
		s.17(1) (defn. of "the national minimum wage") added (*prosp.*)	39, s.47, Sch.2, Pt.I, para.9(2)
		s.17(1A) added (*prosp.*)	39, s.47, Sch.2, Pt.I, para.9(3)
		s.17A added (*prosp.*)	39, s.47, Sch.2, Pt.I, para.10
c.57	Public Registers and Records (Scotland) Act 1948	s.1(1) am. (1.7.1999)	46, s.125, Sch.8, para.8
c.ix	Church of Scotland Trust (Amendment) Order Confirmation Act 1948	rep.	43, s.1(1), Sch.1, Pt.VII, Group 8
1948 (12, 13 & 14 Geo. 6) c.1	Colonial Stock Act 1948	rep.	43, s.1(1), Sch.1, Pt.IV, Group 1
1949 (12, 13 & 14 Geo. 6) c.30	Agricultural Wages (Scotland) Act 1949	excl. (*prosp.*)	39, s.46(3)(4)(b)
		power to am. (*prosp.*)	39, s.47(2)(b)(3)
		s.3(2B)(2C) added (*prosp.*)	39, s.47, Sch.2, Pt.II, para.12(2)
		s.3(8)-(15) added (*prosp.*)	39, s.47, Sch.2, Pt.II, para.12(3)
		s.3A added (*prosp.*)	39, s.47, Sch.2, Pt.II, para.13
		s.4(1) rep.in pt. (*prosp.*)	39, ss.47,53, Sch.2, Pt.II, para.14(a)(ii), Sch.3

Year and Chap. or No. of Measure	Short title	How affected	1998, Chapter of Act or Number of Measure or Statutory Instrument
1949—*cont.*			
		s.4(1)(a)(b)(d) rep. (*prosp.*)	39, ss.47,53, Sch.2, Pt.II, para.14(a)(i), Sch.3
		s.4(2) rep. (*prosp.*)	39, ss.47,53, Sch.2, Pt.II, para.14(b), Sch.3
		s.4(3) rep.in pt. (*prosp.*)	39, ss.47,53, Sch.2, Pt.II, para.14(c), Sch.3
		s.4(4) rep. (*prosp.*)	39, ss.47,53, Sch.2, Pt.II, para.14(d), Sch.3
		s.5(1) am. (*prosp.*)	39, s.47, Sch.2, Pt.II, para.15(2)
		s.5(1A)(1B) added (*prosp.*)	39, s.47, Sch.2, Pt.II, para.15(3)
		s.5(2) am. (*prosp.*)	39, s.47, Sch.2, Pt.II, para.15(4)
		s.7 power to am. (*prosp.*)	39, s.47(4)(b)
		s.11(1)(a) rep. (*prosp.*)	39, ss.47,53, Sch.2, Pt.II, para.16, Sch.3
		s.12(4)(a) rep. (*prosp.*)	39, ss.47,53, Sch.2, Pt.II, para.17(2), Sch.3
		s.12(7)(8) added (*prosp.*)	39, s.47, Sch.2, Pt.II, para.17(3)
		s.15A added (*prosp.*)	39, s.47, Sch.2, Pt.II, para.18
		s.17(1) (defn. of "the national minimum wage") added (*prosp.*)	39, s.47, Sch.2, Pt.II, para.19(2)
		s.17(1A) added (*prosp.*)	39, s.47, Sch.2, Pt.II, para.19(3)
		s.17A added (*prosp.*)	39, s.47, Sch.2, Pt.II, para.20
c.42	Lands Tribunal Act 1949	s.2(9) am. (1.7.1999)	46, s.125, Sch.8, para.9(a)(i)
		s.2(9)(a) am. (1.7.1999)	46, s.125, Sch.8, para.9(a)(ii)
		s.2(10) added (1.7.1999)	46, s.125, Sch.8, para.9(b)
c.54	Wireless Telegraphy Act 1949	power to restrict regulations conferred	6, s.4(4)
		defn. of "wireless telegraphy" appl.	6, s.8
		s.1(2) restr.	6, s.3(7)
		s.1(4) power to restr. conferred	6, s.4(1)
		s.2(1) am.	6, s.7, Sch.1, para.1(a)(b)
		s.3A rep.	6, s.7, Sch.2, Pt.I
		s.4 rep.	6, s.7, Sch.1, para.2, Sch.2, Pt.I
		ss.9-13 (Pt.II) saved (6.5.1999)	46, s.30, Sch.5, Pt.II, s.C10
		ss.9,11,12 referred to	SI 3036
		s.20(3) ext.	6, s.9(2)
		s.2(1), proviso am.	6, s.7, Sch.1, para.1(c)

Year and Chap. or No. of Measure	Short title	How affected	1998, Chapter of Act or Number of Measure or Statutory Instrument
1949—*cont.*			
c.76	Marriage Act 1949	ss.27,32,41,51,57,63,64, 65 am. (1.4.1999)	SI 3171, art.2, Sch.
c.xi	University of Nottingham Act 1949	s.7 rep.	43, s.1(1), Sch.1, Pt.III, Group 2
1950			
(14 Geo. 6) c.6	Statute Law Revision Act 1950	s.3(2) rep.	43, s.1(1), Sch.1, Pt.IX, Group 1
c.xxvi	Merchants House of Glasgow (Crematorium) Order Confiramtion Act 1950	rep.	43, s.1(1), Sch.1, Pt.VII, Group 8
1951			
(14 & 15 Geo. 6) c.65	Reserve and Auxiliary Forces (Protection of Civil Interests) Act 1951	Sch.1, para.1(i) rep.in pt. (1.1.1999)	SI 3086, reg.10(1)
1952			
(15 & 16 Geo. 6 & 1 Eliz. 2) c.39	Motor Vehicles (International Circulation) Act 1952	saved (6.5.1999)	46, s.30, Sch.5, Pt.II, s.E1(a)
c.52	Prison Act 1952	s.43(1)(d) subst. (*prosp.*)	37, s.119, Sch.8, para.6
		s.49(1) am. (*prosp.*)	37, s.119, Sch.8, para.7(1)
		s.49(2) am. (*prosp.*)	37, s.119, Sch.8, para.7(2)
		s.49(5) added (*prosp.*)	37, s.119, Sch.8, para.7(3)
c.66	Defamation Act 1952	s.10 ext.	38, s.77(5)
		s.10 am. (19.11.1998)	46, s.125, Sch.8, para.10
1952			
(1 & 2 Eliz. 2) c.3	Public Works Loans Act 1952	s.6 rep. (*prosp.*)	47, s.100(2), Sch.15
1953			
(1 & 2 Eliz. 2) c.20	Births and Deaths Registration Act 1953	ss.13,30,31,32,33 am. (1.4.1999)	SI 3171, art.2, Sch.
c.iv	University of Southampton Act 1953	s.7 rep.	43, s.1(1), Sch.1, Pt.III, Group 2
c.xix	Clyde Navigation Order Confirmation Act 1953	rep.	43, s.1(1), Sch.1, Pt.VII, Group 6
No.2	Diocesan Stipends Funds Measure 1953	s.4(1)(ba)(bb)(bc) added (1.1.1999)	GSM 1, s.13(1), Sch.5, para.1(a)
		s.5(1)(ab) added (1.1.1999)	GSM 1, s.13(1), Sch.5, para.1(b)
1953			
(2 & 3 Eliz. 2) c.5	Statute Law Revision Act 1953	s.1 rep.	43, s.1(1), Sch.1, Pt.IX, Group 1
1954			
(2 & 3 Eliz. 2) c.17	Royal Irish Constabulary (Widow's Pension) Act 1954	rep. (saving)(*prosp.*)	32, s.74(2)(3), Schs.5,6
c.56	Landlord and Tenant Act 1954	appl. (*prosp.*)	31, s.76, Sch.22, Pt.III, para.10(1)(2)
		s.30(2) excl. (*prosp.*)	v, s.13(1)(a)
		s.59(1) am.	38, s.129, Sch.15, para.1
(2 & 3 Eliz. 2)		ss.59(1B),60B rep.	38, s.152, Sch.18, Pt.IV

Year and Chap. or No. of Measure	Short title	How affected	1998, Chapter of Act or Number of Measure or Statutory Instrument
1954—_cont._			
c.61	Pharmacy Act 1954	saved (6.5.1999)	46, s.30, Sch.5, Pt.II, s.G2(a)
		s.24(1) (defn. of "a registered pharmaceutical chemist") appl.	29, s.69(1)(d)
c.70	Mines and Quarries Act 1954	s.85 rep.	SI 2307, reg.16
		Sch.4 rep.in pt. (the paragraph relating to the Petroleum (Production) Act 1934) (_prosp._)	17, s.51, Sch.5, Pt.I
c.i	Dunoon Burgh (Pavilion Expenditure) Order Confirmation) Act 1954	rep.	43, s.1(1), Sch.1, Pt.VII, Group 5
c.xxxix	Royal Russell School Act 1954	rep. (except ss.1-3,6,12-15,25,26)	SI 2883(L), art.2, Appx.
1955			
(3 & 4 Eliz. 2) c.18	Army Act 1955	cont. (until 31/8/1999)	SI 1499, art.2
		defn. of "Her Majesty's forces" appl.	33, s.5(7)
		am.	42, ss.21(5),22(7)
		s.3(3) am. (1.1.1999)	SI 3086, reg.9(2)
		s.9 mod. (1.1.1999) transtl. provn.	SI 3086, reg.11, Sch., para.1
		s.15 am. (1.1.1999)	SI 3086, reg.9(3)
		s.21(3) am. (1.1.1999)	SI 3086, reg.9(4)
		s.57(2)(a) rep.in pt. (1.1.1999)	SI 3086, reg.4(1)(a)
		s.57(2B)(2C) added (1.1.1999)	SI 3086, reg.4(2)
		s.70(4) am. (_prosp._)	7, s.12(a)
		s.71(5) rep.in pt. (1.1.1999)	SI 3086, reg.3(1)
		s.71(5A)(5B) added (1.1.1999)	SI 3086, reg.3(2)
		s.76C(9) replaced (by s.76C(9)(9A)) (1.1.1999)	SI 3086, reg.3(4)
		s.133A(2) am. (pt. renumbered as para.(a)) (1.1.1999)	SI 3086, reg.5(1)
		s.133A(2)(b) added (1.1.1999)	SI 3086, reg.5(1)
		s.150A(3) am. (_prosp._)	14, s.86(1), Sch.7, para.1
		s.150AA(3) am. (_prosp._)	SI 1506, art.78(1), Sch.6, para.1
		s.167(2) am. (1.1.1999)	SI 3086, reg.9(5)
(3 & 4 Eliz. 2)		s.225(1) (defn. of "service property") subst. (1.1.1999)	SI 3086, reg.7
		s.225(2) rep. (1.1.1999)	SI 3086, reg.9(1)
		Sch.7, paras.4A,4B mod. (1.1.1999) transtl. provn.	SI 3086, reg.11, Sch., para.4
c.19	Air Force Act 1955	cont. (until 31/8/1999)	SI 1499, art.2
		am.	42, ss.21(5),22(7)

Year and Chap. or No. of Measure	Short title	How affected	1998, Chapter of Act or Number of Measure or Statutory Instrument
1955—*cont.*			
		s.9 mod. (1.1.1999) transtl. provn.	SI 3086, reg.11, Sch., para.2
		s.15 am. (1.1.1999)	SI 3086, reg.9(3)
		s.21(3) am. (1.1.1999)	SI 3086, reg.9(4)
		s.57(2)(a) rep.in pt. (1.1.1999)	SI 3086, reg.4(1)(a)
		s.57(2B)(2C) added (1.1.1999)	SI 3086, reg.4(2)
		s.70(4) am. (*prosp.*)	7, s.12(b)
		s.71(5) rep.in pt. (1.1.1999)	SI 3086, reg.3(1)
		s.71(5A)(5B) added (1.1.1999)	SI 3086, reg.3(2)
		s.76C(9) replaced (by s.76C(9)(9A)) (1.1.1999)	SI 3086, reg.3(4)
		s.133A(2) am. (pt.renumbered as para.(a))(1.1.1999)	SI 3086, reg.5(1)
		s.133A(2)(b) added (1.1.1999)	SI 3086, reg.5(1)
		s.150A(3) am. (*prosp.*)	14, s.86(1), Sch.7, para.2
		s.150AA(3) am. (*prosp.*)	SI 1506, art.78(1), Sch.6, para.2
		s.167(2) am. (1.1.1999)	SI 3086, reg.9(6)
		s.223(1) subst. (1.1.1999)	SI 3086, reg.7
		s.223(2) rep. (1.1.1999)	SI 3086, reg.9(1)
1955 (4 & 5 Eliz. 2) c.6	Miscellaneous Financial Provisions Act 1955	s.5 appl.(mods.)	SI 1446, art.22(2)
c.ii	Writers to the Signet Widows' Fund Order Confirmation Act 1955	rep.	43, s.1(1), Sch.1, Pt.VII, Group 6
1956 (4 & 5 Eliz. 2) c.28	Agricultural Research Act 1956	rep.	43, s.1(1), Sch.1, Pt.X, Group 4
c.60	Valuation and Rating (Scotland) Act 1956	s.6(1) mod. (1.4.1997)	SI 947, arts.1(2),7
1957 (5 & 6 Eliz. 2) c.53	Naval Discipline Act 1957	cont. (until 31/8/1999)	SI 1499, art.2
		am.	42, ss.21(5),22(7)
		s.38(3)(a) rep.in pt. (1.1.1999)	SI 3086, reg.4(1)(b)
		s.38(3B)(3C) added (1.1.1999)	SI 3086, reg.4(3)
		s.43(6) rep.in pt. (1.1.1999)	SI 3086, reg.3(1)
		s.43(6A)(6B) added (1.1.1999)	SI 3086, reg.3(3)
		s.48(2) am. (*prosp.*)	7, s.12(c)
		s.128F(2) am. (pt. renumbered as para.(a)) (1.1.1999)	SI 3086, reg.5(1)
		s.128F(2)(b) added (1.1.1999)	SI 3086, reg.5(1)
c.x	City of London (Various Powers) Act 1957	s.4 (defns. of "ward election" and "ward list") appl.	3, s.2(3)

Year and Chap. or No. of Measure	Short title	How affected	1998, Chapter of Act or Number of Measure or Statutory Instrument
1957—cont.			
c.xxviii	Tamar Bridge Act 1957	s.4 (defns. of "the Act of 1998", "tidal work" and "Trinity House") added	iv, s.34(1)(a)
		s.4 (defn. of "the bridge") subst.	iv, s.34(1)(b)
		s.20 appl.	iv, s.16
		s.27 subst.	iv, s.34(2)
		s.33(1) subst.	iv, s.34(3)(a)
		s.33(3) added	iv, s.34(3)(b)
		s.36(1)(2) added	iv, s.34(4)(a)(b)
		s.36(3) subst.	iv, s.34(4)(c)
		ss.37-39 subst.	iv, s.34(5)(6)(7)
		s.40(1) am.	iv, s.34(8)(a)
		s.40(2) subst.	iv, s.34(8)(b)
		s.41 subst.	iv, s.34(9)
		s.46A added	iv, s.34(10)
		s.60(1)(e) am.	iv, s.34(11)
		s.60(4) excl.	iv, s.31(1)
		s.65 excl.	iv, s.36(24)
		s.67(1) replaced (by s.67(1)(1A))	iv, s.34(12)(a)
		s.67(3)(4) am.	iv, s.34(12)(b)
		s.67(7) am.	iv, s.34(12)(c)
		s.67(8) replaced (by s.67(8)(8A)(8B)(8C)	iv, s.34(12)(d)
		s.70(1) am.	iv, s.34(13)(a)-(c)
		s.70(5A) added	iv, s.34(13)(d)
		s.72 am.	iv, s.34(14)
		s.73 am.	iv, s.34(15)
		s.78 am.	iv, s.34(16)
1958			
(6 & 7 Eliz. 2) c.47	Agricultural Marketing Act 1958	s.19A mod. (*prosp.*)	41, s.45(7), Sch.7, Pt.II, para.20(2)(b)
c.51	Public Records Act 1958	restr. (*prosp.*)	38, s.116(1)
		mod. (*prosp.*)	38, s.116(2)
		Sch.1, para.2(2)(e) added (*prosp.*)	38, s.125, Sch.12, para.3(2)
		Sch.1, para.3, Table , Pt.I am. (*prosp.*)	38, s.125, Sch.12, para.3(3)
		Sch.1, para.3, Table , Pt.I rep.in pt. (*prosp.*)	38, s.152, Sch.18, Pt.II
		Sch.1, para.3, Table , Pt.II am.	22, s.7(3), Sch.2 (adding 1993 c.39, Sch.6A)
		Sch.1, para.3, Table , Pt.II am. (*prosp.*)	29, s.74(1), Sch.15, para.1(1)
		Sch.1, para.3, Table , Pt.II rep.in pt. (*prosp.*)	31, s.140(3), Sch.31
		Sch.1, para.3, Table , Pt.II rep.in pt. (*prosp.*)	38, s.152, Sch.18, Pt.II

Year and Chap. or No. of Measure	Short title	How affected	1998, Chapter of Act or Number of Measure or Statutory Instrument
1958—*cont.*			
		Sch.1, para.4(1)(nn) added (insertion of para.4(1)(nn) continued) (*prosp.*)	29, s.74(1), Sch.15, para.1(2)(3)
		Sch.1, para.5 am. (*prosp.*)	38, s.125, Sch.12, para.3(4)
		Sch.1, para.6 am. (*prosp.*)	38, s.125, Sch.12, para.3(5)
		Sch.1, para.7(1) am. (*prosp.*)	38, s.125, Sch.12, para.3(6)
		Sch.1, Table , Pt.II, para.3 am. (*prosp.*)	22, s.1(5), Sch.1, Pt.III, para.8
		Sch.1, Table , Pt.II, para.3 am.	22, s.14(11)
		Sch.1, Table , Pt.II, para.3 am. (*prosp.*)	30, s.44(1), Sch.3, para.1
		Sch.1, Table , Pt.II, para.3 am. (pt.prosp.)	45, s.32, Sch.7, para.1
1960			
(8 & 9 Eliz. 2) c.41	Ghana (Consequential Provisions) Act 1960	s.1(3) rep.	43, s.1(1), Sch.1, Pt.IV, Group 1
c.52	Cyprus Act 1960	Sch., para.9 rep.	43, s.1(1), Sch.1, Pt.IV, Group 1
c.66	Professions Supplementary to Medicine Act 1960	saved (6.5.1999)	46, s.30, Sch.5, Pt.II, s.G2(b)
c.67	Public Bodies (Admission to Meetings) Act 1960	saved (EW)	18, s.12(4)
		s.1(4)(b) saved (EW)	18, s.10(5)(a)
		Sch., para.1(ba) added	38, s.128, Sch.14, Pt.II, para.13
		Sch., para.1(bb) rep.	38, s.152, Sch.18, Pt.V
1961			
(9 & 10 Eliz. 2) c.9	Agricultural Research etc. (Pensions) Act 1961	s.1(1) rep.in pt.	43, s.1(1), Sch.1, Pt.X, Group 4
		s.1(1)(a)(3) rep.	43, s.1(1), Sch.1, Pt.X, Group 4
		s.2(1) rep.in pt.	43, s.1(1), Sch.1, Pt.X, Group 4
c.27	Carriage by Air Act 1961	saved (6.5.1999)	46, s.30, Sch.5, Pt.II, s.E4(a)
		s.1(1A) added	SI 1751, s.3(1)
		s.14(2) subst.	SI 1751, s.3(2)
c.33	Land Compensation Act 1961	appl.	iv, s.8(2)
		appl.(mods.)	iv, s.10(3)
		appl.	38, s.127, Sch.13, para.3 (adding 1975 c.70, Sch.4, at Pt.III, para.5(5))
		mod. (pt.prosp.)	45, s.19(6)-(8), Sch.4, paras.1-5
		appl. (pt.prosp.)	45, s.23, Sch.6, para.1(5)

Year and Chap. or No. of Measure	Short title	How affected	1998, Chapter of Act or Number of Measure or Statutory Instrument
1961—*cont.*			
		ss.1-4 (Pt.I) appl.	SI 1936(L), arts.11(6), 19(6),21(10),32(6),33(7), 36(4)
		ss.1-4 (Pt.I) appl.	SI 2919(L), art.4(2)
		ss.1-4 (Pt.I) appl. (13.1.1999)	SI 3269(L), arts.9(5), 16(7), 18(4),27(3)
		ss.2,4 appl.(mods.)	38, s.127, Sch.13, para.3 (adding 1975 c.70, Sch.4, at Pt.IV, para.15(4))
		ss.23-29 (Pt.IV) excl. (pt.prosp.)	45, s.19(8)
		s.23(3)(aa) rep.	38, s.152, Sch.18, Pt.V
		s.23(3)(za) added	38, s.128, Sch.14, Pt.II, para.14
c.34	Factories Act 1961	ss.22,23,25-27 rep.	SI 2307, reg.15
		ss.74,128,131,132 rep.	SI 543, reg.14(1)
		s.178 am. (1.4.1999)	SI 3171, art.2, Sch.
c.42	Sheriffs' Pensions (Scotland) Act 1961	power to am.	42, s.18(6), Sch.4, paras.3,4
c.cxliv	Bristol Corporation Act 1961	defn.of (" craft") explained	SI 1209(L), art.18(7)
		s.4(1) (defn. of "vessel") subst.	SI 1209(L), art.18(2)
		s.4(1) (defn. of "craft") rep.	SI 1209(L), art.19, Sch.
		s.8 rep.	SI 1209(L), art.19, Sch.
		s.17 appl.	SI 1209(L), art.7(4)
		s.18 rep.in pt. (proviso rep.)	SI 1209(L), art.19, Sch.
		s.18(1) rep.in pt.	SI 1209(L), art.19, Sch.
		s.18(2) am.	SI 1209(L), art.18(3)(a)
		s.18(5) added	SI 1209(L), art.18(3)(b)
		s.22(1)(2) subst.	SI 1209(L), art.18(4)
		s.25, proviso rep.	SI 1209(L), art.19, Sch.
		s.25(1) am.	SI 1209(L), art.18(5)
		s.30 rep.	SI 1209(L), art.19, Sch.
		s.31 subst.	SI 1209(L), art.18(6)
		Schs.3,5 rep.	SI 1209(L), art.19, Sch.
No.3	Clergy Pensions Measure 1961	saved (1.1.1999)	GSM 1, s.5(1)(a)(iv)
		s.21(5) trans.of functions (1.1.1999)	SI 1715, art.2, Sch.1
1962			
(10 & 11 Eliz. 2) c.12	Education Act 1962	power to trans. functions modify etc. in relation to certain savings	30, s.25(3)(a)
		rep. (*prosp.*)	30, s.44(2), Sch.4
		mod. (*prosp.*)	31, s.44(7)
		power to appl.	31, s.144(3)(4)
c.30	Northern Ireland Act 1962	s.25, Sch.2 rep.	43, s.1(1), Sch.1, Pt.I, Group 2

Year and Chap. or No. of Measure	Short title	How affected	1998, Chapter of Act or Number of Measure or Statutory Instrument
1962—*cont.*			
c.43	Carriage by Air (Supplementary Provisions) Act 1962	saved (6.5.1999)	46, s.30, Sch.5, Pt.II, s.E4(b)
c.48	Law Reform (Husband and Wife) Act 1962	s.1(3) rep. (26.4.1999)	SI 2940, art.4
c.58	Pipe-lines Act 1962	saved (6.5.1999)	46, s.30, Sch.5, Pt.II, s.D2(d)
		s.49(1)-(3) mod. (*prosp.*)	17, s.28(4)
		s.49(1)-(3) ext. (as modified) (NI) (*prosp.*)	17, s.28(5)
		s.65 (defn. of "pipelines") appl.	46, s.30, Sch.5, Pt.II, s.D2(d)
1963			
c.14	Corn Rents Act 1963	s.2 rep.	43, s.1(1), Sch.1, Pt.II, Group 2
c.18	Stock Transfer Act 1963	defn. of "registered securities" appl. (*prosp.*)	v, s.9(2)
c.25	Finance Act 1963	s.55(1)(d)(e) am. (24.3.1998)	36, s.149(1)(4)(5)
c.33	London Government Act 1963	s.31 rep. (*prosp.*)	31, s.140(3), Sch.31
c.37	Children and Young Persons Act 1963	s.37(1) am.	SI 276, reg.12(1)(2)
		s.37(2) am.	SI 276, reg.12(1)(3)
		s.37(3) am.	SI 276, reg.12(1)(4)(a)(b)
		s.37(3)(a) am.	SI 276, reg.12(1)(4)(c)
		s.37(3)(b) rep.in pt.	SI 276, reg.12(1)(4)(d)
		s.37(4) am.	SI 276, reg.12(1)(5)
		s.37(6) am.	SI 276, reg.12(1)(6)
		s.38(1) am.	SI 276, reg.13
		s.39(1)(2) am.	SI 276, reg.14(1)(2)
		s.39(3) am.	SI 276, reg.14(1)(3)
		s.39(5) am.	SI 276, reg.14(1)(4)
		s.40(1)(a) am.	SI 276, reg.15
		s.42(1) am.	SI 276, reg.16(1)(2)
		s.42(2) am.	SI 276, reg.16(1)(3)
c.41	Offices, Shops and Railway Premises Act 1963	s.19 rep.	SI 2306, reg.38
No.1	Ecclesiastical Jurisdiction Measure 1963	s.58 saved (1.1.1999)	GSM 1, s.5(1), Sch.2, Pt.I
No.2	Cathedrals Measure 1963	saved (1.1.1999)	GSM 1, s.5(1), Sch.2, Pt.II
1964			
c.16	Industrial Training Act 1964	s.16 rep.	43, s.1(1), Sch.1, Pt.X, Group 5
c.26	Licensing Act 1964	s.8A added	SI 114, art.2
		ss.9A,9B added	SI 114, art.3(1)
		s.115(3) rep.	38, s.152, Sch.18, Pt.IV
		s.193AA added	SI 114, art.4
		s.201(1) (defn. of "interim authority") am.	SI 114, art.3(2)
		Sch.10, para.1(1A) am.	38, s.152, Sch.18, Pt.IV

Year and Chap. or No. of Measure	Short title	How affected	1998, Chapter of Act or Number of Measure or Statutory Instrument
1964—*cont.*			
c.29	Continental Shelf Act 1964	s.1(3) rep. (*prosp.*)	17, ss.50,51, Sch.4, para.2(2), Sch.5, Pt.I
		s.1(8) rep.in pt. (*prosp.*)	17, ss.50,51, Sch.4, para.2(2), Sch.5, Pt.I
		s.6 am.	6, s.7, Sch.1, para.3
		ss.6,7 am. (*prosp.*)	17, s.50, Sch.4, para.2(3)
		s.8(1A) added (*prosp.*)	17, s.50, Sch.4, para.2(4)
c.48	Police Act 1964	defn. of "police authority" appl. (13.1.1999)	SI 3269(L), art.40(3)(a)
c.51	Universities and Colleges Estates Act 1964	s.1(1) rep.in pt.	43, s.1(1), Sch.1, Pt.II, Group 1
c.60	Emergency Laws (Re-enactments and Repeals) Act 1964	s.2 saved (6.5.1999)	46, s.30, Sch.5, Pt.II, s.C15(a)
c.81	Diplomatic Privileges Act 1964	Sch.1 appl. (*prosp.*)	33, s.15(5)
		Sch.1, art.29 appl. (*prosp.*)	7, s.8(1)(a)
		Sch.1, art.30(1)(2) appl. (*prosp.*)	7, s.8(1)(b)
		Sch.1, art.31(1)(2)(3) appl. (*prosp.*)	7, s.8(1)(c)
		Sch.1, art.34 appl. (*prosp.*)	7, s.8(1)(d)
		Sch.1, art.36(1)(b) appl.(mods.) (*prosp.*)	7, s.8(2)
1965			
c.4	Science and Technology Act 1965	defn. of "Research Councils" saved (6.5.1999)	46, s.30, Sch.5, Pt.II, s.C12
		defn. of "Research Councils" appl. (*prosp.*)	47, s.4(1), Sch.3, para.35
		ss.1(1)(a),2(4) rep.in pt.	43, s.1(1), Sch.1, Pt.X, Group 4
		s.2(4) am.	43, s.1(2), Sch.2, para.11
		s.2(5) rep.in pt.	43, s.1(1), Sch.1, Pt.X, Group 4
		s.5 saved (6.5.1999)	46, s.30, Sch.5, Pt.II, s.C12
		s.5 trans.of functions (1.7.1999)	46, ss.53,56(1)(d)
c.19	Teaching Council (Scotland) Act 1965	s.1(3) added	30, s.16
		Sch.1, para.9 added	30, s.17
c.24	Severn Bridge Tolls Act	s.92 appl.	iii, s.1, Sch., O., s.53
		s.92(8) (defn. of "bus services") excl.	iii, s.1, Sch., O., s.53
c.32	Administration of Estates (Small Payments) Act 1965	s.6(1) ext.(mods.)	SI 633, art.J20(3)
		Sch.1, Pt.I, Sch.3 rep.in pt. (entry relating to 1840 c.110 rep.)	43, s.1(1), Sch.1, Pt.IV, Group 4
c.49	Registration of Births, Deaths and Marriages (Scotland) Act 1965	s.1(1) am. (1.7.1999)	46, s.125, Sch.8, para.12

Year and Chap. or No. of Measure	Short title	How affected	1998, Chapter of Act or Number of Measure or Statutory Instrument
1965—*cont.*			
c.51	National Insurance Act 1965	power to mod. (EWS) (*prosp.*)	14, s.11(1)(3)
		s.36(1) am.	SI 470, art.11(1)
c.52	National Insurance (Industrial Injuries) Act 1965	power to mod. (EWS) (*prosp.*)	14, s.11(1)(3)
c.56	Compulsory Purchase Act 1965	mod.	SI 1936(L), art.29(2)(3), Sch.7, paras.3-9
		ext.(mods.) (pt.prosp.)	45, s.20, Sch.5, Pt.II, para.3(1)
		ss.1-32 (Pt.I) appl.(mods.)	SI 1936(L), arts.27(1)(2), 35
		ss.1-32 (Pt.I) appl.(mods.)	SI 2919(L), art.4(1)(2)
		ss.1-32 (Pt.I) appl.(mods.) (13.1.1999)	SI 3269(L), arts.23(1)(2), 24, Sch.7
		ss.1-32 (Pt.I) appl.(mods.) (exc.s.4, Sch.3, para.3(3))	iv, ss.4(2)-(4),5(2)-(4), 6(1),13, Sch.
		ss.1-32 (Pt.I) appl.(mods.)	38, s.127, Sch.13, para.3 (adding 1975 c.70, Sch.4, at Pt.II, para.4)
		ss.1-32 (Pt.I) mod. (pt.prosp.)	45, s.20(6)(7), Sch.5, Pt.II, paras.3,4,5
		ss.1-32 (Pt.I) appl.(mods.) (other than s.31) (pt.prosp.)	45, s.20(7)
		s.7 appl.(mods.)	38, s.127, Sch.13, para.3 (adding 1975 c.70, at Sch.4, Pt.III, para.6(4)(a))
		s.7 ext. (pt.prosp.)	45, s.23, Sch.6, para.2(4)-(8)
		s.10 appl.(mods.)	38, s.127, Sch.13, para.3 (adding 1975 c.70, at Sch.4, Pt.III, para.6(4)(a))
		s.10 ext. (pt.prosp.)	45, s.23, Sch.6, para.2(4)-(8)
		s.10(2) saved	SI 1936(L), arts.21(9)(10), 32(7),33(8)
c.69	Criminal Procedure (Attendance of Witnesses) Act 1965	s.2(4) am. (4.1.1999)	37, s.119, Sch.8, para.8
c.74	Superannuation Act 1965	s.38(2)(a)(b) rep.in pt.	43, s.1(1), Sch.1, Pt.IV, Group 5
c.xii	Writers to the Signet Widows' Fund Order Confirmation Act 1965	rep.	43, s.1(1), Sch.1, Pt.VII, Group 6
1966			
c.4	Mines (Working Facilities and Support) Act 1966	appl.(mods.) (*prosp.*)	17, ss.7(1),9
		ext. (*prosp.*)	17, ss.7(3)(4),9
		s.2(1) saved (*prosp.*)	17, ss.7(3)(4),9
		s.15(5), Sch.2 rep. (*prosp.*)	17, s.51, Sch.5, Pt.I

Year and Chap. or No. of Measure	Short title	How affected	1998, Chapter of Act or Number of Measure or Statutory Instrument
1966—*cont.* c.36	Veterinary Surgeons Act 1966	defn. of "veterinary surgery" defn(s). appl. (11.1.1999)	41, s.3(1)(d), Sch.4, Pt.II, para.12
		saved (6.5.1999)	46, s.30, Sch.5, Pt.II, s.G2(c)
c.45	Armed Forces Act 1966	s.4 appl.(mods.) (1.1.1999)	SI 3086, reg.8(1)(2) (subst. 1981 c.55, Sch.3, para.12)
		ss.4,5 mod. (1.1.1999) transtl. provn.	SI 3086, reg.11, Sch., para.3
c.xli	Lee Valley Regional Park Act 1966	s.15(3) added	SI 458, art.3(1)
		s.23A added	SI 458, art.3(2)
1967 c.1	Land Commission Act 1967	rep.	43, s.1(1), Sch.1, Pt.IV, Group 2
c.10	Forestry Act 1967	power to rep. or am. (*prosp.*)	38, s.105, Sch.7, para.1(2)
c.13	Parliamentary Commissioner Act 1967	s.3(2) am. (*prosp.*)	38, s.125, Sch.12, para.5
		s.4(3A) added (*prosp.*)	38, s.125, Sch.12, para.6
		s.5 mod.	31, s.25, Sch.5, para.9
		s.5(2)(b) excl. (*prosp.*)	47, s.78(2)(a)
		s.5(2A) added (NI) (*prosp.*)	SI 3162, art.105(1), Sch.3
		s.5(8) am. (*prosp.*)	14, s.86(1), Sch.7, para.3(1)
		s.11(2A) am. (*prosp.*)	38, s.125, Sch.12, para.7
		s.11A(1) am. (*prosp.*)	38, s.125, Sch.12, para.8(2)
		s.11A(2) am. (*prosp.*)	38, s.125, Sch.12, para.8(3)
		s.11A, sidenote am. (*prosp.*)	38, s.125, Sch.12, para.8(4)
		Sch.2 am.	SI 1340, reg.9(6), Sch.2, para.7
		Sch.2 rep.in pt. (*prosp.*)	22, ss.1(5),26, Sch.1, Pt.III, para.9(b), Sch.5, Pt.I
		Sch.2 am. (*prosp.*)	22, s.1(5), Sch.1, Pt.III, para.9(a)
		Sch.2 am. (*prosp.*)	29, s.74(1), Sch.15, para.2
		Sch.2 am. (*prosp.*)	38, s.125, Sch.12, para.9(a)
		Sch.2 am.	38, s.129, Sch.15, para.2
		Sch.2 rep.in pt. (*prosp.*)	38, s.152, Sch.18, Pt.I
		Sch.2 rep.in pt.	38, s.152, Sch.18, Pt.IV
		Sch.2 rep.in pt.	38, s.152, Sch.18, Pt.VI
		Sch.2 am. (pt.prosp.)	45, s.32, Sch.7, para.2
		Sch.2, Note 1A am. (*prosp.*)	38, s.125, Sch.12, para.9(b)
		Sch.2, Note 1B added (*prosp.*)	38, s.125, Sch.12, para.9(c)

Year and Chap. or No. of Measure	Short title	How affected	1998, Chapter of Act or Number of Measure or Statutory Instrument
1967—*cont.*			
		Sch.4 rep.in pt. (*prosp.*)	14, s.86(1)(2), Sch.7, para.3(2), Sch.8
		Sch.4 am. (*prosp.*)	29, s.74(1), Sch.15, para.3
c.22	Agriculture Act 1967	s.67 restr. (*prosp.*)	39, s.47, Sch.2, Pt.II, para.12(3) (adding 1949 c.30, s.3(14))
		s.67 power to am. (*prosp.*)	39, s.47(2)(c)(3)
c.41	Marine, &c., Broadcasting (Offences) Act 1967	s.7A(1) rep.in pt. (1.1.1999)	SI 3086, reg.10(2)
c.58	Criminal Law Act 1967	s.5 restr.	35, s.14(2)(c)
c.77	Police (Scotland) Act 1967	appl. (*prosp.*)	32, s.51, Sch.3, para.8(9)
		appl. (*prosp.*)	32, s.73(1)
		defn. of "police force" appl.	40, s.1(1) (adding 1989 c.4, s.2A(11))
		s.38A(1)(ca) added (*prosp.*)	32, s.74(1), Sch.4, para.4(2)
		s.38A(6)(c) am. (*prosp.*)	32, s.74(1), Sch.4, para.4(3)
		s.38A(7)(b) am. (*prosp.*)	32, s.74(1), Sch.4, para.4(4)
c.80	Criminal Justice Act 1967	s.56 ext.	37, s.106, Sch.7, para.29(2) (adding 1980 c.80 s.38(2A))
		s.56 ext.	37, s.106, Sch.7, para.30(3) (adding 1980 c.43 s.38A(5A))
		s.56(1)(b)(i) am.	37, s.106, Sch.7, para.2(1)
		s.56(2) am.	37, s.106, Sch.7, para.2(2)
		s.56(2) am. (*prosp.*)	37, s.119, Sch.8, para.9(1)(a)
		s.56(2) am.	37, s.119, Sch.8, para.9(1)(b)
		s.56(3) rep.	37, ss.106,120(2), Sch.7, para.2(3), Sch.10
		s.56(5) replaced (by s.56(5)(5A)(5B)(5C))	37, s.106, Sch.7, para.2(4)
		s.56(6) rep. (*prosp.*)	37, ss.119,120(2), Sch.8, para.9(2), Sch.10
		s.56(13) rep.	37, ss.106,120(2), Sch.7, para.2(5), Sch.10
		s.67 appl.	37, s.119, Sch.8, para.135(3)(d) (adding 1997 c.43 Sch.1, para.8(6))
		s.67(5)(b) rep.	37, s.119, Sch.8, para.10(a)
		s.67(5)(c) rep. (*prosp.*)	37, ss.119,120(2), Sch.8, para.10(b), Sch.10
		s.104(2) am.	37, ss.119,120(1), Sch.8, para.11, Sch.9, para.15
c.86	Countryside (Scotland) Act 1967	s.72 rep.	43, s.1(1), Sch.1, Pt.IV, Group 2

Year and Chap. or No. of Measure	Short title	How affected	1998, Chapter of Act or Number of Measure or Statutory Instrument
1967—*cont.*			
c.88	Leasehold Reform Act 1967	s.24(2) rep.	43, s.1(1), Sch.1, Pt.IV, Group 2
		ss.28(5)(bb),29(6A) rep.	38, s.152, Sch.18, Pt.IV
		ss.29(7),30(7) rep.in pt.	38, s.152, Sch.18, Pt.IV
		Sch.4, Pt.II, para.6, Sch.4A, para.2(2)(e) rep.	38, s.152, Sch.18, Pt.IV
1968			
c.2	Provisional Collection of Taxes Act 1968	s.1(1) rep.in pt. (6.4.1999)	36, ss.31,165, Sch.3, para.1(2)(3), Sch.27, Pt.III(2), Note
		s.1(1) am.	36, s.148(1)
		s.1(2)(b) appl. (6.5.1999)	46, s.73(5)
		ss.1(6)(7),5(3) mod.	36, s.148(2)(b)
c.7	London Cab Act 1968	ss.4,4A rep. (*prosp.*)	34, s.39(2), Sch.2
c.13	National Loans Act 1968	s.5 appl.	38, s.87
		s.5 appl. (1.7.1999)	46, s.68(1)
		s.20A added	36, s.160, Sch.26, paras.1(2),3
		Sch.1 rep.in pt.	43, s.1(1), Sch.1, Pt.IV, Group 2
		Sch.5A added	36, s.160, Sch.26, paras.1(3),3
c.19	Criminal Appeal Act 1968	s.9(2) am. (4.1.1999)	37, s.119, Sch.8, para.12
		s.10(2) rep.in pt.	37, ss.119,120(2), Sch.8, para.13(1), Sch.10
		s.10(3)(cc) added	37, s.119, Sch.8, para.13(2)
c.27	Firearms Act 1968	saved (6.5.1999)	46, s.30, Sch.5, Pt.II, s.B4
		s.21(2) am. (*prosp.*)	37, s.119, Sch.8, para.14(1)
		s.21(2A)(c) added (*prosp.*)	37, s.119, Sch.8, para.14(2)
		s.52(1) am. (*prosp.*)	37, s.119, Sch.8, para.15
c.34	Agriculture (Miscellaneous Provisions) Act 1968	s.13(2) rep.in pt.	38, s.152, Sch.18, Pt.IV
		s.46 power to am. (*prosp.*)	39, s.47(2)(d)(3)
c.44	Finance Act 1968	s.40 rep.	43, s.1(1), Sch.1, Pt.IV, Group 2
c.49	Social Work (Scotland) Act 1968	s.12(3A)(3B) added (EW)	19, s.2
		s.60(1) am.	25, s.1(2)
		s.61(1)(c)-(e) added	25, s.1(1)
		s.61A am.	25, s.1(3)
c.50	Hearing Aid Council Act 1968	saved (6.5.1999)	46, s.30, Sch.5, Pt.II, s.C7(a)
c.55	Friendly and Industrial and Provident Societies Act 1968	s.4A(3)(b) am.	38, s.140, Sch.16, para.1

Year and Chap. or No. of Measure	Short title	How affected	1998, Chapter of Act or Number of Measure or Statutory Instrument
1968—*cont.*			
c.59	Hovercraft Act 1968	defn. of "hovercraft" appl. (have effect in relation to every chargeable period ending on or after 12.5.1998)	36, s.83(3)(6)(7) (amending 1990 c.1 s.22(10))
		saved (6.5.1999)	46, s.30, Sch.5, Pt.II, s.E3(b)
c.60	Theft Act 1968	s.28 saved	37, s.106, Sch.7, para.18(3) (substituting 1973 c.62 s.11(4))
c.65	Gaming Act 1968	s.20(3) am.	SI 962, art.2
		s.20(8) am.	SI 962, art.3
		s.48(3)(4)(4A) am.	SI 456, art.2, Sch.
c.67	Medicines Act 1968	excl.in pt.	SI 1046, reg.43
		excl. (except ss.32-36 (other than s.35(8)(a)), 38,39)	SI 1047, s.74(1)(2)
		saved (6.5.1999)	46, s.30, Sch.5, Pt.II, s.J4(a)
		s.130(1) (defn. of "Medicinal products") appl. (6.5.1999)	46, s.30, Sch.5, Pt.II, s.J4
c.73	Transport Act 1968	s.14(1)(a) restr. (EW)	18, s.30(2)
		s.14(3) subst. (EW)	18, s.54(1), Sch.3, para.2
		s.95(2)(c) added	SI 2006, reg.2
		s.105(1)(b)(2) saved	SI 1936(L), art.43(16)
c.75	Miscellaneous Financial Provisions Act 1968	s.2 mod. (*prosp.*)	17, s.46(1)
		s.2(5) am. (*prosp.*)	17, s.50, Sch.4, para.3
c.77	Sea Fisheries Act 1968	s.22(6) rep.	43, s.1(1), Sch.1, Pt.X, Group 2
c.i	Airdrie Court House Commissioners (Dissolution) Order Confirmation Act 1968	rep.	43, s.1(1), Sch.1, Pt.VII, Group 8
1969			
c.16	Customs Duties (Dumping and Subsidies) Act 1969	rep.	36, ss.154,165, Sch.27, Pt.V(4)
c.32	Finance Act 1969	ss.43-49 rep.	43, s.1(1), Sch.1, Pt.IV, Group 2
		s.58(4), Table rep.in pt.	38, s.152, Sch.18, Pt.IV
c.48	Post Office Act 1969	s.3(2)-(5) rep.	6, s.7, Sch.2, Pt.I
		s.72 appl.(mods.)	SI 1126, art.6(4)
		s.72 appl.(mods.)	SI 1287, art.3(4)
		s.108(1)(c) rep.	SI 1446, art.30(2), Sch.2, Pt.I
		s.113 rep.	43, s.1(1), Sch.1, Pt.X, Group 5
		Sch.4, Pt.II, paras.84, 93(1)(xxvi)(3)(4)(f), Sch.9, Pt.II, para.27(10) rep.	43, s.1(1), Sch.1, Pt.IV, Group 2
c.51	Development of Tourism Act 1969	ss.7-16 (Pt.II),19(2), Schs.3,4 rep.	43, s.1(1), Sch.1, Pt.IV, Group 3

Year and Chap. or No. of Measure	Short title	How affected	1998, Chapter of Act or Number of Measure or Statutory Instrument
1969—*cont.*			
c.52	Statute Law (Repeals) Act 1969	ss.1,2(3) rep.	43, s.1(1), Sch.1, Pt.IX, Group 2
		s.5(1) rep.in pt.	43, s.1(1), Sch.1, Pt.IX, Group 2
		s.6, Sch. rep.	43, s.1(1), Sch.1, Pt.IX, Group 2
c.54	Children and Young Persons Act 1969	s.7(8) am.	37, s.119, Sch.8, para.16
		s.7(9) added	37, s.106, Sch.7, para.3
		s.11 am. (in force 30.9.1998 for areas sepcified in SI 1998/2327, Sch.1)	37, s.119, Sch.8, para.17
		s.12(4) added	37, s.106, Sch.7, para.4
		s.12A(3)(aa) added (*prosp.*)	37, s.71(1)
		s.12A(5) am. (*prosp.*)	37, s.71(2)
		s.12A(7)(aa) added (*prosp.*)	37, s.71(3)
		s.12AA(6) am. (1.4.1999)	37, s.71(4)
		s.12AA(6)(b)-(d) subst. (1.4.1999)	37, s.71(4)
		s.12B(1) am.	37, s.106, Sch.7, para.5(1) (a)(b)
		s.12B(1)(a) am.	37, s.106, Sch.7, para.5(1) (c)
		s.12B(1)(aa) am.	37, s.106, Sch.7, para.5(1) (d)
		s.12B(1)(b) am.	37, s.106, Sch.7, para.5(1) (e)
		s.12B(1)(c) am.	37, s.106, Sch.7, para.5(1) (f)
		s.12B(1A) added	37, s.106, Sch.7, para.5(2)
		s.12B(3) added	37, s.106, Sch.7, para.5(3)
		s.12D rep.	37, ss.119,120(2), Sch.8, para.18, Sch.10
		s.13(2) rep.	37, ss.71(5),120(2), Sch.10
		s.13(4) added (in force 30.9.1998 for areas specified in SI 1998/2327, Sch.1)	37, s.119, Sch.8, para.19
		s.15(3)(a)(b) replaced (by s.15(3)(a)(b)([c]))	37, s.72(1)
		s.15(4)(5)(6) subst.	37, s.72(2)
		s.15(7)(8) am.	37, s.72(3)
		s.16(8) am.	37, s.119, Sch.8, para.20(1)
		s.16(10) rep.	37, ss.119,120(2), Sch.8, para.20(2), Sch.10
		s.16(11) rep.in pt.	37, ss.106,120(2), Sch.7, para.6, Sch.10
		s.16A(1)(a) am.	37, s.106, Sch.7, para.7(1)
		s.16A(2)(b)(i)(ii) am.	37, s.106, Sch.7, para.7(2)
		s.16B added	37, s.119, Sch.8, para.21

Year and Chap. or No. of Measure	Short title	How affected	1998, Chapter of Act or Number of Measure or Statutory Instrument
1969—*cont.*			
		s.23 (defn. of "secure accommodation") appl. (*prosp.*)	37, s.74(7)
		s.23 mod. (*prosp.*)	37, s.98(1)
		s.23 (defn. of "secure accommodation") appl.	37, s.107(5)
		s.23(4) am. (pt.prosp.)	37, s.97(1)
		s.23(5) am. (pt.prosp.)	37, s.97(2)
		s.23(5A) added (pt.prosp.)	37, s.97(3)
		s.23(12) (defn. of "prescribed description") added (pt.prosp.)	37, s.97(4)
		s.23(14)(a) rep.	37, ss.119,120(2), Sch.8, para.22, Sch.10
		s.34(1)(c) rep.in pt.	37, ss.106,120(2), Sch.7, para.8, Sch.10
		s.69(5) rep.in pt.	37, ss.106,120(2), Sch.7, para.9, Sch.10
		s.70(1) (defn. of "youth offending team") added (in force 30.9.1998 for areas specified in SI 1998/2327, Sch.1)	37, s.119, Sch.8, para.23
		s.70(1A)(1B) subst.	37, s.106, Sch.7, para.10
		Sch.6 rep.in pt.	37, ss.106,120(2), Sch.7, para.11, Sch.10
c.57	Employers'Liability (Compulsory Insurance) Act 1969	referred to	SI 2573, regs.2-4,8,9
		excl. (*prosp.*)	29, s.6(7), Sch.5, para.4(6)
		saved (6.5.1999)	46, s.30, Sch.5, Pt.II, s.H1(a)
c.xliv	Kidderminster Corporation Act 1969	rep. (except ss.1-3.99-106,132,134,136,137,139-141,141(1),143,144 and Schs.1,3 pt.I)	43, s.1(1), Sch.1, Pt.V
c.lvi	Worcestershire County Council Act 1969	rep. (except ss.1,3,18, 85)	43, s.1(1), Sch.1, Pt.V
No.2	Synodical Government Measure 1969	Sch.2, para.4(2) trans.of functions (1.1.1999)	SI 1715, art.2, Sch.1
		Sch.2, para.10 saved (1.1.1999)	GSM 1, s.10
		Sch.2, para.10(2) am. (1.1.1999)	SI 1715, art.4(4), Sch.2, para.1
		Sch.3, rule 18(3) subst.	SI 319, para.1
		Sch.3, rule 18(5A) added	SI 319, para.2
		Sch.3, rule 18(6) am.	SI 319, para.3
		Sch.3, rule 40(1) am. (1.1.1999)	GSM 1, s.13(1), Sch.5, para.2(a)
		Sch.3, rule 42(1)(g) added (1.1.1999)	GSM 1, s.13(1), Sch.5, para.2(b)

Year and Chap. or No. of Measure	Short title	How affected	1998, Chapter of Act or Number of Measure or Statutory Instrument
1969—*cont.*			
		Sch.3, rule 44(8) subst. (1.1.1999)	GSM 1, s.13(1), Sch.5, para.2(c)
		Sch.3, rule 44(9) am. (1.1.1999)	GSM 1, s.13(1), Sch.5, para.2(d)
		Sch.3, rule 54(1)(d) added	SI 319, para.4
		Sch.3, rule 54(8)(a)(c) am. (1.1.1999)	GSM 1, s.13(1), Sch.5, para.2(e)
1970 c.9	Taxes Management Act 1970	ext.(mods.) (6.4.1999)	SI 1870, reg.35(3)-(5)
		power to appl. or extend with mods.	30, s.22(5)(g)
		defn. of "the Taxes Acts" appl.	30, s.22(6)(b)
		defn. of "the Taxes Acts" appl.	30, s.29(2) (adding 1980 c.44, s.73B(4))
		mod. (6.4.1998)	36, s.74(1), Sch.13, Pt.III, para.28 (adding 1992 c.12, Sch.5B, para.1A)
		restr.	36, s.110(8)(10)
		ext.	36, s.113, Sch.17, paras.9(3),37 (adding 1988 c.1 s.754(1A))
		restr.	36, s.113, Sch.17, paras.11,37 (adding 1988 c.1, s.754B)
		appl.(mods.)	36, s.117, Sch.18, Pt.VII, paras.61,62(5)(6)
		am.	36, s.117(2)(4), Sch.18
		ss.7-12 (Pt.II) replaced	36, s.117(1)(a)(4), Sch.18
		s.7(9)(a) am. (6.4.1998)	36, s.86, Sch.14, paras.5(a),7(5)
		s.7(9)(aa) added (6.4.1998)	36, s.86, Sch.14, paras.5(b),7(5)
		s.8 ext.	36, s.56(7)(a)(9)
		s.9(1) am. (year 1998-99 and subsequent years of assessment and shall be deemed to have had effect for the years 1996-97 and 1997-98) (*retrosp.*)	36, s.98(2)
		s.9(1A) added (year 1998- 99 and subsequent years of assessment and shall be deemed to have had effect for the years 1996-97 and 1997-98) (*retrosp.*)	36, s.98(2)(3)
		s.10 rep.	36, ss.117,165, Sch.19, para.1, Sch.27, Pt.III(28), Note
		s.10(4) rep. (6.4.1999)	36, ss.31,165, Sch.3, para.2(2)(3), Sch.27, Pt.III(2), Note

Year and Chap. or No. of Measure	Short title	How affected	1998, Chapter of Act or Number of Measure or Statutory Instrument
1970—*cont.*			
		ss.11,11AA,11AB,11AC-11AE rep.	36, ss.117,165, Sch.19, para.1, Sch.27, Pt.III(28), Note
		s.12(2) rep.in pt.	36, ss.117,165, Sch.19, para.2, Sch.27, Pt.III(28), Note
		s.12AA ext.	36, s.56(7)(b)(9)
		s.12AA(7) am.	36, s.117, Sch.19, para.3
		s.12AB subst.	36, s.117, Sch.19, para.4
		s.12AC subst.	36, s.117, Sch.19, para.5
		s.12B(1) rep.in pt.	36, ss.117,165, Sch.19, para.6, Sch.27, Pt.III(28), Note
		s.19A(1) rep.in pt.	36, ss.117,165, Sch.19, para.7, Sch.27, Pt.III(28), Note
		s.20B(4)(8)-(14)(8C) appl. (2.7.1997) (*retrosp.*)	36, s.115(1)(3) (adding 1988 c.1 s.767C)
		s.28A(1) rep.in pt.	36, ss.117,165, Sch.19, para.8(2), Sch.27, Pt.III(28), Note
		s.28A(7B) rep.in pt.	36, ss.117,165, Sch.19, para.8(3), Sch.27, Pt.III(28), Note
		s.28A(7B)(b) rep.	36, ss.117,165, Sch.19, para.8(3), Sch.27, Pt.III(28), Note
		s.28A(7C) rep.	36, ss.117,165, Sch.19, para.8(4), Sch.27, Pt.III(28), Note
		s.28A(8) subst.	36, s.117, Sch.19, para.8(5)
		ss.28AA,28AB rep.	36, ss.117,165, Sch.19, para.9, Sch.27, Pt.III(28), Note
		s.28B(4) subst.	36, s.117, Sch.19, para.10(2)
		s.28B(6B) subst.	36, s.117, Sch.19, para.10(3)
		ss.28D,28E,28F rep.	36, ss.117,165, Sch.19, para.11, Sch.27, Pt.III(28), Note
		ss.29-43 (Pt.IV) replaced	36, s.117(1)(a)(4), Sch.18
		s.29 am.	36, s.117, Sch.19, para.12(3)
		s.29(1) am.	36, s.117, Sch.19, para.12(2)
		s.29(2)(3) am.	36, s.117, Sch.19, para.12(4)
		s.29(3)(b) rep.in pt.	36, ss.117,165, Sch.19, para.12(5), Sch.27, Pt.III(28), Note

Year and Chap. or No. of Measure	Short title	How affected	1998, Chapter of Act or Number of Measure or Statutory Instrument
1970—*cont.*			
		s.29(5)(a)(6)(a)(7)(a) am.	36, s.117, Sch.19, para.12(4)
		s.29(10) rep.	36, ss.117,165, Sch.19, para.12(6), Sch.27, Pt.III(28), Note
		s.30(1) am.	36, s.117, Sch.19, para.13(2)
		s.30(2)(a) rep.in pt.	36, ss.117,165, Sch.19, para.13(3), Sch.27, Pt.III(28), Note
		s.30(2A) rep.	36, ss.117,165, Sch.19, para.13(4), Sch.27, Pt.III(28), Note
		s.30(3) rep.in pt.	36, ss.117,165, Sch.19, para.13(5), Sch.27, Pt.III(28), Note
		s.30(3A) rep.	36, ss.117,165, Sch.19, para.13(6), Sch.27, Pt.III(28), Note
		s.30(4) subst.	36, s.117, Sch.19, para.13(7)
		s.30(4A) rep.	36, ss.117,165, Sch.19, para.13(8), Sch.27, Pt.III(28), Note
		s.30(5)(a) am.	36, s.117, Sch.19, para.13(9)
		s.30B(2) subst.	36, s.117, Sch.19, para.14(2)
		s.30B(7)(b) am.	36, s.117, Sch.19, para.14(3)
		s.30B(9) (defn. of "profits") subst.	36, s.117, Sch.19, para.14(4)
		s.33(1) subst.	36, s.117, Sch.19, para.15(2)
		s.33(5) am.	36, s.117, Sch.19, para.15(3)
		s.33(5)(c) rep.	36, ss.117,165, Sch.19, para.15(3), Sch.27, Pt.III(28), Note
		s.33A(1) rep.	36, ss.117,165, Sch.19, para.16(2), Sch.27, Pt.III(28), Note
		s.33A(4) subst.	36, s.117, Sch.19, para.16(3)
		s.34(1) am.	36, s.117, Sch.19, para.17
		s.35 rep.	36, s.165, Sch.27, Pt.III(9), Note
		s.36(1) am.	36, s.117, Sch.19, para.18
		s.41A rep.	36, ss.117,165, Sch.19, para.19, Sch.27, Pt.III(28), Note
		s.41A(9)(b) subst.	36, s.38, Sch.5, Pt.III, paras.33,73

Year and Chap. or No. of Measure	Short title	How affected	1998, Chapter of Act or Number of Measure or Statutory Instrument
1970—*cont.*			
		ss.41B,41C rep.	36, ss.117,165, Sch.19, para.19, Sch.27, Pt.III(28), Note
		s.42(2) rep.in pt.	36, ss.117,165, Sch.19, para.20(2), Sch.27, Pt.III(28), Note
		s.42(5) rep.in pt.	36, ss.117,165, Sch.19, para.20(3), Sch.27, Pt.III(28), Note
		s.42(7) rep.in pt.	36, s.165, Sch.27, Pt.III(4), Note
		s.42(9)(11) rep.in pt.	36, ss.117,165, Sch.19, para.20(2), Sch.27, Pt.III(28), Note
		s.42(13) am.	36, s.117, Sch.19, para.20(4)
		s.42(13)(c) rep.	36, ss.117,165, Sch.19, para.20(4), Sch.27, Pt.III(28), Note
		s.43(1) subst.	36, s.117, Sch.19, para.21
		s.43A excl.	36, s.117, Sch.18, Pt.VII, paras.61,63(2)
		s.43A(1)(a) subst.	36, s.117, Sch.19, para.22(2)
		s.43A(2)(3)(4)(5) am.	36, s.117, Sch.19, para.22(3)
		s.46(1) appl.	36, s.117, Sch.18, Pt.XI, para.94(1)
		s.46(2) rep.in pt.	36, ss.117,165, Sch.19, para.23, Sch.27, Pt.III(28), Note
		s.46B(2)(a) subst.	36, s.117, Sch.19, para.24
		s.46C(2)(a) subst.	36, s.117, Sch.19, para.25
		s.46D(2)(a) subst.	36, s.117, Sch.19, para.26
		s.50(6)(a) am.	36, s.117, Sch.19, para.27(2)
		s.50(7)(a) am.	36, s.117, Sch.19, para.27(3)
		s.50(9) subst.	36, s.117, Sch.19, para.27(4)
		s.55(1)(a)(b) subst.	36, s.117, Sch.19, para.28
		s.56A restr.	36, s.117, Sch.18, Pt.VI, para.51(6), Pt.VII, para.59(2)
		ss.59A-59D, head. added	36, s.117, Sch.19, para.29(1)
		ss.59A-59D (Pt.VA) mod.	36, s.117, Sch.18, Pt.V, para.39(2)(a), Pt.VII, para.59(2)
		s.59D replaced (by ss.59D, 59DA)	36, s.117, Sch.19, para.29(2)

Year and Chap. or No. of Measure	Short title	How affected	1998, Chapter of Act or Number of Measure or Statutory Instrument
1970—*cont.*			
		s.59DA saved	36, s.117, Sch.18, Pt.IV, para.31(3), Pt.VII, para.59(2)
		s.59E added	36, s.30(1)
		s.59E restr.	36, s.35, Sch.4, para.5(4)(5)(6) (adding 1988 c.1 s.826(7E))
		s.59E(4) referred to	SI 3175, reg.13
		ss.60A-70 (Pt.VI) mod.	36, s.117, Sch.18, Pt.V, para.39(2)(a), Pt.VII, para.59(2)
		s.65(1) am.	36, s.117, Sch.19, para.30(2)
		s.65(3) rep.in pt.	36, ss.117,165, Sch.19, para.30(3), Sch.27, Pt.III(28), Note
		s.65(5) am.	36, s.117, Sch.19, para.30(4)
		s.69 am.	36, s.35, Sch.4, para.3(2)(3)
		s.69 am.	36, s.117, Sch.19, para.31
		s.70(2)(a) am.	36, s.117, Sch.19, para.32
		ss.86-92 (Pt.IX) mod.	36, s.117, Sch.18, Pt.V, para.39(2)(a), Pt.VII, para.59(2)
		s.87(1) rep.in pt. (6.4.1999)	36, ss.31,165, Sch.3, para.3(2)(6), Sch.27, Pt.III(2), Note
		s.87(2)(a) rep. (6.4.1999)	36, ss.31,165, Sch.3, para.3(3)(6), Sch.27, Pt.III(2), Note
		s.87(6) rep.in pt. (6.4.1999)	36, ss.31,165, Sch.3, para.3(4)(6), Sch.27, Pt.III(2), Note
		s.87(7) rep.in pt. (6.4.1999)	36, ss.31,165, Sch.3, para.3(5)(6), Sch.27, Pt.III(2), Note
		s.87(7) am. (6.4.1999)	36, s.31, Sch.3, para.3(5)(6)
		s.87A appl.(mods.) (7.1.1999)	SI 3175, reg.7
		s.87A(4) rep. (6.4.1999)	36, ss.31,165, Sch.3, para.4(2)(4), Sch.27, Pt.III(2), Note
		s.87A(4)(4A) am.	36, s.35, Sch.4, para.4(2)(5)(6)
		s.87A(4B) rep. (6.4.1999)	36, ss.31,165, Sch.3, para.4(3)(5), Sch.27, Pt.III(2), Note
		s.87A(6) am.	36, s.35, Sch.4, para.4(2)(5)(6)
		s.87A(7) rep. (6.4.1999)	36, ss.31,165, Sch.3, para.4(3)(5), Sch.27, Pt.III(2), Note

Year and Chap. or No. of Measure	Short title	How affected	1998, Chapter of Act or Number of Measure or Statutory Instrument
1970—*cont.*		s.87A(8) added	36, s.35, Sch.4, para.4(3)(5)
		s.87A(9) added	36, s.35, Sch.4, para.4(4)(5)
		s.90 renumbered (as s.90(1))	36, s.33(2)
		s.90(1) am.	36, s.33(2)(3)(5)
		s.90(2) added	36, s.33(4)(5)
		ss.93-107 (Pt.X) replaced (in part)	36, s.117(1)(b)(4), Sch.18
		s.94 rep.	36, ss.117,165, Sch.19, para.33, Sch.27, Pt.III(28), Note
		s.94(8) rep. (6.4.1999)	36, ss.31,165, Sch.3, para.5(2)(3), Sch.27, Pt.III(2), Note
		s.96 rep.	36, ss.117,165, Sch.19, para.34, Sch.27, Pt.III(28), Note
		s.97(1)(2) am.	36, s.117, Sch.19, para.35
		s.97A rep.in pt.	36, ss.117,165, Sch.19, para.37, Sch.27, Pt.III(28), Note
		s.97AA(1) am.	36, s.117, Sch.19, para.36
		s.98, Table am.	36, s.52(2)
		s.98, Table am.	36, s.77(2)
		s.98, Table am. (have effect in relation to every chargeable period ending on or after 12.5.1998)	36, s.83(5)(6)(7)
		s.98, Table am.	36, s.96(3)(a)(c)
		s.98, Table rep.in pt. (*prosp.*)	36, ss.96(3)(b)(4),165, Sch.27, Pt.III(21), Note
		s.98, Table appl. (2.7.1997) (*retrosp.*)	36, s.115(2)(3)
		s.98, Table rep.in pt. (6.4.1999)	36, s.165, Sch.27, Pt.III(2), Note
		s.98, Table rep.in pt. (*prosp.*)	36, s.165, Sch.27, Pt.III(3), Note
		s.98, Table rep.in pt.	36, s.165, Sch.27, Pt.III(4), Note
		s.98, Table rep.in pt.	36, s.165, Sch.27, Pt.III(9), Note
		s.98, Table rep.in pt.	36, s.165, Sch.27, Pt.III(25), Note
		s.100(6)(a) rep.	36, s.117, Sch.19, para.38
		s.101 subst.	36, s.117, Sch.19, para.39
		s.103A am.	36, s.117, Sch.19, para.40
		ss.108-118 (Pt.XI) mod.	36, s.117, Sch.18, Pt.V, para.39(2)(a), Pt.VII, para.59(2)
		s.109(3A) am. (6.4.1999)	36, s.31, Sch.3, para.6(2)(a)(3)

Year and Chap. or No. of Measure	Short title	How affected	1998, Chapter of Act or Number of Measure or Statutory Instrument
1970—*cont.*			
		s.109(3A) am. (6.4.1999)	36, s.31, Sch.3, para.6(2) (c)(d)
		s.109(3A)(b) added (6.4.1999)	36, s.31, Sch.3, para.6(2) (b)(3)
		s.113(1B) am.	36, s.117, Sch.19, para.41
		Sch.1A excl.	36, s.113, Sch.17, paras.4, 37 (replacing 1988 c.1, s.749 at s.749A(4)(b))
		Sch.1A excl.	36, s.113, Sch.17, paras.20(9),37 (adding 1988 c.1, Sch.24, para.9(7))
		Sch.1A excl.	36, s.113, Sch.17, paras.35(7),37 (adding 1988 c.1, Sch.26, para.3(6A))
		Sch.1A appl.	36, s.117, Sch.18, Pt.VII, paras.57(4),59(2),60
		Sch.1A appl.	36, s.117, Sch.18, Pt.VII, paras.58(1)(2),59(2),60
		Sch.1A appl.	36, s.117, Sch.18, Pt.VII, para.59(1)(2)
		Sch.1A, para.1 (defn. of "profits") subst.	36, s.117, Sch.19, para.42(2)
		Sch.1A, para.2(5) ext.	36, s.117, Sch.19, para.48(3) (substituting 1988 c.1, s.488(12))
		Sch.1A, para.2(5)(c) am.	36, s.117, Sch.19, para.42(3)
		Sch.1A, para.2A(3)(5)(a) am.	36, s.117, Sch.19, para.42(4)
		Sch.1A, para.5(3)(b) am.	36, s.117, Sch.19, para.42(5)
		Sch.1A, para.6(3) replaced (by para.6(3A) (3B)(3C))	36, s.117, Sch.19, para.42(6)
		Sch.1A, para.6A added	36, s.117, Sch.19, para.42(7)
		Sch.3A, para.1(4)(a) am.	36, s.117, Sch.19, para.43(2)
		Sch.3A, para.8(2)(a) am.	36, s.117, Sch.19, para.43(3)
c.39	Local Authorities (Goods and Services) Act 1970	saved	SI 633, art.D1(9)
		ext.	31, s.140(1), Sch.30, para.2(1)(2)
		am. (pt.prosp.)	45, s.32, Sch.7, para.3
		s.1(5) ext.	31, s.140(1), Sch.30, para.2(2)
		s.1(5) am.	31, s.140(1), Sch.30, para.2(3)
c.40	Agriculture Act 1970	s.79(5) mod. (NI)	SI 1049, reg.96(2)(a)(ii)
		s.82(1) mod. (NI)	SI 1049, reg.96(2)(b)
		s.110(1) mod. (NI)	SI 1049, reg.96(2)(c)

Year and Chap. or No. of Measure	Short title	How affected	1998, Chapter of Act or Number of Measure or Statutory Instrument
1970—*cont.*			
c.41	Equal Pay Act 1970	saved (6.5.1999)	46, s.30, Sch.5, Pt.II, s.L2(a)-(d)
c.42	Local Authority Social Services Act 1970	defn(s). appl.	29, s.68(1)(c), Sch.12, para.3(5)
c.46	Radiological Protection Act 1970	s.1(9)(10) am. (NI) (*prosp.*)	SI 2795, art.6(1), Sch.1, para.4
c.xxxvi	Midlothian County Council Order Confirmation Act 1970	rep.	43, s.1(1), Sch.1, Pt.VII, Group 5
c.xxxvii	West Lothian County Council Order Confirmation Act 1970	rep.	43, s.1(1), Sch.1, Pt.VII, Group 5
c.lvi	Aberdeen Corporation Order Confirmation Act 1970	rep.	43, s.1(1), Sch.1, Pt.VII, Group 5
c.lix	Dundee Corporation Order Confirmation Act 1970	rep.	43, s.1(1), Sch.1, Pt.VII, Group 5
1971			
c.18	Land Commission (Dissolution) Act 1971	rep.	43, s.1(1), Sch.1, Pt.IV, Group 2
c.19	Carriage of Goods by Sea Act 1971	saved (6.5.1999)	46, s.30, Sch.5, Pt.II, s.E3(c)
c.23	Courts Act 1971	s.18 mod.	42, s.18(4)(d)
		Sch.2, Pt.IA am.	8, s.15, Sch.1, para.1
		Sch.8, para.8 rep.	43, s.1(1), Sch.1, Pt.VIII
c.29	National Savings Bank Act 1971	s.19(1) am.	36, s.162(1)(a)
		s.19(1) am.	36, s.162(2)
		s.19(2) am.	36, s.162(3)
		s.20 am.	36, s.162(4)
c.30	Unsolicited Goods and Services Act 1971	saved (6.5.1999)	46, s.30, Sch.5, Pt.II, s.C7(b)
c.32	Attachment of Earnings Act 1971	s.24(2)(b) am. (1.1.1999)	SI 3086, reg.6(1)
c.38	Misuse of Drugs Act 1971	saved (6.5.1999)	46, s.30, Sch.5, Pt.II, s.B1(a)
		Sch.2, Pt.I, para.1(a) am.	SI 750, art.2(1)(2)
		Sch.2, Pt.II, para.1(a) am.	SI 750, art.2(1)(3)
		Sch.2, Pt.III, para.1(a) am.	SI 750, art.2(1)(4)
c.52	Statute Law (Repeals) Act 1971	rep.	43, s.1(1), Sch.1, Pt.IX, Group 2
c.56	Pensions (Increase) Act 1971	saved (6.5.1999)	46, s.30, Sch.5, Pt.II, s.F3
		Sch.2, Pt.II, para.38AB added (6.5.1999)	46, s.125, Sch.8, para.13
		Sch.2, Pt.II, para.38B added (*prosp.*)	38, s.125, Sch.12, para.10
		Sch.3 mod.	SI 366, reg.90
c.58	Sheriff Courts (Scotland) Act 1971	s.11(1) mod.	42, s.18(5)
c.60	Prevention of Oil Pollution Act 1971	s.23 subst. (*prosp.*)	17, s.50, Sch.4, para.4

Year and Chap. or No. of Measure	Short title	How affected	1998, Chapter of Act or Number of Measure or Statutory Instrument
1971—*cont.*			
c.61	Mineral Workings (Offshore Installations) Act 1971	defn. of "offshore installation" appl. (17.3.1998) (*retrosp.*)	36, s.63(1)(5)(6)(7) (adding 1988 c.1, s.192A)
c.xxxviii	Lanarkshire County Council Order Confirmation Act 1971	rep.	43, s.1(1), Sch.1, Pt.VII, Group 5
1972			
c.6	Summer Time Act 1972	saved (6.5.1999)	46, s.30, Sch.5, Pt.II, s.L5
c.9	Mineral Exploration and Investment Grants Act 1972	s.1 saved (6.5.1999)	46, s.30, Sch.5, Pt.II, s.D2(b)
		s.1 trans.of functions (1.7.1999)	46, ss.53,56(1)(e)
c.11	Superannuation Act 1972	s.1 ext. (*prosp.*)	22, s.1(5), Sch.1, Pt.II, para.7 (adding 1993 c.39, Sch.2A, para.6(5))
		s.1 ext.	30, s.1(9), Sch.1, para.7(1)
		s.1 ext. (*prosp.*)	30, s.37 (adding 1992 c.37, s.59A(3)(a))
		s.1 ext. (NI) (*prosp.*)	32, s.51, Sch.3, para.3(3)
		s.1 ext. (EW)	37, ss.41(11),64(5), Sch.2, para.4(3)
		s.1 ext. (*prosp.*)	38, s.104, Sch.6, para.3(2)
		s.1 ext. (pt.prosp.)	45, s.2, Sch.2, para.5(1)
		s.1 ext. (*prosp.*)	47, s.68(4), Sch.7, para.4(2)
		s.1(2) ext.	38, s.34(5)
		s.1(2) ext. (25.1.1999)	46, s.51(6)
		s.1(3) ext.	38, s.34(5)
		s.1(3) ext. (25.1.1999)	46, s.51(6)
		s.1(6) am. (6.5.1999)	46, s.125, Sch.8, para.14
		Sch.1 am.	SI 1879, art.2
		Sch.1 am. (pt.to 3.10.1994, pt.to 22.9.1997) (*retrosp.*)	SI 3030, arts.2,4
		Sch.1 rep.in pt. & am. (to 1.7.1996) (*retrosp.*)	SI 3030, art.3
		Sch.1 am. (*prosp.*)	29, s.74(1), Sch.15, para.4
		Sch.1 am. (*prosp.*)	30, s.44(1), Sch.3, para.2
		Sch.1 rep.in pt. (*prosp.*)	31, s.140(3), Sch.31
		Sch.1 am. (NI) (*prosp.*)	32, s.51, Sch.3, para.3(3)
		Sch.1 rep.in pt. (NI) (saving)(*prosp.*)	32, s.74(2)(3), Schs.5,6
		Sch.1 am.	37, s.119, Sch.8, para.24
		Sch.1 am.	38, ss.91(3),92(5)
		Sch.1 am. (*prosp.*)	38, s.111, Sch.9, Pt.I, para.4(4)
		Sch.1 am. (*prosp.*)	38, s.112, Sch.10, para.17 (adding 1993 c.46, Sch.1A, at para.5(5))
		Sch.1 am. (pt.prosp.)	45, s.2, Sch.2, para.5(2)

Year and Chap. or No. of Measure	Short title	How affected	1998, Chapter of Act or Number of Measure or Statutory Instrument
1972—*cont.*			
		Sch.1 am. (*prosp.*)	47, s.68(4), Sch.7, para.4(2)
c.22	Northern Ireland (Temporary Provisions) Act 1972	rep. (*prosp.*)	47, s.100(2), Sch.15
c.30	Civil Evidence Act 1972	s.4(2) referred to (26.4.1999)	SI 3132, rule 33.7
c.44	Children Act	s.1(1) rep.	SI 276, reg.17(1)
c.63	Industry Act 1972	ss.10-12 trans.of functions (1.7.1999)	46, ss.53,56(1)(f)
c.65	National Debt Act 1972	s.2(3)(4) replaced (by.s.2(3))	SI 1446, art.30(1), Sch.1, para.1
		s.3(1)(b) rep.in pt.	SI 1446, art.30(2), Sch.2, Pt.I
		s.3(2)(a)(b) rep.	SI 1446, art.30(2), Sch.2, Pt.I
		s.3(2)(c) rep.in pt.	SI 1446, art.30(2), Sch.2, Pt.I
		s.6 rep.	SI 1446, art.30(2), Sch.2, Pt.I
c.66	Poisons Act 1972	saved (6.5.1999)	46, s.30, Sch.5, Pt.II, s.J4(b)
c.68	European Communities Act 1972	s.1 saved (1.7.1999)	46, ss.29,53(4), Sch.4, Pt.I, paras.1(2)(c),9
		s.1(2) defn.of (" "the Treaties" and "the Community Treaties") para.([o]) added	21, s.1
		s.2 saved (1.7.1999)	46, ss.29,53(4), Sch.4, Pt.I, paras.1(2)(c),9
		s.2 ext. (1.7.1999)	46, s.125, Sch.8, para.15(2)
		s.2 mod. (1.7.1999)	46, s.125, Sch.8, para.15(3)
		s.2(2) ext.	38, s.29(2)
		s.3(1)(2) saved (1.7.1999)	46, ss.29,53(4), Sch.4, Pt.I, paras.1(2)(c),9
		s.3(3) power to mod. (*prosp.*)	47, s.7(2)
		s.3(4) ext. (1.7.1999)	46, s.125, Sch.8, para.15(4)
		ss.3(4),11(1) power to mod. (*prosp.*)	47, s.7(2)
		s.11(2), Sch.1 saved (1.7.1999)	46, ss.29,53(4), Sch.4, Pt.I, paras.1(2)(c),9
		Sch.2, para.2(2) am.	38, s.29(3)
c.70	Local Government Act 1972	ss.80(1)(e),86(1)(b),87(1)(d) am.	18, s.54(1), Sch.3, para.3
		ss.100A-100K (Pt.VA) mod.	18, s.10(6)
		s.100B(1) mod.	18, s.10(5)(b)
		s.100B(7) saved	18, s.10(5)(a)
		s.101 excl.	18, s.11(8)(9)
		s.101 mod.	30, s.23(3)(a)
		s.123 excl. (E)	31, s.77(6)(9)

Year and Chap. or No. of Measure	Short title	How affected	1998, Chapter of Act or Number of Measure or Statutory Instrument
1972—*cont.*			
		s.123(2) excl. (*prosp.*)	31, s.22, Sch.3, Pt.III, para.12
		s.127 excl. (E)	31, s.77(6)(9)
		s.134(1)(2) rep.in pt. (*prosp.*)	31, s.140(3), Sch.31
		s.137(7) am.	18, s.54(1), Sch.3, para.3(4)
		s.145(1) appl.	ii, s.5(1)(a)
		s.173(4) mod. (*prosp.*)	31, s.24, Sch.4, para.3(1)
		s.173(4) appl.(mods.) (*prosp.*)	31, s.67, Sch.18, para.3(1)
		s.173(4) appl.(mods.) (*prosp.*)	31, s.94, Sch.24, Pt.I, para.5(1)
		s.174 ext. (*prosp.*)	31, s.67, Sch.18, para.3(1)
		s.174 appl.(mods.) (*prosp.*)	31, s.94, Sch.24, Pt.I, para.5(1)(2)
		s.174(1) mod. (*prosp.*)	31, s.24, Sch.4, para.3(2)
		s.174(1) mod. (*prosp.*)	31, s.67, Sch.18, para.3(2)
		s.174(1) appl.(mods.) (*prosp.*)	31, s.94, Sch.24, Pt.I, para.5(1)(2)
		s.177(1) rep.in pt. (*prosp.*)	31, s.140(1)(3), Sch.30, para.3(2), Sch.31
		s.177(1A) added (*prosp.*)	31, s.140(1), Sch.30, para.3(3)
		s.231 appl.in pt.	iv, s.39
		s.231 ext.	38, s.128, Sch.14, Pt.I, para.9 (subst.1975 c.70, s.25)
		s.233 appl.in pt.	iv, s.39
		s.233 ext.	38, s.128, Sch.14, Pt.I, para.9 (subst.1975 c.70, s.25)
		s.236(3)-(8) appl.	SI 1209(L), art.12(1)
		s.236(7) mod.	SI 1209(L), art.12(2)
		s.238 appl.	SI 1209(L), art.12(1)
		s.246(15) am.	18, s.54(1), Sch.3, para.3(5)
		s.250 ext.	38, s.127, Sch.13, para.3 (adding 1975 c.70, Sch.4, at Pt.IV, para.21)
		s.250(2)-(5) appl.	iv, s.38(2)
		s.250(2)-(5) appl.	38, s.35(2)
		s.250(2)-(5) appl. (pt.prosp.)	45, s.25(5)
		s.250(2)(3) appl.	38, s.2, Sch.1, para.6(5)
		s.270 appl.	18, s.53(2)
		s.270(1) (defn. of "local authority") appl.	37, s.17(3)
c.71	Criminal Justice Act 1972	s.49 rep.	37, ss.106,120(2), Sch.7, para.12, Sch.10
c.xviii	United Reformed Church Act 1972	ext.(mods.) (to Jersey)	SI 751, art.3, Sch.1
No.2	Repair of Benefice Buildings Measure 1972	s.31(1) (defn. of "team vicar's house") rep.in pt.	GSM 1, s.13(1), Sch.5, para.3

Year and Chap. or No. of Measure	Short title	How affected	1998, Chapter of Act or Number of Measure or Statutory Instrument
1972—*cont.*			
No.5	Clergy Pensions (Amendment) Measure 1972	s.6(4A) trans.of functions (1.1.1999)	SI 1715, art.2, Sch.1
1973			
c.15	Administration of Justice Act 1973	s.9(1)(c) mod.	42, s.18(4)(b)
		s.9(1)(d) mod.	42, s.18(4)(c)
c.16	Education Act 1973	s.3 power to trans. functions , modify etc. in relation to certain savings	30, s.25(3)(b)
		s.3 rep. (*prosp.*)	30, s.44(2), Sch.4
c.17	Northern Ireland Assembly Act 1973	rep. (*prosp.*)	47, s.100(2), Sch.15
		s.3(1) restr. (*prosp.*)	47, s.36(2)
c.18	Matrimonial Causes Act 1973	s.31(7D)(7F) mod. (*temp.*)	SI 2572, art.4
c.20	London Cab Act 1973	rep. (*prosp.*)	34, s.39(2), Sch.2
c.21	Overseas Pensions Act 1973	s.2(2)(d)(iii) added (NI) (*prosp.*)	32, s.74(1), Sch.4, para.7
c.24	Employment of Children Act 1973	s.2 excl.	31, s.112(2)
c.26	Land Compensation Act 1973	s.32(7B)(b) rep.in pt.	38, s.152, Sch.18, Pt.VI
		s.39(4)(f)(8)(d) rep.	38, s.152, Sch.18, Pt.IV
		s.44 mod. (pt.prosp.)	45, s.20, Sch.5, Pt.II, para.4
		s.44(1) mod.	SI 1936(L), art.29(3), Sch.7, para.2(1)(2)
		s.58(1) mod.	SI 1936(L), art.29(3), Sch.7, para.2(1)(3)
c.27	Bahamas Independence Act 1973	Sch.2, para.9 rep.	43, s.1(1), Sch.1, Pt.IV, Group 1
c.33	Protection of Wrecks Act 1973	s.2 saved (6.5.1999)	46, s.30, Sch.5, Pt.II, s.E3(d)
c.35	Employment Agencies Act 1973	saved (6.5.1999)	46, s.30, Sch.5, Pt.II, s.H1(b)
c.36	Northern Ireland Constitution Act 1973	ss.1-9,11-30 rep. (*prosp.*)	47, s.100(2), Sch.15
		s.12 saved (*prosp.*)	47, s.100(1), Sch.14, para.20
		ss.17,18 saved (*prosp.*)	47, s.100(1), Sch.14, para.21
		s.19 ext. (*prosp.*)	32, s.1(2)
		s.19 ext. (*prosp.*)	32, s.18(4)
		s.19 excl.	35, s.1, Sch.1, para.10(a)
		s.19 saved (*prosp.*)	47, s.100(1), Sch.14, para.22
		s.31(1)-(3) rep. (*prosp.*)	47, s.100(2), Sch.15
		s.31(4)-(6) rep.	47, s.100(2), Sch.15
		ss.32,33(1),36(1)(d),37(1) ,38-40, Schs.1-5 rep. (*prosp.*)	47, s.100(2), Sch.15

Year and Chap. or No. of Measure	Short title	How affected	1998, Chapter of Act or Number of Measure or Statutory Instrument
1973—*cont.*			
		Sch.6, Pt.I saving rep.in pt. (in part)	36, s.150(5)
c.39	Statute Law (Repeals) Act 1973	s.2(1)(2), Sch.1 rep.in pt.	43, s.1(1), Sch.1, Pt.IX, Group 2
		Sch.2, para.2 rep.	43, s.1(1), Sch.1, Pt.IX, Group 2
c.41	Fair Trading Act 1973	appl.(mods.) (NI) (*prosp.*)	41, s.66(5), Sch.10, Pt.I, para.17(2) (replacing 1992/231 at art.15(8)(9))
		appl.(mods.) (*prosp.*)	41, s.66(5), Sch.10, Pt.IV, para.9(2) (replacing 1984 c.12, s.13(9)(10) at s.13(9))
		appl.(mods.) (*prosp.*)	41, s.66(5), Sch.10, Pt.IV, para.10(2) (replacing 1986 c.44 at s.24(7))
		appl.(mods.) (*prosp.*)	41, s.66(5), Sch.10, Pt.IV, para.13(3) (replacing 1991 c.56 at s.14(7))
		appl.(mods.) (*prosp.*)	41, s.66(5), Sch.10, Pt.IV, para.15(2) (replacing 1993 c.43 at s.13(8))
		appl.(mods.) (*prosp.*)	41, s.66(5), Sch.10, Pt.V, para.18(2) (replacing 1996/275 art.15(9))
		ext. (*prosp.*)	41, s.74(1), Sch.12, para.4(3) (replacing 1980 c.21 at s.11(9))
		mod. (*prosp.*)	41, s.74(1), Sch.12, para.7(2) (replacing 1986 c.31 at s.44(3))
		mod. (*prosp.*)	41, s.74(1), Sch.12, para.14(3) (replacing 1990 c.42 Sch.4,at para.4(7))
		mod. (*prosp.*)	41, s.74(1), Sch.12, para.20(2) (am. SI 1994/426 (NI No.1)
		ss.1-12 (Pt.I) saved (6.5.1999)	46, s.30, Sch.5, Pt.II, s.C7(c)
		s.4 rep. (*prosp.*)	41, s.74(1)(3), Sch.12, para.1(2), Sch.14, Pt.I
		s.10(2) rep. (*prosp.*)	41, s.74(1)(3), Sch.12, para.1(3)(a), Sch.14, Pt.I
		s.10(8) am. (*prosp.*)	41, s.74(1), Sch.12, para.1(4)
		ss.13-33 (Pt.II),34-43 (Pt.III) saved (6.5.1999)	46, s.30, Sch.5, Pt.II, s.C7(c)
		ss.35,37-41 am. (*prosp.*)	41, s.74(1), Sch.12, para.1(5)
		s.41A added (*prosp.*)	41, s.74(1), Sch.12, para.1(6)

Year and Chap. or No. of Measure	Short title	How affected	1998, Chapter of Act or Number of Measure or Statutory Instrument
1973—*cont.*			
		s.42(1) am. (*prosp.*)	41, s.74(1), Sch.12, para.1(7)(a)
		s.42(2)(b) am. (*prosp.*)	41, s.74(1), Sch.12, para.1(7)(b)
		s.42(3) added (*prosp.*)	41, s.74(1), Sch.12, para.1(7)(c)
		s.44(1) am. (*prosp.*)	41, ss.54,66(2)(5), Sch.10, Pt.I, para.1
		s.44(1A) added (*prosp.*)	41, ss.54,66(3)(5), Sch.10, Pt.I, para.1
		s.44(2) subst. (*prosp.*)	41, ss.54,66(4)(5), Sch.10, Pt.I, para.1
		s.45 rep. (*prosp.*)	41, s.74(1)(3), Sch.12, para.1(8), Sch.14, Pt.I
		s.46(1)(2) rep. (*prosp.*)	41, ss.54,66(5),67(2), Sch.10, Pt.I, para.1
		s.46(4)-(8) added (*prosp.*)	41, ss.54,66(5),67(3), Sch.10, Pt.I, para.1
		s.54(5) rep. (*prosp.*)	41, s.74(1)(3), Sch.12, para.1(3)(b), Sch.14, Pt.I
		s.56 mod. (*prosp.*)	41, s.45(7), Sch.7, Pt.II, para.20(2)(a)
		s.65 appl.(mods.) (11.1.1999)	41, ss.3(1)(a),19(1)(a), Sch.1, Pt.I, paras.1(4), 2(2)
		s.70 appl.(mods.) (*prosp.*)	41, s.66(5), Sch.10, Pt.IV, para.9(2) (replacing 1984 c.12, s.13(9)(10) at s.13(9A))
		s.70 appl.(mods.) (*prosp.*)	41, s.66(5), Sch.10, Pt.IV, para.10(2) (replacing 1986 c.44 at s.24(7))
		s.70 appl.(mods.) (*prosp.*)	41, s.66(5), Sch.10, Pt.IV, para.10(2) (replacing 1986 c.44 at s.24(7A))
		s.70 appl.(mods.) (*prosp.*)	41, s.66(5), Sch.10, Pt.IV, para.12(2) (replacing 1989 c.29 at s.12(8))
		s.70 appl.(mods.) (*prosp.*)	41, s.66(5), Sch.10, Pt.IV, para.12(2) (replacing 1989 c.29 at s.12(8A))
		s.70 appl.(mods.) (*prosp.*)	41, s.66(5), Sch.10, Pt.IV, para.13(3) (replacing 1991 c.56 at s.14(7)(7A))
		s.70 appl.(mods.) (*prosp.*)	41, s.66(5), Sch.10, Pt.IV, para.15(2) (replacing 1993 c.43 at s.13(8)(8A))
		s.70 appl.(mods.) (*prosp.*)	41, s.66(5), Sch.10, Pt.V, para.17(2) (replacing 1992/231 at art.15(8)(9))

Year and Chap. or No. of Measure	Short title	How affected	1998, Chapter of Act or Number of Measure or Statutory Instrument
1973—*cont.*			
		s.70 appl.(mods.) (*prosp.*)	41, s.66(5), Sch.10, Pt.VI, para.18(2) (replacing 1996/275 art.15(9))
		s.70 mod. (*prosp.*)	41, s.74(1), Sch.12, para.4(3) (replacing 1980 c.21 s.11(9A))
		s.70 mod. (*prosp.*)	41, s.74(1), Sch.12, para.7(2) (replacing 1986 c.31 at s.44(3))
		s.70 mod. (*prosp.*)	41, s.74(1), Sch.12, para.7(2) (replacing 1986 c.31 at s.44(3A))
		s.70 mod. (*prosp.*)	41, s.74(1), Sch.12, para.20(2) (am. SI 1994/426 (NI No 1)
		s.70 mod. (*prosp.*)	41, s.74(1), Sch.12, para.20(2) (am. SI 1994/426 (NI No.1))
		s.73 mod. (*prosp.*)	41, s.45(7), Sch.7, Pt.II, para.20(2)(a)
		s.75(5) appl. (*prosp.*)	41, s.45(7), Sch.7, Pt.II, para.15(7)(b)
		s.78(3) rep. (*prosp.*)	41, s.74(1)(3), Sch.12, para.1(3)(c), Sch.14, Pt.I
		s.81(1) rep.in pt. (*prosp.*)	41, s.74(1)(3), Sch.12, para.1(9)(a)(i), Sch.14, Pt.I
		s.81(2) rep.in pt. (*prosp.*)	41, s.74(1)(3), Sch.12, para.1(9)(b), Sch.14, Pt.I
		s.81(3) rep.in pt. (*prosp.*)	41, s.74(1)(3), Sch.12, para.1(9)(c), Sch.14, Pt.I
		s.81(b) rep.in pt. (*prosp.*)	41, s.74(1)(3), Sch.12, para.1(9)(a)(ii), Sch.14, Pt.I
		s.83(1) rep.in pt. (11.1.1999)	41, ss.69(a),74(3), Sch.14, Pt.I
		s.83(1A) rep. (11.1.1999)	41, ss.69(b),74(3), Sch.14, Pt.I
		s.84 mod. (*prosp.*)	41, s.74(1), Sch.12, para.4(3) (replacing 1980 c.21 s.11(9A))
		s.85 appl.(mods.) (*prosp.*)	41, s.66(5), Sch.10, Pt.IV, para.9(2) (replacing 1984 c.12, s.13(9)(10) at s.13(9A))
		s.85 appl.(mods.) (*prosp.*)	41, s.66(5), Sch.10, Pt.IV, para.10(2) (replacing 1986 c.44 at s.24(7))
		s.85 appl.(mods.) (*prosp.*)	41, s.66(5), Sch.10, Pt.IV, para.10(2) (replacing 1986 c.44 at s.24(7A))

Year and Chap. or No. of Measure	Short title	How affected	1998, Chapter of Act or Number of Measure or Statutory Instrument
1973—*cont.*		s.85 appl.(mods.) (*prosp.*)	41, s.66(5), Sch.10, Pt.IV, para.12(2) (replacing 1989 c.29 at s.12(8A))
		s.85 appl.(mods.) (*prosp.*)	41, s.66(5), Sch.10, Pt.IV, para.13(3) (replacing 1991 c.56 at s.14(7)(7A))
		s.85 appl.(mods.) (*prosp.*)	41, s.66(5), Sch.10, Pt.IV, para.15(2) (replacing 1993 c.43 at s.13(8)(8A))
		s.85 appl.(mods.) (*prosp.*)	41, s.66(5), Sch.10, Pt.V, para.17(2) (replacing 1992/231 at art.15(8)(9))
		s.85 appl.(mods.) (*prosp.*)	41, s.66(5), Sch.10, Pt.VI, para.18(2) (replacing 1996/275 art.15(9))
		s.85 mod. (*prosp.*)	41, s.74(1), Sch.12, para.4(3) (replacing 1980 c.21 s.11(9A))
		s.85 mod. (*prosp.*)	41, s.74(1), Sch.12, para.7(2) (replacing 1986 c.31 at s.44(3A))
		s.85 mod. (*prosp.*)	41, s.74(1), Sch.12, para.14(3) (replacing 1990 c.42 Sch.4, at para.4(7A))
		s.85 mod. (*prosp.*)	41, s.74(1), Sch.12, para.20(2) (am. SI 1994/426 (NI No.1))
		s.85(1)(b) am. (*prosp.*)	41, s.74(1), Sch.12, para.1(10)(a)
		s.85(1)(b)(ii) added (*prosp.*)	41, s.74(1), Sch.12, para.1(10)(b)
		s.85(1)(c) am. (*prosp.*)	41, s.74(1), Sch.12, para.1(11)
		s.85(1A) added (*prosp.*)	41, s.74(1), Sch.12, para.1(12)
		s.85(2) am. (*prosp.*)	41, s.74(1), Sch.12, para.1(13)
		s.85(6)-(8) mod. (*prosp.*)	41, s.74(1), Sch.12, para.4(4)(b) (replacing 1980 c.21 at s.13(8))
		s.93B mod. (*prosp.*)	41, s.66(5), Sch.10, Pt.IV, para.9(5) (adding 1984 c.12 s.50(6A))
		s.93B mod. (*prosp.*)	41, s.66(5), Sch.10, Pt.IV, para.12(6) (adding 1989 c.29 at s.43(6A))
		s.93B mod. (*prosp.*)	41, s.66(5), Sch.10, Pt.IV, para.13(8) (replacing 1991 c.56 at s.31(8A))

Year and Chap. or No. of Measure	Short title	How affected	1998, Chapter of Act or Number of Measure or Statutory Instrument
1973—*cont.*			
		s.93B mod. (*prosp.*)	41, s.66(5), Sch.10, Pt.V, para.17(6) (adding 1992/231 at art.46(6A))
		ss.118-123 (Pt.XI) saved (6.5.1999)	46, s.30, Sch.5, Pt.II, s.C7(c)
		s.133(2)(a) am. (11.1.1999)	41, s.74(1), Sch.12, para.1(14)
		s.135(1) rep.in pt. (*prosp.*)	41, s.74(1)(3), Sch.12, para.1(15)(a), Sch.14, Pt.I
		s.135(1)(a) rep. (*prosp.*)	41, s.74(1)(3), Sch.12, para.1(15)(b), Sch.14, Pt.I
		s.137(3A)-(3C) added (*prosp.*)	41, s.68
		Sch.3 rep. (*prosp.*)	41, s.74(1)(3), Sch.12, para.1(2), Sch.14, Pt.I
		Sch.7, Pt.II, paras.9,12 rev.	SI 2253, art.2
		Sch.8, para.3(1)(2) rep. (*prosp.*)	41, s.74(1)(3), Sch.12, para.1(3)(d), Sch.14, Pt.I
c.43	Hallmarking Act 1973	s.2(1)(d) added (1.1.1999)	SI 2978, reg.2(2)
		s.2(2) am. (1.1.1999)	SI 2978, reg.2(3)
		s.2(2A) added (1.1.1999)	SI 2978, reg.2(4)
		s.2(3) am. (1.1.1999)	SI 2978, reg.2(5)
		s.2(5)(c) am. (1.1.1999)	SI 2978, reg.2(6)
		s.4(1)(a)(iii) replaced (by sub-paras.(iii)-(v)) (1.1.1999)	SI 2978, reg.2(7)
		s.4(1A)(2) replaced (by s.4(2)) (1.1.1999)	SI 2978, reg.2(8)
		s.4(3)(a)(b)(i) am. (by s.4(2)) (1.1.1999)	SI 2978, reg.2(9)
		s.4(3)(b)(iii) am. (by s.4(2)) (1.1.1999)	SI 2978, reg.2(10)
		s.4(4) rep. (by s.4(2)) (1.1.1999)	SI 2978, reg.2(11)
		s.22(1) (defn. of "EEA hallmark") added (1.1.1999)	SI 2978, reg.2(12)
		s.22(1) (defn. of "minimum fineness") am. (1.1.1999)	SI 2978, reg.2(13)
		s.22(1) (defn. of "sponsor's mark") am. (1.1.1999)	SI 2978, reg.2(14)
		Sch.1, Pt.II, para.10(b) am. (1.1.1999)	SI 2979, art.2
		Sch.2, Pt.I subst. (1.1.1999)	SI 2978, reg.2(15)
c.50	Employment and Training Act 1973	saved (6.5.1999)	46, s.30, Sch.5, Pt.II, s.H3(b)
		s.2 trans.of functions (1.7.1999)	46, ss.53,56(1)(g)
		s.4(3)(e)(ii) rep.in pt.	38, s.152, Sch.18, Pt.IV
		s.4(5)(f) rep.	38, s.152, Sch.18, Pt.IV

Year and Chap. or No. of Measure	Short title	How affected	1998, Chapter of Act or Number of Measure or Statutory Instrument
1973—*cont.*			
		ss.8,9 (defn. of "relevant services") appl.	30, s.35
		ss.11(3),12(4) trans.of functions (1.7.1999)	46, ss.53,56(1)(g)
c.51	Finance Act 1973	s.56 ext.	38, s.29(4)
		s.56(4) restr.	38, s.29(5)
		Sch.15, paras.2,4(1)(a), 4A(1)(a) am. (*prosp.*)	17, s.50, Sch.4, para.5
c.53	Northern Ireland (Emergency Provisions) Act 1973	defn. of "scheduled offence" appl.	35, s.3(7)(b)
		defn. of "scheduled offence" appl.	35, s.17, Sch.3, para.2(1) (c)
		s.1(1) am. (*prosp.*)	SI 1504, art.65(1), Sch.5, para.6(a)
		s.1(3) am. (*prosp.*)	SI 1504, art.65(1), Sch.5, para.6(b)
		s.9(1)-(5) rep. (*prosp.*)	SI 1504, art.65(2), Sch.6
		Sch.1, Pt.II am. (*prosp.*)	SI 1504, art.65(1), Sch.5, para.7
c.55	Statute Law Revision (Northern Ireland) Act 1973	s.1, Sch. rep.	43, s.1(1), Sch.1, Pt.IX, Group 1
c.62	Powers of Criminal Courts Act 1973	defn. of "community service order" appl.	37, s.106, Sch.7, para.51(2) (replacing 1997 c.43 s.37(4)(5) at s.37(4))
		s.1(6) am.	37, ss.106,120(2), Sch.7, para.13(1)
		s.1(8)(a) subst.	37, ss.106,120(2), Sch.7, para.13(2)
		s.1(8)(b)(8A) rep.in pt. (*prosp.*)	37, s.120(2), Sch.10
		s.1A(1)(b) restr. (1.12.1998) (1.4.1999)	37, ss.1(11),2(9)
		s.1A(1)(b) restr. (in force 30.9.1998 for the pupose of warning a person under 1998 c.37, s.65 in any area specified in SI 1998/2327, Sch.3) (pt.prosp.)	37, s.66(4)(a)
		s.1A(1)(b) ext.(mods.)	37, s.106, Sch.7, para.46(11) (adding 1991 c.53, Sch.2, para.8A(3) (5))
		s.1A(1A) added (in force 30.9.1998 for areas specified in SI 1998/2327, Sch.1)	37, s.119, Sch.8, para.25
		s.1A(3) excl.	37, s.106, Sch.7, para.46(11) (adding 1991 c.53, Sch.2, para.8A(7))

Year and Chap. or No. of Measure	Short title	How affected	1998, Chapter of Act or Number of Measure or Statutory Instrument
1973—*cont.*			
		s.1B(9) am.	37, s.106, Sch.7, para.14(1)
		s.1B(9) appl.(mods.)	37, s.106, Sch.7, para.46(12) (adding 1991 c.53, Sch.2, para.11B)
		s.1B(10) rep.	37, ss.106,120(2), Sch.7, para.14(2), Sch.10
		s.1C(1) rep.in pt. (EWS)	37, ss.106,120(2), Sch.7, para.15(b), Sch.10
		s.1C(1)(a) am. (EWS)	37, s.106, Sch.7, para.15(a)
		s.1C(1)(b) rep. (EWS)	37, ss.106,120(2), Sch.7, para.15(b), Sch.10
		s.2(1) rep.in pt. and superseded (pt.prosp.)	37, ss.106,120(2), Sch.7, para.16, Sch.10
		s.2(1) rep.in pt. (in force 30.9.1998 for areas specified in SI 1998/2327, Sch.1)	37, ss.119,120(2), Sch.8, para.26(1), Sch.10
		s.2(1) am. (in force 30.9.1998 for areas specified in SI 1998/2327, Sch.1)	37, s.119, Sch.8, para.26(1)
		s.2(2) am. (in force 30.9.1998 for areas specified in SI 1998/2327, Sch.1)	37, s.119, Sch.8, para.26(2)
		s.2(2A) added (in force 30.9.1998 for areas specified in SI 1998/2327, Sch.1)	37, s.119, Sch.8, para.26(3)
		s.2(4) am. (in force 30.9.1998 for areas specified in SI 1998/2327, Sch.1)	37, s.119, Sch.8, para.26(4)
		s.2(4A) added (in force 30.9.1998 for areas specified in SI 1998/2327, Sch.1)	37, s.119, Sch.8, para.26(5)
		s.2(6) am. (in force 30.9.1998 for areas specified in SI 1998/2327, Sch.1)	37, s.119, Sch.8, para.26(6)
		s.11 rep.in pt. and superseded	37, ss.106,120(2), Sch.7, para.17, Sch.10
		s.12(2) subst.	37, s.106, Sch.7, para.18(1)
		s.12(3) am.	37, s.106, Sch.7, para.18(2)
		s.12(4) subst.	37, s.106, Sch.7, para.18(3)
		s.14(1) am.	37, s.106, Sch.7, para.19(1)(2)

Year and Chap. or No. of Measure	Short title	How affected	1998, Chapter of Act or Number of Measure or Statutory Instrument
1973—*cont.*			
		s.14(4) am. (in force 30.9.1998 for areas specified in SI 1998/2327, Sch.1)	37, s.119, Sch.8, para.27(1)
		s.14(4A) added (in force 30.9.1998 for areas specified in SI 1998/2327, Sch.1)	37, s.119, Sch.8, para.27(2)
		s.14(7) am.	37, s.106, Sch.7, para.19(3)
		s.14(8) rep.	37, ss.106,120(2), Sch.7, para.19(4), Sch.10
		s.14(9) added (in force 30.9.1998 for areas specified in SI 1998/2327, Sch.1)	37, s.119, Sch.8, para.27(3)
		s.15(3) subst.	37, s.106, Sch.7, para.20
		s.21(2) am. (4.1.1999)	37, s.119, Sch.8, para.28
		s.21(3)(b) am.	37, s.106, Sch.7, para.21
		s.22(3) am.	37, s.106, Sch.7, para.22
		s.23 mod.	37, s.106, Sch.7, para.2(4) (replacing 1967 c.80 s.56(5) at s.56(5A))
		s.23(2A) added	37, s.119, Sch.8, para.30
		s.31(3A) rep.	37, ss.106,120(2), Sch.7, para.23(1)(a), Sch.10
		s.31(3B)(3C) rep.	37, ss.106,120(2), Sch.7, para.23(1)(b), Sch.10
		s.31(4) rep.in pt.	37, ss.106,120(2), Sch.7, para.23(1)(c), Sch.10
		s.31(6) rep.in pt.	37, ss.106,120(2), Sch.7, para.23(2)(a), Sch.10
		s.31(6) am.	37, s.106, Sch.7, para.23(2)(b)
		s.31(8) am.	37, s.106, Sch.7, para.23(3)
		s.32(1)(b) am. (4.1.1999)	37, s.119, Sch.8, para.29
		s.32(2) am.	37, s.106, Sch.7, para.24(1)
		s.32(3) am.	37, s.106, Sch.7, para.24(2)
		s.32(4) subst.	37, s.106, Sch.7, para.24(3)
		s.32(5) rep.	37, ss.106,120(2), Sch.7, para.24(4), Sch.10
		s.42(2) rep. (*prosp.*)	37, ss.119,120(2), Sch.8, para.31, Sch.10
		s.46(1) am. (in force 30.9.1998 for areas specified in SI 1998/2329, Sch.1)	37, s.119, Sch.8, para.32
		s.46(3) added	37, s.106, Sch.7, para.25

Year and Chap. or No. of Measure	Short title	How affected	1998, Chapter of Act or Number of Measure or Statutory Instrument
1973—*cont.*		s.57(1) (defn. of "youth offending team") added (in force 30.9.1998 for areas specified in SI 1998/2329, Sch.1)	37, s.119, Sch.8, para.33
		s.57(5) subst.	37, s.106, Sch.7, para.26(1)
		s.57(7) added	37, s.106, Sch.7, para.26(2)
		Sch.1A, para.2(7) subst.	37, s.106, Sch.7, para.27(1)
		Sch.1A, para.3(4) subst.	37, s.106, Sch.7, para.27(2)
		Sch.1A, para.5 am.	37, s.106, Sch.7, para.27(3)
		Sch.1A, para.5(4) am.	37, s.106, Sch.7, para.27(4)
		Sch.1A, para.5(10) (defn. of "registered medical practitioner") added	37, s.106, Sch.7, para.27(5)
		Sch.1A, para.6(1) am.	37, s.119, Sch.8, para.34(1)
		Sch.1A, para.6(1A) am.	37, s.119, Sch.8, para.34(2)
		Sch.1A, para.6(4) am.	37, s.106, Sch.7, para.27(6)
		Sch.1A, para.6(7) rep.	37, ss.106,120(2), Sch.7, para.27(7), Sch.10
		Sch.1A, para.7 added	37, s.119, Sch.8, para.34(3)
		Sch.5, para.35 rep.	37, s.120(2), Sch.10
c.65	Local Government (Scotland) Act 1973	s.210(4)(5) appl.	46, s.1, Sch.1, para.6(5)
		Sch.27, Pt.II, para.194 rep.	43, s.1(1), Sch.1, Pt.IV, Group 3
c.69	Northern Ireland Constitution (Amendment) Act 1973	rep. (*prosp.*)	47, s.100(2), Sch.15
c.vi	Mallaig Harbour Order Confirmation Act 1973	rep.	43, s.1(1), Sch.1, Pt.VII, Group 6
c.xxxii	Tyneside Metropolitan Railway Act 1973	s.58 appl. (13.1.1999)	SI 3269(L), art.38(3)
1974			
c.7	Local Government Act 1974	ss.23-34 (Pt.III) appl.(mods.)	SI 633, art.L
		s.23(2A) added (*prosp.*)	38, s.125, Sch.12, para.12(2)
		s.23(3)(12) am. (*prosp.*)	38, s.125, Sch.12, para.12(3)(4)
		s.25(1)(aa) rep.	38, s.152, Sch.18, Pt.V
		s.25(1)(bc) rep.	38, s.152, Sch.18, Pt.IV
		s.25(5) subst. (*prosp.*)	31, s.140(1), Sch.30, para.4(2)

Year and Chap. or No. of Measure	Short title	How affected	1998, Chapter of Act or Number of Measure or Statutory Instrument
1974—*cont.*			
		s.26(6)(b) am. (*prosp.*)	38, s.125, Sch.12, para.13
		s.26(7)(b) rep.	38, s.152, Sch.18, Pt.IV
		s.26(13) rep.in pt.	38, s.152, Sch.18, Pt.IV
		s.27(1)(a)(b) am. (*prosp.*)	38, s.125, Sch.12, para.14
		s.29(3) am. (*prosp.*)	38, s.125, Sch.12, para.15(2)
		s.29(5)(aa) added (*prosp.*)	38, s.125, Sch.12, para.15(3)
		s.30(2A) rep.	38, s.152, Sch.18, Pt.V
		s.32(5) am. (*prosp.*)	38, s.125, Sch.12, para.16
		s.33(1) am. (*prosp.*)	38, s.125, Sch.12, para.17(2)
		s.33(1)(aa) added (*prosp.*)	38, s.125, Sch.12, para.17(2)
		s.33(2) am. (*prosp.*)	38, s.125, Sch.12, para.17(3)
		s.33(5) rep.in pt. (*prosp.*)	38, ss.125,152, Sch.12, para.17(4)(b), Sch.18, Pt.I
		s.33(5) am. (*prosp.*)	38, s.125, Sch.12, para.17(4)(a)
		Sch.5, para.5(1) rep.	31, s.140(3), Sch.31
		Sch.5, para.6 am.	38, s.129, Sch.15, para.3
c.22	Statute Law (Repeals) Act 1974	s.3(2), Sch. rep.in pt.	43, s.1(1), Sch.1, Pt.IX, Group 2
c.23	Juries Act 1974	Sch.1, Pt.III am. (*prosp.*)	38, s.125, Sch.12, para.18
		Sch.1, Pt.III am. (6.5.1999)	46, s.85(1)
c.28	Northern Ireland Act 1974	interim period cont. (until 16.7.1999)	SI 1677, art.2
		rep. (*prosp.*)	47, s.100(2), Sch.15
		Sch.1, para.1(4) excl.	1, s.4
		Sch.1, para.1(4) excl.	8, s.16(4)
		Sch.1, para.1(4) excl. (*prosp.*)	14, s.85
		Sch.1, para.1(4) excl.	23, s.17
		Sch.1, para.1(4) excl.	24, s.4
		Sch.1, para.1(4) excl.	30, s.45
		Sch.1, para.1(4) excl.	37, s.118
		Sch.1, para.1(5) excl.	1, s.4
		Sch.1, para.1(5) excl.	8, s.16(4)
		Sch.1, para.1(5) excl. (*prosp.*)	14, s.85
		Sch.1, para.1(5) excl.	23, s.17
		Sch.1, para.1(5) excl.	24, s.4
		Sch.1, para.1(5) excl.	30, s.45
		Sch.1, para.1(5) excl.	37, s.118
		Sch.1, para.5(2) rep.in pt.	SI 749, art.9, Sch.
c.37	Health and Safety at Work etc. Act 1974	ss.1-54 (Pt.I) saved (6.5.1999)	46, s.30, Sch.5, Pt.II, s.H2(a)
		s.19(2)(3) excl. (*prosp.*)	17, s.8(2)(c)
		s.20 appl. (*prosp.*)	17, s.8(1)
		s.38 appl. (*prosp.*)	17, s.20(3)

Year and Chap. or No. of Measure	Short title	How affected	1998, Chapter of Act or Number of Measure or Statutory Instrument
1974—*cont.*			
c.39	Consumer Credit Act 1974	ss.55-60 (Pt.II) saved (6.5.1999)	46, s.30, Sch.5, Pt.II, s.H2(b)
		defn. of "consumer credit agreement" appl. (*prosp.*)	20, s.2(7)
		defn. of "credit reference agency" appl.	29, s.70(1)
		saved (6.5.1999)	46, s.30, Sch.5, Pt.II, s.C7(d)
		s.16(3)(f) am.	11, s.23, Sch.5, Pt.I, Ch.III, para.36
		s.16(6B)(a) rep.in pt.	38, s.152, Sch.18, Pt.VI
		ss.70(6),77(1),78(1),79(1),84(1),101(7)(a),107(1),108(1),109(1),110(1),118(1)(b),120(1)(a), 155(1) rev.	SI 997, art.3, Sch.
		s.158 saved (*prosp.*)	29, s.73, Sch.14, para.20
		s.158(1) rev.	SI 997, art.3, Sch.
		s.158(1)(a) am. (*prosp.*)	29, s.62(1)(a)
		s.158(2) am. (*prosp.*)	29, s.62(1)(b)
		s.158(3) am. (*prosp.*)	29, s.62(1)(c)
		s.159(1) subst. (*prosp.*)	29, s.62(2)
		s.159(2)-(6) am. (*prosp.*)	29, s.62(3)
		s.159(7)(8) added (*prosp.*)	29, s.62(4)
		s.160(4) am. (*prosp.*)	29, s.62(5)(a)(i)
		s.160(4)(a)(b) am. (*prosp.*)	29, s.62(5)(a)(ii)
		s.160(7) added (*prosp.*)	29, s.62(5)(b)
		s.174(3A) am.	11, s.23, Sch.5, Pt.IV, Ch.II, para.60
c.40	Control of Pollution Act 1974	s.30A(1) (defns. of "controlled waters" and "inland waters") appl.	iii, s.1, Sch., O., s.29(4)
		s.30A(1) (defn. of "controlled waters") appl. (6.5.1999)	46, s.30, Sch.5, Pt.II, s.D2(f)
		s.30C mod.	SI 250, reg.5
		s.30C mod.	SI 1344, reg.5
		s.30F appl.(mods.)	iii, s.1, Sch., O., s.29(4)
		ss.42A,42B appl.(mods.) (1.4.1999)	SI 2746, reg.14(3)
		s.301(1) appl.(mods.) (1.4.1999)	SI 2746, reg.14(2)
c.47	Solicitors Act 1974	excl.	SI 633, art.K6
c.53	Rehabilitation of Offenders Act 1974	s.5(6A) added (*prosp.*)	37, s.119, Sch.8, para.35
		s.7(2)(bb) added	37, s.119, Sch.8, para.36
c.iv	Renfrew County Council Order Confirmation Act 1974	rep.	43, s.1(1), Sch.1, Pt.VII, Group 5
c.vii	Greenock Corporation Order Confirmation Act 1974	rep.	43, s.1(1), Sch.1, Pt.VII, Group 8

Year and Chap. or No. of Measure	Short title	How affected	1998, Chapter of Act or Number of Measure or Statutory Instrument
1975			
c.4	Biological Standards Act 1975	saved (6.5.1999)	46, s.30, Sch.5, Pt.II, s.J4(c)
c.8	Offshore Petroleum Development (Scotland) Act 1975	s.20(2) (defn. of "petroleum") am. (*prosp.*)	17, s.50, Sch.4, para.6
c.10	Statute Law (Repeals) Act 1975	ss.1(1)(3),2(2), Sch. rep.	43, s.1(1), Sch.1, Pt.IX, Group 2
c.13	Unsolicited Goods and Services (Amendment) Act 1975	saved (6.5.1999)	46, s.30, Sch.5, Pt.II, s.C7(b)
c.14	Social Security Act 1975	power to mod. (EWS) (*prosp.*)	14, s.11(1)(3)
		s.126A am.	SI 470, art.4(4)(c)
c.22	Oil Taxation Act 1975	defn. of "light gases" appl. (*retrosp.*)	36, s.152(3) (adding 1988 c.1 s.493(6))
		s.1(1) am. (*prosp.*)	17, s.50, Sch.4, para.7(2)
		s.12(1) (defn. of "licence") am. (*prosp.*)	17, s.50, Sch.4, para.7(3)
		s.21(5) rep. (*prosp.*)	17, ss.50,51, Sch.4, para.7(4), Sch.5, Pt.I
		Sch.1, para.1(2)(a) am. (*prosp.*)	17, s.50, Sch.4, para.7(5)
		Sch.2, para.2(2)(c) am. (*prosp.*)	17, s.50, Sch.4, para.7(6)
		Sch.3, para.3A(3A) added	36, s.152(1)
		Sch.3, para.4 am. (*prosp.*)	17, s.50, Sch.4, para.7(7)
c.24	House of Commons Disqualification Act 1975	am.	8, ss.1(2),16(3)(a)
		appl.	12, s.4(1)
		s.1(1)(a)-(e) appl.	46, s.15(1)(a)
		s.2 (defn. of "Ministerial office") appl. (6.5.1999)	46, s.44(4)
		Sch.1, Pt.II am.	2, s.18(1), Sch.3, para.1
		Sch.1, Pt.II am. (*prosp.*)	22, s.1(5), Sch.1, Pt.III, para.10(a)
		Sch.1, Pt.II amdt(s). cont. (*prosp.*)	29, s.74(1), Sch.15, para.5(1)
		Sch.1, Pt.II rep.in pt. (saving)(*prosp.*)	32, s.74(2)(3), Schs.5,6
		Sch.1, Pt.II am. (EW)	37, ss.41(11),64(5), Sch.2, para.6
		Sch.1, Pt.II rep.in pt.	38, s.152, Sch.18, Pts.IV-VI
		Sch.1, Pt.II am.	39, s.8, Sch.1, para.5(1)(a)
		Sch.1, Pt.II am. (*prosp.*)	41, s.45(7), Sch.7, Pt.IV, para.28
		Sch.1, Pt.II am. (pt.prosp.)	45, s.32, Sch.7, para.4
		Sch.1, Pt.II am. (*prosp.*)	47, s.73(5), Sch.8, para.9
		Sch.1, Pt.II am. (*prosp.*)	47, s.73(5), Sch.11, para.10
		Sch.1, Pt.II rep.in pt. (*prosp.*)	47, s.100(2), Sch.15

Year and Chap. or No. of Measure	Short title	How affected	1998, Chapter of Act or Number of Measure or Statutory Instrument
1975—*cont.*			
		Sch.1, Pt.III am.	SI 1340, reg.9(6), Sch.2, para.8
		Sch.1, Pt.III am. (NI) (*prosp.*)	SI 2795, art.6(1), Sch.1, para.6
		Sch.1, Pt.III rep.in pt. (NI) (*prosp.*)	SI 2795, art.6(2), Sch.2
		Sch.1, Pt.III am.	11, s.13, Sch.3, para.15
		Sch.1, Pt.III rep.in pt. (*prosp.*)	14, s.86(1)(2), Sch.7, para.4(1)(2), Sch.8
		Sch.1, Pt.III am. (*prosp.*)	14, s.86(1), Sch.7, para.4(3)
		Sch.1, Pt.III amdt(s). cont. (EW)	18, s.1(5), Sch.1, para.6
		Sch.1, Pt.III am. (EW)	18, s.54(1), Sch.3, para.4
		Sch.1, Pt.III rep.in pt. (*prosp.*)	22, ss.1(5),26, Sch.1, Pt.III, para.10(b), Sch.5, Pt.I
		Sch.1, Pt.III am.	22, s.8(3)
		Sch.1, Pt.III am.	22, s.14(12)(a)
		Sch.1, Pt.III am.	22, s.16(2), Sch.4, para.10(1)
		Sch.1, Pt.III am. (*prosp.*)	29, s.74(1), Sch.15, para.5(2)
		Sch.1, Pt.III am. (*prosp.*)	30, s.44(1), Sch.3, para.3
		Sch.1, Pt.III am.	31, s.25, Sch.5, para.8
		Sch.1, Pt.III rep.in pt. (*prosp.*)	31, s.140(3), Sch.31
		Sch.1, Pt.III am. (*prosp.*)	32, s.74(1), Sch.4, para.8
		Sch.1, Pt.III am.	35, s.1, Sch.1, para.7
		Sch.1, Pt.III am. (*prosp.*)	38, s.125, Sch.12, para.19
		Sch.1, Pt.III am. (*prosp.*)	47, s.68(4), Sch.7, para.9
		Sch.1, Pt.III rep.in pt. (*prosp.*)	47, s.100(2), Sch.15
		Sch.2 rep.in pt. (20.5.1999)	46, ss.48(6),125, Sch.9
		Sch.2 am. (20.5.1999)	46, s.87(1)
c.25	Northern Ireland Assembly Disqualification Act 1975	am. (*prosp.*)	47, s.36(1)
		s.5(1) rep. (*prosp.*)	47, s.100(2), Sch.15
		Sch.1, Pt.II rep.in pt. (*prosp.*)	SI 1506, art.78(1), Sch.6, para.3(1)-(3)
		Sch.1, Pt.II am. (*prosp.*)	SI 2795, art.6(1), Sch.1, para.7
		Sch.1, Pt.II rep.in pt. (*prosp.*)	SI 2795, art.6(2), Sch.2
		Sch.1, Pt.II am.	2, s.18(1), Sch.3, para.2
		Sch.1, Pt.II am. (*prosp.*)	22, s.1(5), Sch.1, Pt.III, para.11(a)
		Sch.1, Pt.II amdt(s). cont. (*prosp.*)	29, s.74(1), Sch.15, para.6(1)
		Sch.1, Pt.II rep.in pt. (saving)(*prosp.*)	32, s.74(2)(3), Schs.5,6
		Sch.1, Pt.II am.	39, s.8, Sch.1, para.5(1)(b)

Year and Chap. or No. of Measure	Short title	How affected	1998, Chapter of Act or Number of Measure or Statutory Instrument
1975—*cont.*			
		Sch.1, Pt.II am. (*prosp.*)	41, s.45(7), Sch.7, Pt.IV, para.29
		Sch.1, Pt.II am. (pt.prosp.)	45, s.32, Sch.7, para.5
		Sch.1, Pt.II am. (*prosp.*)	47, s.73(5), Sch.8, para.10
		Sch.1, Pt.II am. (*prosp.*)	47, s.73(5), Sch.11, para.11
		Sch.1, Pt.II rep.in pt. (*prosp.*)	47, s.100(2), Sch.15
		Sch.1, Pt.III rep.in pt. (*prosp.*)	SI 1506, art.78(1), Sch.6, para.3(1)-(3)
		Sch.1, Pt.III am. (entries added) (*prosp.*)	SI 1506, art.78(1), Sch.6, para.3(4)
		Sch.1, Pt.III am.	11, s.13, Sch.3, para.15
		Sch.1, Pt.III rep.in pt. (*prosp.*)	22, ss.1(5),26, Sch.1, Pt.III, para.11(b), Sch.5, Pt.I
		Sch.1, Pt.III am.	22, s.8(4)
		Sch.1, Pt.III am.	22, s.14(12)(b)
		Sch.1, Pt.III am.	22, s.16(2), Sch.4, para.10(2)
		Sch.1, Pt.III am. (*prosp.*)	29, s.74(1), Sch.15, para.6(2)
		Sch.1, Pt.III am. (*prosp.*)	32, s.74(1), Sch.4, para.9
		Sch.1, Pt.III am.	35, s.1, Sch.1, para.8
		Sch.1, Pt.III am. (*prosp.*)	47, s.68(4), Sch.7, para.9
		Sch.1, Pt.III rep.in pt. (*prosp.*)	47, s.100(2), Sch.15
		Sch.2 rep. (*prosp.*)	47, s.100(2), Sch.15
c.26	Ministers of the Crown Act 1975	defn. of "the Ministers" appl. (1.4.1999)	SI 2746, reg.21(5)
		defn. of "Minister of the Crown" appl.	29, s.70(1)
		defn. of "Minister of the Crown" appl. (pt.prosp.)	45, s.41
c.27	Ministerial and other Salaries Act 1975	Sch.1, Pt.III rep.in pt. (20.5.1999)	46, ss.48(6),125, Sch.9
		Sch.1, Pt.III am. (20.5.1999)	46, s.87(1)
c.30	Local Government (Scotland) Act 1975	s.2(1) mod. (1.4.1997)	SI 947, arts.1(2),8(3)
		s.2(1)(c)(iii) mod. (1.4.1997)	SI 947, arts.1(2),8(1)
		s.2(1)(d) mod. (1.4.1997)	SI 947, arts.1(2),8(2)
		s.3(2) mod. (1.4.1997)	SI 947, arts.1(2),8(4)
		s.3(4) mod. (1.4.1997)	SI 947, arts.1(2),8(5)
c.45	Finance (No.2) Act 1975	s.73 excl.	SI 1446, art.16(2)(a)(i)
c.51	Salmon and Freshwater Fisheries Act 1975	defns. of "eels", "freshwater fish", "salmon" and "trout" appl. (6.5.1999)	46, s.111(4)
		s.39 (defns. of "the River Tweed" and "the River Esk") appl. (6.5.1999)	46, s.111(4)

Year and Chap. or No. of Measure	Short title	How affected	1998, Chapter of Act or Number of Measure or Statutory Instrument
1975—*cont.*			
c.55	Statutory Corporations (Financial Provisions) Act 1975	Sch.2 rep.in pt.	38, s.152, Sch.18, Pt.VI
c.60	Social Security Pensions Act 1975	power to am. (*prosp.*)	47, s.87
c.65	Sex Discrimination Act 1975	saved (6.5.1999)	46, s.30, Sch.5, Pt.II, s.L2(a)-(d)
		ss.6,7 mod.	SI 218, art.3, Sch.
		s.7 saved	SI 633, art.J10(2)
		s.9 mod.	SI 218, art.3, Sch.
		s.10(5) am. (*prosp.*)	17, s.50, Sch.4, para.8
		ss.17-27 (Pt.III) appl.	31, s.25, Sch.5, para.6(b)
		ss.22-36 (Pt.III) appl. (*prosp.*)	31, s.24, Sch.4, para.8(a)
		ss.22-36 (Pt.III) appl.	31, s.25, Sch.5, para.6(a)
		s.22, Table , para.3A rep. (*prosp.*)	31, s.140(3), Sch.31
		s.22(1), Table am. (*prosp.*)	31, s.140(1), Sch.30, para.5
		s.23C rep. (*prosp.*)	31, s.140(3), Sch.31
		s.25(2)(4)(6)(c)(i) rep.in pt. (*prosp.*)	31, s.140(3), Sch.31
		s.25(6)(e) rep. (*prosp.*)	31, s.140(3), Sch.31
		s.27 (defn. of "transitional exemption order") appl. (*prosp.*)	31, ss.28,29,31, Sch.6, Pt.IV, para.21(6)
		s.27 appl. (*prosp.*)	31, s.34, Sch.7, Pt.VI, para.16(6)
		s.27(1A) added (*prosp.*)	31, s.140(1), Sch.30, para.6
		s.41 mod.	SI 218, art.3, Sch.
		s.77(4A)(c) am.	8, s.9(1)(2)(a)
		s.77(4A)(d) am.	8, s.10(1)(2)(a)
		s.77(4B)(4C) replaced (by s.77(4B)(4BA)(4BB)(4BC)(4C))	8, s.15, Sch.1, para.2
		s.77(4D) added	8, s.8(1)
		s.82(1A) mod.	SI 218, art.3, Sch.
		Sch.2, para.1 rep. (*prosp.*)	31, s.140(3), Sch.31
c.68	Industry Act 1975	ss.11-20 (Pt.II) saved (6.5.1999)	46, s.30, Sch.5, Pt.II, s.C15(b)
		s.13(7)(8) added	SI 3035, reg.2
c.70	Welsh Development Agency Act 1975	defn. of "business" appl.	38, s.128, Sch.14, Pt.II, para.15 (am.1976 c.75, s.26(2))
		s.1(2)(a)(b)(3)(a)-(d) am.	38, s.126(1)(2)(3)(a)-(c)
		s.1(3)(da) added	38, s.126(1)(3)(d)
		s.1(3)(f)(g)(j) am.	38, s.126(1)(2)(3)(a)-(c)
		s.1(8) am.	38, s.126(4)
		s.1(14) am.	38, s.128, Sch.14, Pt.I, para.2(2)

Year and Chap. or No. of Measure	Short title	How affected	1998, Chapter of Act or Number of Measure or Statutory Instrument
1975—*cont.*			
		s.1(15) am.	38, s.128, Sch.14, Pt.I, para.2(3)
		s.2(1) am.	38, s.128, Sch.14, Pt.I, para.3
		s.2(1A) rep.	38, s.152, Sch.18, Pt.IV
		s.2(2) rep.in pt.	38, s.152, Sch.18, Pt.IV
		s.5(1) am.	38, s.128, Sch.14, Pt.I, para.4
		s.5(1A) rep.	38, s.152, Sch.18, Pt.IV
		s.9(1)(3) am.	38, s.128, Sch.14, Pt.I, para.5(2)(3)
		s.10 am.	38, s.128, Sch.14, Pt.I, para.6
		s.11(2)(a) rep.	38, s.152, Sch.18, Pt.IV
		s.11(2)(b) am.	38, s.129, Sch.15, para.4
		s.15(1)(2) am.	38, s.128, Sch.14, Pt.I, para.7(2)(3)
		s.16(3)(b) rep.in pt.	38, s.152, Sch.18, Pt.III
		s.17(1) am.	38, s.128, Sch.14, Pt.I, para.8
		ss.21A-21C added	38, s.127, Sch.13, para.2
		ss.22,23,24(1)-(5) rep.	38, s.152, Sch.18, Pt.III
		s.25 subst.	38, s.128, Sch.14, Pt.I, para.9
		s.26 rep.	38, s.152, Sch.18, Pt.III
		s.27(1) (defns. of "business", "common", "dispose" and "fuel or field garden allotment") added	38, s.128, Sch.14, Pt.I, para.10(2)
		s.27(1) (defn. of "land") replaced (by defns. "land" & "open space")	38, s.128, Sch.14, Pt.I, para.10(3)
		s.27(1) rep.in pt.	38, s.152, Sch.18, Pt.III
		s.28(1) am.	38, s.128, Sch.14, Pt.I, para.11(2)
		s.28(1A) added	38, s.128, Sch.14, Pt.I, para.11(3)
		s.28(3) added	38, s.128, Sch.14, Pt.I, para.11(4)
		s.28, sidenote am.	38, s.128, Sch.14, Pt.I, para.11(5)
		Sch.1, para.8 rep.in pt.	38, ss.128,152, Sch.14, para.12(2), Sch.18, Pt.III
		Sch.1, para.9 rep.in pt.	38, ss.128,152, Sch.14, para.12(3), Sch.18, Pt.III
		Sch.1, para.10 rep.in pt.	38, ss.128,152, Sch.14, para.12(4), Sch.18, Pt.III

Year and Chap. or No. of Measure	Short title	How affected	1998, Chapter of Act or Number of Measure or Statutory Instrument
1975—*cont.*			
		Sch.1, para.11 rep.in pt.	38, ss.128,152, Sch.14, para.12(5), Sch.18, Pt.III
		Sch.1, para.12(1) rep.in pt.	38, ss.128,152, Sch.14, para.12(6), Sch.18, Pt.III
		Sch.1, paras.19A,19B added	38, s.128, Sch.14, Pt.I, para.12(7)
		Sch.3, para.8(1) mod.	38, s.138(4)
		Sch.4 added	38, s.127, Sch.13, para.3
c.74	Petroleum and Submarine Pipelines Act 1975	rep. (saving)(*prosp.*)	17, ss.49,51, Sch.3, Pt.II, para.10, Sch.5, Pt.I
		s.26 saving (*prosp.*)	17, s.49, Sch.3, Pt.II, para.10
		Sch.2, Pt.II incorp. in pt. (*prosp.*)	17, s.5, Sch.1, para.6
c.75	Policyholders Protection Act 1975	power to H.M.Treasury to contract out certain functions	SI 2842, art.2, Sch., Pt.II, para.63
c.xiii	Fraserburgh Harbour Order Confirmation Act 1975	rep.	43, s.1(1), Sch.1, Pt.VII, Group 6
No.1	Church Commissioners (Miscellaneous Provisions) Measure 1975	saved (1.1.1999)	GSM 1, s.5(1), Sch.2, Pt.I
1976			
c.12	Statute Law Revision (Northern Ireland) Act 1976	rep.	43, s.1(1), Sch.1, Pt.IX, Group 1
c.14	Fatal Accidents and Sudden Deaths Inquiry (Scotland) Act 1976	s.9 am. (*prosp.*)	17, s.50, Sch.4, para.9
c.16	Statute Law (Repeals) Act 1976	ss.1(1),2(3) rep.	43, s.1(1), Sch.1, Pt.IX, Group 2
		s.3(2) rep.in pt.	43, s.1(1), Sch.1, Pt.IX, Group 2
		Sch.1 rep.	43, s.1(1), Sch.1, Pt.IX, Group 2
c.25	Fair Employment (Northern Ireland) Act 1976	rep. (subject to transtl.savings) (*prosp.*)	SI 3162, art.105(2)(4), Sch.4, para.6(b), Sch.5
		s.1(1) am. (*prosp.*)	47, s.99, Sch.13, para.1(2)(a)
		s.1(2) rep. (*prosp.*)	47, ss.99,100(2), Sch.13, para.1(2)(b), Sch.15
		s.2 am. (*prosp.*)	47, s.99, Sch.13, para.1(3)
		s.17 excl.	35, s.1, Sch.1, para.10(b)
		s.49(3) am. (*prosp.*)	17, s.50, Sch.4, para.10
		s.53(4A) added (*prosp.*)	32, s.74(1), Sch.4, para.10(2)
		s.53(5) rep. (saving) (*prosp.*)	32, s.74(2)(3), Schs.5,6
		s.53(6) (defn. of "police force") am. (*prosp.*)	32, s.74(1), Sch.4, para.10(3)

Year and Chap. or No. of Measure	Short title	How affected	1998, Chapter of Act or Number of Measure or Statutory Instrument
1976—*cont.*			
		s.53(6) rep.in pt. (saving)(*prosp.*)	32, s.74(2)(3), Schs.5,6
		s.57(1) am. (*prosp.*)	47, s.99, Sch.13, para.1(4)
		s.57(2)(3) (defns. of "political opinion" and "religious belief") appl.	47, s.98(1)
		s.58(1) rep. (*prosp.*)	47, s.100(2), Sch.15
		Sch.1 rep. (*prosp.*)	47, ss.99,100(2), Sch.13, para.1(5), Sch.15
		Sch.6 rep. (*prosp.*)	47, s.100(2), Sch.15
c.30	Fatal Accidents Act 1976	am. (*prosp.*)	17, s.23(2)(a)(3)
		s.23(2)(a) ext. (*prosp.*)	17, s.49, Sch.3, Pt.II, para.13
		Sch.1, para.2(2) rep.in pt. (*prosp.*)	17, s.51, Sch.5, Pt.I
c.33	Restrictive Practices Court Act 1976	power to exclude or modify (NI)	SI 1762, art.4(1)(n)
		rep. (saving)(*prosp.*)	41, ss.1,74(2)(3), Schs.13, 14, Pt.I
c.34	Restrictive Trade Practices Act 1976	rep. (saving)(*prosp.*)	41, ss.1,74(2)(3), Schs.13, 14, Pt.I
c.53	Resale Prices Act 1976	rep. (saving)(*prosp.*)	41, ss.1,74(2)(3), Schs.13, 14, Pt.I
c.57	Local Government (Miscellaneous Provisions) Act 1976	s.51(1)(b) am.	SI 1946, art.2
		s.59(1A)(b) am.	SI 1946, art.3
		s.75(2B) added (*prosp.*)	34, s.39(1), Sch.1, para.1
c.63	Bail Act 1976	s.1 (defn. of "bail in criminal proceedings") appl.(mods.)	37, s.53 (subst. 1985 c.23 s.7A)
		s.3(5) rep.in pt.	37, ss.54(1),120(2), Sch.10
		s.3(6)(e) added	37, s.54(2)
		s.3(8B) added (4.1.1999)	37, s.119, Sch.8, para.37
		s.3A(2) am.	37, s.54(3)
		Sch.1, para.8(1) am.	37, s.119, Sch.8, para.38
c.74	Race Relations Act 1976	saved (6.5.1999)	46, s.30, Sch.5, Pt.II, s.L2(a)-(d)
		ss.4,5 mod.	SI 218, art.3, Sch.
		s.5 saved	SI 633, art.J10(2)
		s.7 mod.	SI 218, art.3, Sch.
		ss.8(5),9(3) am. (*prosp.*)	17, s.50, Sch.4, para.11
		ss.17-27 (Pt.III) appl. (*prosp.*)	31, s.24, Sch.4, para.8(b)
		s.17, Table , para.3A rep.in pt. (*prosp.*)	31, s.140(3), Sch.31
		s.17(1), Table am.	31, s.140(1), Sch.30, para.7
		s.18C rep. (*prosp.*)	31, s.140(3), Sch.31
		s.19(2)(4)(6)(c)(i) rep.in pt. (*prosp.*)	31, s.140(3), Sch.31
		s.19(6)(e) rep. (*prosp.*)	31, s.140(3), Sch.31
		s.32 mod.	SI 218, art.3, Sch.

Year and Chap. or No. of Measure	Short title	How affected	1998, Chapter of Act or Number of Measure or Statutory Instrument
1976—*cont.*			
		s.72(4A)(c) am.	8, s.9(1)(2)(b)
		s.72(4A)(d) am.	8, s.10(1)(2)(b)
		s.72(4B)(4C) replaced (by (4B)(4BA)(4BB)(4BC)(4C))	8, s.15, Sch.1, para.3
		s.72(4D) added	8, s.8(2)
c.75	Development of Rural Wales Act 1976	ss.1-22,23(3)(4),24,25 rep.	38, s.152, Sch.18, Pt.IV
		s.26(1) rep.in pt.	38, s.152, Sch.18, Pt.IV
		s.26(2) am.	38, s.128, Sch.14, Pt.II, para.15
		ss.27-34,35(2) rep.	38, s.152, Sch.18, Pt.IV
		s.35(3) rep.in pt.	38, s.152, Sch.18, Pt.IV
		Schs.1-7 rep.	38, s.152, Sch.18, Pt.IV
c.76	Energy Act 1976	saved (6.5.1999)	46, s.30, Sch.5, Pt.II, s.D5
		s.5 rep. (*prosp.*)	41, s.74(1)(3), Sch.12, para.2, Sch.14, Pt.I
		s.9(6) am. (*prosp.*)	17, s.50, Sch.4, para.12
c.80	Rent (Agriculture) Act 1976	excl.	38, s.127, Sch.13, para.3 (adding 1975 c.70, Sch.4, at Pt.IV, para.16)
		excl. (pt.prosp.)	45, s.23, Sch.6, para.5
		s.5(3)(da) rep.	38, s.152, Sch.18, Pt.VI
c.86	Fishery Limits Act 1976	Sch.2, para.5 rep.	43, s.1(1), Sch.1, Pt.X, Group 2
c.v	City of Aberdeen District Council Order Confirmation Act 1976	rep.	43, s.1(1), Sch.1, Pt.VII, Group 2
c.xxxvi	Tyne and Wear Act 1976	s.13(4)(aa) added	i, s.3(1)(2)
		s.14(1)(c) am.	i, s.3(1)(3)
		s.36 (defn. of "the tunnel") appl.	i, s.2
No.1	The Cathedrals Measure 1976	saved (1.1.1999)	GSM 1, s.5(1), Sch.2, Pt.II
No.4	Endowments and Glebe Measure 1976	s.35A added (1.1.1999)	GSM 1, s.13(1), Sch.5, para.4
1977			
c.3	Aircraft and Shipbuilding Industries Act 1977	s.3(5) rep.	43, s.1(1), Sch.1, Pt.IV, Group 5
c.5	Social Security (Miscellaneous Provisions) Act 1977	s.1(2) am. (to 25.7.1991) (*retrosp.*)	14, s.66(2)
c.18	Statute Law (Repeals) Act 1977	ss.1(1),4(2) rep.	43, s.1(1), Sch.1, Pt.IX, Group 2
		s.4(3) rep.in pt.	43, s.1(1), Sch.1, Pt.IX, Group 2
		Sch.1 rep.	43, s.1(1), Sch.1, Pt.IX, Group 2
		Sch.2 rep.in pt.	43, s.1(1), Sch.1, Pt.IX, Group 2
c.19	Restrictive Trade Practices Act 1977	power to exclude or modify (NI)	SI 1762, art.4(1)(n)

Year and Chap. or No. of Measure	Short title	How affected	1998, Chapter of Act or Number of Measure or Statutory Instrument
1977—*cont.*			
		rep. (saving)(*prosp.*)	41, ss.1,74(2)(3), Schs.13, 14, Pt.I
c.37	Patents Act 1977	ss.44,45 rep. (*prosp.*)	41, ss.70,74(3), Sch.14, Pt.I
		s.132(4) am. (*prosp.*)	17, s.50, Sch.4, para.14
c.42	Rent Act 1977	excl. 38, s.127, Sch.13, para.3 (adding 1975 c.70, Sch.4, at Pt.IV, para.16)	
		excl. (pt.prosp.) 45, s.23, Sch.6, para.5	
		s.14(f) rep.	38, s.152, Sch.18, Pt.IV
		ss.15(2),86(2),93(1) rep.in pt.	38, s.152, Sch.18, Pt.VI
c.43	Protection From Eviction Act 1977	s.3A(8)(f) rep.	38, s.152, Sch.18, Pt.IV
		s.3A(8)(g) rep.in pt.	38, ss.140,152, Sch.16, para.2(a), Sch.18, Pt.VI
		s.3A(8)(ga) added	38, s.140, Sch.16, para.2(b)
c.45	Criminal Law Act 1977	s.1(1A)(1B) rep.	40, s.9(1)(2), Sch.1, Pt.II, para.4(a), Sch.2, Pt.II
		s.1(4) rep.in pt.	40, s.9(1)(2), Sch.1, Pt.II, para.4(b), Sch.2, Pt.II
		s.1(5)(6) rep.	40, s.9(1)(2), Sch.1, Pt.II, para.4(c), Sch.2, Pt.II
		s.1A added	40, s.5(1)
		s.4(5)(6)(7) added	40, s.5(2)
		s.12A(7) rep.in pt.	38, ss.140,152, Sch.16, para.3(2), Sch.18, Pt.VI
		s.12A(7A) added	38, s.140, Sch.16, para.3(3)
c.49	National Health Service Act 1977	defn. of "the health service" appl.	18, s.53(1)
		saved	38, s.27(10)
		defn. of "health service hospitals" appl. (*prosp.*)	38, s.118(2)(f)
		s.5(1)(a)(1A)(a) rep.in pt. (*prosp.*)	31, s.140(3), Sch.31
		s.8(1) mod.	38, s.27(7)(a)
		s.8(2) am.	38, s.148
		s.8(5)(a) mod.	38, s.27(7)(a)
		s.20 mod.	38, s.27(7)(b)
		s.28A(2)(e) rep.in pt.	38, s.152, Sch.18, Pt.IV
		s.28A(2)(e) rep.in pt.	38, s.152, Sch.18, Pt.VI
		s.28A(2)(e)(vi) rep.	38, s.152, Sch.18, Pt.IV
		s.28A(2)(e)(vii) rep.	38, s.152, Sch.18, Pt.VI
		s.28B(1)(b) rep.in pt.	38, s.152, Sch.18, Pt.IV
		s.28B(1)(b) rep.in pt.	38, s.152, Sch.18, Pt.VI
		s.28B(1)(b)(vi) rep.	38, s.152, Sch.18, Pt.IV
		s.83A(1)(a) am.	SI 2385, art.2
		Sch.1, paras.3,4 am. (*prosp.*)	31, s.140(1), Sch.30, para.8

Year and Chap. or No. of Measure	Short title	How affected	1998, Chapter of Act or Number of Measure or Statutory Instrument
1977—cont.			
c.50	Unfair Contract Terms Act 1977	ss.3(2)(b),17(1)(b) ext. (*prosp.*)	20, s.14(2)
c.xxi	Aberdeen Shoemakers Incorporation Order Confirmation Act 1977	rep.	43, s.1(1), Sch.1, Pt.VII, Group 8
No.1	Incumbents (Vacation of Benefices) Measure 1977	s.18(1)(5) trans.of functions (1.1.1999)	SI 1715, art.2, Sch.1
1978			
c.5	Northern Ireland (Emergency Provisions) Act 1978	appl.	35, s.3(7)(b)
		appl.	35, s.17, Sch.3, para.2(1) (c)
c.10	European Assenbly Elections Act 1978	power to apply or incorporate	38, s.11(3)(a)
		power to appl.	46, s.12(4)(5)
		saved (6.5.1999)	46, s.30, Sch.5, Pt.II, s.B3(a)
		s.3(8)(a) am.	48, s.23, Sch.3, para.1
c.15	Solomon Islands Act 1978	Sch., para.7 rep.	43, s.1(1), Sch.1, Pt.IV, Group 1
c.19	Oaths Act 1978	s.2 rep. (NI) (*prosp.*)	SI 1504, art.65(2), Sch.6
c.20	Tuvalu Act 1978	Sch.2, para.7 rep.	43, s.1(1), Sch.1, Pt.IV, Group 1
c.23	Judicature (Northern Ireland) Act 1978	ss.2(1),3(1) mod.	42, s.18(4)(c)
		s.35(2)(h) appl.(mods.)	SI 1287, art.3(4)
		Sch.5, Pt.II am. (*prosp.*)	SI 1504, art.65(1), Sch.5, para.8
		Sch.5, Pt.II rep.in pt. (saving)(*prosp.*)	32, s.74(2)(3), Schs.5,6
		Sch.5, Pt.II rep.in pt.	43, s.1(1), Sch.1, Pt.VIII
c.29	National Health Service (Scotland) Act 1978	defn. of "a Health Board" appl.	29, s.69(2)(c)
		defn. of "a Special Health Board" appl.	29, s.69(2)(d)
		s.49(3) (defn. of "Medical supplies") appl. (6.5.1999)	46, s.30, Sch.5, Pt.II, s.J4
		s.75A(1)(a) am.	SI 2385, art.3
c.30	Interpretation Act 1978	defn. of "subordinate legislation" appl.	36, s.118(9)
		appl.	36, s.163(6)
		saved (1.7.1999)	46, ss.29,53(4), Sch.4, Pt.II, para.8
		defn. of "subordinate legislation" appl.	46, s.126(1)
		defn. of "subordinate legislation" appl.	47, s.98(1)
		s.14 excl. (*prosp.*)	17, s.25(9)
		s.14 excl. (1.7.1999)	46, s.115, Sch.7, para.5
		s.17(2) excl. (EW)	18, s.54(2), Sch.4, para.6

Year and Chap. or No. of Measure	Short title	How affected	1998, Chapter of Act or Number of Measure or Statutory Instrument
1978—*cont.*			
		s.23A added (1.7.1999)	46, s.125, Sch.8, para.16(2)
		s.24(5)(d)(e) replaced (by s.24(5)(d)(e)(f)(g)) (*prosp.*)	47, s.99, Sch.13, para.3
		Sch.1 (defns. of "Act" and "Enactment") added (1.7.1999)	46, s.125, Sch.8, para.16(3)
c.42	Finance Act 1978	s.6(5)(6)(7)(9), Schs.1, 12, para.26 rep.	36, s.165, Sch.27, Pt.V(4)
c.45	Statute Law (Repeals) Act 1978	s.1(1) rep.	43, s.1(1), Sch.1, Pt.IX, Group 2
		s.3(2) rep.in pt.	43, s.1(1), Sch.1, Pt.IX, Group 2
		Sch.1 rep.	43, s.1(1), Sch.1, Pt.IX, Group 2
c.46	Employment (Continental Shelf) Act 1978	rep. (*prosp.*)	17, s.51, Sch.5, Pt.I
c.47	Civil Liability (Contribution) Act 1978	mod. (*prosp.*)	42, s.8(5)(b)
c.xviii	Cunninghame District Council Order Confirmation Act 1978	rep.	43, s.1(1), Sch.1, Pt.VII, Group 2
c.xx	District Council of Renfrew Order Confirmation Act 1978	rep.	43, s.1(1), Sch.1, Pt.VII, Group 2
No.1	Dioceses Measure 1978	restr. (1.1.1999)	GSM 1, s.5(3)(6)(7)
		ss.1(1),2(1)(2),4(1),5(2)(4),6(2),18(2),19(3) trans.of functions (1.1.1999)	SI 1715, art.2, Sch.1
1979			
c.2	Customs and Excise Management Act 1979	mod. (EWI) (*prosp.*)	33, s.21(4)(5)(7)
		s.1(1) (defn. of "armed forces") rep.in pt. (1.1.1999)	SI 3086, reg.10(3)
		s.138 appl.(mods.)	SI 1531, reg.4(3)
		s.139(4)(c) am. (NI) (*prosp.*)	32, s.74(1), Sch.4, para.14
		ss.145-148 appl.(mods.)	SI 1531, reg.4(4)(5)
		ss.150-155 appl.(mods.)	SI 1531, reg.4(4)
		Sch.4, para.12, Table , Pt.I rep.in pt.	36, s.165, Sch.27, Pt.V(4)
c.4	Alcoholic Liquor Duties Act 1979	s.8(3)(4) added	36, s.20, Sch.2, paras.1, 12
		s.10(3)(4) added	36, s.20, Sch.2, paras.2, 12
		s.11 am.	36, s.20, Sch.2, paras.3(2), 12
		s.11(2)-(4) added	36, s.20, Sch.2, paras.3(3) , 12
		s.36(1) am. (1.1.1999)	36, s.1(1)(2)
		s.42 rep. (*prosp.*)	36, ss.5(1)(2),165, Sch.27, Pt.I(1), Note

Year and Chap. or No. of Measure	Short title	How affected	1998, Chapter of Act or Number of Measure or Statutory Instrument
1979—*cont.*			
		s.62(1A)(a) am. (17.3.1998) (*retrosp.*)	36, s.2(3)(4)
		s.62(1A)(b)(c) subst. (1.1.1999)	36, s.4(1)(2)
		Sch.1, Table , Pt.I am. (17.3.1998) (*retrosp.*)	36, s.2(2)(4)
		Sch.1, Table , Pt.I subst. (1.1.1999)	36, s.3(1)(2)
c.5	Hydrocarbon Oil Duties Act 1979	s.1(6) subst. (17.3.1998) (*retrosp.*)	36, s.8(1)(2)
		s.6(1) am. (*prosp.*)	36, s.6(1)(a)(3)
		s.6(1) rep.in pt. (*prosp.*)	36, ss.6(1)(b)(3),165, Sch.27, Pt.I(2), Note
		s.6(1A)(a)(b)(c) am. (17.3.1998) (*retrosp.*)	36, s.7(1)(a)(b)(c)(5)
		s.6(2) replaced (by s.6(2)(2AA)(2AB)) (*prosp.*)	36, s.6(2)(3)
		s.11(1)(a)(b)(ba) am. (17.3.1998) (*retrosp.*)	36, s.7(2)(a)(b)(5)
		s.13A(1A)(a)(b) am. (17.3.1998) (*retrosp.*)	36, s.7(3)(a)(b)(5)
		s.13AB(1)(a) subst.	36, s.20, Sch.2, paras.4(2), 12
		s.13AB(2)(a) subst.	36, s.20, Sch.2, paras.4(3) , 12
		s.14(1) am. (17.3.1998) (*retrosp.*)	36, s.7(4)(5)
		s.20AAA(2A) added (17.3.1998) (*retrosp.*)	36, s.9(1)(6)
		s.20AAA(3) am. (17.3.1998) (*retrosp.*)	36, s.9(2)(6)
		s.20AAB(1) am. (17.3.1998) (*retrosp.*)	36, s.9(3)(6)
		Sch.2A, para.7A added (17.3.1998) (*retrosp.*)	36, s.9(4)(6)
		Sch.2A, para.9(1A) added (17.3.1998) (*retrosp.*)	36, s.9(5)(6)
c.7	Tobacco Products Duty Act 1979	s.8(2) am.	36, s.20, Sch.2, paras.5, 12
		Sch.1, Table subst. (1.12.1998)	36, s.10(1)(2)
c.10	Public Lending Right Act 1979	saved (6.5.1999)	46, s.30, Sch.5, Pt.II, s.K2
c.17	Vaccine Damage Payments Act 1979	s.3(4) am. (*prosp.*)	14, s.86(1), Sch.7, para.5
		s.3A added (*prosp.*)	14, s.45
		s.4 subst. (*prosp.*)	14, s.46
		s.5(1)-(3)(5) rep. (*prosp.*)	14, s.86(1)(2), Sch.7, para.6, Sch.8
		s.7(3) rep.in pt. (*prosp.*)	14, s.86(1)(2), Sch.7, para.7(1)(b), Sch.8

Year and Chap. or No. of Measure	Short title	How affected	1998, Chapter of Act or Number of Measure or Statutory Instrument
1979—*cont.*			
		s.7(3) am. (*prosp.*)	14, s.86(1), Sch.7, para.7(1)(a)
		s.7(4) am. (*prosp.*)	14, s.86(1), Sch.7, para.7(2)
		s.7A added (*prosp.*)	14, s.47
		s.7B added (*prosp.*)	14, s.86(1), Sch.7, para.8
		s.8(3) am. (*prosp.*)	14, s.86(1), Sch.7, para.9
		s.12(1) rep. (*prosp.*)	14, s.86(1)(2), Sch.7, para.10, Sch.8
c.27	Kiribati Act 1979	Sch., para.8 rep.	43, s.1(1), Sch.1, Pt.IV, Group 1
c.28	Carriage by Air and Road Act 1979	saved (6.5.1999)	46, s.30, Sch.5, Pt.II, s.E4(c)
c.33	Land Registration (Scotland) Act 1979	appt. day(s) for ss.2(1) (2), 3(3) (1.4.1999)	SI 1810, art.2
		appt. day(s) for ss.2(1) (2),3(3) (1.10.1999) [Counties of Berwick, East Lothian, Roxburgh, Selkirk & Peebles)	SI 2980, art.2
c.38	Estate Agents Act 1979	saved (6.5.1999)	46, s.30, Sch.5, Pt.II, s.C7(e)
		s.10(3) rep.in pt. (*prosp.*)	41, s.74(1)(3), Sch.12, para.3(a), Sch.14, Pt.I
		s.10(3)(a) am. (11.1.1999)	41, s.74(1), Sch.12, para.3(b)
c.41	Pneumoconiosis etc. (Workers' Compensation) Act 1979	saved (6.5.1999)	46, s.30, Sch.5, Pt.II, s.H1(c)
c.54	Sale of Goods Act 1979	defns. of "contract of sale of goods" and "goods" appl. (*prosp.*)	20, s.2(7)
c.i	Tyneside Metropolitan Raiway Act 1973	s.5 appl. (13.1.1999)	SI 3269(L), art.38(3)
c.ii	Inverclyde District Council Order Confirmation Act 1979	rep.	43, s.1(1), Sch.1, Pt.VII, Group 2
c.iii	Solicitors in the Supreme Court of Scotland (Amendment) Order Confirmation Act 1979	rep.	43, s.1(1), Sch.1, Pt.VII, Group 8
c.xviii	Dumbarton District Council Order Confirmation Act 1979	rep.	43, s.1(1), Sch.1, Pt.VII, Group 2
c.xxi	Scots Episcopal Fund Order Confirmation Act 1979	rep.	43, s.1(1), Sch.1, Pt.VII, Group 8
1980			
c.2	Papua New Guinea, Western Samoa and Nauru (Miscellaneous Provisions) Act 1980	Sch., para.2 rep.	43, s.1(1), Sch.1, Pt.IV, Group 1
c.9	Reserve Forces Act 1980	s.19 mod. (1.1.1999) transtl. provn.	SI 3086, reg.11, Sch., para.6

Year and Chap. or No. of Measure	Short title	How affected	1998, Chapter of Act or Number of Measure or Statutory Instrument
1980—*cont.*			
		s.21 mod. (1.1.1999) transtl. provn.	SI 3086, reg.11, Sch., para.7
		s.36(3)(b) rep.in pt. (1.1.1999)	SI 3086, reg.12
		ss.83,156(1) mod. (1.1.1999) transtl. provn.	SI 3086, reg.11, Sch., para.8(1)
c.11	Protection of Trading Interests Act 1980	saved (6.5.1999)	46, s.30, Sch.5, Pt.II, s.C15(c)
c.17	National Heritage Act 1980	ss.8,9 saved (6.5.1999)	46, s.30, Sch.5, Pt.II, s.K4
		ss.16,16A saved (6.5.1999)	46, s.30, Sch.5, Pt.II, s.K3
c.20	Education Act 1980	s.19, Sch.5 rep. (*prosp.*)	30, s.44(2), Sch.4
c.21	Competition Act 1980	ss.2-10 rep. (*prosp.*)	41, ss.17,74(3), Sch.14, Pt.I
		s.11(8) rep.in pt. (*prosp.*)	41, s.74(1)(3), Sch.12, para.4(2), Sch.14, Pt.I
		s.11(8)(b) rep. (*prosp.*)	41, s.74(1)(3), Sch.12, para.4(2), Sch.14, Pt.I
		s.11(9) replaced (by s.11(9)(9A)) (*prosp.*)	41, s.74(1), Sch.12, para.4(3)
		s.13(1) rep.in pt. (*prosp.*)	41, s.74(1)(3), Sch.12, para.4(4)(a), Sch.14, Pt.I
		s.13(6) replaced (by s.13(6)(7)(8)) (*prosp.*)	41, s.74(1), Sch.12, para.4(4)(b)
		s.15(2)(b)(3)(4) rep. (*prosp.*)	41, s.74(1)(3), Sch.12, para.4(5), Sch.14, Pt.I
		s.16(3) rep. (*prosp.*)	41, s.74(1)(3), Sch.12, para.4(6), Sch.14, Pt.I
		s.17(1) rep.in pt. (*prosp.*)	41, s.74(1)(3), Sch.12, para.4(7)(a), Sch.14, Pt.I
		s.17(2) rep.in pt. (*prosp.*)	41, s.74(1)(3), Sch.12, para.4(7)(b), Sch.14, Pt.I
		s.17(3)-(5) rep.in pt. (*prosp.*)	41, s.74(1)(3), Sch.12, para.4(7)(a), Sch.14, Pt.I
		s.17(6) am. (*prosp.*)	41, s.74(1), Sch.12, para.4(7)(c)
		s.19(3)(d)(e) rep. (*prosp.*)	41, s.74(1)(3), Sch.12, para.4(8), Sch.14, Pt.I
		s.19(3)(e) rep. (*prosp.*)	41, s.74(1), Sch.12, para.4(8)
		s.19(3)(r) added (11.1.1999)	41, s.74(1), Sch.12, para.4(9)
		s.19(5)(a) rep.in pt. (*prosp.*)	41, s.74(1)(3), Sch.12, para.4(10), Sch.14, Pt.I
		s.22 rep. (11.1.1999)	41, s.74(1)(3), Sch.12, para.4(11), Sch.14, Pt.I
		s.24 appl.(mods.) (*prosp.*)	41, s.66(5), Sch.10, Pt.IV, para.9(2) (replacing 1984 c.12 at s.13(9A))

Year and Chap. or No. of Measure	Short title	How affected	1998, Chapter of Act or Number of Measure or Statutory Instrument
1980—*cont.*			
		s.24 appl.(mods.) (*prosp.*)	41, s.66(5), Sch.10, Pt.IV, para.10(2) (replacing 1986 c.44 at s.24(7A))
		s.24 appl.(mods.) (*prosp.*)	41, s.66(5), Sch.10, Pt.IV, para.12(2) (replacing 1989 c.29 at s.12(8A))
		s.24 appl.(mods.) (*prosp.*)	41, s.66(5), Sch.10, Pt.IV, para.13(3) (replacing 1991 c.56 at s.14(7A))
		s.24 appl.(mods.) (*prosp.*)	41, s.66(5), Sch.10, Pt.IV, para.15(2) (replacing 1993 c.43 at s.13(8A))
		s.24 appl.(mods.) (*prosp.*)	41, s.66(5), Sch.10, Pt.V, para.17(2) (replacing 1992/231 at art.15(8)(9))
		s.24 appl.(mods.) (*prosp.*)	41, s.66(5), Sch.10, Pt.V, para.18(2) (replacing 1996/275 art.15(9))
		s.24 mod. (*prosp.*)	41, s.74(1), Sch.12, para.7(2) (replacing 1986 c.31 at s.44(3A))
		s.24 mod. (*prosp.*)	41, s.74(1), Sch.12, para.14(3) (replacing 1990 c.42 Sch.4, at para.4(7A))
		s.24 mod. (*prosp.*)	41, s.74(1), Sch.12, para.20(2) (am. SI 1994/426 (NI No.1))
		s.24(1) am. (*prosp.*)	41, s.74(1), Sch.12, para.4(12)
		ss.25-30 rep. (*prosp.*)	41, s.74(1)(3), Sch.12, para.4(13), Sch.14, Pt.I
		s.31(2) rep. (*prosp.*)	41, s.74(1)(3), Sch.12, para.4(14)(a), Sch.14, Pt.I
		s.31(3) rep.in pt. (*prosp.*)	41, s.74(1)(3), Sch.12, para.4(14)(b), Sch.14, Pt.I
		s.33(2) am. (*prosp.*)	41, s.74(1), Sch.12, para.4(15)(a)
		s.33(3)(4) rep. (*prosp.*)	41, s.74(1)(3), Sch.12, para.4(15)(b), Sch.14, Pt.I
c.43	Magistrates' Courts Act 1980	appl. (*prosp.*)	34, s.25(3)
		s.10(3A) added	37, s.47(5)
		s.11(3) am. (*prosp.*)	37, s.119, Sch.8, para.39
		s.12(3)(b) subst. (*prosp.*)	15, s.1(1)
		s.12(7)(a) replaced (by s.12(7)(a)(aa)) (*prosp.*)	15, s.1(2)
		s.12(7A)(7B) added (*prosp.*)	15, s.1(3)
		s.13(1) rep.in pt.	15, s.3(1)
		s.13(3) replaced (by 1980 c.43 s.13(3)(3A))	15, s.3(2)

Year and Chap. or No. of Measure	Short title	How affected	1998, Chapter of Act or Number of Measure or Statutory Instrument
1980—*cont.*			
		s.22 (defns. of "the value involved" and "the relevant sum") appl. (4.1.1999)	37, s.52(4)
		s.22 (defns. of "the value involved" and "the relevant sum") appl. (4.1.1999)	37, s.52(4)(6), Sch.3, para.14(7)
		s.24(1)(a) am.	37, s.119, Sch.8, para.40(1)
		s.24(1A) added	37, s.47(6)
		s.24(2) am. (4.1.1999)	37, s.119, Sch.8, para.40(2)
		s.30(2)(a) am.	37, s.106, Sch.7, para.28
		s.37 rep. (*prosp.*)	37, ss.119,120(2), Sch.8, para.41, Sch.10
		s.38(2) rep.in pt.	37, ss.106,120(2), Sch.7, para.29(1), Sch.10
		s.38(2A) added	37, s.106, Sch.7, para.29(2)
		s.38A(2) rep.in pt.	37, ss.106,120(2), Sch.7, para.30(1), Sch.10
		s.38A(5) am.	37, s.106, Sch.7, para.30(2)
		s.38A(5A) added	37, s.106, Sch.7, para.30(3)
		s.39(6)(b) am.	37, s.106, Sch.7, para.31
		s.65 ext.	37, s.11(6)
		s.65(1)(q) added	37, s.119, Sch.8, para.42
		s.85(1)(a) am.	37, s.106, Sch.7, para.32
		s.104 restr.	15, s.2(1) (adding 1988 c.53 s.13(3A)(3B))
		s.108(2) rep.in pt.	37, ss.119,120(2), Sch.8, para.43, Sch.10
		s.120(1)(2) replaced (by s.120(1)(1A)(2))	37, s.55
		s.125(4)(c)(ii) rep.in pt.	37, ss.119,120(2), Sch.8, para.44(a), Sch.10
		s.125(4)(c)(iii) am.	37, s.119, Sch.8, para.44(b)
		s.125(4)(c)(iv) added	37, s.119, Sch.8, para.44(c)
		s.126(c) rep.in pt. (4.1.1999)	37, ss.119,120(2), Sch.8, para.45(a), Sch.10
		s.126(cc) added (4.1.1999)	37, s.119, Sch.8, para.45(b)
		s.126(e) added (4.1.1999)	37, s.119, Sch.8, para.45(c)
		s.127(1) excl. (*prosp.*)	37, s.45 (adding 1985 c.23 s.22B(4))
		s.128 restr.	37, s.47(3)
		s.133(1) am.	37, s.119, Sch.8, para.46

Year and Chap. or No. of Measure	Short title	How affected	1998, Chapter of Act or Number of Measure or Statutory Instrument
1980—*cont.*			
		s.141 appl. (4.1.1999)	37, s.52(6), Sch.3, para.6(11)
		s.141(2) appl.	SI 644, reg.3(5)
		s.144 ext. (in force 1/8/1998 for the purpose of making rules etc. see SI 1998/1883) (pt.prosp.)	37, s.49(2)
		s.144 (defn. of "justices' clerk") appl. (in force 30/9/1998 in areas specified in SI 1998/2327, Sch.2) (pt.prosp.)	37, s.49(5)
		s.144 ext. (4.1.1999)	37, s.52(6), Sch.3, para.4(12)
		Sch.7, para.120(b) rep. (*prosp.*)	37, s.120(2), Sch.10
c.44	Education (Scotland) Act 1980	defns. of "education authority" and "further education" appl.	29, s.30(5)
		defn. of "the proprietor" appl. (*prosp.*)	29, s.30(5)
		defn. of "the managers" appl. (*prosp.*)	29, s.30(5)
		defn. of "the education authority" appl. (*prosp.*)	29, s.30(5)
		defn. of "education authority" appl.	29, s.68(1)(6), Sch.11, para.6(a)
		defn. of "pupil" appl.	29, s.70(1)
		defn. of "school" appl.	29, s.70(1)
		ss.31,33 appl.	39, s.55(4)
		s.66(1B) added	30, s.21
		s.73(f) am.	30, s.29(1)
		ss.73A-73D added	30, s.29(2)
		s.73E added	30, s.30
		s.75A(9A) rep.in pt. (pt.prosp.)	31, ss.130(2)(a),140(3), Sch.31
		s.75A(9A)(c) added	31, s.130(2)(b)
		s.133(2) am.	30, s.44(1), Sch.3, para.4(a)
		s.133(2A)(2B) added	30, s.44(1), Sch.3, para.4(b)
		s.135(1) (defn. of "central institution") appl.	30, s.28(1)
		s.135(1) (defn. of "Her Majesty's inspectors") rep.in pt. (1.7.1999)	46, s.125, Sch.8, para.17, Sch.9
		s.135(2)(b) (defn. of "secondary education") appl. (*prosp.*)	30, s.32 (adding 1996 c.18, s.63A(2)(a)(ii))
c.48	Finance Act 1980	s.97(3)(e) rep.	38, s.152, Sch.18, Pt.IV
		s.120(4) am.	36, s.162(1)(b)(2)
		s.120(5) am.	36, s.162(5)

Year and Chap. or No. of Measure	Short title	How affected	1998, Chapter of Act or Number of Measure or Statutory Instrument
1980—*cont.*			
c.55	Law Reform (Miscellaneous Provisions) (Scotland) Act 1980	Sch.1, Pt.III am. (*prosp.*)	38, s.125, Sch.12, para.20
		Sch.1, Pt.III am. (6.5.1999)	46, s.85(2)
c.59	Statute Law Revision (Northern Ireland) Act 1980	rep.	43, s.1(1), Sch.1, Pt.IX, Group 1
c.63	Overseas Development and Co-operation Act 1980	s.10 saved (NI) (*prosp.*)	32, s.8(6)
		ss.10(2),13(1)(2) restr. (6.4.1998) (except where the payment or other benefit or the right to receive it has been brought into charge to tax before that date) (*retrosp.*)	36, s.58(2)(4), Sch.9, Pt.I, para.6(2) (substituting 1988 c.1 Sch.11 at para.6(2))
c.65	Local Government, Planning and Land Act 1980	Sch.1, Pt.III rep.in pt. appl.(mods.)	38, s.152, Sch.18, Pt.IV iv, s.11
		s.2(7)(b) subst. (EW)	18, s.54(1), Sch.3, para.5(1)
		s.14(1) am. (EW)	18, s.54(1), Sch.3, para.5(2)
		ss.102-104,106-111 rep.	38, s.152, Sch.18, Pt.V
		s.131(5) rep.	38, s.152, Sch.18, Pt.IV
		s.166(1A) added	SI 85, art.4(1)
		Sch.16, para.9A rep.	38, s.152, Sch.18, Pt.VI
		Sch.17, Pt.III, para.4, Pt.IV, para.9, Schs.18- 22 rep.	38, s.152, Sch.18, Pt.V
		Sch.19, para.1(f) rep.	38, s.152, Sch.18, Pt.IV
		Sch.21, para.6 mod.	38, s.138(2)
		Sch.32, para.5 saved (1.7.1999)	46, s.55(2)
		Sch.32, para.5(3)(b) saved (1.7.1999)	46, ss.29,53(4), Sch.4, Pt.I, paras.1(2)(d),9
		Sch.32, para.15 saved (1.7.1999)	46, s.55(2)
		Sch.32, para.15(4)(b) saved (1.7.1999)	46, ss.29,53(4), Sch.4, Pt.I, paras.1(2)(d),9
c.66	Highways Act 1980	defns. of "highway" and "local highway authority" appl. (pt.prosp.)	45, s.24(9)
		ss.205-237 (Pt.XI) (defn. of "private street") appl. (pt.prosp.)	45, s.24(9)
		Sch.24, para.28 rep.	38, s.152, Sch.18, Pt.IV
No.2	Diocese in Europe Measure 1980	saved (1.1.1999)	GSM 1, s.5(1), Sch.2, Pt.I
1981			
c.3	Gas Levy Act 1981	rep. (saving)	36, s.165, Sch.27, Pt.V(3), Note 1

Year and Chap. or No. of Measure	Short title	How affected	1998, Chapter of Act or Number of Measure or Statutory Instrument
1981—*cont.*			
		s.1(3) (defn. of "petroleum production licence") subst. (*prosp.*)	17, s.50, Sch.4, para.15
		s.3 restr. (*retrosp.*)	36, s.153(3)
c.6	Industry Act 1981	ss.2(4),7(5) rep.in pt.	38, s.152, Sch.18, Pt.IV
c.14	Public Passenger Vehicles Act 1981	defn. of "public service vehicle" appl. (*prosp.*)	34, s.36
		saved (6.5.1999)	46, s.30, Sch.5, Pt.II, s.E1(b)
		s.1 (defn. of "service vehicle") appl.	iii, s.1, Sch., O., s.28(6) (b)
		s.79 am. (*prosp.*)	34, s.39(1), Sch.1, para.2
c.20	Judicial Pensions Act 1981	am.	8, ss.1(2),16(3)(b)
		power to am.	42, s.18(6), Sch.4, paras.3,4
		s.13 excl. (EWS) (*prosp.*)	14, s.14(12), Sch.4, para.4(2)
		s.16 am.	8, s.15, Sch.1, para.4
		s.17(4) am.	8, s.15, Sch.1, para.5
		s.32 excl. (EWS) (*prosp.*)	14, s.14(12), Sch.4, para.4(2)
c.22	Animal Health Act 1981	Sch.2, para.4A added	13, s.1
c.35	Finance Act 1981	s.107(3)(ca) rep.	38, s.152, Sch.18, Pt.VI
		s.107(3)(i) rep.	38, s.152, Sch.18, Pt.IV
		s.118(2)(c) am. (*prosp.*)	17, s.50, Sch.4, para.16
		s.137(1)(2) rep. (*prosp.*)	47, s.100(2), Sch.15
c.49	Contempt of Court Act 1981	defns. of "the strict liability rule" and "publication" appl.	38, s.78(2)
		defns. of "strict liability rule" and "publication" appl. (6.5.1999)	46, s.42
		defn. of "the strict liability rule" appl. (*prosp.*)	47, s.50(3)
c.52	Belize Act 1981	Sch.2, para.7 rep.	43, s.1(1), Sch.1, Pt.IV, Group 1
c.54	Supreme Court Act 1981	ss.2(1),4(1),12(1)-(6) mod.	42, s.18(4)(a)
		s.33(2) rep.in pt. (26.4.1999)	SI 2940, art.5(a)
		s.34(1) rep. (26.4.1999)	SI 2940, art.5(b)(i)
		s.34(2)(3) rep.in pt. (26.4.1999)	SI 2940, art.5(b)(ii)
		s.47(1A) added	37, s.119, Sch.8, para.47
		s.81(1)(a) am. (4.1.1999)	37, s.119, Sch.8, para.48
c.55	Armed Forces Act 1981	Sch.3, para.12 subst. (1.1.1999)	SI 3086, reg.8(1)(2)
		Sch.3, para.12 mod. (1.1.1999) transtl. provn.	SI 3086, reg.11, Sch., para.5
c.61	British Nationality Act 1981	defn. of "British protected person" appl. (*prosp.*)	7, s.2(3)(c)
		Sch.3 am. (25.1.1999)	SI 3161, art.2
c.63	Betting and Gaming Duties Act 1981	s.21(3A)(b)(c) subst. (1.4.1998) (*retrosp.*)	36, s.13(1)(2)

Effects of Legislation

Year and Chap. or No. of Measure	Short title	How affected	1998, Chapter of Act or Number of Measure or Statutory Instrument
1981—*cont.*			
		s.21(3A)(d) added	36, s.14(1)(4)
		s.21(3B)-(3E) added	36, s.14(2)(4)
		s.22(2) am.	SI 2207, art.3
		s.23(2), Table subst. (17.3.1998) (*retrosp.*)	36, s.12(1)(2)
		s.25(4)(6) am.	36, s.14(3)(4)
c.64	New Towns Act 1981	ss.1(2),2(5) rep.	38, s.152, Sch.18, Pt.IV
		s.3(1) rep.in pt.	38, s.152, Sch.18, Pt.IV
		s.36(1)(a) am. (subst. in pt. by sub-paras.(i)(ii))	SI 85, art.3(1)
		s.36(2) am.	SI 85, art.3(2)
		s.36(3) am.	SI 85, art.3(3)
		s.36(3A) added	SI 85, art.3(4)
		s.36(4) am.	SI 85, art.3(5)
		s.36(4A) added	SI 85, art.3(6)
		Sch.12, paras.20-22 rep.	38, s.152, Sch.18, Pt.IV
c.66	Compulsory Purchase (Vesting Declarations) Act 1981	appl.(mods.)	SI 1936(L), art.28
		appl.(mods.) (13.1.1999)	SI 3269(L), art.22(1)(2)
		mod. (pt.prosp.)	45, s.19(6), Sch.4, paras.6-9
c.67	Acquisition of Land Act 1981	appl.(mods.)	38, s.127, Sch.13, para.3 (adding 1975 c.70, Sch.4, at Pt.I, para.1(1))
		appl.(mods.) (pt.prosp.)	45, s.20(4)(5), Sch.5, Pt.I
		defn. of "compulsory purchase order" appl. (pt.prosp.)	45, s.20(8)
		defn. of "owner" appl. (pt.prosp.)	45, s.21(10)
		s.4 appl.	iv, s.9
		s.17(3) am.	38, s.128, Sch.14, Pt.II, para.17
		s.17(3) rep.in pt.	38, s.152, Sch.18, Pt.V
		s.17(4)(ab)(ac) rep. (*prosp.*)	31, s.140(3), Sch.31
		s.28(aa) added	38, s.128, Sch.14, Pt.II, para.18
		s.28(c) rep.	38, s.152, Sch.18, Pt.IV
		s.31(1)(b) rep.	38, s.152, Sch.18, Pt.V
		s.31(1)(c) am.	38, s.135(3)
		s.31(1)(d) added	38, s.128, Sch.14, Pt.II, para.19
		Sch.2, Pt.II appl.	iv, s.7(1)
		Sch.2, Pt.III appl.(mods.)	iv, s.7(1)(2)
		Sch.3, para.4(3) am.	38, s.128, Sch.14, Pt.II, para.20
		Sch.3, para.4(3) rep.in pt.	38, s.152, Sch.18, Pt.V
		Sch.4, para.1, Table rep.in pt.	38, s.152, Sch.18, Pt.III
		Sch.4, paras.1, Table , 16(3) rep.in pt.	38, s.152, Sch.18, Pt.IV

Year and Chap. or No. of Measure	Short title	How affected	1998, Chapter of Act or Number of Measure or Statutory Instrument
1981—*cont.*			
		Sch.4, para.27 rep.	38, s.152, Sch.18, Pt.IV
		Sch.4, para.30(2)(3)(10) (11) rep.	38, s.152, Sch.18, Pt.V
c.69	Wildlife and Countryside Act 1981	Sch.5 am.	SI 878, art.2
		Sch.8 am.	SI 878, art.3
c.i	Bearsden and Milngavie District Council Order Confirmation Act 1981	rep.	43, s.1(1), Sch.1, Pt.VII, Group 2
c.xxiv	United Reformed Church Act 1981	ss.1,2,21,24,28,29 ext.(mods.) (to Jersey)	SI 751, art.4, Sch.2
1982			
c.16	Civil Aviation Act 1982	saved (6.5.1999)	46, s.30, Sch.5, Pt.II, s.E4(d)
		Sch.13, Pt.III, para.6(5) restr. (*prosp.*)	17, s.12(2)(b)(3)
c.23	Oil and Gas (Enterprise) Act 1982	rep.in pt. (*prosp.*)	17, s.51, Sch.5, Pt.I
c.27	Civil Jurisdiction and Judgments Act 1982	s.18 excl. (S)	SI 752, art.3(3)
		s.46(3)(aa) added (6.5.1999)	46, s.125, Sch.8, para.18(2)
		s.46(7) am. (6.5.1999)	46, s.125, Sch.8, para.18(3)
		Sch.5, para.9 am.	17, s.50, Sch.4, para.17(a)
		Sch.9, para.10 am.	17, s.50, Sch.4, para.17(b)
c.30	Local Government (Miscellaneous Provisions) Act 1982	Sch.4, para.2(5) rep.in pt.	38, s.152, Sch.18, Pt.IV
		Sch.4, para.2(5)(c) am.	38, s.129, Sch.15, para.5
		Sch.4, para.2(5)(e) rep.	38, s.152, Sch.18, Pt.IV
c.32	Local Government Finance Act 1982	s.9(1) am.	18, s.54(1), Sch.3, para.6
		ss.11-36 (Pt.III),38(5)(6) , Schs.3,5,6, Pt.IV rep.	18, s.54(3), Sch.5
c.34	Forfeiture Act 1982	s.4(2)(b) am. (*prosp.*)	14, s.86(1), Sch.7, para.11(1)
		s.4(5) (defn. of "Commissioner") am. (*prosp.*)	14, s.86(1), Sch.7, para.11(2)
c.36	Aviation Security Act 1982	saved (6.5.1999)	46, s.30, Sch.5, Pt.II, s.E4(e)
c.37	Merchant Shipping (Liner Conferences) Act 1982	saved (6.5.1999)	46, s.30, Sch.5, Pt.II, s.E3(e)
c.38	Northern Ireland Act 1982	rep. (*prosp.*)	47, s.100(2), Sch.15
		Sch.1, para.8(1) rep.in pt.	SI 749, art.9, Sch.
c.39	Finance Act 1982	s.129(1) am.	22, s.24(4)
c.41	Stock Transfer Act 1982	s.4 rep.	SI 1446, art.30(2), Sch.2, Pt.I
		Sch.2, para.6 rep.	43, s.1(1), Sch.1, Pt.IV, Group 1
c.42	Derelict Land Act 1982	ss.1(12),2(3)(4) rep. (*prosp.*)	38, s.152, Sch.18, Pt.III

Year and Chap. or No. of Measure	Short title	How affected	1998, Chapter of Act or Number of Measure or Statutory Instrument
1982—*cont.*			
c.45	Civic Government (Scotland) Act 1982	s.21(3A) added (*prosp.*)	34, s.39(1), Sch.1, para.3
		s.54(2A)-(2C) added	37, s.24(2)
		s.60(5) am.	37, s.24(3)(a)
		s.60(6)(a) am.	37, s.24(3)(b)(i)
		s.60(6)(c) am.	37, s.24(3)(b)(ii)
		Sch.2A added	37, s.24(4), Sch.1
c.48	Criminal Justice Act 1982	s.1(2) am. (4.1.1999)	37, s.119, Sch.8, para.49
		s.1A(1) am. (*prosp.*)	37, s.119, Sch.8, para.50(1)
		s.1A(3) am. (*prosp.*)	37, s.119, Sch.8, para.50(2)
		s.1A(4) am. (*prosp.*)	37, s.119, Sch.8, para.50(3)
		s.1A(4A) rep. (*prosp.*)	37, ss.119,120(2), Sch.8, para.50(4), Sch.10
		s.1A(6) am.	37, s.119, Sch.8, para.50(5)
		s.1B rep. & superseded (*prosp.*)	37, ss.73(7)(a),120(2), Sch.10
		s.1B am.	37, s.116(4)
		s.1C mod. (*prosp.*)	37, s.79(3)(4)
		s.1C(2) rep.in pt. (*prosp.*)	37, ss.119,120(2), Sch.8, para.51, Sch.10
		s.3(1)(a) rep.in pt.	37, ss.106,120(2), Sch.7, para.33(a), Sch.10
		s.3(1)(c) am.	37, s.106, Sch.7, para.33(b)
		s.3(1)(d) am.	37, s.106, Sch.7, para.33(c)
		s.3(1)(e) subst. (*prosp.*)	37, s.119, Sch.8, para.52(1)
		s.3(2) am. (4.1.1999)	37, s.119, Sch.8, para.52(2)
		s.13(3) am.	37, s.106, Sch.7, para.34(1)
		s.13(6) am.	37, s.106, Sch.7, para.34(2)
		s.16(2) am.	37, s.106, Sch.7, para.35
		ss.17-19 appl.(mods.)	37, s.106, Sch.7, para.46(7) (adding 1991 c.53 Sch.2, para.6(6))
		s.17 appl.(mods.)	37, ss.68(3),70(5), Sch.5, para.5(1)
		s.17 ext.	37, s.72(1) (replacing 1969 c.54 s.15(3)(a)(b))
		s.17(1) am.	37, s.106, Sch.7, para.36(1)
		s.17(1)(a) subst.	37, s.106, Sch.7, para.36(2)
		s.17(1)(b) am.	37, s.106, Sch.7, para.36(3)

Year and Chap. or No. of Measure	Short title	How affected	1998, Chapter of Act or Number of Measure or Statutory Instrument
1982—*cont.*			
		s.17(1)(bb) added	37, s.106, Sch.7, para.36(3)
		s.17(1A) added	37, s.106, Sch.7, para.36(4)
		s.17(8) subst.	37, s.106, Sch.7, para.36(5)
		s.18 appl.(mods.)	37, ss.68(3),70(5), Sch.5, para.5(2)
		s.18(4A) replaced (by s.18(4A)(4B))	37, s.106, Sch.7, para.37(1)
		s.18(7) rep.	37, ss.106,120(2), Sch.7, para.37(2), Sch.10
		s.18(10)(11) added	37, s.106, Sch.7, para.37(3)
		s.19 appl.(mods.)	37, ss.68(3),70(5), Sch.5, para.5(2)
		s.19(1) am.	37, s.106, Sch.7, para.38(1)
		s.19(3)(a) rep.in pt.	37, ss.119,120(2), Sch.8, para.53(1), Sch.10
		s.19(5) am.	37, s.106, Sch.7, para.38(2)
		s.19(5) rep.in pt.	37, ss.119,120(2), Sch.8, para.53(2), Sch.10
		s.19(5A)(b) subst.	37, s.119, Sch.8, para.53(3)
		s.19(5B) added	37, s.119, Sch.8, para.53(4)
		s.19(8)(9) added	37, s.106, Sch.7, para.38(3)
		Sch.14, para.28 rep. (*prosp.*)	37, s.120(2), Sch.10
c.50	Insurance Companies Act 1982	power to H.M.Treasury to contract out certain functions	SI 2842, art.2, Sch., Pt.I, paras.1-61
		defn. of "insurance company" appl.	36, s.77(1) (adding 1988 c.1 s.333B)
		s.1 (defns. of "long-term business" and "general business") appl.	SI 3081, reg.2(1)
		s.1 (defn. of "general business") appl.	36, s.113, Sch.17, paras.14,37 (adding 1988 c.1, s.755B)
		s.96(1) (defn. of "insurance company") appl. (year 1998-99 and subsequent years of assessment)	36, s.121, Sch.20 (adding 1992 c.12, Sch.A1)
		s.96(1) (defn. of "insurance company") appl.	36, s.121, Sch.21, para.9 (adding 1992 c.12 s.214C)
		Sch.2B, para.3(1), Table entry 1A added	11, s.23, Sch.5, Pt.IV, Ch.II, para.61(2)
		Sch.2B, para.3(5)(e) added	11, s.23, Sch.5, Pt.IV, Ch.II, para.61(3)

Year and Chap. or No. of Measure	Short title	How affected	1998, Chapter of Act or Number of Measure or Statutory Instrument
1982—*cont.* c.52	Industrial Development Act 1982	s.1 saved (6.5.1999)	46, s.30, Sch.5, Pt.II, s.C13
		ss.7-9,11-13 trans.of functions (1.7.1999)	46, ss.53,56(1)(h)
		Sch.2, Pt.II, para.5 rep.	43, s.1(1), Sch.1, Pt.IV, Group 3
1983 c.2	Representation of the People Act 1983	appl.(mods.)	SI 746, art.12, Sch.1, Table 1
		appl.in pt.(mods.)	SI 1287, art.3(1)(3)(5), Sch.1
		power to apply or incorporate	38, s.11(3)(a)
		power to appl.	46, s.12(4)(5)
		saved (6.5.1999)	46, s.30, Sch.5, Pt.II, s.B3(b)
		s.11(3) appl.	SI 1287, art.5(2)
		ss.18,23 appl. (NI)	SI 1126, art.6, Sch.2
		ss.29,30,49,50 appl.(mods.) (NI)	SI 1126, art.6, Sch.2
		ss.60,61,63,65,66,91,94 appl. (NI)	SI 1126, art.6, Sch.2
		s.95(2)(a) am. (*prosp.*)	31, s.140(1), Sch.30, para.10
		s.96(2)(a) am. (*prosp.*)	31, s.140(1), Sch.30, para.11
		s.97 appl.(mods.) (NI)	SI 1126, art.6, Sch.2
		s.98 appl. (NI)	SI 1126, art.6, Sch.2
		s.100 appl.(mods.) (NI)	SI 1126, art.6, Sch.2
		ss.101-104,109 appl. (NI)	SI 1126, art.6(1), Sch.2
		s.110 appl.(mods.) (NI)	SI 1126, art.6(1), Sch.2
		s.111 appl. (NI)	SI 1126, art.6(1), Sch.2
		s.112 appl.(mods.) (NI)	SI 1126, art.6(1), Sch.2
		ss.113-115 appl. (NI)	SI 1126, art.6(1), Sch.2
		ss.116,117 appl.(mods.) (NI)	SI 1126, art.6(1), Sch.2
		s.118 appl. (NI)	SI 1126, art.6(1), Sch.2
		ss.120-186 (Pt.III) saved	46, s.16(5)(a)
		ss.160(4),167,168,169,170, 173 appl.(mods.) (NI)	SI 1126, art.6(1), Sch.2
		s.174 appl. (NI)	SI 1126, art.6(1), Sch.2
		s.175 appl.(mods.) (NI)	SI 1126, art.6(1), Sch.2
		ss.176,178,179,181 appl. (NI)	SI 1126, art.6(1), Sch.2
		s.184 appl.(mods.) (NI)	SI 1126, art.6(1), Sch.2
		s.185 appl. (NI)	SI 1126, art.6(1), Sch.2
		s.191 (defn. of "local government election") appl.	48, s.22
		ss.200,202 appl. (NI)	SI 1126, art.6(1), Sch.2
		ss.203,204 (defn. of "local government election") appl.	48, s.22

Year and Chap. or No. of Measure	Short title	How affected	1998, Chapter of Act or Number of Measure or Statutory Instrument
1983—*cont.*			
		s.205 appl. (NI)	SI 1126, art.6(1), Sch.2
		Sch.1, rule 6A added (*prosp.*)	48, s.13, Sch.2, para.2
		Sch.1, rule 12(3) am. (*prosp.*)	48, s.13, Sch.2, para.3(2)
		Sch.1, rule 12(3A) added (*prosp.*)	48, s.13, Sch.2, para.3(3)
		Sch.1, rule 12(4) am. (*prosp.*)	48, s.13, Sch.2, para.3(4)
		Sch.1, rule 19(2A)(2B) added (*prosp.*)	48, s.13, Sch.2, para.4
		Sch.1, rules 20,22,23 appl.(mods.) (NI)	SI 1126, art.6(1), Sch.2
		Sch.1, rules 24,25 appl. (NI)	SI 1126, art.6(1), Sch.2
		Sch.1, rules 26,28 appl.(mods.) (NI)	SI 1126, art.6(1), Sch.2
		Sch.1, rule 29 appl. (NI)	SI 1126, art.6(1), Sch.2
		Sch.1, rules 30,31,32 appl.(mods.) (NI)	SI 1126, art.6(1), Sch.2
		Sch.1, rules 33,34 appl. (NI)	SI 1126, art.6(1), Sch.2
		Sch.1, rules 35,36,37 appl.(mods.) (NI)	SI 1126, art.6(1), Sch.2
		Sch.1, rules 38,39,40 appl. (NI)	SI 1126, art.6(1), Sch.2
		Sch.1, rule 40A appl.(mods.) (NI)	SI 1126, art.6(1), Sch.2
		Sch.1, rules 41,42 appl.	SI 1126, art.6(1), Sch.2
		Sch.1, rules 43,44,45,47, 48 appl.(mods.) (NI)	SI 1126, art.6(1), Sch.2
		Sch.1, rule 54 appl. (NI)	SI 1126, art.6(1), Sch.2
		Sch.1, rule 55 appl.(mods.) (NI)	SI 1126, art.6(1), Sch.2
		Sch.1, para.22(1)(i) rep.in pt. (*prosp.*)	31, s.140(3), Sch.31
		Sch.1, Appx.of Forms am. (*prosp.*)	48, s.13, Sch.2, para.5
		Sch.1, Appx.of Forms, Directions, para.2(a) am. (*prosp.*)	48, s.13, Sch.2, para.6(a)
		Sch.1, Appx.of Forms Directions, para.3A added (*prosp.*)	48, s.13, Sch.2, para.6(b)
		Sch.2, para.11A(2) am. (*prosp.*)	29, s.74(1), Sch.15, para.7
		Sch.5, para.1(1) am. (*prosp.*)	31, s.140(1), Sch.30, para.12
		Appendix of Forms appl.(mods.) (NI)	SI 1126, art.6(1), Sch.2
c.20	Mental Health Act 1983	s.37(8) am.	37, s.119, Sch.8, para.54
		s.54(2)(3) ext.	37, s.106, Sch.7, para.5(3) (adding 1969 c.54, s.12B(3))
		s.134(3)(a) am. (*prosp.*)	47, s.99, Sch.13, para.5(2)
		s.134(3)(c) am. (*prosp.*)	38, s.125, Sch.12, para.22
		s.141(8) added (19.11.1998)	46, s.125, Sch.8, para.19

Year and Chap. or No. of Measure	Short title	How affected	1998, Chapter of Act or Number of Measure or Statutory Instrument
1983—*cont.*			
		s.141(9) added (*prosp.*)	38, s.125, Sch.12, para.23
		s.141(10) added (*prosp.*)	47, s.99, Sch.13, para.5(3)
		Sch.3 rep.in pt.	43, s.1(1), Sch.1, Pt.IV, Group 1
c.28	Finance Act 1983	s.45(3) rep.in pt.	38, s.152, Sch.18, Pt.IV
		s.45(3)(b) rep.	38, s.152, Sch.18, Pt.IV
c.29	Miscellaneous Financial Provisions Act 1983	Sch.2 rep.in pt. (the entry relating to the Local Government Finance Act 1982) (EW)	18, s.54(3), Sch.5
		Sch.2 rep.in pt.	38, s.152, Sch.18, Pt.IV
		Sch.2 rep.in pt.	38, s.152, Sch.18, Pt.V
c.40	Education (Fees and Awards) Act 1983	s.1(6) am.	30, s.44(1), Sch.3, para.5
		s.2(3)(a) rep. (*prosp.*)	30, s.44(2), Sch.4
		s.2(3)(b) rep.in pt. (*prosp.*)	30, s.44(2), Sch.4
c.41	Health and Social Services and Social Security Adjudications Act 1983	s.25, Sch.8 rep. (*prosp.*)	14, s.86(2), Sch.8
c.44	National Audit Act 1983	s.6 restr.	22, s.5(1)(2) (adding 1993 c.39, s.33(4))
		s.6 restr.	38, s.101(2)(b)
		s.6 excl. (1.4.2000)	46, s.125, Sch.8, para.20
		s.6(3)(aa) added	38, s.100(5)
		s.7 restr. (*prosp.*)	38, s.111, Sch.9, Pt.I, paras.12,13
		s.7 restr. (*prosp.*)	38, s.112, Sch.10, para.17 (adding 1993 c.46, Sch.1A, at para.14(2))
		s.7 excl. (1.4.2000)	46, s.125, Sch.8, para.20
		s.13 appl. (*prosp.*)	38, s.155(4)
c.54	Medical Act 1983	defn. of "a fully registered person" appl.	37, s.106, Sch.7, para.5(2) (adding 1969 c.54 s.12B(1A))
		defn. of "fully registered person" appl.	37, s.106, Sch.7, para.27(5) (adding 1973 c.62, Sch.1A, para.5(10) defn. of "registered medical practitioner")
		saved (6.5.1999)	46, s.30, Sch.5, Pt.II, s.G2(d)
c.56	Oil Taxation Act 1983	Sch.2, para.12(2)(5) am.	36, s.152(2)
c.59	Petroleum Royalties (Relief) Act 1983	s.1 am. (*prosp.*)	17, s.49, Sch.3, Pt.II, para.8(1)
		s.1(3) (defn. of "petroleum") am. (*prosp.*)	17, s.50, Sch.4, para.18
No.1	Pastoral Measure 1983	restr. (1.1.1999)	GSM 1, s.5(3)(6)(7)
		ss.45(1)(2)(4),53(6A) trans.of functions (1.1.1999)	SI 1715, art.2, Sch.1
		s.78A(2) am. (1.1.1999)	GSM 1, s.13(1), Sch.5, para.5

Year and Chap. or No. of Measure	Short title	How affected	1998, Chapter of Act or Number of Measure or Statutory Instrument
1984			
c.4	Tourism (Overseas Promotion) (Scotland) Act 1984	s.1(2) rep. (1.7.1999)	46, s.125, Sch.8, para.21, Sch.9
c.12	Telecommunications Act 1984	s.1(6) am.	SI 1580, reg.40(1)
		s.1(6) am. (1.5.1999)	SI 3170, reg.3(1), Sch.1, para.1
		s.3(3)(b) am. (pt.prosp.)	41, s.66(5), Sch.10, Pt.II, para.2(3)
		s.3(3B)(3C) added (pt.prosp.)	41, s.66(5), Sch.10, Pt.II, para.2(4)
		s.4(3) defn.of (" telecommunication service") para.(a) appl. in pt.	6, s.2(3)
		s.7 (defn. of "telecommunications code system") appl.	iii, s.1, Sch., O., s.3(2)
		s.13(9)(10) replaced (by s.13(9)(9A)(10)(10A)) (*prosp.*)	41, s.66(5), Sch.10, Pt.IV, para.9(2)
		s.14(2) rep. (*prosp.*)	41, ss.66(5),74(3), Sch.10, Pt.IV, para.9(3), Sch.14, Pt.I
		s.16(5) rep.in pt. (*prosp.*)	41, ss.66(5),74(3), Sch.10, Pt.IV, para.9(4), Sch.14, Pt.I
		s.16(5)(c) added (*prosp.*)	41, s.66(5), Sch.10, Pt.IV, para.9(4)
		s.50(3) restr. (pt.prosp.)	41, s.66(5), Sch.10, Pt.II, para.2(1)
		s.50(3) replaced (by s.50(3)(3A)) (pt.prosp.)	41, s.66(5), Sch.10, Pt.II, para.2(5)(6)
		s.50(4) rep.in pt. (pt.prosp.)	41, ss.66(5),74(3), Sch.10, Pt.II, para.2(5)(7), Sch.14, Pt.I
		s.50(4)(c) rep. (pt.prosp.)	41, ss.66(5),74(3), Sch.10, Pt.II, para.2(5)(7), Sch.14, Pt.I
		s.50(5) rep.in pt. (pt.prosp.)	41, ss.66(5),74(3), Sch.10, Pt.II, para.2(5)(8), Sch.14, Pt.I
		s.50(6)(b) subst. (pt.prosp.)	41, s.66(5), Sch.10, Pt.II, para.2(5)(9)
		s.50(6A) added (*prosp.*)	41, s.66(5), Sch.10, Pt.IV, para.9(5)
		s.50(7) rep.in pt. (pt.prosp.)	41, ss.66(5),74(3), Sch.10, Pt.II, para.2(5)(10), Sch.14, Pt.I
		s.53 am.	SI 1580, reg.40(2)
		s.74 rep.	6, s.7, Sch.2, Pt.I

Year and Chap. or No. of Measure	Short title	How affected	1998, Chapter of Act or Number of Measure or Statutory Instrument
1984—*cont.*			
		s.95(1) rep.in pt. (*prosp.*)	41, ss.66(5),74(3), Sch.10, Pt.IV, para.9(6)(a), Sch.14, Pt.I
		s.95(2) rep.in pt. (*prosp.*)	41, ss.66(5),74(3), Sch.10, Pt.IV, para.9(6)(b)(ii), Sch.14, Pt.I
		s.95(2) am. (*prosp.*)	41, s.66(5), Sch.10, Pt.IV, para.9(6)(b)(i)
		s.95(2)(c) rep. (*prosp.*)	41, ss.66(5),74(3), Sch.10, Pt.IV, para.9(6)(b)(ii), Sch.14, Pt.I
		s.95(3) rep.in pt. (*prosp.*)	41, ss.66(5),74(3), Sch.10, Pt.IV, para.9(6)(c), Sch.14, Pt.I
		s.101(3)(d)(e) rep. (*prosp.*)	41, ss.66(5),74(3), Sch.10, Pt.IV, para.9(7)(a), Sch.14, Pt.I
		s.101(3)(n) added	41, s.66(5), Sch.10, Pt.IV, para.9(7)(b)
		s.101(6) added (*prosp.*)	41, s.66(5), Sch.10, Pt.IV, para.9(8)
		s.107(1) am. (*prosp.*)	17, s.50, Sch.4, para.19(a)
		s.107(3) rep. (*prosp.*)	17, ss.50,51, Sch.4, para.19(b), Sch.5, Pt.I
		Sch.2 saved	iv, s.37(2)
		Sch.2, para.1(1) (defn. of "telecommunications apparatus") appl.	iii, s.1, Sch., O., s.3(2)
		Sch.4, para.1 excl. (pt.prosp.)	45, s.23, Sch.6, para.8(1)(e)
		Sch.4, para.1 defn(s). appl. (pt.prosp.)	45, s.23, Sch.6, para.16(1)
		Sch.4, paras.3(1)(e),67 rep.	38, s.152, Sch.18, Pt.IV
c.22	Public Health (Control of Disease) Act 1984	s.69(2) am.	18, s.54(1), Sch.3, para.7
c.24	Dentists Act 1984	defn. of "dentistry" appl. (11.1.1999)	41, s.3(1)(d), Sch.4, Pt.II, para.10
		saved (6.5.1999)	46, s.30, Sch.5, Pt.II, s.G2(e)
		s.15(4)(d) am.	SI 811, reg.20(1)
		s.15(4A)(4B)(4C) added	SI 811, reg.19
		s.16(2A) added	SI 811, reg.20(2)
		s.17(2)(d) subst.	SI 811, reg.20(3)(a)
		s.17(3A) added	SI 811, reg.20(3)(b)
		s.21A added	SI 811, reg.21(1)
		s.40(2)(ab) added	SI 1546, art.2
		s.53(1) (defn. of "a registered dentist") appl.	29, s.69(1)(b)
		Sch.4, para.2(2)(a) am.	SI 811, reg.21(2)
c.27	Road Traffic Regulation Act 1984	ss.17,25 saved (6.5.1999)	46, s.30, Sch.5, Pt.II, s.E1(c)

Year and Chap. or No. of Measure	Short title	How affected	1998, Chapter of Act or Number of Measure or Statutory Instrument
1984—*cont.*			
		s.46 mod. (Borough of Luton) (19.1.1999)	SI 3207(L), art.5, Sch.2
		s.55 mod.	SI 1134, art.5(1)
		ss.55,63A mod. (Borough of Luton) (19.1.1999)	SI 3207(L), art.5, Sch.2
		ss.64-80 (Pt.V) saved (6.5.1999)	46, s.30, Sch.5, Pt.II, s.E1(c)
		s.64 (defn. of "traffic sign") appl.	iii, s.1, Sch., O., s.3(2)
		ss.81-91 (Pt.VI) saved (6.5.1999)	46, s.30, Sch.5, Pt.II, s.E1(c)
		ss.101,102 mod. (Borough of Luton) (19.1.1999)	SI 3207(L), art.5, Sch.2
		s.102(2) mod.	SI 1134, art.5(2)
		s.142(1) mod. (Borough of Luton) (19.1.1999)	SI 3207(L), art.5, Sch.2
		Sch.4, para.20(a)(iii) am.	43, s.1(2), Sch.2, para.12(1)(2)
		Sch.12 rep.	43, s.1(1), Sch.1, Pt.I, Group 2
c.28	County Courts Act 1984	s.47 rep. (26.4.1999)	SI 2940, art.6(a)
		s.52(2) rep.in pt. (26.4.1999)	SI 2940, art.6(b)
		s.53(1) rep. (26.4.1999)	SI 2940, art.6(c)(i)
		s.53(2)(3) rep.in pt. (26.4.1999)	SI 2940, art.6(c)(ii)
		s.63(1) rep.in pt. (26.4.1999)	SI 2940, art.6(d)(i)
		s.63(2) rep. (26.4.1999)	SI 2940, art.6(d)(ii)
		s.63(3) am. (26.4.1999)	SI 2940, art.6(d)(iii)
		s.63(4) am. (26.4.1999)	SI 2940, art.6(d)(iv)
		s.74 referred to (26.4.1999)	SI 3132, rule 44.12(2)
		s.74 power to excl. (26.4.1999)	SI 3132, rules 47.8(3), 47.14(5)
		s.133(1) rep.in pt. (26.4.1999)	SI 2940, art.6(e)
		s.134 rep. (26.4.1999)	SI 2940, art.6(f)
c.32	London Regional Transport Act 1984	Sch.6, para.26 rep.	18, s.54(3), Sch.5
c.35	Data Protection Act 1984	referred to (*prosp.*)	v, s.6(15)
		rep. (saving)(*prosp.*)	29, ss.73,74(2), Sch.14, paras.3-5,7,8,14-16, Sch.16, Pt.I
		ss.10,13,14,16, Schs.3,4 appl.(mods.) (1.5.1999)	SI 3170, reg.13, Sch.2
c.36	Mental Health (Scotland) Act 1984	s.74(8A) am. (1.1.1998) (*retrosp.*)	37, s.119, Sch.8, para.55
c.39	Video Recordings Act 1984	saved (6.5.1999)	46, s.30, Sch.5, Pt.II, s.B5(a)
c.47	Repatriation of Prisoners Act 1984	s.2(4)(b) mod. (*temp.*)	SI 2327, art.5(3)(a)
		s.2(4)(b)(i) subst.	37, s.119, Sch.8, para.56
		s.2(4)(b)(iii) am. (*prosp.*)	SI 1504, art.65(1), Sch.5, para.22
		s.2(4)(i) mod. (*temp.*)	SI 2327, art.5(3)(a)

Year and Chap. or No. of Measure	Short title	How affected	1998, Chapter of Act or Number of Measure or Statutory Instrument
1984—*cont.*			
		s.3(9) am.	37, s.119, Sch.8, para.57
		s.9(4) ext.	37, s.121(12)
		Sch.2, para.2(4) mod. (*temp.*)	SI 2327, art.5(3)(b)
		Sch., para.2 am.	37, s.119, Sch.8, para.59(1)
		Sch., para.2(2) am.	37, s.119, Sch.8, para.59(1)(2)
		Sch., para.2(4) (defn. of "the enactments relating to release on licence") subst.	37, s.119, Sch.8, paras.58, 59(3)
c.51	Inheritance Tax Act 1984	Sch., para.3 subst. mod.	37, s.119, Sch.8, para.60 36, s.161(2)(c)
		s.23(5) am. (saving)	36, s.143(2)(a)
		s.26 rep. (saving)	36, ss.143(1),165, Sch.27, Pt.IV, Note 1
		s.27(1) am. (saving)	36, s.144(1)(2)
		s.27(1A) added (saving)	36, s.144(1)(2)
		s.29(5) am. (saving)	36, s.143(2)(b)
		s.29A(6) am. (saving)	36, s.143(2)(a)
		s.30(3BA) added (saving)	36, s.142, Sch.25, para.2(1)(2)
		s.31(1)(a) replaced (by s.31(1)(a)(aa))	36, s.142, Sch.25, para.4(1)(4)
		s.31(2)(3) am.	36, s.142, Sch.25, para.4(2)(4)
		s.31(4FA) added	36, s.142, Sch.25, para.5(1)(2)
		s.31(4FB) added	36, s.142, Sch.25, para.6(1)(2)
		s.31(5) subst.	36, s.142, Sch.25, para.4(3)(4)
		s.32(2) am.	36, s.142, Sch.25, para.7(1)(9)
		s.32(5)(b) subst.	36, s.142, Sch.25, para.7(2)(9)
		s.32(5AA) added	36, s.142, Sch.25, para.7(3)(9)
		s.32A(6) am.	36, s.142, Sch.25, para.7(4)(9)
		s.32A(8)(b) subst.	36, s.142, Sch.25, para.7(5)(9)
		s.32A(8A) added	36, s.142, Sch.25, para.7(6)(9)
		s.32A(9) subst.	36, s.142, Sch.25, para.7(7)(9)
		s.35A added	36, s.142, Sch.25, para.8(1)
		s.35A ext.	36, s.142, Sch.25, para.9 (adding 1992 c.12 s.258(8A))
		s.35A appl.(mods.)	36, s.142, Sch.25, para.10
		s.56(4)(7) am. (saving)	36, s.143(3)

Year and Chap. or No. of Measure	Short title	How affected	1998, Chapter of Act or Number of Measure or Statutory Instrument
1984—*cont.*			
		s.65 restr.	36, s.161(3)
		s.76(1)(b) am. (17.3.1998)	36, s.143(4)(a)(5)
		s.76(1)(d)(2) rep. (17.3.1998)	36, ss.143(4)(a)(5),165, Sch.27, Pt.IV, Note 1
		s.76(3) am. (17.3.1998)	36, s.143(4)(b)(5)
		s.76(6)(8) am. (17.3.1998)	36, s.143(4)(c)(5)
		s.78(1A) added (saving)	36, s.142, Sch.25, para.3(1)(2)
		s.79A added	36, s.142, Sch.25, para.8(2)
		s.161(2)(b) am. (17.3.1998)	36, s.143(6)
		Sch.1, Table am. (amounts specified from 6.4.1998)	SI 756, art.2
		Sch.3 am.	22, s.24(3)
		Sch.4, para.3(3A) added	36, s.142, Sch.25, para.8(3)(4)
		Sch.5, para.5 subst.	36, s.142, Sch.25, para.7(8)(9)
c.53	Local Government (Interim Provisions) Act 1984	s.10(2) am.	18, s.54(1), Sch.3, para.8(1)
		s.11(1) am.	18, s.54(1), Sch.3, para.8(2)
c.54	Roads (Scotland)) Act 1984	s.151 (defns. of "footpath", "footway" and "road") appl.	iii, s.1, Sch., O., s.3(2)
c.55	Building Act 1984	appt. day(s) for Sch.1, para.9 (7.8.1998)	SI 1836, art.2
		s.4(1)(a)(ii) rep.in pt. (*prosp.*)	31, s.140(3), Sch.31
		s.4(1)(a)(iii)(iv) rep. (*prosp.*)	31, s.140(3), Sch.31
		s.35 excl. (1.4.1999)	SI 3129, reg.13
		s.115(3) am.	18, s.54(1), Sch.3, para.9
c.60	Police and Criminal Evidence Act 1984	s.24(2) appl.(mods.)	SI 1531, reg.4(2)
		s.24(2)(a) added	37, ss.84(2),120(1), Sch.9, para.9
		s.24(2)(o) added (1.3.1999	37, s.27(1)
		s.24(2)(p) added	37, s.32(2)
		s.27(4A) added (in force 30.9.1998 for the purpose of reprimands and warnings under 1998 c.37 s.65 in any area specified in SI 1998/2327, Sch.3)	37, s.119, Sch.8, para.61
		s.47(3) am. (in force 30/9/1998 in the areas specified in SI 1998/2327, Sch.2) (pt.prosp.)	37, s.46(1)
		s.47(3A) added (in force 30/9/1998 in the areas specified in SI 1998/2327, Sch.2) (pt.prosp.)	37, s.46(2)
		s.47A added	37, s.119, Sch.8, para.62

Year and Chap. or No. of Measure	Short title	How affected	1998, Chapter of Act or Number of Measure or Statutory Instrument
1984—*cont.*			
c.xvi	Shrewsbury and Atcham Borough Council Act 1984	am.	ii, s.3
		s.3 excl.	ii, ss.4,5,7
		s.5 subst.	ii, s.8
		s.6 am.	ii, s.9
		s.8(2) subst.	ii, s.10
1985			
c.2	Elections (Northern Ireland) Act 1985	appl.in pt.(mods.)	SI 1287, art.3(1)(3), Sch.1
		s.3 appl.	SI 1126, art.6(1), Sch.2
c.5	New Towns and Urban Development Corporations Act	s.11, Sch.2, para.1 rep.	38, s.152, Sch.18, Pt.IV
c.6	Companies Act 1985	appl.(mods.)	11, s.7(3)(9)
		defn. of "authorised minimum" appl. (6.4.1998)	36, s.74(1), Sch.13, Pt.III, para.35 (adding 1992 c.12, Sch.5B, paras.10-15 at para 14(5) (a))
		s.259 (defn. of "undertaking") appl.	11, s.17(7)
		s.259(1) (defn. of "body corporate or other undertaking") appl.	38, s.99(4)(a)
		s.259(1) (defn. of "undertaking") appl.	38, s.144(3)(b)
		s.449(1)(f) replaced (by s.449(1)(f)(fa))	11, s.23, Sch.5, Pt.IV, Ch.II, para.62(2)
		s.449(3)(ha) added	11, s.23, Sch.5, Pt.IV, Ch.II, para.62(3)
		s.654 excl. (*prosp.*)	v, s.10(2)
		s.694A referred to (26.4.1999)	SI 3132, rule 6.2(2)(c)
		s.695 referred to (26.4.1999)	SI 3132, rule 6.2(2)(b)
		s.704(2) ext.	48, s.23, Sch.3, para.2
		s.725 referred to (26.4.1999)	SI 3132, rule 6.2(2)(a)
		s.736 (defn. of "subsidiary") appl. (EW)	18, s.31(3)
		s.736 (defn. of "wholly-owned subsidiary") appl. (pt.prosp.)	45, s.19(10)
c.9	Companies Consolidation (Consequential Provisions) Act 1985	Sch.2 rep.in pt. (the entry relating to the Local Government Finance Act 1982) (EW)	18, s.54(3), Sch.5
		Sch.2 rep.in pt. (entry relating to 1969 (c.51) rep.)	43, s.1(1), Sch.1, Pt.IV, Group 3
c.13	Cinemas Act 1985	ss.1-3,5-16 saved (6.5.1999)	46, s.30, Sch.5, Pt.II, s.B5(b)
c.17	Reserve Forces (Safeguard of Employment) Act 1985	s.20(1) (defn. of "permanent service") rep. (1.1.1999)	SI 3086, reg.10(4)
c.22	Dangerous Vessels Act 1985	saved (6.5.1999)	46, s.30, Sch.5, Pt.II, s.E3(f)

Year and Chap. or No. of Measure	Short title	How affected	1998, Chapter of Act or Number of Measure or Statutory Instrument
1985—*cont.*			
c.23	Prosecution of Offences Act 1985	s.7A subst.	37, s.53
		s.22(2)(a)(b) subst.	37, s.43(1)
		s.22(3) subst.	37, s.43(2)
		s.22(4) am.	37, s.43(3)
		s.22(6) am.	37, s.43(4)
		s.22(6A) added	37, s.43(5)
		s.22(7) am.	37, s.43(6)
		s.22(8) am.	37, s.43(7)
		s.22(11A) (defn. of "the start of the trial") appl.	37, s.57(4)
		s.22(11B) appl.	37, s.47(1)
		s.22(11B) (defn. of "the start of the trial") appl.	37, s.57(4)
		s.22(11ZA) added	37, s.43(8)
		s.22A added (*prosp.*)	37, s.44
		s.22B added (*prosp.*)	37, s.45
		s.23(2)(c) added (4.1.1999)	37, s.119, Sch.8, para.63
		s.23A added (4.1.1999)	37, s.119, Sch.8, para.64
c.43	Local Government (Access to Information) Act 1985	Sch.2, para.7 rep.	18, s.54(3), Sch.5
c.47	The Further Education Act 1985	s.3(4) am.	18, s.54(1), Sch.3, para.10
c.48	Food and Environment Protection Act 1985	ss.5-15 power to trans. functions	38, s.22(1)(c)(5), Sch.3, Pt.I, para.4(1)(a)
		ss.5-15 saved (6.5.1999)	46, s.30, Sch.5, Pt.II, s.D2(g)
		s.7A added (*prosp.*)	17, s.50, Sch.4, para.20
		s.15(4)(b) rep. (*prosp.*)	17, s.51, Sch.5, Pt.I
		s.16(2)(g) am.	26, s.1(1)(2)
		s.16(2)(j) subst.	26, s.1(1)(3)
		s.16(2A) added	26, s.1(1)(4)
		s.19(6A)(6B) added	26, s.2(1)
		s.25(2A) added	26, s.1(1)(5)
		Sch.2, para.2A added	26, s.2(2)
		Sch.2, para.4 renumbered (as Sch.2, para.4(1))	26, s.2(3)
		Sch.2, para.4(2)(3) added	26, s.2(3)
c.50	Representation of the People Act 1985	appl.(mods.)	SI 746, art.12, Sch.1, Table 3
		appl.in pt.(mods.)	SI 1287, art.3(1)(3), Sch.1
		saved (6.5.1999)	46, s.30, Sch.5, Pt.II, s.B3(b)
		ss.5,7,8,9 appl.(mods.) (NI)	SI 1126, art.6(1), Sch.2
		s.12 appl. (NI)	SI 1126, art.6(1), Sch.2
		s.27 appl.(mods.) (NI)	SI 1126, art.6(1), Sch.2
c.51	Local Government Act 1985	defn. of "joint authority" appl.	37, s.17(3)
		s.63(1)(2) am.	18, s.54(1), Sch.3, para.11(2)(a)(b)

Year and Chap. or No. of Measure	Short title	How affected	1998, Chapter of Act or Number of Measure or Statutory Instrument
1985—*cont.*			
		s.63(2)(a)(b) am.	18, s.54(1), Sch.3, para.11(2)(b)
		s.63(3) am.	18, s.54(1), Sch.3, para.11(2)(c)
		ss.63(6),72(3) rep.	18, s.54(1)(3), Sch.3, para.11(2)(d), Sch.5
		s.79(1)(2)-(4)(8) am.	18, s.54(1), Sch.3, para.11(3)(a)-(e)
		s.92(7) am.	18, s.54(1), Sch.3, para.11(4)
		Sch.8 rep.in pt. (entry relating to 1840 (c.110) rep.)	43, s.1(1), Sch.1, Pt.IV, Group 4
c.62	Oil and Pipelines Act 1985	s.6 (defn. of "petroleum") subst. (*prosp.*)	17, s.50, Sch.4, para.21
c.66	Bankruptcy (Scotland) Act 1985	s.1 subst. (1.7.1999)	46, s.125, Sch.8, para.22
		s.32(2) saved	SI 366, reg.95(3)
		s.32(2) restr.	SI 2003, reg.13(2)
c.67	Transport Act 1985	saved (6.5.1999)	46, s.30, Sch.5, Pt.II, s.E1(b)
		s.2 (defn. of "local services") excl.	iii, s.1, Sch., O., s.54
		ss.6-9 appl.	iii, s.1, Sch., O., s.54
		s.13(3) (defn. of "licensed hire car") defn(s). am.	34, s.39(1), Sch.1, para.4
		ss.26-30 appl.	iii, s.1, Sch., O., s.54
		s.63(7) excl.	iii, s.1, Sch., O., s.51(1)
		ss.89(1),92(1) excl.	iii, s.1, Sch.O, s.51(2)
		ss.93-102 appl.	iii, s.1, Sch., O., s.52
		s.94(4) (defn. of "eligible services") excl.	iii, s.1, Sch., O., s.52
		s.112 appl.	iii, s.1, Sch., O., s.52
		s.125(7)(8) saved (6.5.1999)	46, s.30, Sch.5, Pt.II, s.E5(a)
		Sch.3, para.8, Sch.7, para.22 rep. (EW)	18, s.54(3), Sch.5
c.68	Housing Act 1985	am.	38, s.140, Sch.16, para.5
		s.4(a) am.	38, s.129, Sch.15, para.7
		s.5(4)(b) am.	38, s.140, Sch.16, para.6
		s.6A(1)(2) am.	38, s.140, Sch.16, para.7
		ss.8-57 (Pt.II) defn(s). appl.	29, s.68(1)(c), Sch.12, para.3(5)
		s.27B(3) rep.in pt.	38, s.152, Sch.18, Pt.IV
		s.45(2) am.	38, s.140, Sch.16, para.8(2)
		s.45(2) rep.in pt.	38, s.152, Sch.18, Pt.IV
		s.45(2A) added	38, s.140, Sch.16, para.8(3)
		s.50(2) am.	38, s.129, Sch.15, para.8
		s.50(2) rep.in pt.	38, s.152, Sch.18, Pt.IV

Year and Chap. or No. of Measure	Short title	How affected	1998, Chapter of Act or Number of Measure or Statutory Instrument
1985—*cont.*			
		s.51(6) am.	38, s.129, Sch.15, para.9
		s.57 rep.in pt.	38, ss.140,152, Sch.16, para.9, Sch.18, Pt.VI
		s.80(1) rep.in pt.	38, s.152, Sch.18, Pt.IV
		s.92(2A)(a) rep.in pt.	38, ss.140,152, Sch.16, para.10, Sch.18, Pt.VI
		s.114(1) am.	38, s.129, Sch.15, para.10
		s.114(1) rep.in pt.	38, s.152, Sch.18, Pt.IV
		s.114(2) am.	38, s.129, Sch.15, para.10
		s.114(2) rep.in pt.	38, s.152, Sch.18, Pt.IV
		s.117 rep.in pt.	38, ss.140,152, Sch.16, para.11(a), Sch.18, Pt.VI
		s.117 am.	38, s.140, Sch.16, para.11(b)
		s.157(1) rep.in pt.	38, s.152, Sch.18, Pt.IV
		s.157(4) am.	38, s.140, Sch.16, para.12
		s.171(2) am.	38, s.140, Sch.16, para.13
		s.171(2) rep.in pt.	38, s.152, Sch.18, Pt.IV
		s.173 rep.	43, s.1(1), Sch.1, Pt.X, Group 5
		s.174 rep.in pt.	43, s.1(1), Sch.1, Pt.X, Group 5
		s.174(b) rep.	43, s.1(1), Sch.1, Pt.X, Group 5
		s.188 rep.in pt.	38, ss.140,152, Sch.16, para.14(a), Sch.18, Pt.VI
		s.188 am.	38, s.140, Sch.16, para.14(b)
		s.421(1) rep.in pt.	38, s.152, Sch.18, Pt.IV
		s.426 rep.	38, s.152, Sch.18, Pt.IV
		ss.427(1),427A rep.in pt.	38, s.152, Sch.18, Pt.IV
		s.429A(2A)(b) rep.	38, ss.140,152, Sch.16, para.15(2), Sch.18, Pt.VI
		s.429A(2B) added	38, s.140, Sch.16, para.15(3)
		s.447(1) rep.in pt.	38, s.152, Sch.18, Pt.IV
		s.450A(1A) added	38, s.140, Sch.16, para.16
		s.450B(1A) added	38, s.140, Sch.16, para.17(2)
		s.450B(3A) added	38, s.140, Sch.16, para.17(3)
		s.458 renumbered (as s.458(1))	38, s.140, Sch.16, para.18(2)
		s.458(1) (defn. of "housing authority") am.	38, s.140, Sch.16, para.18(2)
		s.458(2) added	38, s.140, Sch.16, para.18(3)

Year and Chap. or No. of Measure	Short title	How affected	1998, Chapter of Act or Number of Measure or Statutory Instrument
1985—*cont.*			
		s.459 rep.in pt.	38, ss.140,152, Sch.16, para.19(a), Sch.18, Pt.VI
		s.459 am.	38, s.140, Sch.16, para.19(b)
		s.548(1), Table , para.3 rep.	38, s.152, Sch.18, Pt.IV
		s.573(1) rep.in pt.	38, s.152, Sch.18, Pt.IV
		s.577 rep.in pt.	38, ss.140,152, Sch.16, para.20(a), Sch.18, Pt.VI
		s.577 am.	38, s.140, Sch.16, para.20(b)
		Sch.1, para.2(1), Sch.2, Pt.I, Ground 7 rep.in pt.	38, s.152, Sch.18, Pt.IV
		Sch.2, Pt.II, Ground 10A am.	38, s.140, Sch.16, para.21(2)
		Sch.2, Pt.III, Ground 12 rep.in pt.	38, s.152, Sch.18, Pt.IV
		Sch.2, Pt.V, para.6 am.	38, s.140, Sch.16, para.21(3)
		Sch.3, Ground 5 rep.in pt.	38, s.152, Sch.18, Pt.IV
		Sch.4, para.7(1) am.	38, s.140, Sch.16, para.22
		Sch.5, para.5(1)(b) rep.in pt.	38, s.152, Sch.18, Pt.IV
c.69	Housing Associations Act 1985	s.9(1A)(c) am.	38, s.140, Sch.16, para.24(2)
		s.9(6) rep.in pt.	38, ss.140,152, Sch.16, para.24(3)(a), Sch.18, Pt.VI
		s.9(6) am.	38, s.140, Sch.16, para.24(3)(b)
		s.10(1)(c) am.	38, s.140, Sch.16, para.25
		s.33A am.	38, s.140, Sch.16, para.26
		s.69(1)(a) am.	38, s.140, Sch.16, para.27(2)
		s.69(2) am.	38, s.140, Sch.16, para.27(3)
		s.69(2A) am.	38, s.140, Sch.16, para.27(4)
		ss.74-102 (Pt.III) am.	38, s.140, Sch.16, para.28
		s.74(1) am.	38, s.140, Sch.16, para.29(2)
		s.74(4)(a) am.	38, s.140, Sch.16, para.29(3)
		s.75(5) am.	38, s.140, Sch.16, para.30
		s.76(1)(2)(4) am.	38, s.140, Sch.16, para.31
		s.76A(1)(2) am.	38, s.140, Sch.16, para.32(2)
		s.76A(3) am. (and sidenote am.)	38, s.140, Sch.16, para.32(3)
		s.76A(4) am.	38, s.140, Sch.16, para.32(2)
		s.77(3) am.	38, s.140, Sch.16, para.33

Year and Chap. or No. of Measure	Short title	How affected	1998, Chapter of Act or Number of Measure or Statutory Instrument
1985—*cont.*			
		s.78(1) am.	38, s.140, Sch.16, para.34
		s.78(1)(2) mod.	38, s.142(2)
		s.78(3) appl.	38, s.142(4)
		s.79(1)(2) subst.	38, s.140, Sch.16, para.35(2)
		s.79(4) am.	38, s.140, Sch.16, para.35(3)
		s.80(1) rep.in pt.	38, ss.140,152, Sch.16, para.36(2), Sch.18, Pt.VI
		s.80(3) rep.in pt.	38, ss.140,152, Sch.16, para.36(3), Sch.18, Pt.VI
		s.80(3A) added	38, s.140, Sch.16, para.36(4)
		s.80(4) am.	38, s.140, Sch.16, para.36(5)
		s.83(1) subst.	38, s.140, Sch.16, para.37(2)
		s.83(1A) added	38, s.140, Sch.16, para.37(3)
		s.83(3A) am.	38, s.140, Sch.16, para.37(4)
		s.84(1) rep.in pt.	38, ss.140,152, Sch.16, para.38(2), Sch.18, Pt.VI
		s.84(4) am.	38, s.140, Sch.16, para.38(3)
		s.84(5) am.	38, s.140, Sch.16, para.38(4)
		s.85(4) am.	38, s.140, Sch.16, para.39
		s.85(4) rep.in pt.	38, s.152, Sch.18, Pt.IV
		s.87(2) am.	38, s.140, Sch.16, para.40
		s.88(1) am.	38, s.140, Sch.16, para.41
		s.90(1) am.	38, s.140, Sch.16, para.42(2)
		s.90(2) am.	38, s.140, Sch.16, para.42(3)
		s.90(3) am.	38, s.140, Sch.16, para.42(4)
		s.90(4) am.	38, s.140, Sch.16, para.42(5)
		s.90(5)(a) am.	38, s.140, Sch.16, para.42(6)(a)
		s.90(5)(b) am.	38, s.140, Sch.16, para.42(6)(b)
		s.90(6) am.	38, s.140, Sch.16, para.42(7)
		s.91 am.	38, s.140, Sch.16, para.43
		s.92 am.	38, s.140, Sch.16, para.44
		s.93(1) am.	38, s.140, Sch.16, para.45(2)

Year and Chap. or No. of Measure	Short title	How affected	1998, Chapter of Act or Number of Measure or Statutory Instrument
1985—*cont.*			
		s.93(2) am.	38, s.140, Sch.16, para.45(3)
		s.93(2A) rep.in pt.	38, ss.140,152, Sch.16, para.45(4)(a), Sch.18, Pt.VI
		s.93(2A)(b) rep.	38, ss.140,152, Sch.16, para.45(4)(b), Sch.18, Pt.VI
		s.93(4)(5) am.	38, s.140, Sch.16, para.45(2)
		s.94(1)(4) am.	38, s.140, Sch.16, para.46
		s.95(1) am. (and sidenote am.)	38, s.140, Sch.16, para.47
		s.96(1)(2)(3) am.	38, s.140, Sch.16, para.48(2)
		s.96(3) am.	38, s.140, Sch.16, para.48(3)
		s.96(4) am.	38, s.140, Sch.16, para.48(2)
		s.96(4) am.	38, s.140, Sch.16, para.48(3)
		s.97(1)-(3) mod.	38, s.142(2)
		s.97(1)(2)(3)(4) am.	38, s.140, Sch.16, para.49
		s.97(4) appl.(mods.)	38, s.142(5)
		s.98(1) am.	38, s.140, Sch.16, para.50
		s.99(1)(2) am.	38, s.140, Sch.16, para.51
		Sch.1, para.1 rep.in pt.	38, s.152, Sch.18, Pt.VI
		Sch.5, Pt.I, para.6(2)(b) rep.in pt.	38, ss.140,152, Sch.16, para.52, Sch.18, Pt.VI
		Sch.7, para.2(1) rep.in pt.	38, ss.140,152, Sch.16, para.53(2)(a), Sch.18, Pt.VI
		Sch.7, para.2(2) rep.in pt.	38, ss.140,152, Sch.16, para.53(1)(2)(b), Sch.18, Pt.VI
		Sch.7, para.2(3) added	38, s.140, Sch.16, para.53(2)(c)
		Sch.7, para.3 am.	38, s.140, Sch.16, para.53(3)
		Sch.7, para.4 renumbered (as para.4(1))	38, s.140, Sch.16, para.53(4)
		Sch.7, para.4(1) am.	38, s.140, Sch.16, para.53(4)(a)
		Sch.7, para.4(2) added	38, s.140, Sch.16, para.53(4)(b)
		Sch.7, para.5(1) am.	38, s.140, Sch.16, para.53(5)(a)
		Sch.7, para.5(1A) added	38, s.140, Sch.16, para.53(5)(b)
		Sch.7, para.5(3)(4)(5) am.	38, s.140, Sch.16, para.53(5)(c)

Year and Chap. or No. of Measure	Short title	How affected	1998, Chapter of Act or Number of Measure or Statutory Instrument
1985—*cont.*			
		Sch.7, para.6 added	38, s.140, Sch.16, para.53(5)(d)
c.70	Landlord and Tenant Act 1985	s.26(1) am.	38, s.129, Sch.15, para.12
		s.26(1) rep.in pt.	38, s.152, Sch.18, Pt.IV
		s.28(6) am.	38, s.129, Sch.15, para.13
		Sch., para.9(1) am.	38, s.129, Sch.15, para.14
		Sch., para.9(1) rep.in pt.	38, s.152, Sch.18, Pt.IV
c.xxxvi	Church of Scotland Trust (Amendment) Order Confirmation Act 1985	rep.	43, s.1(1), Sch.1, Pt.VII, Group 8
1986			
c.10	Local Government Act 1986	s.2A(4)(a) am. (*prosp.*)	31, s.140(1), Sch.30, para.13
		s.5(4) am. (EW)	18, s.54(1), Sch.3, para.12
c.14	Animals (Scientific Procedures) Act 1986	saved (6.5.1999)	46, s.30, Sch.5, Pt.II, s.B7
		s.4(4A) added	SI 1974, reg.2, Sch., para.2
		s.5(5) subst.	SI 1974, reg.2, Sch., para.3
		s.10(2A) added	SI 1974, reg.2, Sch., para.4(2)
		s.10(3) am.	SI 1974, reg.2, Sch., para.4(3)(b)
		s.10(3)(d) added	SI 1974, reg.2, Sch., para.4(3)(a)
		s.10(3B)(3C)(3D) added	SI 1974, reg.2, Sch., para.4(4)
		s.10(5A) added	SI 1974, reg.2, Sch., para.4(5)
		s.10(6A)(6B)(6C)(6D) added	SI 1974, reg.2, Sch., para.4(6)
		s.14 subst.	SI 1974, reg.2, Sch., para.5
		Sch.2 am.	SI 1674, art.2
		Sch.2A added	SI 1974, reg.2, Sch., para.6
c.31	Airports Act 1986	defn. of "relevant airport operator" appl. (pt.prosp.)	45, s.19(10)(b)
		saved (6.5.1999)	46, s.30, Sch.5, Pt.II, s.E4(f)
		s.24(3)(a) am. (EW)	18, s.54(1), Sch.3, para.13
		s.44(3) replaced (by s.44(3)(3A)) (*prosp.*)	41, s.74(1), Sch.12, para.7(2)
		s.45(3) rep. (*prosp.*)	41, s.74(1)(3), Sch.12, para.7(3), Sch.14, Pt.I
		s.54(1) rep.in pt. (*prosp.*)	41, s.74(1)(3), Sch.12, para.7(4)(a), Sch.14, Pt.I

Effects of Legislation

Year and Chap. or No. of Measure	Short title	How affected	1998, Chapter of Act or Number of Measure or Statutory Instrument
1986—*cont.*			
		s.54(3) rep.in pt. (*prosp.*)	41, s.74(1)(3), Sch.12, para.7(4)(b), Sch.14, Pt.I
		s.54(3)(c) rep. (*prosp.*)	41, s.74(1)(3), Sch.12, para.7(4)(b), Sch.14, Pt.I
		s.54(4) rep.in pt. (*prosp.*)	41, s.74(1)(3), Sch.12, para.7(4)(c), Sch.14, Pt.I
		s.56(a)(ii) rep. (*prosp.*)	41, s.74(1)(3), Sch.12, para.7(5), Sch.14, Pt.I
		Sch.2, para.1(1) rep.in pt.	38, s.152, Sch.18, Pt.IV
c.41	Finance Act 1986	s.80C mod. (1.1.1999)	SI 3177, reg.25
		s.80C mod. (1.1.1999)	SI 3177, regs.27(2),29(2)
		s.89AA mod. (1.1.1999)	SI 3177, regs.26(2),28(2), 30(2)
		s.90(7)(e) added	22, s.24(5)
		s.95(3) am.	36, s.151(1)(6)
		s.95(5)-(7) added	36, s.151(2)(6)
		s.97(4) am.	36, s.151(3)(6)
		s.97(6)(7) added	36, s.151(4)(6)
		s.99(10) am.	36, s.151(5)(6)
		s.102(5)(g) rep.	36, s.165, Sch.27, Pt.IV, Note 2
c.44	Gas Act 1986	s.4(3A)(3B) added (pt.prosp.)	41, s.66(5), Sch.10, Pt.II, para.3(3)
		s.24(7) replaced (by s.24(7)(7A)) (*prosp.*)	41, s.66(5), Sch.10, Pt.IV, para.10(2)
		s.25(2) rep. (*prosp.*)	41, ss.66(5),74(3), Sch.10, Pt.IV, para.10(3), Sch.14, Pt.I
		s.27(1) rep.in pt. (*prosp.*)	41, ss.66(5),74(3), Sch.10, Pt.IV, para.10(4)(a), Sch.14, Pt.I
		s.27(3)(a) rep.in pt. (*prosp.*)	41, ss.66(5),74(3), Sch.10, Pt.IV, para.10(4)(b), Sch.14, Pt.I
		s.27(6) rep.in pt. (*prosp.*)	41, ss.66(5),74(3), Sch.10, Pt.IV, para.10(4)(c), Sch.14, Pt.I
		s.28(5) rep.in pt. (*prosp.*)	41, ss.66(5),74(3), Sch.10, Pt.IV, para.10(5), Sch.14, Pt.I
		s.28(5)(c) added (*prosp.*)	41, s.66(5), Sch.10, Pt.IV, para.10(5)
		s.36A(3) restr. (pt.prosp.)	41, s.66(5), Sch.10, Pt.II, para.3(1)
		s.36A(3) replaced (by s.36(3A)(3B)) (pt.prosp.)	41, s.66(5), Sch.10, Pt.II, para.3(5)
		s.36A(5) rep.in pt. (pt.prosp.)	41, ss.66(5),74(3), Sch.10, Pt.II, para.3(6)(c), Sch.14, Pt.I

Year and Chap. or No. of Measure	Short title	How affected	1998, Chapter of Act or Number of Measure or Statutory Instrument
1986—*cont.*			
		s.36A(5) am. (pt.prosp.)	41, s.66(5), Sch.10, Pt.II, para.3(6)(a)
		s.36A(5) am. (pt.prosp.)	41, s.66(5), Sch.10, Pt.II, para.3(6)(b)
		s.36A(5)(d) rep. (pt.prosp.)	41, ss.66(5),74(3), Sch.10, Pt.II, para.3(6)(c), Sch.14, Pt.I
		s.36A(6) rep.in pt. (pt.prosp.)	41, ss.66(5),74(3), Sch.10, Pt.II, para.3(7), Sch.14, Pt.I
		s.36A(7)(b) subst. (pt.prosp.)	41, s.66(5), Sch.10, Pt.II, para.3(8)
		s.36A(8) rep.in pt. (pt.prosp.)	41, ss.66(5),74(3), Sch.10, Pt.II, para.3(9)(a), Sch.14, Pt.I
		s.36A(8) am. (pt.prosp.)	41, s.66(5), Sch.10, Pt.II, para.3(9)(b)
		s.36A(9) rep.in pt. (pt.prosp.)	41, ss.66(5),74(3), Sch.10, Pt.II, para.3(10), Sch.14, Pt.I
		s.36A(10) am. (pt.prosp.)	41, s.66(5), Sch.10, Pt.II, para.3(11)
		s.42(3)(e)(f) rep. (*prosp.*)	41, ss.66(5),74(3), Sch.10, Pt.IV, para.10(6)(a), Sch.14, Pt.I
		s.42(3)(o) added (11.1.1999)	41, s.66(5), Sch.10, Pt.IV, para.10(6)(b)
		s.42(7) added (*prosp.*)	41, s.66(5), Sch.10, Pt.IV, para.10(7)
		s.60(1) rep.in pt.	36, s.165, Sch.27, Pt.V(3), Note 1
		s.60(1)(b) rep.	36, s.165, Sch.27, Pt.V(3), Note 1
		s.60(4) rep.	36, s.165, Sch.27, Pt.V(3), Note
		s.62(6) (defn. of "petroleum production licence") am. (*prosp.*)	17, s.50, Sch.4, para.22
		Sch.2B, para.17(1) rev.in pt.	SI 2451, reg.41(2)(a)
		Sch.2B, para.17(2) rev.in pt.	SI 2451, reg.41(2)(b)
		Sch.2B, para.17(5)(6) am.	SI 2451, reg.41(2)(c)
		Sch.6 rep.	36, s.165, Sch.27, Pt.V(3), Note 1
c.45	Insolvency Act 1986	ss.53(1),54(3),61(6),62(5),67(1),69(2),84(3) am. (19.11.1998) (1.7.1999)	46, s.125, Sch.8, para.23(1)-(3)
		s.89(3) am. (1.7.1999)	46, s.125, Sch.8, para.23(5)
		ss.94(3),106(3)(5) am. (19.11.1998) (1.7.1999)	46, s.125, Sch.8, para.23(1)-(3)
		s.109(1) am. (1.7.1999)	46, s.125, Sch.8, para.23(5)

Year and Chap. or No. of Measure	Short title	How affected	1998, Chapter of Act or Number of Measure or Statutory Instrument
1986—*cont.*			
		ss.112(3),130(1),147(3), 170(2) am. (19.11.1998) (1.7.1999)	46, s.125, Sch.8, para.23(1)-(3)
		s.171(5)(6) am. (1.7.1999)	46, s.125, Sch.8, para.23(5)
		s.172(8) am. (19.11.1998) (1.7.1999)	46, s.125, Sch.8, para.23(1)-(3)
		ss.173(2)(a),192(1) am. (1.7.1999)	46, s.125, Sch.8, para.23(5)
		ss.307,310 restr.	SI 2003, reg.13(1)
		s.422(1) am.	11, s.23, Sch.5, Pt.I, Ch.III, para.37
		s.427(6A) added (19.11.1998) (1.7.1998)	46, s.125, Sch.8, para.23(6)
		s.427(6B) added (*prosp.*)	38, s.125, Sch.12, para.24
		s.427(6C) added (*prosp.*)	47, s.99, Sch.13, para.6
		s.428 (defn. of "Insolvency services") defn(s). appl. (11.1.1999)	41, s.3(1)(d), Sch.4, Pt.II, para.19
c.47	Legal Aid (Scotland) Act 1986	s.8(a) am.	SI 971, reg.3
		s.11(2) am.	SI 971, reg.5
		s.11(2)(a) am.	SI 971, reg.4
		s.15(1) am.	SI 970, reg.3
		s.17(2)(a) am.	SI 970, reg.4
c.49	Agriculture Act 1986	appt. day(s) for spec. provns. (1.4.1998)	SI 879, art.2
c.50	Social Security Act 1986	Pt.II power to mod. (EWS) (*prosp.*)	14, s.11(1)(3)
		s.63 am.	SI 470, art.4(4)(c)
		Sch.9, para.6 rep. (*prosp.*)	47, s.100(2), Sch.15
c.53	Building Societies Act 1986	defn. of "building society" appl.	11, s.17(3)(c)
		s.53(5) am.	11, s.23, Sch.5, Pt.IV, Ch.II, para.64(2)(a)
		s.53(5) am.	11, s.23, Sch.5, Pt.IV, Ch.II, para.64(2)(c)
		s.53(5)(b) subst.	11, s.23, Sch.5, Pt.IV, Ch.II, para.64(2)(b)
		s.53(5A) added	11, s.23, Sch.5, Pt.IV, Ch.II, para.64(3)
		s.54(3A) am.	11, s.23, Sch.5, Pt.IV, Ch.II, para.64(4)
		s.101(4) trans.of functions	11, s.21(a)
		s.101(4) am.	11, s.23, Sch.5, Pt.I, Ch.III, para.38(1)(2)
		s.101(6) (defn. of "the Bank") replaced (by the def. "the Authority")	11, s.23, Sch.5, Pt.I, Ch.III, para.38(3)(a)
		s.101(6) defn.of (" financial institution") para.([c]) am.	11, s.23, Sch.5, Pt.I, Ch.III, para.38(3)(b)
		s.122(2) rep. (*prosp.*)	47, s.100(2), Sch.15

Year and Chap. or No. of Measure	Short title	How affected	1998, Chapter of Act or Number of Measure or Statutory Instrument
1986—*cont.*			
		Sch.8A, para.9 am.	SI 212, reg.5(1), Sch.3
		Sch.17, para.2 am.	SI 212, reg.4, Sch.2
c.56	Parliamentary Constituencies Act 1986	ext.	38, s.2, Sch.1, para.3
		mod.	38, s.2, Sch.1, para.9(1)
		saved (6.5.1999)	46, s.30, Sch.5, Pt.II, s.B3(c)
		ext. (*prosp.*)	47, s.33(3)
		s.4 mod.	46, s.1, Sch.1, para.4
		s.27(4) subst.	SI 2169, reg.3
		Sch.2, rule 1(2) rep. (1.7.1999)	46, ss.86(2),125, Sch.9
		Sch.2, rule 3A added (1.7.1999)	46, s.86(3)
		Sch.2, rule 4 am. (1.7.1999)	46, s.86(3)
		Sch.2, rule 5 am. (1.7.1999)	46, s.86(4)
		Sch.2, para.7 am. (1.7.1999)	46, s.86(5)
		Sch.3, paras.1,2 rcp. (*prosp.*)	47, s.100(2), Sch.15
c.60	Financial Services Act 1986	power to H.M.Treasury to contract out certain functions	SI 2842, art.2, Sch., Pt.II, para.64
		defn. of "designated agency" appl.	11, ss.23,42, Sch.5, Pt.IV, Ch.I, para.53(2)(b), Sch.8, para.3 (adding 1987 c.22 s.83(1)(aa))
		defn. of "designated agency" appl.	11, s.23, Sch.1, Pt.III, para.47(4) (adding 1989 c.40, s.171(2A))
		defn. of "designated agency" appl.	11, s.23, Sch.5, Pt.IV, Ch.II, para.62(2) (replacing 1985 c.6, s.449(1)(f))
		defn. of "designated agency" appl.	11, s.23, Sch.5, Pt.IV, Ch.II, para.64(4)(a) (am. 1986 c.53, s.54(3A))
		defn. of "designated agency" defn(s). appl.	11, s.36(1)
		defn. of "designated agency" appl.	11, s.37, Sch.7, para.3(1)
		defn. of "designated agency" appl.	11, s.42, Sch.8, paras.2-5 (modifying 1987 c.22, ss.83-85)
		s.43 trans.of functions	11, s.21(b)
		s.43(1) am.	11, s.23, Sch.1, Pt.II, para.44(2)
		s.43(2) am.	11, s.23, Sch.1, Pt.II, para.44(3)
		s.43(2A)(2B) added	11, s.26(2)
		s.43(3) am.	11, s.23, Sch.1, Pt.II, para.44(3)

Year and Chap. or No. of Measure	Short title	How affected	1998, Chapter of Act or Number of Measure or Statutory Instrument
1986—*cont.*			
		s.43(4) am.	11, s.23, Sch.1, Pt.II, para.44(4)
		s.43(5) added	11, s.25(1)
		s.125 subst. (*prosp.*)	41, s.3(1)(b), Sch.2, Pt.I, para.1(2)
		s.126 rep. (*prosp.*)	41, ss.3(1)(b),74(3), Sch.2, Pt.I, para.1(3), Sch.14, Pt.I
		s.127 subst. (*prosp.*)	41, s.3(1)(b), Sch.2, Pt.I, para.1(4)
		s.127(2) saved (*prosp.*)	41, s.74(2), Sch.13, Pt.IV, Ch.III, para.26
		s.128C(3)(a)(iii) am.	11, s.23, Sch.5, Pt.I, Ch.III, para.39
		s.179(3)(ba) appl.	11, s.23, Sch.5, Pt.IV, Ch.II, para.65(2)(b) (am. 1986 c.53, s.54(3A))
		s.179(3)(f) rep.	11, ss.23,43, Sch.5, Pt.IV, Ch.II, para.65(2)(b), Sch.9, Pt.I
		s.180(1)(ea) added	11, s.23, Sch.5, Pt.IV, Ch.II, para.65(3)(a)
		s.180(1)(f) am.	11, s.23, Sch.5, Pt.IV, Ch.II, para.65(3)(b)
		ss.185(4),186(7) am.	11, s.23, Sch.5, Pt.I, Ch.III, para.39
		s.190 rep. (*prosp.*)	29, s.74(2), Sch.16, Pt.I
		s.209(2) rep. (*prosp.*)	47, s.100(2), Sch.15
		Sch.5, paras.1,4(1)(b)(2), 9(a) am.	11, s.32
		Sch.7, para.1(2) rep.in pt.	11, ss.31,43, Sch.9, Pt.I
		Sch.11, para.12(1) rep.in pt. (*prosp.*)	41, s.74(1), Sch.12, para.8(a)
		Sch.11, para.12(2) rep. (*prosp.*)	41, s.74(1), Sch.12, para.8(b)
c.61	Education (No.2) Act 1986	s.49 excl.	30, s.19(7)
		s.49(3)(b) am. (*prosp.*)	31, s.140(1), Sch.30, para.14(a)
		s.49(3)(ba) rep. (*prosp.*)	31, s.140(1)(3), Sch.30, para.14(b), Sch.31
c.64	Public Order Act 1986	ss.1-16 (Pt.II) (defn. of "public place") appl. (EW)	37, s.14(8)
		s.26(1) am. (6.5.1999)	46, s.125, Sch.8, para.24
No.1	Bishops (Retirement) Measure 1986	saved (1.1.1999)	GSM 1, s.5(1), Sch.2, Pt.I
No.2	Ecclesiastical Fees Measure 1986	s.1 trans.of functions (1.1.1999)	SI 1715, art.3
		s.1 am. (1.1.1999)	SI 1715, art.4(4), Sch.2, para.2(1)
		s.2 trans.of functions (1.1.1999)	SI 1715, art.3

Year and Chap. or No. of Measure	Short title	How affected	1998, Chapter of Act or Number of Measure or Statutory Instrument
1986—*cont.*			
		s.2 am. (1.1.1999)	SI 1715, art.4(4), Sch.2, para.2(1)
		ss.2(3),4 trans.of functions (1.1.1999)	SI 1715, art.2, Sch.1
		s.4(1)(e) subst. (1.1.1999)	SI 1715, art.4(4), Sch.2, para.2(2)
		s.4(4)(b) am. (1.1.1999)	SI 1715, art.4(4), Sch.2, para.2(3)
		ss.5(4),6(4) trans.of functions (1.1.1999)	SI 1715, art.2, Sch.1
		s.8 saved (1.1.1999)	GSM 1, s.5(1), Sch.2, Pt.I
No.3	Patronage (Benefices) Measure 1986	s.38(1)(5), Sch.1, paras.10(1),12(2) trans.of functions (1.1.1999)	SI 1715, art.2, Sch.1
1987			
c.4	Ministry of Defence Police Act 1987	s.1(2)(c) am. (*prosp.*)	32, s.74(1), Sch.4, para.16
c.12	Petroleum Act 1987	s.24(1)(b) am. (*prosp.*)	17, s.50, Sch.4, para.23
c.16	Finance Act 1987	s.55 ext. (20.5.1999)	46, s.123
		s.55(1) am. (*prosp.*)	38, s.125, Sch.12, para.25
c.18	Debtors (Scotland) Act 1987	s.1(5)(f) rep.in pt. (*prosp.*)	14, s.86(1)(2), Sch.7, para.12(a), Sch.8
		s.1(5)(f)(iv) added (*prosp.*)	14, s.86(1), Sch.7, para.12(b)
		s.5(4) rep.in pt. (*prosp.*)	14, s.86(2), Sch.8
		s.73(3)(b) am. (1.1.1999)	SI 3086, reg.6(2)
		s.106 (defn. of "summary warrant") am. (*prosp.*)	14, s.86(1), Sch.7, para.13
		Sch.5, para.35 (defn. of "creditor") am. (*prosp.*)	14, s.86(1), Sch.7, para.14
		Sch.6, para.9 rep.	43, s.1(1), Sch.1, Pt.X, Group 2
c.21	Pilotage Act 1987	Sch.2, para.5 rep. (*prosp.*)	17, s.51, Sch.5, Pt.I
c.22	Banking Act 1987	defns. of "authorised institution" and "former authorised institution" appl.	11, s.17(3)(a)
		trans.of functions	11, ss.21,22, Sch.4
		restr.	11, s.26, Sch.6, para.1(1)
		defns. of "authorised" and "institution" appl.	11, s.26, Sch.6, para.1(5)
		s.1(1)(2)(3) am.	11, s.23, Sch.5, Pt.I, Ch.I, para.2(a)(b)
		s.1(4) am.	11, ss.23,42, Sch.5, Pt.I, Ch.I, para.2(c), Sch.8, para.1
		s.1(4) saved	11, s.42, Sch.8, para.1
		s.2(1)(2) replaced (by s.2(1)(2)(2A))	11, s.28(1)
		s.2(3)(4)(6)(7) am.	11, s.28(2)
		ss.3(1),4(3) am.	11, s.23, Sch.5, Pt.I, Ch.I, para.3

Year and Chap. or No. of Measure	Short title	How affected	1998, Chapter of Act or Number of Measure or Statutory Instrument
1987—*cont.*		ss.7-10 am.	11, s.23, Sch.5, Pt.I, Ch.I, para.4
		s.11 am.	11, s.23, Sch.5, Pt.I, Ch.I, para.5(a)
		s.11(1A)(c) am.	11, s.23, Sch.5, Pt.I, Ch.I, para.5(b)(i)
		s.11(1A)(c)(ii) am.	11, s.23, Sch.5, Pt.I, Ch.I, para.5(b)(ii)
		s.12 am.	11, s.23, Sch.5, Pt.I, Ch.I, para.6(a)
		s.12(1)(a) am.	11, s.23, Sch.5, Pt.I, Ch.I, para.6(b)
		ss.12A-17 am.	11, s.23, Sch.5, Pt.I, Ch.I, para.7
		s.19 am.	11, s.23, Sch.5, Pt.I, Ch.I, para.8(a)
		s.19(3) am.	11, s.23, Sch.5, Pt.I, Ch.I, para.8(b)
		ss.20-27 am.	11, s.23, Sch.5, Pt.I, Ch.I, para.9
		s.29 am.	11, s.23, Sch.5, Pt.I, Ch.I, para.10(a)
		s.29(3) am.	11, s.23, Sch.5, Pt.I, Ch.I, para.10(b)
		ss.30-34,36-42 am.	11, s.23, Sch.5, Pt.I, Ch.I, para.11
		s.39(1)(a) am.	11, s.27
		s.43(1) am.	11, s.23, Sch.5, Pt.I, Ch.I, para.12
		ss.46-49 am.	11, s.23, Sch.5, Pt.I, Ch.I, para.13
		ss.52(2A),58(2A)(b) am.	11, s.23, Sch.5, Pt.I, Ch.I, para.14
		s.58(5) subst.	SI 2169, reg.4
		ss.59(1)(a)(4),65(1),67(6),68(7),69(7) am.	11, s.23, Sch.5, Pt.I, Ch.I, para.14
		ss.70-72,75 am.	11, s.23, Sch.5, Pt.I, Ch.I, para.15
		s.75 restr.	11, s.26, Sch.6, para.1(1)
		s.76 am.	11, s.23, Sch.5, Pt.I, Ch.I, para.16(a)
		s.76(3)(b) am.	11, s.23, Sch.5, Pt.I, Ch.I, para.16(b)
		ss.77-80 am.	11, s.23, Sch.5, Pt.I, Ch.I, para.17
		ss.82-87 (Pt.V) mod.	11, ss.23,36(4), Sch.5, para.57
		ss.82-87 (Pt.V) (defns. of "authorised institutions" and "credit institutions") appl.	11, ss.23,36(4), Sch.5, para.57

Year and Chap. or No. of Measure	Short title	How affected	1998, Chapter of Act or Number of Measure or Statutory Instrument
1987—*cont.*			
		ss.82-87 (Pt.V) mod.	11, s.23, Sch.5, Pt.IV, Ch.1, para.57(2)(3)(4)
		ss.83-85 mod.	11, s.42, Sch.8, paras.2-5
		s.83(1) am.	11, ss.23,42, Sch.5, Pt.IV, Ch.I, para.53(2)(a), Sch.8, para.3
		s.83(1)(aa) added	11, ss.23,42, Sch.5, Pt.IV, Ch.I, para.53(2)(b), Sch.8, para.3
		s.83(1)(b) rep.	11, ss.23,42,43, Sch.5, Pt.IV, Ch.I, para.53(2)(b), Sch.8, para.3, Sch.9, Pt.I
		s.83(1)(c) rep.in pt.	11, ss.23,42,43, Sch.5, Pt.IV, Ch.I, para.53(2)(d), Sch.8, para.3, Sch.9, Pt.I
		s.83(1)(d) rep.in pt.	11, ss.23,42,43, Sch.5, Pt.IV, Ch.I, para.53(2)(e), Sch.8, para.3, Sch.9, Pt.I
		s.83(2)(3) am.	11, ss.23,42, Sch.5, Pt.IV, Ch.I, para.53(3), Sch.8, para.3
		s.84(1) am.	11, ss.23,42, Sch.5, Pt.IV, Ch.I, para.54(2), Sch.8, para.4
		s.84(1), Table , entry 4A added	11, ss.23,42, Sch.5, Pt.IV, Ch.I, para.54(3), Sch.8, para.4
		s.84(1), Table, entry 18 am.	11, ss.23,42, Sch.5, Pt.IV, Ch.1, para.54(4), Sch.8, para.4
		s.84(2)(4)(5)(5A)(6)(7) am.	11, ss.23,42, Sch.5, Pt.IV, Ch.1, para.54(5), Sch.8, para.4
		s.85(1)(2) am.	11, ss.23,42, Sch.5, Pt.IV, Ch.1, para.55, Sch.8, para.5
		s.86 mod.	11, s.23, Sch.5, Pt.IV, Ch.1, para.57(2)
		s.86(1) am.	11, s.23, Sch.5, Pt.IV, Ch.1, paras.56(1)(2),57
		s.86(2)(a) am.	11, ss.23,36(1), Sch.5, para.57
		s.86(2)(a)(3)(4A) am.	11, s.23, Sch.5, Pt.IV, Ch.1, paras.56(1)(2),57
		s.86(5) mod.	11, ss.23,36(2), Sch.5, para.57
		s.86(5) (defn. of "relevant functions") subst.	11, s.23, Sch.5, Pt.IV, Ch.1, paras.56,57(1)
		s.86(5) (defn. of "relevant functions") subst.	11, s.23, Sch.5, Pt.IV, Ch.1, paras.56(3),57

Year and Chap. or No. of Measure	Short title	How affected	1998, Chapter of Act or Number of Measure or Statutory Instrument
1987—*cont.*			
		s.87(2) am.	11, s.23, Sch.5, Pt.IV, Ch.1, paras.58(2),59
		s.87(2) rep.in pt.	11, s.23, Sch.5, Pt.IV, Ch.1, para.59(1)(2)
		s.87(2) mod.	11, s.23, Sch.5, Pt.IV, Ch.1, para.59(1)(4)
		s.87(3) am.	11, s.23, Sch.5, Pt.IV, Ch.1, paras.58(3),59
		s.87(3) rep.in pt.	11, s.23, Sch.5, Pt.IV, Ch.1, para.59(1)(2)
		s.87(3) mod.	11, s.23, Sch.5, Pt.IV, Ch.1, para.59(1)(4)
		s.87(3A) mod.	11, ss.23,36(3), Sch.5, para.57
		s.87(3A) am.	11, s.23, Sch.5, Pt.IV, Ch.1, paras.58(4),59
		s.87(3A) am.	11, s.23, Sch.5, Pt.IV, Ch.1, para.59(1)(3)(b)
		s.87(3A) mod.	11, s.23, Sch.5, Pt.IV, Ch.1, para.59(1)(4)
		s.87(3A)(b) am.	11, s.23, Sch.5, Pt.IV, Ch.1, para.59(1)(3)(a)
		s.87(4) am.	11, s.23, Sch.5, Pt.IV, Ch.1, paras.58(4),59
		ss.92-96,99-101,105 am.	11, s.23, Sch.5, Pt.I, Ch.I, para.18
		s.106(1) (defn. of "authorisation") am.	11, s.23, Sch.5, Pt.I, Ch.I, para.19(a)
		s.106(1) (defn. of "the Authority") added	11, s.23, Sch.5, Pt.I, Ch.I, para.19(b)
		s.106(1) defn.of (" relevant supervisory authority") para.(b) am.	11, s.23, Sch.5, Pt.I, Ch.I, para.19(c)
		s.109(2) rep. (*prosp.*)	47, s.100(2), Sch.15
		Sch.1 am.	11, s.28(3)
		Sch.3 am.	11, s.23, Sch.5, Pt.I, Ch.I, para.20
		Sch.4, para.1(1)(a)-(c) subst.	11, s.29(2)
		Sch.4, para.1(2) subst.	11, s.29(3)
		Sch.4, para.1(3) subst.	11, s.29(4)
		Sch.4, para.1(4)(b) am.	11, s.29(5)
c.26	Housing (Scotland) Act 1987	s.61(11)(h) rep.	38, s.152, Sch.18, Pt.IV
		Sch.3, para.2 subst.	37, s.23(2)
		Sch.3, para.2 restr.	37, s.23(5)
		Sch.3, para.7 subst.	37, s.23(3)
		Sch.3, para.7 restr.	37, s.23(5)
c.31	Landlord and Tenant Act 1987	s.4 excl. (*prosp.*)	v, s.13(1)(a)
		s.58(1)(d) rep.	38, s.152, Sch.18, Pt.IV
		s.58(1)(ea) rep.	38, s.152, Sch.18, Pt.VI
c.37	Access to Personal Files Act 1987	rep. (*prosp.*)	29, s.74(2), Sch.16, Pt.I

Year and Chap. or No. of Measure	Short title	How affected	1998, Chapter of Act or Number of Measure or Statutory Instrument
1987—*cont.*			
c.38	Criminal Justice Act 1987	s.4(4) added (4.1.1999)	37, s.119, Sch.8, para.65
		s.9(3) mod.	40, s.5(1) (adding 1977 c.45, s.1A(10))
c.42	Family Law Reform Act 1987	s.1 appl.	37, s.106, Sch.7, para.1(3) (adding 1933 c.12, s.55(6))
		s.1 appl.	37, s.106, Sch.7, para.3 (adding 1969 c.54 s.7(9))
		s.1 appl.	37, s.106, Sch.7, para.10 (substituting 1969 c.54, s.70(1B))
		s.1 appl.	37, s.106, Sch.7, para.25 (adding 1973 c.62, s.46(3))
		s.8(1), Sch.2, para.26 rep. (*prosp.*)	37, s.120(2), Sch.10
c.43	Consumer Protection Act 1987	ss.14,15,28-35,37,38 appl.(mods.)	SI 1165, reg.13(2)(a)
		s.38(3)(e)(f) rep. (*prosp.*)	41, s.74(1)(3), Sch.12, para.10(a), Sch.14, Pt.I
		s.38(3)(p) added (11.1.1999)	41, s.74(1), Sch.12, para.10(b)
		ss.39,40 appl.(mods.)	SI 1165, reg.13(2)(b)
		ss.44,47 appl.(mods.)	SI 1165, reg.13(2)(a)
		s.49(2) rep. (*prosp.*)	47, s.100(2), Sch.15
c.47	Abolition of Domestic Rates Etc. (Scotland) Act 1987	Sch.2, para.7A(2)(a) am. (*prosp.*)	14, s.86(1), Sch.7, para.15
c.49	Territorial Sea Act 1987	s.2(4)(a)(b) am. (*prosp.*)	17, s.50, Sch.4, para.24
		Sch.1, para.7(1)(2) rep. (*prosp.*)	17, s.51, Sch.5, Pt.I
c.51	Finance (No.2) Act 1987	ss.82,83,88 rep.	36, s.165, Sch.27, Pt.III(28), Note
c.53	Channel Tunnel Act 1987	saved (6.5.1999)	46, s.30, Sch.5, Pt.II, s.E2
		s.33(2) rep.in pt. (*prosp.*)	41, s.74(1)(3), Sch.12, para.11(a), Sch.14, Pt.I
		s.33(2)(c)(5)(b)(c) rep. (*prosp.*)	41, s.74(1)(3), Sch.12, para.11(b), Sch.14, Pt.I
c.viii	West Glamorgan Act 1987	ss.37(3)(a),68 rep.	SI 1562, art.2, Sch.
c.xxviii	British Waterways Act 1987	s.44(6)(b) rep.in pt.	38, s.152, Sch.18, Pt.IV
1988			
c.1	Income and Corporation Taxes Act 1988	mod. (1.1.1999)	SI 3177, reg.21(2)(3)
		defn. of "retirement benefits scheme" appl. (*prosp.*)	v, s.8(1)
		power to appl. or extend with mods. [regulations made under s.203 of 1988 c.1]	30, s.22(5)(g)
		mod.	36, s.30(3)
		mod.	36, s.31(2)

Year and Chap. or No. of Measure	Short title	How affected	1998, Chapter of Act or Number of Measure or Statutory Instrument
1988—*cont.*			
		power to mod.	36, s.32(8)(a)
		power to appl.	36, s.32(8)(b)
		ext.	36, s.38, Sch.5, Pt.I, paras.24,73 (substituting 1088 c.1, s.65A)
		ext.	36, s.38, Sch.5, Pt.I, paras.25,73 (adding 1988 c.1, s.70A)
		defn. of "Schedule A business" appl.	36, s.38, Sch.5, Pt.III, paras.62,63(2)(a),73,(b) (substituting 1992 c.12, s.241(3)(a))
		mod.	36, s.38, Sch.5, Pt.IV, paras.65(2),70,71
		mod.	36, s.46
		mod.	36, s.47(3)(a)(5)
		defn. of "ordinary share capital" appl. (6.4.1998)	36, s.74(1), Sch.13, Pt.II, para.24(7)(8)(e) (adding 1992 c.12, s.150A(10A))
		defn. of "ordinary share capital" appl. (6.4.1998)	36, s.74(1), Sch.13, Pt.III, para.36 (adding 1992 c.12, Sch.5B, paras.16-19 added at para.19(1))
		defn. of "ordinary share capital" appl. (6.4.1998)	36, s.74(1), Sch.13, Pt.IV, para.42(7)(8)(f) (adding 1992 c.12, s.150(12))
		mod. (year 1998-99 and subsequent years of assessment)	36, s.93(3)(4) (adding 1988 c.1 s.596C)
		excl.	36, s.108, Sch.16 (adding 1988 c.1, Sch.28AA at para.6(2)(b))
		am.	36, s.113, Sch.17, paras.9(4),37 (substituting 1988 c.1, s.754(2))
		mod.	36, s.117, Sch.18, Pt.II, para.6(2)
		mod. (as to Corporations)	36, s.117, Sch.18, Pt.V, para.39(2)(c), Pt.VII, para.59(2)
		restr. (as to Corporations)	36, s.117, Sch.18, Pt.VII, paras.54,55,59(2)
		mod. (as to Corporations)	36, s.117, Sch.18, Pt.XI, para.88(2)(7)
		am.	36, s.117(2)(4)
		power to mod.	36, s.118(1)
		defns. of "office" and "employment" appl. (year 1998-99 and subsequent years of assessment)	36, s.121, Sch.20 (adding 1992 c.12, Sch.A1)

Year and Chap. or No. of Measure	Short title	How affected	1998, Chapter of Act or Number of Measure or Statutory Instrument
1988—*cont.*			
		defn. of "trade, profession or vocation" appl. (year 1998-99 and subsequent years of assessment)	36, s.121, Sch.20 (adding 1992 c.12, Sch.A1)
		mod.	36, s.161(2)(b)
		mod. (pt.prosp.)	45, s.38
		defn. of "capital allowance" appl. (pt.prosp.)	45, s.38(10)
		mod. (6.5.1999)	46, s.73(2)
		s.1(2)(aa)(b) am. (amounts specified 1998- 99)	SI 755, art.2(2)
		s.1A(1) am. (year 1998-99 and subsequent years of assessment)	36, s.100(1)(3)
		s.1A(2)(aa) added (year 1998-99 and subsequent years of assessment)	36, s.100(2)(3)
		s.7(2) rep.in pt.	36, s.165, Sch.27, Pt.III(28), Note
		s.7(5)-(7) rep.	36, s.165, Sch.27, Pt.III(28), Note
		s.11(3) rep.in pt.	36, s.165, Sch.27, Pt.III(28), Note
		s.13(2) am. (financial year 1998)	36, s.28(2)(b)
		s.13(2) am. (financial year 1999)	36, s.29(2)(b)
		s.13(7) am. (6.4.1999)	36, s.31, Sch.3, para.7(2)
		s.13(7) am. (6.4.1999)	36, s.31, Sch.3, para.7(2) (4)
		s.13(8AA)(8AB) added (6.4.1999)	36, s.31, Sch.3, para.7(3) (4)
		s.14(1)(3)(4)(5) rep. (6.4.1999)	36, ss.31,165, Sch.3, para.8(2)(3), Sch.27, Pt.III(2), Note
		s.15(1) subst.	36, s.38, Sch.5, Pt.I, paras.1,73
		s.15(1A) added	36, s.38, Sch.5, Pt.I, paras.2,73
		s.15(2) rep.	36, s.165, Sch.27, Pt.III(4), Note
		s.18 ext. (6.4.1999) (Sch.D, Case VI)	36, s.44, Sch.6, paras.1, 2(2)(b),6
		s.18 mod. (Sch.D Cases I, II,VI)	36, s.47(4)
		s.18 ext. (Tax Sch.D, Case VI)	36, s.117, Sch.18, Pt.VI, para.52(4), Pt.VII, para.59(2)
		s.18 mod. (Tax Sch.D)	36, s.117, Sch.18, Pt.X, para.84
		s.18(2) restr. (Sch.D, Cases I,II restr.)	36, s.42

Year and Chap. or No. of Measure	Short title	How affected	1998, Chapter of Act or Number of Measure or Statutory Instrument
1988—*cont.*			
		s.19(1) rep.in pt. (17.3.1998) (*retrosp.*)	36, ss.63(3)(a)(5)(6)(7), 165, Sch.27, Pt.III(11), Note (adding 1988 c.1, s.192A)
		ss.21-43 (Pt.II), head. subst.	36, s.38, Sch.5, Pt.I, paras.3,73
		s.21 replaced (by ss.21, 21A,21B)	36, s.38, Sch.5, Pt.I, paras.4,73
		s.21C added	36, s.38, Sch.5, Pt.I, paras.5,73
		s.24(6) mod.	36, s.47(3)(b)(5)
		s.24(6) rep.in pt.	36, s.165, Sch.27, Pt.III(4), Note
		s.24(6)(c)(7) rep.	36, s.165, Sch.27, Pt.III(4), Note
		s.25 rep.	36, ss.38,165, Sch.5, Pt.I, paras.6,73, Sch.27, Pt.III(4), Note
		s.25(3) restr.	36, s.38, Sch.5, Pt.IV, paras.68,69
		s.26 rep.in pt. (for income tax purposes on and after 6.4.2001)	36, ss.39(a),165, Sch.27, Pt.III(5), Note
		s.26 rep.in pt. for corporation tax purposes, for accounting periods beginning on or after 1.4.2001)	36, ss.39(b),165, Sch.27, Pt.III(5), Note
		s.26(1) am.	36, s.38, Sch.5, Pt.I, paras.7(2)(b),73
		s.26(1)(a) rep.in pt.	36, ss.38,165, Sch.5, Pt.I, paras.7(2)(a),73, Sch.27, Pt.III(4), Note
		s.26(2)(a) rep.	36, ss.38,165, Sch.5, Pt.I, paras.7(3),73, Sch.27, Pt.III(4), Note
		s.26(2A) added	36, s.38, Sch.5, Pt.I, paras.7(4),73
		s.27 rep.in pt. (for income tax purposes on and after 6.4.2001)	36, ss.39(a),165, Sch.27, Pt.III(5), Note
		s.27 rep.in pt. for corporation tax purposes, for accounting periods beginning on or after 1.4.2001)	36, ss.39(b),165, Sch.27, Pt.III(5), Note
		s.27(3) subst.	36, s.38, Sch.5, Pt.I, paras.8,73
		s.28 rep.	36, ss.38,165, Sch.5, Pt.I, paras.9,73, Sch.27, Pt.III(4), Note

Year and Chap. or No. of Measure	Short title	How affected	1998, Chapter of Act or Number of Measure or Statutory Instrument
1988—*cont.*			
		s.29 rep.	36, ss.38,165, Sch.5, Pt.I, paras.10,73, Sch.27, Pt.III(4), Note
		s.30(1) am.	36, s.38, Sch.5, Pt.I, paras.11,73
		s.31 rep.	36, ss.38,165, Sch.5, Pt.I, paras.12,73, Sch.27, Pt.III(4), Note
		s.31(3) restr.	36, s.38, Sch.5, Pt.IV, paras.68,69
		s.33 rep.	36, ss.38,165, Sch.5, Pt.I, paras.13,73, Sch.27, Pt.III(4), Note
		ss.33A,33B rep.	36, ss.38,165, Sch.5, Pt.I, paras.14,73, Sch.27, Pt.III(4), Note
		s.34(1) am. (17.3.1998) (*retrosp.*)	36, s.40(2)(5)
		s.34(3) am.	36, s.38, Sch.5, Pt.I, paras.15(3),73
		s.34(4)(a)(b) am. (17.3.1998) (*retrosp.*)	36, s.40(3)(5)
		s.34(5)(a)(b) am. (17.3.1998) (*retrosp.*)	36, s.40(4)(5)
		s.34(6) am.	36, s.38, Sch.5, Pt.I, paras.15(4),73
		s.34(7A) added	36, s.38, Sch.5, Pt.I, paras.15(5),73
		s.34(8) am.	36, s.38, Sch.5, Pt.I, paras.15(6),73
		s.34 sidenote subst.	36, s.38, Sch.5, Pt.I, paras.15(2),73
		s.35(2) am.	36, s.38, Sch.5, Pt.I, paras.16(3),73
		s.35(2A) added	36, s.38, Sch.5, Pt.I, paras.16(4),73
		s.35 sidenote am.	36, s.38, Sch.5, Pt.I, paras.16(2),73
		s.36(1) am.	36, s.38, Sch.5, Pt.I, paras.17(3),73
		s.36(4A)(4B) added	36, s.38, Sch.5, Pt.I, paras.17(4),73
		s.36 sidenote am.	36, s.38, Sch.5, Pt.I, paras.17(2),73
		s.37(1)(a)(b) subst.	36, s.38, Sch.5, Pt.I, paras.18(1),73
		s.37(2)(b) am.	36, s.38, Sch.5, Pt.I, paras.18(3),73
		s.37(3) am.	36, s.38, Sch.5, Pt.I, paras.18(4),73
		s.37(4) am.	36, s.38, Sch.5, Pt.I, paras.18(5),73

Year and Chap. or No. of Measure	Short title	How affected	1998, Chapter of Act or Number of Measure or Statutory Instrument
1988—*cont.*			
		s.40, head. subst.	36, s.38, Sch.5, Pt.I, paras.19,73
		s.40(1) am.	36, s.38, Sch.5, Pt.I, paras.20(2),73
		s.40(3)(b) am.	36, s.38, Sch.5, Pt.I, paras.20(3),73
		s.40(4A) added	36, s.38, Sch.5, Pt.I, paras.20(4),73
		s.40(5) rep.	36, ss.38,165, Sch.5, Pt.I, paras.20(5),73, Sch.27, Pt.III(4), Note
		s.41 rep.	36, ss.38,165, Sch.5, Pt.I, paras.21(5),73, Sch.27, Pt.III(4), Note
		s.42A(8) rep.	36, ss.38,165, Sch.5, Pt.I, paras.22,73, Sch.27, Pt.III(4), Note
		s.51B rep. (*prosp.*)	36, ss.37(1)(3),165, Sch.27, Pt.III(3), Note
		ss.53(1)(3),55(1),60(1)(2) ,61(1),63A(1)(3)(5) am.	36, s.46(3)(a)(b), Sch.7, para.1
		s.65(2A) rep.	36, ss.38,165, Sch.5, Pt.I, paras.23(a),73, Sch.27, Pt.III(4), Note
		s.65(2A) am.	36, s.46(3)(a)(b), Sch.7, para.1
		s.65(2B) rep.	36, ss.38,165, Sch.5, Pt.I, paras.23(a),73, Sch.27, Pt.III(4), Note
		s.65(4) am.	36, s.38, Sch.5, Pt.I, paras.23(b),73
		s.65(5)(b) am.	36, s.46(3)(a)(b), Sch.7, para.1
		s.65A subst.	36, s.38, Sch.5, Pt.I, paras.24,73
		s.68(1) am.	36, s.46(3)(a)(b), Sch.7, para.1
		s.70A added	36, s.38, Sch.5, Pt.I, paras.25,73
		s.74(1) am.	36, s.46(3)(a)(b), Sch.7, para.1
		s.74(1)(a) ext. (1.1.1999)	SI 3177, reg.5
		s.75(1) ext. (1.1.1999)	SI 3177, reg.6
		s.75(2) rep.in pt. (6.4.1999)	36, ss.31,165, Sch.3, para.9(2)(3), Sch.27, Pt.III(2), Note
		s.76 mod. (1.1.1999)	SI 3177, reg.6
		s.76(1)(d) mod. (6.4.1999)	SI 1871, regs.5,6
		ss.77(1)(2)(a)(i),79(1), 79A(1),80(10),82(1)(5) am.	36, s.46(3)(a)(b), Sch.7, para.1
		s.82(6) rep.in pt.	36, s.165, Sch.27, Pt.III(4), Note

Year and Chap. or No. of Measure	Short title	How affected	1998, Chapter of Act or Number of Measure or Statutory Instrument
1988—*cont.*			
		ss.83,84A(2)(a),85(1)(a), 85A(2)(a) am.	36, s.46(3)(a)(b), Sch.7, para.1
		s.86(2) (defn. of "deductible") am.	36, s.46(3)(a)(b), Sch.7, para.1
		s.86A(2)(a) am.	36, s.46(3)(a)(b), Sch.7, para.1
		s.87(1)(a)(b) subst.	36, s.38, Sch.5, Pt.III, paras.34,73
		s.87(2)(6) am.	36, s.46(3)(a)(b), Sch.7, para.1
		s.87(10) rep.	36, s.165, Sch.27, Pt.III(4), Note
		ss.88(a),89,90(1)(a),91(1) (4)(a)(i),91A(2)(3)(a), 91B(2)(5)(a)(6)(a), 91C(b),94(1),96(7) am.	36, s.46(3)(a)(b), Sch.7, para.1
		s.96(11) rep.in pt.	36, s.165, Sch.27, Pt.III(4), Note
		s.97 am.	36, s.46(3)(a)(b), Sch.7, para.1
		s.98 subst. (17.3.1998) (*retrosp.*)	36, s.41(1)(3)
		ss.99(1)(2),100(1)(1D)(1E) am.	36, s.46(3)(a)(b), Sch.7, para.1
		s.100(2) (defn. of "trading stock") appl.	36, s.117, Sch.18, Pt.II, para.13(3)
		s.100(4) am.	36, s.35, Sch.4, para.7(2) (4)
		s.100(4A) added	36, s.35, Sch.4, para.7(3) (4)
		ss.101(1)(2)(a),102(1), 103(1)(2)(a)(b)(4)(a)(5) ,104(1)(2) am.	36, s.46(3)(a)(b), Sch.7, para.1
		s.104(4) excl. (6.4.1999)	36, s.44(3)(4)
		ss.104(4)(5)(7),105(1)(a) (4),106(2),107,109(1)(b) ,109A(2)(d)(4)(4A), 110(3)(4)(5),110A(1) am.	36, s.46(3)(a)(b), Sch.7, para.1
		s.111 excl. (6.4.1999)	36, s.44, Sch.6, paras.1,6
		ss.111(2)(3)(4)(7)(8)(a) (11),112(1A)(1B),113(1) am.	36, s.46(3)(a)(b), Sch.7, para.1
		s.116(2)(d) rep. (6.4.1999)	36, ss.31,165, Sch.3, para.10(2)(3), Sch.27, Pt.III(2), Note
		s.117(1)(3)(b)(4) am.	36, s.46(3)(a)(b), Sch.7, para.1
		s.118(1) am.	36, s.38, Sch.5, Pt.III, paras.35(a),73
		s.118(1) am.	36, s.46(3)(a)(b), Sch.7, para.1
		s.118(2) (defn. of "the aggregate amount") am.	36, s.38, Sch.5, Pt.III, paras.35(b),73

Year and Chap. or No. of Measure	Short title	How affected	1998, Chapter of Act or Number of Measure or Statutory Instrument
1988—*cont.*			
		s.132(3) am. (17.3.1998) (*retrosp.*)	36, s.63(3)(c)(5)(6)(7)
		s.134(5)(c) rep. (6.4.1998) (*retrosp.*)	36, ss.55(1)(3),165, Sch.27, Pt.III(7), Note
		s.140G added	36, s.52(1)
		s.140H added	36, s.53
		s.144A(2) am. (6.4.1998) (*retrosp.*)	36, s.69(4)(5)
		s.148 subst. (6.4.1998) (except where the payment or other benefit or the right to receive it has been brought into charge to tax before that date) (*retrosp.*)	36, s.58(1)(4)
		s.148 restr. (6.4.1998) (except where the payment or other benefit or the right to receive it has been brought into charge to tax before that date) (*retrosp.*)	36, s.58(2)(4), Sch.9, Pt.II, para.5 (substituting 1995 c.4, s.92(10)
		s.158(2), Table A, Table AB, Table B subst. (year 1998-99 and subsequent years of assessment)	36, s.59(1)(2)
		s.158(6) rep.in pt. (year 1998-99 and subsequent years of assessment)	36, s.165, Sch.27, Pt.III(10), Note
		s.158(7) rep. (year 1998-99 and subsequent years of assessment)	36, s.165, Sch.27, Pt.III(10), Note
		s.160(1C)(b) am.	36, s.46(3)(a)(b), Sch.7, para.1
		s.168A(1) am. (year 1998-99 and subsequent years of assessment)	36, s.60(1)(6)
		s.168A(11) am. (year 1998-99 and subsequent years of assessment)	36, s.60(2)(6)
		s.168AB added (year 1998-99 and subsequent years of assessment)	36, s.60(3)(6)
		s.168B am. (year 1998-99 and subsequent years of assessment)	36, s.60(4)(6)
		s.168C am. (year 1998-99 and subsequent years of assessment)	36, s.60(5)(6)
		ss.169-184 (Pt.V) (Ch.III) defn(s). appl.	36, s.62, Sch.11, para.5
		s.171(4) mod.	36, s.62, Sch.11, paras.2, 5(2)
		s.172(3) am. (*prosp.*)	14, s.86(1), Sch.7, para.16
		s.178(2)(m) am.	36, s.35, Sch.4, para.1(3)

Year and Chap. or No. of Measure	Short title	How affected	1998, Chapter of Act or Number of Measure or Statutory Instrument
1988—*cont.*			
		s.188 rep.	36, s.165, Sch.27, Pt.III(9), Note
		s.189 renumbered (as s.189(1)) (6.4.1998) (except where payment or other benefit or right to receive it has been brought into charge to tax before that date) (*retrosp.*)	36, s.58(2)(4), Sch.9, Pt.II, para.1(1)(2)
		s.189(1)(a) am. (6.4.1998) (except where the payment or other benefit or the right to receive it has been brought into charge to tax before that date) (*retrosp.*)	36, s.58(2)(4), Sch.9, Pt.II, para.1(3)
		s.189(2)(3) added (6.4.1998) (except where the payment or other benefit or the right to receive it has been brought into charge to tax before that date) (*retrosp.*)	36, s.58(2)(4), Sch.9, Pt.II, para.1(4)
		s.190 am. (6.4.1998) (except where the payment or other benefit or the right to receive it has been brought into charge to tax before that date) (*retrosp.*)	36, s.58(2)(4), Sch.9, Pt.II, para.2
		s.192A added (17.3.1998) (*retrosp.*)	36, s.63(2)(5)(6)(7)
		s.193(1) rep. (17.3.1998) (*retrosp.*)	36, ss.63(1)(5)(6)(7),165, Sch.27, Pt.III(11), Note
		s.193(1) saved (17.3.1998) (*retrosp.*)	36, s.63(6)
		s.198(1)-(1B) replaced (by subss.(1)(1A)(1B)) (year 1998-99 and subsequent years of assessment)	36, s.61(1)(3)
		s.198A rep. (year 1998-99 and subsequent years of assessment)	36, s.165, Sch.27, Pt.III(10), Note
		s.202B(8) am. (6.4.1998) (except where the payment or other benefit or the right to receive it has been brought into charge to tax before that date) (*retrosp.*)	36, s.58(2)(4), Sch.9, Pt.II, para.3
		s.203 saved	36, s.64(5)(a)
		s.203 mod.	36, s.64(6)(a)
		s.203 saved	36, s.65(7)(a)
		s.203 saved	36, s.66(3)(a)
		s.203 saved	36, s.67(3)(a)
		s.203 saved	36, s.68(5)(a)
		s.203 mod. (6.5.1999)	46, s.79(3)
		s.203(10) added	36, s.119

Year and Chap. or No. of Measure	Short title	How affected	1998, Chapter of Act or Number of Measure or Statutory Instrument
1988—*cont.*			
		s.203C(1)(b)(c)(d) am. (6.4.1998) (*retrosp.*)	36, s.69(1)(5)
		s.203C(3A)(3B) added (6.4.1998) (*retrosp.*)	36, s.69(2)(5)
		s.203F mod.	36, s.64(1)
		s.203F(1) am.	36, s.65(2)(6)(7)
		s.203F(2)(3) replaced (by s.203F(2)(3)(3A)(3B)(3C))	36, s.65(3)(6)(7)
		s.203F(4)(5) am.	36, s.65(4)(6)(7)
		s.203F(6) added	36, s.65(5)(6)(7)
		s.203FA added (6.4.1998) (*retrosp.*)	36, s.66(1)(2)
		s.203FB added	36, s.67(1)(2)
		s.203G(3)(4) replaced (by s.203G(3)(4)(5) (6.4.1998) (*retrosp.*)	36, s.68(1)(4)(5)
		s.203H(1)(b) subst. (6.4.1998) (*retrosp.*)	36, s.68(2)(4)(5)
		s.203H(2) rep. (6.4.1998) (*retrosp.*)	36, ss.68(2)(4)(5),165, Sch.27, Pt.III(12), Note 1
		s.203I(3) added (6.4.1998) (*retrosp.*)	36, s.68(3)(4)(5)
		s.203J mod.	36, s.64(6)(a)
		s.203J appl.	36, s.64(7)
		s.203J(3) saved	36, s.64(5)(b)
		s.203J(3) saved	36, s.65(7)(b)
		s.203J(3) saved	36, s.66(3)(b)
		s.203J(3) saved	36, s.67(3)(b)
		s.203J(3) saved	36, s.68(5)(b)
		s.203K(1)-(3) rep. (6.4.1998)	36, s.165, Sch.27, Pt.III(12), Note 2
		s.203L(1)(2) replaced (by s.203L(1)(1A)(1B)(1C)(2)) (6.4.1998) (*retrosp.*)	36, s.69(3)(5)
		s.231(1) am. (8.4.1998) (*retrosp.*)	36, s.102(1)(9)
		s.231(1) am. (6.4.1999)	36, s.102(2)(10)
		s.231(2) saved (for specified purpose) (6.4.1999) (*temp.*)	SI 1871, reg.4(1)
		s.231(2) saving (re 1997 repeal)	36, s.90(1)
		s.231AA added (8.4.1998) (*retrosp.*)	36, s.102(1)(9)
		s.231AB added (6.4.1999)	36, s.102(2)(10)
		s.238 rep. (6.4.1999)	36, ss.31,165, Sch.3, para.11(2)(3), Sch.27, Pt.III(2), Note
		s.238(3) appl.	36, s.31(4)
		s.239 rep. (6.4.1999)	36, ss.31,165, Sch.3, para.12(1)(2), Sch.27, Pt.III(2), Note

Year and Chap. or No. of Measure	Short title	How affected	1998, Chapter of Act or Number of Measure or Statutory Instrument
1988—*cont.*			
		s.239(2) mod. (6.4.1999)	36, s.31, Sch.3, para.12(4)(6)
		s.239(4) restr. (6.4.1999)	36, s.31, Sch.3, para.12(3)(5)
		s.240 rep. (6.4.1999)	36, ss.31,165, Sch.3, para.13(1)(2), Sch.27, Pt.III(2), Note
		s.240(1) (defn. of "surrendering company") appl. (6.4.1999)	36, s.31, Sch.3, para.13(2)
		s.240(1) (defn. of "surrendering company") appl. (6.4.1999)	36, s.31, Sch.3, para.30(3)
		s.241 rep. (6.4.1999)	36, ss.31,165, Sch.3, para.14(1)(2), Sch.27, Pt.III(2), Note
		s.245 rep. (6.4.1999)	36, ss.31,165, Sch.3, para.15(1)(2), Sch.27, Pt.III(2), Note
		s.245 (defn. of "changes in ownership") appl. (6.4.1999)	36, s.31, Sch.3, para.15(2)
		s.245A rep. (6.4.1999)	36, ss.31,165, Sch.3, para.16(1)(2), Sch.27, Pt.III(2), Note
		s.245B rep. (6.4.1999)	36, ss.31,165, Sch.3, para.17(1)(2), Sch.27, Pt.III(2), Note
		s.245B(4)(a) mod. (6.4.1999)	36, s.31, Sch.3, para.17(3)
		s.246 rep. (6.4.1999)	36, ss.31,165, Sch.3, para.18(1)(2), Sch.27, Pt.III(2), Note
		s.246Q(6) am.	36, s.117, Sch.19, para.44(2)
		s.246Q(7) am.	36, s.117, Sch.19, para.44(3)
		s.246U(7)(a) subst.	36, s.117, Sch.19, para.45(2)
		s.246U(8) am.	36, s.117, Sch.19, para.45(3)
		s.247(1)(2)(3) rep. (6.4.1999)	36, ss.31,165, Sch.3, para.19(2)(8), Sch.27, Pt.III(2), Note
		s.247(4)(a) subst. (6.4.1999)	36, s.31, Sch.3, para.19(3)(8)
		s.247(5) rep.in pt. (6.4.1999)	36, ss.31,165, Sch.3, para.19(4)(b)(8), Sch.27, Pt.III(2), Note
		s.247(5) am. (6.4.1999)	36, s.31, Sch.3, para.19(4)(a)(8)
		s.247(6) rep.in pt. (6.4.1999)	36, ss.31,165, Sch.3, para.19(5)(b)-(f)(8), Sch.27, Pt.III(2), Note

Year and Chap. or No. of Measure	Short title	How affected	1998, Chapter of Act or Number of Measure or Statutory Instrument
1988—*cont.*		s.247(6)(a) rep. (6.4.1999)	36, ss.31,165, Sch.3, para.19(5)(a)(8), Sch.27, Pt.III(2), Note
		s.247(7) rep.in pt. (6.4.1999)	36, ss.31,165, Sch.3, para.19(6)(8), Sch.27, Pt.III(2), Note
		s.247(10) rep.in pt. (6.4.1999)	36, ss.31,165, Sch.3, para.19(7)(8), Sch.27, Pt.III(2), Note
		s.248(2)(3) rep.in pt. (6.4.1999)	36, ss.31,165, Sch.3, para.20(2)(3), Sch.27, Pt.III(2), Note
		s.252(1)(a) rep. (6.4.1999)	36, ss.31,165, Sch.3, para.21(2)(3), Sch.27, Pt.III(2), Note
		s.253(1) rep.in pt. (6.4.1999)	36, ss.31,165, Sch.3, para.22(2)(b)(5), Sch.27, Pt.III(2), Note
		s.253(1)(b) rep. (6.4.1999)	36, ss.31,165, Sch.3, para.22(2)(a)(5), Sch.27, Pt.III(2), Note
		s.253(2) rep. (6.4.1999)	36, ss.31,165, Sch.3, para.22(3)(5), Sch.27, Pt.III(2), Note
		s.253(3)(a) rep.in pt. (6.4.1999)	36, ss.31,165, Sch.3, para.22(4)(5), Sch.27, Pt.III(2), Note
		s.255 rep. (6.4.1999)	36, ss.31,165, Sch.3, para.23(1)(2), Sch.27, Pt.III(2), Note
		s.256(2)(a) am. (year 1999-00 and subsequent years of assessment)	36, s.27(1)(a)
		s.257 am. (amounts specified 1998-99)	SI 755, art.2(3)
		s.257A am. (amounts specified 1998-99)	SI 755, art.2(4)
		s.257A(2)(3) am. (year 1999-00)	36, s.27(2)
		s.259(1)(c) am. (year 1998-99 and subsequent years of assessment and retrosp. for year 1997-98)	36, s.26(1)(4)
		s.259(4) am. (year 1998-99 and subsequent years of assessment and retrosp. for year 1997-98)	36, s.26(2)(4)
		s.261A(3) am. (year 1998-99 and subsequent years of assessment and retrosp. for year 1997-98)	36, s.26(3)(4)

Year and Chap. or No. of Measure		Short title	How affected	1998, Chapter of Act or Number of Measure or Statutory Instrument
1988—*cont.*				
			ss.289-312 (Pt.VII CH.III) (defn. of "qualifying company") appl. (6.4.1998)	36, s.74(1), Sch.13, Pt.III, para.36 (adding 1992 c.12, Sch.5B, paras.16-19 added at para.19(1))
			s.289(1)(a) am. (6.4.1998)	36, s.74(1), Sch.13, Pt.I, para.1(1)(a)
			s.289(1)(aa) added (6.4.1998)	36, s.74(1), Sch.13, Pt.I, para.1(1)(b)
			s.289(1)(b) am. (6.4.1998)	36, s.74(1), Sch.13, Pt.I, para.1(1)(c)
			s.289(1)(c) am. (6.4.1998)	36, s.74(1), Sch.13, Pt.I, para.1(1)(d)
			s.289(1A)(c) am. (6.4.1998)	36, s.74(1), Sch.13, Pt.I, para.1(2)
			s.289(2) (defn. of "qualifying business activity") appl. (6.4.1998)	36, s.74(1), Sch.13, Pt.III, para.36 (adding 1992 c.12, Sch.5B, paras.16-19 added at para.19(1))
			s.289(6) am. (6.4.1998)	36, s.74(1), Sch.13, Pt.I, para.1(3)
			s.289(7) am. (6.4.1998)	36, s.74(1), Sch.13, Pt.I, para.1(4)
			s.289(7) rep.	36, s.165, Sch.27, Pt.III(14), Note 4
			s.289(9) added (6.4.1998)	36, s.74(1), Sch.13, Pt.I, para.1(5)
			s.289A(4) am. (6.4.1998)	36, s.74(1), Sch.13, Pt.I, para.2
			s.289B(3)(b) am. (6.4.1998)	36, s.74(1), Sch.13, Pt.I, para.3(1)(5)
			s.289B(3A) added (6.4.1998)	36, s.74(1), Sch.13, Pt.I, para.3(2)(5)
			s.289B(4) subst. (6.4.1998)	36, s.74(1), Sch.13, Pt.I, para.3(3)
			s.289B(5) am. (6.4.1998)	36, s.74(1), Sch.13, Pt.I, para.3(4)
			s.290(2) am. (6.4.1998)	36, s.74(1), Sch.13, Pt.I, para.4
			s.290A rep. (6.4.1998)	36, ss.74(1),165, Sch.13, Pt.I, para.5, Sch.27, Pt.III(14), Note 4
			s.291(1) am. (6.4.1998)	36, s.74(1), Sch.13, Pt.I, para.6(1)
			s.291(2) rep.in pt. (6.4.1998)	36, ss.74(1),165, Sch.13, Pt.I, para.6(2), Sch.27, Pt.III(14), Note 4
			s.291(3) subst. (6.4.1998)	36, s.74(1), Sch.13, Pt.I, para.6(3)
			s.291(6) added (6.4.1998)	36, s.74(1), Sch.13, Pt.I, para.6(4)

Year and Chap. or No. of Measure	Short title	How affected	1998, Chapter of Act or Number of Measure or Statutory Instrument
1988—*cont.*			
		s.291(6) (defn. of "seven year period") appl. (6.4.1998)	36, s.74(1), Sch.13, Pt.III, para.36 (adding 1992 c.12, Sch.5B, paras.16-19 added at para.19(1))
		s.291A(1)(a) am. (6.4.1998)	36, s.74(1), Sch.13, Pt.I, para.7(1)
		s.291A(3)(f)(ii) am.	36, s.46(3)(a)(b), Sch.7, para.1
		s.291A(5) rep.in pt. (6.4.1998)	36, ss.74(1),165, Sch.13, Pt.I, para.7(2)(b), Sch.27, Pt.III(14), Note 4
		s.291A(5)(b)(ii) subst. (6.4.1998)	36, s.74(1), Sch.13, Pt.I, para.7(2)(a)
		s.291B(5A) added (6.4.1998)	36, s.74(1), Sch.13, Pt.I, para.8(1)
		s.291B(6) subst. (6.4.1998)	36, s.74(1), Sch.13, Pt.I, para.8(2)
		s.293(3B)(b) am. (6.4.1998)	36, s.74(1), Sch.13, Pt.I, para.9(1)
		s.293(6)(a) rep.in pt. (6.4.1998)	36, ss.74(1),165, Sch.13, Pt.I, para.9(2)(6), Sch.27, Pt.III(14), Note 1
		s.293(6A)-(6D) added (6.4.1998)	36, s.74(1), Sch.13, Pt.I, para.9(3)
		s.293(7) rep. (6.4.1998)	36, ss.74(1),165, Sch.13, Pt.I, para.9(4), Sch.27, Pt.III(14), Note 4
		s.293(8) am. (6.4.1998)	36, s.74(1), Sch.13, Pt.I, para.9(5)
		s.293(8) excl. (6.4.1998)	36, s.74(1), Sch.13, Pt.III, para.34 (adding 1992 c.12, Sch.5B, paras.7-9)
		s.293(8) am. (6.4.1998)	36, s.74(1), Sch.13, Pt.IV, paras.37,38(1)(2)
		s.297(1) rep.in pt. (6.4.1998)	36, ss.74(1),165, Sch.13, Pt.I, para.10, Sch.27, Pt.III(14), Note 4
		s.297(2)(fa)-(fe) mod. (17.3.1998)	36, s.70, Sch.12, paras.1(1),5(1)
		s.297(2)(g) am. (17.3.1998)	36, s.70, Sch.12, paras.1(2),5(1)
		s.297(3A) added (17.3.1998)	36, s.70, Sch.12, paras.1(3),5(1)
		s.298(1) am. (6.4.1998)	36, s.74(1), Sch.13, Pt.I, para.11
		s.298(4) am.	36, s.70(2)(4)
		s.298(5) (defn. of "nursing home") added (17.3.1998)	36, s.70, Sch.12, paras.2(1),5(1)

Year and Chap. or No. of Measure	Short title	How affected	1998, Chapter of Act or Number of Measure or Statutory Instrument
1988—*cont.*			
		s.298(5) (defns. of "property development" and "residential care home") added (17.3.1998)	36, s.70, Sch.12, paras.2(2),5(1)
		s.298(5A)-(5C) added (17.3.1998)	36, s.70, Sch.12, paras.2(3),5(1)
		s.299(1) am. (6.4.1998)	36, s.74(1), Sch.13, Pt.I, para.12(1)(a)(8)
		s.299(1) am. (6.4.1998)	36, s.74(1), Sch.13, Pt.IV, paras.37,39(1)(3)
		s.299(1)(a)(b)(ii) am. (6.4.1998)	36, s.74(1), Sch.13, Pt.I, para.12(1)(b)(8)
		s.299(3) am. (6.4.1998)	36, s.74(1), Sch.13, Pt.I, para.12(2)(8)
		s.299(4) am. (6.4.1998)	36, s.74(1), Sch.13, Pt.I, para.12(3)(8)
		s.299(4) replaced (by s.299(4)(4A)(4B)(4C) (6.4.1998)	36, s.74(1), Sch.13, Pt.IV, paras.37,39(2)(3)
		s.299(5A) added (6.4.1998)	36, s.74(1), Sch.13, Pt.I, para.12(4)(8)
		s.299(6) replaced (by s.299(6)(6A)(6B)(6C)(6D)) (6.4.1998)	36, s.74(1), Sch.13, Pt.I, para.12(5)(8)
		s.299(7) rep. (6.4.1998)	36, ss.74(1),165, Sch.13, Pt.I, para.12(6)(8), Sch.27, Pt.III(14), Note 2
		s.299(8)(a) rep. (6.4.1998)	36, ss.74(1),165, Sch.13, Pt.I, para.12(6)(8), Sch.27, Pt.III(14), Note 4
		s.299B added (2.7.1997) (*retrosp.*)	36, s.71(1)(5)
		s.300(1) subst. (6.4.1998)	36, s.74(1), Sch.13, Pt.I, para.13(1)
		s.300(1C) subst. (6.4.1998)	36, s.74(1), Sch.13, Pt.I, para.13(2)
		s.300(6) added (6.4.1998)	36, s.74(1), Sch.13, Pt.I, para.13(3)(4)
		s.301(4A) added (6.4.1998)	36, s.74(1), Sch.13, Pt.I, para.14(1)(3)
		s.301(5) am. (6.4.1998)	36, s.74(1), Sch.13, Pt.I, para.14(2)
		s.303(1)(2) replaced (by s.303(1)(1A)(1B)(1C)(1D)) (6.4.1998)	36, s.74(1), Sch.13, Pt.I, para.15(1)
		s.303(3) am. (6.4.1998)	36, s.74(1), Sch.13, Pt.I, para.15(2)
		s.303(9A) subst. (6.4.1998)	36, s.74(1), Sch.13, Pt.I, para.15(3)
		s.304(7) added (6.4.1998)	36, s.74(1), Sch.13, Pt.IV, paras.37,40(1)(2)

Year and Chap. or No. of Measure	Short title	How affected	1998, Chapter of Act or Number of Measure or Statutory Instrument
1988—*cont.*			
		s.304A added (6.4.1998)	36, s.74(1), Sch.13, Pt.IV, paras.37,41(1)(2)
		s.306 appl.(mods.) (6.4.1998)	36, s.74(1), Sch.13, Pt.III, para.33 (substituting 1992 c.12, Sch.5B, para.6)
		s.307(6)(a) am. (2.7.1997) (*retrosp.*)	36, s.71(2)(5)
		s.310(1) am. (6.4.1998)	36, s.74(1), Sch.13, Pt.I, para.22(1)
		s.310(2) rep.in pt. (6.4.1998)	36, ss.74(1),165, Sch.13, Pt.I, para.22(2)(b), Sch.27, Pt.III(14), Note 1
		s.310(2) am. (6.4.1998)	36, s.74(1), Sch.13, Pt.I, para.22(2)(a)
		s.310(5) am. (2.7.1997) (*retrosp.*)	36, s.71(3)(5)
		s.310(6) subst. (2.7.1997) (*retrosp.*)	36, s.71(4)(5)
		s.310(7) am. (6.4.1998)	36, s.74(1), Sch.13, Pt.I, para.22(3)
		s.310(9A) added (6.4.1998)	36, s.74(1), Sch.13, Pt.I, para.22(4)(5)
		s.312(1) (defn. of "new consideration") rep. (6.4.1998)	36, ss.74(1),165, Sch.13, Pt.I, para.23(1)(a), Sch.27, Pt.III(14), Note 4
		s.312(1) (defns. of "research and development" and "relief") replaced (by defns."relief" "research and development" "the seven year period") (6.4.1998)	36, s.74(1), Sch.13, Pt.I, para.23(1)(b)
		s.312(1A) rep.in pt. (6.4.1998)	36, ss.74(1),165, Sch.13, Pt.I, para.23(2), Sch.27, Pt.III(14), Note 4
		s.312(1B)(c) rep.in pt. (6.4.1998)	36, ss.74(1),165, Sch.13, Pt.I, para.23(3), Sch.27, Pt.III(14), Note 4
		s.312(2) rep.in pt. (6.4.1998)	36, s.74(1), Sch.13, Pt.I, para.23(4)
		s.312(4A)(4B) added (6.4.1998)	36, s.74(1), Sch.13, Pt.I, para.23(5)
		s.312(7) am. (6.4.1998)	36, s.74(1), Sch.13, Pt.I, para.23(6)
		s.326A(3) am.	36, s.78
		s.333 ext. (17.3.1998) (*retrosp.*)	36, s.123(7)(a)
		s.333(1A) added	36, s.75(1)
		s.333(3)(b) rep.in pt.	36, ss.75(2),165, Sch.27, Pt.III(15)

Year and Chap. or No. of Measure	Short title	How affected	1998, Chapter of Act or Number of Measure or Statutory Instrument
1988—*cont.*			
		s.333(4)(b) am.	36, s.75(3)(a)
		s.333(4)(b)(ii) added	36, s.75(3)(b)
		s.333(4)(c)(iii) am.	36, s.75(4)
		s.333(4)(ca)-(cd) added	36, s.75(5)
		s.333B added	36, s.77(1)
		s.342(2) am.	36, s.35, Sch.4, para.6(2)(4)
		s.342(3A) added	36, s.35, Sch.4, para.6(3)(4)
		s.347B(5A) rep.in pt. (year 1999-00 and subsequent years of assessment)	36, s.165, Sch.27, Pt.III(1), Note
		s.347B(5A)(a) am. (year 1999-00 and subsequent years of assessment)	36, s.27(1)(b)
		s.360(3A) am. (6.4.1998) (*retrosp.*)	36, s.79(1)(2)
		ss.368(3)(4)(a),375A(1)(b) am.	36, s.46(3)(a)(b), Sch.7, para.1
		s.376(4)(ka) added	38, s.140, Sch.16, para.55
		s.376(4)(n) rep.	38, s.152, Sch.18, Pt.IV
		s.379A, head. subst.	36, s.38, Sch.5, Pt.II, paras.26,73
		s.379A(1)(a)(b)(7) am.	36, s.46(3)(a)(b), Sch.7, para.1
		s.379B added	36, s.38, Sch.5, Pt.II, paras.27,73
		ss.380-392 (Pt.X) (Ch.I ext. (6.4.1999)	36, s.44, Sch.6, paras.1,6
		s.382(3) am.	36, s.46(3)(a)(b), Sch.7, para.1
		s.385 mod.	36, s.56(4)(9)
		ss.385(4),386(1),388(1)(4)(5)(7) am.	36, s.46(3)(a)(b), Sch.7, para.1
		s.392A added	36, s.38, Sch.5, Pt.II, paras.28,73
		ss.392A,392B mod.	36, s.38, Sch.5, Pt.IV, para.72(1)(2)
		ss.393-396 (Pt.X) (Ch.II ext. (6.4.1999)	36, s.44, Sch.6, paras.1,6
		s.396 am.	36, s.38, Sch.5, Pt.IV, para.72(1)
		s.400(2) (defn. of "tax losses") appl. (pt.prosp.)	45, s.38(10)
		s.400(2)(bb) added	36, s.38, Sch.5, Pt.III, paras.36,73
		ss.400(6),401(1)(b) am.	36, s.46(3)(a)(b), Sch.7, para.1
		s.401(1B) rep.	36, s.165, Sch.27, Pt.III(4), Note
		ss.402-413 (Pt.X) (Ch.IV) restr.	36, s.117, Sch.18, Pt.VIII, para.66

Year and Chap. or No. of Measure	Short title	How affected	1998, Chapter of Act or Number of Measure or Statutory Instrument
1988—*cont.*			
		s.403 replaced (by ss.403, 403ZA,403ZB,403ZC,403ZD, 403ZD,403ZE)	36, s.38, Sch.5, Pt.II, paras.29,73
		s.403 appl.	36, s.38, Sch.5, Pt.III, paras.64(3),73 (substituting 1996 c.8, Sch.8, para.2(2))
		s.403 mod.	36, s.38, Sch.5, Pt.IV, paras.75,76
		s.403C am. (*retrosp.*)	36, s.81(5)
		s.403C(1)(a) am. (*retrosp.*)	36, s.81(1)(5)
		s.403C(2)(a) am. (*retrosp.*)	36, s.81(3)(5)
		s.403C(3)(a)(b) am. (*retrosp.*)	36, s.81(4)(5)
		s.404(2)(a) replaced (by s.404(2)(a)(aa))	36, s.38, Sch.5, Pt.III, paras.37(2),73
		s.412 subst.	36, s.117, Sch.19, para.46
		s.413(6) am.	36, s.38, Sch.5, Pt.III, paras.38,73
		s.413(6)(c) rep.	36, ss.38,165, Sch.5, Pt.III, paras.37(3),73, Sch.27, Pt.III(4), Note
		s.416 (defn. of "associated companies") appl. (year 1998-99 and subsequent years of assessment)	36, s.121, Sch.20 (adding 1992 c.12, Sch.A1)
		s.416 appl.(mods.)	36, s.131, Sch.22, para.2(2) (adding 1992 c.12, Sch.5, para.2(2A))
		s.417(1) (defn. of "participator") appl. (year 1998-99 and subsequent years of assessment)	36, s.121, Sch.20 (adding 1992 c.12, Sch.A1)
		s.417(1) (defn. of "participator") appl.	36, s.131, Sch.22, para.2(2) (adding 1992 c.12, Sch.5, para.2(2A))
		s.417(1) (defn. of "participator") appl.	36, s.131, Sch.22, para.4(2)(3) (substituting 1992 c.12, Sch.5, at para.9(11))
		s.417(1) (defns. of "participator" and "relevant income") appl.	36, s.132, Sch.23, para.3(12)
		s.419(1) am. (6.4.1999)	36, s.31, Sch.3, para.24(2)(5)
		s.419(3) am.	36, s.117, Sch.19, para.47(2)
		s.419(4) am. (6.4.1999)	36, s.31, Sch.3, para.24(3)(a)(c)(6)
		s.419(4) rep.in pt.	36, ss.117,165, Sch.19, para.47(3), Sch.27, Pt.III(28), Note
		s.419(4)(b) added (6.4.1999)	36, s.31, Sch.3, para.24(3)(b)(6)

Year and Chap. or No. of Measure	Short title	How affected	1998, Chapter of Act or Number of Measure or Statutory Instrument
1988—*cont.*			
		s.419(4A) am. (6.4.1999)	36, s.31, Sch.3, para.24(4) (a)(c)(6)
		s.419(4A)(b) added (6.4.1999)	36, s.31, Sch.3, para.24(4) (b)(6)
		s.419(4B) added	36, s.117, Sch.19, para.47(4)
		ss.431-458 (Pt.XII)(Ch.I) (defn. of "annuity business") appl.	36, s.117, Sch.18, Pt.X, para.84
		s.431(2) mod. (6.4.1999)	SI 1871, regs.5,7
		s.431(2) (defns. of "long term busines" and "insurance company") appl.	36, s.117, Sch.18, Pt.II, para.13(3)
		ss.431C(1),431D(1) mod. (6.4.1999)	SI 1871, regs.5,8
		s.431F mod. (6.4.1999)	SI 1871, regs.5,9
		s.432A(2) mod. (6.4.1999)	SI 1871, regs.5,10
		s.432AA added	36, s.38, Sch.5, Pt.III, paras.39,73
		s.432AA(4) mod. (6.4.1999)	SI 1871, regs.5,11
		s.432AB added	36, s.38, Sch.5, Pt.III, paras.39,73
		ss.432C(1),432D(1) mod. (6.4.1999)	SI 1871, regs.5,12
		s.434(3) rep. (6.4.1999)	36, ss.31,165, Sch.3, para.25(2)(5), Sch.27, Pt.III(2), Note
		s.434(6) rep. (6.4.1999)	36, ss.31,165, Sch.3, para.25(3)(6), Sch.27, Pt.III(2), Note
		s.434(8) rep. (6.4.1999)	36, ss.31,165, Sch.3, para.25(4)(6), Sch.27, Pt.III(2), Note
		s.434C rep. (6.4.1999)	36, ss.31,165, Sch.3, para.26(1)(2), Sch.27, Pt.III(2), Note
		s.434D(4) ext. (1.1.1999)	SI 3177, reg.6
		s.434D(5) mod. (6.4.1999)	SI 1871, regs.5,12
		s.434E(1) subst.	36, s.38, Sch.5, Pt.III, paras.40(2),73
		s.434E(3) rep.	36, ss.38,165, Sch.5, Pt.III, paras.40(3),73, Sch.27, Pt.III(4), Note
		s.434E(6) am.	36, s.38, Sch.5, Pt.III, paras.40(4),73
		s.436 mod. (6.4.1999)	SI 1871, regs.5,13
		s.436 mod. (6.4.1999)	SI 1871, reg.25(1)(3) (adding SI 1997/473, regs.19A,20A)
		s.438(1) mod. (6.4.1999)	SI 1871, regs.5,14
		s.440(4)(a) mod. (6.4.1999)	SI 1871, regs.5,15

Year and Chap. or No. of Measure	Short title	How affected	1998, Chapter of Act or Number of Measure or Statutory Instrument
1988—*cont.*			
		s.440A am. (6.4.1998) (*retrosp.*)	36, s.123(5)(a)(6)
		s.440A(2)(a)(i) mod. (6.4.1999)	SI 1871, regs.5,16
		s.441B(2A) added	36, s.38, Sch.5, Pt.III, paras.41,73
		s.460(2) mod. (6.4.1999)	SI 1871, reg.25(5) (adding SI 1997/473, reg.31)
		s.466(2) mod. (6.4.1999)	SI 1871, regs.5,17
		s.468Q(3) (defns. of "C" and "D") subst. (6.4.1999)	36, s.31, Sch.3, para.27(2) (5)
		s.468Q(3A) added (6.4.1999)	36, s.31, Sch.3, para.27(3) (5)
		s.468Q(5A)-(5C) added (6.4.1999)	36, s.31, Sch.3, para.27(4) (5)
		s.471 rep.	36, ss.101(1)(3),165, Sch.27, Pt.III(23), Note 1
		s.472 rep.	36, ss.101(2)(4),165, Sch.27, Pt.III(23), Note
		s.473(2) rep.in pt.	36, s.165, Sch.27, Pt.III(23), Note 1
		s.486(10) am.	36, s.46(3)(a)(b), Sch.7, para.1
		s.488(3) rep.	36, s.165, Sch.27, Pt.III(4), Note
		s.488(7A) rep.in pt.	38, ss.140,152, Sch.16, para.56, Sch.18, Pt.VI
		s.488(7A)(b) rep.	38, ss.140,152, Sch.16, para.56, Sch.18, Pt.VI
		s.488(11A) am.	36, s.117, Sch.19, para.48(2)(b)
		s.488(11A)(a) am.	36, s.117, Sch.19, para.48(2)(a)
		s.488(12) subst.	36, s.117, Sch.19, para.48(3)
		s.489(5A) rep.in pt.	38, ss.140,152, Sch.16, para.57, Sch.18, Pt.VI
		s.489(5A)(b) rep.	38, ss.140,152, Sch.16, para.57, Sch.18, Pt.VI
		s.489(9A) am.	36, s.117, Sch.19, para.49(b)
		s.489(9A)(a) am.	36, s.117, Sch.19, para.49(a)
		s.491(3)(4)(5)(6)(8)(b) (11) am.	36, s.46(3)(a)(b), Sch.7, para.1
		s.493(6) added (*retrosp.*)	36, s.152(3)
		s.494(4)(5) rep.	36, s.165, Sch.27, Pt.III(4), Note
		s.494A added	36, s.38, Sch.5, Pt.II, paras.30,73

Year and Chap. or No. of Measure	Short title	How affected	1998, Chapter of Act or Number of Measure or Statutory Instrument
1988—*cont.*			
		s.497 rep. (6.4.1999)	36, ss.31,165, Sch.3, para.29(1)(2), Sch.27, Pt.III(2), Note
		s.498(5) am. (6.4.1999)	36, s.31, Sch.3, para.30(3)
		s.499 rep. (6.4.1999)	36, ss.31,165, Sch.3, para.31(1)(2), Sch.27, Pt.III(2), Note
		s.502(1) (defn. of "oil") am. (*prosp.*)	17, s.50, Sch.4, para.25
		s.503 subst.	36, s.38, Sch.5, Pt.III, paras.42,73
		s.506 (defn. of "charity") appl.	36, s.47(9)
		s.507(1)(f) added	22, s.24(1)
		ss.509(1),526(1)(b),528(1)(a) am.	36, s.46(3)(a)(b), Sch.7, para.1
		ss.539-554 (Pt.XIII Ch.II) appl.(mods.) (6.4.1999)	SI 3174, reg.12 (adding reg.36(3)-(7) to 1998/1870)
		s.547(1)(a) rep. & superseded (in pt.) (6.4.1998)	36, ss.86,165, Sch.14, paras.1(2),7(5), Sch.27, Pt.III(19), Note
		s.547(1)(d) added (6.4.1998)	36, s.86, Sch.14, paras.1(3),7(5)
		s.547(1)(d) restr. (6.4.1998)	36, s.86, Sch.14, para.7(1)(2)(5)
		s.547(1)(e) added (6.4.1998)	36, s.86, Sch.14, paras.1(3),7(5)
		s.547(3) rep. & superseded (6.4.1998)	36, ss.86,165, Sch.14, paras.1(4),7(5), Sch.27, Pt.III(19), Note
		s.547(4) am. (6.4.1998)	36, s.86, Sch.14, paras.1(5),7(5)
		s.547(5) am. (6.4.1998)	36, s.86, Sch.14, paras.1(6),7(5)
		s.547(5AA) added (6.4.1998)	36, s.86, Sch.14, paras.1(7),7(5)
		s.547(9)-(12) added (6.4.1998)	36, s.86, Sch.14, paras.1(8),7(5)
		s.547(9) renumbered (as s.547(13) (6.4.1998)	36, s.86, Sch.14, paras.1(8),7(5)
		s.547(13) (defn. of "foreign institution") added (6.4.1998)	36, s.86, Sch.14, paras.1(9),7(5)
		s.547(14) added (6.4.1998)	36, s.86, Sch.14, paras.1(10),7(5)
		s.547A added (6.4.1998)	36, s.86, Sch.14, paras.2, 7(5)
		s.551A added (6.4.1998)	36, s.86, Sch.14, paras.3, 7(5)
		s.552(1) excl. (6.4.1999)	SI 1870, reg.35(6)
		ss.552A,552B added	36, s.87

Year and Chap. or No. of Measure	Short title	How affected	1998, Chapter of Act or Number of Measure or Statutory Instrument
1988—*cont.*			
		s.553(3) am. (6.4.1998)	36, s.86, Sch.14, paras.4(2),7(5)
		s.553(5A) added (6.4.1998)	36, s.86, Sch.14, paras.4(3),7(5)
		s.553(10) (defn. of "foreign institution") added (6.4.1998)	36, s.86, Sch.14, paras.4(4),7(5)
		s.553A added	36, s.88(1)
		s.553B added	36, s.88(2)
		s.553C added	36, s.89
		ss.556(3)(a),557(1)(2)(a) (b)(c), , sidenote am.	36, s.46(3)(a)(b), Sch.7, para.1
		ss.559-567 (Pt.XIII Ch.IV) (defn. of "construction operations") appl.	36, s.56(8)(9)
		s.559(1) am. (6.4.1998) (*retrosp.*)	36, s.55(2)(3)
		s.559(1A) added (6.4.1998) (*retrosp.*)	36, s.55(2)(3)
		s.559(4)(b)(5) am.	36, s.46(3)(a)(b), Sch.7, para.1
		s.559(5A) added	36, s.57, Sch.8, para.2(1) (3)
		s.560(2) added	36, s.57, Sch.8, para.2(2) (3)
		s.560(2)(da) added	38, s.140, Sch.16, para.58(a)
		s.560(2)(e) rep.in pt.	38, ss.140,152, Sch.16, para.58(b), Sch.18, Pt.VI
		s.560(2A)(2B) added	36, s.57, Sch.8, para.2(2) (3)
		s.560(2B) am.	36, s.57, Sch.8, para.2(4)
		s.564(2A) am.	36, s.57, Sch.8, paras.3(1),5
		s.564(2AA) added	36, s.57, Sch.8, paras.3(2),5
		s.564(2C) added	36, s.57, Sch.8, paras.3(3),5
		s.565(2A)(2B) replaced (by s.565(2A)(2B)(2BB))	36, s.57, Sch.8, paras.4(1),5
		s.565(2D) added (by s.565(2A)(2B)(2BB))	36, s.57, Sch.8, paras.4(2),5
		s.566(2)(c) rep.in pt.	36, s.165, Sch.27, Pt.III(8)
		s.566(4)(5) added	36, s.57, Sch.8, para.6
		ss.568(1),570(1) am.	36, s.46(3)(a)(b), Sch.7, para.1
		s.576(1) am. (in relation to disposals made on or after 6.4.1998) (*retrosp.*)	36, s.80(1)(5)(a)

Year and Chap. or No. of Measure	Short title	How affected	1998, Chapter of Act or Number of Measure or Statutory Instrument
1988—*cont.*			
		s.576(1A)(1B) added (in relation to disposals made on or after 6.4.1998) (*retrosp.*)	36, s.80(2)(5)(a)
		s.576(4) replaced (by s.576(4)(4A)(4B)) (in relation to shares issued on or after 6.4.1998) (*retrosp.*)	36, s.80(3)(5)(b)
		s.576(5) (defns. of "excluded company" and "relevant period") am. (in relation to shares issued on or after 6.4.1998) (*retrosp.*)	36, s.80(4)(a)(b)(5)(b)
		s.576(5) (defn. of "shares") subst. (in relation to shares issued on or after 6.4.1998) (*retrosp.*)	36, s.80(4)(c)(5)(b)
		s.576(5) (defn. of "trading group") rep.in pt. (in relation to shares issued on or after 6.4.1998) (*retrosp.*)	36, ss.80(4)(d)(5)(b),165, Sch.27, Pt.III(16), Note
		s.577(1) rep.in pt.	36, s.165, Sch.27, Pt.III(4), Note
		s.577(1)(a)(9) am.	36, s.46(3)(a)(b), Sch.7, para.1
		s.577(9) rep.in pt.	36, s.165, Sch.27, Pt.III(4), Note
		s.577A(1) am.	36, s.46(3)(a)(b), Sch.7, para.1
		s.577A(1) rep.in pt.	36, s.165, Sch.27, Pt.III(4), Note
		s.577A(1A) am.	36, s.46(3)(a)(b), Sch.7, para.1
		s.577A(1A) rep.in pt.	36, s.165, Sch.27, Pt.III(4), Note
		s.579(2) am.	36, s.46(3)(a)(b), Sch.7, para.1
		s.579(4) rep.	36, ss.38,165, Sch.5, Pt.III, paras.43,73, Sch.27, Pt.III(4), Note
		s.579(5) am.	36, s.38, Sch.5, Pt.III, paras.43,73
		s.588(3) am.	36, s.46(3)(a)(b), Sch.7, para.1
		s.588(4A) rep.	36, s.165, Sch.27, Pt.III(4), Note
		s.589A(8) am.	36, s.46(3)(a)(b), Sch.7, para.1
		s.589A(9A) rep.	36, s.165, Sch.27, Pt.III(4), Note

Year and Chap. or No. of Measure	Short title	How affected	1998, Chapter of Act or Number of Measure or Statutory Instrument
1988—*cont.*			
		ss.590-612 (Pt.XIV)(Ch.I) (defns. of "retirement benefits scheme" and "approved") appl.	36, s.92, Sch.15, para.7(6)
		s.590C(4)(5) am. (figure specified for 1998-99)	SI 758, art.2
		s.591A referred to (descriptions of provisions specified)	SI 729, reg.3
		s.591C(3) rep.	36, s.165, Sch.27, Pt.III(20)
		s.591C(4) am. (17.3.1998)	36, s.92, Sch.15, para.1(2) (6)
		s.591C(6A) added (17.3.1998)	36, s.92, Sch.15, para.1(3) (6)
		s.591C(7) am. (17.3.1998)	36, s.92, Sch.15, para.1(4) (6)
		s.591C(8)(9) added (17.3.1998)	36, s.92, Sch.15, para.1(5) (6)
		s.591D(3)(c)(d) subst. (17.3.1998)	36, s.92, Sch.15, para.2(1) (2)
		s.591D(5) appl.	36, s.92, Sch.15, para.7(5)
		s.596A(4)(b) subst. (year 1998-99 and subsequent years of assessment)	36, s.93(1)(4)
		s.596B(9) replaced (by s.596B(9)(b)([c]) (year 1998-99 and subsequent years of assessment)	36, s.93(2)(4)
		s.596C added (year 1998-99 and subsequent years of assessment)	36, s.93(3)(4)
		s.599 appl.	SI 366, regs.48(8),49(3)
		s.604(1) am.	36, s.92, Sch.15, para.3(1) (a)(3)
		s.604(1)(c) am.	36, s.92, Sch.15, para.3(1) (b)(3)
		s.604(1A) added	36, s.92, Sch.15, para.3(2) (3)
		s.605(1B)(b) subst.	36, s.92, Sch.15, para.4
		s.606(9A) added (*retrosp.*)	36, s.92, Sch.15, para.5(1)
		s.606(11A) added (17.3.1998)	36, s.92, Sch.15, para.5(2) (3)
		s.606A added (17.3.1998)	36, s.92, Sch.15, para.6(1) (2)
		s.623(2)(c) ext. (6.4.1999)	36, s.44, Sch.6, paras.2(2) (c),6
		s.631(2) am.	36, s.94(2)
		s.638A added	36, s.94(1)
		s.644(2)(c) ext. (6.4.1999)	36, s.44, Sch.6, paras.2(2) (c),6
		s.650(6) added	36, s.95(2)(4)

Year and Chap. or No. of Measure	Short title	How affected	1998, Chapter of Act or Number of Measure or Statutory Instrument
1988—*cont.*			
		s.650A added	36, s.95(1)(4)
		s.650A(3) (defns. of "the appropriate part" and "the relevant time") appl.	36, s.95(3)(4) (adding 1992 c.12 s.239B)
		s.651A added	36, s.96(1)
		s.652 rep. (*prosp.*)	36, ss.96(2)(4),165, Sch.27, Pt.III(21), Note
		s.653A added	36, s.97(1)(2)
		s.658A added (*retrosp.*)	36, s.98(1)
		s.660G(1)(2) appl. (year 1998-99 and subsequent years of assessment)	36, s.121, Sch.20 (adding 1992 c.12, Sch.A1)
		s.703(3A) added (6.4.1999)	36, s.31, Sch.3, para.32(2)(4)
		s.703(4)-(6) rep. (year 1990-00 and subsequent years of assessment)	36, ss.31,165, Sch.3, para.32(3)(5), Sch.27, Pt.III(2), Note
		s.704(A)(d) rep. (6.4.1999)	36, ss.31,165, Sch.3, para.33(2)(3), Sch.27, Pt.III(2), Note
		s.705(6)-(8) rep. (year 1999-00 and subsequent years of assessment)	36, ss.31,165, Sch.3, para.34(2)(3), Sch.27, Pt.III(2), Note
		ss.711-728 mod.	36, s.161(2)(a)
		s.717 excl. (1.1.1999)	SI 3177, reg.33(2)
		s.717(1) rep.in pt.	36, s.165, Sch.27, Pt.III(22)
		s.717(4)(5) rep.	36, s.165, Sch.27, Pt.III(22)
		ss.727A(1),730A(1) mod. (1.1.1999)	SI 3177, regs.14-18
		s.730C(1) am.	36, s.46(3)(a)(b), Sch.7, para.1
		s.737A(1) mod. (1.1.1999)	SI 3177, regs.14-18
		s.737D(2) rep.in pt. (6.4.1999)	36, ss.102(2)(10),165, Sch.27, Pt.III(24), Note
		ss.747-756 (Pt.XVII CH.IV) (defn. of "accounting period") appl.	36, s.113, Sch.17, para.37(4)
		s.747(1) rep.in pt.	36, ss.113,165, Sch.17, paras.1(2),37, Sch.27, Pt.III(27), Note
		s.747(2) (defn. of "controlled foreign company") appl.	SI 3081, reg.2(1)
		s.747(3) am.	36, s.113, Sch.17, paras.1(3),37
		s.747(4)(a) power to mod.	36, s.32(5)
		s.747(4)(a)(b) am.	36, s.113, Sch.17, paras.1(4),37
		s.747(5) am.	36, s.113, Sch.17, paras.1(5),37
		s.747A(2) mod. (1.1.1999)	SI 3177, reg.40

Year and Chap. or No. of Measure	Short title	How affected	1998, Chapter of Act or Number of Measure or Statutory Instrument
1988—*cont.*			
		s.747A(6) am.	36, s.113, Sch.17, paras.2(2),37
		s.747A(8)(a)(b) subst.	36, s.113, Sch.17, paras.2(3),37
		s.747A(9)(b) am.	36, s.113, Sch.17, paras.2(4),37
		s.748(1) am.	36, s.113, Sch.17, paras.3(2),37
		s.748(1)(d) am.	36, s.113, Sch.17, paras.3(3),37
		s.748(1)(e) referred to	SI 3081, regs.3,4
		s.748(1)(e) added	36, s.113, Sch.17, paras.3(4),37
		s.748(1A) added	36, s.113, Sch.17, paras.3(5),37
		s.748(2) rep.	36, ss.113,165, Sch.17, paras.3(6),37, Sch.27, Pt.III(27), Note
		s.748(3) am.	36, s.113, Sch.17, paras.3(7)(8),37
		s.748(3) sidenote am.	36, s.113, Sch.17, paras.3(9),37
		s.749 replaced (by ss.749, 749A,749B)	36, s.113, Sch.17, paras.4, 37
		s.750(1) am.	36, s.113, Sch.17, paras.5(2),37
		s.750(3)(a) subst.	36, s.113, Sch.17, paras.5(3),37
		s.751(1)(b) rep.in pt.	36, ss.113,165, Sch.17, paras.6(2)(a),37, Sch.27, Pt.III(27), Note
		s.751(1)(b) am.	36, s.113, Sch.17, paras.6(2)(b),37
		s.751(5) am.	36, s.113, Sch.17, paras.6(3),37
		s.751(5) am.	36, s.113, Sch.17, paras.6(4),37
		s.751(5A) added	36, s.113, Sch.17, paras.6(5),37
		s.751(6) am.	36, s.113, Sch.17, paras.6(6),37
		s.752 replaced (by ss.752, 752A,752B,752C)	36, s.113, Sch.17, paras.7, 37
		s.752A (defn. of "relevant interest") appl.	SI 3081, reg.1(2)
		s.753 rep.	36, ss.113,165, Sch.17, paras.8,37, Sch.27, Pt.III(27), Note
		s.754(1) am.	36, s.113, Sch.17, paras.9(2),37
		s.754(1A) added and am.	36, s.113, Sch.17, paras.9(3),37

Year and Chap. or No. of Measure	Short title	How affected	1998, Chapter of Act or Number of Measure or Statutory Instrument
1988—*cont.*			
		s.754(2) subst.	36, s.113, Sch.17, paras.9(4),37
		s.754(2A)-(2E) added	36, s.113, Sch.17, paras.9(5),37
		s.754(3) replaced (by s.754(3)(3A)(3B))	36, s.113, Sch.17, paras.9(6),37
		s.754(4) rep.	36, ss.113,165, Sch.17, paras.9(7),37, Sch.27, Pt.III(27), Note
		s.754(6) am.	36, s.113, Sch.17, paras.9(8)(a)(d),37
		s.754(6)(a)(b) am.	36, s.113, Sch.17, paras.9(8)(b)(c),37
		s.754(7)(a) am.	36, s.113, Sch.17, paras.9(9)(a)(b),37
		s.754(7)(b) am.	36, s.113, Sch.17, paras.9(9)(c),37
		s.754(8) am.	36, s.113, Sch.17, paras.9(10),37
		s.754A added	36, s.113, Sch.17, paras.10,37
		s.754B added	36, s.113, Sch.17, paras.11,37
		s.755 rep.	36, ss.113,165, Sch.17, paras.12,37, Sch.27, Pt.III(27), Note
		s.755A mod. (6.4.1999)	SI 1871, regs.5,18
		s.755A added	36, s.113, Sch.17, paras.13,37
		s.755B added	36, s.113, Sch.17, paras.14,37
		s.755C added	36, s.113, Sch.17, paras.15,37
		s.756(1) (defn. of "company tax return") added	36, s.113, Sch.17, paras.16,37
		s.767A(4) am. (2.7.1997) (*retrosp.*)	36, s.116(3)(6)
		s.767A(10) am. (2.7.1997) (*retrosp.*)	36, s.116(4)(6)
		s.767AA added (2.7.1997) (*retrosp.*)	36, s.114(1)(2)
		s.767B(1A) added (2.7.1997) (*retrosp.*)	36, s.116(1)(6)
		s.767B(2) am. (2.7.1997) (*retrosp.*)	36, s.116(2)(6)
		s.767C added (2.7.1997) (*retrosp.*)	36, s.115(1)(3)
		s.768D added	36, s.38, Sch.5, Pt.II, paras.31,73
		s.769(1) am.	36, s.38, Sch.5, Pt.II, paras.32(a),73
		s.769(1) am. (2.7.1997) (*retrosp.*)	36, s.116(5)(a)(6)

Year and Chap. or No. of Measure	Short title	How affected	1998, Chapter of Act or Number of Measure or Statutory Instrument
1988—*cont.*			
		s.769(2)(d) am.	36, s.38, Sch.5, Pt.II, paras.32(a),73
		s.769(2)(d) am. (2.7.1997) (*retrosp.*)	36, s.116(5)(b)(6)
		s.769(2A) am. (2.7.1997) (*retrosp.*)	36, s.116(5)(c)(6)
		s.769(3) am.	36, s.38, Sch.5, Pt.II, paras.32(b),73
		s.769(4) am.	36, s.38, Sch.5, Pt.II, paras.32(c),73
		s.769(5) am.	36, s.38, Sch.5, Pt.II, paras.32(a),73
		s.769(5) am. (2.7.1997) (*retrosp.*)	36, s.116(5)(a)(6)
		s.769(9) am. (2.7.1997) (*retrosp.*)	36, s.116(5)(c)(6)
		ss.770-773 replaced (by s.770A)	36, s.108(1)(5)(6)
		ss.770(2)(a)(iii)(b)(iii), 776(a)(b),779(13)(b), 780(3)(a),781(4)(a)(5) (b),782(1)(a)(2)(3) am.	36, s.46(3)(a)(b), Sch.7, para.1
		s.785 (defn. of "capital sum") am.	36, s.46(3)(a)(b), Sch.7, para.1
		s.787(3) am.	36, s.38, Sch.5, Pt.III, paras.44,73
		s.797(4)(5) rep. (6.4.1999)	36, ss.31,165, Sch.3, para.35(2)(3), Sch.27, Pt.III(2), Note
		s.798 subst.	36, s.103(1)(2)(3)
		s.798A added	36, ss.103(2)(3),104
		s.798B added	36, ss.103(2)(3),105
		s.802(2)(a) rep.in pt. (6.4.1999)	36, ss.31,165, Sch.3, para.36(2)(3), Sch.27, Pt.III(2), Note
		s.803(1)(b)(c) am. (17.3.1998) (*retrosp.*)	36, s.106(2)(a)(b)(11)(12)
		s.803(1)(d) subst. 17.3.1998 (*retrosp.*)	36, s.106(2)(c)(11)(12)
		s.803(3) am. 17.3.1998 (*retrosp.*)	36, s.106(3)(11)(12)
		s.803(4)(a) am. 17.3.1998 (*retrosp.*)	36, s.106(4)(a)(11)(12)
		s.803(4)(b) subst. 17.3.1998 (*retrosp.*)	36, s.106(4)(b)(11)(12)
		s.803(5) am. 17.3.1998 (*retrosp.*)	36, s.106(5)(11)(12)
		s.803(6) am. 17.3.1998 (*retrosp.*)	36, s.106(6)(11)(12)
		s.803(7) subst. 17.3.1998 (*retrosp.*)	36, s.106(7)(11)(12)
		s.803(8) am. 17.3.1998 (*retrosp.*)	36, s.106(8)(11)(12)

Year and Chap. or No. of Measure	Short title	How affected	1998, Chapter of Act or Number of Measure or Statutory Instrument
1988—*cont.*			
		s.803(9) am. 17.3.1998) (*retrosp.*)	36, s.106(9)(11)(12)
		s.803(10)(11) replaced (by s.803(10)) (17.3.1998) (*retrosp.*)	36, s.106(10)(11)(12)
		s.806(3)-(6) added (17.3.1998)	36, s.107(1)(2)
		s.813(6)(b) rep. (6.4.1999)	36, ss.31,165, Sch.3, para.37(2)(3), Sch.27, Pt.III(2), Note
		s.826 appl.(mods.) (7.1.1999)	SI 3175, reg.8
		s.826(2) am.	36, s.35, Sch.4, para.1(1)
		s.826(2A) rep. (6.4.1999)	36, ss.31,165, Sch.3, para.38(2)(5), Sch.27, Pt.III(2), Note
		s.826(3) am.	36, s.35, Sch.4, para.2(1)(2)
		s.826(5) am.	36, s.34(2)
		s.826(5)(b) am.	36, s.34(3)(5)
		s.826(5A) added	36, s.34(4)(5)
		s.826(7) rep. (6.4.1999)	36, ss.31,165, Sch.3, para.38(3)(6), Sch.27, Pt.III(2), Note
		s.826(7)(7A) am.	36, s.35, Sch.4, para.5(2)(6)
		s.826(7AA) rep. (6.4.1999)	36, ss.31,165, Sch.3, para.38(4)(7), Sch.27, Pt.III(2), Note
		s.826(7B)(7C) am.	36, s.35, Sch.4, para.5(2)(6)
		s.826(7CA) rep. (6.4.1999)	36, ss.31,165, Sch.3, para.38(4)(7), Sch.27, Pt.III(2), Note
		s.826(7D) added	36, s.35, Sch.4, para.5(3)(5)(6)
		s.826(7E) added	36, s.35, Sch.4, para.5(4)(5)(6)
		s.826(8A)-(8C) added	36, s.35, Sch.4, para.3(1)(3)
		s.826A added	36, s.35, Sch.4, para.1(2)
		s.830(4) am.	36, s.46(3)(a)(b), Sch.7, para.1
		s.832(1) (defns. of "franked payment", "group income", "the rate of advance corporation tax" and "surplus of franked investment income") rep. (6.4.1999)	36, ss.31,165, Sch.3, para.39(3)(4)(5)(6)(8)(9), Sch.27, Pt.III(2), Note
		s.832(1) (defn. of "franked investment income") subst. (6.4.1999)	36, s.31, Sch.3, para.39(2)(8)
		s.832(1) (defn. of "overseas property business") added	36, s.38, Sch.5, Pt.III, paras.45,73

Year and Chap. or No. of Measure	Short title	How affected	1998, Chapter of Act or Number of Measure or Statutory Instrument
1988—*cont.*			
		s.832(1) (defn. of "notice") am.	36, s.118(10)
		s.832(4A) added (6.4.1999)	36, s.31, Sch.3, para.39(7) (8)
		s.833(3)(a) am. (6.4.1998) (except where the payment or other benefit or the right to receive it has been brought into charge to tax before that date) (*retrosp.*)	36, s.58(2)(4), Sch.9, Pt.II, para.4
		s.833(4)(c) ext. (6.4.1999)	36, s.44, Sch.6, paras.2(2)(c),6
		s.835(6)(a) am. (6.4.1999)	36, s.31, Sch.3, para.40(2)(3)
		s.838 (defn. of "51 per cent subsidiary") appl. (year 1998-99 and subsequent years of assessment)	36, s.121, Sch.20 (adding 1992 c.12, Sch.A1)
		s.839 appl.	36, s.47(10)
		s.839 appl.	36, s.62, Sch.11, para.3(4)
		s.842AA(14) rep.in pt. (6.4.1998) (*retrosp.*)	36, ss.73(1)(a)(6),165, Sch.27, Pt.III(13), Note 1
		Sch.1 rep.	36, s.165, Sch.27, Pt.III(4), Note
		Sch.5, para.1(1) am.	36, s.46(3)(a)(b), Sch.7, para.1
		Sch.5, para.2(6) am. (meaning of "qualifying year of assessment")	36, s.46(3)(a)(b), Sch.7, para.1
		Sch.5, paras.3(1),4(b), 5(1) am.	36, s.46(3)(a)(b), Sch.7, para.1
		Sch.5, para.6(4) am. (meaning of "qualifying year of assessment")	36, s.46(3)(a)(b), Sch.7, para.1
		Sch.5, paras.6(5),8(7) am.	36, s.46(3)(a)(b), Sch.7, para.1
		Sch.5AA, para.4(6) (defn. of "option") am. (on or after 6.2.1998) (*retrosp.*)	36, s.99(4)(5)
		Sch.5AA, para.4A added (on or after 6.2.1998) (*retrosp.*)	36, s.99(1)(5)
		Sch.5AA, para.9 am. (on or after 6.2.1998) (*retrosp.*)	36, s.99(2)(5)
		Sch.5AA, para.9(3)-(7) added (on or after 6.2.1998) (*retrosp.*)	36, s.99(3)(5)
		Sch.11 subst. (6.4.1998) (except where the payment or other benefit or the right to receive it has been brought into charge to tax before that date) (*retrosp.*)	36, s.58(2)(4), Sch.9

Year and Chap. or No. of Measure	Short title	How affected	1998, Chapter of Act or Number of Measure or Statutory Instrument
1988—*cont.*			
		Sch.11, para.10 am. (17.3.1998) (*retrosp.*)	36, s.63(3)(b)(5)(6)(7)
		Sch.12, paras.1,1A,2(1), 3(1) am. (17.3.1998) (*retrosp.*)	36, s.63(3)(c)(5)(6)(7)
		Sch.12, para.3(2)(a)(b) am. (17.3.1998) (*retrosp.*)	36, s.63(4)(a)(5)(6)(7)
		Sch.12, para.3(2A) rep.	36, s.165, Sch.27, Pt.III(11), Note
		Sch.12, paras.3(3),5 am. (17.3.1998) (*retrosp.*)	36, s.63(3)(c)(5)(6)(7)
		Sch.12, para.5 am. (17.3.1998) (*retrosp.*)	36, s.63(4)(b)(i)(5)(6)(7)
		Sch.12, para.5(a)(b) am. (17.3.1998) (*retrosp.*)	36, s.63(4)(b)(ii)(5)(6)(7)
		Sch.12, para.6 am. (17.3.1998) (*retrosp.*)	36, s.63(3)(c)(5)(6)(7)
		Sch.12, para.7 rep.	36, s.165, Sch.27, Pt.III(11), Note
		Sch.12A added (year 1998-99 and subsequent years of assessment)	36, s.61(2)(3), Sch.10
		Sch.13 rep. (6.4.1999)	36, ss.31,165, Sch.3, para.41(1)(2), Sch.27, Pt.III(2), Note
		Sch.13A rep. (6.4.1999)	36, ss.31,165, Sch.3, para.42(1)(2), Sch.27, Pt.III(2), Note
		Sch.13A, para.5(1) am.	36, s.117, Sch.19, para.50(2)
		Sch.13A, para.5(2) subst.	36, s.117, Sch.19, para.50(3)
		Sch.13A, para.14(1) rep.in pt.	36, ss.117,165, Sch.19, para.50(4), Sch.27, Pt.III(28), Note
		Sch.13A, para.14(6) am.	36, s.117, Sch.19, para.50(5)
		Sch.13A, para.14(8) rep.in pt.	36, ss.117,165, Sch.19, para.50(6), Sch.27, Pt.III(28), Note
		Sch.15B, para.6(1) rep.in pt. (6.4.1998) (*retrosp.*)	36, ss.73(1)(b)(6),165, Sch.27, Pt.III(13), Note 2
		Sch.17A replaced	36, s.117(1)(c)(4), Sch.18
		Sch.17A rep.	36, s.165, Sch.27, Pt.III(28), Note
		Sch.19AA mod. (6.4.1999)	SI 1871, regs.5,19
		Sch.19AB mod. (6.4.1999)	SI 1871, regs.5,20,21
		Sch.19AB, para.1(4) am.	36, s.117, Sch.19, para.51(2)
		Sch.19AB, para.1(6) subst.	36, s.117, Sch.19, para.51(3)
		Sch.19AB, para.1(7) am.	36, s.117, Sch.19, para.51(4)

Year and Chap. or No. of Measure	Short title	How affected	1998, Chapter of Act or Number of Measure or Statutory Instrument
1988—*cont.*			
		Sch.19AB, para.1(10)(11) subst.	36, s.117, Sch.19, para.51(5)
		Sch.19AB, para.2(1)(c) am.	36, s.117, Sch.19, para.51(6)
		Sch.19AB, para.3(1) am.	36, s.117, Sch.19, para.51(7)
		Sch.19AB, para.3(1A) am.	36, s.117, Sch.19, para.51(8)
		Sch.19AB, para.3(1C) rep.in pt. (*prosp.*)	36, ss.37(2)(b)(3),165, Sch.27, Pt.III(3), Note
		Sch.19AB, para.3(1C)(a) am. (*prosp.*)	36, s.37(2)(a)(3)
		Sch.19AB, para.3(1C)(c) rep. (*prosp.*)	36, ss.37(2)(b)(3),165, Sch.27, Pt.III(3), Note
		Sch.19AB, para.3(1D) subst.	36, s.117, Sch.19, para.51(9)
		Sch.19AB, para.3(3) am.	36, s.117, Sch.19, para.51(10)
		Sch.19AB, para.3(7) am.	36, s.117, Sch.19, para.51(11)
		Sch.19AB, para.3(9) am.	36, s.117, Sch.19, para.51(12)
		Sch.19AB, para.6(4)(b) am.	36, s.117, Sch.19, para.51(13)
		Sch.21, para.6(1)(b)(3) am.	36, s.46(3)(a)(b), Sch.7, para.1
		Sch.23A, para.2(2) subst. (6.4.1999)	36, s.102(5)(10)
		Sch.23A, para.2(3)(a) rep. (6.4.1999)	36, ss.102(6)(10),165, Sch.27, Pt.III(24), Note
		Sch.23A, para.2(4)(5) rep. (6.4.1999)	36, ss.102(6)(8)(a)(10), 165, Sch.27, Pt.III(24), Note
		Sch.23A, para.2(6) rep.in pt. (6.4.1999)	36, ss.102(6)(8)(a)(10), 165, Sch.27, Pt.III(24), Note
		Sch.23A, para.2(6) am. (6.4.1999)	36, s.102(7)(10)
		Sch.23A, para.2(6)(b) rep. (6.4.1999)	36, ss.102(6)(8)(a)(10), 165, Sch.27, Pt.III(24), Note
		Sch.23A, para.2A(1) rep.in pt. (6.4.1999)	36, ss.102(6)(8)(b)(10), 165, Sch.27, Pt.III(24), Note
		Sch.23A, para.2A(3) rep. (6.4.1999)	36, ss.102(6)(8)(b)(10), 165, Sch.27, Pt.III(24), Note
		Sch.24, para.1(3A) am.	36, s.113, Sch.17, paras.17(2)(5),37
		Sch.24, para.1(3A)(a) am.	36, s.113, Sch.17, paras.17(2)(3),37
		Sch.24, para.1(3A)(b)(i) subst.	36, s.113, Sch.17, paras.17(2)(4)(a),37

Year and Chap. or No. of Measure	Short title	How affected	1998, Chapter of Act or Number of Measure or Statutory Instrument
1988—*cont.*			
		Sch.24, para.1(3A)(b)(ii) am.	36, s.113, Sch.17, paras.17(2)(4)(b),37
		Sch.24, para.1(4) am.	36, s.113, Sch.17, paras.17(2)(6),37
		Sch.24, para.1(4) am.	36, s.113, Sch.17, paras.17(2)(9),37
		Sch.24, para.1(4)(a) am.	36, s.113, Sch.17, paras.17(2)(7),37
		Sch.24, para.1(4)(b) added	36, s.113, Sch.17, paras.17(2)(8),37
		Sch.24, para.2(1) am.	36, s.113, Sch.17, paras.18(b),37
		Sch.24, para.2(1)(a) am.	36, s.113, Sch.17, paras.18(a),37
		Sch.24, para.4(1A)(a) am.	36, s.113, Sch.17, paras.19(2),37
		Sch.24, para.4(2) am.	36, s.113, Sch.17, paras.19(3),37
		Sch.24, para.4(2A) rep.	36, ss.113,165, Sch.17, paras.19(4),37, Sch.27, Pt.III(27), Note
		Sch.24, para.4(3) am.	36, s.113, Sch.17, paras.19(5),37
		Sch.24, para.4(3A)(a)(b) am.	36, s.113, Sch.17, paras.19(6),37
		Sch.24, para.6(1)(a) rep. (6.4.1999)	36, ss.31,165, Sch.3, para.43(2)(a)(4), Sch.27, Pt.III(2), Note
		Sch.24, para.6(2) rep. (6.4.1999)	36, ss.31,165, Sch.3, para.43(2)(b)(4), Sch.27, Pt.III(2), Note
		Sch.24, para.7 rep. (6.4.1999)	36, ss.31,165, Sch.3, para.43(3)(4), Sch.27, Pt.III(2), Note
		Sch.24, para.9 am.	36, s.113, Sch.17, paras.20(2),37
		Sch.24, para.9(1) rep.in pt.	36, ss.113,165, Sch.17, paras.20(3)(a),37, Sch.27, Pt.III(27), Note
		Sch.24, para.9(1)(a) am.	36, s.113, Sch.17, paras.20(3)(b),37
		Sch.24, para.9(2) rep.	36, ss.113,165, Sch.17, paras.20(4),37, Sch.27, Pt.III(27), Note
		Sch.24, para.9(3) am.	36, s.113, Sch.17, paras.20(5),37
		Sch.24, para.9(4) subst.	36, s.113, Sch.17, paras.20(6),37
		Sch.24, para.9(5)(6) rep.	36, ss.113,165, Sch.17, paras.20(7)(8),37, Sch.27, Pt.III(27), Note
		Sch.24, para.9(7) added	36, s.113, Sch.17, paras.20(9),37

Year and Chap. or No. of Measure	Short title	How affected	1998, Chapter of Act or Number of Measure or Statutory Instrument
1988—*cont.*			
		Sch.24, para.10(1) am.	36, s.113, Sch.17, paras.21(a),37
		Sch.24, para.10(1)(a) am.	36, s.113, Sch.17, paras.21(b),37
		Sch.24, para.11 rep.	36, ss.113,165, Sch.17, paras.22,37, Sch.27, Pt.III(27), Note
		Sch.24, para.11A(3)(6) rep.	36, ss.113,165, Sch.17, paras.23,37, Sch.27, Pt.III(27), Note
		Sch.24, para.20 added	36, s.113, Sch.17, paras.24,37
		Sch.25, Pt.II, para.9(1A) subst.	36, s.112(2)(5)
		Sch.25, Pt.II, para.9(3) am.	36, s.112(4)(a)(5)
		Sch.25, Pt.II, para.11(1) (c) subst.	36, s.112(3)(5)
		Sch.25, Pt.II, para.11(3) am.	36, s.112(4)(b)(5)
		Sch.25, para.1 am.	36, s.113, Sch.17, paras.26,37
		Sch.25, para.2A(2)(a)(b) am.	36, s.113, Sch.17, paras.27(2),37
		Sch.25, para.2A(4) am.	36, s.113, Sch.17, paras.27(3),37
		Sch.25, para.2A(8)(a) am.	36, s.113, Sch.17, paras.27(5),37
		Sch.25, para.2A(8)(aa) added	36, s.113, Sch.17, paras.27(4),37
		Sch.25, para.3(4A)(b) am.	36, s.113, Sch.17, paras.28,37
		Sch.25, para.5(2A) am.	36, s.113, Sch.17, paras.29,37
		Sch.25, para.6(1)(c) am.	36, s.113, Sch.17, paras.30(2),37
		Sch.25, para.6(2)(b) am.	36, s.113, Sch.17, paras.30(3),37
		Sch.25, para.6(3)(b) am.	36, s.113, Sch.17, paras.30(4),37
		Sch.25, para.6(4)(b) am.	36, s.113, Sch.17, paras.30(5),37
		Sch.25, para.6(4A)(4B) added	36, s.113, Sch.17, paras.30(6),37
		Sch.25, para.6(4C) added	36, s.113, Sch.17, paras.30(7),37
		Sch.25, para.6(5) am.	36, s.113, Sch.17, paras.30(8),37
		Sch.25, para.6(5A) added	36, s.113, Sch.17, paras.30(9),37
		Sch.25, para.8(3) am.	36, s.113, Sch.17, paras.31(2),37
		Sch.25, para.12(1) am.	36, s.113, Sch.17, paras.32(2),37

Year and Chap. or No. of Measure	Short title	How affected	1998, Chapter of Act or Number of Measure or Statutory Instrument
1988—*cont.*			
		Sch.25, para.12(5)(a) am.	36, s.113, Sch.17, paras.32(3),37
		Sch.25, para.12A added	36, s.113, Sch.17, paras.33,37
		Sch.25, head. added	36, s.113, Sch.17, paras.25,37
		Sch.26, para.1(1) rep.in pt.	36, ss.113,165, Sch.17, paras.34(2)(a)(b),37, Sch.27, Pt.III(27), Note
		Sch.26, para.1(1)(c) rep.	36, ss.113,165, Sch.17, paras.34(2)(a),37, Sch.27, Pt.III(27), Note
		Sch.26, para.1(2)(a) am.	36, s.113, Sch.17, paras.34(3),37
		Sch.26, para.1(3)(a) am.	36, s.38, Sch.5, Pt.III, paras.46,73
		Sch.26, para.1(4)(6) rep.	36, ss.113,165, Sch.17, paras.34(4)(5),37, Sch.27, Pt.III(27), Note
		Sch.26, para.2 rep. (6.4.1999)	36, ss.31,165, Sch.3, para.44(2)(3), Sch.27, Pt.III(2), Note
		Sch.26, para.2(3) (defn. of "relevant maximum") am. (6.4.1999)	36, s.31, Sch.3, para.44(4)
		Sch.26, para.3(1)(a) rep.	36, s.113, Sch.17, paras.35(2),37
		Sch.26, para.3(1)(b)(c) am.	36, s.113, Sch.17, paras.35(3),37
		Sch.26, para.3(1)(d) am.	36, s.113, Sch.17, paras.35(4),37
		Sch.26, para.3(3) am.	36, s.113, Sch.17, paras.35(5),37
		Sch.26, para.3(4) am.	36, s.113, Sch.17, paras.35(6),37
		Sch.26, para.3(6A) added	36, s.113, Sch.17, paras.35(7),37
		Sch.26, para.4(1)(a) subst.	36, s.113, Sch.17, paras.36(2),37
		Sch.26, para.4(1)(b) subst.	36, s.113, Sch.17, paras.36(3),37
		Sch.26, para.4(2) am.	36, s.113, Sch.17, paras.36(4),37
		Sch.26, para.5(a) am.	36, s.113, Sch.17, paras.36(5),37
		Sch.28, para.6(da) am. (*retrosp.*)	36, s.82(3)(a)(4)
		Sch.28, para.6(db) rep.in pt. (*retrosp.*)	36, ss.82(3)(b)(4),165, Sch.27, Pt.III(17), Note
		Sch.28, para.6(dc) am. (*retrosp.*)	36, s.82(3)(c)(4)
		Sch.28, para.7(1)(b) am. (*retrosp.*)	36, s.82(3)(d)(4)

Year and Chap. or No. of Measure	Short title	How affected	1998, Chapter of Act or Number of Measure or Statutory Instrument
1988—*cont.*			
		Sch.28, para.11(2)(a) rep. (*retrosp.*)	36, ss.82(3)(e)(4),165, Sch.27, Pt.III(17), Note
		Sch.28, para.13(1)(ea) am. (*retrosp.*)	36, s.82(3)(f)(4)
		Sch.28, para.13(1)(eb) rep.in pt. (*retrosp.*)	36, ss.82(3)(g)(4),165, Sch.27, Pt.III(17), Note
		Sch.28, para.13(1)(ec) am. (*retrosp.*)	36, s.82(3)(h)(4)
		Sch.28, para.16(1)(b) am. (*retrosp.*)	36, s.82(3)(i)(4)
		Sch.28A, para.13(1)(eb) rep.in pt.	36, s.165, Sch.27, Pt.III(17), Note
		Sch.28AA added	36, s.108(2), Sch.16
		Sch.28AA excl.	36, s.108(6)
		Sch.28AA appl.	36, s.108(7)
		Sch.28B, para.3 am. (6.4.1998) (*retrosp.*)	36, s.73(3)(6)
		Sch.28B, para.4(2)(ea)- (ee) added (17.3.1998)	36, s.70, Sch.12, paras.3(1),5(1)
		Sch.28B, para.4(2)(f) am. (17.3.1998)	36, s.70, Sch.12, paras.3(2),5(2)
		Sch.28B, para.4(3A) added (17.3.1998)	36, s.70, Sch.12, paras.3(3),5(2)
		Sch.28B, para.5(1) (defn. of "nursing home") added (17.3.1998)	36, s.70, Sch.12, paras.4(1),5(2)
		Sch.28B, para.5(1) (defn. of "property development") added (17.3.1998)	36, s.70, Sch.12, paras.4(2),5(2)
		Sch.28B, para.5(1) (defn. of "residential care home") added (17.3.1998)	36, s.70, Sch.12, paras.4(3),5(2)
		Sch.28B, para.5(5) (defn. of "interest in land") added (17.3.1998)	36, s.70, Sch.12, paras.4(4),5(2)
		Sch.28B, para.5(6)(7) added (17.3.1998)	36, s.70, Sch.12, paras.4(5),5(2)
		Sch.28B, para.6(1)(b)(2A) (c)(2B)(5) am. (6.4.1998) (*retrosp.*)	36, s.73(4)(6)
		Sch.28B, para.8(1) am. (6.4.1998) (*retrosp.*)	36, s.73(5)(6)
		Sch.28B, para.10(3) am. (6.4.1998) (*retrosp.*)	36, s.73(2)(6)
		Sch.28B, para.10A added (2.7.1997) (*retrosp.*)	36, s.72(1)(3)(4)
		Sch.28B, para.10B added (2.7.1997) (*retrosp.*)	36, s.72(2)(3)(4)
		Sch.28B, para.10B mod.	36, s.72(5)(6)
		Sch.28B, para.12(a) am.	36, s.70(3)(4)
		Sch.29, para.10(3) rep.in pt.	36, s.165, Sch.27, Pt.III(28), Note

Year and Chap. or No. of Measure	Short title	How affected	1998, Chapter of Act or Number of Measure or Statutory Instrument
1988—*cont.*			
		Sch.29, para.10(7) rep.	36, s.165, Sch.27, Pt.III(28), Note
		Sch.A subst.	36, s.38, Sch.5, Pt.I, paras.1,73
c.4	Norfolk and Suffolk Broads Act 1988	s.17(10) rep.	18, s.54(3), Sch.5
		s.17(11) am.	18, s.54(1), Sch.3, para.14
		s.17(12) rep.	18, s.54(3), Sch.5
		s.25 (defn. of "participating authority") appl.	18, s.53(4)(a)
c.9	Local Government Act 1988	s.16(1) am. (EW)	18, s.54(1), Sch.3, para.15
		s.30 rep. (EW)	18, s.54(3), Sch.5
		Sch.1, para.8(5) am. (*prosp.*)	31, s.140(1), Sch.30, para.15
		Sch.4 rep. (EW)	18, s.54(3), Sch.5
c.13	Coroners Act 1988	s.1(1)(a)(c) am.	SI 465, reg.2(2)(3)
		s.1(1A)(a)(b) am.	SI 465, reg.2(4)(5)
		s.2(2) am.	SI 465, reg.2(6)
		s.4(1) am.	SI 465, reg.2(7)
		s.4(5A) am.	SI 465, reg.2(8)
		s.27(4)(a) am.	SI 465, reg.2(9)
		s.31(aa) added	SI 465, reg.2(10)
c.28	Access to Medical Reports Act 1988	s.2(1) (defn. of "health professional") am. (*prosp.*)	29, s.74(1), Sch.15, para.8
c.33	Criminal Justice Act 1988	s.40 mod. (4.1.1999)	37, s.52(6), Sch.3, para.6(8)
		s.40(1) am. (4.1.1999)	37, s.119, Sch.8, para.66
		s.69(2) rep. (*prosp.*)	37, s.120(2), Sch.10
		s.71(9A) added	37, ss.83,120(1), Sch.9, para.8
		s.74(2)(c) rep.in pt.	40, s.9(1)(2), Sch.1, Pt.I, para.1, Sch.2, Pt.I
		s.74(2)(e) added	40, s.9(1), Sch.1, Pt.I, para.1
		ss.93H,93I restr.	35, s.14(3)(b)
		s.93J restr.	35, s.14(3)(c)
		Sch.11, para.8 rep.	18, s.54(3), Sch.5
		Sch.15, para.40 rep.	37, ss.106,120(2), Sch.7, para.39, Sch.10
c.34	Legal Aid Act 1988	ss.19-26 (Pt.V) mod. (in force 30/9/1998 in areas specified in SI 1998/2327, Sch.2) (pt.prosp.)	37, s.49(1)
		s.20(4)(aa) added (4.1.1999)	37, s.119, Sch.8, para.67(1)
		s.20(5A) added (4.1.1999)	37, s.119, Sch.8, para.67(2)
		s.21(3)(a) am. (4.1.1999)	37, s.119, Sch.8, para.67(3)
		s.21(4) am. (4.1.1999)	37, s.119, Sch.8, para.67(4)

Year and Chap. or No. of Measure	Short title	How affected	1998, Chapter of Act or Number of Measure or Statutory Instrument
1988—_cont._ c.36	Court of Session Act 1988	s.1(1) mod.	42, s.18(4)(b)
		Sch.18 restr.	36, s.113, Sch.17, paras.11,37 (adding 1988 c.1, s.754B)
		Sch.18, para.10 excl.	36, s.113, Sch.17, paras.35(7),37 (adding 1988 c.1, Sch.26, para.3(6A))
c.39	Finance Act 1988	s.42 appl.	36, s.38, Sch.5, Pt.I, paras.4,73 (replacing 1988 c.1, s.21 at s.21A(2))
		s.44 appl.	36, s.38, Sch.5, Pt.I, paras.4,73 (replacing 1988 c.1, s.21 at s.21B)
		s.46(1)(2) appl.	36, s.38, Sch.5, Pt.I, paras.4,73 (replacing 1988 c.1, s.21 at s.21A(2))
		s.67 rep.	36, s.165, Sch.27, Pt.III(11), Note
		s.73(2) appl.	36, s.38, Sch.5, Pt.I, paras.4,73 (replacing 1988 c.1, s.21 at s.21A(2))
		s.73(2) am.	36, s.46(3), Sch.7, para.2
		s.74 rep.	36, s.165, Sch.27, Pt.III(9), Note
		s.121 rep.	36, s.165, Sch.27, Pt.III(28), Note
		Sch.6 appl.	36, s.38, Sch.5, Pt.I, paras.4,73 (replacing 1988 c.1, s.21 at s.21B)
		Sch.12, para.2(2) am.	36, s.46(3), Sch.7, para.2
c.40	Education Reform Act 1988	defn. of "higher education corporation" appl.	30, s.44(1), Sch.3, para.9 (adding 1993 c.10, s.3(5A)(a))
		power to am. (_prosp._)	31, s.137(2)
		s.125A added	30, s.41(1)
		ss.166,167 rep. (_prosp._)	31, s.140(3), Sch.31
		s.182(1)(2)(3) am.	18, s.54(1), Sch.3, para.16(2)(3)(4)
		s.191(5) am.	18, s.54(1), Sch.3, para.17
		s.197 power to am. (_prosp._)	31, s.137(4)
		s.197(7) rep.in pt. (_prosp._)	31, s.140(3), Sch.31
		s.198 appl.(mods.) (_prosp._)	31, s.74, Sch.21, Pt.I, para.2(3)
		s.198 power to am. (_prosp._)	31, s.137(4)
		s.198(1)-(4) replaced (by s.198(1)(1A)(2)(3)(4)) (_prosp._)	31, s.137, Sch.29, para.2(1)(2)
		s.198(5)(6) am. (_prosp._)	31, s.137, Sch.29, para.2(1)(3)

Year and Chap. or No. of Measure	Short title	How affected	1998, Chapter of Act or Number of Measure or Statutory Instrument
1988—*cont.*			
		s.209 rep. (*prosp.*)	30, s.44(2), Sch.4
		s.218(1)(aa) added (*prosp.*)	30, s.11
		s.218(1)(ab) added (*prosp.*)	30, s.18(1)(2)
		s.218(1)(c) rep.in pt.	30, s.44(2), Sch.4
		s.218(2) (defn. of "qualified teacher") appl. (*prosp.*)	30, s.3(3)
		s.218(2AA) added (*prosp.*)	30, s.13
		s.218(2C)-(2F) added (*prosp.*)	30, s.18(3)
		s.218(9)(b) am. (*prosp.*)	30, s.18(4)
		s.218(12) subst. (*prosp.*)	31, s.140(1), Sch.30, para.17
		s.218(14) added (*prosp.*)	30, s.18(5)
		s.220 rep.	18, s.54(3), Sch.5
		s.221(1)(b) am. (*prosp.*)	31, s.140(1), Sch.30, para.18
		s.223 rep.in pt.	29, s.74(2), Sch.16
		s.226(4) am. (*prosp.*)	31, s.140(1), Sch.30, para.19
		s.232(6) rep.in pt.	30, s.44(1)(2), Sch.3, para.6, Sch.4
		s.236(1) rep.in pt. (*prosp.*)	31, s.140(3), Sch.31
		Sch.8 power to am. (*prosp.*)	31, s.137(4)
		Sch.8, para.6(3) rep.	31, s.140(1)(3), Sch.30, para.20(a), Sch.31
		Sch.8, para.8(4) rep.in pt.	31, s.140(1)(3), Sch.30, para.20(b)(i), Sch.31
		Sch.8, para.8(7) rep.	31, s.140(1), Sch.30, para.20(b)(ii)
		Sch.10 appl.(mods.) (*prosp.*)	31, s.74, Sch.21, Pt.I, para.2(3)
		Sch.10 am. (*prosp.*)	31, s.137, Sch.29, para.10
		Sch.10 power to am. (*prosp.*)	31, s.137(4)
		Sch.10, para.1 subst. (*prosp.*)	31, s.137, Sch.29, para.3
		Sch.10, para.2 subst. (*prosp.*)	31, s.137, Sch.29, para.4
		Sch.10, para.3 subst. (*prosp.*)	31, s.137, Sch.29, para.5
		Sch.10, para.5 am. (*prosp.*)	31, s.137, Sch.29, para.6
		Sch.10, paras.6-8 appl. (*prosp.*)	31, s.76, Sch.22, Pt.III, para.9(2)
		Sch.10, para.7 am. (*prosp.*)	31, s.137, Sch.29, para.7
		Sch.10, para.9(6)(a)(b) am. (*prosp.*)	31, s.137, Sch.29, para.8(a)(b)
		Sch.10, para.9(9) am. (*prosp.*)	31, s.137, Sch.29, para.8(c)
		Sch.10, para.10 am. (*prosp.*)	31, s.137, Sch.29, para.9
		Sch.12, paras.11,13,15,16, 18-22,30,31,36 rep. (*prosp.*)	31, s.140(3), Sch.31
c.41	Local Government Finance Act 1988	ss.41-67 (Pt.III) mod. (*prosp.*)	31, s.78
		s.79 appl. (defn. of "Revenue Support Grant")	SI 655, reg.5(2)
		ss.114-116 saved	18, s.11(9)

Year and Chap. or No. of Measure	Short title	How affected	1998, Chapter of Act or Number of Measure or Statutory Instrument
1988—*cont.*			
		Sch.4, para.6(2)(a) am. (*prosp.*)	14, s.86(1), Sch.7, para.17
		Sch.12, para.3 rep. (EW)	18, s.54(3), Sch.5
c.43	Housing (Scotland) Act 1988	Sch.5, Ground 15 subst.	37, s.23(4)
		Sch.5, Ground 15 restr.	37, s.23(5)
c.48	Copyright, Designs and Patents Act 1988	s.12(9) am. (6.5.1999)	46, s.125, Sch.8, para.25(2)
		s.12(9) am. (*prosp.*)	47, s.99, Sch.13, para.8(2)
		s.49 am. (*prosp.*)	38, s.125, Sch.12, para.27
		s.153(2) am. (6.5.1999)	46, s.125, Sch.8, para.25(3)
		s.153(2) am. (*prosp.*)	47, s.99, Sch.13, para.8(3)
		s.163(1A) added (*prosp.*)	38, s.125, Sch.12, para.28
		s.163(6) am. (6.5.1999)	46, s.125, Sch.8, para.25(4)
		s.163(6) am. (*prosp.*)	47, s.99, Sch.13, para.8(4)
		s.164(1) am. (6.5.1999)	46, s.125, Sch.8, para.25(5)
		s.164(1) am. (*prosp.*)	47, s.99, Sch.13, para.8(5)
		s.166A added (6.5.1999)	46, s.125, Sch.8, para.25(6)
		s.166B added (*prosp.*)	47, s.99, Sch.13, para.8(6)
		s.178 (defn. of "parliamentary proceedings") am.	12, s.1, Sch., para.9
		s.178 (defns. of "the Crown" and "parliamentary proceedings") am. (6.5.1999)	46, s.125, Sch.8, para.25(7)
		s.178 (defn. of "parliamentary proceedings") rep.in pt. (*prosp.*)	47, s.99, Sch.13, para.8(7)
		s.179 am. (6.5.1999)	46, s.125, Sch.8, para.25(8)
		s.179 am. (*prosp.*)	47, s.99, Sch.13, para.8(8)
		ss.274-286 (Pt.V) (defn. of "registered patent agents") appl. (11.1.1999)	41, s.3(1)(d), Sch.4, Pt.II, para.20
		ss.274-286 (Pt.V) (defn. of "European list") appl. (11.1.1999)	41, s.3(1)(d), Sch.4, Pt.II, para.21
		Sch.2, para.10(1) am. (*prosp.*)	38, s.125, Sch.12, para.29
c.50	Housing Act 1988	excl.	38, s.127, Sch.13, para.3 (adding 1975 c.70, Sch.4, at Pt.IV, para.16)
		excl. (pt.prosp.)	45, s.23, Sch.6, para.5
		s.35(4)(a) am.	38, s.129, Sch.15, para.15
		s.35(5) am.	38, s.140, Sch.16, para.60
		s.38(5)(c) rep.	38, s.152, Sch.18, Pt.IV
		ss.46-59 (Pt.II) am. (EW)	38, s.140, Sch.16, para.61

Year and Chap. or No. of Measure	Short title	How affected	1998, Chapter of Act or Number of Measure or Statutory Instrument
1988—*cont.*			
		s.46 rep.	38, ss.140,152, Sch.16, para.62, Sch.18, Pt.VI
		s.47 rep.	38, ss.140,152, Sch.16, para.63, Sch.18, Pt.VI
		s.50(5) subst. (EW)	38, s.140, Sch.16, para.64(2)
		s.50(8) am. (EW)	38, s.140, Sch.16, para.64(3)
		s.53(2) am. (EW)	38, s.140, Sch.16, para.65
		s.57 am. (EW)	38, s.140, Sch.16, para.66
		s.59(2)(b) rep.in pt.	38, ss.140,152, Sch.16, para.67(a), Sch.18, Pt.VI
		s.59(2)(c) am.	38, s.140, Sch.16, para.67(b)
		s.81(6) am.	38, s.140, Sch.16, para.68(a)
		s.81(7) am.	38, s.140, Sch.16, para.68(b)
		s.82(2)(3)(4) am.	38, s.140, Sch.16, para.69(2)
		s.82(5) am.	38, s.140, Sch.16, para.69(3)
		s.82 sidenote am.	38, s.140, Sch.16, para.69(2)
		s.92(2) rep.	38, ss.140,152, Sch.16, para.70, Sch.18, Pt.VI
		s.133(6) rep.in pt.	38, ss.140,152, Sch.16, para.71(a), Sch.18, Pt.VI
		s.133(7) am.	38, s.140, Sch.16, para.71(b)
		s.140(1) rep.in pt.	38, ss.140,152, Sch.16, para.72, Sch.18, Pt.VI
		Sch.1, Pt.I, para.12(1)(c) rep.	38, s.152, Sch.18, Pt.IV
		Sch.5 rep.	38, ss.140,152, Sch.16, para.73, Sch.18, Pt.VI
		Sch.6, Pt.I, para.2 rep.	38, s.152, Sch.18, Pt.VI
		Sch.6, Pt.II, para.30(1) rep.in pt.	38, s.152, Sch.18, Pt.VI
		Sch.6, Pt.II, para.30(1) (b) rep.	38, s.152, Sch.18, Pt.VI
		Sch.17, Pt.II, para.91 rep.	43, s.1(1), Sch.1, Pt.IV, Group 2
		Sch.17, Pt.II, para.97 rep.	38, s.152, Sch.18, Pt.IV
		Sch.17, para.80 rep. (*prosp.*)	29, s.74(2), Sch.16, Pt.I
c.52	Road Traffic Act 1988	saved (6.5.1999)	46, s.30, Sch.5, Pt.II, s.E1(d)
		ss.39,40 trans.of functions (1.7.1999)	46, ss.53,56(1)(i)
		s.88(1)(b)(ii) subst.	SI 1420, reg.3(1)(2)
		s.88(2) am.	SI 1420, reg.3(1)(3)

Year and Chap. or No. of Measure	Short title	How affected	1998, Chapter of Act or Number of Measure or Statutory Instrument
1988—*cont.*			
		s.92(5)(a) rep.in pt.	SI 1420, reg.17, Sch.
		s.92(5)(c) added	SI 1420, reg.4(1)(2)
		s.92(7)(7A) replaced (by (7)(7ZA)(7ZB)(7A))	SI 1420, reg.4(1)(3)
		s.93(2A) added	SI 1420, reg.5
		s.97(1A) added	SI 1420, reg.6(1)(2)
		s.97(3)(e) am.	SI 1420, reg.6(1)(3)
		s.97(3A) am.	SI 1420, reg.6(1)(4)
		s.97(4) am.	SI 1420, reg.6(1)(5)
		s.98(1) replaced (by (1) (1A))	SI 1420, reg.7(1)(2)
		s.98(3)(c) am.	SI 1420, reg.7(1)(3)
		s.99(2) am.	SI 1420, reg.8(1)(2)
		s.99(2A) added	SI 1420, reg.8(1)(3)
		s.99(4) rep.in pt.	SI 1420, reg.8(1)(4)
		s.99(5) am.	SI 1420, reg.8(1)(5)
		s.99(7)(8) replaced (by (7)(7A)(7B)(8))	SI 1420, reg.8(1)(6)
		s.99A(4)(a) subst.	SI 1420, reg.9
		s.105(2)(e) rev.in pt. & am.	SI 1420, reg.10(1)(2)
		s.105(2)(e) rep.in pt.	SI 1420, reg.17, Sch.
		s.105(4) am.	SI 1420, reg.10(1)(3)
		s.108(1) (defn. of "motor bicycle") am.	SI 1420, reg.11
		s.108(1) am.	SI 1917, art.2(2)
		s.108(2) replaced (by s.108(2)(2A)(2B))	SI 1917, art.2(3)
		s.117A(3) replaced (by (3) (3A))	SI 1420, reg.12
		s.118(4A) added	SI 1420, reg.13
		s.164(3) am.	SI 1420, reg.14
		s.170 saved (*prosp.*)	34, s.8(3)
		s.183(4) am.	SI 1420, reg.15
c.53	Road Traffic Offenders Act 1988	saved (6.5.1999)	46, s.30, Sch.5, Pt.II, s.E1(d)
		s.8 am.	15, s.4(1)(a)
		s.13(3A)(3B) added	15, s.2(1)
		s.13(4)(a) am.	15, s.2(2)
		s.25(2)(a) am.	15, s.4(1)(a)
		s.36(11A) subst.	SI 1917, art.3
		Schs.1,2, Pt.I am.	SI 1420, reg.16
c.54	Road Traffic (Consequential Provisions) Act 1988	Sch.3, para.19 rep. (*prosp.*)	41, s.74(1)(3), Sch.12, para.12, Sch.14, Pt.I
c.i	Greater Manchester (Light Rapid Transit System) Act 1988	s.41 excl.	SI 1936(L), art.42(23)(a)
		s.42 appl.(mods.)	SI 1936(L), art.42(23)(b)
		s.47 ext.	SI 2919(L), art.10(8)

Year and Chap. or No. of Measure	Short title	How affected	1998, Chapter of Act or Number of Measure or Statutory Instrument
1989			
c.1	Petroleum Royalties (Relief) and Continental Shelf Act 1989	s.1 am. (*prosp.*)	17, s.49, Sch.3, Pt.II, para.8(1)
		s.1(3) (defn. of "petroleum") am. (*prosp.*)	17, s.50, Sch.4, para.26
		s.2 am. (*prosp.*)	17, s.49, Sch.3, Pt.II, para.8(1)
c.4	Prevention of Terrorism (Temporary Provisions) Act 1989	s.2(1) restr.	35, s.14(2)(a)
		ss.2A,2B added	40, s.1(1)
		ss.3,9,10,11 restr.	35, s.14(2)(a)
		s.14(1)(a) am.	40, s.3(1)(2)
		s.15(7)(c) subst. (*prosp.*)	SI 1504, art.65(1), Sch.5, para.39
		s.18 restr.	35, s.14(2)(a)
		s.27 am.	40, s.1(2)
		s.27(5) appl.(mods.)	40, s.4(9)(a)
		s.27(11) am.	9, s.7(1), Sch.1, para.1
		Sch.3, para.3(3)(a)(i) am.	40, s.9(1), Sch.1, Pt.I, para.2
		Sch.4 appl.(mods.)	40, s.4(7)
		Sch.7, paras.2,2A,3,5,6, 11A,12,14,15 restr.	35, s.14(3)(a)
c.6	Official Secrets Act 1989	ext.	38, s.53(4)
		ext.	38, s.90(7)
		ext.	38, s.92(7)
		ext. (*prosp.*)	38, s.111, Sch.9, Pt.I, para.2(3)
		ext. (*prosp.*)	38, s.112, Sch.10, para.17 (adding 1993 c.46 Sch.1A, at para.2(2))
		saved (6.5.1999)	46, s.30, Sch.5, Pt.II, s.B8(b)
		s.12(1)(aa) added (6.5.1999)	46, s.125, Sch.8, para.26(2)
		s.12(1)(b) rep. (*prosp.*)	47, ss.99,100(2), Sch.13, para.9(2), Sch.15
		s.12(1)(e) am. (*prosp.*)	32, s.74(1), Sch.4, para.17
		s.12(2)(a) am. (6.5.1999)	46, s.125, Sch.8, para.26(3)
		s.12(2)(aa) added (*prosp.*)	38, s.125, Sch.12, para.30
		s.12(4) added (6.5.1999)	46, s.125, Sch.8, para.26(4)
		s.12(5) added (*prosp.*)	47, s.99, Sch.13, para.9(3)
c.15	Water Act 1989	s.174(3)(d)(e) rep. (*prosp.*)	41, ss.66(5),74(3), Sch.10, Pt.IV, para.11(a), Sch.14, Pt.I
		s.174(3)(ll) added (11.1.1999)	41, s.66(5), Sch.10, Pt.IV, para.11(b)
		Sch.25, para.1(2)(xxii) rep.	38, s.152, Sch.18, Pt.IV
		Sch.25, para.1(2)(xxiv) am.	38, s.135(2)(a)

Year and Chap. or No. of Measure	Short title	How affected	1998, Chapter of Act or Number of Measure or Statutory Instrument
1989—*cont.*			
		Sch.25, para.3 rep.	43, s.1(1), Sch.1, Pt.X, Group 3
		Sch.25, para.54 rep.	38, s.152, Sch.18, Pt.IV
		Sch.25, para.61(3)(7) rep.	38, s.152, Sch.18, Pt.V
		Sch.25, para.(10)(vi) rep.	38, s.152, Sch.18, Pt.IV
		Sch.26, para.46 rep.	43, s.1(1), Sch.1, Pt.X, Group 3
c.22	Road Traffic (Driver Licensing and Information Systems) Act 1989	s.5(3) rep.	SI 1420, reg.17, Sch.
		Sch.3, paras.27(d),28(b) rep.in pt.	SI 1420, reg.17, Sch.
c.24	Social Security Act 1989	power to am. (*prosp.*)	47, s.87
		s.25 (defn. of "war pension") appl.	14, s.2(3)
c.26	Finance Act 1989	appt. day(s) for s.178(1) [9.3.1998] (for ss.59C & 103A of 1970 c.9)	SI 311, s.2
		s.43 appl.	36, s.38, Sch.5, Pt.I, paras.4,73 (replacing 1988 c.1, s.21 at s.21A(2))
		s.43 excl.	36, s.38, Sch.5, Pt.IV, paras.66(2),69
		s.67(2)(a) am.	36, s.46(3), Sch.7, para.3
		s.76 appl.	36, s.38, Sch.5, Pt.I, paras.4,73 (replacing 1988 c.1, s.21 at s.21A(2))
		s.76(1)(4)(a) am.	36, s.46(3), Sch.7, para.3
		s.80 rep.	36, s.165, Sch.27, Pt.III(23)
		ss.97,98,99(2) rep. (6.4.1999)	36, s.165, Sch.27, Pt.III(2), Note
		s.102 appl.(mods.) (7.1.1999)	SI 3175, reg.9
		s.112 appl.	36, s.38, Sch.5, Pt.I, paras.4,73 (replacing 1988 c.1, s.21 at s.21A(2))
		s.112(1) am.	36, s.46(3), Sch.7, para.3
		s.113 appl.	36, s.38, Sch.5, Pt.I, paras.4,73 (replacing 1988 c.1, s.21 at s.21A(2))
		s.149(3)(c) rep. (6.4.1999)	36, s.165, Sch.27, Pt.III(2), Note
		s.151(2) subst. (6.4.1998)	36, s.86, Sch.14, paras.6, 7(3)(4)(5)
		s.182(4)(a)(i) rep.in pt. (*prosp.*)	38, s.152, Sch.18, Pt.I
		s.182(4)(a)(iii)(iv) added (*prosp.*)	38, s.125, Sch.12, para.31(2)

Year and Chap. or No. of Measure	Short title	How affected	1998, Chapter of Act or Number of Measure or Statutory Instrument
1989—*cont.*			
		s.182(6) am. (*prosp.*)	38, s.125, Sch.12, para.31(3)
		Sch.17, Pt.II rep.	SI 1446, art.30(2), Sch.2, Pt.I
c.29	Electricity Act 1989	ss.1-64 (Pt.I) defn(s). appl. (*prosp.*)	41, s.74(2), Sch.13, Pt.IV, Ch.IV, para.28(7)
		s.3(6A)(6B) added (pt.prosp.)	41, s.66(5), Sch.10, Pt.II, para.4(3)
		s.12(8)(9) replaced (by s.12(8)(8A)(9)(9A)) (*prosp.*)	41, s.66(5), Sch.10, Pt.IV, para.12(2)
		s.13(2) rep. (*prosp.*)	41, ss.66(5),74(3), Sch.10, Pt.IV, para.12(3), Sch.14, Pt.I
		s.15(1) rep.in pt. (*prosp.*)	41, ss.66(5),74(3), Sch.10, Pt.IV, para.12(4)(a), Sch.14, Pt.I
		s.15(1)(b) rep. (*prosp.*)	41, ss.66(5),74(3), Sch.10, Pt.IV, para.12(4)(a), Sch.14, Pt.I
		s.15(2) rep.in pt. (*prosp.*)	41, ss.66(5),74(3), Sch.10, Pt.IV, para.12(4)(b)(ii), Sch.14, Pt.I
		s.15(2) am. (*prosp.*)	41, s.66(5), Sch.10, Pt.IV, para.12(4)(b)(i)
		s.15(2)(c) rep. (*prosp.*)	41, ss.66(5),74(3), Sch.10, Pt.IV, para.12(4)(b)(ii), Sch.14, Pt.I
		s.15(3) rep.in pt. (*prosp.*)	41, ss.66(5),74(3), Sch.10, Pt.IV, para.12(4)(c), Sch.14, Pt.I
		s.25(5) rep.in pt. (*prosp.*)	41, ss.66(5),74(3), Sch.10, Pt.IV, para.12(5), Sch.14, Pt.I
		s.25(5)(d) added (*prosp.*)	41, s.66(5), Sch.10, Pt.IV, para.12(5)
		s.33(8) (defns. of "leviable electricity" and "non-fossil fuel generating station") replaced (by defn. "leviable electricity")	5, s.1(2)
		s.33(9) added	5, s.1(3)
		s.43(3) restr. (pt.prosp.)	41, s.66(5), Sch.10, Pt.II, para.4(1)
		s.43(3) replaced (by s.43(3)(3A)) (pt.prosp.)	41, s.66(5), Sch.10, Pt.II, para.4(5)
		s.43(4) rep.in pt. (pt.prosp.)	41, ss.66(5),74(3), Sch.10, Pt.II, para.4(6), Sch.14, Pt.I
		s.43(4)(c) rep. (pt.prosp.)	41, ss.66(5),74(3), Sch.10, Pt.II, para.4(6), Sch.14, Pt.I

Year and Chap. or No. of Measure	Short title	How affected	1998, Chapter of Act or Number of Measure or Statutory Instrument
1989—*cont.*			
		s.43(5) rep.in pt. (pt.prosp.)	41, ss.66(5),74(3), Sch.10, Pt.II, para.4(7), Sch.14, Pt.I
		s.43(6)(b) subst. (pt.prosp.)	41, s.66(5), Sch.10, Pt.II, para.4(8)
		s.43(6A) added (*prosp.*)	41, s.66(5), Sch.10, Pt.IV, para.12(6)
		s.43(7) rep.in pt. (pt.prosp.)	41, ss.66(5),74(3), Sch.10, Pt.II, para.4(9), Sch.14, Pt.I
		s.57(3)(d)(e) rep. (*prosp.*)	41, ss.66(5),74(3), Sch.10, Pt.IV, para.12(7)(a), Sch.14, Pt.I
		s.57(3)(nop) added (11.1.1999)	41, s.66(5), Sch.10, Pt.IV, para.12(7)(b)
		s.57(7) added (*prosp.*)	41, s.66(5), Sch.10, Pt.IV, para.12(8)
		ss.65-95 (Pt.II) saved (6.5.1999)	46, s.30, Sch.5, Pt.II, s.D1
		Sch.16, para.1(1)(xxxi) rep.	38, s.152, Sch.18, Pt.IV
		Sch.16, para.1(1)(xxxiv) am.	38, s.135(2)(b)
		Sch.16, para.3(1)(f) rep.	38, s.152, Sch.18, Pt.IV
c.32	Fair Employment (Northern Ireland) Act 1989	rep. (*prosp.*)	SI 3162, art.105(4), Sch.5
		s.1 subst. (*prosp.*)	47, s.99, Sch.13, para.10(2)
		s.9(6) am. (*prosp.*)	47, s.99, Sch.13, para.10(3)
		s.21(1) (defn. of "the Commission") rep. (*prosp.*)	47, s.100(2), Sch.15
		Sch.2, paras.5,6,22-28 rep. (*prosp.*)	47, ss.99,100(2), Sch.13, para.10(4), Sch.15
c.37	Football Spectators Act 1989	s.5(5)(6) am. (*prosp.*)	29, s.74(1), Sch.15, para.9
		s.16(5) am.	37, ss.84(1),120(1), Sch.9, para.9
c.38	Employment Act 1989	Sch.6, para.17 rep.	38, s.152, Sch.18, Pt.IV
c.39	Self-Governing Schools etc.(Scotland) Act 1989	defn. of "board of management" appl. (*prosp.*)	29, s.30(5)
		defn. of "board of management" appl.	29, s.68(1)(6), Sch.11, para.6(a)
c.40	Companies Act 1989	appt. day(s) for ss.185, 186 (10.8.1998) (insofar as tehy are not yet in force)	SI 1747, art.2
		s.82(2)(a)(ii) am.	11, s.23, Sch.5, Pt.IV, Ch.II, para.66(2)(a)
		s.82(5) am.	11, s.23, Sch.5, Pt.IV, Ch.II, para.66(2)(b)
		s.87(4), Table am.	11, s.23, Sch.5, Pt.IV, Ch.II, para.66(3)
		s.155(2)(a) am.	SI 1748, reg.3(a)
		s.155(2)(b) subst.	SI 1748, reg.3(b)

Year and Chap. or No. of Measure	Short title	How affected	1998, Chapter of Act or Number of Measure or Statutory Instrument
1989—*cont.*			
		s.155(3) subst.	SI 1748, reg.4
		s.171 trans.of functions	11, s.21(c)
		s.171(1)(2) am.	11, s.23, Sch.1, Pt.III, para.47(2)(3)
		s.171(2A) added	11, s.23, Sch.1, Pt.III, para.47(4)
		s.171(3)(a) am.	11, s.23, Sch.1, Pt.III, para.47(5)
		s.171(3A)(3B) added	11, s.26(3)
		s.171(3C) added	11, s.23, Sch.1, Pt.III, para.47(6)
		s.171(4) am.	11, s.23, Sch.1, Pt.III, para.47(7)
		s.171(6) am.	11, s.23, Sch.1, Pt.III, para.47(8)
		s.171(6A) added	11, s.25(3)
		s.176(2)(b) am.	11, s.23, Sch.1, Pt.III, para.48(2)
		s.176(6) replaced (by s.176(6)(6A))	11, s.23, Sch.1, Pt.III, para.48(3)
		s.207(10) added	11, s.35
		s.213(7) rep.in pt. (*prosp.*)	47, s.100(2), Sch.15
		Sch.14, para.9 subst. (*prosp.*)	41, s.3(1)(b), Sch.2, Pt.II, para.2(2)
		Sch.20, paras.21-24 rep. (*prosp.*)	41, s.74(1)(3), Sch.12, para.13, Sch.14, Pt.I
		Sch.21, para.1(4)(5) am.	SI 1748, reg.5(1)(2)
		Sch.21, para.7 subst.	SI 1748, reg.6
c.41	Children Act 1989	ext.	37, s.11(6)
		defn. of "local authority" appl.	37, s.11(7)
		defn. of "local authority" appl.	37, ss.68(3),70(5), Sch.5, para.1
		defn. of "local authority" appl.	37, s.116(2) (modifying 1994 c.33, ss.2,4)
		defn. of "local authority" appl.	37, s.116(5)
		s.8(1) (defn. of "residence order") appl.	37, s.106, Sch.7, para.10 (substituting 1969 c.54, s.70(1B))
		s.8(4)(i) added	37, s.119, Sch.8, para.68
		s.31(1)(a) ext.	37, s.12(6)(7)
		s.31(2) mod.	37, s.12(7)
		s.47(1) am.	37, s.15(4)(b)
		s.47(1)(a)(iii) added	37, s.15(4)(a)
		s.47(3) am.	37, s.119, Sch.8, para.69
		Sch.9, para.3(1)(f) rep. (*prosp.*)	31, s.140(3), Sch.31
		Sch.9, para.3(3) (defns. of "assisted" and "maintained") subst. (*prosp.*)	31, s.140(1), Sch.30, para.21

Effects of Legislation

Year and Chap. or No. of Measure	Short title	How affected	1998, Chapter of Act or Number of Measure or Statutory Instrument
1989—*cont.*			
		Sch.9, para.3(3) (defn. of "grant maintained") rep. (*prosp.*)	31, s.140(3), Sch.31
c.42	Local Government and Housing Act 1989	s.5 saved (EW)	18, s.11(9)
		s.11(1) rep.in pt.	18, s.54(1)(3), Sch.3, para.18(1)(a), Sch.5
		s.11(3) (defn. of "relevant body") am.	18, s.54(1), Sch.3, para.18(1)(b)
		s.13(5) am. (*prosp.*)	31, s.140(1), Sch.30, para.22
		s.19 referred to	SI 633, art.E7(1)
		s.66(5)(b) rep.in pt.	18, s.54(1)(3), Sch.3, para.18(2), Sch.5
		s.68(1) appl.	18, s.45(5)
		s.70(2)(4) am.	18, s.54(1), Sch.3, para.18(3)
		s.80 power to restr.	38, s.22(5), Sch.3, Pt.II, para.8
		s.90(2) rep.in pt.	38, s.152, Sch.18, Pt.IV
		s.90(2)(c) am.	38, s.129, Sch.15, para.16
		s.90(2)(e) rep.	38, s.152, Sch.18, Pt.IV
		s.172(2)(b) rep.in pt.	38, ss.140,152, Sch.16, para.75, Sch.18, Pt.VI
		s.172(8) rep.in pt.	38, s.152, Sch.18, Pt.IV
		s.173(6) rep.in pt.	38, ss.140,152, Sch.16, para.76(2), Sch.18, Pt.VI
		s.173(7) am.	38, s.140, Sch.16, para.76(3)
		s.184(2) rep.	18, s.54(3), Sch.5
		Sch.11, para.82 rep.	38, s.152, Sch.18, Pt.IV
c.44	Opticians Act 1989	saved (6.5.1999)	46, s.30, Sch.5, Pt.II, s.G2(f)
		s.36(1) (defn. of "a registered optician") appl.	29, s.69(1)(c)
		Sch.1, para.1(a) am. (1.1.1999)	SI 3117, art.2(2)(a)
		Sch.1, para.1(b) am. (1.1.2002)	SI 3117, art.3(2)(a)
		Sch.1, para.1(c) am. (1.1.2002)	SI 3117, art.3(2)(b)
		Sch.1, para.1(d) am. (1.1.1999)	SI 3117, art.2(2)(a)
		Sch.1, para.1(d) am. (1.1.1999)	SI 3117, art.2(2)(b)
		Sch.1, para.1(d) added (1.1.2002)	SI 3117, art.3(2)(c)
		Sch.1, para.1(e) am. (1.1.1999)	SI 3117, art.2(2)(c)
		Sch.1, para.4 rep.in pt. (1.1.2002)	SI 3117, art.3(2)(d)

Year and Chap. or No. of Measure	Short title	How affected	1998, Chapter of Act or Number of Measure or Statutory Instrument
1989—*cont.*			
		Sch.1, para.4(a) am. (1.1.1999)	SI 3117, art.2(2)(d)(i)
		Sch.1, para.4(b) rep. (1.1.2002)	SI 3117, art.3(2)(d)
		Sch.1, para.4(c) subst. (1.1.1999)	SI 3117, art.2(2)(d)(ii)
		Sch.1, para.4(d) added (1.1.2002)	SI 3117, art.3(2)(e)
		Sch.1, para.5 subst. (1.1.1999)	SI 3117, art.2(2)(e)
		Sch.1, para.6(1)(c) am. (1.1.1999)	SI 3117, art.2(2)(f)
		Sch.1, para.6(2) am. (1.1.1999)	SI 3117, art.2(2)(g)
		Sch.1, para.6(2A) added (1.1.1999)	SI 3117, art.2(2)(h)
c.45	Prisons (Scotland) Act 1989	s.2 rep. (1.7.1999)	46, s.125, Sch.8, para.27(2), Sch.9
		s.3(1) am. (1.7.1999)	46, s.125, Sch.8, para.27(3)
		s.3(1A) added (1.7.1999)	46, s.125, Sch.8, para.27(3)
		s.3(2) excl.	SI 2251, art.16(1)
		s.3A mod.	SI 2251, art.16(2)
		s.3A(2) am. (1.7.1999)	46, s.125, Sch.8, para.27(4)(a)
		s.3A(4) am. (1.7.1999)	46, s.125, Sch.8, para.27(4)(b)
		ss.7,8,9 excl.	SI 2251, art.16(1)
		s.10 excl.	SI 2251, art.16(5)
		s.16(1) am.	37, s.119, Sch.8, para.70(2)
		s.16(3) added	37, s.119, Sch.8, para.70(3)
		s.34 mod.	SI 2251, art.16(3)
		ss.36-38 excl.	SI 2251, art.16(1)
		s.39(7) rep.in pt.	37, ss.119,120(2), Sch.8, para.71(a), Sch.10
		s.39(7) am.	37, s.119, Sch.8, para.71(a)
		s.39(7A)(7B) added	37, s.119, Sch.8, para.71(b)
		ss.40,40A,41,41A excl.	SI 2251, art.16(1)
c.xviii	Scottish Episcopal Clergy Widows' and Orphans' Fund Order Confirmation Act 1989	rep.	43, s.1(1), Sch.1, Pt.VII, Group 1
1990			
c.1	Capital Allowances Act 1990	saved	36, s.108, Sch.16 (adding 1988 c.1, Sch.28AA at para.13)

Year and Chap. or No. of Measure	Short title	How affected	1998, Chapter of Act or Number of Measure or Statutory Instrument
1990—*cont.*			
		restr.	36, s.117, Sch.18, Pt.IX, para.78
		s.9 subst.	36, s.38, Sch.5, Pt.III, paras.47,73
		s.12 am.	36, s.46(3), Sch.7, para.4
		s.15(2)(2A)(3) rep.	36, ss.38,165, Sch.5, Pt.III, paras.48,73, Sch.27, Pt.III(4), Note
		s.15A rep.	36, ss.38,165, Sch.5, Pt.III, paras.50,73, Sch.27, Pt.III(4), Note
		s.15ZA rep.	36, s.38, Sch.5, Pt.III, paras.49,73
		ss.17(1),18(13) am.	36, s.46(3), Sch.7, para.4
		s.22(1) am. (every chargeable period ending on or after 2.7.1998)	36, s.84(1)(3)
		s.22(3CA)-(3CC) added (have effect in relation to every chargeable period ending on or after 12.5.1998)	36, s.83(1)(6)(7)
		s.22(3D) added (every chargeable period ending on or after 2.7.1998)	36, s.84(2)(3)
		s.22(4)(6B)(6C) am. (every chargeable period ending on or after 12.5.1998)	36, s.85(1)(9)
		s.22(6D)(6E) added (have effect in relation to every chargeable period ending on or after 12.5.1998)	36, s.83(2)(6)(7)
		s.22(10) am. (have effect in relation to every chargeable period ending on or after 12.5.1998)	36, s.83(3)(6)(7)
		s.22A(4)(6) am. (in relation to expenditure incurred on or after 12.5.1998)	36, s.85(2)(10)
		s.22A(8) am. (in relation to expenditure incurred on or after 12.5.1998)	36, s.85(3)(10)
		s.22B added (have effect in relation to every chargeable period ending on or after 12.5.1998)	36, s.83(4)(6)(7)
		s.23(1)(c) am.	36, s.46(3), Sch.7, para.4
		s.23(6) am. (every chargeable period ending on or after 12.5.1998)	36, s.85(4)(9)
		s.28A(2) rep.	36, s.165, Sch.27, Pt.III(4), Note

Year and Chap. or No. of Measure	Short title	How affected	1998, Chapter of Act or Number of Measure or Statutory Instrument
1990—*cont.*			
		s.29 excl.	36, s.38, Sch.5, Pt.I, paras.25,73 (adding 1988 c.1, s.70A)
		s.29(1) rep.in pt.	36, ss.38,165, Sch.5, Pt.III, paras.51(a),73, Sch.27, Pt.III(4), Note
		s.29(1A) rep.	36, ss.38,165, Sch.5, Pt.III, paras.51(b),73, Sch.27, Pt.III(4), Note
		ss.30(4),31(10) am.	36, s.38, Sch.5, Pt.III, paras.52,73
		ss.33A(3),35(2) am.	36, s.46(3), Sch.7, para.4
		s.39(2)(a) am. (every chargeable period ending on or after 12.5.1998)	36, s.85(6)(9)
		s.42(1)(b) am.	36, s.46(3), Sch.7, para.4
		s.42(9) am. (every chargeable period ending on or after 12.5.1998)	36, s.85(4)(9)
		s.43(2) am.	36, s.46(3), Sch.7, para.4
		s.43(5) am. (every chargeable period ending on or after 12.5.1998)	36, s.85(7)(9)
		s.44(2)(a) am.	36, s.46(3), Sch.7, para.4
		s.44(5) am. (every chargeable period ending on or after 12.5.1998)	36, s.85(5)(9)
		s.45(2)(4)(5) am.	36, s.46(3), Sch.7, para.4
		ss.46(8),48(7) am. (every chargeable period ending on or after 12.5.1998)	36, s.85(5)(9)
		s.50(3)(4A) am. (every chargeable period ending on or after 12.5.1998)	36, s.85(4)(9)
		s.52(1)(a) am.	36, s.38, Sch.5, Pt.III, paras.53,73
		s.53(1)(b) rep.in pt.	36, ss.38,165, Sch.5, Pt.III, paras.54(2),73, Sch.27, Pt.III(4), Note
		s.53(1)(bb) subst.	36, s.38, Sch.5, Pt.III, paras.54(3),73
		s.53(1B)(a) am.	36, s.38, Sch.5, Pt.III, paras.54(4),73
		s.61(6) rep.	36, ss.38,165, Sch.5, Pt.III, paras.55(2),73, Sch.27, Pt.III(4), Note
		s.61(7) am.	36, s.38, Sch.5, Pt.III, paras.55(3),73
		s.62A(3)(a) am. (*prosp.*)	17, s.50, Sch.4, para.27(2)
		s.65(3) am.	36, s.46(3), Sch.7, para.4
		s.67(2)(3)(3A) rep.	36, ss.38,165, Sch.5, Pt.III, paras.56,73, Sch.27, Pt.III(4), Note

Year and Chap. or No. of Measure	Short title	How affected	1998, Chapter of Act or Number of Measure or Statutory Instrument
1990—*cont.*			
		ss.68(7)(10),69(1)(2), 70(1),71(1) am.	36, s.46(3), Sch.7, para.4
		s.73(1) am.	36, s.38, Sch.5, Pt.III, paras.57(a),73
		s.73(1A) rep.	36, ss.38,165, Sch.5, Pt.III, paras.57(b),73, Sch.27, Pt.III(4), Note
		s.73(2) rep.in pt.	36, ss.38,165, Sch.5, Pt.III, paras.57(c),73, Sch.27, Pt.III(4), Note
		s.76(3) rep. (every chargeable period ending on or after 12.5.1998)	36, ss.85(8)(9),165, Sch.27, Pt.III(18), Note 1
		s.76(4) am. (every chargeable period ending on or after 12.5.1998)	36, s.85(8)(9)
		s.80(1)(b) am.	36, s.46(3), Sch.7, para.4
		s.92(A1) subst.	36, s.38, Sch.5, Pt.III, paras.58,73
		ss.109(1)(c),115(2A) am.	36, s.46(3), Sch.7, para.4
		s.116(2) am. (*prosp.*)	17, s.50, Sch.4, para.27(3)
		s.132 subst.	36, s.38, Sch.5, Pt.III, paras.59,73
		s.136 am.	36, s.46(3), Sch.7, para.4
		s.138A(4) (defns. of "overseas petroleum" and "petroleum") am. (*prosp.*)	17, s.50, Sch.4, para.27(4)
		s.145A rep.	36, s.165, Sch.27, Pt.III(28), Note
		s.153(2)(b) am.	36, s.46(3), Sch.7, para.4
		s.159(1A) rep.in pt.	36, ss.38,165, Sch.5, Pt.III, paras.60,73, Sch.27, Pt.III(4), Note
		s.161(2A) subst.	36, s.38, Sch.5, Pt.III, paras.61,73
		Sch.1, para.8(3) rep.	36, s.165, Sch.27, Pt.III(4), Note
		Sch.1, para.8(32) rep.	36, s.165, Sch.27, Pt.III(25), Note
		Sch.1, para.8(39) rep.	36, s.165, Sch.27, Pt.III(9), Note
		Sch.A1 replaced	36, s.117(1)(d)(4), Sch.18
		Sch.A1 rep.	36, s.165, Sch.27, Pt.III(28), Note
c.5	Criminal Justice (International Co-operation) Act 1990	ss.12-14 saved (6.5.1999)	46, s.30, Sch.5, Pt.II, s.B1(b)
		s.12(1A) added	27, s.1
c.6	Education (Student Loans) Act 1990	power to trans. functions , modify etc. in relation to certain savings	30, s.25(3)(c)
		rep.	30, s.44(2), Sch.4

Year and Chap. or No. of Measure	Short title	How affected	1998, Chapter of Act or Number of Measure or Statutory Instrument
1990—*cont.*			
		s.1A added	1, s.1
		Sch.2 am. (*prosp.*)	29, s.74(1), Sch.15, para.10
		Sch.2, para.1(1)(b)(c) replaced (by para.1(1) (b))	1, s.2(2)
		Sch.2, para.1(3) am.	1, s.2(3)
		Sch.2, para.1(4)(5) subst.	1, s.2(4)
		Sch.2, para.1(6) added	1, s.2(5)(7)
		Sch.2, para.1(6) mod.	1, s.2(7)
		Sch.2, para.3 subst. (saving)	1, s.3(1)(4)(5)
		Sch.2, para.3A(a) am.	1, s.3(2)
		Sch.2, para.4(1) subst.	1, s.3(3)
c.8	Town and Country Planning Act 1990	appl.in pt.	SI 1936(L), art.41, Sch.10, para.1
		defn. of "local planning authority" appl.	43, s.1(2), Sch.2, para.10 (subst. 1931 c.28, Sch.2, para.2(a))
		s.2(6A) am.	18, s.54(1), Sch.3, para.19
		s.8 saved (13.1.1999)	SI 3269(L), art.19(3)
		s.118 appl. (pt.prosp.)	45, s.21(9)
		ss.262-283 (Pt.XI) appl. (pt.prosp.)	45, s.23, Sch.6, para.16(2) (3)
		s.262 appl. (pt.prosp.)	45, s.23, Sch.6, para.16(2)
		ss.271-274 appl.(mods.)	SI 1936(L), art.41, Sch.10, para.1
		s.271 saved	SI 1936(L), art.36(5)
		s.271 appl.(mods.) (13.1.1999)	SI 3269(L), art.34(4)
		s.272 saved	SI 1936(L), art.36(5)
		s.272 appl.(mods.) (13.1.1999)	SI 3269(L), art.34(4)
		s.280 appl.	38, s.127, Sch.13, para.3 (adding 1975 c.70, Sch.4, at Pt.III, paras.11(7), 13(9))
		s.280 appl. (pt.prosp.)	45, s.23, Sch.6, paras.9(6) ,11(8)
		s.282 appl.	38, s.127, Sch.13, para.3 (adding 1975 c.70, Sch.4, at Pt.III, paras.11(7), 13(9))
		s.282 appl. (pt.prosp.)	45, s.23, Sch.6, paras.9(6) ,11(8)
		s.293(2) appl.	38, s.127, Sch.13, para.3 (adding 1975 c.70, Sch.4, ar Pt.Iv para.22(2)(e))
		s.325(9) defn(s). appl. (pt.prosp.)	45, s.21(11)
c.11	Planning (Consequential Provisions) Act 1990	Sch.2, para.1 rep.	43, s.1(1), Sch.1, Pt.IV, Group 2
		Sch.2, para.34(2) rep.	38, s.152, Sch.18, Pt.III

Year and Chap. or No. of Measure	Short title	How affected	1998, Chapter of Act or Number of Measure or Statutory Instrument
1990—*cont.*			
		Sch.2, para.37 rep.	38, s.152, Sch.18, Pt.IV
		Sch.2, para.44(3)(4)(9) (10) rep.	38, s.152, Sch.18, Pt.V
c.16	Food Safety Act 1990	s.2 appl.	SI 141, reg.10
		s.2 appl.	SI 616, reg.6(1)
		s.2 appl.	SI 2424, reg.8
		s.3 appl.	SI 141, reg.10
		s.3 appl.	SI 2424, reg.8
		s.3(4) appl.	SI 1376, reg.12(2)
		s.6(3) appl.	SI 994, reg.55(2)
		s.9(2)-(9) appl.(mods.)	SI 1277, art.4(1)(a)(2)
		s.20 appl.	SI 141, reg.10
		s.20 appl.	SI 616, reg.6(1)
		s.20 appl.	SI 2424, reg.8
		s.21 appl.	SI 141, reg.10
		s.21 appl.	SI 616, reg.6(1)
		s.21 appl.	SI 2424, reg.8
		s.22 appl.	SI 141, reg.10
		ss.29,30 mod.	SI 1376, reg.12(3)
		s.30(8) appl.	SI 141, reg.10
		s.30(8) appl.	SI 616, reg.6(1)
		s.30(8) appl.	SI 2424, reg.8
		s.32 appl.	SI 616, reg.6(2)
		s.32 appl.(mods.)	SI 994, reg.3
		s.33 appl.	SI 141, reg.10
		s.33 appl.	SI 616, reg.6(2)
		s.33 appl.	SI 1277, art.4(1)(b)(c)(d)
		s.33 appl.	SI 2424, reg.8
		s.35(1)-(3) appl.	SI 616, reg.6(1)
		s.35(1)-(3) appl.	SI 2424, reg.8
		s.35(1) appl.	SI 141, reg.10
		s.35(1) appl.	SI 1277, art.4(1)(b)(c)(d)
		ss.35(2)(3),36 appl.	SI 141, reg.10
		s.36 appl.	SI 616, reg.6(1)
		s.36 appl.	SI 2424, reg.8
		s.44 appl.	SI 141, reg.10
		s.44 appl.	SI 616, reg.6(1)
		s.44 appl.	SI 1277, art.4(1)(b)(c)(d)
		s.44 appl.	SI 2424, reg.8
		s.58(1) appl.(mods.)	SI 994, reg.4
		s.58(2) am. (*prosp.*)	17, s.50, Sch.4, para.28(a)
		s.58(4) (defn. of "installation") am. (*prosp.*)	17, s.50, Sch.4, para.28(b)
c.18	Computer Misuse Act 1990	s.7(1)(2) rep.	40, s.9(2), Sch.2, Pt.II
		s.8(2) rep.	40, s.9(1)(2), Sch.1, Pt.II, para.6(1)(a), Sch.2, Pt.II
		s.8(5) am.	40, s.9(1)(2), Sch.1, Pt.II, para.6(1)(b), Sch.2, Pt.II

Year and Chap. or No. of Measure	Short title	How affected	1998, Chapter of Act or Number of Measure or Statutory Instrument
1990—*cont.*			
		s.8(6)(b) rep.	40, s.9(1)(2), Sch.1, Pt.II, para.6(1)(c), Sch.2, Pt.II
		s.9(2)(b) rep.	40, s.9(1)(2), Sch.1, Pt.II, para.6(2), Sch.2, Pt.II
		s.16(4) am.	40, s.9(1), Sch.1, Pt.II, para.6(3)(a)
		s.16(5)(6)(8)(a) rep.	40, s.9(1)(2), Sch.1, Pt.II, para.6(3)(b), Sch.2, Pt.II
c.19	National Health Service and Community Care Act 1990	s.14 appl.	18, s.53(1)
		s.20(1)(3)-(8) rep. (EW)	18, s.54(3), Sch.5
		Sch.2, para.7(2) am.	18, s.54(1), Sch.3, para.20
		Sch.4 rep. (EW)	18, s.54(3), Sch.5
c.23	Access to Health Records Act 1990	s.1(1) rep.in pt. (*prosp.*)	29, s.74(2), Sch.16, Pt.I
		s.2 subst. (*prosp.*)	29, s.74(1), Sch.15, para.11
		s.3(1)(a)-(e) rep. (saving)(*prosp.*)	29, s.74(2), Sch.1, Pt.I
		s.3(4)(a) am. (*prosp.*)	29, s.74(1), Sch.15, para.12
		s.3(6)(a) rep.in pt. (saving)(*prosp.*)	29, ss.73,74, Sch.4, para.17(1), Sch.16, Pt.I
		s.4(1)(2) rep. (saving) (*prosp.*)	29, ss.73,74, Sch.14, para.17(1), Sch.16, Pt.I
		s.5(1)(a)(i) rep.in pt. (*prosp.*)	29, s.74(2), Sch.16, Pt.I
		s.5(3) am. (*prosp.*)	29, s.74(1), Sch.15, para.13
		s.10(2)(3) rep.in pt. (*prosp.*)	29, s.74(2), Sch.16, Pt.I
		s.11 (defns. of "child" and "parental responsibility") appl.	29, s.74(2), Sch.16, Pt.I
c.29	Finance Act 1990	s.25 mod.	36, s.48(4)
		s.25 appl.	36, s.48(10)
		s.25(2)(e) appl.	36, s.48(4)(d)
		s.25(2)(g) mod.	36, s.48(3)
		s.45(6) rep. (6.4.1999)	36, s.165, Sch.27, Pt.III(2), Note
		ss.91,95,98(3),100,102 rep.	36, s.165, Sch.27, Pt.III(28), Note
		s.123 rep.	36, s.165, Sch.27, Pt.V(3), Note 1
		s.126(2) am.	36, s.46(3), Sch.7, para.5
		Sch.14, para.2(a)(b) rep.	36, s.165, Sch.27, Pt.III(4), Note
		Sch.14, para.12 rep.	36, s.165, Sch.27, Pt.III(25), Note
		Schs.15,16 rep.	36, s.165, Sch.27, Pt.III(28), Note
c.31	Aviation and Maritime Security Act 1990	saved (6.5.1999) (other than Pt.I)	46, s.30, Sch.5, Pt.II, s.E3(g)

Year and Chap. or No. of Measure	Short title	How affected	1998, Chapter of Act or Number of Measure or Statutory Instrument
1990—*cont.*			
		s.1 saved (6.5.1999)	46, s.30, Sch.5, Pt.II, s.E4(g)
		s.14(3) am. (*prosp.*)	17, s.50, Sch.4, para.29
		s.48 saved (6.5.1999)	46, s.30, Sch.5, Pt.II, s.E4(g)
c.37	Human Fertilisation and Embryology Act 1990	s.33(8) rep. (*prosp.*)	29, s.74(2), Sch.16, Pt.I
		s.48(2) rep. (*prosp.*)	47, s.100(2), Sch.15
c.40	Law Reform (Miscellaneous Provisions) (Scotland) Act 1990	ss.16–44 (Pt.II) (defns. of "advocates", "solicitors", "qualified conveyancers" and "executry practitioners") appl. (6.5.1999)	46, s.30, Sch.5, Pt.II, s.C3
c.41	Courts and Legal Services Act 1990	defn. of "authorised litigator" appl. (26.4.1999)	SI 3132, rule 48.6(6)(b)
		defns. of "authorised advocate" and "authorised litigator" appl.	8, s.15, Sch.1, para.2 (replacing 1975 c.65 s.77(4BB)(a))
		defn. of "authorised advocate or authorised litigator" appl.	8, s.15, Sch.1, para.3 (replacing 1976 c.74 s.72(4BB)(a))
		defn. of "authorised advocate or authorised litigator" appl.	8, s.15, Sch.1, para.9(1)(3) (replacing 1992 c.52 s.288(4))
		defn. of "authorised advocate or authorised litigator" appl.	8, s.15, Sch.1, para.11 (replacing 1995 c.50 s.9(4))
		defn. of "authorised advocate or authorised litigator" appl.	8, s.15, Sch.1, para.24(3)
		defns. of "authorised advocate" and "authorised litigator" appl.	39, s.49(7)(a)(iii)
		s.11 referred to (26.4.1999)	SI 3132, rule 27.14(4)
		ss.37(8)(a),48(4)(a) rep.in pt.	11, ss.23,43, Sch.5, Pt.I, Ch.III, para.41(1)(2), Sch.9, Pt.I
		s.50(2)(fa) added	11, s.23, Sch.5, Pt.IV, Ch.II, para.67(a)
		s.50(2)(p)(i) am.	11, s.23, Sch.5, Pt.IV, Ch.II, para.67(b)
		s.52(6) rep.in pt.	11, ss.23,43, Sch.5, Pt.I, Ch.III, para.41(1)(3)(a), Sch.9, Pt.I
		s.52(6) am.	11, s.23, Sch.5, Pt.I, Ch.III, para.41(1)(3)(b)
		s.71 (defn. of "general qualification") appl. (EWS) (*prosp.*)	14, s.5(2)(a)
		s.71 (defn. of "general qualification") appl. (*prosp.*)	14, s.7(2)(a)

Year and Chap. or No. of Measure	Short title	How affected	1998, Chapter of Act or Number of Measure or Statutory Instrument
1990—*cont.*			
		s.71 (defn. of "general qualification") appl. (EWS) (*prosp.*)	14, s.14(12), Sch.4, para.1(3)
		s.71 (defn. of "7 year general qualification") appl.	29, s.6(5)(a)
		s.71 (defn. of "ten year general qualification") appl. (*prosp.*)	41, s.45(7), Sch.7, Pt.I, para.4(3)(a)
		s.71 mod. (*prosp.*)	41, s.45(7), Sch.7, Pt.III, para.26(2)(a)
		s.119(1) (defn. of "authorised litigator") appl.	37, s.54(2)
		Sch.10, para.58 rep. (*prosp.*)	29, s.74(2), Sch.16, Pt.I
		Sch.11 am.	8, s.15, Sch.1, para.6
c.42	Broadcasting Act 1990	defn. of "programme service" appl. (4.1.1999)	37, s.52(6), Sch.3, para.3(13)
		saved (6.5.1999)	46, s.30, Sch.5, Pt.II, s.K1
		s.2(1)(a) am.	SI 3196, reg.2, Sch., para.1(2)(a)
		s.2(1)(cc) added	SI 3196, reg.2, Sch., para.1(2)(b)
		s.2(1)(d) subst.	SI 3196, reg.2, Sch., para.1(2)(c)
		s.27(1)(a) am.	SI 2915, art.2
		s.36(3) am. (*prosp.*)	48, s.23, Sch.3, para.3
		s.43 subst.	SI 3196, reg.2, Sch., para.2
		s.46(6)(b) subst.	SI 3196, reg.2, Sch., para.3
		s.79(5)(a)(ii) subst.	SI 3196, reg.2, Sch., para.4
		s.107(2) am. (*prosp.*)	48, s.23, Sch.3, para.3
		s.177(6) (defn. of "foreign satellite service") subst.	SI 3196, reg.2, Sch., para.5
		s.180(2) subst.	6, s.7, Sch.1, para.4
		s.193(2) rep.in pt. (*prosp.*)	41, s.74(1)(3), Sch.12, para.14(2)(a), Sch.14, Pt.I
		s.193(2)(c) rep. (*prosp.*)	41, s.74(1)(3), Sch.12, para.14(2)(a), Sch.14, Pt.I
		s.193(4) rep.in pt. (*prosp.*)	41, s.74(1)(3), Sch.12, para.14(2)(b), Sch.14, Pt.I
		s.194A saved (*prosp.*)	41, s.74(2), Sch.13, Ch.III, para.26
		s.194A(2)-(6) replaced (by s.194A(2)-(11)) (*prosp.*)	41, s.3(1)(b), Sch.2, Pt.III, para.4(2)
		s.202(4A) added	SI 3196, reg.2, Sch., para.6(2)
		s.202(5A) rep.	SI 3196, reg.2, Sch., para.6(3)

Year and Chap. or No. of Measure	Short title	How affected	1998, Chapter of Act or Number of Measure or Statutory Instrument
1990—*cont.*			
		Sch.2, Pt.III, para.2(2) (a) am.	SI 3196, reg.2, Sch., para.7(2)(a)
		Sch.2, Pt.III, para.2(2) (aa) added	SI 3196, reg.2, Sch., para.7(2)(b)
		Sch.2, Pt.III, para.2(2) (b) am.	SI 3196, reg.2, Sch., para.7(2)(a)
		Sch.2, Pt.III, para.2(2) (bb) added	SI 3196, reg.2, Sch., para.7(2)(c)
		Sch.2, Pt.III, para.7(5) am.	SI 3196, reg.2, Sch., para.7(3)(a)
		Sch.2, Pt.III, para.7(7) am.	SI 3196, reg.2, Sch., para.7(3)(b)
		Sch.2, Pt.III, para.7(7) (b)(c) am.	SI 2770, art.2
		Sch.2, Pt.III, para.7(8) subst.	SI 3196, reg.2, Sch., para.7(3)(c)
		Sch.4, para.4(7) replaced (by Sch.4, para.4(7)) (*prosp.*)	41, s.74(1), Sch.12, para.14(3)
		Sch.18, Pt.I, para.2(2) rep.	6, s.7, Sch.2, Pt.I
		Sch.20, para.10 rep. (*prosp.*)	34, s.39(2), Sch.2
		Sch.20, para.15(3)(4) rep. (NI) (*prosp.*)	SI 1504, art.65(2), Sch.6
		Sch.20, para.19 rep. (*prosp.*)	47, s.100(2), Sch.15
c.43	Environmental Protection Act 1990	ss.1-28 (Pt.I) saved (6.5.1999)	46, s.30, Sch.5, Pt.II, s.D1
		s.3(8) rep. (*prosp.*)	47, s.100(2), Sch.15
		s.6(1) excl. transtl. provn.	SI 767, reg.3
		s.63A added	44, s.1
		s.71 appl.(mods.) (1.4.1999)	SI 2746, reg.15
		s.98(2)(f)(g) subst. (*prosp.*)	31, s.140(1), Sch.30, para.23
		s.153(1)(gg) added	SI 538, art.2
		s.153(1)(hh) added	SI 1001, art.2
		s.153(1)(ii) added (27.1.1999)	SI 3234, art.2
		s.153(5) rep. (*prosp.*)	47, s.100(2), Sch.15
		Sch.3, para.5 am. (EW)	18, s.54(1), Sch.3, para.21
		Sch.6, para.23(a) rep. (*prosp.*)	38, s.152, Sch.18, Pt.I
c.xix	River Tees Barrage and Crossing Act 1990	s.50(9) appl.	SI 570, art.4(2)
c.xxix	Zetland Masonic Sick and Widows and Orphans Fund Order Confirmation Act 1990	rep.	43, s.1(1), Sch.1, Pt.VII, Group 1
No.2	Care of Cathedrals Measure 1990	s.18(1)(2)(3)(5), Sch.1, para.2 trans.of functions (1.1.1999)	SI 1715, art.2, Sch.1
1991			
c.1	Development Board for Rural Wales Act 1991	rep.	38, s.152, Sch.18, Pt.IV
c.15	Local Government Finance (Publicity for Auditors' Reports) Act 1991	rep.	18, s.54(3), Sch.5

Year and Chap. or No. of Measure	Short title	How affected	1998, Chapter of Act or Number of Measure or Statutory Instrument
1991—*cont.*			
c.22	New Roads and Street Works Act 1991	appl.in pt.	SI 1936(L), art.4(2)(3)
		ss.48-106 ext.	iv, s.3
		ss.48-106 (Pt.III) saved	SI 1936(L), art.4(4)(a)(b)
		ss.48-106 (Pt.III) (defn. of "apparatus") appl.	SI 1936(L), art.9(2)(a)
		ss.48-106 (Pt.III) appl.	SI 1936(L), art.41, Sch.10, paras.2(8),3(2)
		ss.48-106 (Pt.III) saved (13.1.1999)	SI 3269(L), art.12(4)
		s.54 appl.	SI 1936(L), art.4(3)
		s.54 appl. (13.1.1999)	SI 3269(L), art.4(2)(3)(4)
		s.55 appl.	SI 1936(L), art.4(3)
		s.55 appl. (13.1.1999)	SI 3269(L), art.4(2)(3)(4)
		s.56 excl.	SI 1936(L), art.4(1)
		s.57 appl.	SI 1936(L), art.4(3)
		s.58 excl.	SI 1936(L), art.4(1)
		s.59 appl.	SI 1936(L), art.4(3)
		s.59 appl. (13.1.1999)	SI 3269(L), art.4(2)(3)
		s.60 appl.	SI 1936(L), art.4(3)
		s.60 appl. (13.1.1999)	SI 3269(L), art.4(2)(3)
		s.64(1) (defn. of "electric line") appl.	SI 1936(L), art.9(2)(b)
		ss.68,69 appl.	SI 1936(L), art.4(3)
		s.69 appl. (13.1.1999)	SI 3269(L), art.4(2)(3)
		ss.75,76 appl.	SI 1936(L), art.4(3)
		s.76 appl. (13.1.1999)	SI 3269(L), art.4(2)(3)
		s.77 appl.	SI 1936(L), art.4(3)
		s.77 appl. (13.1.1999)	SI 3269(L), art.4(2)(3)
		s.86(3) ext. (13.1.1999)	SI 3269(L), art.4(1)(a)
		s.87 saved	SI 1936(L), art.4(4)(a)
		s.87 saved (13.1.1999)	SI 3269(L), art.12(4)
		Sch.8, Pt.IV, para.107 rep.	38, s.152, Sch.18, Pt.IV
c.24	Northern Ireland (Emergency Provisions) Act 1991	appl.	35, s.3(7)(b)
		appl.	35, s.17, Sch.3, para.2(1)(c)
c.27	Radioactive Material (Road Transport) Act 1991	defn. of "Radioactive material" appl. (6.5.1999)	46, s.30, Sch.5, Pt.II, s.E5
c.31	Finance Act 1991	s.45 rep.	36, s.165, Sch.27, Pt.III(11), Note
		s.121 am.	36, s.46(3), Sch.7, para.6
		Sch.2, para.9 rep. (*prosp.*)	36, s.165, Sch.27, Pt.I(1), Note
		Sch.15, paras.13,26 rep.	36, s.165, Sch.27, Pt.III(4), Note
c.40	Road Traffic Act 1991	appt. day(s) for spec. provns. (10.4.1998)	SI 967, art.1
		am.	SI 2018, art.2 (extending 1996/500 to S.)

Year and Chap. or No. of Measure	Short title	How affected	1998, Chapter of Act or Number of Measure or Statutory Instrument
1991—*cont.*			
		ss.66,69-74 appl.(mods.) (in relation to the Borough of Luton) (19.1.1999)	SI 3207(L), art.4, Sch.1
		s.70 mod.	SI 1134, art.6(1)
		s.71 mod.	SI 1134, art.6(2)
		s.74(8) mod.	SI 1134, art.6(3)
		ss.78,79 appl.(mods.) (in relation to the Borough of Luton) (19.1.1999)	SI 3207(L), art.4, Sch.1
		s.79(2) mod.	SI 1134, art.6(4)
		s.82 appl.(mods.) (in relation to the Borough of Luton) (19.1.1999)	SI 3207(L), art.4, Sch.1
		Sch.6 mod.	SI 1134, art.6(5)
		Sch.6 appl.(mods.) (in relation to the Borough of Luton) (19.1.1999)	SI 3207(L), art.4, Sch.1
c.48	Child Support Act 1991	mod.	14, s.2(1)(2)(d)
		saved (6.5.1999)	46, s.30, Sch.5, Pt.II, s.F1
		saved (6.5.1999)	46, s.30, Sch.5, Pt.II, s.F2
		power to am. (*prosp.*)	47, s.87
		s.2 rep.in pt. (*prosp.*)	14, s.86(1)(2), Sch.7, para.18, Sch.8
		s.4 am. (*prosp.*)	14, s.4(2)(c)
		s.4(4) rep.in pt. (*prosp.*)	14, s.86(1)(2), Sch.7, para.19, Sch.8
		s.6(9) rep.in pt. (*prosp.*)	14, s.86(1)(2), Sch.7, para.20, Sch.8
		s.7(5) rep.in pt. (*prosp.*)	14, s.86(1)(2), Sch.7, para.21, Sch.8
		s.8(1)(2) rep.in pt. (*prosp.*)	14, s.86(1), Sch.7, para.22
		s.10(4) am. (*prosp.*)	14, s.86(1), Sch.7, para.23(1)
		s.10(5) am. (*prosp.*)	14, s.86(1), Sch.7, para.23(2)
		s.11 am. (*prosp.*)	14, s.4(2)(d)
		s.11(1) am. (*prosp.*)	14, s.86(1), Sch.7, para.24(1)
		s.11(1A) am. (*prosp.*)	14, s.86(1), Sch.7, para.24(2)
		s.12(1)(1A) replaced (by s.12(1)) (*prosp.*)	14, s.86(1), Sch.7, para.25(1)
		s.12(4)(5) am. (*prosp.*)	14, s.86(1), Sch.7, para.25(2)
		s.13 trans.of functions (*prosp.*)	14, s.1(c)
		s.13 rep. (*prosp.*)	14, s.86(1)(2), Sch.7, para.26, Sch.8
		s.14(2)(2A) rep.	14, s.86(1)(2), Sch.7, para.27(a), Sch.8
		s.14(3) rep.in pt. & am. (*prosp.*)	14, s.86(1)(2), Sch.7, para.27(b), Sch.8

Year and Chap. or No. of Measure	Short title	How affected	1998, Chapter of Act or Number of Measure or Statutory Instrument
1991—*cont.*			
		s.15(1) rep.in pt. (*prosp.*)	14, s.86(1)(2), Sch.7, para.28, Sch.8
		s.16 subst.	14, s.40
		ss.17-19 replaced (by s.17) (*prosp.*)	14, s.41
		s.20 am. (*prosp.*)	14, s.4(2)(b)
		s.20 replaced (by s.20) (*prosp.*)	14, s.42
		s.20 mod. (*temp.*)	14, s.83, Sch.6, para.9
		s.21 trans.of functions (*prosp.*)	14, s.4(1)(b)
		s.21 replaced (by s.20) (*prosp.*)	14, s.42
		s.22(4)(a) am. (*prosp.*)	14, s.86(1), Sch.7, para.29
		s.23(4)(5) rep. (*prosp.*)	47, s.100(2), Sch.15
		s.24 am. (*prosp.*)	14, s.86(1), Sch.7, para.30(1)(3)-(7)
		s.24(1A) rep. (*prosp.*)	14, s.86(1)(2), Sch.7, para.30(2), Sch.8
		s.26(1) am. (*prosp.*)	14, s.86(1), Sch.7, para.31(1)
		s.26(2) am. (Case E am.) (*prosp.*)	14, s.86(1), Sch.7, para.31(2)
		s.27(1) am. (*prosp.*)	14, s.86(1), Sch.7, para.32
		s.28(1) am. (*prosp.*)	14, s.86(1), Sch.7, para.33
		s.28A(4) am. (*prosp.*)	14, s.86(1), Sch.7, para.34
		s.28B(4)(5) rep. (*prosp.*)	14, s.86(1)(2), Sch.7, para.35(1), Sch.8
		s.28B(6) subst. (*prosp.*)	14, s.86(1), Sch.7, para.35(2)
		s.28D(1)(3) am. (*prosp.*)	14, s.86(1), Sch.7, para.36
		s.28F(6) am. (*prosp.*)	14, s.86(1), Sch.7, para.37
		s.28G(1) rep. (*prosp.*)	14, s.86(1)(2), Sch.7, para.38, Sch.8
		s.28H subst. (*prosp.*)	14, s.86(1), Sch.7, para.39
		ss.28ZA,28ZB added (EWS) (*prosp.*)	14, s.43
		ss.28ZC,28ZD added (EWS) (*prosp.*)	14, s.44
		s.43(3) added (*prosp.*)	14, s.86(1), Sch.7, para.40
		s.44(1) am. (*prosp.*)	14, s.86(1), Sch.7, para.41
		s.45(1) am. (*prosp.*)	14, s.86(1), Sch.7, para.42(1)
		s.45(6) am. (*prosp.*)	14, s.86(1), Sch.7, para.42(2)
		s.46(2) am. (*prosp.*)	14, s.86(1), Sch.7, para.43(1)
		s.46(3)-(6) am. (*prosp.*)	14, s.86(1), Sch.7, para.43(2)
		s.46(7)(8) replaced (by s.46(7)) (*prosp.*)	14, s.86(1), Sch.7, para.43(3)

Year and Chap. or No. of Measure	Short title	How affected	1998, Chapter of Act or Number of Measure or Statutory Instrument
1991—*cont.*		s.46(11) (defn. of "reduced benefit direction") rep.in pt.	14, s.86(1)(2), Sch.7, para.43(4), Sch.8
		ss.46A,46B added (*prosp.*)	14, s.86(1), Sch.7, para.44
		s.50(5)(c) added (*prosp.*)	14, s.86(1), Sch.7, para.45
		s.51(2)(a)(iii) subst.	14, s.86(1), Sch.7, para.46(a)
		s.51(2)(b) am. (*prosp.*)	14, s.86(1), Sch.7, para.46(b)
		s.54 (defns. of "adjudication officer", "Chief Adjudication Officer", "Chief Child Support Officer", "child support appeal tribunal" and "child support officer") rep.	14, s.86(1)(2), Sch.7, para.47(b), Sch.8
		s.54 (defn. of "appeal tribunal") added (*prosp.*)	14, s.86(1), Sch.7, para.47(a)
		s.56(2)-(4) rep. & superseded (*prosp.*)	47, s.87(8)(c)
		s.56(2)-(4) rep. (*prosp.*)	47, s.100(2), Sch.15
		Sch.1, para.8 am. (*prosp.*)	14, s.86(1), Sch.7, para.48(1)
		Sch.1, para.9 am. (*prosp.*)	14, s.86(1), Sch.7, para.48(2)
		Sch.1, para.13 am. (*prosp.*)	14, s.86(1), Sch.7, para.48(3)
		Sch.1, para.15 am. (*prosp.*)	14, s.86(1), Sch.7, para.48(4)
		Sch.1, para.16(2)-(6)(4A)(7)(8) am. (*prosp.*)	14, s.86(1), Sch.7, para.48(5)(a)-(c)
		Sch.1, para.16(10) rep.in pt. (*prosp.*)	14, s.86(1)(2), Sch.7, para.48(5)(d), Sch.8
		Sch.2, para.2 rep.	14, s.86(1)(2), Sch.7, para.49, Sch.8
		Sch.3 rep. (*prosp.*)	14, s.86(1)(2), Sch.7, para.50, Sch.8
		Sch.4, para.2A(1) subst. (*prosp.*)	14, s.86(1), Sch.7, para.51
		Sch.4, para.5 am. (*prosp.*)	14, s.86(1), Sch.7, para.52(1)-(3)
		Sch.4, para.6(2) subst. (*prosp.*)	14, s.86(1), Sch.7, para.52(4)
		Sch.4A, para.1 (defn. of "review") rep.	14, s.86(1)(2), Sch.7, para.53(1), Sch.8
		Sch.4A, para.2(b)(c) am. (*prosp.*)	14, s.86(1), Sch.7, para.53(2)
		Sch.4A, para.4(1) rep.in pt. (*prosp.*)	14, s.86(1)(2), Sch.7, para.53(3), Sch.8
		Sch.4A, para.6 rep. (*prosp.*)	14, s.86(1)(2), Sch.7, para.53(4), Sch.8

Year and Chap. or No. of Measure	Short title	How affected	1998, Chapter of Act or Number of Measure or Statutory Instrument
1991—*cont.*			
		Sch.4A, para.8 am. (*prosp.*)	14, s.86(1), Sch.7, para.53(5)
		Sch.4A, para.9, head. am. (*prosp.*)	14, s.86(1), Sch.7, para.53(6)(a)
		Sch.4A, para.9(1) am. (*prosp.*)	14, s.86(1), Sch.7, para.53(6)(b)
		Sch.4C added (*prosp.*)	14, s.86(1), Sch.7, para.54
		Sch.5, para.2 rep. (*prosp.*)	47, s.100(2), Sch.15
		Sch.5, para.3(3) rep. (*prosp.*)	14, s.86(2), Sch.8
c.49	School Teachers' Pay and Conditions Act 1991	s.1(5) rep.in pt. (*prosp.*)	31, s.140(1)(3), Sch.30, para.25(a)(ii), Sch.31
		s.1(5)(b) am. (*prosp.*)	31, s.140(1), Sch.30, para.25(a)(i)
		s.1(6) rep. (*prosp.*)	31, s.140(1)(3), Sch.30, para.25(b), Sch.31
		s.2(1)(b) subst. (*prosp.*)	31, s.140(1), Sch.30, para.26(a)
		s.2(2) rep. (*prosp.*)	31, s.140(1)(3), Sch.30, para.26(b), Sch.31
		s.2(3) am.	31, s.140(1), Sch.30, para.26(c)
		s.2(4)(a) rep.in pt.	31, s.140(1)(3), Sch.30, para.26(d)(i), Sch.31
		s.2(4)(g) am.	31, s.140(1), Sch.30, para.26(d)(ii)
		s.2(4)(h) rep.	31, s.140(1)(3), Sch.30, para.26(d)(iii), Sch.31
		s.2(5) rep.in pt. (*prosp.*)	31, s.140(1)(3), Sch.30, para.26(e), Sch.31
		s.2(6)(a) rep.in pt. (*prosp.*)	31, s.140(1)(3), Sch.30, para.26(f), Sch.31
		s.3 saved (amendment excl.) (*temp.*)	SI 2115, reg.3
		s.3 subst. (saving)	31, s.13, Sch.32, Pt.II, para.7
		s.3A(1) subst. (*prosp.*)	31, s.140(1), Sch.30, para.27(a)
		s.3A(3) am. (*prosp.*)	31, s.140(1), Sch.30, para.27(b)
		s.5(1) (defns. of "school teacher" and "school which has a delegated budget") am. (*prosp.*)	31, s.140(1), Sch.30, para.28(2)(a)(b)
		s.5(1) am. (*prosp.*)	31, s.140(1), Sch.30, para.28(2)(c)
		s.5, sidenote am. (*prosp.*)	31, s.140(1), Sch.30, para.28(3)
c.53	Criminal Justice Act 1991	ss.1-4 appl. (*prosp.*)	37, s.73(4)
		ss.1-31 (Pt.I) appl.	37, s.18(2)
		ss.1-31 (Pt.I) (defn. of "violent offence") appl.	37, ss.58(8),120(1), Sch.9, para.3

Year and Chap. or No. of Measure	Short title	How affected	1998, Chapter of Act or Number of Measure or Statutory Instrument
1991—*cont.*			
		ss.1-31 (Pt.I) ext.(mods.)	37, ss.61(4),120(1), Sch.9, para.4
		ss.1-31 (Pt.I) ext.(mods.)	37, s.69(11)
		ss.1-31 (Pt.I) ext. (*prosp.*)	37, s.73(4)
		ss.1-31 (Pt.I) defn(s). appl.	37, s.85(5)
		ss.1-31 (Pt.I) (defn. of "community order") appl.	37, s.106, Sch.7, para.4 (adding 1969 c.54 s.12(4))
		ss.1-31 (Pt.I) (defn. of "community order") am.	37, s.106, Sch.7, para.20
		ss.1-31 (Pt.I) (defn. of "community sentence") appl.	37, s.106, Sch.7, para.22 (amending 1973 c.62 s.22(3))
		ss.1-31 (Pt.I) (defn. of "community order") appl.	37, s.106, Sch.7, para.27(1) (substituting 1973 c.62, Sch.1A, para.2(7))
		ss.1-31 (Pt.I) (defn. of "community order") appl.	37, s.106, Sch.7, para.27(2) (substituting 1973 c.62, Sch.1a, para.3(4))
		ss.1-31 (Pt.I) (defn. of "community order") appl.	37, s.106, Sch.7, para.36(5) (substituting 1982 c.48 s.17(8))
		ss.1-31 (Pt.I) appl.	37, s.106, Sch.7, para.51(2) (replacing 1997 c.43 s.37(4)(5))
		ss.1-31 (Pt.I) ext.	37, s.106, Sch.7, para.51(2) (replacing 1997 c.43 s.37(4)(5))
		ss.1-31 (Pt.I) (defn. of "custodial sentence") appl.	37, s.117(1)
		ss.1-31 (Pt.I) (defn. of "community order") appl.	37, s.119, Sch.8, para.54 (amending 1983 c.20, s.37(8))
		s.1(2) excl.	37, s.63(6)
		s.1(2) excl.	37, s.119, Sch.8, para.53(3) (substituting 1982 c.48, s.19(5A)(b))
		s.1(3) subst.	37, s.119, Sch.8, para.72
		s.2(2) mod.	37, ss.58(6),120(1), Sch.9, para.3
		s.3(5)(a) am.	37, s.119, Sch.8, para.73
		s.6(4) rep.in pt.	37, ss.119,120(2), Sch.8, para.74(b), Sch.10
		s.6(4)(aa) added	37, s.119, Sch.8, para.74(a)
		s.6(4)(g) added	37, s.119, Sch.8, para.74(c)
		s.7(3)(aa) added	37, s.119, Sch.8, para.75(c)

Year and Chap. or No. of Measure	Short title	How affected	1998, Chapter of Act or Number of Measure or Statutory Instrument
1991—*cont.*			
		s.11(1) am. (in force 30.9.1998 for areas specified in SI/1998 2327, Sch.1)	37, s.119, Sch.8, para.76
		s.11(1A) added	37, s.106, Sch.7, para.40
		s.12 appl.(mods.)	37, ss.68(3),70(5), Sch.5, para.5(3)
		s.12 ext.	37, s.72(1) (replacing 1969 c.54 s.15(3)(a)(b))
		s.12 appl.(mods.)	37, s.119, Sch.8, para.21 (adding 1969 c.54 s.16B)
		s.12(5)(c) am.	37, s.106, Sch.7, para.41(1)
		s.12(6) ext.	37, s.106, Sch.7, para.51(2) (replacing 1997 c.43 s.37(4)(5))
		s.12(6B) added	37, s.106, Sch.7, para.41(2)
		s.12(8) added	37, s.106, Sch.7, para.41(3)
		s.15(3)(a) am. (in force 30.9.1998 for areas specified in SI 1998/2327, Sch.1)	37, s.119, Sch.8, para.77(a)
		s.15(3)(aa) added	37, s.119, Sch.8, para.77(b)
		s.24(2)(b) am. (*prosp.*)	14, s.86(1), Sch.7, para.55
		s.31(1) mod. (*temp.*)	SI 2327, art.5(2)(b)
		s.31(1) defn.of (" custodial sentence") para.(b) am.	37, s.106, Sch.7, para.42
		s.31(1) defn.of (" custodial sentence") para.(b) rep. in pt. (*prosp.*)	37, ss.119,120(2), Sch.8, para.78(b), Sch.10
		s.31(1) added	37, s.119, Sch.8, para.78(a)
		s.31(1) defn.of (" custodial sentence") para.(b) am. (*prosp.*)	37, s.119, Sch.8, para.78(b)
		s.31(1) (defns. of "detention and training order" and "drug treatment and testing order") added	37, s.119, Sch.8, para.78(c)
		ss.32-51 (Pt.II) (defn. of "licence") appl.	37, ss.58(8),120(1), Sch.9, para.3
		ss.32-51 (Pt.II) mod. (*prosp.*)	37, s.79(3)(4)
		ss.32-51 (Pt.II) appl.	37, s.102
		s.32(1)(b) am.	37, s.119, Sch.8, para.79(1)
		s.32(3)(4)(6) am.	37, s.119, Sch.8, para.79(2)
		s.33 mod.	37, s.120(1), Sch.9, para.12(3)(9)

Year and Chap. or No. of Measure	Short title		How affected	1998, Chapter of Act or Number of Measure or Statutory Instrument
1991—*cont.*				
			s.33(3) am.	37, ss.104(1),120(1), Sch.9, para.13
			s.33(3)(a)(b) am.	37, s.119, Sch.8, para.80(1)(a)(b)
			s.33(3A) added	37, s.119, Sch.8, para.80(2)
			s.33(4) rep.	37, ss.119,120(2), Sch.8, para.80(3), Sch.10
			s.33A mod. (*temp.*)	SI 2327, art.5(3)(c)
			s.33A added	37, s.119, Sch.8, para.81
			s.33A mod.	37, s.120(1), Sch.9, para.12(4)(9)
			s.34A added (28.1.1999)	37, ss.99,120(1), Sch.9, para.10
			s.34A mod.	37, s.120(1), Sch.9, para.12(5)(9)
			s.36(1) am.	37, s.119, Sch.8, para.82
			s.37 mod. (*temp.*)	SI 2327, art.5(3)(d)
			s.37(1) rep.in pt. (1.1.1999) (in so far as not already in force)	37, ss.119,120(1)(2), Sch.8, para.83(1)(b), Sch.9, para.12, Sch.10
			s.37(1) am.	37, ss.119,120(1), Sch.8, para.83(1)(a), Sch.9, para.12
			s.37(1A) added	37, ss.104(2),120(1), Sch.9, para.13
			s.37(1B) added (1.1.1999) (in so far as not already in force)	37, s.119, Sch.8, para.83(2)
			s.37(2) am. (1.1.1999) (in so far as not already in force)	37, s.119, Sch.8, para.83(3)
			s.37(4) rep.in pt.	37, ss.119,120(2), Sch.8, para.83(4)(b), Sch.10
			s.37(4) am.	37, s.119, Sch.8, para.83(4)(a)
			s.37(4A) mod. (*temp.*)	SI 2327, art.5(1)(a)
			s.37(4A) added	37, s.119, Sch.8, para.83(5)
			s.37(5) subst.	37, s.119, Sch.8, para.83(6)
			s.37A added (30.9.1998) (for the purpose of making orders under 1991 c.53,s.37A) (28.1.1999) (to the extent not already in force)	37, s.100(1)
			s.38 rep. (1.1.1999)	37, ss.103(1)(2),120(1)(2), Sch.9, para.12, Sch.10
			s.38A added (28.1.1999) (to the extent not already in force)	37, s.100(2)
			s.39(1) am. (1.1.1999)	37, ss.103(3),120(1), Sch.9, para.12

Year and Chap. or No. of Measure	Short title	How affected	1998, Chapter of Act or Number of Measure or Statutory Instrument
1991—*cont.*			
		s.39(5A) added	37, s.119, Sch.8, para.84
		s.40 (defn. of "the new offence") appl.	37, s.120(1), Sch.9, para.14(2)
		s.40(3) am.	37, s.106, Sch.7, para.43(1)
		s.40(3A)(3B) added	37, s.106, Sch.7, para.43(2)
		s.40(4) am.	37, s.106, Sch.7, para.43(3)
		s.40(5)(6) added	37, s.119, Sch.8, para.85
		s.40A added	37, ss.105,120(1), Sch.9, para.14
		s.40A mod.	37, s.120(1), Sch.9, para.12(6)(9)
		s.41(1)(2) subst. (*prosp.*)	37, s.119, Sch.8, para.86(1)
		s.41(4) added (*prosp.*)	37, s.119, Sch.8, para.86(2)
		s.43(3) am.	37, s.119, Sch.8, para.87(1)
		s.43(5) am.	37, s.119, Sch.8, para.87(2)
		s.44 subst.	37, s.59
		s.44 mod.	37, s.120(1), Sch.9, para.12(7)(9)
		s.44A added	37, s.60
		s.45 mod. (*temp.*)	SI 2327, art.5(3)(e)
		s.45 am.	37, s.120(1), Sch.9, para.12(8)(9)
		s.45(1) am.	37, s.119, Sch.8, para.88(1)
		s.45(3) am.	37, s.119, Sch.8, para.88(2)
		s.45(4) rep.in pt. (1.1.1999)	37, ss.119,120(1)(2), Sch.8, para.88(3)(a), Sch.9, para.12, Sch.10
		s.45(4) am.	37, s.119, Sch.8, para.88(3)(b)
		s.46(2) am.	37, s.119, Sch.8, para.89
		s.47(2) subst.	37, s.119, Sch.8, para.90
		s.50(3) subst.	37, s.119, Sch.8, para.91
		s.51(2) replaced (by s.51(2)(2A)(2B)(2C)(2D))	37, ss.101(1),120(1), Sch.9, para.11
		s.51(4) am.	37, s.119, Sch.8, para.92
		s.53(8) added (4.1.1999)	37, s.119, Sch.8, para.93
		s.57(3)(a)(4)(a) am.	37, s.106, Sch.7, para.44
		s.58(9) added	37, s.106, Sch.7, para.45
		s.62 rep. & superseded (*prosp.*)	37, ss.98(7),120(1), Sch.10
		s.65(1) am. (30.9.1998 for areas specified in SI 1998/2327, Sch.1)	37, s.119, Sch.8, para.94(1)

Year and Chap. or No. of Measure	Short title	How affected	1998, Chapter of Act or Number of Measure or Statutory Instrument
1991—*cont.*			
		s.65(1A)(1B) added (30.9.1998 for areas specified in SI 1998/2327, Sch.1)	37, s.119, Sch.8, para.94(2)
		s.99(1) (defn. of "youth offending team") added (30.9.1998 for areas specified in SI 1998/2327, Sch.1)	37, s.119, Sch.8, para.95
		Sch.2 appl.(mods.)	37, ss.68(3),70(5), Sch.5, para.5(4)(5)
		Sch.2 appl.(mods.)	37, s.119, Sch.8, para.21 (adding 1969 c.54 s.16B)
		Sch.2, para.1(1) am.	37, s.64(5), Sch.4, para.2(1)(a)
		Sch.2, para.1(1)(a) am.	37, s.64(5), Sch.4, para.2(1)(b)
		Sch.2, para.1(4) added	37, s.64(5), Sch.4, para.2(2)
		Sch.2, para.1(6) added	37, s.119, Sch.8, para.96(1)
		Sch.2, para.2(2) am.	37, s.64(5), Sch.4, para.3
		Sch.2, para.3(1)(d) rep.in pt.	37, ss.119,120(2), Sch.8, para.96(2), Sch.10
		Sch.2, para.3(2A) added	37, s.119, Sch.8, para.96(3)
		Sch.2, para.4(1) am.	37, s.64(5), Sch.4, para.4
		Sch.2, para.4(1)(d) rep.in pt.	37, ss.119,120(2), Sch.8, para.96(4), Sch.10
		Sch.2, para.4(2A) added	37, s.119, Sch.8, para.96(5)
		Sch.2, para.5(2) am.	37, s.64(5), Sch.4, para.5
		Sch.2, para.6(6A) added	37, s.106, Sch.7, para.46(8)
		Sch.2, para.7(1) am.	37, s.64(5), Sch.4, para.6(1)
		Sch.2, para.7(3) am.	37, s.64(5), Sch.4, para.6(2)
		Sch.2, para.7(5) am.	37, s.106, Sch.7, para.46(9)
		Sch.2, para.8(1A) added	37, s.64(5), Sch.4, para.7(1)
		Sch.2, para.8(2)(b) subst.	37, s.106, Sch.7, para.46(10)
		Sch.2, para.8(3) am.	37, s.64(5), Sch.4, para.7(2)
		Sch.2, para.8A added	37, s.106, Sch.7, para.46(11)
		Sch.2, para.9(1)(a) subst.	37, s.64(5), Sch.4, para.8
		Sch.2, paras.11A,11B added	37, s.106, Sch.7, para.46(12)
		Sch.2, para.12(1) am.	37, s.64(5), Sch.4, para.9

Year and Chap. or No. of Measure	Short title	How affected	1998, Chapter of Act or Number of Measure or Statutory Instrument
1991—*cont.*			
		Sch.2, para.12(5)(6) added (partly in force 30.9.1998 for areas specified in Si 1998/2327, Sch.1)	37, s.119, Sch.8, para.96(6)
		Sch.2, para.14A added	37, s.64(5), Sch.4, para.10
		Sch.2, para.16 am.	37, s.64(5), Sch.4, para.11
		Sch.2, para.17(1) rep.in pt.	37, ss.119,120(1), Sch.8, para.96(7), Sch.10
		Sch.2, para.18(1) am.	37, s.64(5), Sch.4, para.12(1)
		Sch.2, para.18(1A) added	37, s.64(5), Sch.4, para.12(2)
		Sch.2, para.18(2) am.	37, s.64(5), Sch.4, para.12(3)
		Sch.5, para.1(2) am.	37, s.119, Sch.8, para.97
		Sch.11, paras.10,11,14 rep.	37, s.120(2), Sch.10
		Sch.12, para.1(5) added	37, s.106, Sch.7, para.46(1)
		Sch.12, para.3(1)(c) subst.	37, s.106, Sch.7, para.46(2)
		Sch.12, para.4(1) am.	37, s.106, Sch.7, para.46(3)(a)
		Sch.12, para.4(1)(c) subst.	37, s.106, Sch.7, para.46(2)
		Sch.12, para.4(1)(d) am.	37, s.106, Sch.7, para.46(3)(b)
		Sch.12, para.6(1) am.	37, s.106, Sch.7, para.46(4)
		Sch.12, para.6(3A) added	37, s.106, Sch.7, para.46(5)
		Sch.12, para.6(5) subst.	37, s.106, Sch.7, para.46(6)
		Sch.12, para.6(6) added	37, s.106, Sch.7, para.46(7)
		Sch.12, para.17(3) rep. (*prosp.*)	37, s.120(2), Sch.10
c.56	Water Industry Act 1991	s.2(6)(a) am. (pt.prosp.)	41, ss.54,66(5), Sch.10, Pt.II, para.5(3)
		s.2(6A)(6B) added (pt.prosp.)	41, s.66(5), Sch.10, Pt.II, para.5(4)
		s.12(5) rep.in pt. (*prosp.*)	41, ss.66(5),74(3), Sch.10, Pt.IV, para.13(2)(b), Sch.14, Pt.I
		s.12(5) am. (*prosp.*)	41, s.66(5), Sch.10, Pt.IV, para.13(2)(a)
		s.14(7)(8) replaced (by s.14(7)(7A)(8)(8A)) (*prosp.*)	41, s.66(5), Sch.10, Pt.IV, para.13(3)
		s.15(2) rep. (*prosp.*)	41, ss.66(5),74(3), Sch.10, Pt.IV, para.13(4), Sch.14, Pt.I
		s.17(1) rep.in pt. (*prosp.*)	41, ss.66(5),74(3), Sch.10, Pt.IV, para.13(5)(a), Sch.14, Pt.I

Effects of Legislation

Year and Chap. or No. of Measure	Short title	How affected	1998, Chapter of Act or Number of Measure or Statutory Instrument
1991—*cont.*			
		s.17(1)(b) rep. (*prosp.*)	41, ss.66(5),74(3), Sch.10, Pt.IV, para.13(5)(a), Sch.14, Pt.I
		s.17(2) rep.in pt. (*prosp.*)	41, ss.66(5),74(3), Sch.10, Pt.IV, para.13(5)(b)(ii), Sch.14, Pt.I
		s.17(2) am. (*prosp.*)	41, s.66(5), Sch.10, Pt.IV, para.13(5)(b)(i)
		s.17(2)(c) rep. (*prosp.*)	41, ss.66(5),74(3), Sch.10, Pt.IV, para.13(5)(b)(ii), Sch.14, Pt.I
		s.17(4) rep.in pt. (*prosp.*)	41, ss.66(5),74(3), Sch.10, Pt.IV, para.13(5)(c), Sch.14, Pt.I
		s.19(1A) added (*prosp.*)	41, s.66(5), Sch.10, Pt.IV, para.13(6)
		s.19(3) am. (*prosp.*)	41, s.66(5), Sch.10, Pt.IV, para.13(7)
		s.31(3) restr. (pt.prosp.)	41, s.66(5), Sch.10, Pt.II, para.5(1)
		s.31(3) subst. (pt.prosp.)	41, s.66(5), Sch.10, Pt.II, para.5(6)
		s.31(4) rep.in pt. (pt.prosp.)	41, ss.66(5),74(3), Sch.10, Pt.II, para.5(7)(a), Sch.14, Pt.I
		s.31(4) am. (pt.prosp.)	41, s.66(5), Sch.10, Pt.II, para.5(5)(7)(a)
		s.31(4)(c) rep. (pt.prosp.)	41, ss.66(5),74(3), Sch.10, Pt.II, para.5(7)(a), Sch.14, Pt.I
		s.31(4A) added (pt.prosp.)	41, s.66(5), Sch.10, Pt.II, para.5(8)
		s.31(5) rep.in pt. (pt.prosp.)	41, ss.66(5),74(3), Sch.10, Pt.II, para.5(9), Sch.14, Pt.I
		s.31(6) rep.in pt. (pt.prosp.)	41, ss.66(5),74(3), Sch.10, Pt.II, para.5(10), Sch.14, Pt.I
		s.31(7) rep.in pt. (pt.prosp.)	41, ss.66(5),74(3), Sch.10, Pt.II, para.5(11), Sch.14, Pt.I
		s.31(8)(b) subst. (pt.prosp.)	41, s.66(5), Sch.10, Pt.II, para.5(12)
		s.31(8A) added (*prosp.*)	41, s.66(5), Sch.10, Pt.IV, para.13(8)
		s.31(9) rep.in pt. (pt.prosp.)	41, ss.66(5),74(3), Sch.10, Pt.II, para.5(13), Sch.14, Pt.I
		s.41(2)(d)(ii) rep.in pt.	38, s.152, Sch.18, Pt.IV
		s.97(5) defn.of (" relevant area") para.(d) rep.	38, s.152, Sch.18, Pt.IV
		s.97(5)(b) defn.of (" relevant authority") para.(b) am.	38, s.129, Sch.15, para.17(b)

Year and Chap. or No. of Measure	Short title	How affected	1998, Chapter of Act or Number of Measure or Statutory Instrument
1991—*cont.*			
		s.97(5)(c) defn.of ('' relevant area'') para.([c]) am.	38, s.129, Sch.15, para.17(a)
		s.97(6) rep.	43, s.1(1), Sch.1, Pt.X, Group 3
		s.98(2)(d)(ii) rep.in pt.	38, s.152, Sch.18, Pt.IV
		s.206(9A) added (*prosp.*)	41, s.66(5), Sch.10, Pt.IV, para.13(9)
		Sch.15, Pt.II rep.in pt. (*prosp.*)	41, ss.66(5),74(3), Sch.10, Pt.IV, para.13(10)(a), Sch.14, Pt.I
		Sch.15, Pt.II am. (11.1.1999)	41, s.66(5), Sch.10, Pt.IV, para.13(10)(b)
c.57	Water Resources Act 1991	defn. of "flood defence functions" appl.	38, s.111, Sch.9, Pt.II, para.15(1)
		s.83 mod.	SI 389, reg.5
		s.85 appl.(mods.)	iv, s.22(4)(a)
		s.85(1) saved	SI 1936(L), art.20(6)
		s.85(1) saved (13.1.1999)	SI 3269(L), art.15(6)
		s.85(2) saved	SI 1936(L), art.20(6)
		s.85(2) saved (13.1.1999)	SI 3269(L), art.15(6)
		s.85(3) saved	SI 1936(L), art.20(6)
		s.85(3) saved (13.1.1999)	SI 3269(L), art.15(6)
		s.88(1) appl.(mods.) (1.4.1999)	SI 2746, reg.14(2)
		s.109 saved	SI 1209(L), art.5(10)
		s.109 mod.	iv, s.35(13)
		ss.191A,191B appl.(mods.) (1.4.1999)	SI 2746, reg.14(3)
		Sch.10, para.11 appl.(mods.) (1.4.1999)	SI 2746, reg.14(4)
		Sch.24, Pt.II rep.in pt. (*prosp.*)	41, ss.66(5),74(3), Sch.10, Pt.IV, para.14(a), Sch.14, Pt.I
		Sch.24, Pt.II am. (11.1.1999)	41, s.66(5), Sch.10, Pt.IV, para.14(b)
c.59	Land Drainage Act 1991	s.23 saved	SI 1209(L), art.5(10)
c.xiii	London Local Authorities Act 1991	s.23(11B) am.	18, s.54(1), Sch.3, para.22
c.xvi	Greater Manchester (Light Rapid Transit System) Act 1991	s.19 appl.	SI 2919(L), art.9
		s.19 appl.(mods.)	SI 2919(L), art.10(7)
		ss.43,44 appl.	SI 2919(L), art.9
No.1	Care of Churches and Ecclesiastical Jurisdiction Measure 1991	ss.25(2)(b),27(3) trans.of functions (1.1.1999)	SI 1715, art.2, Sch.1
No.2	Diocesan Boards of Education Measure 1991	s.3(1)(2) am. (*prosp.*)	31, s.140(1), Sch.30, para.30(a)(b)
		s.3(4)(5) rep. (*prosp.*)	31, s.140(1)(3), Sch.30, para.30(c), Sch.31
		s.3(6) rep.in pt. (*prosp.*)	31, s.140(1)(3), Sch.30, para.30(d)(i), Sch.31

Year and Chap. or No. of Measure	Short title	How affected	1998, Chapter of Act or Number of Measure or Statutory Instrument
1991—*cont.*			
		s.3(6) am. (*prosp.*)	31, s.140(1), Sch.30, para.30(d)(ii)
		ss.5,6(2) rep. (*prosp.*)	31, s.140(3), Sch.31
		s.7(1) replaced (by s.7(1) (1A)) (*prosp.*)	31, s.140(1), Sch.30, para.31(a)
		s.7(2) am. (*prosp.*)	31, s.140(1), Sch.30, para.31(b)
		s.7(3) am. (*prosp.*)	31, s.140(1), Sch.30, para.31(c)
		s.7(5) rep. (*prosp.*)	31, s.140(1)(3), Sch.30, para.31(d), Sch.31
		s.7, sidenote subst. (*prosp.*)	31, s.140(1), Sch.30, para.31(e)
		s.9 rep. (*prosp.*)	31, s.140(3), Sch.31
		s.10(1) (defn. of "Church of England voluntary school") rep. (*prosp.*)	31, s.140(1)(3), Sch.30, para.32(2)(a), Sch.31
		s.10(1) (defn. of "church school") subst. (*prosp.*)	31, s.140(1), Sch.30, para.32(2)(b)
		s.10(2) rep. (*prosp.*)	31, s.140(1)(3), Sch.30, para.32(3), Sch.31
		s.10(3) subst. (*prosp.*)	31, s.140(1), Sch.30, para.32(4)
1992 c.4	Social Security Contributions and Benefits Act 1992	mod.	SI 263, art.2, Sch.
		mod.	14, s.2(1)(2)(b)
		mod. (EWS) (*prosp.*)	14, s.8(1)(c)(4)(5)
		power to mod. (EWS) (*prosp.*)	14, s.11(1)(3)
		power to am. (*prosp.*)	47, s.87
		Pts.II-V mod. (*prosp.*)	14, s.8(1)(a)(2)(3)(a)
		s.1(2) am. (6.4.1999)	14, s.86(1), Sch.7, para.56(1)
		s.1(2)(bb) added (6.4.1999)	14, s.86(1), Sch.7, para.56(1)
		s.1(4)(a) am. (6.4.1999)	14, s.86(1), Sch.7, para.56(2)
		s.1(6) am. (6.4.1999)	14, s.86(1), Sch.7, para.56(3)
		s.3(2A) added	14, s.48
		s.3(4)(5) added	14, s.49
		s.4(4) subst.	14, s.50(1)(3)
		s.4(6) added (*prosp.*)	14, s.50(2)
		s.4(6) restr. (*prosp.*)	14, s.50(4)(a)
		s.4(6) ext. (*prosp.*)	14, s.50(4)(b)
		s.5(1) subst. (*prosp.*)	14, s.51(1)
		s.6(1) subst. (*prosp.*)	14, s.51(2)
		s.6(2A) added (6.4.1999)	14, s.86(1), Sch.7, para.57
		s.8(1)(2) subst. (*prosp.*)	14, s.51(3)
		s.9 subst. (*prosp.*)	14, s.51(4)

Year and Chap. or No. of Measure	Short title	How affected	1998, Chapter of Act or Number of Measure or Statutory Instrument
1992—*cont.*			
		s.10(2)(b) subst.	14, s.52
		s.10(5) am. (*prosp.*)	14, s.86(1), Sch.7, para.58(1)
		s.10(8A) added (6.4.1999)	14, s.86(1), Sch.7, para.58(2)
		s.10A added (6.4.1999)	14, s.53
		s.11(1)(4) am.	SI 469, art.2
		s.13(1) am.	SI 469, art.3
		s.14(4) added (*prosp.*)	14, s.86(1), Sch.7, para.59
		ss.15(3),18(1) am.	SI 469, art.4
		s.19A added (*prosp.*)	14, s.54
		s.21(5A) added (*prosp.*)	14, s.86(1), Sch.7, para.60
		s.22(4) am. (*prosp.*)	14, s.86(1), Sch.7, para.61
		ss.22(5)(a),30C am.	14, s.77(1)-(7)(8)(a)-(d)
		s.35(5) am. (paras.(a)(b) replaced) (*prosp.*)	14, s.67
		s.44(4) am.	SI 470, art.4(3)
		s.44(4) subst.	14, s.68
		s.54(2) am. (*prosp.*)	14, s.86(1), Sch.7, para.62
		ss.68,69 am.	14, s.77(1)-(7)(8)(a)-(d)
		s.80(4) am.	SI 470, art.8
		s.95(5)(c) am. (*prosp.*)	14, s.86(1), Sch.7, para.63
		s.97(1)(b) am. (*prosp.*)	14, s.86(1), Sch.7, para.64
		s.109(2) am. (*prosp.*)	14, s.86(1), Sch.7, para.65
		s.113(3) am. (*prosp.*)	14, s.86(1), Sch.7, para.66
		s.116(2) am. (*prosp.*)	14, s.86(1), Sch.7, para.67
		s.117(1) am. (*prosp.*)	14, s.86(1), Sch.7, para.68
		s.119 am. (*prosp.*)	14, s.86(1), Sch.7, para.69
		s.120(1) am. (*prosp.*)	14, s.86(1), Sch.7, para.70
		s.120(2) am. (*prosp.*)	17, s.50, Sch.4, para.30
		s.122(1) (defns. of "initial primary percentage" and "main primary percentage") rep.	14, s.86(1)(2), Sch.7, para.71(b), Sch.8
		s.122(1) (defn. of "entitled") am. (*prosp.*)	14, s.86(1), Sch.7, para.71(a)
		s.122(1) (defns. of "lower earnings limit" and "upper earnings limit") replaced (*prosp.*)	14, s.86(1), Sch.7, para.71(c)
		s.122(1) (defn. of "PAYE settlement agreement") added (6.4.1999)	14, s.86(1), Sch.7, para.71(d)
		s.122(1) (defn. of "primary percentage") am. (*prosp.*)	14, s.86(1), Sch.7, para.71(e)
		s.124(1)(e) am.	14, s.77(1)-(7)(8)(a)-(d)
		s.126(7) am.	SI 470, art.20
		s.135(1) am.	14, s.77(1)-(7)(8)(a)-(d)
		s.138(1) subst. (*prosp.*)	14, s.70(1)
		s.138(1)(a)(b)(2) mod. (*prosp.*)	14, s.8(1)(b)(3)(f)

Year and Chap. or No. of Measure	Short title	How affected	1998, Chapter of Act or Number of Measure or Statutory Instrument
1992—*cont.*			
		s.138(5) added (*prosp.*)	14, s.70(2)
		s.139(1) subst. (*prosp.*)	14, s.86(1), Sch.7, para.72(1)
		s.139(2) am. (*prosp.*)	14, s.86(1), Sch.7, para.72(2)
		s.139(3) rep. (*prosp.*)	14, s.86(1)(2), Sch.7, para.72(3), Sch.8
		s.139(4) am. (*prosp.*)	14, s.86(1), Sch.7, para.72(4)
		s.139(5) am. (*prosp.*)	14, s.86(1), Sch.7, para.72(5)
		s.140(1)-(5) am. (*prosp.*)	14, s.86(1), Sch.7, para.73
		s.140(1) am. (*prosp.*)	14, s.71(1)
		s.140(1A) added (*prosp.*)	14, s.71(2)
		s.140(4)(aa) added (*prosp.*)	14, s.71(3)
		s.140(4)(e) rep. (*prosp.*)	14, ss.71(3),86(2), Sch.8
		s.145(4) excl.	14, s.72(1)
		s.148 mod. (*prosp.*)	14, s.33(1)
		s.150 appl. (*prosp.*)	14, s.33(2)
		s.157(1) am.	SI 470, art.9
		s.163(1) (defn. of "employer") am. (*prosp.*)	14, s.86(1), Sch.7, para.74
		s.163(1) (defn. of "employer") am. (*prosp.*)	14, Sch.7, para.74
		s.171(1) (defn. of "employer") am. (*prosp.*)	14, s.86(1), Sch.7, para.75
		ss.171A-171G (Pt.XIIA) am.	14, s.77(1)-(7)(8)(e)
		s.171E(2) am. (*prosp.*)	14, s.86(1), Sch.7, para.76
		Sch.1, para.1(2) subst. (*prosp.*)	14, s.86(1), Sch.7, para.77(2)
		Sch.1, para.1(3) am. (*prosp.*)	14, s.86(1), Sch.7, para.77(3)
		Sch.1, para.1(6)(a) am. (*prosp.*)	14, s.86(1), Sch.7, para.77(4)
		Sch.1, para.3(1) am. (*prosp.*)	14, s.86(1), Sch.7, para.77(5)
		Sch.1, para.3(3) am.	14, s.55(a)
		Sch.1, para.3(4)(5) added	14, s.55(b)
		Sch.1, para.5 subst.	14, s.86(1), Sch.7, para.77(6)
		Sch.1, para.5A added (6.4.1999)	14, s.86(1), Sch.7, para.77(7)
		Sch.1, para.6(1) subst. (6.4.1999)	14, s.86(1), Sch.7, para.77(8)
		Sch.1, para.6(2) am. (6.4.1999)	14, s.86(1), Sch.7, para.77(9)(a)
		Sch.1, para.6(2)(b) rep.in pt. (6.4.1999)	14, s.86(1)(2), Sch.7, para.77(9)(b), Sch.8
		Sch.1, para.6(4) subst. (*prosp.*)	14, s.86(1), Sch.7, para.77(10)
		Sch.1, para.6(4A) added (6.4.1999)	14, s.86(1), Sch.7, para.77(11)

Year and Chap. or No. of Measure	Short title	How affected	1998, Chapter of Act or Number of Measure or Statutory Instrument
1992—*cont.*			
		Sch.1, para.7(3) am. (*prosp.*)	14, s.56(1)
		Sch.1, para.7(11)(a) am.	14, s.86(1), Sch.7, para.77(12)
		Sch.1, para.7(12) subst. (*prosp.*)	14, s.86(1), Sch.7, para.77(13)
		Sch.1, para.7A added (*prosp.*)	14, s.56(2)
		Sch.1, para.7B added (*prosp.*)	14, s.57
		Sch.1, para.7C added (*prosp.*)	14, s.58
		Sch.1, para.8(1)(b) am. (6.4.1999)	14, s.86(1), Sch.7, para.77(14)
		Sch.1, para.8(1)(ia) added (6.4.1999)	14, s.86(1), Sch.7, para.77(15)
		Sch.1, para.8(1)(l) am. (6.4.1999)	14, s.86(1), Sch.7, para.77(16)
		Sch.1, head. am. (*prosp.*)	14, s.86(1), Sch.7, para.77(1)
		Sch.2 am.	14, s.59(1)
		Sch.2, para.2 am.	14, s.59(2)
		Sch.2, para.3 rep.	14, ss.59(3),86(2), Sch.8
		Sch.2, para.4(2) am.	14, s.59(4)
		Sch.2, para.6(1) am.	14, s.59(5)(a)
		Sch.2, para.6(1) am.	14, s.59(5)(b)
		Sch.2, para.6(2) rep.in pt.	14, ss.59(6)(a),86(2), Sch.8
		Sch.2, para.6(2) rep.in pt.	14, s.59(6)(b)
		Sch.4, Pts.I,III,IV,V am.	SI 470, art.3(1), Sch.1
		Sch.7, para.4(a)(b) am.	SI 520, art.2
		Sch.7, para.13(4) am.	SI 470, art.4(2)
		Sch.8, paras.2(6)(c),6(2) (b) am.	SI 470, art.7
		Sch.11, para.2(d) rep.in pt. (6.4.1999)	14, ss.73,86(2), Sch.8
c.5	Social Security Administration Act 1992	mod.	SI 263, art.2, Sch.
		mod.	14, s.2(1)(2)(c)
		mod. (EWS) (*prosp.*)	14, s.8(1)(c)(4)(5)
		power to am. (*prosp.*)	47, s.87
		Pt.II trans.of functions (EWS) (*prosp.*)	14, s.4(1)(a)
		Pt.II rep. & superseded (EWS) (*prosp.*)	14, s.39(3)
		s.3(2) am. (*prosp.*)	14, s.86(1), Sch.7, para.78(b)
		s.3(2)(a) subst. (*prosp.*)	14, s.86(1), Sch.7, para.78(a)
		s.5(1) am. (*temp.*)	14, s.83, Sch.6, para.5(1)
		s.5(1)(e) am. (*prosp.*)	14, s.86(1), Sch.7, para.79(1)(a)
		s.5(1)(hh) added (*prosp.*)	14, s.74
		s.5(1)(n)(o) rep. (*prosp.*)	14, s.86(1)(2), Sch.7, para.79(1)(b), Sch.8

Year and Chap. or No. of Measure	Short title	How affected	1998, Chapter of Act or Number of Measure or Statutory Instrument
1992—*cont.*			
		s.5(4) rep. (*prosp.*)	14, s.86(1)(2), Sch.7, para.79(2), Sch.8
		s.6(1)(n)(o) rep. (*prosp.*)	14, s.86(1)(2), Sch.7, para.80, Sch.8
		ss.17-70 (Pt.II) rep. (*prosp.*)	14, s.86(2), Sch.8
		s.21 am. (subsection (7) added)	14, s.83, Sch.6, para.2
		s.22 mod. (*temp.*)	14, s.83, Sch.6, para.3(1)
		s.23 am. (*temp.*)	14, s.83, Sch.6, para.4(1)
		s.33 mod. (*temp.*)	14, s.83, Sch.6, para.3(2)
		s.34 am. (*temp.*)	14, s.83, Sch.6, para.4(2)
		s.38 trans.of functions (*prosp.*)	14, s.1(a)
		s.41 am. (*temp.*)	14, s.83, Sch.6, para.1
		s.48 am. (*temp.*)	14, s.83, Sch.6, para.4(3)
		s.61A am.	14, s.77(1)-(7)(8)(f)
		s.64 trans.of functions (*prosp.*)	14, s.1(b)
		s.66 am. (*temp.*)	14, s.83, Sch.6, para.7
		s.69 am. (*temp.*)	14, s.83, Sch.6, para.6
		s.71(2) am. (*prosp.*)	14, s.86(1), Sch.7, para.81(1)
		s.71(5)(a)(b) am. (*prosp.*)	14, s.86(1), Sch.7, para.81(2)
		s.71(5A) am. (*prosp.*)	14, s.86(1), Sch.7, para.81(3)
		s.71A(1) am. (*prosp.*)	14, s.86(1), Sch.7, para.82
		s.71ZA added	14, s.75(1)(2)
		s.71ZA am. (*temp.*)	14, s.83, Sch.6, para.8
		s.113 subst. (*prosp.*)	14, s.60
		s.114 replaced (by ss.114, 114A) (*prosp.*)	14, s.61
		s.116(6) rep. (*prosp.*)	14, s.86(1)(2), Sch.7, para.83, Sch.8
		s.117 subst. (*prosp.*)	14, s.86(1), Sch.7, para.84
		s.118(1) replaced (by s.118(1)(1A)) (*prosp.*)	14, s.62(1)
		s.118(3) am. (*prosp.*)	14, s.62(2)
		s.118(4) rep.in pt. (*prosp.*)	14, ss.62(3),86(2), Sch.8
		s.118(7) added (*prosp.*)	14, s.62(4)
		s.119(2) rep. (*prosp.*)	14, s.86(1)(2), Sch.7, para.85, Sch.8
		s.120(1) rep.in pt. (*prosp.*)	14, s.86(1)(2), Sch.7, para.86(1), Sch.8
		s.120(3) am. (*prosp.*)	14, s.86(1), Sch.7, para.86(2)
		s.120(4) am. (*prosp.*)	14, s.86(1), Sch.7, para.86(3)
		s.120(4A) added (*prosp.*)	14, s.86(1), Sch.7, para.86(4)

Year and Chap. or No. of Measure	Short title	How affected	1998, Chapter of Act or Number of Measure or Statutory Instrument
1992—*cont.*			
		s.120(5) rep.in pt. (*prosp.*)	14, s.86(1)(2), Sch.7, para.86(5)(a), Sch.8
		s.120(5) am. (*prosp.*)	14, s.86(1), Sch.7, para.86(5)(b)
		s.120(5)(b) rep. (*prosp.*)	14, s.86(1)(2), Sch.7, para.86(5)(a), Sch.8
		s.120(6) am. (*prosp.*)	14, s.86(1), Sch.7, para.86(6)
		s.121(1) rep.in pt. (*prosp.*)	14, s.86(1)(2), Sch.7, para.87, Sch.8
		s.121(1) am.	15, s.4(2)(a)
		s.121(2) rep.in pt. (*prosp.*)	14, s.86(1)(2), Sch.7, para.87, Sch.8
		ss.121A-121B added (*prosp.*)	14, s.63
		ss.121C-121D added (*prosp.*)	14, s.64
		ss.122C,122D ext.	14, s.3(3)
		s.123(6A) am. (*prosp.*)	14, s.86(1), Sch.7, para.88
		s.123(8)(ba)(hd) added (*prosp.*)	38, s.125, Sch.12, para.32
		s.124 am. (1.4.1999)	SI 3171, art.2, Sch.
		s.125(1) am. (*prosp.*)	14, s.86(1), Sch.7, para.89
		s.139D(1)(b)(d) am. (EW)	18, s.54(1), Sch.3, para.23(2)(3)
		ss.140A-140G saved (1.7.1999)	46, ss.29,53(4), Sch.4, Pt.I, paras.1(2)(e),9
		s.140D(1)(c) rep.in pt.	38, s.152, Sch.18, Pt.IV
		s.143(1)(a)(b) subst. (*prosp.*)	14, s.86(1), Sch.7, para.90(1)
		s.143(4)(a) subst. (*prosp.*)	14, s.86(1), Sch.7, para.90(2)
		s.143A added	14, s.65
		s.144 am. (6.4.1999)	14, s.86(1), Sch.7, para.91
		s.145(1)-(3) subst. (*prosp.*)	14, s.86(1), Sch.7, para.92
		s.146 rep. (*prosp.*)	14, s.86(1)(2), Sch.7, para.93, Sch.8
		s.147(1)-(3) rep.in pt. (*prosp.*)	14, s.86(1)(2), Sch.7, para.94, Sch.8
		s.150(1)(e) am.	SI 470, art.4(4)(c)
		s.155(3) excl.	SI 521, reg.2
		s.155A added	14, s.76
		s.159(2) am. (*prosp.*)	14, s.86(1), Sch.7, para.95
		s.159A(3) am. (*prosp.*)	14, s.86(1), Sch.7, para.96
		s.160(2) am. (*prosp.*)	14, s.86(1), Sch.7, para.97
		s.160A(2) am. (*prosp.*)	14, s.86(1), Sch.7, para.98
		s.162(2A) added	14, s.86(1), Sch.7, para.99(1)
		s.162(4A) added	14, s.86(1), Sch.7, para.99(2)
		s.162(5)(b) am. (*prosp.*)	14, s.86(1), Sch.7, para.99(3)
		s.162(5)(ca) added (6.4.1999)	14, s.65(2)

Year and Chap. or No. of Measure	Short title	How affected	1998, Chapter of Act or Number of Measure or Statutory Instrument
1992—*cont.*			
		s.162(8)(b) am. (6.4.1999)	14, s.86(1), Sch.7, para.99(4)
		s.163(4) am. (*retrosp.*)	14, s.66(1)
		s.163(4) am. (6.4.1999)	14, s.86(1), Sch.7, para.100(1)
		s.163(5) am. (*prosp.*)	14, s.86(1), Sch.7, para.100(2)
		s.164(5)(a) rep. (6.4.1999)	14, s.86(1)(2), Sch.7, para.101, Sch.8
		s.166(1)(d) am. (*prosp.*)	14, s.86(1), Sch.7, para.102(1)
		s.166(2)(c) am. (*prosp.*)	14, s.86(1), Sch.7, para.102(2)
		s.168(3)(a) am. (*prosp.*)	14, s.86(1), Sch.7, para.103(1)
		s.168(5) am. (*prosp.*)	14, s.86(1), Sch.7, para.103(2)
		s.168(6) added (*prosp.*)	14, s.86(1), Sch.7, para.103(3)
		s.170 defn.of (" the relevant Northern Ireland enactments2) para.(ad) added (*prosp.*)	14, s.86(1), Sch.7, para.104(b)
		s.170(5) defn.of (" the relevant enactments") para.(ad) added (*prosp.*)	14, s.86(1), Sch.7, para.104(a)
		s.177 rep. & superseded (*prosp.*)	47, s.87(8)(a)
		s.177 rep. (*prosp.*)	47, s.100(2), Sch.15
		s.177(2) mod. (*prosp.*)	47, s.88
		s.177(5)(a)(b) am. (*prosp.*)	14, s.86(1), Sch.7, para.105
		s.178 rep. & superseded (*prosp.*)	47, s.87(8)(a)
		s.178 rep. (*prosp.*)	47, s.100(2), Sch.15
		s.178(1)(3) am. (*prosp.*)	14, s.86(1), Sch.7, para.106
		s.179(3)(a) am. (*prosp.*)	14, s.86(1), Sch.7, para.107(1)
		s.179(4)(ab) added (*prosp.*)	14, s.86(1), Sch.7, para.107(2)
		s.180(a)(b)(i) am. (*prosp.*)	14, s.86(1), Sch.7, para.108
		s.189 appl. (*prosp.*)	47, s.87(9)
		s.189(1) rep.in pt. (*prosp.*)	14, s.86(1)(2), Sch.7, para.109(a), Sch.8
		s.189(2) rep. (*prosp.*)	14, s.86(1)(2), Sch.7, para.109(b), Sch.8
		s.189(4) rep.in pt. (*prosp.*)	14, s.86(1)(2), Sch.7, para.109(c), Sch.8
		s.189(5) rep.in pt. (*prosp.*)	14, s.86(1)(2), Sch.7, para.109(d), Sch.8

Year and Chap. or No. of Measure	Short title	How affected	1998, Chapter of Act or Number of Measure or Statutory Instrument
1992—*cont.*			
		s.189(6) rep.in pt. (*prosp.*)	14, s.86(1)(2), Sch.7, para.109(e), Sch.8
		s.189(9) am. (*prosp.*)	47, s.99, Sch.13, para.11
		s.189(10) rep. (*prosp.*)	14, s.86(1)(2), Sch.7, para.109(f), Sch.8
		s.189(11) am. (*prosp.*)	47, s.99, Sch.13, para.11
		s.190(1)(a) rep.in pt. (6.4.1999)	14, s.86(1)(2), Sch.7, para.110(1)(b), Sch.8
		s.190(1)(a) am. (6.4.1999)	14, s.86(1), Sch.7, para.110(1)(a)
		s.190(4) rep. (*prosp.*)	14, s.86(1)(2), Sch.7, para.110(2), Sch.8
		s.191 appl. (*prosp.*)	14, s.39(2)
		s.191 (defn. of "Commissioner") rep.	14, s.86(1)(2), Sch.7, para.111(a), Sch.8
		s.191 (defn. of "claimant") am. (*prosp.*)	14, s.86(1), Sch.7, para.111(b)
		s.191 (defn. of "housing authority") am.	38, s.129, Sch.15, para.18
		s.192(5) rep.in pt. (*prosp.*)	14, s.86(1)(2), Sch.7, para.112, Sch.8
		s.192(5) am. (*prosp.*)	47, s.89(9)
		Sch.4, Pt.I rep.in pt. (*prosp.*)	14, s.86(1)(2), Sch.7, para.113, Sch.8
		Sch.4, Pt.I am. (*prosp.*)	14, s.86(1), Sch.7, para.113
		Sch.7, Pt.I am. (6.4.1999)	14, s.86(1), Sch.7, para.114(1)
		Sch.7, Pt.II am. (6.4.1999)	14, s.86(1), Sch.7, para.114(2)
		Sch.8 rep. (*prosp.*)	47, s.100(2), Sch.15
		Sch.9, para.1(6) am. (*prosp.*)	14, s.86(1), Sch.7, para.115
		Sch.10, para.3(1)(2) am. (*prosp.*)	14, s.86(1), Sch.7, para.116
c.6	Social Security (Consequential Provisions) Act 1992	mod. (EWS) (*prosp.*)	14, s.8(1)(c)(4)(5)
		Sch.4, para.12 rep. (*prosp.*)	14, s.86(2), Sch.8
c.7	Social Security Contributions and Benefits (Northern Ireland) Act 1992	power to am. (*prosp.*)	47, s.87
		s.1(2) am. (*prosp.*)	SI 1506, art.78(1), Sch.6, para.38(1)
		s.1(4)(a) am. (*prosp.*)	SI 1506, art.78(1), Sch.6, para.38(2)
		s.1(6) am. (*prosp.*)	SI 1506, art.78(1), Sch.6, para.38(3)
		s.6(2A) added (*prosp.*)	SI 1506, art.78(1), Sch.6, para.39
		s.10(5) am. (*prosp.*)	SI 1506, art.78(1), Sch.6, para.40(1)

Year and Chap. or No. of Measure	Short title	How affected	1998, Chapter of Act or Number of Measure or Statutory Instrument
1992—*cont.*			
		s.10(8A) added (*prosp.*)	SI 1506, art.78(1), Sch.6, para.40(2)
		s.14(4) added (*prosp.*)	SI 1506, art.78(1), Sch.6, para.41
		s.21(5A) added (*prosp.*)	SI 1506, art.78(1), Sch.6, para.42
		s.22(4)(a) am. (*prosp.*)	SI 1506, art.78(1), Sch.6, para.43
		s.54(2) am. (*prosp.*)	SI 1506, art.78(1), Sch.6, para.44
		s.95(5)(c) am. (*prosp.*)	SI 1506, art.78(1), Sch.6, para.45
		s.97(1)(b) am. (*prosp.*)	SI 1506, art.78(1), Sch.6, para.46
		s.109(2) am. (*prosp.*)	SI 1506, art.78(1), Sch.6, para.47
		s.166(3) am. (*prosp.*)	17, s.50, Sch.4, para.31
		Sch.2 am.	14, s.59(1)
		Sch.2, para.2 am.	14, s.59(2)
		Sch.2, para.3 rep.	14, ss.59(3),86(2), Sch.8
		Sch.2, para.4(2) am.	14, s.59(4)
		Sch.2, para.6(1) am.	14, s.59(5)
		Sch.2, para.6(1) am.	14, s.59(5)(b)
		Sch.2, para.6(2) rep.in pt.	14, ss.59(6),86(2), Sch.8
		Sch.9, para.1(1) am. (*prosp.*)	SI 1504, art.65(1), Sch.5, para.40
		Sch.9, para.1(1)(e) rep. (*prosp.*)	SI 1504, art.65(2), Sch.6
c.8	Social Security Administration (Northern Ireland) Act 1992	power to am. (*prosp.*)	47, s.87
		ss.5(1),19-21,32,39,64,67, 69ZA mod. (*temp.*)	SI 1506, art.77, Sch.5
		s.149(1) subst. (*prosp.*)	47, s.89(1)
		s.149(2A) subst. (*prosp.*)	47, s.89(2)
		s.149(3) am. (*prosp.*)	47, s.89(3)
		s.149(3A) added (*prosp.*)	47, s.89(4)
		s.150(1)(2) am. (*prosp.*)	47, s.89(5)
		s.150(3) am. (*prosp.*)	47, s.89(6)
		s.150(5) am. (*prosp.*)	47, s.89(5)
		s.150(6) (defn. of "the Council") added (*prosp.*)	47, s.89(7)
		s.153 rep. & superseded (*prosp.*)	47, s.87(8)(b)
		s.153 rep. (*prosp.*)	47, s.100(2), Sch.15
		s.154 rep. & superseded (*prosp.*)	47, s.87(8)(b)
		s.154 rep. (*prosp.*)	47, s.100(2), Sch.15
		s.165 ext. (*prosp.*)	47, s.87(10)
		s.165(10)(11) am. (*prosp.*)	47, s.99, Sch.13, para.12

Year and Chap. or No. of Measure	Short title	How affected	1998, Chapter of Act or Number of Measure or Statutory Instrument
1992—*cont.*			
		s.167(1) (defn. of "Joint Authority") rep. (*prosp.*)	47, s.100(2), Sch.15
		Sch.5A added (*prosp.*)	47, s.89(8)
c.12	Taxation of Chargeable Gains Act 1992	saved	36, s.108, Sch.16 (adding 1988 c.1, Sch.28AA at para.13)
		defn(s). appl.	36, s.132, Sch.23, para.6(7)
		s.2(4)(5) added	36, s.121, Sch.21, para.2
		s.2A added (year 1998-99 and subsequent years of assessment)	36, s.121(1)(4)
		s.3 am. (amount specified for 1998-99)	SI 757, art.2
		s.3(5) replaced (by s.3(5)(5A)(5B)(5C))	36, s.121, Sch.21, para.3
		s.4(1) rep.in pt. (year 1998-99 and subsequent years of assessment)	36, s.165, Sch.27, Pt.III(29), Note
		s.4(1AA) added (year 1998-99 and subsequent years of assessment)	36, s.120(1)(2)
		s.5 rep. (year 1998-99 and subsequent years of assessment)	36, s.165, Sch.27, Pt.III(29), Note
		s.9(3) am. (year 1997-98, year 1998-99)	36, s.127(2)(4)
		s.10A added (year 1997-98, year 1998-99)	36, s.127(1)(4)
		s.13(10A) added	36, s.121, Sch.21, para.4
		s.13(11A) added (6.4.1998) (*retrosp.*)	36, s.122(4)(6)(7)
		ss.39(1)(2),41(4)(5) am.	36, s.46(3), Sch.7, para.7
		s.53(1A) added (6.4.1998) (*retrosp.*)	36, s.122(1)(6)(7)
		s.53(4) am. (6.4.1998) (*retrosp.*)	36, s.125(3)(4)
		s.54(1) am. (6.4.1998) (*retrosp.*)	36, s.122(2)(6)(7)
		s.54(1A) added (6.4.1998) (*retrosp.*)	36, s.122(3)(6)(7)
		s.62(2A)(2B) added	36, s.121, Sch.21, para.5
		s.64 rep.in pt.	38, ss.140,152, Sch.16, para.95(a), Sch.18, Pt.VI
		s.76(1) am. (6.3.1998) (*retrosp.*)	36, s.128(1)(a)(4)
		s.76(1A)(1B) added (6.3.1998) (*retrosp.*)	36, s.128(1)(b)(2)(4)
		s.76(3) added (6.3.1998) (*retrosp.*)	36, s.128(1)(c)(3)(4)
		s.77(6A) added	36, s.121, Sch.21, para.6(1)

Year and Chap. or No. of Measure	Short title	How affected	1998, Chapter of Act or Number of Measure or Statutory Instrument
1992—*cont.*			
		s.86 mod.	36, s.132, Sch.23, para.1(2)(3)
		s.86 mod.	36, s.132, Sch.23, para.2(3)(5)(6)
		s.86 mod.	36, s.132, Sch.23, para.2(4)(5)(6)
		s.86 mod.	36, s.132, Sch.23, para.3(2)(3)(4)(6)
		s.86(1)(e) mod.	36, s.132, Sch.23, para.4(1)
		s.86(1)(e) mod.	36, s.132(5)
		s.86(4A) added	36, s.121, Sch.21, para.6(2)
		s.86A added (year of departure is 1997-98 or any subsequent year of assessment)	36, s.129(1)(3)
		s.87 mod.	36, s.130(4)
		s.87(1) rep.in pt. (year 1998-99 and subsequent years of assessment and shall be deemed to have applied for the year 1997-98)	36, ss.130(1)(3),165, Sch.27, Pt.III(30), Note 1
		s.87(2) mod.	36, s.132, Sch.23, para.5(1)
		s.87(3) mod.	36, s.132, Sch.23, para.4(6)
		s.87(3) mod.	36, s.132, Sch.23, para.5(2)
		s.87(6A) added	36, s.121, Sch.21, para.6(3)
		s.88(1) rep.in pt. (year 1998-99 and subsequent years of assessment and shall be deemed to have applied for the year 1997-98)	36, ss.130(2)(b)(3),165, Sch.27, Pt.III(30), Note 1
		s.88(1)(a) am. (year 1998- 99 and subsequent years of assessment and shall be deemed to have applied for the year 1997-98)	36, s.130(2)(a)(3)
		s.88(1)(c) rep. (year 1998-99 and subsequent years of assessment and shall be deemed to have applied for the year 1997-98)	36, ss.130(2)(b)(3),165, Sch.27, Pt.III(30), Note 1
		s.89(3) am.	36, s.121, Sch.21, para.6(4)
		s.96(9A)(9B) added (year 1997-98, year 1998-99)	36, s.127(3)(4)

Year and Chap. or No. of Measure	Short title	How affected	1998, Chapter of Act or Number of Measure or Statutory Instrument
1992—*cont.*			
		s.97(1)-(5)(7)(8) added (year of departure is 1997-98 or any subsequent year of assessment)	36, s.129(2)(3)
		s.101(1B) added (17.3.1998) (*retrosp.*)	36, s.134(3)(5)
		s.101A added (17.3.1998) (*retrosp.*)	36, s.133(1)(3)
		s.101B added (17.3.1998) (*retrosp.*)	36, s.134(2)(5)
		s.101C added (17.3.1998) (*retrosp.*)	36, s.135(2)(5)
		ss.104-114 mod.	SI 1869, reg.12 (replacing 1989/469 at reg.27(2))
		ss.104-114 mod. (6.4.1999)	SI 1870, reg.34(2)
		s.104 (defn. of "securities") appl. (17.3.1998) (*retrosp.*)	36, s.124(9)
		s.104(1) restr. (17.3.1998) (*retrosp.*)	36, s.124(8)(c)
		s.104(2)(aa) added (6.4.1998) (*retrosp.*)	36, s.123(1)(6)
		s.104(2A) added (6.4.1998) (*retrosp.*)	36, s.123(2)(6)
		s.104(3) am. (6.4.1998) (*retrosp.*)	36, s.123(3)(6)
		s.104(3) am. (6.4.1998) (*retrosp.*)	36, s.125(3)(4)
		s.104(4) subst. (6.4.1998) (*retrosp.*)	36, s.123(4)(6)
		s.104(5) am. (6.4.1998) (*retrosp.*)	36, s.125(3)(4)
		s.104(6) am. (6.4.1998) (*retrosp.*)	36, s.123(5)(b)(6)
		s.105(1) am. (6.4.1998) (*retrosp.*)	36, s.124(2)(7)
		s.105(2) subst. (6.4.1998) (*retrosp.*)	36, s.124(2)(7)
		s.106A mod.	SI 1869, reg.12 (replacing 1989/469 at reg.27(3))
		s.106A mod. (6.4.1999)	SI 1870, reg.34(3)
		s.106A added (6.4.1998) (*retrosp.*)	36, s.124(1)(7)
		s.106A(5) mod. (17.3.1998) (*retrosp.*)	36, s.124(8)(a)(b)
		s.107 am. (6.4.1998) (*retrosp.*)	36, s.123(5)(b)(6)
		s.107(1)(2) replaced (by s.107(1)(1A)(2)) (6.4.1998) (*retrosp.*)	36, s.124(3)(7)
		s.108 (defn. of "securities") appl. (17.3.1998) (*retrosp.*)	36, s.124(9)
		s.108(2) am. (6.4.1998) (*retrosp.*)	36, s.124(5)(a)(b)(7)

Year and Chap. or No. of Measure	Short title	How affected	1998, Chapter of Act or Number of Measure or Statutory Instrument
1992—*cont.*		s.108(7) am. (6.4.1998) (*retrosp.*)	36, s.124(5)(a)(7)
		s.108(A1) added (6.4.1998) (*retrosp.*)	36, s.124(4)(7)
		s.110 am. (6.4.1998) (*retrosp.*)	36, s.123(5)(b)(6)
		s.110(1) am. (6.4.1998) (*retrosp.*)	36, s.125(1)(4)
		s.110A added (6.4.1998) (*retrosp.*)	36, s.125(2)(4)
		s.120(5A)(5B) added (17.3.1998) (*retrosp.*)	36, s.54(2)(6)
		s.120(7) am. (17.3.1998) (*retrosp.*)	36, s.54(3)(6)
		s.120(8) added (17.3.1998) (*retrosp.*)	36, s.54(4)(6)
		ss.126-140 (Pt.IV) (Ch.II) mod. (1.1.1999)	SI 3177, reg.39
		ss.127-131 restr.	SI 1869, reg.12 (replacing 1989/469 at reg.27(4))
		ss.127-131 restr. (6.4.1999)	SI 1870, reg.34(4)
		s.139(4) am. (17.3.1998) (*retrosp.*)	36, s.134(1)(4)
		ss.141,142 replaced (by s.142) (6.4.1998) (*retrosp.*)	36, s.126(1)(2)
		s.145(1) am. (6.4.1998) (*retrosp.*)	36, s.122(5)(6)(7)
		s.145(1A) added (6.4.1998) (*retrosp.*)	36, s.122(5)(6)(7)
		s.149B added (17.3.1998) (*retrosp.*)	36, s.54(5)(6)
		s.150(4)(a) am. (6.4.1998)	36, s.74(1), Sch.13, Pt.IV, para.42(1)(8)(a)
		s.150(5) am. (6.4.1998)	36, s.74(1), Sch.13, Pt.IV, para.42(2)(8)(a)
		s.150(7) am. (6.4.1998)	36, s.74(1), Sch.13, Pt.IV, para.42(3)(8)(b)
		s.150(8) rep.in pt. (6.4.1998)	36, ss.74(1),165, Sch.13, Pt.IV, para.42(4)(8)(c), Sch.27, Pt.III(14), Note 1
		s.150(8A)(a) am. (6.4.1998)	36, s.74(1), Sch.13, Pt.IV, para.42(5)(8)(d)
		s.150(8A)(a) rep.in pt.	36, s.165, Sch.27, Pt.III(14), Note 3
		s.150(8D) added (6.4.1998)	36, s.74(1), Sch.13, Pt.IV, para.42(6)(8)(e)
		s.150(12) added (6.4.1998)	36, s.74(1), Sch.13, Pt.IV, para.42(7)(8)(f)
		s.150A(1)(2) rep.in pt. (6.4.1998)	36, ss.74(1),165, Sch.13, Pt.II, para.24(1)(8)(a), Sch.27, Pt.III(14), Note 2

Year and Chap. or No. of Measure	Short title	How affected	1998, Chapter of Act or Number of Measure or Statutory Instrument
1992—*cont.*			
		s.150A(4)(a) am. (6.4.1998)	36, s.74(1), Sch.13, Pt.II, para.24(2)(8)(a)
		s.150A(5) am. (6.4.1998)	36, s.74(1), Sch.13, Pt.II, para.24(3)(8)(a)
		s.150A(6) replaced (by s.150A(6)(6A)) (6.4.1998)	36, s.74(1), Sch.13, Pt.II, para.24(4)(8)(b)
		s.150A(8A)(a) rep.in pt. (6.4.1998)	36, ss.74(1),165, Sch.13, Pt.II, para.24(5)(8)(c) (54), Sch.27, Pt.III(14), Note 3
		s.150A(8D) added (6.4.1998)	36, s.74(1), Sch.13, Pt.II, para.24(6)(8)(c)
		s.150A(10A) added (6.4.1998)	36, s.74(1), Sch.13, Pt.II, para.24(7)(8)(e)
		s.150B(1) rep.in pt. (6.4.1998)	36, ss.74(1),165, Sch.13, Pt.II, para.25(1)(2), Sch.27, Pt.III(14), Note 2
		s.151 ext. (17.3.1998)	36, s.123(7)(b)
		s.151(2) am.	36, s.75(6)
		s.151(2)(2A) rep.in pt.	36, s.165, Sch.27, Pt.III(15)
		s.151B(1)(7) am. (6.4.1998) (*retrosp.*)	36, s.124(6)(7)
		s.156(4) subst. (17.3.1998) (*retrosp.*)	36, s.41(2)(3)
		s.157 am. (2003-04 and subsequent years of assessment)	36, s.140(3)(6)
		ss.163,164 rep. (2003-04 and subsequent years of assessment)	36, ss.140(2)(a)(b),165, Sch.27, Pt.III(31), Note
		ss.164A-164N (Pt.V) (Ch.1A) rep. (has effect in relation to acquisitions made on or after 6.4.1998)	36, ss.141(1)(a)(2)(a),165, Sch.27, Pt.III(32), Note 1
		s.164L(8) am.	36, s.46(3), Sch.7, para.7
		s.165(3)(a)(b)(6) rep. (year 2003-04 and subsequent years of assessment)	36, s.165, Sch.27, Pt.III(31), Note
		s.165(8)(a) replaced (by s.165(8)(a)(aa)) (2003- 04 and subsequent years of assessment)	36, s.140(4)(6)
		s.170(9)(cc) added (17.3.1998) (*retrosp.*)	36, s.136(1)(4)
		s.171(2)(cc) added (17.3.1998) (*retrosp.*)	36, s.135(1)(4)
		s.171(2)(cd) added (17.3.1998) (*retrosp.*)	36, s.136(2)(5)
		s.171(5) added (17.3.1998) (*retrosp.*)	36, s.136(3)(5)

Year and Chap. or No. of Measure	Short title	How affected	1998, Chapter of Act or Number of Measure or Statutory Instrument
1992—*cont.*			
		s.177B added (17.3.1998) (*retrosp.*)	36, s.137(1)(5)
		s.179(2B)(b)(c) am. (17.3.1998) (*retrosp.*)	36, s.139(1)(2)
		s.179(2C) added (17.3.1998) (*retrosp.*)	36, s.133(2)(3)
		s.179(2D) added (17.3.1998) (*retrosp.*)	36, s.135(3)(5)
		s.193(1) am. (*prosp.*)	17, s.50, Sch.4, para.32(2)
		s.196(5) (defns. of "oil" and "overseas petroleum") am. (*prosp.*)	17, s.50, Sch.4, para.32(3)
		s.212(2) mod. (6.4.1999)	SI 1871, regs.22,23
		s.213(3) am. (17.3.1998) (*retrosp.*)	36, s.137(3)(a)(b)(6)
		s.213(3)(ca) added (17.3.1998) (*retrosp.*)	36, s.137(3)(b)(6)
		s.213(3A)(3B) added (17.3.1998) (*retrosp.*)	36, s.137(4)(7)
		s.214A(11) mod. (6.4.1999)	SI 1871, regs.22,23
		s.214C added	36, s.121, Sch.21, para.7
		s.218 am. (heading preceding section and sidenote amended)	38, s.140, Sch.16, para.80
		s.218(3) am.	38, s.140, Sch.16, para.78
		s.219(2) am.	38, s.140, Sch.16, para.79
		s.219 sidenote am.	38, s.140, Sch.16, para.80
		s.228(8) am. (2003-04 and subsequent years of assessment)	36, s.140(5)(a)(6)
		s.239B added	36, s.95(3)(4)
		s.241(3) am.	36, s.121, Sch.21, para.8
		s.241(3) rep.in pt. (year 2003-04 and subsequent years of assessment)	36, s.165, Sch.27, Pt.III(31), Note
		s.241(3)(a) subst.	36, s.38, Sch.5, Pt.III, paras.62,73
		s.253(14)(b) am. (2003-04 and subsequent years of assessment)	36, s.140(5)(b)(6)
		ss.254,255 rep. (has effect in relation to loans made on or after 17.3.1998)	36, ss.141(1)(b)(2)(b),165, Sch.27, Pt.III(32), Note 2
		s.258(1) rep.	36, s.165, Sch.27, Pt.IV, Note 2
		s.258(2)(a) am. (in relation to any disposal on or after 17.3.1998)	36, s.143(7)
		s.258(8A) added	36, s.142, Sch.25, para.9(1)(2)
		s.260(2)(b)(ii) rep.	36, s.165, Sch.27, Pt.IV, Note 2

Year and Chap. or No. of Measure	Short title	How affected	1998, Chapter of Act or Number of Measure or Statutory Instrument
1992—*cont.*			
		s.260(5) rep.in pt. (year 2003-04 and subsequent years of assessment)	36, s.165, Sch.27, Pt.III(31), Note
		s.263A(1) mod. (1.1.1999)	SI 3177, regs.14-18
		s.263B mod. (1.1.1999)	SI 3177, reg.22(2)
		s.263B (defn. of "stock lending arrangement") appl. (8.4.1998) (*retrosp.*)	36, s.102(1)(9) (adding 1988 c.1 s.231AA)
		s.271(7) am.	22, s.24(2)
		s.272 (defn. of "market value") appl.	36, s.95(1)(4) (adding 1988 c.1 s.650A)
		s.279(2)(a) am.	36, s.121, Sch.21, para.9
		Sch.1, paras.12(6),13(7) am.	38, s.140, Sch.16, para.96(3)
		Sch.1, para.15(5) subst.	38, s.140, Sch.16, para.96(4)
		Sch.3, para.7(2)(c) am. (*prosp.*)	17, s.50, Sch.4, para.32(4)
		Sch.5 (defn. of "settlor") appl.	36, s.132, Sch.23, para.6(1)
		Sch.5, para.2(1) am.	36, s.131, Sch.22, para.2(1)
		Sch.5, para.2(3)(da)(db) added (year 1998-99 and subsequent years of assessment and shall be deemed to ahve applied for the year 1997-98)	36, s.131(1)(a)(3)
		Sch.5, para.2(3)(e) am. (year 1998-99 and subsequent years of assessment and shall bc dccmed to ahve applied for the year 1997-98)	36, s.131(1)(b)(3)
		Sch.5, para.2(7) subst. (year 1998-99 and subsequent years of assessment and shall be deemed to ahve applied for the year 1997-98)	36, s.131(2)(3)
		Sch.5, para.2A added	36, s.131, Sch.22, para.2(2)
		Sch.5, para.4(1)(a) am.	36, s.131, Sch.22, para.3(1)
		Sch.5, para.4(4) am.	36, s.131, Sch.22, para.3(2)(b)
		Sch.5, para.4(4)(b) am.	36, s.131, Sch.22, para.3(2)(a)
		Sch.5, para.5(1)(a) am.	36, s.131, Sch.22, para.3(1)
		Sch.5, para.8 appl.	36, s.132, Sch.23, para.6(6)
		Sch.5, para.9(1A)(1B) added	36, s.132(1)

Year and Chap. or No. of Measure	Short title	How affected	1998, Chapter of Act or Number of Measure or Statutory Instrument
1992—*cont.*			
		Sch.5, para.9(2) restr.	36, s.132(2)
		Sch.5, para.9(2) rep. (year 1998-99 and subsequent years of assessment)	36, s.165, Sch.27, Pt.III(30), Notes 2-3
		Sch.5, para.9(6A) added	36, s.132(3)
		Sch.5, para.9(7)(da)(db) added	36, s.131, Sch.22, para.4(1)(a)(3)
		Sch.5, para.9(7)(e) am.	36, s.131, Sch.22, para.4(1)(b)(3)
		Sch.5, para.9(8) rep. (year 1998-99 and subsequent years of assessment)	36, s.165, Sch.27, Pt.III(30), Notes 2-3
		Sch.5, para.9(10A)-(10D) added	36, s.132(4)
		Sch.5, para.9(10A) (defn. of "protected settlement") appl.	36, s.132, Sch.23, para.6(2)(a)
		Sch.5, para.9(10A)(a) appl.(mods.)	36, s.132, Sch.23, para.6(3)
		Sch.5, para.9(11) subst.	36, s.131, Sch.22, para.4(2)(3)
		Sch.5A, para.2(1)(a) am.	36, s.131, Sch.22, para.5(1)(2)
		Sch.5B, para.1(1)(b) am. (6.4.1998)	36, s.74(1), Sch.13, Pt.III, para.27(1)
		Sch.5B, para.1(2)(3) subst. (6.4.1998)	36, s.74(1), Sch.13, Pt.III, para.27(2)
		Sch.5B, para.1A added (6.4.1998)	36, s.74(1), Sch.13, Pt.III, para.28
		Sch.5B, para.2(3)(a) subst. (6.4.1998)	36, s.74(1), Sch.13, Pt.III, para.29 (adding 1992 c.12, Sch.5B, para.1A)
		Sch.5B, para.3(1)(c)(d) am. (6.4.1998)	36, s.74(1), Sch.13, Pt.III, para.30(1)(a) (adding 1992 c.12, Sch.5B, para.1A)
		Sch.5B, para.3(1)(e)(f) replaced (Sch.5B, para.3(1)(e)(f) replaced by para.3(1)(e)) (6.4.1998)	36, s.74(1), Sch.13, Pt.III, para.30(1)(b)
		Sch.5B, para.3(2) rep. (6.4.1998)	36, ss.74(1),165, Sch.13, Pt.III, para.30(2), Sch.27, Pt.III(14), Note 4
		Sch.5B, para.3(6) added (6.4.1998)	36, s.74(1), Sch.13, Pt.III, para.30(3)
		Sch.5B, para.4(2)-(4) replaced (by Sch.5B, para.4(2)-(4C)) (6.4.1998)	36, s.74(1), Sch.13, Pt.III, para.31(1)(3)
		Sch.5B, para.4(5)(b) am. (6.4.1998)	36, s.74(1), Sch.13, Pt.III, para.31(2)(3)
		Sch.5B, para.5(1)(c)(d) subst. (6.4.1998)	36, s.74(1), Sch.13, Pt.III, para.32

Year and Chap. or No. of Measure	Short title	How affected	1998, Chapter of Act or Number of Measure or Statutory Instrument
1992—*cont.*			
		Sch.5B, para.6 subst. (6.4.1998)	36, s.74(1), Sch.13, Pt.III, para.33
		Sch.5B, paras.7-9 added (6.4.1998)	36, s.74(1), Sch.13, Pt.III, para.34
		Sch.5B, paras.10-15 added (6.4.1998)	36, s.74(1), Sch.13, Pt.III, para.35
		Sch.5B, para.14(4) (defn. of "qualifying chargeable event") appl. (6.4.1998)	36, s.74(1), Sch.13, Pt.I, para.15(3) (replacing 1988 s.303(1)(2) at s.303(1B))
		Sch.5B, paras.16-19 added (6.4.1998)	36, s.74(1), Sch.13, Pt.III, para.36
		Sch.5C, para.4(2) am. (6.4.1998) (*retrosp.*)	36, s.124(6)(7)
		Sch.6 rep. (2003-04 and subsequent years of assessment)	36, ss.140(2)(c),165, Sch.27, Pt.III(31), Note
		Sch.6, para.13(1) mod. (*retrosp.*)	36, s.140(1)
		Sch.7, para.8 rep. (year 2003-04 and subsequent years of assessment)	36, s.165, Sch.27, Pt.III(31), Note
		Sch.7A, para.9(6) am. (17.3.1998) (*retrosp.*)	36, s.138(1)(2)
		Sch.7AA added (17.3.1998) (*retrosp.*)	36, s.137(2)(5), Sch.24
		Sch.8, para.5(1)(2) am.	36, s.38, Sch.5, Pt.III, paras.63(2)(a),73
		Sch.8, para.5(3) am.	36, s.38, Sch.5, Pt.III, paras.63(2)(b),73
		Sch.8, para.6(2) am.	36, s.38, Sch.5, Pt.III, paras.63(3),73
		Sch.8, para.7 am.	36, s.38, Sch.5, Pt.III, paras.63(4),73
		Sch.8, para.7A subst.	36, s.38, Sch.5, Pt.III, paras.63(5),73
		Sch.10, para.14(15) rep. (6.4.1999)	36, s.165, Sch.27, Pt.III(2), Note
		Sch.A1 added (year 1998-99 and subsequent years of assessment)	36, s.121, Sch.20
		Sch.A1 added (year 1998-99 and subsequent years of assessment)	36, s.121(2)(4)
c.13	Further and Higher Education Act 1992	defns. of "higher education corporation" and "further education corporation" appl.	18, s.36(4)(a)
		ext.	30, s.26(11)
		defn. of "further education corporation" appl.	30, s.44(1), Sch.3, para.9 (adding 1993 c.10, s.3(5A)(b))

Year and Chap. or No. of Measure	Short title	How affected	1998, Chapter of Act or Number of Measure or Statutory Instrument
1992—*cont.*			
		s.1(6) (defn. of "the appropriate further education funding council") appl.	31, s.142(1)
		s.2(2)(6) rep.in pt. (*prosp.*)	31, s.140(3), Sch.31
		s.3(3) subst. (*prosp.*)	30, s.36(1)(2)
		s.3(5) am. (*prosp.*)	30, s.36(1)(3)
		s.5(4) am. (*prosp.*)	31, s.140(1), Sch.30, para.34
		s.5(5A) added (*prosp.*)	31, s.125(2)
		s.7(1) ext.	30, s.26(1)
		s.16(2)(3)(a) rep.in pt. (*prosp.*)	31, s.140(3), Sch.31
		s.17(1) am.	30, s.44(1), Sch.3, para.7
		s.18(1) rep.in pt. (*prosp.*)	31, s.125(3)(a)
		s.18(1)(aa) added	31, s.113(1)
		s.18(4)(5)(6) added (*prosp.*)	31, s.125(3)(b)
		s.21(1) rep.in pt. (*prosp.*)	31, s.140(1)(3), Sch.30, para.35(a)(ii), Sch.31
		s.21(1)(a) rep. (*prosp.*)	31, s.140(1)(3), Sch.30, para.35(a)(i), Sch.31
		s.21(2) rep.in pt. (*prosp.*)	31, s.140(1)(3), Sch.30, para.35(b), Sch.31
		s.21(2)(a)(b) rep.in pt. (*prosp.*)	31, s.140(1), Sch.30, para.35(b)
		s.21(3) am. (*prosp.*)	31, s.140(1), Sch.30, para.35(c)
		s.22A added	30, s.41(2)
		s.25 subst. (*prosp.*)	31, s.140(1), Sch.30, para.36
		s.26(1) rep.in pt. (*prosp.*)	31, s.140(1)(3), Sch.30, para.37(a), Sch.31
		s.26(2)-(4) appl.	SI 1656, art.3
		s.26(2) appl.(mods.)	SI 156, art.3
		s.26(2) appl.(mods.)	SI 1651, art.3
		s.26(2) appl.(mods.)	SI 1652, art.3
		s.26(2) appl.(mods.)	SI 1653, art.3
		s.26(2) appl.(mods.)	SI 1654, art.3
		s.26(2) appl.(mods.)	SI 1655, art.3
		s.26(2) appl.	SI 1657, art.3
		s.26(3) appl.(mods.)	SI 156, art.3
		s.26(3) appl.(mods.)	SI 1651, art.3
		s.26(3) appl.(mods.)	SI 1652, art.3
		s.26(3) appl.(mods.)	SI 1653, art.3
		s.26(3) appl.(mods.)	SI 1654, art.3
		s.26(3) appl.(mods.)	SI 1655, art.3
		s.26(3) appl.	SI 1657, art.3
		s.26(4) appl.(mods.)	SI 156, art.3
		s.26(4) appl.(mods.)	SI 1651, art.3
		s.26(4) appl.(mods.)	SI 1652, art.3
		s.26(4) appl.(mods.)	SI 1653, art.3

Year and Chap. or No. of Measure	Short title	How affected	1998, Chapter of Act or Number of Measure or Statutory Instrument
1992—*cont.*			
		s.26(4) appl.(mods.)	SI 1654, art.3
		s.26(4) appl.(mods.)	SI 1655, art.3
		s.26(4) appl.	SI 1657, art.3
		s.26(6) am. (*prosp.*)	31, s.140(1), Sch.30, para.37(b)(i)
		s.26(6)(b)(c) replaced (by s.26(6)(b)) (*prosp.*)	31, s.140(1), Sch.30, para.37(b)(ii)
		s.28(2)(a) am. (*prosp.*)	31, s.140(1), Sch.30, para.38
		s.32(2A) added (*prosp.*)	31, s.140(1), Sch.30, para.39
		s.37(1) am.	31, s.140(1), Sch.30, para.40(a)
		s.37(7) (defn. of "budget share") am.	31, s.140(1), Sch.30, para.40(b)
		s.44(1) am. (*prosp.*)	31, s.140(1), Sch.30, para.41
		s.45(1) am. (*prosp.*)	31, s.140(1), Sch.30, para.42
		s.47(2) am. (*prosp.*)	31, s.140(1), Sch.30, para.43
		s.48(1)(a)(2)(a) am. (*prosp.*)	31, s.140(1), Sch.30, para.44
		s.52A added	31, s.113(2)
		s.54(1)(b) rep.in pt. (*prosp.*)	31, s.140(3), Sch.31
		s.58(3)(b) subst. (*prosp.*)	31, s.140(1), Sch.30, para.45
		s.60A added (*prosp.*)	31, s.125(4)
		s.65(3A)(3B) added (*retrosp.*)	30, s.27
		s.68(1) ext.	30, s.26(3)
		s.77(4) am.	30, s.40
		s.86 rep. (*prosp.*)	29, s.74(2), Sch.16, Pt.I
		s.90(3) am.	30, s.44(1), Sch.3, para.8
		s.90(3A) added (*prosp.*)	31, s.140(1), Sch.30, para.46(a)
		s.90(5) am. (*prosp.*)	31, s.140(1), Sch.30, para.46(b)
		s.91(3)(5) (defns. of "further education sector" and "higher education sector") appl. (*prosp.*)	30, s.39(7)
		Sch.5A added (1.4.1999) (Sch.27 to the extent that it relates to the power to make regulations)	31, s.125(5), Sch.27
		Sch.8, para.51 rep. (EW)	18, s.54(3), Sch.5
		Sch.8, paras.61-64 rep. (*prosp.*)	31, s.140(3), Sch.31
c.14	Local Government Finance Act 1992	s.13(5) mod.	SI 214, reg.4
		s.32(12) subst.	SI 213, reg.2
		s.41(4) mod.	SI 119, reg.5(2)

Year and Chap. or No. of Measure	Short title	How affected	1998, Chapter of Act or Number of Measure or Statutory Instrument
1992—*cont.*			
		s.42(2) mod.	SI 119, reg.5(3)
		ss.54(4),64(2) mod.	SI 119, reg.6
		Sch.4, para.6(2)(a) am. (*prosp.*)	14, s.86(1), Sch.7, para.117
		Sch.9, para.14 rep. (*prosp.*)	14, s.86(2), Sch.8
		Sch.13, para.29 rep.	43, s.1(1), Sch.1, Pt.IV, Group 3
		Sch.13, para.94 rep. (*prosp.*)	14, s.86(2), Sch.8
c.15	Offshore Safety Act 1992	s.1(2)(b) saving (*prosp.*)	17, s.49, Sch.3, Pt.II, para.11(1)
		s.1(3)(b) subst. (*prosp.*)	17, ss.49,50, Sch.3, para.11(1), Sch.4, para.33(2)(a)
		s.1(3)(c) rep.in pt. (*prosp.*)	17, ss.49,50,51, Sch.3, para.11(1), Sch.4, para.33(2)(a), Sch.5, Pt.I
		s.1(4) (defns. of "pipe- line" and "pipe-line works") subst. (*prosp.*)	17, s.50, Sch.4, para.33(2)(b)
		s.1(4A) added (*prosp.*)	17, s.50, Sch.4, para.33(2)(c)
		s.1(4A) appl.(mods.) (*prosp.*)	17, s.50, Sch.4, para.35 (adding 1992/1728, art.3(4A))
		s.1(4B) added (*prosp.*)	17, s.50, Sch.4, para.33(2)(c)
		s.1(4B) appl.(mods.) (*prosp.*)	17, s.50, Sch.4, para.35 (adding 1992/1728, art.3(4A))
		s.1(5)(b) rep. (*prosp.*)	17, ss.50,51, Sch.4, para.33(2)(d), Sch.5, Pt.I
		s.1(5)(c) rep.in pt. (*prosp.*)	17, ss.50,51, Sch.4, para.33(2)(d), Sch.5, Pt.I
		s.1(5)(d) added (*prosp.*)	17, s.50, Sch.4, para.33(2)(d)
		s.3(1)(c)(d) rep. (*prosp.*)	17, s.51, Sch.5, Pt.I
		s.3(2)(b)(4) am. (*prosp.*)	17, s.50, Sch.4, para.33(2)(3)
		s.5(7) am. (*prosp.*)	17, s.50, Sch.4, para.33(2)(4)
c.19	Local Government Act 1992	ss.1-7 rep.	18, s.54(3), Sch.5
		s.16(1)(2) am.	18, s.54(1), Sch.3, para.24(1)
		s.16(4)(5) added	18, s.54(1), Sch.3, para.24(2)
		s.28 (defns. of "the 1982 Act", "the Audit Commission" and "auditor") appl.	18, s.54(3), Sch.5
		ss.28(2),29(1),30(2) rep.	18, s.54(3), Sch.5

Year and Chap. or No. of Measure	Short title	How affected	1998, Chapter of Act or Number of Measure or Statutory Instrument
1992—*cont.*			
c.35	Timeshare Act 1992	saved (6.5.1999)	46, s.30, Sch.5, Pt.II, s.C7(f)
c.37	Further and Higher Education (Scotland) Act 1992	appt. day(s) for spec. provns. (21.11.1998)	SI 2886, art.2
		defn. of "the higher education sector" appl.	30, s.21 (adding 1980 c.44, s.66(1B))
		s.1(3) (defn. of "further education") appl. (*prosp.*)	30, s.32 (adding 1996 c.18, s.63A(2)(b)(ii))
		s.10(2A)-(2E) added	30, s.31(1)
		s.36(1) (defn. of "college of further education") appl.	30, s.28(1)
		s.42(3A)-(3G) added	30, s.31(2)
		s.59 rep. (*prosp.*)	29, s.74(2), Sch.16, Pt.I
		s.59A added (*prosp.*)	30, s.37
c.40	Friendly Societies Act 1992	power to H.M.Treasury to contract out certain functions	SI 2842, art.2, Sch., Pt.II, para.65
		s.64(5), Table am.	11, s.23, Sch.5, Pt.IV, Ch.II, para.68
		s.124(2) rep. (*prosp.*)	47, s.100(2), Sch.15
		Sch.7, para.1A added	SI 2328, art.2
		Sch.7, para.10 am.	SI 2696, art.2(a)
		Sch.7, para.13 am.	SI 2696, art.2(b)
		Sch.7, para.15 added	SI 2696, art.2(c)
c.42	Transport and Works Act 1992	appt. day(s) for spec. provns. (26.2.1998)	SI 274, art.2
		ss.1,3 restr.	38, s.37(3)
		s.6(2A) added	SI 2226, reg.2(a)
		s.6(3) am.	SI 2226, reg.2(b)
		s.6(7) added	SI 2226, reg.2(c)
		s.6A added	SI 2226, reg.3
		s.14(3AA) added	SI 2226, reg.4(a)
		s.14(3B)(a)(b) am.	SI 2226, reg.4(b)
		s.20 restr.	38, s.37(3)
		s.62(2) rep. (*prosp.*)	34, s.39(2), Sch.2
c.44	Museums and Galleries Act 1992	Sch.5, Pt.II am.	SI 613, art.2
c.48	Finance (No.2) Act 1992	s.2(3) rep.in pt. (*prosp.*)	36, ss.20,165, Sch.2, paras.6(2),12, Sch.27, Pt.I(5), Note
		s.2(3)(b) rep. (*prosp.*)	36, ss.20,165, Sch.2, paras.6(2),12, Sch.27, Pt.I(5), Note
		s.2(3A)(3B) added (*prosp.*)	36, s.20, Sch.2, paras.6(3),12
		s.42(8) am.	36, s.46(3), Sch.7, para.8
		ss.57,58 rep.	36, s.165, Sch.27, Pt.III(4), Note
		s.78 rep.	36, s.165, Sch.27, Pt.V(3), Note 1

Year and Chap. or No. of Measure	Short title	How affected	1998, Chapter of Act or Number of Measure or Statutory Instrument
1992—*cont.*			
		s.79 rep. (*prosp.*)	36, s.165, Sch.27, Pt.VI(1) , Note
		Sch.12, paras.3(3)(c),4(2) am.	36, s.46(3), Sch.7, para.8
c.50	Carriage of Goods by Sea Act 1992	saved (6.5.1999)	46, s.30, Sch.5, Pt.II, s.E3(h)
c.52	Trade Union and Labour Relations (Consolidation) Act 1992	defn. of "trade dispute" ext.	SI 218, art.5
		defn. of "independent trade union" appl.	8, s.15, Sch.1, para.2 (replacing 1975 c.65 s.77(4BC)
		defn. of "independent trade union" appl.	8, s.15, Sch.1, para.3 (replacing 1976 c.74 s.72(4B))
		defn. of "independent trade union" appl.	8, s.15, Sch.1, para.11 (replacing 1995 c.50 s.9(4))
		defn. of "trade union" appl.	29, s.2(d)
		saved (6.5.1999)	46, s.30, Sch.5, Pt.II, s.H1(e)
		s.68 subst.	SI 1529, arts.2(1),3
		s.68A(2) subst.	SI 1529, arts.2(2),3
		s.87 subst.	8, s.6
		s.88 rep.	8, s.15, Sch.2
		ss.146-147,152-154 mod.	SI 218, art.3, Sch.
		ss.156(1),158(1)(2) am.	SI 924, arts.3,4, Sch.
		ss.179,180 saved (1.1.1999)	GSM 1, s.6(1), Sch.3, para.2
		ss.181-185 mod.	SI 218, art.3, Sch.
		s.212A added	8, s.7
		s.212B added	8, s.15, Sch.1, para.7
		s.219 excl.	SI 218, art.5
		s.237(1A) am.	SI 1833, reg.32(8)
		s.237(1A) am. (*prosp.*)	23, s.16
		s.238(2A) am.	SI 1833, reg.32(8)
		s.273(2) am.	8, s.15, Sch.1, para.8
		s.287(1) subst. (*prosp.*)	17, s.50, Sch.4, para.34(2)
		s.287(5) rep. (*prosp.*)	17, ss.50,51, Sch.4, para.34(3), Sch.5, Pt.I
		s.288 am.	8, s.15, Sch.1, para.9(1)
		s.288(2B)(b) am.	8, s.15, Sch.1, para.9(1) (2)
		s.288(2B)(c) am.	8, s.9(1)(2)(c)
		s.288(2B)(d) am.	8, s.10(1)(2)(c)
		s.288(4)(5) replaced (by s.288(4)(4A)(4B)(4C)(5))	8, s.15, Sch.1, para.9(1) (3)
		s.288(6) added	8, s.8(3)
		s.301(1) am.	8, s.15, Sch.1, para.10
		Sch.2, para.29 rep. (*prosp.*)	17, s.51, Sch.5, Pt.I

Year and Chap. or No. of Measure	Short title	How affected	1998, Chapter of Act or Number of Measure or Statutory Instrument
1992—*cont.*			
c.53	Tribunals and Inquiries Act 1992	am.	8, ss.1(2),16(3)(c)
		s.6(3) am. (*prosp.*)	14, s.86(1), Sch.7, para.118(1)
		s.6(4) rep. (*prosp.*)	14, s.86(1)(2), Sch.7, para.118(2), Sch.8
		s.7(2) am. (*prosp.*)	14, s.86(1), Sch.7, para.119
		s.7(2) rep.in pt. (*prosp.*)	22, ss.1(5),26, Sch.1, Pt.III, para.12(2)(b), Sch.5, Pt.I
		s.7(2) am. (*prosp.*)	22, s.1(5), Sch.1, Pt.III, para.12(2)(a)
		s.7(2) am.	31, s.25, Sch.5, para.10(1)
		s.13(5)(a) am. (*prosp.*)	14, s.86(1), Sch.7, para.120(a)
		s.13(5)(b) rep. (*prosp.*)	14, s.86(1)(2), Sch.7, para.120(b), Sch.8
		s.16(1) (defn. of "Minister") am. (*prosp.*)	38, s.125, Sch.12, para.33
		Sch.1, Pt.I, para.14 subst. (*prosp.*)	29, s.74(1), Sch.15, para.16
		Sch.1, para.7(a) subst. (*prosp.*)	14, s.86(1), Sch.7, para.121(1)(a)
		Sch.1, para.7(b) am. (*prosp.*)	14, s.86(1), Sch.7, para.121(1)(b)
		Sch.1, para.9A added (*prosp.*)	41, s.74(1), Sch.12, para.15
		Sch.1, para.15(b)(c) subst. (*prosp.*)	31, s.140(1), Sch.30, para.47(a)
		Sch.1, para.15(d) am. (*prosp.*)	31, s.140(1), Sch.30, para.47(b)
		Sch.1, para.15(f) added	31, s.25, Sch.5, para.10(2)
		Sch.1, para.33A rep. (*prosp.*)	22, ss.1(5),26, Sch.1, Pt.III, para.12(3), Sch.5, Pt.I
		Sch.1, para.33AA added (*prosp.*)	22, s.1(5), Sch.1, Pt.III, para.12(3)
		Sch.1, para.41(a) subst. (*prosp.*)	14, s.86(1), Sch.7, para.121(2)(a)
		Sch.1, para.41(b)(c) rep. (*prosp.*)	14, s.86(1)(2), Sch.7, para.121(2)(b), Sch.8
		Sch.1, para.41(d) am. (*prosp.*)	14, s.86(1), Sch.7, para.121(2)(c)
		Sch.1, para.41(e) rep. (*prosp.*)	14, s.86(1)(2), Sch.7, para.121(2)(b), Sch.8
		Sch.2, para.3 rep. (*prosp.*)	14, s.86(1)(2), Sch.7, para.122(1), Sch.8
		Sch.2, para.4(a)(b) am. (*prosp.*)	14, s.86(1), Sch.7, para.122(2)
		Sch.2, para.5 rep.	43, s.1(1), Sch.1, Pt.I, Group 2

Year and Chap. or No. of Measure	Short title	How affected	1998, Chapter of Act or Number of Measure or Statutory Instrument
1992—*cont.*			
		Sch.3, para.36 rep. (*prosp.*)	14, s.86(2), Sch.8
c.61	Civil Service (Management Functions) Act 1992	s.1 ext. (25.1.1999)	46, s.51(4)(9)
		s.1(2) ext.	38, s.34(4)
c.xxi	City of Bristol (Portishead Docks) Act 1992	defn. of "Portishead Pier estate" appl.	SI 1209(L), art.2
1993			
c.8	Judicial Pensions and Retirement Act 1993	am.	8, ss.1(2),16(3)(d)
		power to am.	42, s.18(6), Sch.4, paras.3,4
		s.26(4)-(6) saved (*prosp.*)	SI 1506, arts.6(3),8(7), Sch.1, para.1
		s.26(4)-(6) saved (NI) (*prosp.*)	SI 3162, art.82(3)
		Sch.1, Pt.II am. (NI) (*prosp.*)	SI 3162, art.105(1), Sch.3
		Sch.1, Pt.II rep.in pt. (*prosp.*)	14, s.86(1)(2), Sch.7, para.123(2), Sch.8
		Sch.1, Pt.II am. (*prosp.*)	14, s.86(1), Sch.7, para.123(1)
		Sch.5 am. (NI) (*prosp.*)	SI 3162, art.105(1), Sch.3
		Sch.5 rep.in pt. (*prosp.*)	14, s.86(1)(2), Sch.7, para.124(2), Sch.8
		Sch.5 am. (*prosp.*)	14, s.86(1), Sch.7, para.124(1)
		Sch.6, paras.21,23(1) rep. (*prosp.*)	14, s.86(2), Sch.8
		Sch.6, para.28(1) rep. (NI) (*prosp.*)	SI 3162, art.105(4), Sch.5
		Sch.6, para.50 rep. (*prosp.*)	29, s.74(2), Sch.16, Pt.I
		Sch.7, para.5 am. (NI) (*prosp.*)	SI 3162, art.105(1), Sch.3
		Sch.7, para.5(5)(iii)(iv) rep. (*prosp.*)	14, s.86(1)(2), Sch.7, para.125, Sch.8
		Sch.8, paras.21(1),23 rep. (*prosp.*)	14, s.86(2), Sch.8
c.9	Prisoners and Criminal Proceedings (Scotland) Act 1993	ss.1-27 (Pt.I) (defns. of "licence" and "relevant officer") appl.	37, s.86(1) (adding 1995 c.46 s.210A(10)
		s.1(1) am.	37, s.119, Sch.8, para.98(1)
		s.1(2) am.	37, s.119, Sch.8, para.98(2)
		s.1(3A) added	37, s.119, Sch.8, para.98(3)
		s.1A added	37, s.111(1)
		s.3A added	37, s.88
		s.4(1A) added (1.1.1998) (*retrosp.*)	37, s.119, Sch.8, para.99(1)(2)
		s.5(1) am.	37, s.119, Sch.8, para.100(a)
		s.5(4) added	37, s.119, Sch.8, para.100(b)

Year and Chap. or No. of Measure	Short title	How affected	1998, Chapter of Act or Number of Measure or Statutory Instrument
1993—*cont.*			
		s.7(1)(b) am.	37, s.119, Sch.8, para.101(a)
		s.7(2A)(2B)(2C) added	37, s.119, Sch.8, para.101(b)
		s.7(4A) added	37, s.119, Sch.8, para.101(c)
		s.7(5) am.	37, s.119, Sch.8, para.101(d)
		s.11(3)(b)(4) rep.	37, ss.119,120(2), Sch.8, para.102, Sch.10
		s.14(2)(3) rep.	37, ss.119,120(2), Sch.8, para.103, Sch.10
		s.16(1) am.	37, s.119, Sch.8, para.104(1)
		s.16(7)(a) am.	37, s.119, Sch.8, para.104(2)
		s.16(7)(b) rep.	37, ss.119,120(2), Sch.8, para.104(3), Sch.10
		s.16(8) added	37, s.111(2)
		s.17(1)(a) mod.	37, s.111(7)
		s.17(4A) added	37, s.119, Sch.8, para.105
		s.20(4) am.	37, s.119, Sch.8, para.106
		s.26A added	37, s.87
		s.27(5) subst.	37, s.111(3)
		s.27(8) am.	37, s.119, Sch.8, para.107
		Sch.6 defn(s). appl.	37, s.112 (adding 1995 c.46, s.204A)
		Sch.6 am.	37, s.119, Sch.8, para.70(1)
		Sch.6, para.6B(1) am.	37, s.111(4)(a)
		Sch.6, para.6B(1) rep.in pt.	37, ss.111(4)(b),120(2), Sch.10
		Sch.6, para.6B(1), head.(b) am.	37, s.111(4)(c)
		Sch.6, para.6B(1), head.(c) added	37, s.111(4)(d)
		Sch.6, para.6C added	37, s.111(5)(6)
		Sch.6, para.6D added	37, s.119, Sch.8, para.108
c.10	Charities Act 1993	defns. of "charity" and "institution" appl.	30, s.41(1) (adding 1988 c.40, s.125A(1)(2))
		ext.	30, s.41(2) (adding 1992 c.13, s.22A(1)(2))
		mod.	31, s.11, Sch.1, para.10
		am. (*prosp.*)	31, s.23(1)(2)
		excl. (*prosp.*)	31, s.23(3)
		defns. of "charity" and "institution" appl. (*prosp.*)	31, s.23(4)(a)
		s.3(5A) added	30, s.44(1), Sch.3, para.9
		s.3(5B) added (*prosp.*)	31, s.140(1), Sch.30, para.48
		s.12 rep. (*prosp.*)	29, s.74(2), Sch.16, Pt.I

Year and Chap. or No. of Measure	Short title	How affected	1998, Chapter of Act or Number of Measure or Statutory Instrument
1993—*cont.*			
		s.28(8)(b)(ii) am.	11, s.23, Sch.5, Pt.I, Ch.III, para.42
		ss.41-48 (Pt.VI) saved (1.1.1999)	GSM 1, s.3(1)
		ss.41-48 (Pt.VI) mod. (1.1.1999)	GSM 1, s.3(3)
		s.79(9) am. (*prosp.*)	31, s.140(1), Sch.30, para.49
		Sch.2, para.(d) rep. (*prosp.*)	31, s.140(3), Sch.31
		Sch.2, para.(h)(j) rep. (*prosp.*)	30, s.44(2), Sch.4
c.11	Clean Air Act 1993	s.30(4) rep.in pt.	43, s.1(1), Sch.1, Pt.X, Group 5
		s.30(4) am.	43, s.1(2), Sch.2, para.13
c.14	Disability Grants Act 1993	power to am. (*prosp.*)	47, s.87
c.19	Trade Union Reform and Employment Rights Act 1993	Sch.6, para.4 rep.in pt.	8, s.15, Sch.2
		Sch.6, para.4(b) rep.	8, s.15, Sch.2
c.21	Osteopaths Act 1993	appt. day(s) for spec. provns. (1.4.1998)	SI 872, art.2
		appt. day(s) for spec. provns. (9.5.1998)	SI 1138, art.2
		saved (6.5.1999)	46, s.30, Sch.5, Pt.II, s.G3(g)
		s.33(4) rep.in pt. (*prosp.*)	41, s.74(1)(3), Sch.12, para.16(a), Sch.14, Pt.I
		s.33(4)(b) rep. (*prosp.*)	41, s.74(1)(3), Sch.12, para.16(a), Sch.14, Pt.I
		s.33(5) rep.in pt. (*prosp.*)	41, s.74(1)(3), Sch.12, para.16(b), Sch.14, Pt.I
		s.38 rep. (*prosp.*)	29, s.74(2), Sch.16, Pt.I
		s.41 (defn. of "a registered osteopath") appl.	29, s.69(1)(f)
c.28	Leasehold Reform, Housing and Urban Development Act 1993	s.160(1) ext.	SI 569, art.4
		s.160(2)(b) excl.	SI 569, art.4
		s.181(2)(4) rep.	38, s.152, Sch.18, Pt.V
c.32	European Communities (Amendment) Act 1993	s.6 am. (*prosp.*)	38, s.125, Sch.12, para.34
		s.6 am. (6.5.1999)	46, s.125, Sch.8, para.28
c.34	Finance Act 1993	s.4(2)(c)(d) rep. (*prosp.*)	36, s.165, Sch.27, Pt.I(1), Note
		ss.78,81 rep. (6.4.1999)	36, s.165, Sch.27, Pt.III(2), Note
		s.94A(3)(a) am. (*prosp.*)	17, s.50, Sch.4, para.36
		ss.125-170 (Pt.II CH.II) restr.	36, s.108, Sch.16 (adding 1988 c.1, Sch.28AA at para.8(1)(2))
		s.126 referred to (1.1.1999)	SI 3177, reg.10
		s.126(1) appl.	SI 3081, reg.7(8)

Year and Chap. or No. of Measure	Short title	How affected	1998, Chapter of Act or Number of Measure or Statutory Instrument
1993—*cont.*			
		s.135(1) rep.in pt.	36, ss.109(1)(a)(4)(5),165, Sch.27, Pt.III(26), Note
		s.135(1)(b) am.	36, s.109(2)(a)(4)(5)
		s.135(1)(d) rep.in pt.	36, ss.109(1)(a)(4)(5),165, Sch.27, Pt.III(26), Note
		s.136(1) rep.in pt.	36, ss.109(1)(b)(i)(4)(5), 165, Sch.27, Pt.III(26), Note
		s.136(1)(b) am.	36, s.109(2)(b)(4)(5)
		s.136(1)(d) rep.	36, ss.109(1)(b)(i)(4)(5), 165, Sch.27, Pt.III(26), Note
		s.136(5) rep.in pt.	36, ss.109(1)(b)(ii)(4)(5), 165, Sch.27, Pt.III(26), Note
		s.136(7)(8) am.	36, s.108(3)(a)
		s.136(9) rep.in pt.	36, ss.109(1)(b)(ii)(4)(5), 165, Sch.27, Pt.III(26), Note
		s.136A(3) rep.in pt.	36, ss.109(1)(c)(4)(5),165, Sch.27, Pt.III(26), Note
		s.136A(5) am.	36, s.108(3)(a)
		s.136A(6) am.	36, s.108(3)(b)
		s.136A(7) rep.in pt.	36, ss.109(1)(c)(4)(5),165, Sch.27, Pt.III(26), Note
		s.137(1) rep.in pt.	36, ss.109(1)(d)(4)(5),165, Sch.27, Pt.III(26), Note
		s.137(1)(b) am.	36, s.109(2)(c)(4)(5)
		s.137(1)(d) rep.	36, ss.109(1)(d)(4)(5),165, Sch.27, Pt.III(26), Note
		ss.139-143 mod. (saving for s.143(7)) (1.1.1999)	SI 3177, reg.7
		s.152 (defn. of "qualifying company") appl.	SI 3081, reg.7(8)
		ss.171-184 (Pt.II Ch.III) (defn. of "ancillary trust fund") appl. (year 1998-99 and subsequent years of assessment)	36, s.121, Sch.20 (adding 1992 c.12, Sch.A1)
		s.209 rep.	36, s.165, Sch.27, Pt.V(3), Notes 1-2
		s.211 rep.	36, ss.160,165, Sch.26, paras.2,3, Sch.27, Pt.VI(2), Note
		Sch.6, paras.12,16 rep. (6.4.1999)	36, s.165, Sch.27, Pt.III(2), Note
		Sch.6, para.23 rep. (year 1998-99 and subsequent years of assessment)	36, s.165, Sch.27, Pt.III(29), Note
		Sch.7, paras.1(2),2 rep. (year 2003-04 and subsequent years of assessment)	36, s.165, Sch.27, Pt.III(31), Note

Year and Chap. or No. of Measure	Short title	How affected	1998, Chapter of Act or Number of Measure or Statutory Instrument
1993—*cont.*			
		Sch.14, paras.1,2 rep.	36, s.165, Sch.27, Pt.III(28), Note
		Sch.14, para.4(1) rep. (6.4.1999)	36, s.165, Sch.27, Pt.III(2), Note
		Sch.14, para.6 rep.	36, s.165, Sch.27, Pt.III(28), Note
		Sch.14, para.10(1)(3)(5) (6) rep. (6.4.1999)	36, s.165, Sch.27, Pt.III(2), Note
c.35	Education Act 1993	s.154(4) am.	18, s.54(1), Sch.3, para.25
c.36	Criminal Justice Act 1993	s.5(1) rep.	40, s.9(1)(2), Sch.1, Pt.II, para.7(1), Sch.2, Pt.II
		s.6(1) rep.in pt.	40, s.9(1)(2), Sch.1, Pt.II, para.7(2), Sch.2, Pt.II
		s.79(11) rep. (*prosp.*)	47, s.100(2), Sch.15
c.38	Welsh Language Act 1993	s.6(1)(l) subst. (*prosp.*)	31, s.140(1), Sch.30, para.50
		Sch.1, para.5 rep. (*prosp.*)	38, s.152, Sch.18, Pt.I
c.39	National Lottery etc. Act 1993	trans.of functions (*prosp.*)	22, s.1(4)
		defn. of "the National Lottery Distribution Fund" appl.	22, s.25(1)
		s.3 rep. (*prosp.*)	22, ss.1(2),26, Sch.5, Pt.I
		s.3A added (*prosp.*)	22, s.1(3)
		s.10A added	22, s.2(1)(5)
		s.10B added	22, s.3
		s.11 am.	22, s.2(2)
		s.14 trans.of functions (*prosp.*)	22, s.1(5), Sch.1, Pt.I, para.6(1)(b)
		s.14(2)(a) rep. (*prosp.*)	22, ss.1(5),26, Sch.1, Pt.I, para.6(5), Pt.III, para.13(a), Sch.5, Pt.I
		s.14(2)(aa) added (*prosp.*)	22, s.1(5), Sch.1, Pt.I, para.6(5), Pt.III, para.13(b)
		s.20 (defn. of "the Director General") rep. (*prosp.*)	22, ss.1(5),26, Sch.1, Pt.III, para.14(b), Sch.5, Pt.I
		s.20 (defn. of "the Commission") added (*prosp.*)	22, s.1(5), Sch.1, Pt.III, para.14(a)
		s.21(2) am.	22, s.2(3)
		s.22(3)(a) am.	22, s.6(3)(9)
		s.22(3)(b) am.	22, s.6(4)(9)
		s.22(3)(c) am.	22, s.6(5)(9)
		s.22(3)(d) am.	22, s.6(6)(9)
		s.22(3)(d) rep.in pt.	22, s.26, Sch.5, Pt.II
		s.22(3)(f) added	22, s.6(2)(9)
		s.22(4) added	22, s.19(7)
		s.23(6) added	22, s.7(1)
		s.25(1A) added	22, s.9(1)
		s.25(2A)(2B) added	22, s.10

Year and Chap. or No. of Measure	Short title	How affected	1998, Chapter of Act or Number of Measure or Statutory Instrument
1993—*cont.*			
		s.25A added	22, s.11(1)
		s.25B added	22, s.12(1)
		s.25C added	22, s.13
		s.26(3A) added	22, s.11(2)
		s.26(4) am.	22, s.11(3)
		s.26(4A) added	22, s.11(4)
		s.30(1)(b) am.	22, s.6(7)(9)
		s.31 ext.	22, s.8(7)
		s.31 ext.	22, s.16(2), Sch.4, para.11
		s.31(2)(a) rep. (*prosp.*)	22, ss.1(5),26, Sch.1, Pt.III, para.15(2)(a), Sch.5, Pt.I
		s.31(2)(aa) added (*prosp.*)	22, s.1(5), Sch.1, Pt.III, para.15(2)(b)
		s.31(3) rep. (*prosp.*)	22, ss.1(5),26, Sch.1, Pt.III, para.15(3), Sch.5, Pt.I
		s.31(4) added (*prosp.*)	22, s.1(5), Sch.1, Pt.III, para.15(4)
		s.32(4) (defn. of "the proceeds") appl.	22, s.6(10)(c)
		s.33(4)-(10) added	22, s.5(1)(2)(3)
		s.35(7) am.	22, s.8(1)
		s.38(3) added	22, s.14(1)
		ss.43A-43D added	22, s.7(2)
		s.44 (defn. of "joint scheme") added	22, s.12(2)
		s.44(1) (defns. of "education" and "the environment") added	22, s.6(8)(9)
		s.44(3) added	22, s.8(2)
		s.44(4) added	22, s.9(2)
		s.60(2) excl.	22, s.8(6)
		s.60(2) am.	22, s.15(2)
		s.60(2A) added	22, s.15(3)
		s.60(3) am.	22, s.15(4)
		s.60(3A)(3B) added	22, s.15(5)
		s.60(6) added	22, s.15(6)
		s.63(2) rep. (*prosp.*)	47, s.100(2), Sch.15
		Sch.1, para.33A am.	22, s.2(4)
		Sch.2 rep. (*prosp.*)	22, ss.1(2),26, Sch.5, Pt.I
		Sch.2A added (*prosp.*)	22, s.1(5), Sch.1, Pt.II, para.7
		Sch.3, Pt.II, para.6(1)(c) rep.in pt.	22, ss.4(2),26, Sch.5, Pt.II
		Sch.3, Pt.II, para.6(1) (cc) added	22, s.4(2)
		Sch.3, Pt.II, para.7(2)(a) am.	22, s.4(3)
		Sch.3, Pt.II, para.9(2)(b) subst.	22, s.4(4)
		Sch.3, Pt.II, para.10 rep.	22, ss.4(5),26, Sch.5, Pt.II

Year and Chap. or No. of Measure	Short title	How affected	1998, Chapter of Act or Number of Measure or Statutory Instrument
1993—*cont.*			
		Sch.3, Pt.II, para.11 added	22, s.4(6)
		Sch.3A added	22, s.12(3), Sch.3
		Sch.5, para.2(4)-(6) rep.	22, ss.11(5),26, Sch.5, Pt.II
		Sch.5, para.2(7) added	22, s.11(5)
		Sch.5, para.3(1)-(6) rep.in pt.	22, s.26, Sch.5, Pt.II
		Sch.5, para.3(4)(a) am.	22, s.11(6)
		Sch.5, para.4(1)(a) am.	22, s.14(2)(3)
		Sch.5, para.4(2) am.	22, s.14(2)(4)
		Sch.5, para.4(3) am.	22, s.14(2)(5)
		Sch.5, para.4(4) rep.	22, ss.14(2)(6),26, Sch.5, Pt.II
		Sch.5, para.5(1) subst.	22, s.14(7)(8)
		Sch.5, para.5(2) am.	22, s.14(7)(9)(a)
		Sch.5, para.5(2) rep.in pt.	22, ss.14(7)(9)(b),26, Sch.5, Pt.II
		Sch.5, para.5(4) rep.	22, ss.14(7)(10),26, Sch.5, Pt.II
		Sch.5, para.6(3) rep.	22, s.26, Sch.5, Pt.II
		Sch.6A added	22, s.7(3), Sch.2
c.40	Noise and Statutory Nuisance Act 1993	Sch.3, para.12 am. (EW)	18, s.54(1), Sch.3, para.26
c.43	Railways Act 1993	s.4(7A)(7B) added (pt.prosp.)	41, s.66(5), Sch.10, Pt.II, para.6(3)
		s.6(1A) added	SI 1340, reg.21(2)
		s.6(2) (defns. of "international licence" and "international services") added	SI 1340, reg.21(3)
		s.6(2A) added	SI 1340, reg.21(4)
		s.13(8) replaced (by s.13(8)(8A)) (*prosp.*)	41, s.66(5), Sch.10, Pt.IV, para.15(2)
		s.14(2) rep. (*prosp.*)	41, ss.66(5),74(3), Sch.10, Pt.IV, para.15(3), Sch.14, Pt.I
		s.16(1) rep.in pt. (*prosp.*)	41, ss.66(5),74(3), Sch.10, Pt.IV, para.15(4)(a), Sch.14, Pt.I
		s.16(1)(b) rep. (*prosp.*)	41, ss.66(5),74(3), Sch.10, Pt.IV, para.15(4)(a), Sch.14, Pt.I
		s.16(2) rep.in pt. (*prosp.*)	41, ss.66(5),74(3), Sch.10, Pt.IV, para.15(4)(b)(ii), Sch.14, Pt.I
		s.16(2) am. (*prosp.*)	41, s.66(5), Sch.10, Pt.IV, para.15(4)(b)(i)
		s.16(2)(c) rep. (*prosp.*)	41, ss.66(5),74(3), Sch.10, Pt.IV, para.15(4)(b)(ii), Sch.14, Pt.I
		s.16(5) rep.in pt. (*prosp.*)	41, ss.66(5),74(3), Sch.10, Pt.IV, para.15(4)(c), Sch.14, Pt.I

Year and Chap. or No. of Measure	Short title	How affected	1998, Chapter of Act or Number of Measure or Statutory Instrument
1993—*cont.*			
		s.17(1)(d) added	SI 1340, reg.21(5)
		s.17(7) (defn. of "the Directive") replaced (by the defn. "the Directives"	SI 1340, reg.21(6)
		s.17(7) (defn. of "implementing regulation") am.	SI 1340, reg.21(7)
		s.17(7) (defn. of "international railway access contract") am.	SI 1340, reg.21(8)
		s.22(6A)(6B) added (*prosp.*)	41, s.66(5), Sch.10, Pt.IV, para.15(5)
		s.55(5A) added (*prosp.*)	41, s.66(5), Sch.10, Pt.IV, para.15(6)
		s.55(6) am. (*prosp.*)	41, s.66(5), Sch.10, Pt.IV, para.15(7)(a)
		s.55(11) am. (*prosp.*)	41, s.66(5), Sch.10, Pt.IV, para.15(7)(b)
		s.63 saved (6.5.1999)	46, s.30, Sch.5, Pt.II, s.E2(a)
		s.67(3) restr. (pt.prosp.)	41, s.66(5), Sch.10, Pt.II, para.6(1)
		s.67(3) replaced (by s.67(3)(3A)) (pt.prosp.)	41, s.66(5), Sch.10, Pt.II, para.6(5)
		s.67(3) restr. (*prosp.*)	41, s.66(5), Sch.10, Pt.IV, para.16(3) (substituting 1996 c.61 s.22(3))
		s.67(4) rep.in pt. (pt.prosp.)	41, ss.66(5),74(3), Sch.10, Pt.II, para.6(6), Sch.14, Pt.I
		s.67(4)(c) rep. (pt.prosp.)	41, ss.66(5),74(3), Sch.10, Pt.II, para.6(6), Sch.14, Pt.I
		s.67(6)(a) rep. (pt.prosp.)	41, ss.66(5),74(3), Sch.10, Pt.II, para.6(7), Sch.14, Pt.I
		s.67(8)(b) subst. (pt.prosp.)	41, s.66(5), Sch.10, Pt.II, para.6(8)
		s.67(9) rep.in pt. (pt.prosp.)	41, ss.66(5),74(3), Sch.10, Pt.II, para.6(9)(a), Sch.14, Pt.I
		s.67(9) am. (pt.prosp.)	41, s.66(5), Sch.10, Pt.II, para.6(9)(b)
		s.82 (defn. of "Railway services") appl. (6.5.1999)	46, s.30, Sch.5, Pt.II, s.E2
		s.82(1)(b) (defn. of "railway services") appl. (6.5.1999)	46, s.30, Sch.5, Pt.II, s.E2(b)
		s.83(1) am.	SI 1340, reg.21(9)
		s.131 rep. (*prosp.*)	41, ss.66(5),74(3), Sch.10, Pt.IV, para.15(8), Sch.14, Pt.I
		s.136 saved (6.5.1999)	46, s.30, Sch.5, Pt.II, s.E2(c)

Year and Chap. or No. of Measure	Short title	How affected	1998, Chapter of Act or Number of Measure or Statutory Instrument
1993—*cont.*			
		s.145(2)(g) am.	SI 1340, reg.21(10)
		s.145(3)(d)(e) rep. (*prosp.*)	41, ss.66(5),74(3), Sch.10, Pt.IV, para.15(9)(a), Sch.14, Pt.I
		s.145(3)(qq) added (11.1.1999)	41, s.66(5), Sch.10, Pt.IV, para.15(9)(b)
		s.145(6A) added (*prosp.*)	41, s.66(5), Sch.10, Pt.IV, para.15(10)
c.45	Scottish Land Court Act 1993	s.1(2) am. (1.7.1999)	46, s.125, Sch.8, para.29(a)
		s.1(2A) added (1.7.1999)	46, s.125, Sch.8, para.29(b)
c.46	Health Service Commissioners Act 1993	s.1(3) am. (*prosp.*)	38, s.112, Sch.10, para.2
		s.2(2)(b) rep.in pt. (*prosp.*)	38, s.152, Sch.18, Pt.I
		s.2(2)(ca) added (*prosp.*)	38, s.112, Sch.10, para.3(2)
		s.2(5) rep.in pt. (*prosp.*)	38, ss.112,152, Sch.10, para.3(3), Sch.18, Pt.I
		s.2(6) subst. (*prosp.*)	38, s.112, Sch.10, para.3(4)
		s.2B(2A) added (*prosp.*)	38, s.112, Sch.10, para.4
		s.3(1YA) added (*prosp.*)	38, s.112, Sch.10, para.5
		s.7(1) am. (*prosp.*)	38, s.112, Sch.10, para.6
		s.8(2)(a) am. (*prosp.*)	38, s.112, Sch.10, para.7(a)
		s.8(2)(c) am. (*prosp.*)	38, s.112, Sch.10, para.7(b)
		s.10(2A) added (*prosp.*)	38, s.112, Sch.10, para.8
		s.11(4) am. (*prosp.*)	38, s.112, Sch.10, para.9
		s.14 am. (*prosp.*)	38, s.112, Sch.10, para.10(2)
		s.14(4) am. (*prosp.*)	38, s.112, Sch.10, para.10(3)
		s.14, sidenote am. (*prosp.*)	38, s.112, Sch.10, para.10(4)
		ss.14A,14B,14C added (*prosp.*)	38, s.112, Sch.10, para.11
		s.15(3) am. (*prosp.*)	38, s.112, Sch.10, para.12
		s.17(1) am. (*prosp.*)	38, s.112, Sch.10, para.13
		s.18(1) am. (*prosp.*)	38, s.112, Sch.10, para.14(2)
		s.18(1)(ba) added (*prosp.*)	38, s.112, Sch.10, para.14(2)
		s.18(2) am. (*prosp.*)	38, s.112, Sch.10, para.14(3)
		s.18(3) rep.in pt. (*prosp.*)	38, ss.112,152, Sch.10, para.14(4), Sch.18, Pt.I

Year and Chap. or No. of Measure	Short title	How affected	1998, Chapter of Act or Number of Measure or Statutory Instrument
1993—*cont.*			
		s.19 (defns. of "the Assembly", "financial year" and "first financial year of the Assembly") added (*prosp.*)	38, s.112, Sch.10, para.15(2)(3)
		s.19 (defn. of "officer") am. (*prosp.*)	38, s.112, Sch.10, para.15(4)
		Sch.1 am. (*prosp.*)	38, s.112, Sch.10, para.16(1)(3)
		Sch.1, para.2(1) am. (*prosp.*)	38, s.112, Sch.10, para.16(4)
		Sch.1, paras.3(2)(a),3A(2) (a) rep.in pt. (*prosp.*)	38, ss.112,152, Sch.10, para.16(5), Sch.18, Pt.I
		Sch.1, para.6(1)(b) am. (*prosp.*)	38, s.112, Sch.10, para.16(1)(6)(a)
		Sch.1, para.6(2) am. (*prosp.*)	38, s.112, Sch.10, para.16(6)(b)
		Sch.1, para.11(2) rep. (*prosp.*)	38, ss.112,152, Sch.10, para.16(7), Sch.18, Pt.I
		Sch.1, para.12 am. (*prosp.*)	38, s.112, Sch.10, para.16(8)
		Sch.1, head. am. (*prosp.*)	38, s.112, Sch.10, para.16(2)
		Sch.1A added (*prosp.*)	38, s.112, Sch.10, para.17
c.47	Probation Service Act 1993	defn. of "approved probation hostel" appl. (30.9.1998) (for the purpose of making orders under 1991 c.53, s.37A) (28.1.1999) (to the extent not already in force)	37, s.100(1) (adding 1991 c.53 s.37A)
		s.4(1)(dd) am. (*prosp.*)	37, s.119, Sch.8, para.109
		s.17(1) am. (*prosp.*)	37, s.119, Sch.8, para.110(1)
		s.17(5A) rep. (*prosp.*)	37, ss.119,120(2), Sch.8, para.110(2), Sch.10
		Sch.3, para.6 rep.	18, s.54(3), Sch.5
c.48	Pension Schemes Act 1993	defns. of "occupational pension scheme", "personal scheme" and "public service pension scheme" appl.	46, s.126(1)
		power to am. (*prosp.*)	47, s.87
		s.8(2) am. (*prosp.*)	14, s.86(1), Sch.7, para.126
		s.12C appl.	SI 366, reg.58(5)(6)
		s.14(2) mod.	SI 366, reg.36(1)
		s.14(8) (defn. of "relevant year") appl.	SI 366, reg.36(3)
		s.15(1) am.	SI 470, art.5(2)
		s.16(5) (defn. of "final relevant year") appl.	SI 366, reg.36(3)

Year and Chap. or No. of Measure	Short title	How affected	1998, Chapter of Act or Number of Measure or Statutory Instrument
1993—*cont.*			
		s.19 (defn. of "appropriately secured") appl.	SI 366, reg.36(3)
		ss.19,21 appl.	SI 366, reg.58(5)(6)
		s.37(2) mod.	SI 1466, reg.2
		s.41(1)(1A) replaced (by s.41(1)(1A)(1B)(1C)) (*prosp.*)	14, s.86(1), Sch.7, para.127
		s.42A(1)(2) replaced (by s.42A(1)(2)(2A)(2B)) (*prosp.*)	14, s.86(1), Sch.7, para.128
		s.68(1) am.	15, s.4(2)(b)
		s.77 appl.	SI 366, reg.58(5)(6)
		ss.93-101 mod.	SI 366, regs.116-118
		s.149(6)(e) am.	11, s.23, Sch.5, Pt.IV, Ch.II, para.69(2)
		s.158(6)(c) am. (*prosp.*)	14, s.86(1), Sch.7, para.129
		s.158A(1), Table am.	11, s.23, Sch.5, Pt.IV, Ch.II, para.69(3)
		s.165(8) (defn. of "continental shelf operations") am. (*prosp.*)	17, s.50, Sch.4, para.37
		s.167(2) rep.in pt. (*prosp.*)	47, s.100(2), Sch.15
		s.167(3) am. (*prosp.*)	14, s.86(1), Sch.7, para.130(1)
		s.167(4) rep. (*prosp.*)	14, s.86(1)(2), Sch.7, para.130(2), Sch.8
		s.170 subst. (*prosp.*)	14, s.86(1), Sch.7, para.131
		s.171(1) am. (*prosp.*)	14, s.86(1), Sch.7, para.132(1)
		s.171(2)(3) subst. (*prosp.*)	14, s.86(1), Sch.7, para.132(2)
		s.187 rep. (*prosp.*)	47, s.100(2), Sch.15
		Sch.8, paras.25,33,34 rep. (*prosp.*)	14, s.86(2), Sch.8
c.49	Pension Schemes (Northern Ireland) Act 1993	power to am. (*prosp.*)	47, s.87
		s.145(6)(e) am.	11, s.23, Sch.5, Pt.IV, Ch.II, para.70(2)
		s.154A(1), Table am.	11, s.23, Sch.5, Pt.IV, Ch.II, para.70(3)
		s.163(2) rep.in pt. (*prosp.*)	47, s.100(2), Sch.15
c.50	Statute Law (Repeals) Act 1993	s.3(3) rep.in pt. (*prosp.*)	43, s.1(1), Sch.1, Pt.X, Group 5
No.3	Ordination of Women (Financial Provisions) Measure 1993	s.10(4)(5)(7) trans.of functions (1.1.1999)	SI 1715, art.2, Sch.1
1994			
c.9	Finance Act 1994	appt. day(s) for Pt.IV Ch.III (corporation tax self-assessment) (1.7.1999)	SI 3173, art.2

Year and Chap. or No. of Measure	Short title	How affected	1998, Chapter of Act or Number of Measure or Statutory Instrument
1994—*cont.*			
		s.12(1A) added	36, s.20, Sch.2, paras.7, 12
		s.12A(3)(b) rep.in pt. (*prosp.*)	36, s.165, Sch.27, Pt.I(5), Note
		s.12A(3)(bb) added	36, s.20, Sch.2, paras.8(2),12
		s.12A(3)(c) am.	36, s.20, Sch.2, paras.8(3),12
		s.12A(3)(d)(e) added (pt.prosp.)	36, s.20, Sch.2, paras.8(3),12
		s.12B(2)(ea)(eb) added	36, s.20, Sch.2, paras.9(2),12
		s.12B(2)(f) am.	36, s.20, Sch.2, paras.9(3),12
		s.12B(2)(ga)(gb) added (pt.prosp.)	36, s.20, Sch.2, paras.9(4),12
		s.14(1)(ba) am.	36, s.20, Sch.2, paras.10(a)(b),12
		s.14(1)(ba) am. (*prosp.*)	36, s.20, Sch.2, paras.10(c),12
		s.16(3A) added	36, s.20, Sch.2, paras.11, 12
		s.34(4) am.	36, s.15(2)
		s.34A added	36, s.15(1)
		s.52A(5) am.	36, s.147(2)(5)
		s.52A(6)(7) replaced (by s.52A)(6)(6A))	36, s.147(3)(5)
		s.52A(9) rep.in pt.	36, ss.147(4)(5),165, Sch.27, Pt.V(1), Note
		ss.67A-67C subst.	36, s.146(5)
		s.92 rep. (year 2003-04 and subsequent years of assessment)	36, s.165, Sch.27, Pt.III(31), Note
		ss.147-177 (Pt.IV Ch.II) restr.	36, s.108, Sch.16 (adding 1988 c.1, Sch.28AA at para.8(1)(2))
		s.147(1) (defn. of "qualifying contract") appl.	SI 3081, reg.7(8)
		s.149(2) referred to (1.1.1999)	SI 3177, reg.8
		s.150 referred to (1.1.1999)	SI 3177, reg.10
		s.150(3) referred to (1.1.1999)	SI 3177, reg.9
		s.150A referred to (1.1.1999)	SI 3177, reg.11
		s.154 (defn. of "qualifying company") appl.	SI 3081, reg.7(8)
		s.167(2) rep.in pt.	36, ss.109(3)(4)(5),165, Sch.27, Pt.III(26), Note
		s.167(2)(b) rep.	36, ss.109(3)(4)(5),165, Sch.27, Pt.III(26), Note
		ss.181-183,195,197 rep.	36, s.165, Sch.27, Pt.III(28), Note
		Sch.6A, para.4 subst.	36, s.146(1)(3)
		Sch.15, para.25(d) rep.	36, s.165, Sch.27, Pt.III(13), Note 2

Year and Chap. or No. of Measure	Short title	How affected	1998, Chapter of Act or Number of Measure or Statutory Instrument
1994—*cont.*			
		Sch.16, paras.2,3(1)-(4) (11)(13),20(3) rep. (6.4.1999)	36, s.165, Sch.27, Pt.III(2), Note
		Sch.19, paras.8(1),10,14-16,17(3),19 rep.	36, s.165, Sch.27, Pt.III(28), Note
		Sch.20, para.3(2) restr.	36, s.56(5)(9)
		Sch.24, para.12(2) am.	36, s.46(3), Sch.7, para.9
c.17	Chiropractors Act 1994	appt. day(s) for spec. provns. (14.8.1998)	SI 2031, art.2, Sch.
		saved (6.5.1999)	46, s.30, Sch.5, Pt.II, s.G2(h)
		s.33(4) rep.in pt. (*prosp.*)	41, s.74(1)(3), Sch.12, para.17(a), Sch.14, Pt.I
		s.33(4)(b) rep. (*prosp.*)	41, s.74(1)(3), Sch.12, para.17(a), Sch.14, Pt.I
		s.33(5) rep.in pt. (*prosp.*)	41, s.74(1)(3), Sch.12, para.17(b), Sch.14, Pt.I
		s.38 rep. (*prosp.*)	29, s.74(2), Sch.16, Pt.I
		s.43 (defn. of "a registered chiropractor") appl.	29, s.69(1)(g)
		Sch.1, para.5 am. (until such time as a person appointed to be registrar under s.2(1) of 1994 c.17 takes office) (*temp.*)	SI 2031, art.3(a)
		Sch.1, para.14(2) am. (until such time as a person appointed to be registrar under s.2(1) of 1994 c.17 takes office) (*temp.*)	SI 2031, art.3(b)
c.18	Social Security (Incapacity for Work) Act 1994	mod.	14, s.2(1)(2)(e)
		power to am. (*prosp.*)	47, s.87
		s.6(2), Sch.1, paras.11, 46-48 rep. (*prosp.*)	14, s.86(2), Sch.8
c.19	Local Government (Wales) Act 1994	Sch.9, para.17(1) rep.in pt.	43, s.1(1), Sch.1, Pt.X, Group 5
		Sch.13, para.6(1)-(4) am.	18, s.54(1), Sch.3, para.27
		Sch.13, para.18(2) am.	38, s.150(2)
		Sch.13, para.18(3) rep.in pt.	38, ss.150(3)(a),152, Sch.18, Pt.VII
		Sch.13, para.18(4) rep.	38, ss.150(3)(b),152, Sch.18, Pt.VII
		Sch.13, para.18(5)-(7) subst.	38, s.150(4)
		Sch.13, para.30 rep. (*prosp.*)	29, s.74(2), Sch.16, Pt.I
		Sch.16, paras.11,40(2)(b) rep.	43, s.1(1), Sch.1, Pt.X, Group 5
		Sch.16, para.53 rep.	38, s.152, Sch.18, Pt.IV
		Sch.16, para.57(6) rep.	43, s.1(1), Sch.1, Pt.X, Group 5
		Sch.16, paras.58,59(6)-(8) rep.	38, s.152, Sch.18, Pt.V

Year and Chap. or No. of Measure	Short title	How affected	1998, Chapter of Act or Number of Measure or Statutory Instrument
1994—cont.			
		Sch.16, paras.67,70,93 rep.	43, s.1(1), Sch.1, Pt.X, Group 5
		Sch.17, para.12(3)(a) am.	18, s.54(1), Sch.3, para.28(2)
		Sch.17, para.12(4) am.	18, s.54(1), Sch.3, para.28(3)(a)
		Sch.17, para.12(4)(a)(b) am.	18, s.54(1), Sch.3, para.28(3)(b)(c)
		Sch.17, para.12(5) am.	18, s.54(1), Sch.3, para.28(4)
c.21	Coal Industry Act 1994	s.3(6) am. (*prosp.*)	17, s.50, Sch.4, para.38(2)
		s.9(1) am. (*prosp.*)	17, s.50, Sch.4, para.38(3)(a)
		s.9(1)(b) am. (*prosp.*)	17, s.50, Sch.4, para.38(3)(b)
		s.9(4) am. (*prosp.*)	17, s.50, Sch.4, para.38(3)(c)
		s.10(3)(a)(b) appl.	iii, s.1, Sch., O., s.40(2)
		s.57(4)(a)(ii) am. (*prosp.*)	17, s.50, Sch.4, para.38(4)
		s.59(4)(e)(f) rep. (*prosp.*)	41, s.74(1)(3), Sch.12, para.18(a), Sch.14, Pt.I
		s.59(4)(n) added (11.1.1999)	41, s.74(1), Sch.12, para.18(b)
		s.68(2)(d)(iii), Sch.9, para.11 rep.	43, s.1(1), Sch.1, Pt.IV, Group 2
		Sch.9, para.19 rep.	38, s.152, Sch.18, Pt.IV
c.22	Vehicle Excise and Registration Act 1994	Sch.9, para.25(1) rep.in pt. saved (6.5.1999)	38, s.152, Sch.18, Pt.V 46, s.30, Sch.5, Pt.II, s.E1(e)
		s.15(2A) added (in relation to licences issued on or after 1.1.1999)	36, s.16, Sch.1, paras.13, 17(1)
		s.16(1)(8)-(10) am. (in relation to licences issued on or after 1.1.1999)	36, s.16, Sch.1, paras.14, 17(1)
		s.22(2A)(a) rep.in pt. (*prosp.*)	36, s.165, Sch.27, Pt.I(4), Note
		s.22(2A)(c)(d) added	36, s.18
		s.35A(1)(a)(b) am.	36, s.19(1)
		s.35A(3)-(6) added	36, s.19(2)
		s.36(4) replaced (by s.36(4)(4A))	36, s.19(3)
		s.36(6) added	36, s.19(4)
		s.45(3A)(3B) am. (in relation to licences issued on or after 1.1.1999)	36, s.16, Sch.1, paras.15, 17(2)
		s.55(1) am.	15, s.4(2)(c)
		s.55(5) am.	15, s.4(1)(b)
		s.61B added	36, s.16, Sch.1, paras.2, 17(2)

Year and Chap. or No. of Measure	Short title	How affected	1998, Chapter of Act or Number of Measure or Statutory Instrument
1994—*cont.*			
		Sch.1, para.3(1) am. (in relation to licences issued on or after 1.1.1999)	36, s.16, Sch.1, paras.3(1),17(1)
		Sch.1, para.3(1A) added (in relation to licences issued on or after 1.1.1999)	36, s.16, Sch.1, paras.3(2),17(1)
		Sch.1, para.3(6) am. (in relation to licences issued on or after 1.1.1999)	36, s.16, Sch.1, paras.3(3),17(1)
		Sch.1, para.4(7) am. (in relation to licences issued on or after 1.1.1999)	36, s.16, Sch.1, paras.4,17(1)
		Sch.1, para.5(6) am. (in relation to licences issued on or after 1.1.1999)	36, s.16, Sch.1, paras.5, 17(1)
		Sch.1, para.6(2) am. (in relation to licences issued on or after 1.1.1999)	36, s.16, Sch.1, paras.6(1),17(1)
		Sch.1, para.6(2A) added (in relation to licences issued on or after 1.1.1999)	36, s.16, Sch.1, paras.6(2),17(1)
		Sch.1, para.6(3A) rep. (in relation to licences issued on or after 1.1.1999)	36, ss.16,165, Sch.1, paras.6(3),17(1), Sch.27, Pt.I(3), Note
		Sch.1, para.7(1)(b) am. (in relation to licences issued on or after 1.1.1999)	36, s.16, Sch.1, paras.7(1),17(1)
		Sch.1, para.7(3) am. (in relation to licences issued on or after 1.1.1999)	36, s.16, Sch.1, paras.7(2),17(1)
		Sch.1, para.7(3A) added and am. (in relation to licences issued on or after 1.1.1999)	36, s.16, Sch.1, paras.7(3),17(1)
		Sch.1, para.7(4)(5)(6) rep. (in relation to licences issued on or after 1.1.1999)	36, ss.16,165, Sch.1, paras.7(4),17(1), Sch.27, Pt.I(3), Note
		Sch.1, para.9(1) am. (in relation to licences issued on or after 1.1.1999)	36, s.16, Sch.1, paras.8(1),17(1)
		Sch.1, para.9(3) am. (in relation to licences issued on or after 1.1.1999)	36, s.16, Sch.1, paras.8(2),17(1)
		Sch.1, para.9(4) am. (in relation to licences issued on or after 1.1.1999)	36, s.16, Sch.1, paras.8(3),17(1)
		Sch.1, para.9(5) rep. (in relation to licences issued on or after 1.1.1999)	36, ss.16,165, Sch.1, paras.8(4),17(1), Sch.27, Pt.I(3), Note
		Sch.1, paras.9A,9B added (in relation to licences issued on or after 1.1.1999)	36, s.16, Sch.1, paras.9, 17(1)
		Sch.1, para.10(1) am. (in relation to licences issued on or after 1.1.1999)	36, s.16, Sch.1, paras.10, 17(1)

Year and Chap. or No. of Measure	Short title	How affected	1998, Chapter of Act or Number of Measure or Statutory Instrument
1994—*cont.*			
		Sch.1, para.11(1) am. (in relation to licences issued on or after 1.1.1999)	36, s.16, Sch.1, paras.11(1),17(1)
		Sch.1, para.11(3) am. (in relation to licences issued on or after 1.1.1999)	36, s.16, Sch.1, paras.11(2),17(1)
		Sch.1, para.11(4) am. (in relation to licences issued on or after 1.1.1999)	36, s.16, Sch.1, paras.11(3),17(1)
		Sch.1, para.11(5) rep. (in relation to licences issued on or after 1.1.1999)	36, ss.16,165, Sch.1, paras.11(4),17(1), Sch.27, Pt.I(3), Note
		Sch.1, paras.11A,11B added (in relation to licences issued on or after 1.1.1999)	36, s.16, Sch.1, paras.12, 17(1)
		Sch.2, para.1A(1) am.	36, s.17
		Sch.2, para.22(1)(a)(b) am. (in relation to licences issued on or after 1.1.1999)	36, s.16, Sch.1, paras.16(2),17(2)
		Sch.2, para.22(2) am. (in relation to licences issued on or after 1.1.1999)	36, s.16, Sch.1, paras.16(3),17(2)
		Sch.2, para.22(2A) am. (in relation to licences issued on or after 1.1.1999)	36, s.16, Sch.1, paras.16(4),17(2)
		Sch.2, para.22(3) am. (in relation to licences issued on or after 1.1.1999)	36, s.16, Sch.1, paras.16(5),17(2)
		Sch.2, para.22(6AA) added (in relation to licences issued on or after 1.1.1999)	36, s.16, Sch.1, paras.16(6),17(2)
		Sch.2, para.22(6B) am. (in relation to licences issued on or after 1.1.1999)	36, s.16, Sch.1, paras.16(7),17(2)
		Sch.2, para.22(8) am. (in relation to licences issued on or after 1.1.1999)	36, s.16, Sch.1, paras.16(8),17(2)
		Sch.2, para.22(8)(d) added (in relation to licences issued on or after 1.1.1999)	36, s.16, Sch.1, paras.16(8),17(2)
		Sch.2, para.22(9) am. (in relation to licences issued on or after 1.1.1999)	36, s.16, Sch.1, paras.16(8),17(2)
		Sch.2, para.22(9)(d) added (in relation to licences issued on or after 1.1.1999)	36, s.16, Sch.1, paras.16(8),17(2)
c.23	Value Added Tax Act 1994	s.6(14A) added (17.3.1998) (*retrosp.*)	36, s.22(2)(3)
		s.36(1)(a) rep.in pt.	36, ss.23(1)(7),165, Sch.27, Pt.II, Note
		s.36(3)(a)(b) am.	36, s.23(2)(7)
		s.36(3A) added	36, s.23(3)(7)
		s.36(5)(c)(e) am.	36, s.23(4)(a)(b)

Year and Chap. or No. of Measure	Short title	How affected	1998, Chapter of Act or Number of Measure or Statutory Instrument
1994—*cont.*			
		s.36(6)(b)(c) am.	36, s.23(5)
		s.36(7) am.	36, s.23(6)
		s.41(6) am. (*prosp.*)	38, s.125, Sch.12, para.35
		s.41(6) am. (6.5.1999)	46, s.125, Sch.8, para.30
		s.57(3) subst.	SI 788, art.2
		s.96(1)(b) (defn. of "major interest") am.	36, s.24
		s.97A added (17.3.1998) (*retrosp.*)	36, s.22(1)(3)
		Sch.1, para.1(1)(2) am.	SI 761, art.2(a)
		Sch.1, paras.1(3),4(1)(2) am.	SI 761, art.2(b)
		Sch.3, paras.1(1)(2),2(1) (2) am.	SI 761, art.3
		Sch.4, para.5(2)(a) am. (17.3.1998) (*retrosp.*)	36, s.21(1)(2)(6)
		Sch.4, para.5(2A) added (17.3.1998) (*retrosp.*)	36, s.21(1)(3)(6)
		Sch.4, para.5(5) am. (17.3.1998) (*retrosp.*)	36, s.21(1)(4)(6)
		Sch.4, para.5(5A) added (17.3.1998) (*retrosp.*)	36, s.21(1)(5)(6)
		Sch.9, Group 6, Note (1) (a)(iii) am. (*prosp.*)	31, s.140(1), Sch.30, para.51(a)
		Sch.9, Group 6, Note (1) (a)(v)(vii) rep. (*prosp.*)	31, s.140(1)(3), Sch.30, para.51(b), Sch.31
		Sch.9, Group 6, Note (1) (a)(viii) am. (NI) (*prosp.*)	SI 1759, art.91(1), Sch.5, Pt.II
		Sch.9, Group 7, Item 1, para.(ca) added	SI 1294, art.2
		Sch.9, Group 10, Note (2A) added	SI 764, arts.2,3
		Sch.9, Group 10, Note (2B) added	SI 764, arts.2,4
		Sch.9, Group 10, Notes (4) ,(5),(6),(7) added	SI 764, arts.2,5
		Sch.A1, para.1(1) replaced (by para.1(1) (1A)(1B))	SI 1375, art.3
		Sch.A1, para.2(c) am.	SI 1375, art.4
		Sch.A1, para.4(1)(2)(3) am.	SI 1375, art.5
		Sch.A1, para.5 added	SI 1375, art.6
c.26	Trade Marks Act 1994	Sch.4, para.1(2) rep.in pt. (*prosp.*)	47, s.100(2), Sch.15
c.29	Police and Magistrates' Courts Act 1994	ss.66-68 (Pt.III) rep. (saving)(*prosp.*)	32, s.74(2)(3), Schs.5,6
		s.96(3) rep.in pt. (saving)(*prosp.*)	32, s.74(2)(3), Schs.5,6
		Sch.4, paras.25-28 rep.	18, s.54(3), Sch.5
c.30	Education Act 1994	ext.	30, s.26(11)
		s.7(1) ext.	30, s.26(3)
		s.11A rep.in pt. (*prosp.*)	31, s.140(1)(3), Sch.30, para.53, Sch.31

Year and Chap. or No. of Measure	Short title	How affected	1998, Chapter of Act or Number of Measure or Statutory Instrument
1994—*cont.*			
		s.12(1) am. (*prosp.*)	31, s.140(1), Sch.30, para.54(a)
		s.12(4)(5) rep. (*prosp.*)	31, s.140(1)(3), Sch.30, para.54(b), Sch.31
		s.12(6) rep. (1.4.1999)	31, s.140(1), Sch.30, para.54(c)
		s.18(1)(a) rep. (*prosp.*)	31, s.140(3), Sch.31
		s.18A added	30, s.20
		Sch.2, para.8(1)(5) rep.	18, s.54(3), Sch.5
c.33	Criminal Justice and Public Order Act 1994	appt. day(s) for ss.1-4 (1.3.1998)	SI 277, art.3(1)
		appt. day(s) for s.168(2) , Sch.10 (so far as not already in force) [1.3.1998]	SI 277, art.3(2)
		appt. day(s) for s.168(3) (so far as not already in force), Sch.11 (in part) [1.3.1998]	SI 277, art.3(3)
		ss.1-4 rep. & superseded (*prosp.*)	37, ss.73(7)(b),120(2), Sch.10
		s.1 power to restr.	37, s.116(1)(a)
		s.2 mod. (*temp.*)	SI 1928, art.3
		s.2 power to mod.	37, s.116(2)
		s.4 mod. (*temp.*)	SI 1928, art.3
		s.4 power to mod.	37, s.116(2)
		s.4 am.	37, s.116(3)
		s.4(3)(a) power to restr.	37, s.116(1)(b)
		s.12(3) am. (*prosp.*)	37, s.119, Sch.8, para.111
		s.20 rep. & superseded (pt.prosp.)	37, ss.97(5),120(2), Sch.10
		s.25(1) am.	37, s.56
		s.35(1) rep.in pt.	37, ss.35(a),120(1)(2), Sch.9, para.2, Sch.10
		s.35(6) rep.	37, ss.35(b),120(1)(2), Sch.9, para.2, Sch.10
		s.60(4A) added (1.3.1999)	37, s.25(1)
		s.60(5) am. (1.3.1999)	37, s.25(2)
		s.60(8) am. (1.3.1999)	37, s.25(3)
		s.60A added (1.12.1998) (part) (1.3.1999 (residue)	37, s.26
		s.60B added (1.3.1999	37, s.27(2)
		s.130(4) rep.	37, s.120(2), Sch.10
		s.161 rep.	29, s.74(2), Sch.16, Pt.I
		s.170(1)(3) am. (*prosp.*)	48, s.15(1)(2)
		s.170(5) added (*prosp.*)	48, s.15(1)(3)
		Sch.1, para.4 (defn. of "offender") am. (*prosp.*)	37, s.119, Sch.8, para.112
		Sch.2, para.3(1)(b)(c) am.	37, s.119, Sch.8, para.113(1)
		Sch.2, para.3(2) am.	37, s.119, Sch.8, para.113(2)

Year and Chap. or No. of Measure	Short title	How affected	1998, Chapter of Act or Number of Measure or Statutory Instrument
1994—*cont.*			
c.36	Law of Property (Miscellaneous Provisions) Act 1994	Sch.10, para.42 rep. (*prosp.*)	37, s.120(2), Sch.10
		Sch.1, para.4 rep.	43, s.1(1), Sch.1, Pt.IV, Group 2
c.37	Drug Trafficking Act 1994	s.2(7)(a) rep. (*prosp.*)	37, ss.119,120(2), Sch.8, para.114, Sch.10
		s.6(3)(f) added	40, s.9(1), Sch.1, Pt.I, para.3
c.39	Local Government etc. (Scotland) Act 1994	appl. (1.4.1999)	37, s.19(8)
		defn. of "local government area" appl.	37, s.95(1) (adding 1995 c.46 s.234K)
		Sch.13, para.154 rep. (*prosp.*)	29, s.74(2), Sch.16, Pt.I
c.40	Deregulation and Contracting Out Act 1994	ss.10,11 rep. (*prosp.*)	41, s.74(1)(3), Sch.12, para.19(2), Sch.14, Pt.I
		s.12(1)-(6) rep. (*prosp.*)	41, s.74(1)(3), Sch.12, para.19(3), Sch.14, Pt.I
		s.70 mod.	30, s.23(3)(b)
		s.74(4)(a) appl.	48, s.23, Sch.3, para.4
		s.79(1) (defn. of "office-holder") am. (*prosp.*)	38, s.125, Sch.12, para.36
		Sch.4, para.1 rep. (*prosp.*)	41, s.74(1)(3), Sch.12, para.19(4), Sch.14, Pt.I
		Sch.11, para.4(3)-(7) rep. (*prosp.*)	41, s.74(1)(3), Sch.12, para.19(5), Sch.14, Pt.I
		Sch.16, para.20(1) rep. (*prosp.*)	14, s.86(2), Sch.8
c.xiii	London Docklands Development Corporation Act 1994	am. (saving)	SI 293(L), art.2(2)
No.2	Care of Cathedrals (Supplementary Provisions) Measure 1994	saved (1.1.1999)	GSM 1, s.5(1), Sch.2, Pt.II
No.3	Church of England (Legal Aid) Measure 1994	ss.1(2)(4),4(1)(2)(5) trans.of functions (1.1.1999)	SI 1715, art.2, Sch.1
1995			
c.4	Finance Act 1995	appt. day(s) for Sch.27, para.3(2)(3)(b) (23.11.1998)	SI 2620, art.2
		appt. day(s) for Sch.27, paras.1,2,3(1), 4-7 (1.8.1999)	SI 2620, art.3
		ss.39,41 rep.	36, s.165, Sch.27, Pt.III(4), Note
		s.78 rep. (*prosp.*)	36, s.165, Sch.27, Pt.III(3), Note
		s.92(10) subst. (6.4.1998) (except where the payment or other benefit or the right to receive it has been brought into charge to tax before that date) (*retrosp.*)	36, s.58(2)(4), Sch.9, Pt.II, para.5

Year and Chap. or No. of Measure	Short title	How affected	1998, Chapter of Act or Number of Measure or Statutory Instrument
1995—*cont.*			
		ss.104(5),107(5)(6) rep.	36, s.165, Sch.27, Pt.III(28), Note
		s.126(6)(7) am.	36, s.46(3), Sch.7, para.10
		s.139(3) ext.	36, s.57, Sch.8, para.7
		s.160 rep.	43, s.1(1), Sch.1, Pt.IV, Group 5
		Sch.4, para.12 rep. (*prosp.*)	36, s.165, Sch.27, Pt.I(3), Note
		Sch.6, paras.1,4-7,9-16, 20-25,29,30,32,34-37 rep.	36, s.165, Sch.27, Pt.III(4), Note
		Sch.8, paras.18,19(3),22, Sch.24, paras.9,12(1)(2)(4)(5) rep. (6.4.1999)	36, s.165, Sch.27, Pt.III(2), Note
		Sch.27, para.1(1) rep. (6.4.1998)	36, s.165, Sch.27, Pt.III(7), Note
c.7	Requirements of Writing (Scotland) Act 1995	s.12(1) (defn. of "Minister") am. (6.5.1999)	46, s.125, Sch.8, para.31(a)
		s.12(1) defn.of (" officer") para.(a) am. (6.5.1999)	46, s.125, Sch.8, para.31(b)
		Sch.4, paras.48,50 rep. (*prosp.*)	17, s.51, Sch.5, Pt.I
c.13	Road Traffic (New Drivers) Act 1995	saved (6.5.1999)	46, s.30, Sch.5, Pt.II, s.E1(f)
c.17	Health Authorities Act 1995	Sch.1, para.106 rep.	18, s.54(3), Sch.5
		Sch.1, para.126(2)(b) rep.in pt. (*prosp.*)	38, s.152, Sch.18, Pt.I
c.18	Jobseekers Act 1995	mod.	14, s.2(1)(2)(f)
		mod. (EWS) (*prosp.*)	14, s.8(1)(c)(4)(5)
		power to mod. (EWS) (*prosp.*)	14, s.11(1)(3)
		power to am. (*prosp.*)	47, s.87
		s.2(3A) added (*prosp.*)	14, s.86(1), Sch.7, para.133
		s.6(6) rep.in pt. (*prosp.*)	14, s.86(1)(2), Sch.7, para.134(1)(a), Sch.8
		s.6(6) am. (*prosp.*)	14, s.86(1), Sch.7, para.134(1)(b)
		s.6(8) am. (*prosp.*)	14, s.86(1), Sch.7, para.134(2)
		s.7(7) rep.in pt. (*prosp.*)	14, s.86(1)(2), Sch.7, para.135, Sch.8
		s.9(6) am. (*prosp.*)	14, s.86(1), Sch.7, para.136(1)
		s.9(7) am. (*prosp.*)	14, s.86(1), Sch.7, para.136(2)
		s.9(8) am. (*prosp.*)	14, s.86(1), Sch.7, para.136(3)
		s.9(9) rep. (*prosp.*)	14, s.86(1)(2), Sch.7, para.136(4), Sch.8
		s.10(5) am. (*prosp.*)	14, s.86(1), Sch.7, para.137(1)

Year and Chap. or No. of Measure	Short title	How affected	1998, Chapter of Act or Number of Measure or Statutory Instrument
1995—*cont.*			
		s.10(6) am. (*prosp.*)	14, s.86(1), Sch.7, para.137(2)
		s.10(7) am. (*prosp.*)	14, s.86(1), Sch.7, para.137(3)
		s.10(8) rep. (*prosp.*)	14, s.86(1)(2), Sch.7, para.137(4), Sch.8
		s.11 rep. (*prosp.*)	14, s.86(1)(2), Sch.7, para.138, Sch.8
		s.16(3)(b) subst. (*prosp.*)	14, s.86(1), Sch.7, para.139(1)
		s.16(4) subst. (*prosp.*)	14, s.86(1), Sch.7, para.139(2)
		s.17(2) am. (*prosp.*)	14, s.86(1), Sch.7, para.140(1)
		s.17(3)(b) replaced (by s.17(3)(b)(c)) (*prosp.*)	14, s.86(1), Sch.7, para.140(2)
		s.17(4)(5) subst. (*prosp.*)	14, s.86(1), Sch.7, para.140(3)
		s.19(3) am. (*prosp.*)	14, s.86(1), Sch.7, para.141(1)
		s.19(4) am. (*prosp.*)	14, s.86(1), Sch.7, para.141(2)
		s.20(2)(b)(ii) am. (*prosp.*)	14, s.86(1), Sch.7, para.142
		s.20(3) rep.	14, s.86(2), Sch.8
		s.28(1)(b)(3) rep. (*prosp.*)	14, s.86(2), Sch.8
		s.31(1)(2) am. (*prosp.*)	14, s.86(1), Sch.7, para.143
		s.35(1) (defn. of "adjudication officer") rep.	14, s.86(1)(2), Sch.7, para.144(a), Sch.8
		s.35(1) (defn. of "entitled") am. (*prosp.*)	14, s.86(1), Sch.7, para.144(b)
		s.36(1) am. (*prosp.*)	14, s.86(1), Sch.7, para.145
		Sch.1, para.10(2) am. (*temp.*)	14, s.83, Sch.6, para.5(2)
		Sch.1, para.10(2) am. (*prosp.*)	14, s.86(1), Sch.7, para.146
		Sch.2, paras.41-47,57 rep. (*prosp.*)	14, s.86(2), Sch.8
c.21	Merchant Shipping Act 1995	saved (6.5.1999)	46, s.30, Sch.5, Pt.II, s.E3(i)
		s.55(1) excl.	31, s.112(2)
		s.89 rep.	SI 2241, reg.3(1)(a)
		s.90 rep.	SI 2647, reg.1(2)(a)
		s.93 sidenote am.	SI 1691, reg.2(7)
		s.93(1) am.	SI 1691, reg.2(1)(2)
		s.93(2) rep.	SI 1691, reg.2(3)
		s.93(3) am.	SI 1691, reg.2(4)
		s.93(4) rep.	SI 1691, reg.2(5)
		s.93(5) rep.in pt.	SI 1691, reg.2(6)
		s.96 appl.	SI 2411, reg.16
		s.96 appl.	SI 2857, reg.13

Year and Chap. or No. of Measure	Short title	How affected	1998, Chapter of Act or Number of Measure or Statutory Instrument
1995—*cont.*			
		s.97 appl.	SI 2411, reg.16
		s.97 appl.	SI 2857, reg.13
		s.131(3) appl.	SI 1377, reg.14(2)
		s.143(6) appl.(mods.)	SI 1377, reg.15(1)
		s.146 appl.(mods.)	SI 1377, reg.15(2)
		ss.152-170 ext.(mods.) (Guernsey)	SI 260, art.2, Sch.1
		ss.152-170 ext.(mods.) (Cayman Islands)	SI 1261, art.2, Sch.
		ss.152-170 ext.(mods.) (Montserrat)	SI 1262, art.2, Sch.
		ss.152-170 ext.(mods.) (Saint Helena)	SI 1263, art.2, Sch.
		ss.172-181 ext.(mods.) (Guernsey)	SI 260, art.2, Sch.1
		ss.172-181 ext.(mods.) (Cayman Islands)	SI 1261, art.2, Sch.
		ss.172-181 ext.(mods.) (Montserrat)	SI 1262, art.2, Sch.
		ss.172-181 ext.(mods.) (Saint Helena)	SI 1263, art.2, Sch.
		s.185 saved	SI 209, reg.4(3)
		s.261(4)(a) rep.in pt.	SI 2241, reg.3(1)(b)
		s.261(4)(a) rep.in pt.	SI 2647, reg.1(2)(b)
		s.277 ext.(mods.) (Guernsey)	SI 260, art.2, Sch.1
		s.277A added (Guernsey)	SI 260, art.3
		ss.279,281 ext.(mods.) (Guernsey)	SI 260, art.2, Sch.1
		s.284 appl.(mods.)	SI 209, reg.9
		s.284 ext.(mods.) (Guernsey)	SI 260, art.2, Sch.1
		s.284 appl.(mods.)	SI 1012, reg.106
		s.284 mod.	SI 1419, reg.9
		s.284 appl.(mods.)	SI 2514, reg.92
		s.284 appl.(mods.)	SI 2515, reg.74
		s.284 appl.(mods.)	SI 2647, reg.8
		s.284 ext.(mods.)	SI 2771, reg.9
		s.284(1)-(5) appl.(mods.)	SI 2857, reg.12
		s.284(1)-(6)(8) appl.(mods.)	SI 1609, reg.10
		s.284(8) appl.(mods.)	SI 2857, reg.12
		s.293(5) (defn. of "pipeline") am.	17, s.50, Sch.4, para.39
		s.306(3) rep.in pt.	SI 2241, reg.3(1)(c)
		ss.308,313,316 ext.(mods.) (Guernsey)	SI 260, art.2, Sch.1
		Sch.3 rep.	SI 2241, reg.3(1)(d)
		Sch.5 ext.(mods.) (Cayman Islands)	SI 1261, art.2, Sch.
		Sch.5 ext.(mods.) (Montserrat)	SI 1262, art.2, Sch.
		Sch.5 ext.(mods.) (Saint Helena)	SI 1263, art.2, Sch.

Year and Chap. or No. of Measure	Short title	How affected	1998, Chapter of Act or Number of Measure or Statutory Instrument
1995—*cont.*			
		Sch.5, Pt.I ext.(mods.) (Guernsey)	SI 260, art.2, Sch.1
		Sch.7, Pts.I,II am. (*prosp.*)	SI 1258, arts.3-7,8, Sch.
		Sch.13, para.4 rep.	43, s.1(1), Sch.1, Pt.VIII
		Sch.13, para.65 rep. (*prosp.*)	17, s.51, Sch.5, Pt.I
c.22	Shipping and Trading Interests (Protection) Act 1995	saved (6.5.1999)	46, s.30, Sch.5, Pt.II, s.E3(j)
c.23	Goods Vehicles (Licensing of Operators) Act 1995	saved (6.5.1999)	46, s.30, Sch.5, Pt.II, s.E1(g)
c.25	Environment Act 1995	appt. day(s) for spec. provns. (1.4.1998) (1.7.1998)	SI 604, arts.2,3
		appt. day(s) for s.116 (insofar as it relates to Sch.21,para.4) (8.4.1998)	SI 781, arts.2,3
		appt. day(s) for s.59 (residue)(1.1.1999)	SI 3272, art.2
		ss.41,42 appl.(mods.)	SI 2746, reg.16(1)
		s.94(1)(oa) added (11.1.1999)	41, s.3(1)(b), Sch.2, Pt.IV, para.6(2)
		s.94(6A) added (11.1.1999)	41, s.3(1)(b), Sch.2, Pt.IV, para.6(3)
		s.94A added (11.1.1999)	41, s.3(1)(b), Sch.2, Pt.IV, para.6(4)
		s.123 appl.(mods.) (1.4.1999)	SI 2746, reg.16(2)
		Sch.5, Pt.I, paras.3(1)(d) 4(1)(c) am.	18, s.54(1), Sch.3, para.29
		Sch.7, para.19 rep.	18, s.54(3), Sch.5
		Sch.10, para.1 rep.	43, s.1(1), Sch.1, Pt.IV, Group 2
		Sch.10, para.16 rep.	38, s.152, Sch.18, Pt.IV
		Sch.10, para.20 rep.	38, s.152, Sch.18, Pt.V
c.26	Pensions Act 1995	power to am. (*prosp.*)	47, s.87
		s.107(1), Table am.	11, s.23, Sch.5, Pt.IV, Ch.II, para.71
		s.137(2), Sch.5, para.70 rep. (*prosp.*)	14, s.86(2), Sch.8
c.27	Geneva Conventions (Amendment)) Act 1995	appt. day (20.7.1998)	SI 1505, art.2
c.32	Olympic Symbols etc. (Protection) Act 1995	s.4(16) (defn. of "Royal Commission") am. (*prosp.*)	47, s.99, Sch.13, para.15
c.34	Child Support Act 1995	mod.	14, s.2(1)(2)(g)
		saved (6.5.1999)	46, s.30, Sch.5, Pt.II, s.F1
		saved (6.5.1999)	46, s.30, Sch.5, Pt.II, s.F2
		power to am. (*prosp.*)	47, s.87
		ss.12,13,14(1),15,16 rep. (*prosp.*)	14, s.86(2), Sch.8
		s.29(2)-(4) rep. & superseded (*prosp.*)	47, s.87(3)(e)
		s.29(2)-(4) rep. (*prosp.*)	47, s.100(2), Sch.15
		Sch.3, para.3(2) rep.	14, s.86(2), Sch.8

Year and Chap. or No. of Measure	Short title	How affected	1998, Chapter of Act or Number of Measure or Statutory Instrument
1995—*cont.*			
		Sch.3, paras.4-6,7(2),17, 19(2) rep. (*prosp.*)	14, s.86(2), Sch.8
c.38	Civil Evidence Act 1995	s.9 referred to (26.4.1999)	SI 3132, rule 33.6(2)
c.39	Criminal Law (Consolidation) (Scotland) Act 1995	s.16A(1)(2) rep.in pt.	40, s.9(1)(2), Sch.1, Pt.II, para.8(a)(b), Sch.2, Pt.II
		s.16A(3) rep.in pt.	40, s.9(1)(2), Sch.1, Pt.II, para.8(c), Sch.2, Pt.II
		s.16A(3)(a) rep.	40, s.9(1)(2), Sch.1, Pt.II, para.8(c), Sch.2, Pt.II
		s.16A(5) rep.in pt.	40, s.9(1)(2), Sch.1, Pt.II, para.8(d), Sch.2, Pt.II
		s.16A(5)(a) rep.	40, s.9(1)(2), Sch.1, Pt.II, para.8(d), Sch.2, Pt.II
		s.24(4) am.	37, s.110
		ss.31-43 (Pt.V) saved (6.5.1999)	46, s.30, Sch.5, Pt.II, s.B1(c)
		s.50A mod.	37, s.33
c.40	Criminal Procedure (Consequential Provisions) (Scotland) Act 1995	Sch.4, para.40 rep. (*prosp.*)	17, s.51, Sch.5, Pt.I
c.43	Proceeds of Crime (Scotland) Act 1995	s.11A added	40, s.7
		s.18 restr.	35, s.14(3)(b)
		s.18(12) added	37, s.119, Sch.8, para.115
		s.19 restr.	35, s.14(3)(b)
		s.19(6) am.	37, s.119, Sch.8, para.116
		s.20 restr.	35, s.14(3)(c)
		s.28(1) appl.	37, s.24(4), Sch.1 (adding 1982 c.45, Sch.2A)
		s.29(3)(a) mod.	SI 752, art.3(1)(f)
		Sch.1, para.4(4) mod.	SI 752, art.3(1)(g)
c.45	Gas Act 1995	Sch.4, para.2(1)(xxv) rep.	38, s.152, Sch.18, Pt.IV
		Sch.4, para.2(1)(xxviii) am.	38, s.135(2)(c)
		Sch.4, para.(10)(f) rep.	38, s.152, Sch.18, Pt.IV
		Sch.5, para.11 rep.in pt.	36, s.165, Sch.27, Pt.V(3), Note 1
		Sch.5, para.11(b) rep.	36, s.165, Sch.27, Pt.V(3), Note 1
c.46	Criminal Procedure (Scotland) Act 1995	s.18(3) subst. (1.8.1997) (*retrosp.*)	37, s.119, Sch.8, para.117(2)
		s.37(9) am.	SI 2635, para.2
		s.49(3)(b) am. (*retrosp.*)	37, s.119, Sch.8, para.118
		s.106(1)(bb) am. (*retrosp.*)	37, s.119, Sch.8, para.119
		s.106(d) am.	37, s.94(2), Sch.6, Pt.II, para.5
		s.108(1)(dd) added	37, s.94(2), Sch.6, Pt.II, para.6(2)
		s.108(2)(b)(iii) am.	37, s.94(2), Sch.6, Pt.II, para.6(3)
		s.108A am. (*retrosp.*)	37, s.119, Sch.8, para.120

Year and Chap. or No. of Measure	Short title	How affected	1998, Chapter of Act or Number of Measure or Statutory Instrument
1995—*cont.*			
		s.118(4A)(c)(iii) rep.in pt. (*retrosp.*)	37, ss.119,120(2), Sch.8, para.121, Sch.10
		s.136 excl. (1.4.1999)	39, s.33(4)
		s.136(3) appl. (S)	SI 955, reg.8(4)
		s.136(3) appl. (1.4.1999)	39, s.33(5)(b)
		s.148(1)(7)(a) am. (*retrosp.*)	10, s.1(1)(2)
		s.167(7) am.	37, s.119, Sch.8, para.122
		s.175(2)(c) am.	37, s.94(2), Sch.6, Pt.II, para.7(2)
		s.175(4)(dd) added	37, s.94(2), Sch.6, Pt.II, para.7(3)
		s.175(4A)(b)(iii) am.	37, s.94(2), Sch.6, Pt.II, para.7(4)
		s.175(5C) rep.in pt.	37, ss.119,120(2), Sch.8, para.123, Sch.10
		s.204A added	37, s.112
		s.209(1) am.	37, s.86(2)(a)(b)
		s.209(1) rep.in pt.	37, ss.86(2)(c),120(2), Sch.10
		s.210A added	37, s.86(1)
		s.210A (defn. of "extended sentence") appl.	37, s.87 (adding 1993 c.9 s.26A(1))
		s.210A (defns. of "custodial term", "extension period" and "imprisonment") appl.	37, s.87 (adding 1993 c.9 s.26A)
		s.210A (defn. of "an extended sentence") appl.	37, s.119, Sch.8, para.71(b) (adding 1989 c.45, s.39(7A)(7B))
		s.228(1) am.	37, s.94(2), Sch.6, Pt.I, para.1
		s.232(3A) am.	37, s.94(2), Sch.6, Pt.I, para.2(2)
		s.232(3B) added	37, s.94(2), Sch.6, Pt.I, para.2(3)
		s.234B added	37, s.89
		s.234C added	37, s.90
		s.234D added	37, s.91
		ss.234E,234F added	37, s.92
		ss.234G,234H added	37, s.93
		s.234J added	37, s.94
		s.234K added	37, s.95(1)
		s.245D subst.	37, s.94(2), Sch.6, Pt.I, para.3
		s.245G(2) subst.	37, s.94(2), Sch.6, Pt.I, para.4(2)
		s.245G(3)(4) added	37, s.94(2), Sch.6, Pt.I, para.4(3)
		s.287 saved (20.5.1999)	46, s.48(4)
		ss.288A,288B added (20.5.1999)	46, s.125, Sch.8, para.32(2)
		s.307 (defn. of "a justice") appl. (*prosp.*)	7, s.10(1)(b)

Year and Chap. or No. of Measure	Short title	How affected	1998, Chapter of Act or Number of Measure or Statutory Instrument
1995—*cont.*			
		s.307 (defn. of "a justice") appl. (*prosp.*)	33, ss.8(2)(b),10(7)(b), 18(1)(b)
		s.307(1) (defn. of "drug treatment and testing order") added	37, s.95(2)
		s.307(1) defn.of (" officer of law") para.(ba) added	37, s.119, Sch.8, para.124(a)
		s.307(1) defn.of (" officer of law") para.(e) am.	37, s.119, Sch.8, para.124(b)
		s.307(1) (defn. of "devolution issue") added (20.5.1999)	46, s.125, Sch.8, para.32(3)
		s.337A(1) subst. (*retrosp.*)	10, s.1(3)
c.47	Northern Ireland (Remission of Sentences) Act 1995	s.3(2) restr.	35, s.18
c.50	Disability Discrimination Act 1995	appt. day(s) for ss.46, 47 and (insofar as it relates to s.46) s.48 (13.5.1998)	SI 1282, art.2
		defn. of "act of discrimination" appl.	8, s.14(1) (adding 1996 c.18, s.117(6)([c]))
		saved (6.5.1999)	46, s.30, Sch.5, Pt.II, s.L2(a)-(d)
		defn. of "disability" appl. (*prosp.*)	47, s.75(5)
		ss.4-6 mod.	SI 218, arts.1(2),3, Sch.
		ss.5,6 saved	SI 633, art.J10(2)
		s.7(1) am.	SI 2618, art.2
		s.9(3)(a) am.	8, s.9(1)(2)(d)
		s.9(3)(b) am. (NI)	SI 1265, art.11(2)(c)
		s.9(3)(b) am.	8, s.10(1)(2)(d)
		s.9(4) replaced (by s.9(4) (4A)(4B)(4C)(5)) (NI)	SI 1265, art.16, Sch.1, para.6
		s.9(4) replaced (by (4) (4A)(4B)(4C))	8, s.15, Sch.1, para.11
		s.9(5) replaced (by s.9(4) (4A)(4B)(4C)(5)) (NI)	SI 1265, art.16, Sch.1, para.6
		s.9(5) replaced (by (4) (4A)(4B)(4C))	8, s.15, Sch.1, para.11
		s.9(6) added (NI)	SI 1265, art.9(3)
		s.9(6) added	8, s.8(4)
		ss.11-12,16 mod.	SI 218, arts.1(2),3, Sch.
		s.19(6)(c)(d) rep. (*prosp.*)	31, s.140(3), Sch.31
		s.19(6)(ff) added (*prosp.*)	30, s.38
		ss.32-49 (Pt.V) saved (6.5.1999)	46, s.30, Sch.5, Pt.II, s.E5(b)
		ss.55,57,58 mod.	SI 218, arts.1(2),3, Sch.
		Sch.8 am. (*prosp.*)	47, s.99, Sch.13, para.16(2)(a)
		Sch.8, para.6(2) rep. (NI) (*prosp.*)	SI 1265, art.16, Sch.2
		Sch.8, para.33(1) replaced (by para.33(1) (1A)) (*prosp.*)	47, s.99, Sch.13, para.16(2)(b)

Year and Chap. or No. of Measure	Short title	How affected	1998, Chapter of Act or Number of Measure or Statutory Instrument
1995—*cont.*			
		Sch.8, para.52 subst. (*prosp.*)	47, s.99, Sch.13, para.16(2)(c)
c.x	London Local Authorities Act 1995	Sch., Pt.I rep.in pt.	18, s.54(1)(3), Sch.3, para.30, Sch.5
		Sch., Pt.I am.	18, s.54(1), Sch.3, para.30
No.2	Church of England (Miscellaneous Provisions) Measure 1995	s.6 rep. (1.1.1999)	GSM 1, s.13(3)
1996			
c.4	Consolidated Fund Act 1996	rep.	28, s.3, Sch.(C)
c.6	Chemical Weapons Act 1996	ext.(mods.) (Isle of Man)	SI 2794, arts.2,3, Sch.
		ss.1-32 ext.(mods.) (Bailiwick of Jersey)	SI 2565, art.4, Sch.
		s.2 ext.(mods.) (Bailiwick of Jersey)	SI 2565, art.3
		ss.34-36,38,39, Sch. ext.(mods.) (Bailiwick of Jersey)	SI 2565, art.4, Sch.
c.8	Finance Act 1996	ss.39-71 appl.	36, s.148(4)
		s.80(2) am.	36, s.46(3), Sch.7, para.11
		s.80(5) excl.	36, ss.103(2)(3),104 (adding 1988 c.1 s.798A)
		s.82(2)(a)(b) am.	36, s.46(3), Sch.7, para.11
		s.83(3)(4) subst. (*retrosp.*)	36, s.82(1)(4)
		s.100(3) am.	36, s.108(4)(a)
		s.121(5) rep.	36, s.165, Sch.27, Pt.III(28), Note
		s.139 rep. (6.4.1999)	36, s.165, Sch.27, Pt.III(2), Note
		s.170 rep.	36, s.165, Sch.27, Pt.III(28), Note
		s.176 rep. (year 2003-04 and subsequent years of assessment)	36, s.165, Sch.27, Pt.III(31), Note
		s.797(3B)(b) rep.in pt. (*retrosp.*)	36, ss.82(2)(a)(4),165, Sch.27, Pt.III(17), Note
		s.797A(5) rep. (*retrosp.*)	36, ss.82(2)(b)(4),165, Sch.27, Pt.III(17), Note
		s.797A(5) am. (*retrosp.*)	36, s.82(2)(c)(4)
		s.797A(5)(a) am. (*retrosp.*)	36, s.82(2)(b)(4)
		s.797A(5)(c) rep. (*retrosp.*)	36, ss.82(2)(b)(4),165, Sch.27, Pt.III(17), Note
		s.797A(6) am. (*retrosp.*)	36, s.82(2)(d)(4)
		s.797A(7) am. (*retrosp.*)	36, s.82(2)(e)(4)
		Sch.1, para.5(6) am.	SI 1200, art.2
		Sch.6, para.4 rep. (*prosp.*)	36, s.165, Sch.27, Pt.III(3), Note
		Sch.8, para.1(3)(b)(i) subst.	36, s.38, Sch.5, Pt.III, paras.64(2),73
		Sch.8, para.2(2) subst.	36, s.38, Sch.5, Pt.III, paras.64(3),73

Year and Chap. or No. of Measure	Short title	How affected	1998, Chapter of Act or Number of Measure or Statutory Instrument
1996—*cont.*			
		Sch.9, para.15 (defn. of "repo or stock-lending") mod. (1.1.1999)	SI 3177, reg.19
		Sch.9, para.16(1)(2) am.	36, s.108(4)(b)
		Sch.13, paras.4,5 referred to (1.1.1999)	SI 3177, reg.12
		Sch.14, para.1(2) rep. (6.4.1999)	36, s.165, Sch.27, Pt.III(2), Note
		Sch.14, para.32(4) rep.	36, s.165, Sch.27, Pt.III(4), Note
		Sch.14, para.48(2) rep. (6.4.1999)	36, s.165, Sch.27, Pt.III(2), Note
		Sch.19, para.2 rep.in pt.	36, s.165, Sch.27, Pt.III(28), Note
		Sch.20, para.28(5) rep.	36, s.165, Sch.27, Pt.III(28), Note
		Sch.20, para.30 rep.	36, s.165, Sch.27, Pt.III(4), Note
		Sch.20, para.66 rep. (year 2003-04 and subsequent years of assessment)	36, s.165, Sch.27, Pt.III(31), Note
		Sch.21, paras.12,13 rep.	36, s.165, Sch.27, Pt.III(23), Notes 1-2
		Sch.21, para.24 rep.	36, s.165, Sch.27, Pt.III(9), Note
		Sch.21, para.44 rep. (year 2003-04 and subsequent years of assessment)	36, s.165, Sch.27, Pt.III(31), Note
		Sch.23, paras.1-3,5,7-9 rep. (6.4.1999)	36, s.165, Sch.27, Pt.III(2), Note
		Sch.24, paras.2-4,6,7,8(2) ,13 rep.	36, s.165, Sch.27, Pt.III(28), Note
		Sch.25 rep. (6.4.1999)	36, s.165, Sch.27, Pt.III(2), Note
		Sch.34, para.1(8) rep.	36, s.165, Sch.27, Pt.III(28), Note
		Sch.36, para.3(6) rep.in pt.	36, s.165, Sch.27, Pt.III(27), Note
		Sch.36, para.3(6)(b)(7) rep.	36, s.165, Sch.27, Pt.III(27), Note
		Sch.39, para.1(2) rep.	36, s.165, Sch.27, Pt.III(4), Note
		Sch.39, para.1(4) rep.in pt.	36, s.165, Sch.27, Pt.III(4), Note
		Sch.39, para.7 rep. (year 2003-04 and subsequent years of assessment)	36, s.165, Sch.27, Pt.III(31), Note
c.9	Education (Student Loans) Act 1996	rep.	30, s.44(2), Sch.4
		Sch., para.3(4)(6)(a) rep.	1, s.6(2), Sch.
c.10	Audit (Miscellaneous Provisions) Act 1996	ss.1,2,3,5,6 rep.	18, s.54(3), Sch.5

Year and Chap. or No. of Measure	Short title	How affected	1998, Chapter of Act or Number of Measure or Statutory Instrument
1996—*cont.*			
c.11	Northern Ireland (Entry to Negotiations, etc) Act 1996	rep. (*prosp.*)	47, s.100(2), Sch.15
		s.3 rep.	SI 1127, art.2
c.14	Reserve Forces Act 1996	s.127(1) (defn. of "permanent service") rep. (1.1.1999)	SI 3086, reg.10(5)
c.16	Police Act 1996	appl. (UK) (*prosp.*)	32, s.51, Sch.3, para.8(8)
		defn. of "police force" appl. (*prosp.*)	32, s.73(1)
		defn. of "police force" appl.	40, s.1(1) (adding 1989 c.4, s.2A(11))
		s.1(2) (defn. of "police area") appl.	37, s.18(1)
		s.10(1) (defns. of "chief officer of police" and "police authority") appl.	37, s.42(1)
		s.62(1)(c) subst. (*prosp.*)	32, s.34(1)
		s.62(3) am. (*prosp.*)	32, s.34(2)
		s.63(1A) am. (*prosp.*)	32, s.74(1), Sch.4, para.20(2)
		s.97(1)(ea) added (*prosp.*)	32, s.74(1), Sch.4, para.20(3)
		s.97(6)(c) am. (*prosp.*)	32, s.74(1), Sch.4, para.20(4)
		s.97(7)(b) am. (*prosp.*)	32, s.74(1), Sch.4, para.20(5)
		s.99(8) am. (*prosp.*)	32, s.74(1), Sch.4, para.20(6)
		s.101(1) (defn. of "chief officer of police") appl.	37, s.18(1)
		s.101(1) (defn. of "police authority") appl.	37, s.18(1)
		s.101(1) (defn. of "police authority") appl.	37, s.115(2)(c)
		Sch.2, para.8 excl. (*temp.*)	SI 1432, art.5, Sch., para.4(7)
		Sch.7, para.1(2)(s) rep.	18, s.54(3), Sch.5
		Sch.7, para.17 rep. (saving)(*prosp.*)	32, s.74(2)(3), Schs.5,6
c.17	Employment Tribunals Act 1996	excl.	SI 218, art.6
		citation amended	8, ss.1(2)(3),16(2)(3)
		saved (6.5.1999)	46, s.30, Sch.5, Pt.II, s.H1(f)
		s.1(2) rep.in pt.	8, s.15, Sch.2
		s.4(1) am.	8, s.15, Sch.1, para.12(1)(2)(3)(4)
		s.4(1)(b) replaced (*prosp.*)	8, s.4
		s.4(3)(a) am.	8, s.3(1)-(3)
		s.4(3)(a) am.	8, s.15, Sch.1, para.12(1)(2)(3)(4)
		s.4(3)(c) am.	8, s.3(1)-(3)
		s.4(3)(ca) added	8, s.3(4)

Year and Chap. or No. of Measure	Short title	How affected	1998, Chapter of Act or Number of Measure or Statutory Instrument
1996—*cont.*			
		s.4(3)(cc)(cd) added (1.4.1999)	39, s.27(1)
		s.4(3)(f) rep.in pt.	8, ss.3(5),15, Sch.2
		s.4(6) am.	8, s.15, Sch.1, para.12(1) (2)(3)(4)
		s.4(6A) added	8, s.3(6)
		s.4(6B)(6C) added	8, s.5
		s.5(1)(b) rep.in pt.	8, s.15, Sch.2
		s.5(1)(d) added	8, s.15, Sch.1, para.13
		s.7(3)(f)(i) rep.	8, s.15, Sch.1, para.14(1) (2), Sch.2
		s.7(3A)(3C) added	8, s.2
		s.7(4)(c) added	8, s.15, Sch.1, para.14(1) (3)
		s.9(4) am.	8, s.15, Sch.1, para.15
		s.10(5)(a) am.	SI 1833, reg.32(9)
		s.16(5)(a) rep.in pt. (*prosp.*)	14, s.86(1)(2), Sch.7, para.147(a), Sch.8
		s.16(5)(d) replaced (by s.16(5)(cc)(d)) (*prosp.*)	14, s.86(1), Sch.7, para.147(b)
		s.18(1)(b) am.	8, s.15, Sch.1, para.16
		s.18(1)(d) am.	8, s.11(1)
		s.18(1)(dd) added	39, s.30(1)
		s.18(1)(ff) added	SI 1833, reg.33(b)
		s.21(1) am.	SI 1833, reg.34(a)
		s.21(1)(e) rep.in pt.	8, s.15, Sch.2
		s.21(1)(f) rep.in pt.	39, s.53, Sch.3
		s.21(1)(ff) added	39, s.29
		s.21(1)(g) added (*retrosp.*)	8, s.15, Sch.1, para.17(1) (2)
		s.21(2) am.	SI 1833, reg.34(b)
		s.21(4) added	8, s.15, Sch.1, para.17(3)
		Sch.1, para.7, Sch.3, para.54 rep. (*prosp.*)	14, s.86(2), Sch.8
c.18	Employment Rights Act 1996	defn. of "dismissal procedures agreements" appl.	8, s.15, Sch.1, para.7 (adding 1992 c.52 s.212B)
		mod. (EW)	18, s.54(2), Sch.4, para.9(2)
		appl. (*prosp.*)	31, s.54, Sch.16, para.27(3)(b)
		appl. (*prosp.*)	31, s.55, Sch.17, paras.24(4)(b),27
		defns. of "contract of employment", "employee" and "employer" appl.	31, s.142(1)
		mod. (pt.prosp.)	45, s.6, Sch.3, para.9(3)
		restr. (pt.prosp.)	45, s.6, Sch.3, para.10
		saved (6.5.1999)	46, s.30, Sch.5, Pt.II, s.H1(g)
		ss.11,12 power to appl.	39, s.12(4)(a)

Year and Chap. or No. of Measure	Short title	How affected	1998, Chapter of Act or Number of Measure or Statutory Instrument
1996—*cont.*			
		ss.13-27 (Pt.II) mod. (1.4.1999)	39, s.18(1)(a)(2)
		s.23 (defn. of "Crown employment") appl.	38, s.24(2)
		s.23(1)(a) ext. (1.4.1999)	39, s.20(1)(a)
		s.23(5) added	8, s.15, Sch.1, para.18
		s.31(1) am.	SI 924, arts.3,4, Sch.
		ss.43A-43L (Pt.IVA) added (pt.prosp.)	23, s.1
		s.45A added	SI 1833, reg.31(1)
		s.47A added (*prosp.*)	30, s.44(1), Sch.3, para.10
		s.47B added (*prosp.*)	23, s.2
		s.48(1) am. (*prosp.*)	30, s.44(1), Sch.3, para.11(a)
		s.48(1A) added (*prosp.*)	23, s.3
		s.48(1ZA) added	SI 1833, reg.31(2)
		s.48(2)(3)(4) appl.(mods.)	39, s.24(2)(a)
		s.48(5) added (*prosp.*)	30, s.44(1), Sch.3, para.11(b)
		s.49 appl.(mods.)	39, s.24(2)(a)
		s.49 restr.	39, s.24(3)
		s.49(2) am.	SI 1833, reg.31(3)(a)
		s.49(2) am. (*prosp.*)	23, s.4(2)
		s.49(5A) added	SI 1833, reg.31(3)(b)
		s.49(6) added (*prosp.*)	23, s.4(3)
		s.50(3) appl.	SI 633, art.J12(2)
		s.50(4) excl.	SI 633, art.J12(1)
		s.50(9)(b) rep.in pt. (*prosp.*)	31, s.140(3), Sch.31
		s.58(3)(c) added (*prosp.*)	30, s.44(1), Sch.3, para.12
		s.63A added (*prosp.*)	30, s.32
		ss.63B,63C added (*prosp.*)	30, s.33
		ss.66-68,70-71,92-93 mod.	SI 218, art.3, Sch.
		s.92 appl.(mods.)	SI 218, art.4(a)
		ss.94-134 (Pt.X) mod.	SI 218, art.3, Sch.
		ss.94-134 (Pt.X) appl.(mods.)	SI 218, art.4(b)
		ss.94-134 (Pt.X) mod. (1.1.1999)	GSM 1, s.6(1), Sch.3, para.3(1)(2)
		ss.94-134 (Pt.X) (defn. of "dismissal") appl.	39, s.23(4)
		s.98(1) mod. (1.1.1999)	GSM 1, s.6(1), Sch.3, para.3(2)(b)
		s.98(4) saved (1.1.1999)	GSM 1, s.6(1), Sch.3, para.3(2)(b)
		s.101A added	SI 1833, reg.32(1)
		s.103A added (*prosp.*)	23, s.5
		s.104(4)(d) added	SI 1833, reg.32(2)(b)
		s.104(5) added (*prosp.*)	30, s.44(1), Sch.3, para.13
		s.104A added	39, s.25(1)
		s.104A mod. (*prosp.*)	39, s.47, Sch.2, Pt.I, para.3 (adding 1948 c.47, s.3A(5))

Year and Chap. or No. of Measure	Short title	How affected	1998, Chapter of Act or Number of Measure or Statutory Instrument
1996—*cont.*			
		s.104A ext. (*prosp.*)	39, s.47, Sch.2, Pt.II, para.13 (adding 1949 c.30, s.3A(4))
		s.105(1)(c) am.	39, s.25(2)
		s.105(4A) added	SI 1833, reg.32(3)
		s.105(6A) added (*prosp.*)	23, s.6
		s.105(7A) added	39, s.25(2)
		s.108(3)(dd) added	SI 1833, reg.32(4)
		s.108(3)(ff) added (*prosp.*)	23, s.7(1)
		s.108(3)(g) rep.in pt.	39, ss.25(3),53, Sch.3
		s.108(3)(gg) added	39, s.25(3)
		s.109(2)(dd) added	SI 1833, reg.32(4)
		s.109(2)(ff) added	23, s.7(2)
		s.109(2)(g) rep.in pt.	39, ss.25(4),53, Sch.3
		s.109(2)(gg) added	39, s.25(4)
		s.110(2) subst.	8, s.12(1)(5)
		s.110(3)(e) subst.	8, s.12(2)(5)
		s.110(6) added	8, s.12(3)
		s.112(4) am. (1.1.1999)	8, s.15, Sch.1, para.19
		s.112(4) am. (pt.prosp.)	23, s.8(1)
		s.117 powcr to mod.	8, s.7 (adding 1992 c.52, s.212A(8)(a))
		s.117(2)(3) am. (pt.prosp.)	23, s.8(2)
		s.117(3)(a) am. (1.1.1999)	8, s.15, Sch.1, para.20
		s.117(4)(b) am.	SI 1833, reg.32(5)
		s.117(6)(a) rep.in pt.	8, s.15, Sch.2
		s.117(6)(c) added	8, s.14(1)
		s.117(8) rep.in pt.	8, s.15, Sch.2
		s.118(1) am. (pt.prosp.)	23, s.8(3)
		s.118(1)(b) am. (1.1.1999)	8, s.15, Sch.1, para.21(1)(2)
		s.118(3) am.	SI 1833, reg.32(5)
		s.118(4) added (1.1.1999)	8, s.15, Sch.1, para.21(1)(3)
		s.119 appl.	39, s.24(4)(a)
		s.120(1) am.	SI 924, arts.3,4, Sch.
		ss.120(1),122(3) am.	SI 1833, reg.32(5)
		s.122(3A) added	8, s.15, Sch.1, para.22
		s.123 appl.	39, s.24(4)(b)
		s.123(1) am. (1.1.1999)	8, s.15, Sch.1, para.23
		s.124(1) am.	SI 924, arts.3,4, Sch.
		s.124(1) appl.	39, s.24(4)(b)
		s.125(1)(2) am.	SI 924, arts.3,4, Sch.
		s.126(1)(b) subst.	8, s.14(2)(3)
		s.126(2) rep.in pt.	8, ss.14(2)(4)(a),15, Sch.2
		s.126(2) am.	8, s.14(2)(4)(b)
		s.127A added (1.1.1999)	8, s.13
		s.127B added (pt.prosp.)	23, s.8(4)
		s.128(1)(b) am.	SI 1833, reg.32(5)
		s.128(1)(b) am. (*prosp.*)	23, s.9

Year and Chap. or No. of Measure	Short title	How affected	1998, Chapter of Act or Number of Measure or Statutory Instrument
1996—*cont.*			
		s.129(1) am.	SI 1833, reg.32(5)
		s.129(1) am. (*prosp.*)	23, s.9
		s.134(1) am. (*prosp.*)	31, s.140(1), Sch.30, para.55
		ss.135-181 (Pt.XI) mod. (pt.prosp.)	45, s.34, Sch.8, para.9(3)(4)
		ss.135-181 (Pt.XI) mod. (pt.prosp.)	45, s.36, Sch.9, para.9(3)(4)
		s.139 appl. (*prosp.*)	31, s.57(6)(7)
		s.166(2)(a) rep.in pt.	8, s.15, Sch.2
		s.166(2)(aa) added	8, s.11(2)
		s.168(1)(a) rep.in pt.	8, s.15, Sch.2
		s.168(1)(aa) added	8, s.11(3)
		s.184(1)(d) power to mod.	8, s.7 (adding 1992 c.52, s.212A(9))
		s.184(1)(d) am.	8, s.12(4)
		s.186(1) am.	SI 924, arts.3,4, Sch.
		s.191(2)(aa) added (*prosp.*)	23, s.10
		s.191(3) (defn. of "Crown employment") appl. (1.7.1999)	46, s.23(3)(b)
		s.192(2)(aa) added	SI 1833, reg.31(4)
		s.193(2)(bb)(bc) added (*prosp.*)	23, s.11(2)
		s.193(4) added (*prosp.*)	23, s.11(3)
		ss.194(2)(c),195(2)(c) am.	SI 1833, reg.31(5)
		s.196(3A) added (*prosp.*)	23, s.12(2)
		s.196(5) am. (*prosp.*)	23, s.12(3)
		s.200(1) am.	SI 1833, reg.31(6)
		s.200(1) am. (*prosp.*)	23, s.13(a)(b)
		s.201(1) subst. (*prosp.*)	17, s.50, Sch.4, para.40(2)
		s.201(5) rep. (*prosp.*)	17, ss.50,51, Sch.4, para.40(3), Sch.5, Pt.I
		s.202(2)(b) am.	SI 1833, reg.31(5)
		s.202(2)(g)(i) am.	SI 1833, reg.32(6)(a)
		s.202(2)(g)(ii) am.	SI 1833, reg.32(6)(b)
		s.203(2)(f) rep.in pt.	8, s.15, Sch.2
		s.203(3)(b) am.	8, s.24(1)(2)
		s.203(3)(c) am.	8, s.9(1)(2)(e)
		s.203(3)(d) am.	8, s.10(1)(2)(e)
		s.203(4) replaced (by s.203(3A)(3B)(4))	8, s.24(1)(3)
		s.203(5) added	8, s.8(5)
		s.205(1A) added (*prosp.*)	23, s.14
		s.205(1ZA) added	SI 1833, reg.31(7)
		s.209(2)(e) am.	SI 1833, reg.32(7)
		ss.210-219 (Pt.XIV) (Ch.I) appl.	SI 366, reg.13(7)
		s.215(5) am. (*prosp.*)	14, s.86(1), Sch.7, para.148

Year and Chap. or No. of Measure	Short title	How affected	1998, Chapter of Act or Number of Measure or Statutory Instrument
1996—*cont.*			
		s.219(1) rep.in pt.	8, s.15, Sch.1, para.25(1) (2)(a), Sch.2
		s.219(1) am.	8, s.15, Sch.1, para.25(1) (2)(b)(c)
		s.219(2)-(4) rep.	8, s.15, Sch.1, para.25(1) (3), Sch.2
		ss.220-224 appl.(mods.)	SI 192, reg.37(1)
		ss.220-229 (Pt.XIV) (Ch.II) appl.(mods.)	8, s.6 (subst. 1992 c.52, s.87(8))
		s.225(4A) added (*prosp.*)	30, s.44(1), Sch.3, para.14
		ss.226-229 appl.(mods.)	SI 192, reg.37(1)
		s.226(3) am. (1.1.1999)	8, s.15, Sch.1, para.26
		s.227(1) am.	SI 924, arts.3,4, Sch.
		s.230(2) (defn. of "contract of employment") appl. (*prosp.*)	29, s.56(10)(a)
		s.230(3)(b) appl.	39, s.24(5)
		s.230(6) added (*prosp.*)	23, s.15(1)
		s.235 (defn. of "protected disclosure") added (*prosp.*)	23, s.15(2)
		Sch.1, para.11 rep.	38, s.152, Sch.18, Pt.IV
		Sch.1, para.18 rep. (*prosp.*)	17, s.51, Sch.5, Pt.I
		Sch.1, para.19 rep. (EW)	18, s.54(3), Sch.5
		Sch.1, para.41 rep.	38, s.152, Sch.18, Pt.VI
		Sch.1, para.45(3)(a) rep. (EW)	18, s.54(3), Sch.5
		Sch.1, para.56(5), Sch.2, Pt.II, para.18 rep.	8, s.15, Sch.2
c.22	Northern Ireland (Emergency Provisions) Act 1996	appl.	35, s.3(7)(b)
		appl.	35, s.17, Sch.3, para.2(1) (c)
		s.3 saved (*prosp.*)	SI 1504, art.12(4)
		s.14 subst. (*prosp.*)	SI 1504, art.65(1), Sch.5, para.47
		ss.29,30(1) restr.	35, s.14(2)(b)
		ss.30A,30B added	40, s.2
		ss.31,35 restr.	35, s.14(2)(b)
		s.36 rep.	9, ss.3,7(2), Sch.2
		s.53(2) subst.	9, s.4
		s.53A added	9, s.5
		s.54(1) am.	9, s.7(1), Sch.1, para.3(2)
		s.60(2) am.	9, s.6(2)
		s.60(4) rep.in pt.	9, s.7(1)(2), Sch.1, para.3(3)(a), Sch.2
		s.60(5) rep.in pt.	9, ss.6(3),7(2), Sch.2
		s.60(5) am.	9, s.7(1), Sch.1, para.3(3) (b)
		s.62 am.	40, s.4(10)
		s.62(2) am.	9, s.1

Year and Chap. or No. of Measure	Short title	How affected	1998, Chapter of Act or Number of Measure or Statutory Instrument
1996—*cont.*			
		s.62(5) rep.	9, s.7(1)(2), Sch.1, para.3(4), Sch.2
		s.62(10) am.	9, s.1
		Sch.1, para.3 am.	9, s.2(1)
		Sch.1, para.7 am. & rep. in pt.	9, s.2(2)
		Sch.1, para.7(a)(b)(c)(d) (f) rep.in pt.	9, s.7(2), Sch.2
		Sch.1, para.8 am.	9, s.2(3)
		Sch.1, para.11 am. & rep. in pt.	9, s.2(2)
		Sch.1, para.11(a) rep.in pt.	9, s.7(2), Sch.2
		Sch.1, paras.12,13 am.	9, s.2(1)
		Sch.1, para.16 am. & rep. in pt.	9, s.2(2)
		Sch.1, para.16(a)(b)(c) rep.in pt.	9, s.7(2), Sch.2
		Sch.1, para.16(g) am.	9, s.7(1), Sch.1, para.3(5) (a)
		Sch.1, para.16(h) rep.in pt.	9, s.7(2), Sch.2
		Sch.1, paras.17,18 am.	9, s.2(1)
		Sch.1, paras.20,21 am.	9, s.2(3)
		Sch.1, para.22(a)(i) am.	9, s.2(1)
		Sch.1, para.22(j) rep.	9, s.7(1)(2), Sch.1, para.3(5)(b), Sch.2
		Sch.3 rep.	9, ss.3,7(2), Sch.2
		Sch.3 rep.	9, s.7(2), Sch.2
		Sch.6, para.1 rep. (*prosp.*)	47, s.100(2), Sch.15
c.23	Arbitration Act 1996	excl. (NI) (*prosp.*)	SI 3162, art.89(6)
		excl.	8, s.7 (adding 1992 c.52, s.212A(6))
		Pt.I excl. (EWS) (*prosp.*)	14, s.16(9)
		s.42 appl.(mods.)	SI 649, art.2, Sch., Pt.I, para.24
		Sch.3, para.51 rep. (NI) (*prosp.*)	SI 3162, art.105(4), Sch.5
		Sch.3, para.55 rep. (NI) (*prosp.*)	SI 1506, art.78(2), Sch.7
c.25	Criminal Procedure and Investigations Act 1996	appt. day(s) for s.45 (insofar as that section relates to notices of transfer served under section 53 of Criminal Justice Act 1991 c.53) (1.4.1998)	SI 851, art.2
		s.1(2)(cc) added (4.1.1999)	37, s.119, Sch.8, para.125(a)
		s.1(2)(f) added (*prosp.*)	37, s.119, Sch.8, para.125(b)
		s.5(3A) added	37, s.119, Sch.8, para.126
		s.13(1) am. (*prosp.*)	37, s.119, Sch.8, para.127(b)

Year and Chap. or No. of Measure	Short title	How affected	1998, Chapter of Act or Number of Measure or Statutory Instrument
1996—*cont.*			
		s.13(1)(cc) added (4.1.1999)	37, s.119, Sch.8, para.127(a)
		s.28(1)(a) am. (4.1.1999)	37, s.119, Sch.8, para.128
		s.31(3) mod.	40, s.5(1) (adding 1977 c.45, s.1A(10))
		s.39(1) am. (4.1.1999)	37, s.119, Sch.8, para.129
c.27	Family Law Act 1996	appt. day(s) for Sch.8, para.16(5)(a)(6)(b)(7) (1.11.1998)	SI 2572, art.3
c.29	Sexual Offences (Conspiracy and Incitement) Act 1996	s.1 rep.	40, s.9(1)(2), Sch.1, Pt.II, para.9(1), Sch.2, Pt.II
		s.3(1) am.	40, s.9(1), Sch.1, Pt.II, para.9(2)(a)
		s.3(2) rep.in pt.	40, s.9(1)(2), Sch.1, Pt.II, para.9(2)(b)(i), Sch.2, Pt.II
		s.3(2) am.	40, s.9(1), Sch.1, Pt.II, para.9(2)(b)(ii)
		s.3(3) rep.	40, s.9(1)(2), Sch.1, Pt.II, para.9(2)(c), Sch.2, Pt.II
		s.3(6) rep.in pt.	40, s.9(1)(2), Sch.1, Pt.II, para.9(2)(d), Sch.2, Pt.II
		s.3(7) rep.	40, s.9(1)(2), Sch.1, Pt.II, para.9(2)(e), Sch.2, Pt.II
		s.3(9) am.	40, s.9(1), Sch.1, Pt.II, para.9(2)(f)
		s.4(b)(c) rep.	40, s.9(1)(2), Sch.1, Pt.II, para.9(3), Sch.2, Pt.II
		s.7(3) rep.in pt.	40, s.9(1)(2), Sch.1, Pt.II, para.9(4), Sch.2, Pt.II
c.31	Defamation Act 1996	defn. of "statement" appl.	38, s.77(3)
		defn. of "statement" appl. (pt.6.5.1999) (pt.1.7.1999)	46, s.41
		defn. of "statement" appl. (*prosp.*)	47, s.50(3)
		defn. of "statement" appl.	47, s.99, Sch.13, para.20 (substituting 1998 c.12, Sch.1, para.8)
		s.17(1) defn.of (" statutory provision") para.(aa) added (6.5.1999)	46, s.125, Sch.8, para.33(2)
		Sch.1 ext.	38, s.77(4)(a)
		Sch.1, para.11(1)(c) mod.	38, s.77(4)(b)
		Sch.1, para.11(1)(c) am. (6.5.1999)	46, s.125, Sch.8, para.33(3)
c.37	Noise Act 1996	s.12(2) am. (EW)	18, s.54(1), Sch.3, para.31
c.42	Railway Heritage Act 1996	saved (6.5.1999)	46, s.30, Sch.5, Pt.II, s.E2
c.45	Appropriation Act 1996	rep.	28, s.3, Sch.(C)
c.48	Damages Act 1996	s.6(8A) added (1.7.1999)	46, s.125, Sch.8, para.34
c.49	Asylum and Immigration Act 1996	s.4 ext.(mods.) (to Bailiwick of Jersey)	SI 1070, art.3, Sch.

Year and Chap. or No. of Measure	Short title	How affected	1998, Chapter of Act or Number of Measure or Statutory Instrument
1996—*cont.*			
		s.4 ext.(mods.) (Guernsey)	SI 1264, art.3, Sch.
		s.5 ext.(mods.) (to Bailiwick of Jersey)	SI 1070, art.3, Sch.
		s.5 ext.(mods.) (Guernsey)	SI 1264, art.3, Sch.
		s.7 ext.(mods.) (to Bailiwick of Jersey)	SI 1070, art.3, Sch.
		s.7 ext.(mods.) (Guernsey)	SI 1264, art.3, Sch.
		s.12(1) ext.(mods.) (to Bailiwick of Jersey)	SI 1070, art.3, Sch.
		s.12(1) ext.(mods.) (Guernsey)	SI 1264, art.3, Sch.
		s.13(1) ext.(mods.) (to Bailiwick of Jersey)	SI 1070, art.3, Sch.
		s.13(1) ext.(mods.) (Guernsey)	SI 1264, art.3, Sch.
		s.13(2) ext.(mods.) (to Bailiwick of Jersey)	SI 1070, art.3, Sch.
		s.13(2) ext.(mods.) (Guernsey)	SI 1264, art.3, Sch.
		Sch.2, para.1 ext.(mods.) (to Bailiwick of Jersey)	SI 1070, art.3, Sch.
		Sch.2, para.1 ext.(mods.) (Guernsey)	SI 1264, art.3, Sch.
		Sch.2, para.2 ext.(mods.) (to Bailiwick of Jersey)	SI 1070, art.3, Sch.
		Sch.2, para.2 ext.(mods.) (Guernsey)	SI 1264, art.3, Sch.
		Sch.2, paras.4-6 ext.(mods.) (to Bailiwick of Jersey)	SI 1070, art.3, Sch.
		Sch.2, paras.4-6 ext.(mods.) (Guernsey)	SI 1264, art.3, Sch.
		Sch.2, paras.8-10 ext.(mods.) (to Bailiwick of Jersey)	SI 1070, art.3, Sch.
		Sch.2, paras.8,10 ext.(mods.) (Guernsey)	SI 1264, art.3, Sch.
		Sch.2, para.13 ext.(mods.) (to Bailiwick of Jersey)	SI 1070, art.3, Sch.
		Sch.2, para.13 ext.(mods.) (Guernsey)	SI 1264, art.3, Sch.
c.50	Nursery Education and Grant-Maintained Schools Act 1996	s.1(2)(a)(b) power exercised	SI 655, reg.3(1)(2)
		s.1(3)(a) referred to	SI 655, reg.4
		s.4(1) am. (*prosp.*)	31, s.140(1), Sch.30, para.56
		s.5 rep.	31, s.140(3), Sch.31
		Sch.1 rep. & superseded	31, s.122(1)(2), Sch.26
		Sch.1 rep.	31, s.140(3), Sch.31
		Sch.1, para.6(1)(a) power exercised	SI 655, reg.10
		Sch.1, para.8(3) am. (*prosp.*)	31, s.135, Sch.28, Pt.II, para.6

Year and Chap. or No. of Measure	Short title	How affected	1998, Chapter of Act or Number of Measure or Statutory Instrument
1996—*cont.*			
		Sch.1, para.10(4)(a) rep.in pt. (*prosp.*)	31, s.135, Sch.28, Pt.II, para.7
		Sch.1, para.13(1)(2) power exercised	SI 655, reg.9(1)(4)
		Sch.1, para.13(3) added	31, s.134(2)
		Sch.1, para.18 added (*prosp.*)	31, s.135, Sch.28, Pt.II, para.8
		Sch.2, para.1(2) referred to	SI 655, reg.8(1)
c.52	Housing Act 1996	appt. day(s) for s.86 (11.8.1998) (to the extent that it does not already have effect)	SI 1768, arts.2,3
		ss.1-64 (Pt.I) (defns. of "the Corporation" and "registered social landlord") appl.	18, s.43
		ss.1-64 (Pt.I) am.	38, s.140, Sch.16, para.82(1)(2)
		s.1(1) rep.in pt.	38, ss.140,152, Sch.16, para.83(2), Sch.18, Pt.VI
		s.1(1A)(1B) added	38, s.140, Sch.16, para.83(3)
		s.1(2) rep.	38, ss.140,152, Sch.16, para.83(4), Sch.18, Pt.VI
		s.9(1) rep.in pt.	38, ss.140,152, Sch.16, para.84(2), Sch.18, Pt.VI
		s.9(1A) added	38, s.140, Sch.16, para.84(3)
		s.18(5) subst.	38, s.140, Sch.16, para.85(2)
		s.18(8) am.	38, s.140, Sch.16, para.85(3)
		s.30(5) subst.	38, s.140, Sch.16, para.86
		s.36(3)(4) subst.	38, s.140, Sch.16, para.87
		s.46(1)(6) rep.in pt.	38, ss.140,152, Sch.16, para.88(2), Sch.18, Pt.VI
		s.46(7) added	38, s.140, Sch.16, para.88(3)
		s.49(3) am.	38, s.140, Sch.16, para.89
		s.51(2)(a) am.	38, s.140, Sch.16, para.90(a)
		s.51(2)(d) am.	38, s.140, Sch.16, para.90(b)
		s.52(1) am.	38, s.140, Sch.16, para.91
		s.53(1)(4)(5) am.	38, s.140, Sch.16, para.92
		s.54 am.	38, s.140, Sch.16, para.93
		s.56(1)(2)(4) am.	38, s.140, Sch.16, para.94

Year and Chap. or No. of Measure	Short title	How affected	1998, Chapter of Act or Number of Measure or Statutory Instrument
1996—*cont.*			
		s.64 rep.in pt.	38, ss.140,152, Sch.16, para.95(a), Sch.18, Pt.VI
		s.64 am.	38, s.140, Sch.16, para.95(b)
		Sch.1, para.9(3) rep.in pt.	38, ss.140,152, Sch.16, para.96(2)(a), Sch.18, Pt.VI
		Sch.1, para.9(3A) added	38, s.140, Sch.16, para.96(2)(b)
		Sch.1, para.11(3) rep.in pt.	38, ss.140,152, Sch.16, para.96(2)(a), Sch.18, Pt.VI
		Sch.1, para.11(3A) added	38, s.140, Sch.16, para.96(2)(b)
		Sch.1, para.20(3) am.	38, s.140, Sch.16, para.96(5)
		Sch.1, para.27(1) rep.in pt.	38, ss.140,152, Sch.16, para.96(6)(a), Sch.18, Pt.VI
		Sch.1, para.27(1) am.	38, s.140, Sch.16, para.96(6)(b)
		Sch.1, para.27(4) am.	38, s.140, Sch.16, para.96(7)
		Sch.1, para.28(2) am.	38, s.140, Sch.16, para.96(8)
		Sch.2, para.6(2) am.	38, s.140, Sch.16, para.97(2)
		Sch.2, para.11(4) am.	38, s.140, Sch.16, para.97(3)
		Sch.3, para.2 rep.	18, s.54(3), Sch.5
c.53	Housing Grants, Construction and Regeneration Act 1996	appt. day(s) for ss.104- 117 (1.5.1998) (in so far as they are not already in force)	SI 650, s.2
		appt. day(s) for ss.104- 117 (in so far as they are not already in force) (1.5.1998)	SI 894, art.2
		ss.3(2)(e),64(7)(c) rep.	38, s.152, Sch.18, Pt.IV
		ss.104-117 (Pt.II) referred to (power to excl. construction contracts exercised)	SI 648, art.2
c.55	Broadcasting Act 1996	appt. day(s) for s.41 (29.1.1998)	SI 188, art.3
		saved (6.5.1999)	46, s.30, Sch.5, Pt.II, s.K1
		s.1(1A) subst.	SI 3196, reg.2, Sch., para.8(2)
		s.1(4A) added	SI 3196, reg.2, Sch., para.8(3)
		s.1(7) (defn. of "general reception") rep.	SI 3196, reg.2, Sch., para.8(4)
		s.1(7) rep.in pt.	SI 3196, reg.2, Sch., para.8(4)

Year and Chap. or No. of Measure	Short title	How affected	1998, Chapter of Act or Number of Measure or Statutory Instrument
1996—*cont.*			
		s.12(1)(c) am.	SI 3196, reg.2, Sch., para.9(2)
		s.12(1)(d) am.	SI 3196, reg.2, Sch., para.9(3)
		s.12(3A) added	SI 3196, reg.2, Sch., para.9(4)
		s.24(1)(a) subst.	SI 3196, reg.2, Sch., para.10
		s.25(5) am.	SI 3196, reg.2, Sch., para.11
		s.54(1)(h) am.	SI 1326, art.2
		s.77(2) rep. (*prosp.*)	41, s.74(1)(3), Sch.12, para.21, Sch.14, Pt.I
c.56	Education Act 1996	mod.	SI 1948, reg.3(1)(2), Sch.
		constr. with	18, s.36(6)
		defn. of "proprietor" appl. (*prosp.*)	29, s.30(5)
		defn. of "registered pupil" appl.	29, s.70(1)
		defn. of "school" appl.	29, s.70(1)
		defn. of "independent school" appl.	30, s.19(10)(c)
		defn. of "secondary education" appl. (*prosp.*)	30, s.32 (adding 1996 c.18, s.63A(2)(a)(i))
		defn. of "further education" appl. (*prosp.*)	30, s.32 (adding 1996 c.18, s.63A(2)(b)(i))
		defns. of "a county school", "a controlled, aided or special agreement school" and "a maintained special school" appl.	31, s.20, Sch.2, para.1
		defns. of "a grant-maintained school" and "a grant-maintained special school" appl.	31, s.20, Sch.2, para.2
		defn(s). appl.	31, s.20, Sch.2, para.3
		defns. of "county, voluntary or maintained special schools" and "grant-maintained or grant-maintained special schools" appl. (saving)	31, s.20(3)
		defns. of "voluntary school" and "grant-maintained school" appl. (saving)	31, s.21(2)(c)

Effects of Legislation

Year and Chap. or No. of Measure	Short title	How affected	1998, Chapter of Act or Number of Measure or Statutory Instrument
1996—*cont.*			
		defns. of "county controlled,aided or special agreement school", "maintained special school" and "grant-maintained or grant-maintained special school" appl. (pt.prosp.)	31, s.36(2), Sch.10, para.1(7)
		defn. of "county, voluntary or maintained special school" appl.	31, s.48, Sch.14, para.1(3)(a)
		defn. of "grant-maintained school" appl. (pt.prosp.)	31, s.69, Sch.19, para.2(4)
		defn. of "grant-maintained school" appl. (pt.prosp.)	31, s.69, Sch.19, para.3(4)
		defns. of "special agreement school", "grant-maintained school" and "grant- maintained special school" appl. (*prosp.*)	31, s.73(8)
		defns. of "grant-maintained school" and "grant-maintained special school" appl. (*prosp.*)	31, s.74, Sch.21, Pt.I, para.1
		defn. of "controlled school" appl. (*prosp.*)	31, s.76, Sch.22, Pt.I, para.3(2)
		defns. of "voluntary school", "grant-maintained school" and "grant-maintained special school" appl. (*prosp.*)	31, s.76, Sch.22, Pt.III, para.10(3)(4)
		defns. of "grant-maintained school" and "grant-maintained special school" appl. (*prosp.*)	31, s.87(5)(b)
		defns. of "county school", "voluntary school" and "grant- maintained school" appl. (*prosp.*)	31, s.93, Sch.23, Pt.I, para.1(1)
		defns. of "county school", "voluntary school" and "grant- maintained school" appl. (pt.prosp.)	31, s.100(2)
		defns. of "county or voluntary school" and "grant-maintained school" appl.	31, s.104(6)
		defns. of "grant-maintained school" and "grant-maintained special school" appl.	31, s.105(10)

Year and Chap. or No. of Measure	Short title	How affected	1998, Chapter of Act or Number of Measure or Statutory Instrument
1996—*cont.*		defn. of "grant-maintained special school" appl.	31, s.107(5)(b)
		mod.	31, s.126
		defn. of "assisted" appl. (*prosp.*)	31, s.140(1), Sch.30, para.21 (subst. defns. in 1989 c.41, Sch.9, para.3(3))
		defn. of "voluntary school" appl. (*prosp.*)	31, s.140(1), Sch.30, para.41 (am 1992 c.13, s.44(1))
		constr. with	31, s.142(8)(9)
		defns. of "grant-maintained school" and "grant-maintained special school" appl.	31, s.144, Sch.32, Pt.I, para.5(7)(a)
		defns. of "any county or voluntary school" and "any grant-maintained school" appl.	31, s.144, Sch.32, Pt.II, para.6(3)
		defn. of "voluntary school" appl.	31, s.144, Sch.32, Pt.II, para.9(3)
		defn. of "local education authority" appl.	31, s.144(3)(a)
		s.1(2) rep.in pt. (*prosp.*)	31, s.140(1)(3), Sch.30, para.58, Sch.31
		s.1(2)(b) rep. (*prosp.*)	31, s.140(1)(3), Sch.30, para.58, Sch.31
		s.1(3)(a) mod.	SI 2670, reg.9
		s.4(3) (defn. of "further education sector") appl. (*prosp.*)	31, s.76, Sch.22, Pt.I, para.3(7)
		s.5(3)(5) am. (*prosp.*)	31, s.140(1), Sch.30, para.59
		s.6(2) am. (*prosp.*)	31, s.140(1), Sch.30, para.60
		s.9 am. (*prosp.*)	31, s.140(1), Sch.30, para.61
		s.13A added	31, s.5
		s.14(5) rep. (*prosp.*)	31, s.140(1)(3), Sch.30, para.62, Sch.31
		s.15A added (*prosp.*)	31, s.140(1), Sch.30, para.63
		s.16, sidenote subst. (*prosp.*)	31, s.140(1), Sch.30, para.64(4)
		s.16(1) rep.in pt. (*prosp.*)	31, s.140(1)(3), Sch.30, para.64(2)(b), Sch.31
		s.16(1)(a) am. (*prosp.*)	31, s.140(1), Sch.30, para.64(2)(a)
		s.16(1)(c) rep. (*prosp.*)	31, ss.128(2),140(1)(3), Sch.30, para.64(2)(b), Sch.31

Year and Chap. or No. of Measure	Short title	How affected	1998, Chapter of Act or Number of Measure or Statutory Instrument
1996—*cont.*			
		s.16(1)(c) rep. (*prosp.*)	31, ss.128(2),140(3), Sch.31
		s.16(2) am. (*prosp.*)	31, s.140(1), Sch.30, para.64(3)
		s.17(2) am. (*prosp.*)	31, s.140(1), Sch.30, para.65
		s.18 subst. (*prosp.*)	31, s.128(1)
		ss.20-28 rep. (*prosp.*)	31, s.140(1)(3), Sch.30, para.66, Sch.31
		s.21 rep. (*prosp.*)	31, s.133
		s.24 power to mod. (*prosp.*)	31, s.132(4)
		s.29(2) rep. (*prosp.*)	31, s.140(1)(3), Sch.30, para.67(a), Sch.31
		s.29(3) rep.in pt. (*prosp.*)	31, s.140(1)(3), Sch.30, para.67(b), Sch.31
		s.30 rep. (*prosp.*)	31, s.140(1)(3), Sch.30, para.68, Sch.31
		ss.31-182 (Pt.II) (defn. of "new school") appl.	31, s.48, Sch.14, para.1(3)(b)
		ss.31-182 (Pt.II) (defn. of "delegated budget") appl.	31, s.107(5)(a)
		ss.31-182 (Pt.II) rep. (repeal of s.155(1)(4) (1.10.1998) (repeal of ss.101-126 (Pt.II) (Ch.V)(1.4.1999)) (pt.prosp.)	31, s.140(1)(3), Sch.30, para.69, Sch.31
		s.32(5) (defn. of "special agreement") appl. (*prosp.*)	31, s.76, Sch.22, Pt.I, para.3(1)(g)
		ss.76-100 (Pt.II) (Ch.IV) referred to	SI 2763, reg.3(b)
		s.76 excl. (1.1.1999)	SI 3097, reg.3
		ss.89-95 excl. (1.1.1999)	SI 3097, reg.8(a)-(d)
		s.89 appl. (pt.prosp.)	31, s.36(2), Sch.10, para.1(7)
		s.96(1)(3) mod. (until 1.9.1999) (*temp.*)	SI 3097, reg.4
		s.96(5) excl. (1.1.1999)	SI 3097, reg.8(a)-(d)
		s.97(1)(2) mod. (until 1.9.1999) (*temp.*)	SI 3097, reg.4
		ss.97(8),100 excl. (1.1.1999)	SI 3097, reg.8(a)-(d)
		s.117 mod.	SI 2670, reg.6
		s.123(2) am.	18, s.54(1), Sch.3, para.32(1)(2)(a)(b)
		ss.183-311 (Pt.III) (defn. of "promoters") appl.	31, s.20, Sch.2, para.3
		ss.183-311 (Pt.III) rep. (repeal of ss.184-199, 200(4),202,203,209,212, 213(2)(3),232-240,290 (1.10.1998)) (pt.prosp.)	31, s.140(1)(3), Sch.30, para.70, Sch.31
		ss.244-254 saved	31, s.144, Sch.32, Pt.I, para.2

Year and Chap. or No. of Measure	Short title	How affected	1998, Chapter of Act or Number of Measure or Statutory Instrument
1996—*cont.*			
		s.246 mod.	SI 2670, reg.7(1)
		s.247 mod.	SI 2670, reg.7(2)
		s.248(1)-(4) mod.	SI 2670, reg.7(3)
		ss.256-258 saved	31, s.144, Sch.32, Pt.I, para.2
		s.280 appl. (pt.prosp.)	31, s.36(2), Sch.10, para.1(7)
		ss.304,305 saved (*prosp.*)	31, s.60(7)
		s.310(4) am.	18, s.54(1), Sch.3, para.32(3)
		s.312(4)(a) rep.in pt. (*prosp.*)	31, s.140(1)(3), Sch.30, para.71(a), Sch.31
		s.312(5) (defn. of "maintained school") subst. (*prosp.*)	31, s.140(1), Sch.30, para.71(b)
		s.313(1) am. (*prosp.*)	31, s.140(1), Sch.30, para.72
		s.315(2) am. (*prosp.*)	31, s.140(1), Sch.30, para.73
		s.317(1)(2) am. (*prosp.*)	31, s.140(1), Sch.30, para.74(2)(3)
		s.317(3)(a) rep.in pt. (*prosp.*)	31, s.140(1)(3), Sch.30, para.74(4)(a)(ii), Sch.31
		s.317(3)(a) am. (*prosp.*)	31, s.140(1), Sch.30, para.74(4)(a)(i)
		s.317(3)(b) am. (*prosp.*)	31, s.140(1), Sch.30, para.74(4)(b)
		s.317(4) am. (*prosp.*)	31, s.140(1), Sch.30, para.74(5)
		s.317(5) am. (*prosp.*)	31, s.140(1), Sch.30, para.74(6)
		s.317(6) am. (*prosp.*)	31, s.140(1), Sch.30, para.74(7)
		s.317(7) am. (*prosp.*)	31, s.140(1), Sch.30, para.74(8)
		s.318(1)(a)(b) am. (*prosp.*)	31, s.140(1), Sch.30, para.75(2)
		s.318(2) am. (*prosp.*)	31, s.140(1), Sch.30, para.75(3)
		s.318(3) replaced (by s.318(3)(3A))	31, s.140(1), Sch.30, para.75(4)
		s.321(3)(a) am. (*prosp.*)	31, s.140(1), Sch.30, para.76(a)
		s.321(3)(b) subst. (*prosp.*)	31, s.140(1), Sch.30, para.76(b)
		s.324(5)(b) am. (*prosp.*)	31, s.140(1), Sch.30, para.77(a)
		s.324(5A) added	31, s.140(1), Sch.30, para.77(b)
		s.327(1)(b) subst. (*prosp.*)	31, s.140(1), Sch.30, para.78

Year and Chap. or No. of Measure	Short title	How affected	1998, Chapter of Act or Number of Measure or Statutory Instrument
1996—*cont.*			
		s.330 rep. (*prosp.*)	31, s.140(1)(3), Sch.30, para.79, Sch.31
		s.337 subst. (*prosp.*)	31, s.140(1), Sch.30, para.80
		ss.338-341 rep. (*prosp.*)	31, s.140(1)(3), Sch.30, para.81, Sch.31
		s.342 subst. (*prosp.*)	31, s.140(1), Sch.30, para.82
		ss.343-346 rep. (s.346 in force 1.10.1998) (pt.prosp.)	31, s.140(1)(3), Sch.30, para.83, Sch.31
		s.348(3) subst. (*prosp.*)	31, s.140(1), Sch.30, para.84
		s.350(1) subst. (*prosp.*)	31, s.140(1), Sch.30, para.85
		s.352(1)(a) mod. (pt.prosp.)	31, s.69, Sch.19, para.2(2)(4)
		s.352(1)(a) mod. (pt.prosp.)	31, s.69, Sch.19, para.3(2)(4)
		s.352(1)(a) mod. (*prosp.*)	31, s.69, Sch.19, para.4(2)
		s.352(1)(a) expld.	31, s.69(2)
		s.352(1)(a) am. (*prosp.*)	31, s.140(1), Sch.30, para.86
		s.356(4) am. (*prosp.*)	31, s.140(1), Sch.30, para.87(a)
		s.356(5)(a)(ii) rep.in pt. (*prosp.*)	31, s.140(1)(3), Sch.30, para.87(b), Sch.31
		s.356(8) am. (*prosp.*)	31, s.140(1), Sch.30, para.87(a)
		s.357(2) rep.	31, s.140(1)(3), Sch.30, para.88, Sch.31
		s.362(3) am. (*prosp.*)	31, s.140(1), Sch.30, para.89(a)
		s.362(4) am. (*prosp.*)	31, s.140(1), Sch.30, para.89(b)
		s.366(1)(b) rep.in pt. (*prosp.*)	31, s.140(1)(3), Sch.30, para.90(a), Sch.31
		s.366(4) am. (*prosp.*)	31, s.140(1), Sch.30, para.90(b)
		s.366(5) rep. (*prosp.*)	31, s.140(1)(3), Sch.30, para.90(c), Sch.31
		s.366(6) am. (*prosp.*)	31, s.140(1), Sch.30, para.90(d)
		ss.370-374 rep. (repeal of ss.370-373 in force 1.10.1998) (pt.prosp.)	31, s.140(1)(3), Sch.30, para.91, Sch.31
		s.375(2) (defn. of "agreed syllabus") appl.	31, s.69, Sch.19, para.1(2)
		ss.376-389 rep. (*prosp.*)	31, s.140(1)(3), Sch.30, para.92, Sch.31
		s.382 (defn. of "appropriate agreed syllabus") appl. (pt.prosp.)	31, s.69, Sch.19, para.3(4)

Year and Chap. or No. of Measure	Short title	How affected	1998, Chapter of Act or Number of Measure or Statutory Instrument
1996—*cont.*			
		s.390(2) subst. (*prosp.*)	31, s.140(1), Sch.30, para.93
		s.391(1)(a) subst. (*prosp.*)	31, s.140(1), Sch.30, para.94(2)
		s.391(8)(9) rep. (*prosp.*)	31, s.140(1)(3), Sch.30, para.94(3), Sch.31
		s.392(4) rep. (*prosp.*)	31, s.140(1)(3), Sch.30, para.95, Sch.31
		s.393 rep. (*prosp.*)	31, s.140(1)(3), Sch.30, para.96, Sch.31
		s.394(1) am. (*prosp.*)	31, s.140(1), Sch.30, para.97(2)(c)
		s.394(1)(a) am. (*prosp.*)	31, s.140(1), Sch.30, para.97(2)(a)
		s.394(1)(b) subst. (*prosp.*)	31, s.140(1), Sch.30, para.97(2)(b)
		s.394(4) am. (*prosp.*)	31, s.140(1), Sch.30, para.97(3)
		s.394(8) am. (*prosp.*)	31, s.140(1), Sch.30, para.97(4)
		s.395(1) am. (*prosp.*)	31, s.140(1), Sch.30, para.98
		s.396(1) am. (*prosp.*)	31, s.140(1), Sch.30, para.99
		s.399 am. (*prosp.*)	31, s.140(1), Sch.30, para.100
		s.402(6) am. (*prosp.*)	31, s.140(1), Sch.30, para.101
		s.403(2) am. (*prosp.*)	31, s.140(1), Sch.30, para.102
		s.404(2) am. (*prosp.*)	31, s.140(1), Sch.30, para.103(a)
		s.404(3) rep.	31, s.140(1)(3), Sch.30, para.103(b), Sch.31
		s.406(3) am. (*prosp.*)	31, s.140(1), Sch.30, para.104
		s.407(2) am. (*prosp.*)	31, s.140(1), Sch.30, para.105
		s.408(1)(b) rep. (*prosp.*)	31, s.140(1)(3), Sch.30, para.106(a), Sch.31
		s.408(2)(d) rep.in pt.	31, s.140(1), Sch.30, para.106(b)
		s.408(3) rep. (*prosp.*)	31, s.140(1)(3), Sch.30, para.106(c), Sch.31
		s.408(4)(b)(c) rep. (*prosp.*)	31, s.140(1)(3), Sch.30, para.106(d)(i), Sch.31
		s.408(4)(d) am. (*prosp.*)	31, s.140(1), Sch.30, para.106(d)(ii)
		s.409, sidenote subst. (*prosp.*)	31, s.140(1), Sch.30, para.107(d)
		s.409(1) am. (*prosp.*)	31, s.140(1), Sch.30, para.107(a)

Year and Chap. or No. of Measure	Short title	How affected	1998, Chapter of Act or Number of Measure or Statutory Instrument
1996—*cont.*			
		s.409(2) am. (*prosp.*)	31, s.140(1), Sch.30, para.107(b)
		s.409(3)(b) rep.in pt. (*prosp.*)	31, s.140(1)(3), Sch.30, para.107(c), Sch.31
		ss.411-432 rep. (*prosp.*)	31, s.140(1)(3), Sch.30, para.109, Sch.31
		s.411 mod. (*temp.*)	SI 1948, reg.3(1)(2), Sch., para.1(1)-(4)
		s.411(6) power to restr.	31, s.144, Sch.32, Pt.II, para.6(1)(a)
		s.411, crossheading subst. (*prosp.*)	31, s.140(1), Sch.30, para.108
		s.416(1) power to restr.	31, s.144, Sch.32, Pt.II, para.6(1)(a)
		s.421 mod. (mod. by insertion of s.421A) (*temp.*)	SI 1948, reg.3(1)(2), Sch., para.2(1)(2)
		s.425A mod. (mod. by insertion of s.425B) (*temp.*)	SI 1948, reg.3(1)(2), Sch., para.3(1)(2)
		s.426 mod. (*temp.*)	SI 1948, reg.3(1)(2), Sch., para.4(1)(2)
		s.426 mod. (mod. by insertion of s.426A) (*temp.*)	SI 1948, reg.3(1)(2), Sch., para.5(1)(2)
		s.426(1) power to restr.	31, s.144, Sch.32, Pt.II, para.6(1)(a)
		s.431 mod. (*temp.*)	SI 1948, reg.3(1)(2), Sch., para.6(1)(2)
		s.432 mod. (*temp.*)	SI 1948, reg.3(1)(2), Sch., para.7(1)(2)
		s.433(4) rep.	31, s.140(1)(3), Sch.30, para.110, Sch.31
		s.434(4)(c)(i) am. (*prosp.*)	31, s.140(1), Sch.30, para.111(a)
		s.434(4)(c)(ii) rep. (*prosp.*)	31, s.140(1)(3), Sch.30, para.111(b), Sch.31
		s.436 rep. (*prosp.*)	31, s.140(1)(3), Sch.30, para.112, Sch.31
		s.437(5)(6) rep.in pt. (*prosp.*)	31, s.140(1)(3), Sch.30, para.113(a), Sch.31
		s.437(8) (defn. of "maintained school") subst. (*prosp.*)	31, s.140(1), Sch.30, para.113(b)
		s.438(4)(a) subst. (*prosp.*)	31, s.140(1), Sch.30, para.114(a)
		s.438(5) subst. (*prosp.*)	31, s.140(1), Sch.30, para.114(b)
		s.438(6)(a)(i) rep.in pt. (*prosp.*)	31, s.140(1)(3), Sch.30, para.114(c), Sch.31
		s.439 mod. (*temp.*)	SI 1948, reg.3(1)(2), Sch., para.8(1)(2)
		s.439(2) am. (*prosp.*)	31, s.140(1), Sch.30, para.115(2)
		s.439(3) rep.in pt. (*prosp.*)	31, s.140(1)(3), Sch.30, para.115(3), Sch.31

Year and Chap. or No. of Measure	Short title	How affected	1998, Chapter of Act or Number of Measure or Statutory Instrument
1996—*cont.*			
		s.439(4A) added (*prosp.*)	31, s.140(1), Sch.30, para.115(4)
		s.439(5)(6) rep.in pt. (*prosp.*)	31, s.140(1)(3), Sch.30, para.115(3), Sch.31
		s.440(2)(a) rep.in pt. (*prosp.*)	31, s.140(1)(3), Sch.30, para.116(a), Sch.31
		s.440(3)(a)(b) subst. (*prosp.*)	31, s.140(1), Sch.30, para.116(b)
		s.440(4)(a) rep.in pt. (*prosp.*)	31, s.140(1)(3), Sch.30, para.116(c), Sch.31
		s.444(4)(b) rep.in pt. (*prosp.*)	31, s.140(1)(3), Sch.30, para.117, Sch.31
		s.448 rep. (*prosp.*)	31, s.140(1)(3), Sch.30, para.118, Sch.31
		s.449, cross-headings subst. (*prosp.*)	31, s.140(1), Sch.30, para.119
		s.451(1) rep.in pt. (*prosp.*)	31, s.140(1)(3), Sch.30, para.120(a), Sch.31
		s.451(3)(b) am. (*prosp.*)	31, s.140(1), Sch.30, para.120(b)
		s.451(4)(b) am. (*prosp.*)	31, s.140(1), Sch.30, para.120(c)
		s.451(5) rep. (*prosp.*)	31, s.140(1)(3), Sch.30, para.120(d), Sch.31
		s.456(1) rep.in pt. (*prosp.*)	31, s.140(1)(3), Sch.30, para.121, Sch.31
		s.457(1) rep.in pt. (*prosp.*)	31, s.140(1)(3), Sch.30, para.122(a), Sch.31
		s.457(3) rep.in pt. (*prosp.*)	31, s.140(1)(3), Sch.30, para.122(b), Sch.31
		s.458(1) rep.in pt. (*prosp.*)	31, s.140(1)(3), Sch.30, para.123(a)(ii), Sch.31
		s.458(1) am. (*prosp.*)	31, s.140(1), Sch.30, para.123(a)(i)
		s.458(2)(a) rep. (*prosp.*)	31, s.140(1)(3), Sch.30, para.123(b)(i), Sch.31
		s.458(2)(b) am. (*prosp.*)	31, s.140(1), Sch.30, para.123(b)(ii)
		s.458(3) rep. (*prosp.*)	31, s.140(1)(3), Sch.30, para.123(c), Sch.31
		s.458(4)(b) rep.in pt. (*prosp.*)	31, s.140(1)(3), Sch.30, para.123(d), Sch.31
		s.463 rep.in pt. (*prosp.*)	31, s.140(1)(3), Sch.30, para.124(b), Sch.31
		s.463(b) am. (*prosp.*)	31, s.140(1), Sch.30, para.124(a)
		s.463(c) rep. (*prosp.*)	31, s.140(1)(3), Sch.30, para.124(b), Sch.31
		s.484 power to ext.	30, s.19(8)
		s.484 am.	31, s.7(10)
		s.484(1) am. (*prosp.*)	31, s.140(1), Sch.30, para.125(a)

Year and Chap. or No. of Measure	Short title	How affected	1998, Chapter of Act or Number of Measure or Statutory Instrument
1996—*cont.*			
		s.484(3)(4) am. (*prosp.*)	31, s.140(1), Sch.30, para.125(b)
		s.484, sidenote subst. (*prosp.*)	31, s.140(1), Sch.30, para.125(c)
		s.489(2)(a) am. (*prosp.*)	31, s.140(1), Sch.30, para.126
		s.490(1)(a) rep. (*prosp.*)	31, s.140(1)(3), Sch.30, para.127, Sch.31
		s.494 mod.	SI 2670, reg.8
		s.494 subst. (1.4.1999)	31, s.140(1), Sch.30, para.128
		ss.495-498 mod. (*prosp.*)	31, s.44(7)
		s.496 ext. (*prosp.*)	31, s.24, Sch.4, para.10
		s.496 power to appl.	31, s.105(7)
		s.496(2)(a) am. (*prosp.*)	31, s.140(1), Sch.30, para.129(a)
		s.496(2)(b)(c) replaced (by s.496(2)(b)) (*prosp.*)	31, s.140(1), Sch.30, para.129(b)
		s.497 appl.	SI 2876, reg.21
		s.497 ext. (*prosp.*)	31, s.24, Sch.4, para.10
		s.497 power to appl.	31, s.105(7)
		s.497(2)(a) am. (*prosp.*)	31, s.140(1), Sch.30, para.130(a)
		s.497(2)(b)(c) replaced (by s.497(b)) (*prosp.*)	31, s.140(1), Sch.30, para.130(b)
		s.497A mod. (12.1.1999)	SI 3217, reg.2(b)
		s.497A added	31, s.8
		s.497B mod. (12.1.1999)	SI 3217, reg.2(b)
		s.497B added	31, s.8
		s.498(2) subst. (*prosp.*)	31, s.140(1), Sch.30, para.131
		s.499(6)-(9) added	31, s.9
		ss.500-505 rep. (*prosp.*)	31, s.140(1)(3), Sch.30, para.132, Sch.31
		s.509(5)(a) rep. (*prosp.*)	31, s.140(1)(3), Sch.30, para.133(a), Sch.31
		s.509(6) subst. (1.4.1999)	31, s.140(1)(3), Sch.30, para.133(b), Sch.31
		s.509A added (1.4.1999)	31, s.124
		s.510(1)(a)(c) rep.in pt. (*prosp.*)	31, s.140(1)(3), Sch.30, para.134(a), Sch.31
		s.510(3)(a) rep.in pt. (*prosp.*)	31, s.140(1)(3), Sch.30, para.134(b), Sch.31
		s.510(4)(a) rep.in pt. (*prosp.*)	31, s.140(1)(3), Sch.30, para.134(c), Sch.31
		s.510(5)(a) rep.in pt. (*prosp.*)	31, s.140(1)(3), Sch.30, para.134(d), Sch.31
		s.512(1A)(1B) added (*prosp.*)	31, s.115(1)
		s.512(2) am. (*prosp.*)	31, s.115(3)
		s.512(3)(a)(b) subst. (*prosp.*)	31, s.115(4)
		s.512(6) added (*prosp.*)	31, s.115(5)

Year and Chap. or No. of Measure	Short title	How affected	1998, Chapter of Act or Number of Measure or Statutory Instrument
1996—*cont.*			
		s.512A added (1.2.1999)	31, s.116
		s.514(1)(a) am. (*prosp.*)	31, s.140(1), Sch.30, para.135
		s.515(2) am. (*prosp.*)	31, s.140(1), Sch.30, para.136
		s.516 rep. (1.4.1999)	31, s.140(1)(3), Sch.30, para.137, Sch.31
		s.517 rep. (*prosp.*)	31, s.140(1)(3), Sch.30, para.138, Sch.31
		s.518 subst. (*prosp.*)	31, s.129
		s.519(1) am. (20.11.1998) (making schemes) 1.4.1999 (for all other purposes)	31, s.140(1), Sch.30, para.139(2)
		s.519(3) am. (20.11.1998) (making schemes) 1.4.1999 (for all other purposes)	31, s.140(1), Sch.30, para.139(3)
		s.519(7) added (20.11.1998) (making schemes) 1.4.1999 (for all other purposes)	31, s.140(1), Sch.30, para.139(4)
		s.520(3) rep. (*prosp.*)	31, s.140(1)(3), Sch.30, para.140, Sch.31
		s.521(4) rep.in pt. (*prosp.*)	31, s.140(1)(3), Sch.30, para.141, Sch.31
		s.521(4)(b) rep. (*prosp.*)	31, s.140(1)(3), Sch.30, para.141, Sch.31
		s.524(1) am. (*prosp.*)	31, s.140(1), Sch.30, para.142(a)
		s.524(3) rep.in pt. (*prosp.*)	31, s.140(1)(3), Sch.30, para.142(b), Sch.31
		s.524(3)(b) rep. (*prosp.*)	31, s.140(1)(3), Sch.30, para.142(b), Sch.31
		s.524, sidenote subst. (*prosp.*)	31, s.140(1), Sch.30, para.142(c)
		s.525(3) rep.in pt. (*prosp.*)	31, s.140(1)(3), Sch.30, para.143, Sch.31
		s.527A(7) subst. (*prosp.*)	31, s.140(1), Sch.30, para.144
		s.529(2)(3) am. (*prosp.*)	31, s.140(1), Sch.30, para.145
		s.530(2)(3) am. (*prosp.*)	31, s.140(1), Sch.30, para.146
		s.531(2) am. (*prosp.*)	31, s.140(1), Sch.30, para.147
		s.533(2)(3) am. (*prosp.*)	31, s.140(1), Sch.30, para.148
		s.534 rep. (*prosp.*)	31, s.140(1)(3), Sch.30, para.149, Sch.31
		s.535(1) am. (*prosp.*)	31, s.140(1), Sch.30, para.150
		s.536 rep. (*prosp.*)	31, s.140(1)(3), Sch.30, para.151, Sch.31
		s.537(1) subst. (*prosp.*)	31, s.140(1), Sch.30, para.152(a)

Year and Chap. or No. of Measure	Short title	How affected	1998, Chapter of Act or Number of Measure or Statutory Instrument
1996—*cont.*			
		s.537(7)(a) rep.in pt. (*prosp.*)	31, s.140(1)(3), Sch.30, para.152(b), Sch.31
		s.537A subst.	31, s.140(1), Sch.30, para.153
		s.538 am. (*prosp.*)	31, s.140(1), Sch.30, para.154
		s.539 rep. (*prosp.*)	31, s.140(1)(3), Sch.30, para.155, Sch.31
		s.540(2) subst. (*prosp.*)	31, s.140(1), Sch.30, para.156
		s.541(4) subst. (*prosp.*)	31, s.140(1), Sch.30, para.157
		s.542(1) rep.in pt. (*prosp.*)	31, s.140(1)(3), Sch.30, para.158(a), Sch.31
		s.542(2) rep.in pt. (*prosp.*)	31, s.140(1)(3), Sch.30, para.161, Sch.31
		s.542(2)(b) rep. (*prosp.*)	31, s.140(1)(3), Sch.30, para.161, Sch.31
		s.542(3) rep. (*prosp.*)	31, s.140(1)(3), Sch.30, para.158(b), Sch.31
		s.542(4) am. (*prosp.*)	31, s.140(1), Sch.30, para.158(c), Sch.31
		s.543(1) am. (1.2.1999)	31, s.140(1), Sch.30, para.159(a)
		s.543(4A) added (1.2.1999)	31, s.140(1), Sch.30, para.159(b)
		s.544(1) rep.in pt. (*prosp.*)	31, s.140(1)(3), Sch.30, para.160(a), Sch.31
		s.544(3)(a) am. (*prosp.*)	31, s.140(1), Sch.30, para.160(b)(i)
		s.544(3)(b) rep. (*prosp.*)	31, s.140(1)(3), Sch.30, para.160(b)(ii), Sch.31
		s.546(2)(a) am. (*prosp.*)	31, s.140(1), Sch.30, para.162(a)
		s.546(2)(b) rep. (*prosp.*)	31, s.140(1)(3), Sch.30, para.162(b), Sch.31
		s.547(2) rep.in pt. (*prosp.*)	31, s.140(1)(3), Sch.30, para.163(a), Sch.31
		s.547(2)(b) rep. (*prosp.*)	31, s.140(1)(3), Sch.30, para.163(a), Sch.31
		s.547(4) am. (*prosp.*)	31, s.140(1), Sch.30, para.163(b)
		s.547(5) am. (*prosp.*)	31, s.140(1), Sch.30, para.163(c)
		s.547(7) am. (*prosp.*)	31, s.140(1), Sch.30, para.163(b)
		s.547(8) am. (*prosp.*)	31, s.140(1), Sch.30, para.163(c)
		s.548 subst. (*prosp.*)	31, s.131(1)
		ss.549,550 rep. (*prosp.*)	31, ss.131(2),140(1)(3), Sch.30, para.164, Sch.31

Year and Chap. or No. of Measure	Short title	How affected	1998, Chapter of Act or Number of Measure or Statutory Instrument
1996—*cont.*			
		s.550B(2) rep.in pt. (*prosp.*)	31, s.140(1)(3), Sch.30, para.165, Sch.31
		s.551(2)(a) am. (*prosp.*)	31, s.140(1), Sch.30, para.166(a)
		s.551(2)(b) rep. (*prosp.*)	31, s.140(1)(3), Sch.30, para.166(b), Sch.31
		s.552 rep. (*prosp.*)	31, s.140(1)(3), Sch.30, para.167, Sch.31
		s.554(1) subst. (*prosp.*)	31, s.140(1), Sch.30, para.168(2)
		s.554(3)(a) subst. (*prosp.*)	31, s.140(1), Sch.30, para.168(3)(a)
		s.554(3)(b) am. (*prosp.*)	31, s.140(1), Sch.30, para.168(3)(b)
		s.554(4)(b) subst. (*prosp.*)	31, s.140(1), Sch.30, para.168(4)
		s.556(2)(a)(b) am. (*prosp.*)	31, s.140(1), Sch.30, para.169(a)(b)
		s.557(9) (defn. of "relevant school") am. (*prosp.*)	31, s.140(1), Sch.30, para.170
		s.559(1)(2) am. (*prosp.*)	31, s.140(1), Sch.30, para.171
		s.560(1)(2) subst.	31, s.112(2)
		s.560(6) rep.in pt. (*prosp.*)	31, ss.112(3),140(3), Sch.31
		s.563(a) am. (*prosp.*)	31, s.140(1), Sch.30, para.172(a)
		s.563(b) rep. (*prosp.*)	31, s.140(1)(3), Sch.30, para.172(b), Sch.31
		s.564 am. (1.4.1999)	SI 3171, art.2, Sch.
		s.566(1)(b) am. (*prosp.*)	31, s.140(1), Sch.30, para.173
		s.567 rep. (*prosp.*)	31, s.140(1)(3), Sch.30, para.174, Sch.31
		s.568(2) subst. (*prosp.*)	31, s.140(1), Sch.30, para.175(a)
		s.568(3) rep.in pt. (*prosp.*)	31, s.140(1)(3), Sch.30, para.175(b), Sch.31
		s.568(5) rep.in pt. (*prosp.*)	31, s.140(1)(3), Sch.30, para.175(c), Sch.31
		s.568(5)(b) rep. (*prosp.*)	31, s.140(1)(3), Sch.30, para.175(c), Sch.31
		s.569(2)(3) am. (*prosp.*)	31, s.140(1), Sch.30, para.176
		s.570(1)(a) am. (*prosp.*)	31, s.140(1), Sch.30, para.177(a)(i)
		s.570(1)(b) rep. (*prosp.*)	31, s.140(1)(3), Sch.30, para.177(a)(ii), Sch.31
		s.570(2) rep.in pt. (*prosp.*)	31, s.140(1)(3), Sch.30, para.177(b), Sch.31
		s.573(2) rep.in pt. (*prosp.*)	31, s.140(1)(3), Sch.30, para.178(a), Sch.31

Year and Chap. or No. of Measure	Short title	How affected	1998, Chapter of Act or Number of Measure or Statutory Instrument
1996—*cont.*		s.573(4)(5)(6) rep. (*prosp.*)	31, s.140(1)(3), Sch.30, para.178(b), Sch.31
		s.575 rep. (*prosp.*)	31, s.140(1)(3), Sch.30, para.179, Sch.31
		s.576(1) am. (*prosp.*)	31, s.140(1), Sch.30, para.180(a)
		s.576(1) appl.(mods.)	31, s.142(10)
		s.576(2) rep. (*prosp.*)	31, s.140(1)(3), Sch.30, para.180(b), Sch.31
		s.577 rep. (*prosp.*)	31, s.140(1)(3), Sch.30, para.181, Sch.31
		s.578 am.	1, ss.6(1),7(2)
		s.578 am.	30, s.44(1), Sch.3, para.15
		s.578 rep.in pt. (*prosp.*)	30, s.44(2), Sch.4
		s.578 am.	30, s.46(2)
		s.578 am. (*prosp.*)	31, s.140(1), Sch.30, para.182
		s.578 am.	31, s.145(2)
		s.579(1) (defns. of "the appropriate further education funding council", "exclude", "governing body (and governors)", "the local education authority", "reception class" and "relevant age group") rep. (*prosp.*)	31, s.140(1)(3), Sch.30, para.183(a)(ii), Sch.31
		s.579(1) am. (*prosp.*)	31, s.140(1), Sch.30, para.183(a)(i)
		s.579(1) (defn. of "proprietor") am. (*prosp.*)	31, s.140(1), Sch.30, para.183(a)(iii)
		s.579(1) (defn. of "trust deed") subst. (*prosp.*)	31, s.140(1), Sch.30, para.183(a)(iv)
		s.579(3) rep. (*prosp.*)	31, s.140(1)(3), Sch.30, para.183(b), Sch.31
		Sch.1, para.6(1)(2) subst.	31, s.140(1), Sch.30, para.184(a)(i)
		Sch.1, para.6(3)(a) am.	31, s.140(1), Sch.30, para.184(a)(ii)
		Sch.1, paras.12,13 rep. (*prosp.*)	31, s.140(1)(3), Sch.30, para.184(b), Sch.31
		Sch.1, para.15(2)(c) rep.in pt. (*prosp.*)	31, s.140(1)(3), Sch.30, para.184(c), Sch.31
		Schs.2A-25 rep. (in force 1.10.1998 to the extent that it relates to the omission of Sch.4, paras.7,8, Sch.20,Pt.I and Sch.21) (pt.prosp.)	31, s.140(1)(3), Sch.30, para.185, Sch.31
		Sch.10 excl. (1.1.1999)	SI 3097, reg.8(e)
		Sch.12 excl.in pt. (until 1.9.1999) (*temp.*)	SI 3097, reg.5

Year and Chap. or No. of Measure	Short title	How affected	1998, Chapter of Act or Number of Measure or Statutory Instrument
1996—*cont.*			
		Sch.19, para.1(1) mod. (1.1.1999)	SI 3097, reg.6
		Sch.19, para.3 mod. (1.1.1999)	SI 3097, reg.7
		Sch.19, paras.11(2),15(2) excl. (1.1.1999)	SI 3097, reg.8(f)
		Sch.23 mod. (*temp.*)	SI 1948, reg.3(1)(2), Sch., para.9(1)(2)
		Sch.27, para.3(1)(4) am. (*prosp.*)	31, s.140(1), Sch.30, para.186(2)(a)(b)
		Sch.27, para.8(1)(a) am. (*prosp.*)	31, s.140(1), Sch.30, para.186(3)
		Sch.28 rep. (*prosp.*)	31, s.140(1)(3), Sch.30, para.187, Sch.31
		Sch.31, paras.11,15 rep. (*prosp.*)	31, s.140(1)(3), Sch.30, para.188, Sch.31
		Sch.32 mod. (*temp.*)	SI 1948, reg.3(1)(2), Sch., para.10(1)-(4)
		Sch.32 rep. (*prosp.*)	31, s.140(1)(3), Sch.30, para.189(a)(b)(c)(d), Sch.31
		Sch.33 mod. (*temp.*)	SI 1948, reg.3(1)(2), Sch., para.11(1)(3)
		Schs.33,33A,33B rep. (*prosp.*)	31, s.140(1)(3), Sch.30, para.189(a)(b)(c)(d), Sch.31
		Sch.37, paras.4-7 rep. (*prosp.*)	30, s.44(2), Sch.4
		Sch.37, paras.9,27,33, 37(a),41,42(4)(b),75 rep. (*prosp.*)	31, s.140(1)(3), Sch.30, para.189(e), Sch.31
		Sch.37, para.78 rep.	18, s.54(3), Sch.5
		Sch.37, para.82(1) rep.in pt. (*prosp.*)	31, s.140(1)(3), Sch.30, para.189(e), Sch.31
		Sch.37, para.82(1)(b) rep. (*prosp.*)	31, s.140(1)(3), Sch.30, para.189(e), Sch.31
		Sch.37, para.82(2) rep.in pt. (*prosp.*)	31, s.140(1)(3), Sch.30, para.189(e), Sch.31
		Sch.37, paras.82(2)(a)(c) (3),96(2),97 rep. (*prosp.*)	31, s.140(1)(3), Sch.30, para.189(e), Sch.31
		Sch.37, para.98 rep. (*prosp.*)	30, s.44(2), Sch.4
		Sch.37, paras.102,103, 104(3),105-108,110(2)(3) (a),122,125(c)(d) rep. (*prosp.*)	31, s.140(1)(3), Sch.30, para.189(e), Sch.31
		Sch.39, paras.1,2 appl.	31, s.142(8)(9)
		Sch.39, paras.2(3),15 rep. (*prosp.*)	31, s.140(1)(3), Sch.30, para.189(f), Sch.31
		Sch.40 rep.	31, s.140(1)(3), Sch.30, para.189(g), Sch.31
c.57	School Inspections Act 1996	defn(s). appl. (certain defns. appld.)	31, s.14
		s.2 saved	30, s.20 (adding 1994 c.30, s.18A(12))

Year and Chap. or No. of Measure	Short title	How affected	1998, Chapter of Act or Number of Measure or Statutory Instrument
1996—*cont.*			
		s.2(7)(a) mod.	31, s.122, Sch.26, para.14
		s.2(7)(b) ext.	31, s.122, Sch.26, para.14
		s.5 saved	30, s.20 (adding 1994 c.30, s.18A(12))
		s.5(7)(a) mod.	31, s.122, Sch.26, para.14
		s.5(7)(b) ext.	31, s.122, Sch.26, para.14
		s.7(3) am.	31, s.135, Sch.28, Pt.I, para.2
		s.9(3)(a) rep.in pt.	31, ss.135,140(3), Sch.28, Pt.I, para.3, Sch.31
		s.10(3) rep.in pt. (*prosp.*)	31, s.140(1)(3), Sch.30, para.191(2)(a), Sch.31
		s.10(3)(a) subst. (*prosp.*)	31, s.140(1), Sch.30, para.191(2)(b)
		s.10(3)(b) rep. (*prosp.*)	31, s.140(1)(3), Sch.30, para.191(2)(c), Sch.31
		s.10(3)(c) rep. (*prosp.*)	31, s.140(1), Sch.30, para.191(2)(d)
		s.10(3)(d) subst. (*prosp.*)	31, s.140(1), Sch.30, para.191(2)(e)
		s.10(4) rep. (*prosp.*)	31, s.140(1)(3), Sch.30, para.191(3), Sch.31
		s.10(4B) subst. (*prosp.*)	31, s.140(1), Sch.30, para.191(4)
		s.11(2) am. (*prosp.*)	31, s.140(1), Sch.30, para.192(2)
		s.11(4) (defn. of "appropriate appointing authority") am. (*prosp.*)	31, s.140(1), Sch.30, para.192(3)(a)
		s.11(4) (defn. of "appropriate authority") subst. (*prosp.*)	31, s.140(1), Sch.30, para.192(3)(b)
		s.11(5)(a) am. (*prosp.*)	31, s.140(1), Sch.30, para.192(4)(a)
		s.11(5)(b) rep.in pt. (*prosp.*)	31, s.140(1)(3), Sch.30, para.192(4)(b), Sch.31
		s.15(3)(b) am. (*prosp.*)	31, s.140(1), Sch.30, para.193
		s.16(1)(a) rep.in pt. (*prosp.*)	31, s.140(1)(3), Sch.30, para.194(2)(a), Sch.31
		s.16(1)(b) am. (*prosp.*)	31, s.140(1), Sch.30, para.194(2)(b)
		s.16(3)(c) am. (*prosp.*)	31, s.140(1), Sch.30, para.194(3)(a)
		s.16(3)(e)(f) rep. (*prosp.*)	31, s.140(1)(3), Sch.30, para.194(3)(b), Sch.31
		s.17(3)(b) am. (*prosp.*)	31, s.140(1), Sch.30, para.195(2)(a)
		s.17(3)(c) rep. (*prosp.*)	31, s.140(1)(3), Sch.30, para.195(2)(b), Sch.31
		s.17(4) am. (*prosp.*)	31, s.140(1), Sch.30, para.195(3)

Year and Chap. or No. of Measure	Short title	How affected	1998, Chapter of Act or Number of Measure or Statutory Instrument
1996—*cont.*			
		s.17(5)(b)(c) rep. (*prosp.*)	31, s.140(1)(3), Sch.30, para.195(4), Sch.31
		s.17(7) am. (*prosp.*)	31, s.140(1), Sch.30, para.195(5)
		s.18(1)(a)(2)(b) am. (*prosp.*)	31, s.140(1), Sch.30, para.196
		s.20(3) rep.in pt. (*prosp.*)	31, s.140(1)(3), Sch.30, para.197(b), Sch.31
		s.20(3)(a) am. (*prosp.*)	31, s.140(1), Sch.30, para.197(a)
		s.21(4) rep.in pt. (*prosp.*)	31, s.140(1)(3), Sch.30, para.198(b), Sch.31
		s.21(4) am. (*prosp.*)	31, s.140(1), Sch.30, para.198(a)
		s.23(1) subst. (*prosp.*)	31, s.140(1), Sch.30, para.199(2)
		s.23(2)(3) rep. (*prosp.*)	31, s.140(1)(3), Sch.30, para.199(3), Sch.31
		s.23(4)(ii) am. (*prosp.*)	31, s.140(1), Sch.30, para.199(4)
		s.23(5)(a) am. (*prosp.*)	31, s.140(1), Sch.30, para.199(5)
		s.23(8)(a)(b) rep.in pt. (*prosp.*)	31, s.140(1)(3), Sch.30, para.199(6), Sch.31
		ss.26-30 rep.	31, s.140(1)(3), Sch.30, para.200(a), Sch.31
		ss.31-41 rep.	31, s.140(1)(3), Sch.30, para.200(b), Sch.31
		s.42 ext.	30, s.20 (adding 1994 c.30, s.18A(5))
		s.42 appl.	31, s.122, Sch.26, para.18(3)
		s.42 appl. (*prosp.*)	31, s.135, Sch.28, Pt.II, para.8 (adding 1996 c.50, Sch.1, para.18)
		s.42A added	31, s.134(1)
		s.42A(2)-(4) ext.	30, s.20 (adding 1994 c.30, s.18A(4))
		s.42A(2)-(4) ext.	30, s.34(1)(8)
		s.42A(2)-(4) appl.	31, s.134(2) (adding 1996 c.50, Sch.1, para.13(3))
		s.42A(2)-(4) appl.	31, s.134(3)
		s.42A(2)(3) appl.	31, s.122, Sch.26, para.13(3)
		s.44 rep.	31, s.140(1)(3), Sch.30, para.200(c), Sch.31
		s.45(1)(2) rep.	31, s.140(1)(3), Sch.30, para.201, Sch.31
		s.46(1) (defn. of "transfer date") rep. (*prosp.*)	31, s.140(1)(3), Sch.30, para.202(4), Sch.31
		s.46(1) (defn. of "Church in Wales") am. (*prosp.*)	31, s.140(1), Sch.30, para.202(2)

Year and Chap. or No. of Measure	Short title	How affected	1998, Chapter of Act or Number of Measure or Statutory Instrument
1996—*cont.*			
		s.46(1) (defn. of "delegated budget") am. (*prosp.*)	31, s.140(1), Sch.30, para.202(3)
		Sch.1, para.5(1)(2) saved	30, s.20 (adding 1994 c.30, s.18A(12))
		Sch.2, paras.2,3 appl.	31, s.122, Sch.26, para.10(2)
		Sch.3, para.1 (defn. of "appropriate authority") subst. (*prosp.*)	31, s.140(1), Sch.30, para.203
		Sch.3, para.3(1) subst. (*prosp.*)	31, s.135, Sch.28, Pt.I, para.4(1)
		Sch.3, para.3A added	31, s.135, Sch.28, Pt.I, para.4(2)
		Sch.3, para.9 added	31, s.135, Sch.28, Pt.I, para.5
		Sch.4, para.3(2)(5) am. (*prosp.*)	31, s.140(1), Sch.30, para.204
		Sch.5 rep. (*prosp.*)	31, s.140(1)(3), Sch.30, para.205, Sch.31
		Sch.6, para.1 rep.in pt. (*prosp.*)	38, s.152, Sch.18, Pt.I
		Sch.6, para.7 rep. (*prosp.*)	31, s.140(1)(3), Sch.30, para.206, Sch.31
c.60	Consolidated Fund (No.2) Act 1996	rep.	28, s.3, Sch.(C)
c.61	Channel Tunnel Rail Link Act 1996	s.21(6) am. (*prosp.*)	41, s.66(5), Sch.10, Pt.IV, para.16(2)
		s.22(3) subst. (*prosp.*)	41, s.66(5), Sch.10, Pt.IV, para.16(3)
1997			
c.7	Northern Ireland Arms Decommissioning Act 1997	appt. day(s) for s.2(2) (b) (27.2.1999)	SI 893, art.2
c.8	Town and Country Planning (Scotland) Act 1997	defn. of "statutory undertaker" appl.	iii, s.1, Sch., O., s.30(3)
		appl.	43, s.1(2), Sch.2, para.10 (subst. 1931 c.28, Sch.2, para.2(b))
		s.83 mod. (conditionally) (25.1.1999)	SI 2914, reg.5
		s.83 mod. (25.1.1999)	SI 2914, reg.6
		s.215 (defn. of "operational land") appl.	iii, s.1, Sch., O., s.3(2)
		s.242 (defn. of "Crown land") appl. (1.7.1999)	46, s.122(2)
c.11	Planning (Consequential Provisions) (Scotland) Act 1997	Sch.2, paras.1,12 rep.	43, s.1(1), Sch.1, Pt.IV, Group 2
c.13	United Nations Personnel Act 1997	ss.1-6 ext.(mods.) (to Bailiwick of Guernsey)	SI 1075, art.2, Sch.
		ss.1-8 ext.(mods.) (Jersey)	SI 1267, art.2, Sch.

Year and Chap. or No. of Measure	Short title	How affected	1998, Chapter of Act or Number of Measure or Statutory Instrument
1997—*cont.*			
		ss.1-8 ext.(mods.) (to Isle of Man)	SI 1509, art.2, Sch.
		s.8 ext.(mods.) (to Bailiwick of Guernsey)	SI 1075, art.2, Sch.
		s.10 ext.(mods.) (to Isle of Man)	SI 1509, art.2, Sch.
		Sch. ext.(mods.) (Jersey)	SI 1267, art.2, Sch.
		Sch. ext.(mods.) (to Isle of Man)	SI 1509, art.2, Sch.
c.14	National Heritage Act 1997	appt. day (4.3.1998)	SI 292, art.2
c.16	Finance Act 1997	appt. day(s) for Sch.3 (1.4.1998)	SI 560, art.2
		s.11(2), Table subst. (1.4.1998) (*retrosp.*)	36, s.11(1)(3)
		s.11(3) am. (1.4.1998) (*retrosp.*)	36, s.11(2)(3)
		s.62(1)-(3) rep. (year 1998-99 and subsequent years of assessment)	36, s.165, Sch.27, Pt.III(10), Note
		s.111 rep.	43, s.1(1), Sch.1, Pt.IV, Group 5
		Sch.12, para.3(6) excl.	36, s.38, Sch.5, Pt.IV, para.74(1)
		Sch.12, para.3(6) rep.	36, s.165, Sch.27, Pt.III(4), Note
		Sch.12, para.6(9)(b) excl.	36, s.38, Sch.5, Pt.IV, para.74(1)
		Sch.12, paras.6(9)(b),8 rep.	36, s.165, Sch.27, Pt.III(4), Note
		Sch.12, para.8(1)-(7) excl.	36, s.38, Sch.5, Pt.IV, para.74(1)
		Sch.12, para.8(4)(a) am.	36, s.46(3), Sch.7, para.12
		Sch.12, para.8(8) excl.	36, s.38, Sch.5, Pt.IV, para.74(3)
		Sch.12, para.8(9) excl.	36, s.38, Sch.5, Pt.IV, para.74(4)
		Sch.12, para.13(7) rep.	36, s.165, Sch.27, Pt.III(4), Note
		Sch.12, para.20(b) excl.	36, s.38, Sch.5, Pt.IV, para.74(1)
		Sch.12, para.20(b), Sch.15, paras.2(2),5(1) (2),6 rep.	36, s.165, Sch.27, Pt.III(4), Note
c.18	Policyholders Protection Act 1997	power to H.M.Treasury to contract out certain functions	SI 2842, art.2, Sch., Pt.II, para.66
c.23	Lieutenancies Act 1997	saved (6.5.1999)	46, s.30, Sch.5, Pt.II, s.B12
c.24	Nurses, Midwives and Health Visitors Act 1997	saved (6.5.1999)	46, s.30, Sch.5, Pt.II, s.G2(i)
c.25	Justices of the Peace Act 1997	defn. of "commission area" appl.	37, s.117(1)
		s.18(4)(a) rep.	SI 276, reg.17(2)

Year and Chap. or No. of Measure	Short title	How affected	1998, Chapter of Act or Number of Measure or Statutory Instrument
1997—*cont.*			
		ss.55(9),56(2) power to exercise functions	SI 2664, art.6(5)
c.27	Social Security (Recovery of Benefits) Act 1997	mod.	14, s.2(1)(2)(h)
		power to mod. (EWS) (*prosp.*)	14, s.11(1)(3)
		power to am. (*prosp.*)	47, s.87
		s.1 (defns. of "compensation payment" and "recoverable benefit") appl. (26.4.1999)	SI 3132, rule 36.23
		s.10(1) subst. (*prosp.*)	14, s.86(1), Sch.7, para.149(1)
		s.10(2)(c) added (*prosp.*)	14, s.86(1), Sch.7, para.149(2)
		s.11(1)(c)(d) added (*prosp.*)	14, s.86(1), Sch.7, para.150(1)
		s.11(2)(aa) added (*prosp.*)	14, s.86(1), Sch.7, para.150(2)
		s.11(6) rep. (*prosp.*)	14, s.86(1)(2), Sch.7, para.150(3), Sch.8
		s.12(1)(2) replaced (by s.12(1)) (*prosp.*)	14, s.86(1), Sch.7, para.151(1)
		s.12(3) am. (*prosp.*)	14, s.86(1), Sch.7, para.151(2)
		s.12(4) am. (*prosp.*)	14, s.86(1), Sch.7, para.151(3)(a)
		s.12(4)(c) added (*prosp.*)	14, s.86(1), Sch.7, para.151(3)(b)
		s.12(5) am. (*prosp.*)	14, s.86(1), Sch.7, para.151(4)(a)
		s.12(5)(c) added (*prosp.*)	14, s.86(1), Sch.7, para.151(4)(b)
		s.12(6) rep. (*prosp.*)	14, s.86(1)(2), Sch.7, para.151(5)(a), Sch.8
		s.12(7) rep.in pt. (*prosp.*)	14, s.86(1)(2), Sch.7, para.151(5)(b), Sch.8
		s.12(8) rep. (*prosp.*)	14, s.86(1)(2), Sch.7, para.151(5)(c), Sch.8
		s.13(1) am. (*prosp.*)	14, s.86(1), Sch.7, para.152(1)
		s.13(2)(b) am. (*prosp.*)	14, s.86(1)(2), Sch.7, para.152(2)(a), Sch.8
		s.13(2)(bb) added (*prosp.*)	14, s.86(1), Sch.7, para.152(2)(b)
		s.13(3) am. (*prosp.*)	14, s.86(1), Sch.7, para.152(3)
		s.13(4) rep. (*prosp.*)	14, s.86(1)(2), Sch.7, para.152(4), Sch.8
		s.29 (defns. of "appeal tribunal" and "Commissioner") added	14, s.86(1), Sch.7, para.153

Year and Chap. or No. of Measure	Short title	How affected	1998, Chapter of Act or Number of Measure or Statutory Instrument
1997—*cont.*			
c.28	Merchant Shipping and Maritime Security Act 1997	ss.24,26,27,28 saved (6.5.1999)	46, s.30, Sch.5, Pt.II, s.E3(k)
c.29	Local Government and Rating Act 1997	appt. day(s) for spec. provns. (18.3.1998)	SI 694, art.2
		appt. day(s) for spec. provns. (1.10.1998) (1.4.2000)	SI 2329, arts.2,3
c.30	Police (Property) Act 1997	rep. (saving)(*prosp.*)	32, s.74(2)(3), Schs.5,6
c.32	Building Societies Act 1997	s.32(1) am.	11, s.23, Sch.5, Pt.I, Ch.III, para.43(2)
		s.32(3)(a) am.	11, s.23, Sch.5, Pt.I, Ch.III, para.43(3)
		s.32(7) (defn. of "the Bank") replaced (by defn. "the Authority")	11, s.23, Sch.5, Pt.I, Ch.III, para.43(4)
c.35	Scottish Legal Services Ombudsman and Commissioner for Local Administration in Scotland Act 1997	appt. day for residue (1.4.1998)	SI 252, art.2
c.40	Protection from Harassment Act 1997	appt. day(s) for s.3(3)- (9) (1.9.1998)	SI 1902, art.2
		s.5 mod.	37, s.32(7)
c.42	Police (Health and Safety) Act 1997	appt. day for residue (1.7.1998)	SI 1542, art.2
c.43	Crime (Sentences) Act 1997	s.1 rep.	37, ss.106,120(2), Sch.7, para.47, Sch.10
		s.3(2) am.	37, s.106, Sch.7, para.48(1)
		s.3(3) am.	37, s.106, Sch.7, para.48(2)
		s.4(2) am.	37, s.106, Sch.7, para.49(1)
		s.4(3) am.	37, s.106, Sch.7, para.49(2)
		s.8 rep.	37, ss.107(2),120(2), Sch.10
		s.9 mod.	37, s.119, Sch.8, para.90 (substituting 1991 c.53 s.47(2))
		s.9(7A) added	37, s.107(3)
		s.9(11)(12) added	37, s.107(4)
		s.9A added	37, s.107(5)
		s.9A mod.	37, s.120(1), Sch.9, para.6
		ss.10-27 rep.	37, ss.107(2),120(2), Sch.10
		ss.28-34 (Pt.II) (Ch.II) (defn. of "life prisoners") appl.	37, s.119, Sch.8, para.97 (amending 1991 c.53 Sch.5, para.1(2))
		s.28(3)(c) added	37, s.119, Sch.8, para.130(1)

Year and Chap. or No. of Measure	Short title	How affected	1998, Chapter of Act or Number of Measure or Statutory Instrument
1997—*cont.*			
		s.28(7)(c) am.	37, s.119, Sch.8, para.130(2)
		s.31(2) rep.in pt. (in force 30.9.1998 for areas specified in SI 1998/2327, Sch.1)	37, ss.119,120(2), Sch.8, para.131(1), Sch.10
		s.31(2A) added (in force 30.9.1998 for areas specified in SI 1998/2327, Sch.1)	37, s.119, Sch.8, para.131(2)
		s.31(6) mod. (*temp.*)	SI 2327, art.5(1)(b)
		s.31(6) am.	37, s.119, Sch.8, para.131(3)
		s.34 (defn. of "life sentences") appl.	37, ss.101(1),120(1), Sch.9, para.11
		s.34(4) added	37, ss.101(2),120(1), Sch.9, para.11
		s.35(1) am.	37, s.119, Sch.8, para.132(1)
		s.35(2)(a) am.	37, s.106, Sch.7, para.50(1)
		s.35(5)(c) rep.	37, ss.106,120(2), Sch.7, para.50(2), Sch.10
		s.35(5)(d) rep.	37, ss.106,120(2), Sch.7, para.50(3), Sch.10
		s.35(5)(e) am.	37, s.119, Sch.8, para.132(2)
		s.35(5)(f)-(h) added	37, s.106, Sch.7, para.50(3)
		s.35(7) am.	37, s.106, Sch.7, para.50(4)
		s.35(8)(a) rep.in pt.	37, ss.106,120(2), Sch.7, para.50(5), Sch.10
		s.35(8)(a) rep.in pt.	37, ss.119,120(2), Sch.8, para.132(3)(a), Sch.10
		s.35(8)(b) am.	37, s.119, Sch.8, para.132(3)(b)
		s.35(8)(c)-(e) added	37, s.106, Sch.7, para.50(5)
		s.35(10) am.	37, s.106, Sch.7, para.50(6)
		s.37(3)(a) am.	37, s.106, Sch.7, para.51(1)(a)
		s.37(3)(b) am.	37, s.106, Sch.7, para.51(1)(b)
		s.37(4)(5) replaced (by s.37(4)(5)(5A))	37, s.106, Sch.7, para.51(2)
		s.50(7) added	37, s.106, Sch.7, para.52
		s.54(2) rep.	37, ss.119,120(2), Sch.8, para.133, Sch.10
		s.54(4) added	37, s.106, Sch.7, para.53
		s.55(2) am.	37, s.106, Sch.7, para.54

Year and Chap. or No. of Measure	Short title	How affected	1998, Chapter of Act or Number of Measure or Statutory Instrument
1997—*cont.*			
		s.57(5)(b) am.	37, s.119, Sch.8, para.134
		Sch.1 excl.	SI 2251, art.16(5)
		Sch.1, Pt.I ext.(mods.) (and related amending Acts ext. (mods.) (Channel Is. and I.of Man)	SI 2798, arts.2,3, Schs.1, 2
		Sch.1, Pt.I, para.15 mod.	35, s.17, Sch.3, para.9(5)
		Sch.1, Pt.II excl.	35, s.17, Sch.3, para.9(1)
		Sch.1, para.6(3)(aa) added	37, s.119, Sch.8, para.135(1)(2)(a)
		Sch.1, para.6(3)(b) am.	37, s.119, Sch.8, para.135(1)(2)(b)
		Sch.1, para.8(2) mod. (*temp.*)	SI 2327, art.5(2)(c)(d)
		Sch.1, para.8(2) am.	37, s.119, Sch.8, para.135(3)(a)(b)(c)
		Sch.1, para.8(4) mod. (*temp.*)	SI 2327, art.5(2)(c)(d)
		Sch.1, para.8(4)(5) am.	37, s.119, Sch.8, para.135(3)(a)(b)(c)
		Sch.1, para.8(6)(7) added	37, s.119, Sch.8, para.135(3)(d)
		Sch.1, para.9(1)(a) rep.	37, ss.119,120(2), Sch.8, para.135(4)(a), Sch.10
		Sch.1, para.9(1)(b) rep.in pt.	37, ss.119,120(2), Sch.8, para.135(4)(a), Sch.10
		Sch.1, para.9(2) mod. (*temp.*)	SI 2327, art.5(2)(c)(d)
		Sch.1, para.9(2) am.	37, s.119, Sch.8, para.135(4)(b)(c)
		Sch.1, para.9(4) mod. (*temp.*)	SI 2327, art.5(2)(c)(d)
		Sch.1, para.9(4) am.	37, s.119, Sch.8, para.135(4)(b)(c)
		Sch.1, para.9(5) rep.	37, ss.119,120(2), Sch.8, para.135(4)(d), Sch.10
		Sch.1, para.9(6) am.	37, s.119, Sch.8, para.135(4)(e)
		Sch.1, para.9(7)(8) added	37, s.119, Sch.8, para.135(4)(f)
		Sch.1, para.10(2)(a) am.	37, s.119, Sch.8, para.135(5)(a)
		Sch.1, para.10(2)(b) am.	37, s.119, Sch.8, para.135(5)(b)
		Sch.1, para.10(4) rep.	37, ss.119,120(2), Sch.8, para.135(5)(c), Sch.10
		Sch.1, para.10(5)(a) rep.	37, s.119, Sch.8, para.135(5)(d)
		Sch.1, para.10(6)(b) subst.	37, s.119, Sch.8, para.135(5)(e)
		Sch.1, para.10(7) subst.	37, s.119, Sch.8, para.135(5)(f)
		Sch.1, para.11(2)(a) am.	37, s.119, Sch.8, para.135(6)(a)
		Sch.1, para.11(4)(a) am.	37, s.119, Sch.8, para.135(6)(b)

Year and Chap. or No. of Measure	Short title	How affected	1998, Chapter of Act or Number of Measure or Statutory Instrument
1997—*cont.*			
		Sch.1, para.11(5) am.	37, s.119, Sch.8, para.135(6)(c)
		Sch.1, para.11(6) rep.in pt.	37, ss.119,120(2), Sch.8, para.135(6)(d), Sch.10
		Sch.1, para.11(6), Table am.	37, s.119, Sch.8, para.135(6)(d)
		Sch.1, para.12(5), Table rep.in pt.	37, ss.119,120(2), Sch.8, para.135(7), Sch.10
		Sch.1, para.13(5), Table rep.in pt.	37, ss.119,120(2), Sch.8, para.135(8), Sch.10
		Sch.1, para.14 ext.	37, s.121(12)
		Sch.1, para.17(1)(a) am. (*prosp.*)	37, s.119, Sch.8, para.135(9)
		Sch.1, para.19 ext.	37, s.121(12)
		Sch.1, para.20(1) (defn. of "supervision") am. (*prosp.*)	37, s.119, Sch.8, para.135(10)
		Sch.2, paras.4,8 rep.	37, ss.119,120(2), Sch.8, para.136, Sch.10
		Sch.4, para.6(1)(b) rep.	37, ss.119,120(2), Sch.8, para.137(a), Sch.10
		Sch.4, paras.9,11 rep.	37, ss.119,120(2), Sch.8, para.137(b), Sch.10
		Sch.4, para.12(4) rep.	37, ss.119,120(2), Sch.8, para.137(c), Sch.10
		Sch.5, paras.1-4 rep.	37, ss.119,120(2), Sch.8, para.138(1), Sch.10
		Sch.5, para.5(2) rep.	37, ss.119,120(2), Sch.8, para.138(1)(a), Sch.10
		Sch.5, para.6 rep.	37, ss.119,120(2), Sch.8, para.138(1), Sch.10
		Sch.5, paras.8,9(1),10(1) rep.	37, ss.119,120(2), Sch.8, para.138(1)(b), Sch.10
		Sch.5, para.11(1) rep.	37, ss.119,120(2), Sch.8, para.138(1)(c), Sch.10
		Sch.5, para.11(2)(a) am.	37, s.119, Sch.8, para.138(2)(a)
		Sch.5, para.11(2)(b) am.	37, s.119, Sch.8, para.138(3)(a)
		Sch.5, para.11(2)(c)(3) rep.in pt.	37, ss.119,120(2), Sch.8, para.138(1)(c), Sch.10
		Sch.5, para.12(1) rep.	37, ss.119,120(2), Sch.8, para.138(1)(d), Sch.10
		Sch.5, para.12(2)(a) am.	37, s.119, Sch.8, para.138(3)(a)
		Sch.5, para.12(2)(b) am.	37, s.119, Sch.8, para.138(3)(b)
		Sch.5, para.12(2)(c) rep.in pt.	37, ss.119,120(2), Sch.8, para.138(1)(d), Sch.10
		Sch.6 rep.in pt.	37, ss.119,120(2), Sch.8, para.139, Sch.10
c.44	Education Act 1997	appt. day(s) for spec. provns. (1.4.1998)	SI 386, arts.2,4, Sch.1, Pt.II, Sch.2, Pt.I

Year and Chap. or No. of Measure	Short title	How affected	1998, Chapter of Act or Number of Measure or Statutory Instrument
1997—*cont.*			
		appt. day(s) for spec. provns. (1.9.1998)	SI 386, arts.2,4, Sch.1, Pt.IV, Sch.2, Pt.II
		appt. day(s) for spec. provns. (1.3.1998)	SI 386, art.2, Sch.1, Pt.I
		appt. day(s) for spec. provns. (1.8.1998)	SI 386, art.2, Sch.1, Pt.III
		appt. day(s) for spec. provns. (1.11.1998)	SI 386, art.2, Sch.1, Pt.V
		appt. day(s) for spec. provns. (1.4.1999)	SI 386, art.2, Sch.1, Pt.VI
		appt. day(s) for spec. provns. (1.9.1999)	SI 386, art.2, Sch.1, Pt.VII
		ss.2,3 rep. (*prosp.*)	31, s.140(1)(3), Sch.30, para.208(a), Sch.31
		ss.6-8 rep. (*prosp.*)	31, s.140(1)(3), Sch.30, para.208(b), Sch.31
		ss.10-14 rep. (in force 1.2.1999 to the extent that it relates to the omission of 1997 c.44 s.13) (pt.prosp.)	31, s.140(1)(3), Sch.30, para.208(c), Sch.31
		s.15 defn.of (" maintained primary school") paras.(a)-([c]) replaced (by paras.(a) (b)) (*prosp.*)	31, s.140(1), Sch.30, para.209
		s.16(5) am. (*prosp.*)	31, s.140(1), Sch.30, para.210
		s.17(5)(b) subst. (*prosp.*)	31, s.140(1), Sch.30, para.211(a)
		s.17(7)(a) rep.in pt. (*prosp.*)	31, s.140(1)(3), Sch.30, para.211(b), Sch.31
		s.18(1)(b) rep.in pt. (*prosp.*)	31, s.140(1)(3), Sch.30, para.212(a), Sch.31
		s.18(2)(a) rep.in pt. (*prosp.*)	31, s.140(1)(3), Sch.30, para.212(b), Sch.31
		s.19(3) subst. (*prosp.*)	31, s.140(1), Sch.30, para.213
		s.23(3) am. (*prosp.*)	31, s.140(1), Sch.30, para.214(a)
		s.23(5) defn.of (" maintained school") paras.(a)-([c]) replaced (by pars.(a)- (b)) (*prosp.*)	31, s.140(1), Sch.30, para.214(b)
		s.29(3) am. (*prosp.*)	31, s.140(1), Sch.30, para.215
		s.39(4) am.	31, s.134(3)
		s.41 restr.	18, s.1(5), Sch.1, para.8(2)(e)
		s.42 am.	31, s.140(1)(3), Sch.30, para.216, Sch.31
		s.43(2)(a) subst.	31, s.140(1), Sch.30, para.217(a)
		s.43(2)(b) rep.	31, s.140(1)(3), Sch.30, para.217(b), Sch.31

Year and Chap. or No. of Measure	Short title	How affected	1998, Chapter of Act or Number of Measure or Statutory Instrument
1997—*cont.*			
		s.43(2)(c) subst.	31, s.140(1), Sch.30, para.217(c)
		s.50 rep. (*prosp.*)	31, s.140(1)(3), Sch.30, para.218, Sch.31
		s.52(4)(5) rep.	31, s.140(1)(3), Sch.30, para.219, Sch.31
		s.57(2)(3) rep. (*prosp.*)	31, s.140(1)(3), Sch.30, para.220, Sch.31
		s.58(4) rep.in pt. (*prosp.*)	31, s.140(1)(3), Sch.30, para.221, Sch.31
		Schs.1-3 rep. (in force in part 1.2.1999 -see SI 1998/2212, Sch.1, Pt.III) (pt.prosp.)	31, s.140(1)(3), Sch.30, para.222(a), Sch.31
		Sch.6, para.5 rep.	31, s.140(1)(3), Sch.30, para.222(b), Sch.31
		Sch.7, para.5 rep.	18, s.54(3), Sch.5
		Sch.7, paras.15-22,25,31-35,40,45-51 rep. (*prosp.*)	31, s.140(1)(3), Sch.30, para.223, Sch.31
c.46	National Health Service (Primary Care) Act 1997	appt. day(s) for spec. provns. (1.4.1998) (11.5.1998)	SI 631, arts.2-5, Schs.1,2
		appt. day(s) for spec. provns. (1.10.1998)	SI 1998, arts.2,3
		appt. day(s) for spec. provns. (18.11.1998) (10.12.1998)	SI 2840, arts.2,3, Sch.
		ss.97,97A saved	SI 631, art.5
		Sch.1, paras.1(2)(c),2(2) (4) mod.	SI 631, art.4
c.47	Social Security Administration (Fraud) Act 1997	s.6 rep. (EW)	18, s.54(3), Sch.5
		ss.17,18 rep. (*prosp.*)	14, s.86(2), Sch.8
		Sch.1, para.1 rep. (EW)	18, s.54(3), Sch.5
		Sch.1, para.2 rep. (*prosp.*)	14, s.86(2), Sch.8
c.48	Crime and Punishment (Scotland) Act 1997	s.4 rep.	37, ss.119,120(2), Sch.8, para.140, Sch.10
		s.16(2) am. (*retrosp.*)	37, s.109(1)(2)
		s.16(3A)(3B)(3C) added (*retrosp.*)	37, s.109(1)(3)
		s.18(1) am.	37, s.119, Sch.8, para.119
		s.18(2) am.	37, s.119, Sch.8, para.120
		s.18(5) am.	37, s.119, Sch.8, para.121
		ss.33-41 (Pt.III) (Ch.I) rep.	37, ss.108,120(2), Sch.10
		Sch.1, paras.1,9(7),10(2) (a),13(3) rep.	37, ss.119,120(2), Sch.8, para.141(1)(a), Sch.10
		Sch.1, para.14(2)(a)(3)(e) (4)(5)(6)(7)(9)(10)(a) (11)(b)(12)(13)(14)(15) rep.	37, ss.119,120(2), Sch.8, para.141(1)(b), Sch.10
		Sch.1, para.14(16) subst.	37, s.119, Sch.8, para.141(2)

Year and Chap. or No. of Measure	Short title	How affected	1998, Chapter of Act or Number of Measure or Statutory Instrument
1997—*cont.*			
		Sch.1, para.14(17) rep.	37, ss.119,120(2), Sch.8, para.141(1)(b), Sch.10
		Sch.1, para.21(3) rep.	37, ss.119,120(2), Sch.8, para.141(1)(a), Sch.10
		Sch.2 rep.	37, ss.119,120(2), Sch.8, para.142, Sch.10
		Sch.3 rep.in pt.	37, ss.119,120(2), Sch.8, para.143, Sch.10
c.49	Public Entertainments Licences (Drug Misuse) Act 1997	appt. day(s) for ss.1-3 (subject to transitional provns) (1.5.1998)	SI 1009, arts.2,3
c.50	Police Act 1997	appt. day(s) for spec. provns. (1.4.1998)	SI 354, art.2
		s.6(3)(d) am. (*prosp.*)	32, s.74(1), Sch.4, para.22(2)
		s.9(2)(b) am. (*prosp.*)	32, s.74(1), Sch.4, para.22(3)
		s.9(3)(c) am. (*prosp.*)	32, s.74(1), Sch.4, para.22(4)
		s.21(3) am. (*prosp.*)	32, s.74(1), Sch.4, para.22(5)
		s.23(5) am. (*prosp.*)	32, s.74(1), Sch.4, para.22(6)
		s.30(1)(c) am. (*prosp.*)	32, s.74(1), Sch.4, para.22(7)
		s.39(2)(b) am. (*prosp.*)	32, s.74(1), Sch.4, para.22(8)
		s.40 am. (*prosp.*)	32, s.74(1), Sch.4, para.22(7)
		ss.52(3)(d),55(3)(c) am. (*prosp.*)	32, s.74(1), Sch.4, para.22(9)
		ss.91-108 (Pt.III) saved (6.5.1999)	46, s.30, Sch.5, Pt.II, s.C10
		s.94(1) am.	37, s.113(1)
		s.94(3)(a)(b) replaced	37, s.113(2)
		s.94(4) rep.in pt.	37, ss.113(3),120(2), Sch.10
		s.94(4)(d) added	37, s.113(3)
		ss.112-127 (Pt.V) expld. (*prosp.*)	29, s.56(4)
		ss.112-127 (Pt.V) (defn. of "caution") appl.	37, s.117(1)
		ss.112-127 (Pt.V) (defn. of "a caution") appl. (in force 30.9.1998 for reprimands and warnings under 1998 c.37 s.65 in areas specified in SI 1998/2327, Sch.3)	37, s.119, Sch.8, para.61 (adding 1984 c.60 s.27(4A))
		ss.130-132,137(3) rep. (saving)(*prosp.*)	32, s.74(2)(3), Schs.5,6
		Sch.4, para.(f) am. (EW)	18, s.54(1), Sch.3, para.33
		Sch.6, paras.19-22 rep. (EW)	18, s.54(3), Sch.5

Year and Chap. or No. of Measure	Short title	How affected	1998, Chapter of Act or Number of Measure or Statutory Instrument
1997—*cont.*			
		Sch.9, paras.21,22 rep. (saving)(*prosp.*)	32, s.74(2)(3), Schs.5,6
c.51	Sex Offenders Act 1997	ss.1-6 (Pt.I) mod. (NI) (*prosp.*)	SI 2839, art.6(5)
		ss.1-6 (Pt.I) mod. (EW)	37, s.2(5)
		ss.1-6 (Pt.I) mod.	37, s.20(6)
		s.4(1)(a) am.	37, s.119, Sch.8, para.144
		s.6(2) appl. (NI) (*prosp.*)	SI 2839, art.7(3)
		s.6(2) appl. (EW)	37, s.3(3)
		s.6(3) appl. (NI) (*prosp.*)	SI 2839, art.7(3)
		s.6(3) appl. (EW)	37, s.3(3)
c.58	Finance (No.2) Act 1997	s.30 mod. (if it is a distribution made before 6.4.2004)	36, s.76(1)(2)
		s.30(4) excl. (6.4.1999) (*temp.*)	SI 1871, reg.4(1)
		s.30(4) power to mod.	36, s.77(1) (adding 1988 c.1 s.333B)
		s.30(4) restr. (repeal of 1988 c.1 s.231(2))	36, s.90(1)
		s.37(6) rep. (*prosp.*)	36, s.165, Sch.27, Pt.III(3), Note
		s.37(11) rep.in pt. (*prosp.*)	36, s.165, Sch.27, Pt.III(3), Note
		s.42(6)(7) rep.	36, s.165, Sch.27, Pt.III(18), Note 2
		s.50(2), Sch.3, para.3(3)(4)(6)(7) rep. (6.4.1999)	36, s.165, Sch.27, Pt.III(2), Note
		Sch.3, para.12 mod.	36, s.90(3)
		Sch.4 appl.(mods.) (6.4.1999) (*temp.*)	SI 1871, reg.4(2)
		Sch.4, para.2 mod.	36, s.90(2)(b)
		Sch.4, para.3 mod.	36, s.90(2)(a)
		Sch.4, para.3 rep.	36, s.165, Sch.27, Pt.III(28), Note
		Sch.4, para.8 rep.	36, ss.31,165, Sch.3, para.45, Sch.27, Pt.III(2), Note
		Sch.4, para.18 rep.	36, ss.31,165, Sch.3, para.47, Sch.27, Pt.III(2), Note
		Sch.4, para.23 rep.	36, ss.31,165, Sch.3, para.48, Sch.27, Pt.III(2), Note
		Sch.4, para.98 rep.	36, ss.31,165, Sch.3, para.46, Sch.27, Pt.III(2), Note
		Sch.7 am. (*retrosp.*)	36, s.81(5)
		Sch.7, para.3 rep.	36, s.165, Sch.27, Pt.III(4), Note
		Sch.8 restr.	36, s.76(5)
		Sch.8 restr.	36, s.90(4)

Year and Chap. or No. of Measure	Short title	How affected	1998, Chapter of Act or Number of Measure or Statutory Instrument
1997—*cont.*			
c.59	Education (Schools) Act 1997	s.2(7) added	31, s.140(1), Sch.30, para.224
		s.3(2)(g) added	31, s.130(1)
		ss.6(1),7(3)(a)(4)(a) rep. (*prosp.*)	31, s.140(3), Sch.31
c.65	Local Government (Contracts) Act 1997	power to appl.	38, s.39
		s.8(1)(a)(b)(c)(2) am. (EW)	18, s.54(1), Sch.3, para.34
c.66	Plant Varieties Act 1997	appt. day for residue (8.5.1998)	SI 1028, art.2
c.68	Special Immigration Appeals Commission Act 1997	appt. day(s) for ss.5,8 (11.6.1998)	SI 1336, art.2
		appt. day for residue (3.8.1998)	SI 1892, art.2
1998			
c.1	Education (Student Loans) Act 1998	rep.	30, s.44(2), Sch.4
		appt. day(s) for ss.2,3, 6(2) [1.3.1998]	SI 210, art.2
		Pt.IV, Ch.VI, head. rep.in pt. (6.4.1999)	36, s.165, Sch.27, Pt.III(6), Note
		s.77(1) am. (17.3.1998) (*retrosp.*)	36, s.50(2)(4)
		s.79(6A) added (17.3.1998) (*retrosp.*)	36, s.50(3)(4)
		s.79(6B) added (17.3.1998) (*retrosp.*)	36, s.51(2)(3)
		s.104(4)(5)(7) rep. (6.4.1999)	36, s.165, Sch.27, Pt.III(6), Note
		s.104 sidenote rep.in pt. (6.4.1999)	36, s.165, Sch.27, Pt.III(6), Note
		s.105(4) rep. (6.4.1999)	36, s.165, Sch.27, Pt.III(6), Note
		s.135(2)(5) am. (6.4.1998)	36, s.49(1)(2)
		ss.140A-140C added (17.3.1998) (*retrosp.*)	36, s.50(1)(4)
		ss.140D-140F added (17.3.1998) (*retrosp.*)	36, s.51(1)(3)
		s.231(4) appl.	36, s.76(4)
		s.304(4) added (6.4.1998)	36, s.74(1), Sch.13, Pt.I, para.16(1)(2)
		s.304A added (6.4.1998)	36, s.74(1), Sch.13, Pt.I, para.17(1)(2)
		s.304A (defn. of "new shares") appl. (6.4.1998)	36, s.74(1), Sch.13, Pt.I, para.17(2)
		s.305A(2) am. (6.4.1998)	36, s.74(1), Sch.13, Pt.I, para.18(2)
		s.306(1) am. (6.4.1998)	36, s.74(1), Sch.13, Pt.I, para.19(1)
		s.306(2) am. (6.4.1998)	36, s.74(1), Sch.13, Pt.I, para.19(2)

Year and Chap. or No. of Measure	Short title	How affected	1998, Chapter of Act or Number of Measure or Statutory Instrument
1998—*cont.*			
		s.306(3) subst. (6.4.1998)	36, s.74(1), Sch.13, Pt.I, para.19(3)
		s.306(3A) rep. (6.4.1998)	36, ss.74(1),165, Sch.13, Pt.I, para.19(4), Sch.27, Pt.III(14), Note 4
		s.306(4)(5) subst. (6.4.1998)	36, s.74(1), Sch.13, Pt.I, para.19(5)
		s.307(1A) am. (6.4.1998)	36, s.74(1), Sch.13, Pt.I, para.20(1)
		s.307(1C) added (6.4.1998)	36, s.74(1), Sch.13, Pt.I, para.20(2)
		s.307(4) am. (6.4.1998)	36, s.74(1), Sch.13, Pt.I, para.20(3)
		s.307(6)(b) am. (6.4.1998)	36, s.74(1), Sch.13, Pt.I, para.20(4)
		s.308(2) am. (6.4.1998)	36, s.74(1), Sch.13, Pt.I, para.21
		Sch.19AB, para.3(1ZA) added (specified accounting periods)	36, s.91(1)(2)
c.2	Public Processions (Northern Ireland) Act 1998	appt. day for residue (2.3.1998)	SI 717, art.2
		s.6 excl.	SI 956, art.3
c.5	Fossil Fuel Levy Act 1998	appt. day (1.4.1998)	SI 930, art.2
c.6	Wireless Telegraphy Act 1998	ss.1-8 ext.(mods.) (to Isle of Man)	SI 1510, art.2
		ss.1-8 ext.(mods.) (to Bailiwick of Guernsey)	SI 1511, art.2
		ss.1-8 ext.(mods.) (to Bailiwick of Jersey)	SI 1512, art.2
		s.10(1) ext.(mods.) (to Isle of Man)	SI 1510, art.2
		s.10(1) ext.(mods.) (to Bailiwick of Guernsey)	SI 1511, art.2
		s.10(1) ext.(mods.) (to Bailiwick of Jersey)	SI 1512, art.2
		Sch.1 ext.(mods.) (to Isle of Man)	SI 1510, art.2
		Sch.1 ext.(mods.) (to Bailiwick of Guernsey)	SI 1511, art.2
		Sch.1 ext.(mods.) (to Bailiwick of Jersey)	SI 1512, art.2
		Sch.2 ext.(mods.) (to Isle of Man)	SI 1510, art.2
		Sch.2 ext.(mods.) (to Bailiwick of Guernsey)	SI 1511, art.2
		Sch.2 ext.(mods.) (to Bailiwick of Jersey)	SI 1512, art.2
c.8	Employment Rights (Dispute Resolution) Act 1998	appt. day(s) for spec. provns. (1.8.1998) (1.10.1998) (1.1.1999)	SI 1658, arts.2,3, Schs.1, 2
c.11	Bank of England Act 1998	appt. day (1.6.1998)	SI 1120, art.2

Year and Chap. or No. of Measure	Short title	How affected	1998, Chapter of Act or Number of Measure or Statutory Instrument
1998—*cont.*			
c.12	Northern Ireland (Elections) Act 1998	rep. (*prosp.*)	47, s.100(2), Sch.15
		appt. day(s) for spec. provns. (28.5.1998)	SI 1313, art.2
		s.2(2)(3)(4) appl.	SI 1287, art.7(3)
		s.4(4A) added	35, s.1, Sch.1, para.9
		Sch.1, para.8 subst.	47, s.99, Sch.13, para.20
c.14	Social Security Act 1998	appt. day(s) for spec. provns. (8.9.1998) (5.10.1998) (6.4.1999)	SI 2209, arts.2,3, Sch.
		appt. day(s) for spec. provns. (16.11.1998) (7.12.1998)	SI 2780, arts.2,3
		power to am. (*prosp.*)	47, s.87
		s.2 appl.(mods.) (*prosp.*)	14, s.86(1), Sch.7, para.131 (substituting 1993 c.48 at s.170(1))
		ss.8-10 appl.(mods.) (*prosp.*)	14, s.86(1), Sch.7, para.131 (substituting 1993 c.48 at s.170(2))
		s.12 appl.(mods.) (*prosp.*)	14, s.86(1), Sch.7, para.131 (substituting 1993 c.48 at s.170(4))
		s.83 rep. (*prosp.*)	14, s.86(2), Sch.8
		Sch.5 power to appl. (*prosp.*)	14, s.42 (replacing 1991 c.48 ss.20,21 at s.20(6))
		Sch.6 rep. (*prosp.*)	14, s.86(2), Sch.8
c.15	Magistrates' Courts (Procedure) Act 1998	appt. day(s) for ss.2,3, 4 (1.9.1998)	SI 1837, arts.2,3,4
c.17	Petroleum Act 1998	ss.29-45 (Pt.IV) power to trans. functions	38, s.22(1)(c)(5), Sch.3, Pt.I, para.4(1)(b)
		Sch.4, para.10 rep. (NI) (*prosp.*)	SI 3162, art.105(4), Sch.5
c.18	Audit Commission Act 1998	s.10(4)-(6) saved	18, s.12(4)
		s.19 mod. (*temp.*)	SI 2825, regs.1(2),6(1)(2), 7,9,10
		s.28(1)(d) mod. (1.4.1999)	31, s.53(1)
		s.36(1) rep.in pt. (*prosp.*)	31, s.140(3), Sch.31
		s.36(3) am.	31, s.140(1), Sch.30, para.225(a)
		s.36(3)(b) rep.in pt.	31, s.140(1)(3), Sch.30, para.225(b), Sch.31
		s.40(1) am.	38, s.140, Sch.16, para.99(2)
		s.40(2) am.	38, s.140, Sch.16, para.99(3)
		s.40(2A) added	38, s.140, Sch.16, para.99(4)
		s.40(4)(6) am.	38, s.140, Sch.16, para.99(5)
		s.41(1)(4) am.	38, s.140, Sch.16, para.100
		s.42 am.	38, s.140, Sch.16, para.101

Year and Chap. or No. of Measure	Short title	How affected	1998, Chapter of Act or Number of Measure or Statutory Instrument
1998—*cont.*			
		s.43 am.	38, s.140, Sch.16, para.102
		Sch.3, paras.25,32 rep. (*prosp.*)	31, s.140(3), Sch.31
c.19	Community Care (Residential Accommodation) Act 1998	s.35(1) (defns. of "special non- metropolitan county" and "special non- metropolitan district") defn(s). added	SI 465, reg.2(11)
c.20	Late Payment of Commercial Debts (Interest) Act 1998	appt. day(s) for spec. provns. (1.11.1998)	SI 2479, arts.2,3, Schs.1, 2
c.22	National Lottery Act 1998	s.2(4) rep. (*prosp.*)	22, s.26, Sch.5, Pt.I
c.29	Data Protection Act 1998	saved (6.5.1999)	46, s.30, Sch.5, Pt.II, s.B2(a)
		s.12A added (to 24.10.2007) (*temp.*) (*prosp.*)	29, s.72, Sch.13, para.1
		s.32(2)(dd) added (to 24.10.2007) (*temp.*) (*prosp.*)	29, s.72, Sch.13, para.2(a)
		s.32(4) am. (to 24.10.2007) (*temp.*) (*prosp.*)	29, s.72, Sch.13, para.2(b)
		s.34 am. (to 24.10.2007) (*temp.*)(*prosp.*)	29, s.72, Sch.13, para.3
		s.53(1) am. (to 24.10.2007) (*temp.*) (*prosp.*)	29, s.72, Sch.13, para.4
		Sch.1, Pt.II, para.8(c) rep. (to 24.10.2007) (*temp.*)(*prosp.*)	29, s.72, Sch.13, para.5
		Sch.1, Pt.II, para.8(e) added (to 24.10.2007) (*temp.*)(*prosp.*)	29, s.72, Sch.13, para.5
		Sch.7, para.4 am. (*prosp.*)	47, s.99, Sch.13, para.21(1)
		Sch.7, para.4 renumbered (as para.4(1)) (*prosp.*)	47, s.99, Sch.13, para.21(2)
		Sch.7, para.4(2) added (*prosp.*)	47, s.99, Sch.13, para.21(2)
c.30	Teaching and Higher Education Act 1998	appt. day(s) for s.44(1) (18.7.1998) (for the purpose of bringing into force the provisions of Sch.3, para.4 to that Act on that day)	SI 1729, art.2
		appt. day(s) for spec. provns. (13.8.1998) (transtl. savings)	SI 2004, arts.2-7
		appt. day(s) for spec. provns. (1.10.1998) (1.4.1999)	SI 2215, arts.2,3
		appt. day(s) for s.44(2) (partially) (1.1.1999)	SI 3237, arts.2-4
		power to mod. (EW)	30, s.6, Sch.2, para.7(3)
		s.1(2)(4)-(9) appl. (General Teaching Council for Wales)	SI 2911, art.3
		s.22(1) referred to	SI 2003, regs.3,4

Year and Chap. or No. of Measure	Short title	How affected	1998, Chapter of Act or Number of Measure or Statutory Instrument
1998—*cont.*			
		Sch.1 appl. (General Teaching Council for Wales)	SI 2911, art.3
c.31	School Standards and Framework Act 1998	am. (E)	SI 1973, reg.3(6)
		appt. day(s) for spec. provns. (8.8.1998) (1.9.1998)	SI 2048, arts.2,3
		appt. day(s) for spec. provns. (1.10.1998) (1.12.1998) (1.2.1999) (1.4.1999)	SI 2212, arts.2,3,4, Schs.1,2
		mod. (to 1.9.1999) (*temp.*)	SI 2248, reg.2
		appt. day(s) for Sch.30, para.139 (20.11.1998) (1.4.1999) (transtl. savings)	SI 2791, arts.2,4
		appt. day(s) for Sch.30, para.153 (20.11.1998) (transtl. savings)	SI 2791, arts.3,5
		appt. day(s) for s.110 (1.9.1999)	SI 2877, art.2
		appt. day(s) for s.89 (6.1.1999)	SI 3198, art.2(1)
		appt. day(s) for spec. provns. (1.2.1999)	SI 3198, art.2(2), Sch.
		ss.2,3 mod. (*temp.*)	SI 1968, reg.2
		s.6 mod. (12.1.1999)	SI 3217, reg.2(a)
		s.10(1) mod.	SI 1878, reg.2
		s.13 excl. (*temp.*)	SI 2115, reg.3
		s.44(5) mod.	SI 2670, reg.3(1)
		s.44(5) mod.	SI 2670, reg.3(2)
		s.44(6) mod.	SI 2670, reg.3(1)
		ss.45-53 (Pt.II) (Ch.IV) mod.	SI 2670, reg.3(1)(3)
		s.45(3)(4) mod.	SI 2670, reg.3(4)
		s.49(6)(b) mod.	SI 2670, reg.3(5)
		s.84(6) mod. (6.1.1999)	SI 3130, reg.2
		s.88 mod. (6.1.1999)	SI 3130, reg.3
		s.89 excl. (shall not apply in relation to the determination of admission arrangements for any school earlier than the school year 2000/2001) (*temp.*)	SI 3198, arts.3,4
		s.89(2) referred to	SI 3165, regs.7,8,9
		s.89(2)(b) mod. (2000/2001 School Year)	SI 3165, reg.5
		s.89(2)(b) mod. (2000/2001 School Year)	SI 3165, reg.6
		s.99(5) mod. (until 1.9.1999) (*temp.*)	SI 2230, reg.2
		s.101 mod. (*temp.*)	SI 2230, reg.3

Year and Chap. or No. of Measure	Short title	How affected	1998, Chapter of Act or Number of Measure or Statutory Instrument
1998—*cont.*			
		s.105 expld.	SI 2876, reg.11(1)
		s.107(5) mod.	SI 2670, reg.4
		s.110(1)(a) mod. (until 1.9.1999)	SI 2834, reg.2
		s.141 appl.(mods.)	SI 2763, reg.6(2)
		ss.213,214(1)(3)(5),216(1),217 cont.(mod.) transtl. provn.	SI 3172, reg.2(1)(3)
		Sch.2 excl. (*temp.*)	SI 1969, art.18
		Sch.2, paras.4-7 excl. (*temp.*)	SI 1969, reg.19(2)
		Sch.2, para.7 excl.	SI 1969, reg.17
		Sch.9, para.15 appl.(mods.)	SI 2763, reg.6(2)
		Sch.9, para.15(1) appl.(mods.)	SI 2763, reg.6(3)
		Sch.9, para.15(1) appl.(mods.)	SI 2763, reg.7(2)
		Sch.11, Pt.I mod.	SI 2670, reg.3(1)(3)
		Sch.11, Pt.II, para.6 mod.	SI 2670, reg.3(1)
		Sch.12, para.1 appl.(mods.)	SI 2763, reg.6(4)
		Sch.12, para.1 appl.(mods.)	SI 2763, reg.7(3)
		Sch.12, para.3 appl.(mods.)	SI 2763, reg.6(5)
		Sch.12, para.3 appl.(mods.)	SI 2763, reg.7(4)
		Sch.15, paras.1,3(1)(a) mod.	SI 2670, reg.6
		Sch.20, para.10 cont.(mod.) transtl. provn.	SI 3172, reg.2(1)(3)
		Sch.32, para.5(5)(a) mod.	SI 2670, reg.5(2)
		Sch.32, para.7 mod. (until 1.9.1999) (*temp.*)	SI 2115, reg.2
		Sch.32, para.7 appl.(mods.) (*temp.*)	SI 2115, regs.3,4(1)(2)
c.32	Police (Northern Ireland) Act 1998	ss.1(2),18(4) rep. (*prosp.*)	47, s.100(2), Sch.15
		Sch.4, para.10 rep. (*prosp.*)	SI 3162, art.105(4), Sch.5
c.35	Northern Ireland (Sentences) Act 1998	appt. day (28.7.1998)	SI 1858, art.2
c.36	Finance Act 1998	appt. day(s) for Sch.2 (in part) (1.10.1998)	SI 2243, art.2
		appt. day(s) for s.145 (4.11.1998)	SI 2703, art.2
		appt. day(s) for Sch.1, paras.3-14 in relation to licences issued on or after 1.1.1999	SI 3092, art.2
		s.490(1) rep.in pt. (6.4.1998)	36, ss.31,165, Sch.3, para.28(2)(3), Sch.27, Pt.III(2), Note
		s.498 rep. (6.4.1998)	36, ss.31,165, Sch.3, para.30(1)(2), Sch.27, Pt.III(2), Note
		Sch.3, para.5 rep.	36, s.165, Sch.27, Pt.III(28), Note

Year and Chap. or No. of Measure	Short title	How affected	1998, Chapter of Act or Number of Measure or Statutory Instrument
1998—*cont.*			
		Sch.5, paras.6,7 rep.	36, s.165, Sch.27, Pt.III(5), Note
		Sch.5, para.33 rep.	36, s.165, Sch.27, Pt.III(28), Note
		Sch.18, para.3 ext.	36, s.117, Sch.19, para.48(3) (substituting 1988 c.1, s.488(12))
		Sch.18, para.10 excl.	36, s.113, Sch.17, paras.4, 37 (replacing 1988 c.1, s.749 at s.749A(4)(a))
		Sch.18, para.10 excl.	36, s.113, Sch.17, paras.20(9),37 (adding 1988 c.1, Sch.24, para.9(7))
		Sch.18, paras.57-60 excl.	36, s.117, Sch.19, para.51(3) (substituting 1988 c.1, Sch.19AB, para.1(6))
c.37	Crime and Disorder Act 1998	appt. day(s) for spec. provns. (1.8.1998) (7.8.1998)	SI 1883, arts.2,3
		appt. day(s) for spec. provns. (30.9.1998)	SI 2327, art.2
		appt. day(s) for spec. provns. (in areas indicated) (30.9.1998) (saving)	SI 2327, arts.3,6-9, Schs.1-3
		appt. day(s) for spec. provns. (1.12.1998) (saving)	SI 2327, arts.4(1),6-8
		appt. day(s) for spec. provns. (in relation to spec. purpose) (4.1.1999) (saving)	SI 2327, arts.4(2),6-8
		appt. day(s) for spec. provns. (1.1.1999) (28.1.1999) (1.3.1999) (1.4.1999) (1.7.1999)	SI 3263, arts.2-7
		s.1 referred to (Form prescribed) (1.4.1999)	SI 2682, rule 6(1), Sch.4
		s.1(11) mod.	37, s.106, Sch.7, para.46(11) (adding 1991 c.53, Sch.2, para.8A(10))
		s.2 referred to (Form prescribed)	SI 2682, rule 2(1)
		ss.2(9),66(4) mod.	37, s.106, Sch.7, para.46(11) (adding 1991 c.53, Sch.2, para.8A(10))
		Sch.3, paras.1,2(1)(4) referred to	SI 3048, rules 2-4
c.38	Government of Wales Act 1998	appt. day(s) for spec. provns. (2.9.1998) (1.10.1998) (1.11.1998)	SI 2244, arts.3,4,5

Year and Chap. or No. of Measure	Short title	How affected	1998, Chapter of Act or Number of Measure or Statutory Instrument
1998—*cont.*			
		appt. day(s) for spec. provns. (1.12.1998)	SI 2789, art.2
		s.4(8) am.	48, s.23, Sch.3, para.5
c.39	National Minimum Wage Act 1998	appt. day(s) for spec. provns. (1.11.1998) (1.4.1999)	SI 2574, art.2, Schs.1,2
		excl. (saving for ss.46, 47) (*prosp.*)	39, s.47, Sch.2, Pt.I, para.10 (adding 1948 c.47, s.17A)
		excl. (saving for ss.46, 47) (*prosp.*)	39, s.47, Sch.2, Pt.III (adding SI 1977/2151 (NI 22) art.2A)
		excl. (saving for ss.46, 47) (*prosp.*)	39, s.47, Sch.2, Pt.III, para.23 (adding 1949 c.30, s.17A)
		saved (6.5.1999)	46, s.30, Sch.5, Pt.II, s.H1(h)
		restr.	47, s.98(3)
		ss.9-11 mod. (*prosp.*)	39, s.47, Sch.2, Pt.I, para.3 (adding 1948 c.47, s.3A(1)-(4))
		ss.9-11 mod. (*prosp.*)	39, s.47, Sch.2, Pt.II, para.13 (adding 1949 c.30, s.3A(1)-(3))
		ss.9-11 ext.(mods.) (*prosp.*)	39, s.47, Sch.2, Pt.III, para.26 (adding SI 1977/2151 (NI 22) art.8A)
		s.14 mod. (*prosp.*)	39, s.47, Sch.2, Pt.I, para.3 (adding 1948 c.47, s.3A(1)-(4))
		s.14 mod. (*prosp.*)	39, s.47, Sch.2, Pt.II, para.13 (adding 1949 c.30, s.3A(1)-(3))
		s.14 ext.(mods.) (*prosp.*)	39, s.47, Sch.2, Pt.III, para.26 (adding SI 1977/2151 (NI 22) art.8A)
		s.17 mod. (*prosp.*)	39, s.47, Sch.2, Pt.I, para.3 (adding 1948 c.47, s.3A(1)-(4))
		s.17 mod. (*prosp.*)	39, s.47, Sch.2, Pt.II, para.13 (adding 1949 c.30, s.3A(1)-(3))
		s.17 ext.(mods.) (*prosp.*)	39, s.47, Sch.2, Pt.III, para.26 (adding SI 1977/2151 (NI 22) art.8A)
		ss.19-22 mod. (*prosp.*)	39, s.47, Sch.2, Pt.I, para.3 (adding 1948 c.47, s.3A(1)-(4))
		ss.19-22 mod. (*prosp.*)	39, s.47, Sch.2, Pt.II, para.13 (adding 1949 c.30, s.3A(1)-(3))

Year and Chap. or No. of Measure	Short title	How affected	1998, Chapter of Act or Number of Measure or Statutory Instrument
1998—*cont.*			
		ss.19-22 ext.(mods.) (*prosp.*)	39, s.47, Sch.2, Pt.III, para.26 (adding SI 1977/2151 (NI 22) art.8A)
		s.23 mod. (*prosp.*)	39, s.47, Sch.2, Pt.I, para.3 (adding 1948 c.47, s.3A(1)-(4))
		s.23 mod. (*prosp.*)	39, s.47, Sch.2, Pt.II, para.13 (adding 1949 c.30, s.3A(1)-(3))
		s.23 ext.(mods.) (*prosp.*)	39, s.47, Sch.2, Pt.III, para.26 (adding SI 1977/2151 (NI 22) art.8A)
		s.24 mod. (*prosp.*)	39, s.47, Sch.2, Pt.I, para.3 (adding 1948 c.47, s.3A(1)-(4))
		s.24 mod. (*prosp.*)	39, s.47, Sch.2, Pt.II, para.13 (adding 1949 c.30, s.3A(1)-(3))
		s.24 ext.(mods.) (*prosp.*)	39, s.47, Sch.2, Pt.III, para.26 (adding SI 1977/2151 (NI 22) art.8A)
		s.28 mod. (*prosp.*)	39, s.47, Sch.2, Pt.I, para.3 (adding 1948 c.47, s.3A(1)-(4))
		s.28 mod. (*prosp.*)	39, s.47, Sch.2, Pt.II, para.13 (adding 1949 c.30, s.3A(1)-(3))
		s.28 ext.(mods.) (*prosp.*)	39, s.47, Sch.2, Pt.III, para.26 (adding SI 1977/2151 (NI 22) art.8A)
		ss.31-33 mod. (*prosp.*)	39, s.47, Sch.2, Pt.I, para.3 (adding 1948 c.47, s.3A(1)-(4))
		ss.31-33 ext.(mods.) (*prosp.*)	39, s.47, Sch.2, Pt.III, para.26 (adding SI 1977/2151 (NI 22) art.8A)
		ss.31,32,33(4)(5) mod. (*prosp.*)	39, s.47, Sch.2, Pt.II, para.13 (adding 1949 c.30, s.3A(1)-(3))
		s.48 mod. (*prosp.*)	39, s.47, Sch.2, Pt.I, para.3 (adding 1948 c.47, s.3A(1)-(4))
		s.48 mod. (*prosp.*)	39, s.47, Sch.2, Pt.II, para.13 (adding 1949 c.30, s.3A(1)-(3))
		s.48 ext.(mods.) (*prosp.*)	39, s.47, Sch.2, Pt.III, para.26 (adding SI 1977/2151 (NI 22) art.8A)

Year and Chap. or No. of Measure	Short title	How affected	1998, Chapter of Act or Number of Measure or Statutory Instrument
1998—*cont.*			
		s.49 mod. (*prosp.*)	39, s.47, Sch.2, Pt.I, para.3 (adding 1948 c.47, s.3A(1)-(4))
		s.49 mod. (*prosp.*)	39, s.47, Sch.2, Pt.II, para.13 (adding 1949 c.30, s.3A(1)-(3))
		s.49 ext.(mods.) (*prosp.*)	39, s.47, Sch.2, Pt.III, para.26 (adding SI 1977/2151 (NI 22) art.8A)
c.41	Competition Act 1998	appt. day(s) for spec. provns. (26.11.1998)	SI 2750, art.2
		appt. day(s) for spec. provns. (11.1.1999)	SI 3166, art.2
		ss.1-60 (Pt.I) cert. functs. made exercisable concurrently (pt.prosp.)	41, s.66(5), Sch.10, Pt.I, para.2(6) (replacing 1984 c.12 at s.50(3))
		Sch.7, Pt.II appl.(mods.) (*prosp.*)	41, s.66(5), Sch.10, Pt.IV, para.9(2) (replacing 1984 c.12 at s.13(9A))
		Sch.7, Pt.II appl.(mods.) (*prosp.*)	41, s.66(5), Sch.10, Pt.IV, para.10(2) (replacing 1986 c.44 at s.24(7A))
		Sch.7, Pt.II appl.(mods.) (*prosp.*)	41, s.66(5), Sch.10, Pt.IV, para.12(2) (replacing 1989 c.29 at s.12(8A))
		Sch.7, Pt.II appl.(mods.) (*prosp.*)	41, s.66(5), Sch.10, Pt.IV, para.13(3) (replacing 1991 c.56 at s.14(7A))
		Sch.7, Pt.II appl.(mods.) (*prosp.*)	41, s.66(5), Sch.10, Pt.IV, para.15(2) (replacing 1993 c.43 at s.13(8A))
		Sch.7, Pt.II appl.(mods.) (*prosp.*)	41, s.66(5), Sch.10, Pt.V, para.17(2) (replacing 1992/231 at art.15(8)(9))
		Sch.7, Pt.II appl.(mods.) (*prosp.*)	41, s.66(5), Sch.10, Pt.V, para.18(2) (replacing 1996/275 art.15(9))
		Sch.7, Pt.II mod. (*prosp.*)	41, s.74(1), Sch.12, para.4(3) (replacing 1980 c.21 s.11(9A))
		Sch.7, Pt.II mod. (*prosp.*)	41, s.74(1), Sch.12, para.7(2) (replacing 1986 c.31 at s.44(3A))
		Sch.7, Pt.II mod. (*prosp.*)	41, s.74(1), Sch.12, para.14(3) (replacing 1990 c.42 Sch.7, at para.4(7A))
		Sch.7, Pt.II mod. (*prosp.*)	41, s.74(1), Sch.12, para.20(2) (am. SI 1994/426 (NI No.1)
		Sch.7, para.20(2)(a) mod. (*prosp.*)	41, s.74(1), Sch.12, para.4(3) (replacing 1980 c.21 at s.11(9))

Year and Chap. or No. of Measure	Short title	How affected	1998, Chapter of Act or Number of Measure or Statutory Instrument
1998—*cont.*			
c.42	Human Rights Act 1998	appt. day(s) for s.19 (24.11.1998)	SI 2882, art.2
		defn. of "the Convention" appl. (*prosp.*)	38, s.107(5)
		saved (1.7.1999)	46, ss.29,53(4), Sch.4, Pt.I, paras.1(2)(f),9
		defn. of "the Convention rights" appl.	46, s.126(1)
		defn. of "the Convention" appl. (*prosp.*)	47, s.71(5)
		defn. of "the Convention rights" appl.	47, s.98(1)
c.45	Regional Development Agencies Act 1998	appt. day(s) for spec. provns. (25.11.1998)	SI 2952, art.2
c.46	Scotland Act 1998	appt. day(s) for spec. provns. (25.1.1999) (1.4.1999) (6.5.1999) (20.5.1999) (1.4.2000)	SI 3178, art.2(2)
		appt. day(s) for spec. provns. (1.7.1999)	SI 3178, art.3
		referred to transtl. provn.	SI 3216
c.47	Northern Ireland Act 1998	defn. of "transferred matters" appl. (*prosp.*)	42, s.21(1)
		defn. of "Northern Ireland legislation" appl.	46, s.126(1)
		ss.24(2),76(4) am. (NI) (*prosp.*)	SI 3162, art.105(1), Sch.3
		ss.91,92 appl. (*prosp.*)	SI 3162, art.80(5)
		s.98(1) (defns. of "political opinion" and "religious belief") am. (NI) (*prosp.*)	SI 3162, art.105(1), Sch.3
		Sch.8, para.5 saved (*prosp.*)	SI 3162, art.18(4)(a)
		Sch.13, paras.1,10 rep. (*prosp.*)	SI 3162, art.105(4), Sch.5
		Sch.13, para.18 rep. (*prosp.*)	47, s.100(2), Sch.15
c.48	Registration of Political Parties Act 1998	s.2(2)(e) rep.in pt. (*prosp.*)	47, s.100(2), Sch.15
c.iii	City of Edinburgh (Guided Busways) Order Confirmation Act 1998	Sch., O., s.11 excl.	iii, s.1, Sch., O., s.37(5) (a)(ii)
		Sch., O., s.27 appl.(mods.)	iii, s.1, Sch., O., s.39(3) (4)
		Sch., O., s.28 excl.	iii, s.1, Sch., O., s.39(2)
		Sch., O. ss.20,31 power to am.	iii, s.1, Sch., O., s.59(1)
c.iv	Tamar Bridge Act 1998	s.37(6)-(9) excl.	iv, s.37(10)
c.v	Lloyds TSB Act 1998	s.13(1)(a) subst. (NI) (*prosp.*)	v, s.14(2)(c)

INDEX

TO THE

PUBLIC GENERAL ACTS

AND

GENERAL SYNOD MEASURES 1998

B

BANK OF ENGLAND ACT 1998 (c. 11) ... ... I p. 97

PART I

CONSTITUTION, REGULATION AND FINANCIAL ARRANGEMENTS
Constitution and regulation

Financial arrangements

Supplementary

PART II

MONETARY POLICY
Role of the Bank

Monetary Policy Committee of the Bank

Information and reports

Treasury's reserve powers

Supplementary

PART III

TRANSFER OF SUPERVISORY FUNCTIONS OF THE BANK TO THE FINANCIAL SERVICES AUTHORITY
Transfer of functions to the Authority

Authority's position in relation to transferred functions

Consequential changes to banking bodies

PART I

PREVENTION OF CRIME AND DISORDER

CHAPTER I

ENGLAND AND WALES

Crime and disorder: general

§ 1. Anti-social behaviour orders.
2. Sex offender orders.
3. Sex offender orders: supplemental.
4. Appeals against orders.

Crime and disorder strategies

5. Authorities responsible for strategies.
6. Formulation and implementation of strategies.
7. Supplemental.

Youth crime and disorder

8. Parenting orders.
9. Parenting orders: supplemental.
10. Appeals against parenting orders.
11. Child safety orders.
12. Child safety orders: supplemental.
13. Appeals against child safety orders.
14. Local child curfew schemes.
15. Contravention of curfew notices.
16. Removal of truants to designated premises etc.

D

Part III—Exemptions available after 23rd October 2001 but before 24th October 2007.
Part IV—Exemptions after 23rd October 2001 for historical research.
Part V—Exemption from section 22.
Schedule 9—Powers of entry and inspection.
Schedule 10—Further provisions relating to assistance under section 53.
Schedule 11—Educational records.
Schedule 12—Accessible public records.
Schedule 13—Modifications of Act having effect before 24th October 2007.
Schedule 14—Transitional provisions and savings.
Schedule 15—Minor and consequential amendments.
Schedule 16—Repeals and revocations.
Part I—Repeals.
Part II—Revocations.

E

Transfer of loans to private sector

§ 1. Transfer of public sector student loans to the private sector.

Terms of loans

2. Regulations to prescribe certain terms of student loan agreements.

Administration of loans

3. Administration of public sector student loans.

General

4. Corresponding provision for Northern Ireland.
5. Financial provisions.
6. Consequential amendment and repeals.
7. Short title, interpretation, commencement and extent.

Schedules:—Repeals.

PART I

EMPLOYMENT TRIBUNALS

Renaming of tribunals

§ 1. Industrial tribunals to be known as employment tribunals.

Hearings etc.

2. Determinations without a hearing or full hearing.
3. Hearings etc. by chairman alone.
4. Hearings by chairman and one other member.

Other provisions

5. Legal officers.
6. Jurisdiction in cases about political fund contributions.

PART II

OTHER METHODS OF DISPUTE RESOLUTION

Arbitration

7. ACAS arbitration scheme.
8. Effect of arbitration agreements.

Compromise agreements

9. Advice of non-lawyer.
10. Indemnity cover.

Other provisions

11. Settlements of redundancy cases.
12. Dismissal procedures agreements.

PART III

AWARDS OF COMPENSATION

13. Internal appeal procedures and unfair dismissal awards.
14. Acts which are both unfair dismissal and disability discrimination.

F

65. Payment in the form of a readily convertible asset.
66. Enhancing the value of an asset.
67. Gains from share options etc.
68. Vouchers and credit-tokens.
69. Intermediaries, non-UK employers, agencies etc.

The enterprise investment scheme and venture capital trusts

70. Qualifying trades for EIS and VCTs.
71. Pre-arranged exits from EIS.
72. Qualifying holdings for VCTs after 2nd July 1997.
73. Other changes to requirements for VCTs.
74. Other changes to EIS etc.

Individual savings accounts etc.

75. Use of PEPs powers to provide for accounts.
76. Tax credits for accounts and for PEPs.
77. The insurance element etc.
78. Phasing out of TESSAs.

Relief for interest and losses etc.

79. Relief for loan to acquire interest in a close company.
80. Relief for losses on unlisted shares in trading companies.
81. Group relief: special rules for consortium cases.
82. Carry forward of non-trading deficit on loan relationships.

Capital allowances

83. First-year allowances for investment in Northern Ireland.
84. First-year allowances for small businesses etc.
85. First-year allowances: consequential amendments etc.

Insurance, insurance companies and friendly societies

86. Life policies etc.
87. Non-resident insurance companies: tax representatives.
88. Overseas life assurance business.
89. Personal portfolio bonds.
90. Distributions to friendly societies.
91. Provisional repayments in connection with pension business.

Pensions

92. Approved retirement benefit schemes etc.
93. Benefits received under non-approved retirement benefits scheme.
94. Approval of personal pension schemes.
95. Personal pensions: charge on withdrawal of approval.
96. Information relating to personal pension schemes etc.
97. Notices to be given to scheme administrator.
98. Assessments on scheme administrators.

Futures and options

99. Extension of provisions relating to guaranteed returns.

Securities

100. Accrued income scheme.
101. Dealers in securities etc.
102. Manufactured dividends.

Double taxation relief

103. Restriction of relief on certain interest and dividends.
104. Adjustments of interest and dividends for spared tax etc.
105. Meaning of "financial expenditure".
106. Underlying tax reflecting interest or dividends.
107. Notification of foreign tax adjustment.

Transfer pricing, FOREX and financial instruments

108. New regime for transfer pricing etc.
109. Abolition of requirements for direction.
110. Determinations requiring the sanction of the Board.
111. Notice to potential claimants.

Controlled foreign companies

112. Exempt activities.
113. Miscellaneous amendments.

G

Part I

The National Assembly for Wales
The Assembly

§ 1. The Assembly.
2. Membership.

Ordinary elections

3. Time of ordinary elections.
4. Voting at ordinary elections.
5. Party lists and individual candidates.
6. Calculation of electoral region figures.
7. Return of electoral region members.

Vacancies

8. Constituency seats.
9. Electoral region seats.

The franchise and conduct of elections

10. Entitlement to vote.
11. Power to make provision about elections etc.

Disqualification

12. Disqualification from being Assembly member.
13. Exceptions and relief from disqualification.
14. Effect of disqualification.
15. Judicial proceedings as to disqualification.

Remuneration, oaths etc.

16. Salaries and allowances.
17. Limit on salaries of members of other public bodies.
18. Pensions etc.
19. Publication of information about remuneration paid.
20. Oath or affirmation of allegiance.

Part II

Assembly Functions
Introduction

21. Introductory.

Transfer of Ministerial functions to Assembly

22. Transfer of Ministerial functions.
23. General transfer of property, rights and liabilities etc.
24. General transfer: supplementary.
25. Power to make specific transfers etc.

26.   Transfers of property: supplementary.

Other functions

27.   Reform of Welsh health authorities.
28.   Reform of other Welsh public bodies.
29.   Implementation of Community law.
30.   Consultation about public appointments.
31.   Consultation about government's legislative programme.
32.   Support of culture etc.
33.   Consideration of matters affecting Wales.

Ancillary powers etc.

34.   Staff.
35.   Inquiries.
36.   Polls for ascertaining views of the public.
37.   Private bills.
38.   Legal proceedings.
39.   Contracts.
40.   Supplementary powers.
41.   Agency arrangements and provision of services.

Supplementary

42.   Different exercise of functions by Assembly.
43.   Construction of references to Ministers and departments.
44.   Parliamentary procedures for subordinate legislation.
45.   Laying of reports and statements.

PART III

ASSEMBLY PROCEDURE

Introductory

46.   Regulation of procedure.
47.   Equal treatment of English and Welsh languages.
48.   Equal opportunities in conduct of business.

Initial provisions

49.   First meeting.
50.   First standing orders.
51.   The Commissioners.

Offices and committees

52.   Presiding officer and deputy.
53.   Assembly First Secretary and Assembly Secretaries.
54.   Committees.
55.   Sub-committees.

The statutory committees

56.   Executive committee.
57.   Subject committees.
58.   Subordinate legislation scrutiny committee.
59.   Members of scrutiny committee etc.
60.   Audit Committee.
61.   Regional committees.

Delegation

62.   Delegation of functions.
63.   Exercise of functions by Assembly staff.

Procedures relating to subordinate legislation

64.   Standing orders to provide procedures.
65.   Regulatory appraisals.
66.   Making of Assembly general subordinate legislation.
67.   Disapplication of procedural requirements.
68.   Financial initiative.

Other provisions about standing orders

69.   Preservation of order.
70.   Openness.
71.   Participation of Assembly members.
72.   Integrity.
73.   Publication.

PART I

THE REFERENDUM

1. Referendum.
2. Entitlement to vote.
3. Counting officers.
4. Referendum: supplementary.
5. Grants towards referendum expenditure.
6. Exclusion of legal proceedings.

PART II

ADVICE ON ELECTORAL ARRANGEMENTS FOR GREATER LONDON AUTHORITY

7. Functions of the Local Government Commission.
8. Preparation and submission of report.
9. Supplementary report.
10. Directions.
11. Payments by Secretary of State to Commission.

PART III

GENERAL

12. Expenditure.
13. Short title.

Schedule:—Form of ballot paper.

H

Introduction

1. The Convention Rights.
2. Interpretation of Convention rights.

Legislation

3. Interpretation of legislation.
4. Declaration of incompatibility.
5. Right of Crown to intervene.

Public authorities

6. Acts of public authorities.
7. Proceedings.
8. Judicial remedies.
9. Judicial acts.

Remedial action

10. Power to take remedial action.

Other rights and proceedings

11. Safeguard for existing human rights.
12. Freedom of expression.
13. Freedom of thought, conscience and religion.

Derogations and reservations

14. Derogations.
15. Reservations.
16. Period for which designated derogations have effect.
17. Periodic review of designated reservations.

Judges of the European Court of Human Rights

18. Appointment to European Court of Human Rights.

Parliamentary procedure

19. Statements of compatibility.

Supplemental

20. Orders etc. under this Act.
21. Interpretation, etc.
22. Short title, commencement, application and extent.
    Schedule 1—The Articles.
        Part I—The Convention.
        Part II—The First Protocol.
        Part III—The Sixth Protocol.
    Schedule 2—Remedial Orders.
    Schedule 3—Derogation and Reservation.
        Part I—Derogation.
        Part II—Reservation.
    Schedule 4—Judicial Pensions.

L

Introduction

§ 1. Mines and components to which Act applies.

Offences relating to anti-personnel mines

2. Prohibited conduct.
3. Application of prohibitions to places outside the UK.
4. Conduct that is permitted.
5. International military operations.
6. Other defences to offences under section 2.

Securing the destruction of anti-personnel mines

7. Suspicious objects.
8. Power to remove or immobilise objects.
9. Power to destroy removed objects.
10. Power to enter premises and destroy objects.
11. Compensation for destruction.

M

4.   Up-dating of references to s. 12 of Magistrates' Courts Act 1980.
5.   Short title, commencement and extent.

N

Archbishops' Council

§ 1.   Establishment of the Archbishops' Council.
  2.   Application of funds.
  3.   Accounts and audit.
  4.   Reports and budgets.

Transfer of functions and officers

  5.   Transfer of functions.
  6.   Transfer of officers.

Church Commissioners

  7.   Amendment of Church Commissioners Measure 1947.
  8.   Management of assets.

General provisions

  9.   Standing Orders of the General Synod.
10.   Committees.
11.   Restriction on elected membership of certain bodies.
12.   Interpretation.
13.   Amendments and repeals.
14.   Extent.
15.   Short title and commencement.
Schedule 1—The Archbishops' Council.
  Part I—Constitution and membership.
  Part II—General provisions.
Schedule 2—Functions of Church Commissioners excluded from section 5.
  Part I—Functions relating to bishops.
  Part II—Functions relating to cathedrals.
Schedule 3—Transfer of officers.
Schedule 4—Amendments of Church Commissioners Measure 1947.
Schedule 5—Amendment of enactments.

PART I

PROVISIONS RELATING TO THE NATIONAL LOTTERY

The Director General and the National Lottery Commission

§ 1.   Replacement of Director General by National Lottery Commission.

Licensees

  2.   Financial penalties for breach of conditions in licences.
  3.   Appeals against financial penalties.
  4.   Appeals against revocation of licences.
  5.   Access by Comptroller and Auditor General to documents etc.

The new good cause

  6.   The new good cause and the re-allocation of lottery money.
  7.   The New Opportunities Fund.
  8.   Provisions supplemental to section 7.

Distributing bodies

  9.   Manner of distribution.
10.   Power of distributing bodies to solicit applications.
11.   Delegation by distributing bodies of their powers of distribution.
12.   Joint schemes for distribution of money by distributing bodies.
13.   Strategic plans for distributing bodies.
14.   The National Lottery Charities Board.

Supplemental provision

15.   Orders and regulations.

Civil procedure, evidence and appeals

27. Tribunal hearings etc by chairman alone.
28. Reversal of burden of proof.
29. Appeals to the Employment Appeal Tribunal.

Conciliation

30. Conciliation.

Offences

31. Offences.
32. Offences by bodies corporate etc.
33. Proceedings for offences.

Special classes of person

34. Agency workers who are not otherwise "workers".
35. Home workers who are not otherwise "workers".
36. Crown employment.
37. Armed forces.
38. House of Lords staff.
39. House of Commons staff.
40. Mariners.

Extensions

41. Power to apply Act to individuals who are not otherwise "workers".
42. Power to apply Act to offshore employment.

Exclusions

43. Share fishermen.
44. Voluntary workers.
45. Prisoners.

Agricultural workers

46. Relationship of this Act and agricultural wages legislation.
47. Amendments relating to remuneration etc of agricultural workers.

Miscellaneous

48. Application of Act to superior employers.
49. Restrictions on contracting out.
50. Publicity.

Supplementary

51. Regulations and orders.
52. Expenses.
53. Repeals and revocations.
54. Meaning of "worker", "employee" etc.
55. Interpretation.
56. Short title, commencement and extent.
    Schedule 1—The Low Pay Commission.
    Schedule 2—Amendments relating to remuneration etc of agricultural workers.
        Part I—The Agricultural Wages Act 1948.
        Part II—The Agricultural Wages (Scotland) Act 1949.
        Part III—The Agricultural Wages (Regulation) (Northern Ireland) Order 1977.
    Schedule 3—Repeals and revocations.

PART I

PRELIMINARY

§ 1. Status of Northern Ireland.
  2. Previous enactments.
  3. Devolution order.
  4. Transferred, excepted and reserved matters.

PART II

LEGISLATIVE POWERS

General

5. Acts of the Northern Ireland Assembly.
6. Legislative competence.
7. Entrenched enactments.
8. Consent of Secretary of State required in certain cases.

PART I

THE POLICE AUTHORITY FOR NORTHERN IRELAND

PART II

POLICING OBJECTIVES, PERFORMANCE TARGETS AND PLANS

PART III

THE POLICE FORCE

PART IV

POLICE REPRESENTATIVE INSTITUTIONS

PART V

FUNCTIONS OF SECRETARY OF STATE

R

S

PART I

THE SCOTTISH PARLIAMENT
The Scottish Parliament

§ 1. The Scottish Parliament.

General elections

2. Ordinary general elections.
3. Extraordinary general elections.
4. Calculating time for meeting of the Parliament.
5. Candidates.
6. Poll for regional members.
7. Calculation of regional figures.
8. Allocation of seats to regional members.

Vacancies

9. Constituency vacancies.
10. Regional vacancies.

Franchise and conduct of elections

11. Electors.
12. Power to make provision about elections.

Duration of membership

13. Term of office of members.
14. Resignation of members.

Disqualification

15. Disqualification from membership of the Parliament.
16. Exceptions and relief from disqualification.
17. Effect of disqualification.
18. Judicial proceedings as to disqualification.

Presiding Officer and administration

19. Presiding Officer.
20. Clerk of the Parliament.
21. Scottish Parliamentary Corporate Body.

Proceedings etc.

22. Standing orders.
23. Power to call for witnesses and documents.
24. Witnesses and documents: notice.
25. Witnesses and documents: offences.
26. Witnesses and documents: general.
27. Participation of the Scottish Law Officers.

Legislation

28. Acts of the Scottish Parliament.
29. Legislative competence.
30. Legislative competence: supplementary.
31. Scrutiny of Bills before introduction.
32. Submission of Bills for Royal Assent.

PART I

DECISIONS AND APPEALS

CHAPTER I

GENERAL

Decisions

§ 1. Transfer of functions to Secretary of State.
 2. Use of computers.
 3. Use of information.

Appeals

 4. Unified appeal tribunals.
 5. President of appeal tribunals.
 6. Panel for appointment to appeal tribunals.
 7. Constitution of appeal tribunals.

CHAPTER II

SOCIAL SECURITY DECISIONS AND APPEALS

Decisions

 8. Decisions by Secretary of State.
 9. Revision of decisions.
10. Decisions superseding earlier decisions.
11. Regulations with respect to decisions.

Appeals

12. Appeal to appeal tribunal.
13. Redetermination etc. of appeals by tribunal.
14. Appeal from tribunal to Commissioner.
15. Appeal from Commissioner on point of law.

T

PART I

THE TEACHING PROFESSION

CHAPTER I

THE GENERAL TEACHING COUNCILS

The General Teaching Council for England

§ 1. The General Teaching Council for England.

Functions of the General Teaching Council for England

2. Advisory functions of General Teaching Council for England.
3. Registration of teachers.
4. Regulations relating to registration.
5. Code of practice for registered teachers.
6. Disciplinary powers of Council in relation to registered teachers.
7. Additional and ancillary functions of Council.

The General Teaching Council for Wales

8. The General Teaching Council for Wales.

Functions of the General Teaching Council for Wales

9. Functions of General Teaching Council for Wales: general.
10. Further functions of General Teaching Council for Wales in relation to teachers.

Supplementary

11. Registration requirement for teachers at schools.
12. Deduction of fees from salaries, etc.
13. Consultation about qualified teacher status.
14. Supply of information relating to teachers: general.
15. Supply of information relating to dismissal or resignation of teachers.

The General Teaching Council for Scotland

16. Duty to have regard to needs of disabled persons.
17. Representation of special educational needs teachers on General Teaching Council for Scotland.

CHAPTER II

HEAD TEACHERS

18. Qualifications of head teachers.

CHAPTER III

TEACHER TRAINING

Induction periods

19. Requirement to serve induction period.

Inspection of teacher training institutions

20. Inspection of institutions training teachers for schools.
21. Inspection of institutions training teachers for schools: Scotland.

PART II

FINANCIAL PROVISION FOR HIGHER AND FURTHER EDUCATION

CHAPTER I

ENGLAND AND WALES

Student support

22. New arrangements for giving financial support to students.
23. Transfer or delegation of functions relating to student support.
24. Supply of information in connection with student loans.
25. Transitional arrangements.

Student fees

26. Imposition of conditions as to fees at further or higher education institutions.

W